WE THE PEOPLE

A CONCISE INTRODUCTION
TO AMERICAN POLITICS

WE THE PEOPLE

A CONCISE INTRODUCTION
TO AMERICAN POLITICS

Second Edition

Thomas E. Patterson

Bradlee Professor of Government and the Press
John F. Kennedy School of Government
Harvard University

Overture
Books

The McGraw-Hill Companies, Inc.
New York   St. Louis   San Francisco   Auckland   Bogotá   Caracas
Lisbon   London   Madrid   Mexico City   Milan   Montreal   New Delhi
San Juan   Singapore   Sydney   Tokyo   Toronto

McGraw-Hill

A Division of The McGraw·Hill Companies

WE THE PEOPLE
A Concise Introduction to American Politics

This book is printed on acid-free paper.

1 2 3 4 5 6 7 8 9 0 QPF QPF 9 0 9 8 7

ISBN 0-07-049400-2

This book was set in Jansen by ComCom, Inc.

Sponsoring editor: Lyn Uhl
Editing supervisor: David A. Damstra
Designer: Wanda Siedlecka
Production supervisor: Paula Keller
Project supervision: Karen L. Osborne
Cover photo: Charles Kennard/Stock/Boston
Printer: Quebecor: Fairfield

Patterson, Thomas E.
    We the people : a concise introduction to American politics /
Thomas E. Patterson. — 2nd ed.
        p.   cm.
    Includes bibliographical references and index.
    ISBN 0-07-049400-2
    1. United States—Politics and government.   I. Title.
JK274.P36   1998
320.473—dc21   97-11441

http://www.mhhe.com

To My Children,
Alex and Leigh

About the Author

Thomas E. Patterson is Bradlee Professor of Government and the Press in the John F. Kennedy School of Government at Harvard University. He was previously distinguished professor of political science in the Maxwell School of Citizenship at Syracuse University. Raised in a small Minnesota town near the Iowa and South Dakota borders, he was educated at South Dakota State University and the University of Minnesota, where he received his Ph.D. in 1971.

He is the author of six books and dozens of articles, which focus primarily on the media and elections. His recent book, *Out of Order* (1994), received national attention when President Clinton said every politician and journalist should be required to read it. An earlier book, *The Mass Media Election* (1980), received a *Choice* award as Outstanding Academic Book, 1980–1981. Another of Patterson's books, *The Unseeing Eye* (1976), was recently selected by the American Association for Public Opinion Research as one of the fifty most influential books of the past half century in the field of public opinion.

His current research includes a five-country study of the news media's political role. His work has been funded by major grants from the National Science Foundation, the Ford Foundation, and the Markle Foundation.

Contents

CHAPTER SIX   Public Opinion and Political Socialization   170

CHAPTER SEVEN   VOTING AND PARTICIPATION   202

Preface

The story of American politics is a compelling one. It is about the struggle of real people to find mutually beneficial ways of living together. The title of this book, *We the People*, is a recognition of this struggle and its lofty goal—a government of and for *all* the people.

The writer Theodore White aptly described the United States as "a nation in search of itself." The American people have created a remarkably stable political system but have never regarded their work as finished. Each generation has had to redefine how their government will work in practice. This imperative is as powerful today as at nearly any time in the nation's history. The late twentieth century has been a period of extraordinary change in America, which has raised new challenges to the practice of government. Minorities and women, long denied access to political and economic power, are seeking a fairer share. New people in the millions from Asia and Latin America have joined the American community, bringing with them cultural traditions that have made our society richer and fuller, but also more fragmented and contentious. Traditional institutions, from political parties to families, have declined dramatically, weakening the fabric of our politics but also creating the possibility of adaptive new arrangements. America's workers and businesses have built a highly productive economy but are now facing the risks and opportunities of a global marketplace. The cold war that dominated our attention in foreign policy for decades has been replaced by ethnic rivalries and localized conflicts that raise troubling new issues of world insecurity which, so far, have defied most attempts to resolve them.

Scholars have endeavored to keep pace with the great changes that are taking place in today's politics. Never before has scholarship been so closely tied to the real world. If much of what political scientists study is arcane, we have tried increasingly to connect our work to the realities of everyday politics. The result has been the gradual emergence of a clearer and more complex picture of how American government operates. I have tried in this book to convey this advancement in knowledge in a faithful and interesting way.

In writing this book, I rejected the impulse to impose a single framework on the analysis. The U.S. political system and scholarship on it are both remarkably pluralistic, and any attempt at orthodoxy distorts their rich nature. Accordingly, this text relies upon the several forms of analysis that have informed the work of political scientists—the philosophical, historical, behavioral, legal, policy-analytic, and institutional. Each perspective has its strengths and its place in a telling of the story of American government.

Nevertheless, the book has a unifying core. The American political system is characterized by a few major tendencies, which are the key to understanding how it operates, namely:

- An enduring set of cultural ideals that are its people's common bond and a source of their political goals.
- An extreme fragmentation of governing authority that is based on an elaborate system of checks and balances.
- A great many competing interests that are the result of the nation's great size, population diversity, and economic complexity.
- A strong emphasis on individual rights that is a consequence of the nation's political traditions.
- A sharp separation of the political and economic spheres that has the effect of placing many economic issues outside the reach of political majorities.

These tendencies are introduced in the first chapter and are woven into subsequent chapters at numerous points. If students soon forget many of the points made in this book, as they invariably will, they may at least retain an awareness of the deep underpinnings of the American political system.

This book originated in my larger text, *The American Democracy*, which was first published in 1990 and will soon enter its fourth edition. This shorter text, however, is not a mere abridgment of the longer one. It is meant to stand on its own and thus was created by a process of revision and reorganization rather than the deletion of whole sections or chapters. Yet throughout the writing of the original edition and now the second edition of *We the People*, I have labored to maintain what readers of the larger text say is one of its greatest strengths: the extensive use of narrative. Nothing dulls a student's interest more quickly than a text that piles fact upon fact and list upon list. Narrative themes are more likely to hold the reader's attention; they have also been shown to heighten learning.

A novel feature of *We the People* is its set of selected readings; each chapter is followed by a reading that develops a major point of the chapter. These readings are intended to deepen the student's understanding of American politics and to add flexibility to the instructor's use of the material. For the instructor who prefers to supplement the course text with a book of read-ings, this text offers both. On the other hand, the instructor who wants to limit reading assignments to the text itself can simply skip the end-of-chapter readings or suggest them as optional reading for students who have the time and interest. The readings, with the exception of James Madison's *Federalist* No. 10, are contemporary ones. The authors, in order of their appear-ance, are distinguished scholars and public servants: Jennifer L. Hochschild; R. Kent Weaver; Benjamin I. Page and Robert Y. Shapiro; Sidney Verba; Kay Lehman Schlozman and Henry E. Banks; Alan Ehrenhalt; Jonathan Rauch; Thomas E. Patterson; Paul S. Herrnson; Richard Rose; David Osborne and Ted Gaebler; William J. Brennan, Jr.; Alice M. Rivlin; B. Guy Peters; and Kenichi Ohmae.

Another feature is a pair of boxed inserts in each chapter. One is enti-tled "How the United States Compares." The United States in many ways is the world's preeminent democracy, but it also has distinctive policies and practices. American students invariably gain a deeper understanding of their own society when they recognize the ways in which it differs from others. Each chapter also has a boxed insert entitled "States in the Nation." This material is designed to alert students to similarities and differences in the politics of the American states.

This book owes a great debt to others. Editions of my larger text were strengthened immeasurably by the suggestions of more than 300 scholars at U.S. colleges and universities of all types—public and private, large and small, two-year and four-year. Their sound advice helped shape every page of that book, which in turn has affected the pages here. I am also deeply thankful to the smaller group of scholars who advised me directly on the con-tent of the first or second edition of *We the People:* Paul Blanchard, Eastern Kentucky University; John Bookman, University of Northern Colorado; Didrick Castberg, University of Hawaii at Hilo; John Cavanaugh, Univer-sity of South Carolina; Paul Chardoul, Grand Rapids Community College; Linda Beail Coleman, Point Loma Nazarene College; Delmer Dunn, Uni-versity of Georgia; Richard Logan Fox, University of Wyoming; Stephen Frank, St. Cloud State University; Lawrence Giventer, California State Uni-versity, Stanislaus; Daniel Gregory, El Camino College; Nancy Haanstad, Weber State College; William Hastings, San Diego Mesa College; Eric Herzik, University of Nevada; Richard Keiser, University of Denver; William Kelly, Auburn University; Donald Kerle, Pittsburgh State Univer-sity; Thomas Marshall, University of Texas at Arlington; Richard Miller, Sacramento City College; John Nickerson, University of Maine; Kenneth Payne, San Diego Mesa College; Linda Potter, Sul Ross State University;

Robert Spitzer, State University of New York, Cortland; Martin Sutton, Bucks County Community College; Miguel Tirado, Sonoma State University; T. Phillip Wolf, Indiana University; and Larry Wright, Florida A&M University.

I also wish to thank Lyn Uhl, my editor at McGraw-Hill. She offered several helpful suggestions for the second edition and provided ample support and constructive criticism at every stage of the writing process. Lyn is a delight to work with, as were my two previous McGraw-Hill editors, Bert Lummus and Peter Labella. David Damstra of McGraw-Hill carefully oversaw the laborious process of turning a rough-hewn manuscript into a well-crafted and, to my mind, beautifully designed book. David has been part of every McGraw-Hill text edition I have written but recently left the company. I am deeply thankful for his help and patience over the years and will greatly miss working with him. Karen Osborne of McGraw-Hill is also owed a deep thanks; her careful copyediting improved the book's prose and substance. Barbara Salz contributed through her careful and imaginative photo research. I am also indebted to McGraw-Hill's Katrina Redmond. Finally, I wish to thank my student assistant, Matthew Malady. He spent a summer helping me update this edition. His many contributions made my job much easier.

Looking ahead, I invite from instructors and students any comments and criticisms that might inform future editions of this text. The strengths and weaknesses of a text are best discovered in its use, and I hope readers will share their thoughts with me. Suggestions can be mailed to me at the John F. Kennedy School of Government, Harvard University, Cambridge, Massachusetts 02138. I can also be reached through e-mail: thomas_patterson@harvard.edu.

Finally, there is an Internet Web site devoted to this text. The site offers instructors and students up-to-date information on American politics that is keyed to the text's chapters. The site is located at:

http://www.mhcollege.com/social/poli/patterson.htm

Thomas E. Patterson

WE THE PEOPLE

A CONCISE INTRODUCTION
TO AMERICAN POLITICS

CHAPTER ONE

The American Heritage

One hears people say that it is inherent in the habits and nature of democracies to change feelings and thoughts at every moment. . . . But I have never seen anything like that happening in the great democracy on the other side of the ocean. What struck me most in the United States was the difficulty experienced in getting an idea, once conceived, out of the head of the majority.

ALEXIS DE TOCQUEVILLE[1]

T MIDDAY on January 20, 1997, Bill Clinton took the oath of office for a second term as president of the United States. Clinton's speech, if not for its contemporary statements, would have sounded familiar to any generation of Americans.[2] His address was punctuated with references to time-honored American principles: democracy, liberty, opportunity for all, diversity, unity, self-reliance. The same ideals had filled the speeches of Ronald Reagan and John Kennedy, Franklin Roosevelt and Abraham Lincoln, and Andrew Jackson and Thomas Jefferson.[3] The same ideals had been used to take America to war, to negotiate peace, to assert new rights, to declare major policies, and to memorialize national holidays.

Of course, the practice of these ideals has changed greatly during the two centuries that the United States has been a nation. When America's founders proclaimed in 1776 that "all men are created equal," they did not have in mind women or slaves. And the assumption that Americans are one people with a common vision has always obscured deep divisions in society.[4] The claim that America is a gigantic melting pot has always been as much fable as fact. When Irish, Italian, and Polish immigrants reached this country's shores, they encountered nativist elements that scorned their ways of life and attacked their religion. The Latinos and Asians who have come here more recently have also been made to feel less than fully welcome. The "English-first" movement includes the not-very-subtle message that "true" Americans do not speak Spanish or Vietnamese or Cambodian.

Yet the American political experience has been remarkably enduring.

U.S. politics is remarkable for its historical continuity, which is celebrated here in a ceremony at the Capitol in Washington D.C. (Joseph Sohm/Stock, Boston)

Throughout their history, Americans have embraced the same core principles. The United States has been settled by diverse peoples who have maintained many of their cultural differences. But they have shared an idealized image of what it means to be an American. They have quarreled over other matters, and over the practice of these principles, but they seem never to have questioned the principles themselves. As Clinton Rossiter concluded, "There has been, in a doctrinal sense, only one America."[5]

This is a book about contemporary American politics, not U.S. history or culture. Yet American politics today cannot be understood apart from the nation's heritage. Government does not begin anew with each generation; it builds on the past. In the case of the United States, the most significant link between past and present lies in the nation's founding ideals. This chapter briefly examines the principles that have shaped American politics since the country's earliest years.

The chapter also explains basic concepts, such as power and authority, that are important in the study of government and politics, and describes the underlying rules and theories of the American governing system, such as constitutionalism and pluralism. The main points made in this chapter are the following:

★ *The American political culture centers on a set of core ideals—liberty, equality, self-government, individualism, diversity, and unity—that serve as the people's common bond.*

★ *Politics is the process that determines whose values will prevail in society. The play of politics in the United States takes place in the context of democratic procedures, constitutionalism, and capitalism, and involves elements of majority, pluralist, and elite rule.*

★ *Politics in the United States is characterized by a number of major patterns, including a highly fragmented governing system, a high degree of pluralism, an extraordinary emphasis on individual rights, and a pronounced separation of the political and economic spheres.*

POLITICAL CULTURE: THE CORE PRINCIPLES OF AMERICAN GOVERNMENT

The people of every nation have a few great ideals that characterize their political life, but, as James Bryce observed, Americans are a special case.[6] Their ideals are the basis of their national identity. Other people take their identity from the common ancestry that led them gradually to gather under one flag. Thus, long before there was a France or a Japan, there were French and Japanese people, each a kinship group united through blood. Not so for Americans. They are a multitude of peoples linked by a political tradition. The United States is a nation that was founded abruptly in 1776 on a set of principles that became its people's common bond.[7]

A strong bond of some kind was a necessity. Nationalities that warred constantly in Europe had to find a way to live together in the New World. Their search for common ground has been replayed many times during America's history. The United States is, and always has been, a nation of immigrant peoples (see Figure 1-1). Yet they are also one people, brought together through allegiance to a set of commonly held ideals.

America's principles are habits of mind, a customary way of thinking about the world. They are part of what social scientists call **political culture,** a term that refers to the characteristic and deep-seated beliefs of a particular people.[8] The American political culture is said to include the following beliefs in idealized form:

- **Liberty** is the principle that individuals should be free to act and think as they choose, provided they do not infringe unreasonably on the freedom and well-being of others.

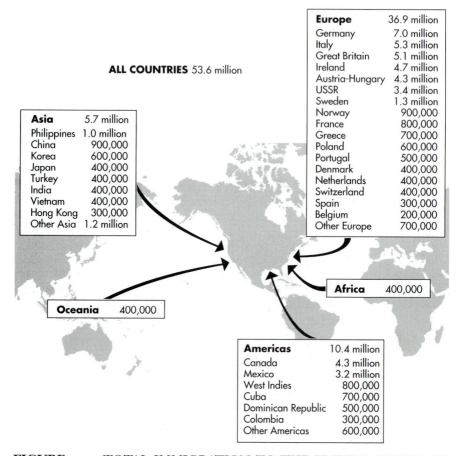

FIGURE 1-1 TOTAL IMMIGRATION TO THE UNITED STATES, BY CONTINENT AND COUNTRY OF ORIGIN (1820–1990)
America is a nation of immigrants who are joined together through a common set of ideals. Source: U.S. Immigration and Naturalization Service.

- **Self-government** is the principle that the people are the ultimate source of governing authority and that their general welfare is the only legitimate purpose of government.

- **Equality** holds that all individuals have moral worth, are entitled to fair treatment under the law, and should have equal opportunity for material gain and political influence.

- **Individualism** is a commitment to personal initiative, self-sufficiency, and material accumulation. This principle upholds the superiority of a private-enterprise economic system and includes the idea of the individual as the foundation of society.

- **Diversity** holds that individual differences should be respected and that these differences are a source of strength and a legitimate basis of self-interest.
- **Unity** is the principle that Americans are one people and form an indivisible union.

These ideals, taken together, are sometimes called "the American creed." In practice, they mean different things to different people, and it is not useful to provide more complex definitions of these values at this point in the book. Few observers would argue, however, with the proposition that *a defining characteristic of the American political system is its enduring and powerful set of cultural ideals.* The Frenchman Alexis de Tocqueville was among the first to see that the main tendencies of American politics cannot be explained without taking into account the country's core beliefs. "Habits of the heart" was Tocqueville's description of Americans' ideals.[9]

The Power of Ideals

America's ideals have had a strong impact on its politics. Ideals serve to define the boundaries of action. They do not determine exactly what people will do, but they have a marked influence on what people will regard as reasonable and desirable. If people believe, as Americans do, that politics exists to promote liberty and equality, they will attempt to realize these values through their political actions.

Why, for example, does the United States spend relatively less money on government programs for the poor and disadvantaged than do other fully industrialized democracies, including Germany, France, Switzerland, the Netherlands, Spain, Britain, Sweden, Italy, and Japan? Are Americans so much better off than these other people that we have less need for welfare programs? The answer is no. Of all these countries, the United States has in both relative and absolute terms the greatest number of hungry, homeless, and poor people. The reason the United States spends less on social welfare lies chiefly in the emphasis that American culture places on *individualism*. We have resisted giving government a larger social welfare role because of our deep-seated cultural belief that able-bodied individuals should take responsibility for themselves (see box: How the United States Compares).

HOW THE UNITED STATES COMPARES

Capitalism, Self-Reliance, and Personal Success

The United States was labeled "the country of individualism *par excellence*" by William Watts and Lloyd Free in their book *State of the Nation*. They were referring to the emphasis that Americans place on self-reliance and the trust they have in the marketplace as a basis of economic security.

Such views also prevail in European democracies but are moderated by a greater acceptance of welfare programs. The difference between the American and European cultures reflects their differing political traditions. America was an open country ruled by a foreign power, and its revolution was fought largely over the issue of personal freedom. In European revolutions, equality was also at issue since wealth was held by hereditary aristocracies. Europeans' concern with equality was gradually translated into a willingness to use government as a means of redistributing wealth. An example is government-paid medical care for all citizens.

Even today, Europeans are more likely to feel that their social and economic status is determined by the circumstances of birth. This outlook is evident in a recent Times-Mirror survey that asked respondents whether "success in life is pretty much determined by forces outside our control." The percentage of Americans and Europeans agreeing with the statement are shown in the accompanying chart.

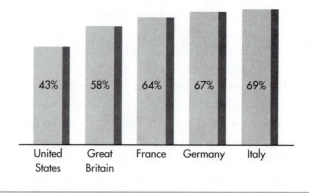

United States	Great Britain	France	Germany	Italy
43%	58%	64%	67%	69%

Of course, social welfare policy is not simply an issue of cultural differences. The welfare issue, like all other issues, is part of the rough and tumble of everyday politics everywhere. There are always powerful interests aligned on both sides of important issues. In the United States, the Republican party, business groups, antitax groups, and others have resisted the expansion of the government's social welfare role, while liberal Democrats, unions, minority groups, and others have from time to time argued for greater intervention. Nevertheless, Americans' belief in individualism, which has no exact equivalent in European society, has played a defining role in shaping U.S. welfare policy.

The distinctiveness of this cultural belief is evident in a Times-Mirror Center survey of opinions in Europe and the United States.[10] When asked whether it is the responsibility of the government "to take care of very poor people who can't take care of themselves," only 23 percent of Americans said they completely agreed. The Germans were the closest to the Americans in their response to this question, but more than twice as many of them, 50 percent, said they believed that the state should take care of the very poor. More than 60 percent of the British, French, and Italians held the same opinion. Americans do not necessarily have less sympathy for the poor; rather, they place more emphasis on personal responsibility than the Europeans do.[11]

The American ideal of equality has meant better employment opportunities for women in recent years. (Robert Rathe/Stock, Boston)

The importance of individualism to American society is also evident in the emphasis on equal opportunity. If individuals are to be entrusted with their own welfare, they must be given a fair chance to succeed on their own. Nowhere is this philosophy more evident than in the country's elaborate system of higher education, which includes nearly 3,000 two-year and four-year institutions. The system is designed to accommodate nearly every individual who wants to pursue a college education. More than a third of the nation's young people enter college, the world's highest rate. Even western Europe has nothing comparable to the American system; fewer than one in ten adults in these countries holds a bachelor's degree. Two in ten adult Americans have the degree. Even the states that rank lowest by this standard have more college graduates than the European average (see box: States in the Nation).

Of course, the idea that success is within the reach of all Americans who strive for it is far from accurate. Young people who grow up in abject poverty and without adequate guidance know all too well the limits on their lives. In some inner-city areas, teenage boys are more likely to spend time in prison than in college.

The Limits of Ideals

Cultural beliefs originate in a country's political and social practices, but they are not perfect representatives of these practices. They are mythic ideas— symbolic positions taken by a people to justify and give meaning to their way of life.[12] Myths contain elements of truth, but they are far from the full truth.

High ideals do not come with a guarantee that a people will live up to them. The clearest proof of this failing in the American case is the human tragedy that began nearly four centuries ago and continues today. In 1619 the first black slaves were brought in chains to America. Slavery lasted 250 years. Slaves in the field worked from dawn to dark (from "can see, 'til can't"), whether in the heat of summer or the cold of winter. The Civil War changed the future of African Americans but did not assure their equality. Slavery was followed by the Jim Crow era of legal segregation: black people in the South were forbidden by law to use the same schools, hospitals, restaurants, and restrooms as white people. For those who got uppish with their white superiors, there were beatings, firebombings, castrations, rapes, and worse—hundreds of African Americans were lynched by white vigilantes in the early 1900s. Today African Americans have equal rights under the law, but in fact they are far from equal. Compared with whites, blacks are three times as likely to live in poverty, twice as likely to be unable to find a job,

STATES IN THE NATION

Percentage of State Residents with a Bachelor's Degree

Reflecting cultural beliefs in equality and individualism, the United States has the world's largest system of college education. Even the state that ranks lowest (West Virginia, 12.3 percent) has a higher percentage of residents with a bachelor's degree than do most west European countries.

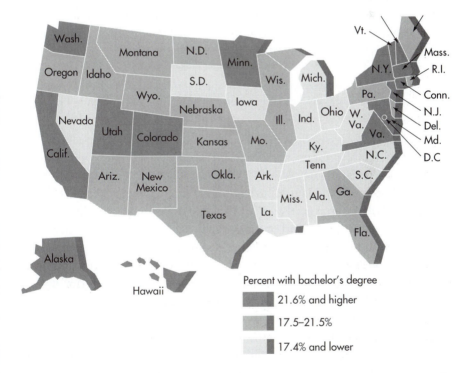

Percent with bachelor's degree

■ 21.6% and higher

■ 17.5–21.5%

■ 17.4% and lower

SOURCE: U.S. Bureau of Census

Even as early Americans were expressing their commitment to the principle of equality, they were allowing slavery to persist. This is the only drawing known to have been made aboard a slave ship as it sailed to America. (National Maritime Museum, London)

twice as likely to die in infancy, seven times as likely to be sentenced to death if convicted of an interracial murder.[13] There have always been at least two Americas, one for whites and one for blacks.

Despite the lofty claim that "all men are created equal," equality has never been an American birthright. In 1892 Congress suspended Chinese immigration on the assumption that the Chinese were an inferior people. Calvin Coolidge in 1923 asked Congress for a permanent ban on Chinese immigration, saying that people "who do not want to be partakers of the American spirit ought not to settle in America."[14] Not until 1965 was discrimination against the Chinese and other Asian peoples effectively eliminated from U.S. immigration laws.

The discrimination against the Chinese is not among the stories that we like to tell about ourselves. Such lapses of historical memory can be found among all peoples, but the tendency to recast history is perhaps exaggerated in the case of Americans because our beliefs are so idealistic. How could a people that upholds the ideal of human equality have barred the Chinese, enslaved the blacks, stolen the Indians' lands, subordinated women, and interned the Japanese?

Cultural beliefs can even lull a people into a false sense of what they have accomplished. Some Americans think that by saying they believe in equality, they have achieved it. A Harris poll showed that two-thirds of white people believe that blacks "get equal pay for equal work." In fact, as U.S. Department of Labor statistics show, blacks in every occupational category are paid less than whites.

One reason America's ideals do not match reality is that they are general principles, not fixed rules of conduct. They derive from somewhat different experiences and philosophical traditions, and there are points at which they conflict. Equality and diversity, for instance, emphasize fairness and a full opportunity for all to partake of society's benefits, whereas liberty and individualism emphasize personal freedom and threats posed to it by political power. Conflict between these sets of beliefs is inevitable. Both are commendable, but the advancement of one set comes only at some cost to the other. Take the issue of affirmative action. Proponents say that only through aggressive affirmative action programs will women and minorities receive the equal treatment in the job market to which they are entitled. Opponents say that aggressive affirmative action infringes unreasonably on the liberty of the employer and the initiative of the work force. Each side can say that it has America's ideals on its side, and no resort to logic can persuade either side that the opposing viewpoint should prevail.

Despite their inexact meanings, conflicting implications, and unfulfilled promise, the ideals of Americans have had a strong impact on the nation's politics. America's broad-based system of public education, for example, stems from an amalgam of its egalitarian and individualistic beliefs. Leon Sampson, a nineteenth-century American socialist, noted the stark difference between the philosophy of public education in the United States and that in Europe. "The European ruling classes," he said, "were open in their contempt for the proletariat. But in the United States equality, and even classlessness, the creation of wealth for all and political liberty were extolled in the public schools." Sampson concluded that American schools embodied a unique conception of equality: everyone was being trained in much the same way so that each person would have the opportunity to succeed. "It is," he said, "a socialist conception of capitalism."[15] In such ways do cultural beliefs lend context and direction to a nation's politics.

POLITICS: THE PROCESS OF DECIDING
UPON SOCIETY'S GOALS

Cultural ideals help shape what people expect from politics and how they conduct their politics. However, politics is more than the pursuit of shared ideals; it is also about getting one's own way. Commenting on the competitive nature of politics, Harold Lasswell described politics as the struggle over "who gets what, when, and how."[16]

Political conflict is rooted in two general conditions of society. One is *scarcity*. Society's resources are finite, but people's appetites are not. There is not enough wealth in even the richest of countries to satisfy everyone's desires. Conflict over the distribution of resources is the inevitable result. This conflict is evident, for example, in policy disputes over the financing of public schools. The quality of American schools varies widely. Affluent suburban districts have better schools and teachers than poor inner-city districts, which reflects differences in their local tax base. In order to equalize quality, less affluent communities have pressed for the statewide funding of public schools, an approach that more affluent communities have resisted.

Differences in values are the other main source of political conflict. People see things in different ways. The right of abortion is freedom of choice to some and murder to others. People bring to politics a wide range of conflicting values—about abortion, about the environment, about the level of defense spending, about crime and punishment, about the poor, about the economy, about almost everything imaginable.

Politics in the United States is not the life-and-death struggle between opposing groups that typifies some countries, but there are many sources of contention. Perhaps no country has more competing interests than does the United States. Its settlement by people of many lands and religions, its enormous size and geographical diversity, and its economic complexity have made the United States a pluralistic nation. *This feature—competition for power among a great many interests of all kinds—is a major characteristic of American politics.*

It is a mistake to assume, however, that conflict is the sum of politics. At base, **government** is the effort of people to find agreeable ways of living together.[17] For government to work, people must have ways of advancing their collective interests as well as their separate ones. Government is not solely about winners and losers. It is also about problem solving. Public safety, public education, and national security are prime examples of people working together for an agreed-upon purpose.

In sum, politics is a process that includes conflict *and* consensus, competition *and* cooperation. Accordingly, we shall define **politics** as, simply, the process through which a society makes its governing decisions.

Power, Authority, and Policy

Those who decide issues are said to have **power,** a term that refers to the ability of persons or institutions to control policy decisions.[18] Power is a basic concept of politics. Power determines which interests will decide policy. Those who have sufficient power can impose taxes, permit or prohibit abortions, protect or take private property, provide or refuse welfare benefits, impose or relax trade barriers. With so much at stake, it is perhaps not surprising that power is widely sought and tightly guarded.

When power is exercised through the laws and institutions of government, the concept of authority applies. **Authority** can be defined as the recognized right of an individual, organization, or institution to make binding decisions. By this definition, government is not the only source of authority: parents have authority over their children; professors have authority over their students; firms have authority over their employees. However, government is a special case in that its authority is more encompassing in scope and more final in nature. Government's authority extends to all within its geographical boundaries. It can be used to redefine the authority of the parent, the professor, or the firm. Government's authority is also the most coercive. It includes the power to arrest and imprison, even to punish by death those who violate its rules.

Government needs coercive power to ensure that its laws will be obeyed, but this power can also be abused. In a perfect world, political power would be used in evenhanded ways for the benefit of all. But the world is imperfect, and those with power can use it for selfish ends, whether to enrich themselves personally or to advance the interests of their side against all others. "Power tends to corrupt, and absolute power tends to corrupt absolutely," was how Lord Acton described the problem.

Although no governing system can assure that power will be applied fairly, the U.S. system strengthens this prospect through an elaborate system of *checks and balances.* This system includes the division of authority among the executive, legislative, and judicial branches of government. Each branch acts as a check on the power of the others and balances their power by exercising power of its own. Many other democratic countries have no comparable fragmentation of power. *Extreme fragmentation of governing authority is a major characteristic of the American political system. This fact, as we will see in subsequent chapters, has profound implications for how politics is conducted, who wins out, and what policies result.*

Governments exercise authority through policy. In its most general sense, **policy** refers to any broad course of action undertaken by government. U.S. policy toward Japan, for example, consists of a wide range of activities, from trade relations to diplomatic overtures. But policy is also used more narrowly to refer to specific programs or initiatives. The Head Start program for improving the educational prospects of poor children, for example, is a policy of government. The general view of policy is the more evocative, because it acknowledges that government exercises authority by not making decisions as well as by making them. In choosing not to decide, a government accepts the existing situation as well as the distribution of benefits and costs embedded in it.

The Rules of the Game of Politics

The play of politics takes place according to rules that the participants accept. The rules establish the process by which power is exercised, define the legitimate uses of power, and establish the basis for allocating costs and benefits among the participants. In the American case, the rules of the game of politics include democracy, constitutionalism, and capitalism.

DEMOCRACY   Democracy is a set of rules for determining who will exercise the authority of government. Democracy comes from the Greek words *demos*, which means "the people," and *kratis*, meaning "to rule." In simple terms, **democracy** is a form of government in which the people govern, either directly or through elected representatives.

Democratic government is based on the idea of the consent of the governed, which in practice has come to mean majority rule. The principle of majority rule, in turn, is based on the notion that the view of the many should prevail over the opinion of the few. The idea also reflects a kind of political equality in that the vote of each citizen counts equally, a principle expressed by the phrase "one person, one vote." In practice, democracy in America works primarily through elections. There are other, more direct forms of democracy, such as the town meeting and the initiative, but ours is a mainly representative system of government in which the people rule indirectly, through the officials they elect.

CONSTITUTIONALISM   For many Americans, "democracy" has the same meaning as "liberty"—the freedom to think, talk, and act as one chooses. However, the terms are not synonymous. The concept of democracy implies that the will of the majority should prevail over the wishes of the minority, whereas the concept of liberty implies that the minority has rights and liberties that cannot be taken away by the majority. The democratic model of government has long been accompanied by a fear of tyranny by the majority—the concern that a majority might ruthlessly impose its will on the minority. A more general concern about all government is the possibility of abuse of power.[19]

Constitutionalism is a set of rules that restricts the lawful uses of power. In its original sense, constitutionalism in western society referred to a government based on laws and constitutional powers.[20] **Constitutionalism** has since come to refer specifically to the idea that there are limits on the rightful power of government over citizens. In a constitutional system, officials govern according to law and citizens have basic rights which government cannot take away or deny.[21] An example of constitutionalism in the United States is freedom of speech. Government is prohibited from interfering with the lawful exercise of free speech. No right is absolute, which means that some restrictions are permissible. For example, a person could be forcibly removed from the visitors' gallery overlooking the floor of the U.S. Senate for shouting at the lawmakers during debate. Nevertheless, free speech is broadly protected by the courts. During the war in the Persian Gulf (1990–1991), there were hundreds of demonstrations against U.S. policy without a single arrest and conviction for spoken words alone. There were instances in which protesters were harassed by officials or other citizens, but those who opposed the war had the opportunity to express their views publicly.

The constitutional tradition in America is at least as strong as the democratic tradition. In fact, *a major characteristic of the American political system is its extraordinary emphasis on individual rights.* Issues that in other democratic countries would be resolved through elections and in legislatures are, in the United States, worked out through court action as well. As Tocqueville noted, there is hardly a political issue in America that does not sooner or later become a judicial issue.[22] Abortion rights, nuclear power, busing, toxic waste disposal, and welfare services are among the scores of issues that in recent years have been played out in part as questions of individual rights to be settled through judicial action.

CAPITALISM   Just as democracy and constitutionalism are systems of rules for allocating society's costs and benefits in American society, so is capitalism. Societies have adopted alternative ways of organizing their

Free speech is a familiar aspect of constitutionalism. This anti–gun control rally
took place in Austin, Texas. (Bob Daemmrich/The Image Works)

economies. One way is socialism, which assigns government a large role in
the ownership of the means of production, in regulating economic decisions,
and in providing for the economic security of the individual. Under the form
of socialism practiced in democratic countries, such as Sweden, the government does not attempt to manage the overall economy. In communist-style
socialism, the government does take responsibility for overall management.

Capitalism is an alternative method for distributing economic costs and
benefits. **Capitalism** holds that the government should interfere with the
economy as little as possible. Free enterprise and self-reliance are the principles of capitalism. Firms are allowed to operate in a free and open marketplace, and individuals are expected to rely on their own initiative to establish their economic security.

As is the case with the rules of democracy and constitutionalism, the rules
of capitalism are not neutral. If democracy responds to numbers and constitutionalism responds to rights, capitalism responds to wealth. Economic
power is largely a function of accumulated wealth, whether in the hands of
the individual or the firm. "Money talks" in a capitalist system, which means,

among other things, that wealthier people will have by far the greater say in the distribution of costs and benefits through the economic system.

The United States does not have a purely capitalist system, in that the government plays a role in regulating and stimulating the economy (see Chapter 15). The term "mixed economy" is used to define this hybrid form of economic system, with its combination of socialist and capitalist elements. The United States has more elements of the capitalist model and fewer elements of the socialist model than do the countries of Europe. Because of their strong tradition of individualism, Americans tend to restrict the scope of governmental action in the area of the economy. *A major characteristic of the American system is a sharp distinction between what is political, and therefore to be decided in the public arena, and what is economic, and therefore to be settled in the private realm.*

For all practical purposes, this outlook places many kinds of choices, which in other countries are decided collectively, beyond the reach of political majorities in the United States. Although Americans complain that their taxes are too high, they actually pay relatively fewer taxes than citizens

Capitalism, the organizing principle of our economic system, emphasizes marketplace competition and self-initiative. As a result, economic wealth and power are very unequally distributed among Americans. This homeless man is on a sidewalk outside the White House. (Larry Downing/Woodfin Camp & Associates)

of European democracies. This situation testifies to the extent to which Americans believe that wealth is more properly allocated through the marketplace than through government.

Theories of Power

The rules of the political game help decide who will exercise power and to what ends. The ultimate question about any political system is the issue of who governs. Is power widely shared and used for the benefit of the many? Or is power narrowly held and used to the advantage of the few? Although this entire book is in some respects an answer to these questions, it is useful here to consider what analysts have concluded about the American political system. Three broad theories predominate (see Table 1-1). None of them describes every aspect of American politics, but each has some validity.

RULE BY THE PEOPLE: MAJORITARIANISM   A basic principle of democracy, as discussed previously, is the idea of majority rule. **Majoritarianism** is the notion that the majority prevails not only in the counting of votes but also in the determination of public policy.

Majorities do sometimes rule in America. Their power is perhaps most evident in those states that offer voters the opportunity to decide directly on policy initiatives, which then become law if they receive a majority vote. The majority's influence is also felt indirectly through the decisions of elected representatives. When Congress in 1996 passed a welfare reform bill that included provisions requiring able-bodied welfare recipients to accept a job or

---

TABLE 1-1   THEORIES OF POWER: WHO GOVERNS AMERICA?
There are three theories of power in America, each of which must be taken into account in any full explanation of the nation's policies.

Theory	Description
Majoritarianism	Holds that numerical majorities determine issues of policy
Pluralism	Holds that policies are effectively decided through power wielded by special interests that dominate particular policy areas
Elitism	Holds that policy is controlled by a small number of well-positioned, highly influential individuals

job training after a two-year period or face a loss of their welfare benefits, it was acting in accord with the thinking of the majority of Americans who believe that employable individuals should be self-reliant. A more systematic assessment of the power of majorities is provided by Benjamin Page and Robert Shapiro's study of the relationship between majority opinions and more than 300 policy issues in the 1935–1979 period. On major issues particularly, they found that policy tended to change in the direction of change in majority opinion.[23]

Majorities do not always rule, however. There are many policy areas in which majority opinion is nonexistent or is ignored by policymakers. In these cases, other explanations of power and policy are necessary.

RULE BY GROUPS: PLURALISM   One of these explanations is provided by the theory of **pluralism,** which focuses on group activity and holds that many policies are effectively decided through power wielded by diverse (plural) interests.

Many policies are in fact more responsive to the interests of particular groups than to majority opinion. Agricultural subsidies, broadcast regulations, and corporate tax incentives are examples. In many cases, the general public has no real knowledge or opinion of issues that concern particular groups. For pluralists, the issue of whether interest-group politics serves the public good centers on whether a great many interests of a diverse nature achieve their goals. Pluralists contend that it is misleading to view society only in terms of majorities that may or may not form around given issues. They see society as primarily a collection of separate interests. Farmers, broadcasters, and multinational corporations have different needs and desires and, according to the pluralist view, should have a large say in policies directly affecting them. Thus, as long as many groups have influence in their own area of interest, government is responding to the interests of most Americans. Pluralists such as Robert Dahl have argued that this is in fact the way the American political system operates most of the time.[24]

Some critics argue that pluralists wrongly assume that nearly all of society's interests are able to compete effectively through group politics. They see a system biased toward a small number of powerful groups. These critics are proponents of elite theory.

RULE BY A FEW: ELITISM   Elite theory offers a pessimistic view of the U.S. political system. **Elitism** holds that power in America is held by a small number of well-positioned, highly influential individuals who control policy for their own purposes. A leading proponent of elite theory was the sociologist C. Wright Mills, who argued that key policies are decided by an overlapping coalition of select leaders, including corporate executives, top military officers, and centrally placed public officials.[25] Other proponents of elite theory have defined the core group somewhat differently, but their contention is the same: America is essentially run not by majorities or a plurality of groups but by a small number of well-placed and privileged individuals.

Some elite theorists offer a conspiratorial view of the policy process. They see elites as operating behind the scenes, and thus, even when there is the appearance of majority rule, actual power is wielded by a tiny group. In support of this contention, they note that key positions of political power are occupied by a relatively few people who often also have power in other realms, particularly industry.

Although some of the claims about a "power elite" are exaggerated, there is no question that certain policy areas are controlled by a tiny circle of influential people. The nation's monetary policy, for example, is set by the decisions of the Federal Reserve Board, which meets in secrecy and is highly responsive to the concerns of bankers and financiers (see Chapter 15).

WHO GOVERNS AMERICA?   The perspective of this book is that each of these theories—majoritarianism, pluralism, and elitism—must be taken into account in any full explanation of politics and power in America. Some policies are decided by majority influence, whereas others reflect the influence of special interests and elites. The challenge is to distinguish the situations in which each of these forms of influence predominates. Subsequent chapters will attempt that task.

THE CONCEPT OF A POLITICAL SYSTEM AND THE BOOK'S ORGANIZATION

As the foregoing discussion suggests, American government is based on a great many related parts. For this reason, it is useful to regard these components as constituting a **political system.** The parts are separate but they connect with each other, affecting how each performs. The political scientist David Easton, who was a pioneer in this conception of politics, said that it makes little sense to study political relations piecemeal when they are, in reality, "interrelated."[26]

The complexity of government has kept political scientists from developing a dynamic explanatory model of the full political system, but the concept of politics as a system is useful for instructional purposes. The concept emphasizes the actual workings of government rather than its institutional structures alone. This approach characterizes this book, beginning with its organizational sequence.

As Figure 1-2 indicates, the political system operates against the backdrop of a constitutional framework that defines how power is to be obtained and exercised. This framework is the focus of Chapters 1–5, which examine the governmental structure and individual rights. *Inputs* are another part of the political system; these are the demands that people and groups place on government and the supports they provide for its institutions, leaders, and policies. These inputs are the subject of Chapters 6–10) which examine public opinion, political participation, voting, political parties, interest groups, and the news media. The functioning of the system itself is the focus of Chapters 11–14, which examine the nation's elective and appointive institutions—Congress, the presidency, the courts, and the government bureaucracy. Some of the discussion in these chapters is devoted simply to describing these institutions, but most of it explores their relationships and how their actions are affected by inputs and the constitutional framework. Building on all the previous units, Chapters 15–17 examine the major areas of public policy: the economy, social welfare, and foreign affairs. These are the system's *outputs:* its binding decisions on society.

The chapters are collectively designed to convey a reliable body of knowledge that will enable the reader to think broadly and systematically

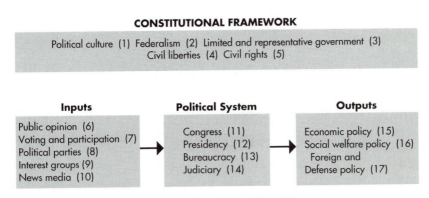

CONSTITUTIONAL FRAMEWORK
Political culture (1) Federalism (2) Limited and representative government (3) Civil liberties (4) Civil rights (5)

Inputs	Political System	Outputs
Public opinion (6) Voting and participation (7) Political parties (8) Interest groups (9) News media (10)	Congress (11) Presidency (12) Bureaucracy (13) Judiciary (14)	Economic policy (15) Social welfare policy (16) Foreign and Defense policy (17)

FIGURE 1-2 THE AMERICAN DEMOCRACY
The book's chapters are organized within a political systems framework.

about the nature of the American political system. To assist in this process, this chapter has identified five encompassing tendencies of American politics that will be examined more closely in later chapters. The United States has:

- An enduring set of cultural ideals that are its people's common bond and a source of their political goals
- An extreme fragmentation of governing authority that is based on an elaborate system of checks and balances
- A great many competing interests that are the result of the nation's great size, population diversity, and economic complexity
- A strong emphasis on individual rights that is a consequence of the nation's political traditions
- A sharp separation of the political and economic spheres that has the effect of placing many economic issues outside the reach of political majorities

Underlying this book's concern with the broad patterns of the American political system is a question that must be asked of any democracy: What is the relationship of the people to their government? The answer to this question is the foundation not only of a reasonable assessment of the state of American democracy but also of good citizenship. Responsible citizenship depends finally on an informed perspective, on a recognition of how difficult it is to govern effectively and yet how important it is to try. It cannot be said too often that the issue of governing is the most difficult issue facing any society. Nor can it be said too often that governing is a quest and a search, not a resolved issue. The Constitution's opening phrase, "We, the People," is a call to Americans to join that quest. E. E. Schattschneider said it clearly: "In the course of centuries, there has come a great deal of agreement about what democracy is, but nobody has a monopoly of it and the last word has not been spoken."[27]

SUMMARY

The United States is a nation that was formed on a set of ideals that include liberty, equality, self-government, individualism, diversity, and unity. These ideals became Americans' common bond and today are the basis of their political culture. Although they are mythic, inexact, and conflicting, these ideals have had a powerful effect on what generation after generation of Americans have tried to achieve politically for themselves and others.

Politics is the process by which it is determined whose values will prevail in society. The basis of politics is conflict over scarce resources and competing values. Those who have power win out in this conflict and are able to control governing authority and policy choices. In the case of the United States, no one faction controls all power and policy. Majorities govern on some issues, while groups and elites each govern on other issues.

The play of politics in the United States takes place through rules of the game, which include democracy, constitutionalism, and capitalism. Democracy is rule by the people, which, in practice, refers to a representative system of government in which the people rule through their elected officials. Constitutionalism refers to rules that limit the rightful power of government over citizens. Capitalism is an economic system based on a free market principle that allows the government only a limited role in determining how economic costs and benefits will be allocated.

MAJOR CONCEPTS

authority
capitalism
constitutionalism
democracy
diversity
elitism
equality
government
individualism
liberty

majoritarianism
pluralism
policy
political culture
political system
politics
power
self-government
unity

SUGGESTED READINGS

Bronfenbrenner, Urie, Peter McClelland, Stephen Ceci, Phyllis Moen, and Elaine Wethington. *The State of Americans: This Generation and the Next.* New York: Free Press, 1996. A comprehensive statistical examination of the American people and the issues they face.

Dahl, Robert. *Democracy and Its Critics.* New Haven, Conn.: Yale University Press, 1989. An analysis of democratic politics by a leading advocate of pluralism.

Domhoff, G. William. *The Power Elite and the State: How Policy Is Made in America.* New York: Aldine de Gruyter, 1990. A critical assessment of American government by a leading proponent of elite theory.

Ellis, Richard J. *American Political Cultures.* New York: Oxford University Press, 1993. An assessment of the American political culture which concludes that individualism and egalitarianism are the main dimensions.

Fischer, William, David Gerber, Jorge Guitart, and Maxine Seller. *Identity, Community, and Pluralism in American Life.* New York: Oxford University Press, 1996. Primary source readings on cultural diversity and pluralism in American life.

Fliegelman, Jay. *Declaring Independence: Jefferson, Natural Language, and the Culture of Performance.* Stanford, Calif.: Stanford University Press, 1993. An analysis of the role of language in the forging of a national identity at the founding of the American state.

Lipset, Seymour Martin. *American Exceptionalism: A Double-Edged Sword.* New York: Norton, 1996. Argues that Americans' tendency to view society in idealized terms is a source of both alienation and progress.

Norton, Anne. *Republic of Signs: Liberal Theory and American Popular Culture.* Chicago: University of Chicago Press, 1993. An insightful study of just how deeply American ideals have seeped into the country's symbols and language.

Salins, Peter D. *Assimilation, American Style.* New York: Basic Books, 1996. A study of immigration and its impact on American culture.

Spinner, Jeff. *The Boundaries of Citizenship: Race, Ethnicity, and Nationality in the Liberal State.* Baltimore: Johns Hopkins University Press, 1994. An account of how liberal societies, especially the United States, shape the cultural identity of their citizens.

READING I

The Future of the American Dream
JENNIFER L. HOCHSCHILD

Perhaps like all dreams, the American dream is open to more interpretations than there are interpreters. . . . [People respond to] the phrase by denying it distinctive meaning beyond general human yearnings for a better life, by affirming that it is what distinguishes Americans from Europeans, by celebrating it as the essence of our ideals, and by denouncing it as a hypocritical sham.

The American dream is all of those things and yet is more than a shapeless muddle. As an ideology, it performs brilliantly. It has distinctive boundaries but capacious content. It provides a unifying vision but allows infinite variations within that vision. It can be used to club the poor into accepting their lot, but it can also be used to make the rich squirm about their luxuries. It encourages people not even to see those aspects of society that make the dream impossible to fulfill for all Americans. It can turn "foreigners" into "Americans" whether they wish such a transformation or not. . . .

Ambiguities in the American dream matter to more than philosophers debating its logic or individuals seeking to live by its precepts. They matter to its ability to function as the dominant ideology of a large and complex society. Like paper money, the American dream will succeed only so long as people believe in it. If the gap between praise for winners and blindness to losers, or the contradictory messages about equality and success, become worrisome to all or incapacitating to some, then the dream will lose its power to order social relations.

Its internal ambiguities are one Achilles heel of the American dream. A more simple loss of faith in either its global vision or each tenet is another. Let us consider the faith necessary to accept each tenet first before turning, in final summary, to the global vision.

Americans' proudest rallying cry, embodied in the first tenet of the American dream, is that "all men [*sic*] are created equal." They seek to reconcile that belief with obvious disparities of life circumstances in several ways: some inequalities are temporary but correctable anomalies in an otherwise well-functioning system; some are chosen by or the fault of the less fortunate themselves; some are mere differences. However they explain away inequalities, no American believer in the dream can any longer query as a point of pride, "How much would it be *worth* to a young man entering upon the practice of law, to be regarded as a *white* man rather than a colored one? . . . Indeed, is it [recognition as white] not the most valuable sort of property, being the master-key that unlocks the golden door of opportunity?" Americans must not believe that the United States has immutable caste or class barriers; otherwise, the rest of the American dream is incoherent.

Americans must believe equally in the second tenet for the dream to bear its ideological weight. . . . Americans must blur the distinction between a reasonable anticipation of success and the expectation of it. If they do not, if they engage in too much rational calculation, then too many will reject the ideology as a bad bet.

Third, Americans must believe that talent and effort will eventually yield their due recompense in order to continue to work hard in the face of little reward. They must also believe that *they* have enough talent for their efforts to be rewarded; thus early manuals for success assured readers that "the most completely provable fact in business [is] that brilliance is more likely to be a curse than an asset, and a hard-hitting mediocrity is almost certain to score over genius." Conversely, they must believe that losers deserve to be at the bottom, lest those who later prove to be losers rebel. . . .

The genius of the American dream is the mutual reinforcement of all tenets; its vulnerability is the same. If a substantial number of Americans lose faith in any foundational precept or the whole gestalt, as racial and class antagonism or white modeling of black disillusionment make possible, the American dream can collapse in upon itself as thoroughly as any savings and loan bank. . . .

Should we be sorry if direct racial conflict and indirect racial modeling and influence together make the flaws and ambiguities of the American dream so intolerable that people lose their faith in it? (Precision has its rhetorical costs!)

Certainly the ideology can be used in defense of atomism, materialism, self-righteousness, and priggishness. More fundamentally, it is flawed at the core: in a capitalist economic system, a majoritarian political system, and a status-driven social system, not all Americans can achieve their dreams no matter how hard they try. But the American dream obscures those structural facts under a cloak of individual agency, thus giving people unjustified hopes and unwarranted feelings of failure.

But debased interpretations can be contested, and it is that very insistence on hope and agency that is the glory as well as the shame of the American dream. No matter who they are, people can make a real difference, as *they* define it, in their own lives and the lives of those they love—I, along with millions of others, find that simple and powerful assertion hard to reject *as a matter of belief, not of fact.*

And anyway, I do not see an alternative that is both plausible and preferable. On plausibility: the American dream is deeply embedded in most Americans' images of themselves and their society, even—or especially—among those most critical of its practice. It has outlasted powerful contenders for ideological domination; it has been embodied in institutions ranging from western land grants to the Civil Rights Act; its protagonists have honed its internal symmetries of optimism and discipline, self-aggrandizement and self-control, morality and hypocrisy into a brilliant balance.

I see only two plausible alternatives to the dominance of the American dream, and neither in my view is preferable. One is ascriptive Americanism, defined as racial, class, and gender hierarchy rationalized by a claim that those on top have "an identity that has inherent and transcendent worth, thanks to nature, history, and God." This whole book is devoted to the eradication of that alternative (although my refusal to make predictions indicates my fear that ascriptive Americanism will prove stronger than the American dream, at least in the arena of race).

The second plausible alternative to the American dream, at least in the arena of race, is black nationalism, whether in the guise of Afrocentrism, the Nation of Islam, or something else. It is not a plausible alternative for more than a tiny fraction of whites, and so far it has not persistently attracted more than a small minority of blacks. But it could, if the American dream yields to ascriptive Americanism among many white Americans.

Those moves—to symmetrical black nationalism and white ascriptivism—would be unfortunate, for two reasons. First, I still hold out the hope that the American dream itself will solve many of the problems of the dream. If Americans faced up to their situation, they could use the optimistic, inclusive, generous elements of their dominant ideology to override the harsh, exclusionary, hypocritical elements of it. Ideally, all Americans will fight their own worst instincts by mobilizing their best; that was Gunnar Myrdal's vision, and Martin Luther King, Jr.,'s after him. Alternatively, some Americans will use the dream's best features to contest other Americans taking advantage of its worst.

My other reason for preferring that African Americans not turn to nationalism or whites to ascriptive Americanism was best articulated by James Baldwin. Let me allow him the last word:

> Each of us, helplessly and forever, contains the other—male in female, female in male, white in black, and black in white. We are part of each other. Many of my countrymen appear to find this fact exceedingly inconvenient and even unfair, and so, very often, do I. But none of us can do anything about it.

SOURCE: Jennifer L. Hochschild, *Facing Up to the American Dream: Race, Class, and the Soul of the Nation* (Princeton, N.J.: Princeton University Press, 1995). Reprinted by permission.
Jennifer L. Hochschild is professor of political science at Princeton University.

CHAPTER TWO

Federal Government

The question of the relation of the states to the federal government is the cardinal
question of our Constitutional system. It cannot be settled by the opinion of one
generation, because it is a question of growth, and each successive stage of our
political and economic development gives it a new aspect, makes it a new question.

WOODROW WILSON[1]

ENATE MAJORITY Leader Trent Lott declared it a great day for
those who believe that the answers to America's problems are more
likely to be found in Albany, Sacramento, and Jackson than in Washington.
His counterpart in the House of Representatives, Newt Gingrich, said the
legislation would restore Americans' faith in work and responsibility.

Senator Daniel Patrick Moynihan, an outspoken critic of the legislation,
called it "the most brutal act of social policy since Reconstruction." The
Urban Institute estimated that within a decade the legislation would push
more than 1 million children into poverty.[2]

At issue was the nation's program of assistance for poor families and
whether the program would be directed by the national government or the
states. Since the 1930s, the program had been run out of Washington as an
entitlement policy, which meant that every American family who met the eligibility criteria was entitled to assistance. For many liberal Democrats, it
was the cornerstone of the idea that no needy American family, wherever it
resided, would be denied help. Individual states had some leeway in deciding the amount of support a needy family would receive each month, but they
had to participate in the program and contribute to its funding.

The new legislation ended the six-decades federal guarantee of cash assistance, replacing it with a system of cash grants to the states, which would
assume responsibility for caring for welfare recipients and getting them into
jobs. The legislation fulfilled the long-held desire of conservative Republicans to reduce welfare dependency and move welfare recipients into taxpaying jobs. It also met their goal of reducing the power of the federal government. Under the new program, states would have to support a needy

family for five years but could deny benefits if, after two years, an able-bodied adult refused to accept a job or job training. And after five years, a state could unconditionally deny benefits to poor families.

The welfare reform bill of 1996 is one of thousands of controversies during American history that have hinged on whether national or state authority should prevail. Americans possess what amounts to dual citizenship: they are citizens both of the United States and of the state where they reside. The American political system is a **federal system,** one in which constitutional authority is divided between a national government and state governments: each is assumed to derive its powers directly from the people and therefore to have sovereignty (final authority) over the policy responsibilities assigned to it. The federal system consists of nation and states, indivisible and yet separate.[3]

This initial chapter on American constitutionalism focuses on federalism. The nature of the relationship between the nation and the states was the question that dominated all others when the Constitution was written in 1787, and this chapter describes how the issue helped form the Constitution. The chapter's concluding sections discuss the evolution of federalism over the course of the nation's history and end with a brief overview of contemporary federalism. The chapter's main points are the following:

* *The power of government must be equal to its responsibilities. The Constitution was needed because the nation's preceding system (under the Articles of Confederation) was too weak to accomplish its expected goals.*

* *Federalism—the Constitution's division of governing authority between two levels, nation and states—was the result of political bargaining.*

* *Federalism is not a fixed principle for allocating power between the national and state governments, but a principle that has changed over the course of time in response to changing political needs.*

* *Contemporary American federalism tilts toward cooperative action between states and nation, reflecting the increased interdependence of American society. However, there is a current trend toward reducing the role of the federal government, a process that is termed devolution.*

BEFORE THE CONSTITUTION: THE ARTICLES OF CONFEDERATION

On June 12, 1776, as the thirteen American colonies braced for full-scale revolutionary war against England, the Continental Congress appointed a committee composed of a member from each colony to decide the form of a central government. The task would be difficult. The colonies had always been governed separately, and their residents considered themselves Virginians, New Yorkers, or Pennsylvanians as much as they thought of themselves as Americans.

This concern led to the formation of a very weak national government that was subordinate to the states. Under the Articles of Confederation, each state kept its "sovereignty, freedom, and independence." There was a national Congress, in which each of the thirteen states had one vote, but the agreement of nine states was required to pass legislation.

The American union held together during the Revolutionary War out of necessity: the states had either to cooperate or to surrender to the British. But once the war ended in 1783, the states felt free to go their separate ways. Several states sent representatives abroad to negotiate trade agreements. New Hampshire, with its eighteen-mile coastline, even established its own navy. In a melancholy letter to Thomas Jefferson, George Washington wondered whether the United States deserved to be called a nation.

A Lack of National Power

Under the Articles of Confederation, Congress was denied the powers it needed if it was to achieve national goals. Although Congress had responsibility for defense of the states, it was not granted the power to tax, so it had to rely on the states for money. During the first six years under the Articles, Congress asked the states for $12 million but received only $3 million—not even enough to pay the interest on Revolutionary War debts. Georgia and North Carolina contributed no money at all to the national treasury between 1781 and 1786. By 1786 the national government was so desperate for funds that it had fewer than 1,000 soldiers in uniform—this at a time when England still had an army in Canada.

Congress was also expected to shape a national economy, yet it was powerless to do so because the Articles forbade Congress from interfering in the states' commerce policies. States imposed trade barriers among themselves. Connecticut, for instance, placed a higher tariff on finished goods from Massachusetts than it did on the same goods shipped from England.

The Articles of Confederation showed the fallacy of the adage "That government is best which governs least." The consequences of an overly weak authority were abundantly clear: public disorder, economic chaos, and inadequate defense.

A Nation in Disarray

By 1784 the nation was unraveling. Congress was so weak that its members often did not bother to attend its sessions.[4] Finally, in late 1786, a revolt in western Massachusetts prompted leading Americans to conclude that the country's government had to be changed. A ragtag army of 2,000 farmers, armed with pitchforks, marched on county courthouses to prevent foreclosures on their land. Many of the farmers were veterans of the Revolutionary War; their leader, Daniel Shays, had been a captain in the Revolutionary army. They had been given assurances during the Revolution that their land, which lay fallow because they were away at war, would not be confiscated for reasons of unpaid debts and taxes.

Although many Americans sympathized with the farmers, Shays' Rebellion scared propertied interests, and they called upon the governor of Massachusetts to put down the revolt. He asked Congress for help, but it had no army to send.[5] He finally raised enough money to hire a militia that put down the revolt, but Shays' Rebellion made it clear that a stronger national government was necessary if the United States was to be saved. At the

The Constitution was written during the summer of 1787 in the East Room of the Old Pennsylvania State House, where the Declaration of Independence had been signed a decade earlier. The room was shuttered to keep eavesdroppers from listening in on the debate. Today, the building is a historical site. (Werner Krutein/Gamma-Liaison International)

urging of the legislatures of several states, Congress authorized a constitutional convention to be held in late spring of 1787 in Philadelphia. Congress planned a limited convention: the delegates were to meet for "the sole and express purpose of revising the Articles of Confederation."

NEGOTIATING TOWARD A CONSTITUTION

The delegates to the Philadelphia constitutional convention ignored the instructions of Congress. They drafted a plan for an entirely new form of government. Prominent delegates (among them George Washington, Benjamin Franklin, and James Madison) were determined from the outset to establish an American nation built upon a strong central government. Recognizing what was likely to happen in Philadelphia, Patrick Henry, a fervent believer in state-level government, said that he "smelt a rat." When the convention adjourned, he realized that his fears were justified. "Who authorized them" he asked, "to speak the language of 'We, the People,' instead of 'We, the States'?"[6]

That question—"people or states?"—was the central one confronting the Philadelphia convention. If the national government was to be effective, as Pennsylvania's James Wilson argued, it had to be a government of the people, not of the states. The Confederation was inherently weak because the central government had no sure way short of war on a state to make it comply with the laws.

The process of writing the Constitution was a contentious one. All the delegates were men of means: they were for the most part lawyers, large landowners, and merchants. They shared a commitment to the interests of the propertied class, but they also had their differences. The Constitution is sometimes portrayed as the work of intellectual geniuses who put politics aside to create a document that would endure the test of time. In reality, the Framers of the Constitution fought like any other group of politicians, each promoting the ideas and values in which he believed. What set the Framers apart was the nature of the times in which they lived. They had experienced the American Revolution and the problems of nation building. They had thought long about and worked hard at the problems of government, and the Philadelphia convention gave them a unique opportunity to apply the constitutional opinions they had formed.

The Framers were astute politicians. After the Constitution was written, they decreed that it would take effect if ratified in special conventions by nine of the thirteen states. In establishing this process the Framers ignored their mandate from Congress, which required any change in the Articles to be confirmed by all the states. The Constitution would not have been adopted if Congress's procedure had been followed. North Carolina and Rhode Island were steadfastly opposed to the Constitution until it was clear that the other states would form a union without them, leaving them weak and isolated.

The Great Compromise: A Two-Chamber Congress

Debate at the constitutional convention of 1787 began over a plan put forward by the Virginia delegation, which was dominated by strong nationalists. The Virginia Plan (also called the large-state plan) called for a two-chamber Congress that would have supreme authority in all areas "in which the separate states are incompetent," particularly defense and interstate trade. The Virginia Plan also provided that the states would have numerical representation in Congress in proportion to their populations or tax contributions. Either way, the larger states would have the more powerful role in the national government.

Not surprisingly, delegates from the smaller states attacked the Virginia Plan. They rallied around a counterproposal made by New Jersey's William Paterson. The New Jersey Plan (also called the small-state plan) called for a stronger national government with the power to tax and to regulate commerce among the states. In most other respects, however, the Articles would remain in effect. Congress would have a single chamber in which each state, large or small, would have a single vote.

The debate over the New Jersey and Virginia plans dragged on for weeks before the delegates reached what is now known as the Great Compromise. It provided for a bicameral (two-chamber) Congress: the House of Representatives would be apportioned among the states on the basis of population and the Senate on the basis of an equal number of votes (two) for each state. The small states would never have agreed to join a union in which their vote was always weaker than that of large states,[7] a fact reflected in Article V of the Constitution: "No state, without its consent, shall be deprived of its equal suffrage in the Senate."

The North–South Compromise: The Issue of Slavery

The separate interests of the states were also the basis for a second major compromise: a North–South bargain over economic issues. The South had a slave-based agricultural economy, and its delegates feared that the North, which had a stronger manufacturing sector, would gain a numerical majority in Congress and then proceed to enact unfair tax policies. Its delegates also worried that northern representatives in Congress might bar the importation of slaves.

After extended debate, a compromise was reached. Congress was to be prohibited from taxing exports but could tax imports. In addition, Congress would be prohibited from passing laws to end the slave trade until 1808. A final bargain was the infamous "Three-fifths Compromise": for purposes of both taxation and representation in Congress, five slaves were to be considered the equivalent of three white people; in effect, a slave was to be counted as three-fifths of a human being. Although the Philadelphia convention has been criticized for the compromise over slavery, the issue of slavery was a pow-

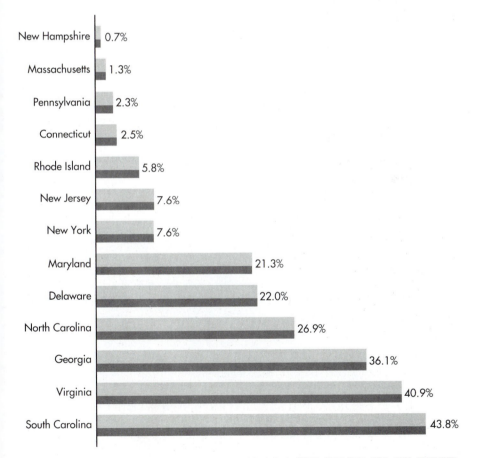

FIGURE 2-1 AFRICAN AMERICANS AS A PERCENTAGE OF STATE POPULATION, 1790. Source: U.S. Bureau of the Census, 1996.

erful argument against a union. Southern states had based their economies on large slave populations (see Figure 2-1). John Rutledge of South Carolina asked during the convention debate whether the North regarded southerners as "fools." Southern delegates declared that they would bolt the convention and form their own union rather than join one that prohibited slavery.

FEDERALISM: NATIONAL AND STATE SOVEREIGNTY

Viewed historically, the most important constitutional decision of the Philadelphia convention was one that underpinned all the deliberations but was not itself debated at great length. This decision was the establishment of **federalism,** which is a system in which **sovereignty,** or the ultimate governing authority, is divided between a national government and regional (that is, state) governments. Because of federalism, the U.S. national government must act with due regard for the states, which are protected constitutionally from being abolished and from unwarranted interference in their policies.

American federalism is a system for dividing power between the national and state governments (see Figure 2-2). The national government has primary responsibility, for example, for national defense and the currency, while

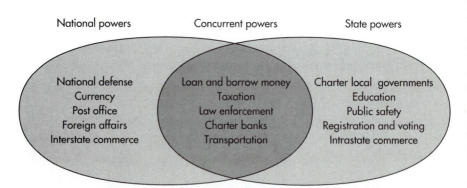

National powers	Concurrent powers	State powers
National defense Currency Post office Foreign affairs Interstate commerce	Loan and borrow money Taxation Law enforcement Charter banks Transportation	Charter local governments Education Public safety Registration and voting Intrastate commerce

FIGURE 2-2 FEDERALISM AS A GOVERNING SYSTEM: EXAMPLES OF NATIONAL, STATE, AND CONCURRENT POWERS
The American federal system divides sovereignty between a national government and the state governments. Each is constitutionally protected in its existence and authority, even though their powers overlap in some cases.

the states have primary responsibility for public education and public safety, among others. The national and state governments also have some concurrent powers; for example, each has the power to raise taxes and borrow money.

Unlike many other features of the U.S. Constitution, the provisions for federalism had no basis in political theory. Indeed, federalism did not exist anywhere in the world before 1787. The United States had been governed as a **confederacy,** in which sovereignty was vested entirely in the state governments. Other countries had unitary systems of government. A **unitary system** vests sovereignty solely in the national government, which has the authority to determine the structure and powers of the governments under it (see box: How the United States Compares).

Within the U.S. federal system, there is a form of unitary government in the relationship between the states and their local governments. Although local units often have considerable autonomy, it is granted at the discretion of the state government, which can overturn local policy and in some circumstances can even abolish a local unit.

Federalism was an accommodation between the ideals of unity and diversity. The states already existed and had the loyalty of their people. When Virginia's George Mason said that he would never consent to a union that abolished the states, he was speaking for nearly all the delegates in Philadelphia. Americans would be governed as one people through their national government and as separate peoples through their respective state governments.

The Powers of the Nation

The Philadelphia convention met to decide the powers of the national government. Accordingly, the U.S. Constitution focuses primarily on the lawful authority of the national government, which is provided through *enumerated* and *implied powers.* Authority that is not in this way granted to the national government is left—or "reserved"—to the states. Thus the states have *reserved powers.*

ENUMERATED POWERS   The primary goal of the writers of the Constitution was to establish a national government strong enough to forge a union that was secure in its defense and open in its commerce. The powers necessary to the achievement of this goal were granted to Congress, which would make the laws. The president would execute the laws and the judiciary would rule upon them.

Congress's lawmaking powers are listed in Article I, section 8, of the Constitution. Seventeen in number, these **enumerated** (or **expressed**) **powers** include, for instance, the powers to tax, to establish an army and navy, to declare war, to regulate commerce among the states, to create a national currency, and to borrow money. In theory at least, these powers would enable the national government to achieve the goals that the government of

HOW THE UNITED STATES COMPARES

Federal versus Unitary Governments

Federalism involves the division of sovereignty between a national government and subnational (such as state) governments. It was invented in 1787 in order to maintain the preexisting American states while establishing an effective central government. Since then a number of other countries have established a *federal* government, but most countries have a *unitary* government, in which all sovereignty is vested in a national government. In some cases, countries have developed hybrid versions. Great Britain's government is formally unitary, but Parliament has granted some autonomy to regions. Mexico's system is formally federal, but in actuality nearly all power is concentrated in the national government.

Country	*Form of Government*
Canada	Federal
France	Unitary
Germany	Federal
Great Britain	Modified unitary
Italy	Modified unitary
Japan	Unitary
Mexico	Modified federal
United States	Federal
Sweden	Unitary

the Articles of Confederation had been unable to achieve. Congress's powers of commerce and currency, for example, would allow it to create a foundation for a viable national economy.

The writers of the Constitution recognized that the lawful exercise of national authority would at times conflict with the actions of the states. In such instances, national law was intended to prevail. Article VI of the Constitution grants this dominance in the so-called **supremacy clause,** which provides that "the laws of the United States . . . shall be the supreme law of the land."

IMPLIED POWERS   The Framers also recognized that an overly narrow definition of national authority would result in a government incapable of adapting to change. Under the Articles of Confederation, Congress was limited to those powers expressly granted to it, inhibiting its ability to respond effectively to the country's changing needs after the Revolutionary War. Concerned that the enumerated powers by themselves might be too restrictive of national authority, the Framers added the **"necessary and proper" clause,** or, as it later came to be known, the **elastic clause.** Article I, section 8, gives Congress the power "to make all laws which shall be necessary and proper for carrying into execution the foregoing [enumerated] powers." This grant gave the national government **implied powers:** the authority to take action that is not expressly authorized by the Constitution but that supports actions that are so authorized.

The Powers of the States

The Framers' preference for a sovereign national government was not shared in 1787 by all Americans. Although Anti-Federalists (as opponents of the Constitution were called) recognized a need to strengthen defense and interstate commerce, they feared the consequences of a strong central government. The interests of the people of New Hampshire were not identical to those of Georgians or Pennsylvanians, and the Anti-Federalists argued that only state-centered government would protect and preserve this diversity.

The Federalists (supporters of the Constitution) responded by asserting that the national government would have no interest in submerging the states. The national government would take responsibility for establishing a strong defense and for promoting a sound economy, while the states would retain nearly all other governing functions, including oversight of public morals, education, and safety. The national government, James Madison said, would neither want these responsibilities nor have the competence to fulfill them.[8]

This argument did not persuade the Anti-Federalists that their fears of an intrusive national government were unfounded. Even some of the Americans who were otherwise inclined to support the proposed constitution worried that it would lead to an overly powerful national government. The supremacy and "necessary and proper" clauses were particularly worrisome, since they provided a constitutional basis for future expansions of national authority. Such concerns led to demands for a constitutional amendment that would protect the states against encroachment by the national government. Ratified in 1791 as the Tenth Amendment to the Constitution, it reads: "The powers not delegated to the United States by the Constitution, nor prohibited by it to the States, are reserved to the States. . . ." The states' powers under the U.S. Constitution are thus called **reserved powers.**

FEDERALISM IN HISTORICAL PERSPECTIVE

Since ratification of the Constitution two centuries ago, no aspect of it has provoked more frequent or bitter conflict than federalism. By establishing two levels of sovereign authority, the Constitution created competing centers of power and ambition, each of which was sure to claim disputed areas as belonging within its realm of authority.

Conflict between national and state authority was also ensured by the brevity of the Constitution. The Framers deliberately avoided detailed provisions, recognizing that brief phrases would give flexibility to the government they were creating. The document does not define what is meant by the "necessary and proper" clause, does not list any of the states' reserved powers, does not indicate whether the supremacy clause allows the states discretionary authority in areas where state and national responsibilities overlap, and does not indicate how *inter*state commerce (which the national government is empowered to regulate) differs from *intra*state commerce (which presumably is reserved for regulation by the states).

Not surprisingly, federalism has been a contentious and dynamic system, its development determined less by constitutional language than by the strength of contending interests and by the country's changing needs. Federalism can be viewed as having progressed through three historical eras, each of which has involved a different relationship between nation and states.

An Indestructible Union (c. 1789–1865)

The issue during the first era, which lasted from the Constitution's beginnings in 1789 through the end of the Civil War in 1865, was the Union's survival. Given the state-centered history of America before the Constitution, it was inevitable that the states would dispute national policies that they perceived as inimical to their separate interests.[9]

THE NATIONALIST VIEW: *McCulloch v. Maryland*   A first dispute over federalism arose early in George Washington's presidency when his secretary of the treasury, Alexander Hamilton, proposed the creation of a national bank. Thomas Jefferson, Washington's secretary of state, opposed the bank on the grounds that its activities would benefit commercial interests and would harm small farmers, who in Jefferson's view were the backbone of the new nation. Jefferson rejected Hamilton's claim that because the government had constitutional authority to regulate currency, the "necessary and proper" clause allowed it to establish a national bank.

Hamilton's view prevailed when Congress in 1791 established the First Bank of the United States, granting it a twenty-year charter. Congress did

Alexander Hamilton (1757–1804), a strong nationalist, was just thirty-two years old when he served as a delegate to the Constitutional Convention. (Courtesy of the New York Historical Society, NYC)

not renew the charter when it lapsed in 1811 but, in 1816, established the Second Bank of the United States over the objections of state and local bankers. Responding to their complaints, several states, including Maryland, attempted to drive the Second Bank of the United States out of existence by levying taxes on its operations within their borders. Edwin McCulloch, who was in charge of the U.S. Bank in Maryland, refused to pay the Maryland tax, and the resulting dispute reached the Supreme Court.

John Marshall, the chief justice of the Supreme Court, was, like Hamilton, a strong nationalist, and in *McCulloch* v. *Maryland* (1819) the Court ruled decisively in favor of national authority. It was reasonable, Marshall concluded, to infer that a government with powers to tax, borrow money, and regulate commerce could establish a bank in order to exercise those powers properly. Marshall's argument was a clear statement of implied powers—the idea that, through the "necessary and proper" clause, the national government's powers extend beyond a narrow reading of its enumerated powers.

Marshall also addressed the meaning of the Constitution's supremacy clause. The state of Maryland argued that it had the sovereign authority to tax the national bank even if the bank was a legal entity. The Supreme Court rejected Maryland's position, concluding that valid national law prevailed over conflicting state law. Because the national government had the power to create the bank, it could also protect the bank from actions by the states, such as taxation, that might destroy it.[10]

The *McCulloch* decision served as precedent for future assertions of national authority.[11] This constitutional interpretation was of the utmost significance: as Justice Oliver Wendell Holmes, Jr., noted a century later, the Union could not have survived if each state had been allowed its own interpretation of national law.[12]

THE STATES'-RIGHTS VIEW Although John Marshall's ruling in the *McCulloch* case helped strengthen national authority, the issue of slavery posed a growing threat to the Union's survival. Fearful that Congress might move to abolish slavery, southerners consequently did what others have done throughout American history: they devised a constitutional argument to fit their political needs. John C. Calhoun of South Carolina argued that the Constitution had created "a government of states . . . not a government of individuals."[13] This reasoning led Calhoun to his famed "doctrine of nullification," which declared that each state had the constitutional right to nullify a national law.

In 1832 South Carolina invoked this doctrine, declaring "null and void" a tariff law that favored northern interests. President Andrew Jackson retorted that South Carolina's action was "incompatible with the existence of the Union," a position that was strengthened when Congress authorized Jackson to use military force against South Carolina. The state backed down when Congress agreed to amend the tariff act slightly.

The clash foreshadowed a confrontation of far greater scope and consequence: the Civil War. The war between the states would not break out for another thirty years, but, in the interim, conflicts over states' rights intensified.[14] Westward expansion and immigration into the northern states were tilting power in Congress toward the free states, which increasingly signaled their intention to outlaw slavery in the United States at some future time. Attempts to find a compromise acceptable to both the North and the South were fruitless. Slavery was too large and too fundamental an issue to be settled peaceably.

The election in 1860 of the Republican Abraham Lincoln was the occasion for war. A sectional split in the majority Democratic party enabled Lincoln to win the presidency with only 40 percent of the popular vote. He had campaigned on a platform that called for the gradual, compensated abolition of slavery,[15] but even a slow step-by-step process was unacceptable to southern interests. By the time Lincoln took office, seven states had already left the Union. Lincoln chose to wage war on the secessionists, saying in his inaugural address that "The Union is older than the states." In 1865 the superior strength of the Union army settled by force the question of whether national authority would be binding on the states.

Dual Federalism and Laissez-Faire Capitalism (c. 1865–1937)

Although the Civil War preserved the Union, a new challenge to federalism was surfacing. Constitutional doctrine held that certain policy areas, such as interstate commerce and defense, were the clear and exclusive province of national authority, while other policy areas, such as public health and intrastate commerce, belonged clearly and exclusively to the states. This doctrine, known as **dual federalism,** was based on the idea that a precise separation of national and state authority was both possible and desirable. "The power which one possesses," said the Supreme Court, "the other does not."[16]

The Industrial Revolution, however, raised questions about the usefulness of dual federalism as a governing concept. The rapid growth of industry had given rise to large firms, which used their economic power to exploit markets and workers. Government was the only possible counterforce against their economic power. Which level of government—state or national—would regulate business?

JUDICIAL PROTECTION OF BUSINESS   For the most part, the answer was that neither level of government would be permitted to do so. The Supreme Court was dominated by adherents of the doctrine of laissez-faire capitalism (which holds that business should be "allowed to act" without interference), and they interpreted the Constitution in ways that frustrated government's attempts to regulate business activity. In 1886, for example, the Court decided that corporations were "persons" within the meaning of the Fourteenth Amendment, and thus their property rights were protected from substantial regulation by the state governments.[17] The Fourteenth Amendment had been ratified after the Civil War to protect citizens (especially the newly freed slaves) from discriminatory actions by state governments. It was not intended as protection for business.

The Court also weakened the national government's regulatory power by narrowly interpreting its commerce power. The Constitution's **commerce clause** says that Congress shall have the power "to regulate commerce" among the states but does not spell out the economic activities included in the grant of power. When the federal government invoked the Sherman Antitrust Act (1890) in an attempt to break up a monopoly on the manufacture of sugar, the Supreme Court blocked the action, claiming that interstate commerce covered only the "transportation" of goods, not their "manufacture."[18] Manufacturing was deemed part of intrastate commerce and thus, according to the dual federalism doctrine, subject to state regulation only. However, since the Court had previously decided that the states' regulatory powers were restricted by the Fourteenth Amendment, they were relatively powerless to control manufacturing activity.

Although the national government subsequently made some headway in business regulation, the Supreme Court remained an obstacle. An example is the case of *Hammer* v. *Dagenhart* (1918), which arose from a 1916 federal act that prohibited the interstate shipment of goods produced by child labor. The act was popular because factory owners were working children for long hours at very low pay. Citing the Tenth Amendment, the Court invalidated the law, ruling that factory practices could be regulated only by the states.[19] However, in an earlier case, *Lochner* v. *New York* (1905), the Court had prevented a state from regulating labor practices, concluding that such action was a violation of firms' property rights.[20]

Between 1865 and 1937, the Supreme Court's rulings severely restricted national power. Narrowly interpreting Congress's constitutional power to regulate commerce, the Court forbade Congress to regulate child labor and other aspects of manufacturing. (Library of Congress)

In effect, the Supreme Court had denied lawmaking majorities the authority to decide economic issues.[21] Neither Congress nor the state legislatures were permitted to substantially regulate business. As the constitutional scholars Alfred Kelly and Winifred Harbison have concluded, "No more complete perversion of the principles of effective federal government can be imagined."[22]

NATIONAL AUTHORITY PREVAILS   Judicial supremacy in the economic sphere ended abruptly in 1937. For nearly a decade, the United States had been mired in the Great Depression, which President Franklin D. Roosevelt's New Deal was designed to alleviate. The Supreme Court, however, had ruled much of the New Deal's economic recovery legislation to be unconstitutional. A constitutional crisis of historic proportions seemed inevitable until the Court suddenly reversed its position. In the process, American federalism was fundamentally and forever changed.

The Great Depression revealed clearly that Americans had become a national community with national economic needs. By the 1930s, more than half of the population lived in cities (only 20 percent did so in 1860) and more than 10 million workers were employed by industry (only 1 million were so employed in 1860). Urban workers were typically dependent on landlords for their housing, on farmers and grocers for their food, and on corporations for their jobs. Farmers were more independent, but they, too, were increasingly a part of a larger economic network. Their income depended on market prices and shipping costs.[23]

This economic interdependence meant that no area of the economy was immune if things went wrong. When the Depression hit in 1929, its effects could not be contained. A decline in spending was followed by a drop in production, a loss of jobs, unpaid rents and grocery bills, and a shrinking market for foodstuffs, which led to a further decline in spending and so on, creating a relentless downward spiral. At the depths of the Great Depression, one-fourth of the nation's work force was unemployed.

The states by tradition had responsibility for welfare, but they were nearly penniless because of declining tax revenues and the growing ranks of poor people. The New Deal programs offered a way out of the crisis; for example, the National Industrial Recovery Act (NIRA) of 1933 called for a massive public works program to create jobs and for coordinated action by major industries. However, the New Deal was opposed by economic conservatives (who accused Roosevelt of leading the nation down the road to communism) and by justices of the Supreme Court. In *Schechter* v. *United States* (1935) the Court invalidated the Recovery Act by a 5–4 vote, ruling that it usurped powers reserved to the states.[24]

Frustrated by the Court's posture, Roosevelt in 1937 proposed his controversial "Court-packing" plan that would permit an additional justice to be appointed to the Supreme Court whenever a seated member passed the age of seventy. The number of justices would increase, and Roosevelt's appointees would presumably be more sympathetic to his programs. The controversy ended when, for reasons that have never become fully clear, Justice Owen Roberts abandoned his opposition to Roosevelt's policies and thus gave the president a 5–4 majority on the Court.

Within months the Court upheld the 1935 National Labor Relations Act, which awarded employees the right to organize and bargain collectively.[25] In passing the act, Congress had argued that labor–management disputes were disruptive of the national economy and therefore could be regulated through the commerce clause. The Supreme Court's ruling upholding the act effectively marked the end of the Court's interference in Congress's

Hundreds of men wait in a food line for a sandwich and cup of coffee, the gift of a New York City newspaper. State and local governments could not cope with the enormous problems created by the Great Depression, so the federal government stepped in with its New Deal programs, greatly changing the nature of federal–state relations. (AP/Wide World Photos)

commerce decisions.[26] Soon thereafter, the Court also lifted its restrictions on the federal government's taxing and spending decisions.[27]

In effect, the Supreme Court had finally recognized the obvious: that an industrial economy is not confined by state boundaries and must be subject to some level of national regulation if it is to serve the nation's needs and interests.[28] It was a principle that business itself also increasingly accepted. The nation's banking industry, for example, was saved in the 1930s from almost complete collapse by the creation of a federal regulatory agency, the Federal Deposit Insurance Corporation (FDIC). By insuring depositors' savings against loss, the FDIC gave depositors the confidence to keep their money in banks, enabling many banks to remain solvent despite the Depression.

FEDERALISM TODAY

Since the 1930s, the relation of the nation to the states has changed so fundamentally that dual federalism is no longer even a roughly accurate description of the American situation.[29] The national government operates in many policy areas that were once almost exclusively within the control of states and localities. The national government does not dominate these policy areas, but it does have a significant role. Much of this influence stems from social welfare policies that were enacted in the 1960s as part of President Lyndon Johnson's Great Society program, which included initiatives in health care, public housing, nutrition, welfare, urban development, and other areas reserved previously to states and localities.

An understanding of the nature of federalism today requires a recognition of two countervailing trends. The first is a long-term *expansion* of national authority that began in the 1930s and continued for the next half century. The second trend is more recent and involves a partial *contraction* of national authority. Known as "devolution," the recent trend involves "the passing down" of authority from the national government to the state and local levels. Devolution has reversed the decades-long increase in federal authority but only in some areas and then only to some degree. Stated differently, the national government's policy authority has expanded greatly since the 1930s even though that authority has been reduced somewhat in recent years.

We will start with an explanation of the first of these trends: the expansion of federal authority since the New Deal era.

Interdependency and Intergovernmental Relations

Interdependency is a primary reason why national authority has increased so dramatically in the twentieth century. Modern systems of transportation, commerce, and communication transcend local and state boundaries. These systems are national, even international, in scope, which means that problems affecting Americans in one part of the country are likely also to affect Americans living elsewhere. This situation has required Washington to assume a larger policy role: national problems ordinarily require national solutions.

The situation has also encouraged national, state, and local policymakers to work together to solve policy problems. This collaborative effort has been described as **cooperative federalism**.[30] The difference between this system of federalism and the older dual federalism system has been likened to the difference between a marble cake, whose levels flow together, and a layer cake, whose levels are separate.[31] Cooperative federalism is based on shared policy responsibilities rather than sharply divided ones. An example is Medicaid, which provides health care for the poor. The program is jointly funded by the national and state governments, operates within eligibility standards set by the national government, and gives states some latitude in determining the benefits recipients receive. The Medicaid program is not an isolated example. There are literally hundreds of policy programs today that are run jointly by the national and state governments. In many cases, local governments are also involved.

Cooperative federalism should not be interpreted to indicate that the states are now powerless and dependent. States have retained most of their traditional authority. In fact, the states have a larger influence than Washington in many policy areas (see Table 2-1). Nearly 95 percent of the funding for public schools, for example, is provided by states and localities, which also set most of the education standards, from teachers' qualifications to

TABLE 2-1   FEDERAL AND STATE/LOCAL GOVERNMENT
EMPLOYEES, AS PERCENT OF TOTAL GOVERNMENT
EMPLOYEES WHO WORK IN SELECTED POLICY AREAS
Although federal authority has reached into areas traditionally dominated by the state governments, state and local governments still dominate many policy areas. One indicator is the high percentage of government employees in selected areas who work for state or local governments.

Policy Area	Percent of Government Employees Who Are:	
	Federal	State/Local
Education	1%*	99%
Highways	1%*	99%
Health and hospitals	18%	82%
Welfare	2%	98%
Police and fire	7%	93%
Sanitation	1%	99%
National resources	52%	48%
Judicial and legal	13%	87%

SOURCE: U.S. Bureau of the Census, 1996. An asterisk indicates that the number was rounded up to 1 percent.

Cooperative federalism brings federal and state government officials together to try to solve major problems. President Clinton is shown here addressing a meeting of state governors. (Paul Conklin/PhotoEdit)

course requirements to the length of the school day. Further, the policy areas dominated by the states—such as education, law enforcement, and transportation—tend to be those that have the most impact on people's daily lives.

Nevertheless, the federal government's involvement in policy areas traditionally reserved for the states has increased its policy influence and has diminished state-to-state policy differences.[32] Before the enactment of the federal Medicaid program in 1965, for example, poor people in many states were not entitled to government-paid health care. Now most poor people are eligible, regardless of where in the United States they live.

Government Revenues and Intergovernmental Relations

The interdependence of different sectors of modern American society is one of two factors that have compelled the federal government to assume a larger domestic policy role. The other is the federal government's superior ability to tax and borrow.[33] States and localities are in an inherently competitive situation with regard to taxation. People and businesses faced with state or local tax increases can move to another state or locality where taxes are lower. Moreover, the federal government depends almost entirely on forms of taxation, such as personal and corporate income taxes, that automatically increase revenues as the economy expands. State and local governments depend more heavily than Washington on revenue sources, such as license fees and property taxes, that are comparatively inflexible. The overall result is that the federal government raises more tax revenues than do all fifty states and the thousands of local governments combined (see Figure 2-3). Finally, because it controls the American dollar, the federal government has a nearly unlimited ability to borrow money to cover its deficits. States and localities can go bankrupt and therefore cannot as easily find the credit to cover their budget deficits.

FISCAL FEDERALISM   The federal government's revenue-raising advantage has helped make money the basis for many of the relations between the national government and the states and localities. **Fiscal federalism** refers to the expenditure of federal funds on programs run in part through state and local government.[34] The federal government provides some or all of the money for a program, while the states and localities administer it.

The pattern of federal assistance to states and localities during the last four decades is shown in Figure 2-4. Federal grants-in-aid increased tenfold during this period. The sharpest rise occurred in the 1960s and early 1970s as a result of President Johnson's Great Society programs. Even at the height of the New Deal, federal aid had accounted for less than 10 percent of state and local spending. With Johnson's Great Society, however, the figure rose above 20 percent and has remained in that range ever since. In other words,

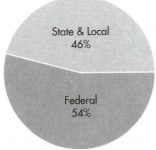

FIGURE 2-3 FEDERAL, STATE, AND LOCAL SHARES OF GOVERNMENT REVENUE
The federal government raises more revenues than all state and local governments combined. Source: U.S. Bureau of the Census, 1996.

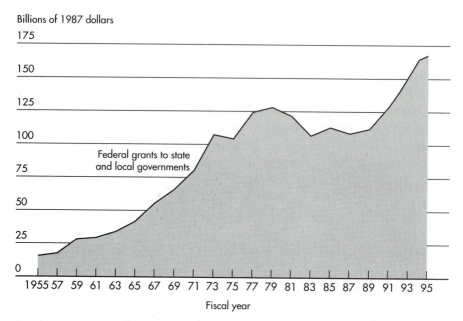

FIGURE 2-4 FEDERAL GRANTS TO STATE AND LOCAL GOVERN-
MENTS IN CONSTANT (1987) DOLLARS, 1955–1995
Federal aid to states and localities has increased dramatically since the 1950s.
Source: U.S. Bureau of the Census, 1996.

about one in every five dollars spent by local and state governments in recent decades was raised not by them, but by the government in Washington
(see box: States in the Nation)

Cash grants to the states and localities have extended Washington's influence over policy.[35] Through its funds and the conditions attached to their
use, the federal government affects the policy choices of state and local governments. They can reject a grant-in-aid, but if they accept it, they must
spend it in the way specified by the federal government. And since most
grants require the states to contribute matching funds, the federal programs
also determine how states will spend some of their own tax dollars.

Nevertheless, federal grants-in-aid also serve the policy interests of state
and local officials. They have often complained that federal grants contain
too many restrictions and infringe too much on their authority, but they have
been eager to get the money since it permits them to offer services they could
not otherwise provide. An example is a 1994 federal grant program that enabled financially strapped local governments to put more than 50,000 additional police officers on the streets.

S T A T E S   I N   T H E   N A T I O N

Federal Grants-in-Aid as a Percent of Total State Revenue

Federal assistance accounts for a significant share of state revenue but the state-to-state variation is considerable. Louisiana is at one extreme: 34.6 percent of its total revenue comes from federal grants. Nevada is at the other extreme: only 14.5 percent of its revenue comes from federal assistance. Ironically, states in regions (the South and Great Plains) where anti-Washington sentiment is relatively high tend to get a larger percentage of their revenue through federal grants than other states do.

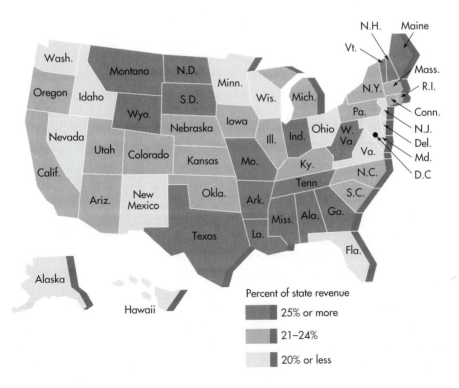

Percent of state revenue

- 25% or more
- 21–24%
- 20% or less

SOURCE: U.S. Bureau of the Census, 1995.

States and localities have the organizational resources to make fiscal federalism a workable arrangement. The national government could not operate the programs on its own because it does not have enough local offices or employees to do the job. States and localities have these resources. In fact, contrary to what many Americans might think, states and localities have nearly five times as many employees as the federal government. Furthermore, all the growth in public employment in the past decade has occurred at the state and local levels; their employment roles have increased by more than 2 million workers, while the number of federal employees has actually declined during this period (see Figure 2-5).

CATEGORICAL AND BLOCK GRANTS State and local governments receive two major types of assistance, categorical grants and block grants, which are differentiated by the extent to which Washington defines the conditions of their use.

Categorical grants are the more restrictive; they can be used only for a designated activity. An example is funds directed for use in school-lunch programs. These funds can be used only in support of school lunches; they cannot be diverted for other school purposes, such as the purchase of text-

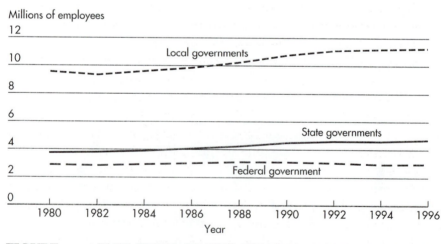

FIGURE 2-5 EMPLOYEES OF THE FEDERAL, STATE, AND LOCAL GOVERNMENTS
Levels of employment in state and local governments have increased in recent years, whereas the number of federal government employees has actually declined somewhat. Source: U.S. Bureau of the Census, 1996.

books or the hiring of teachers. **Block grants** are less restrictive. The federal government specifies the general area in which the funds must be used, but state and local officials select the specific projects. A block grant targeted for health care, for example, might give state and local officials leeway in deciding whether to invest in hospital construction, medical equipment, or some other health-related activity.

State and local officials naturally prefer federal money that comes with few strings attached, so they have favored block grants. On the other hand, members of Congress have at times strongly preferred categorical grants, since this form of assistance gives them more control over how state and local officials will spend federal funds. Recently, however, officials at all levels have looked to block grants as the key to a more workable form of federalism. This tendency is part of a larger trend—that of "devolution."

A New Federalism: Devolution

Devolution is the idea that American federalism will be improved by a shift in authority from the federal government to state and local governments.[36] Devolution, which is reshaping American federalism, is attributable to both practical and political developments.

BUDGETARY PRESSURES AND PUBLIC OPINION   As a practical matter, fiscal federalism peaked in the late 1970s. After that, the federal government's growing budget deficits made grants-in-aid to states and localities an increasingly difficult policy issue. Although assistance levels went up thereafter, the increase was largely attributable to rising program costs (particularly in the health care area) rather than to the creation of expensive new programs.

As budgetary pressures intensified, relations among national, state, and local officials became increasingly strained. Cuts in some federal grants had forced states and localities to pay an increasing share of the costs of joint programs. As they raised taxes or cut other services to meet the costs, taxpayer anger intensified. Some of the grant programs, such as food stamps and Aid to Families with Dependent Children (AFDC), had been unpopular before the budget crunch and now came under even heavier criticism.

By the early 1990s, American federalism was positioned for a major change. Two decades earlier, three-fourths of Americans had expressed confidence in the national government. Less than half of the public now held this view, and most people were more inclined to entrust policy to the state and local governments (see Figure 2-6).

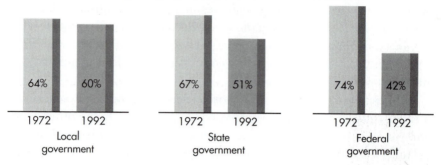

Percent expressing a great deal or a fair amount of confidence:

1972	1992		1972	1992		1972	1992
64%	60%		67%	51%		74%	42%
Local government			State government			Federal government		

FIGURE 2-6 CHANGES IN THE PUBLIC'S CONFIDENCE IN THE FEDERAL, STATE, AND LOCAL GOVERNMENTS
The public's trust in government, particularly at the national level, has declined in recent decades. Source: Surveys for the U.S. Advisory Commission on Intergovernment Relations (ACIR) by the Opinion Research Corporation (1972) and the Gallup Organization (1992).

THE REPUBLICAN REVOLUTION: INNOVATIVE SOLUTIONS OR A RACE TO THE BOTTOM? When the Republican party took control of Congress in 1995, Newt Gingrich declared that "1960s-style federalism is dead." Republicans called for sharp cutbacks in federal grant-in-aid programs, particularly in the welfare area. The Republican majority also proposed to lump dozens of categorical grants into a few block grants, thus giving states more control of how the money would be spent.

These proposals were consistent with the GOP's philosophical stance as the party of smaller government. Although both parties contributed to the expansion of federal authority during the twentieth century, Republicans had more often questioned the overall result. Republican presidents Richard Nixon, Ronald Reagan, and George Bush all advocated some version of a "new federalism" in which some areas of public policy for which the federal government had assumed responsibility would be returned to states and localities.[37]

When Republicans in 1995 took control of both houses of Congress for the first time in forty years, they quickly banned the practice ("unfunded mandates") of imposing costly new programs on the states without also providing the funding to support these programs.[38] But their most significant action in the area of federal–state relations was the sweeping welfare reform bill discussed in the chapter's introduction. Enacted in 1996 and entitled the Personal Responsibility and Work Opportunity Act, the legislation gives states wide latitude in setting benefit levels, eligibility criteria, and other regulations affecting aid for poor families. Its key element is the Temporary Assistance for Needy Families block grant (TANF), which ended the decades-old AFDC program that granted cash assistance to every eligible poor family with children. TANF restricts a family's eligibility for assistance to five years, after which each state can determine what, if any, assistance it will receive. TANF also makes assistance contingent in many instances on the family head's willingness to accept a job or job training.

Advocates of TANF claimed that the states are "laboratories of democracy" and would find innovative ways to provide needy families with assistance and to move able-bodied recipients from welfare to work. Critics painted a darker picture, arguing that the states would engage in "a race to the bottom," competing with each other to slash programs to the bone in order to save money.

In truth, no one is quite sure what the long-term effects of TANF will be, or even whether devolution itself will prove to be a workable idea. What is clear, however, is that American federalism has reached a new stage, where answers to the nation's problems will be sought less in Washington than in the states and localities. (TANF and other aspects of the 1996 welfare reform legislation are discussed further in Chapter 16).

THE PUBLIC'S INFLUENCE: SETTING THE BOUNDARIES OF FEDERAL–STATE POWER   The ebb and flow in Washington's power in the twentieth century has coincided closely with public opinion. The American people have had a decisive voice in determining the relationship between the federal and state governments.

During the Great Depression, when it was clear that the states would be unable to help, Americans turned to Washington for relief. For people without jobs and money, the fine points of the Constitution were of little consequence. President Roosevelt's welfare and public jobs programs were a radical departure from the past but quickly gained widespread support.[39] The second great wave of federal social programs—President Lyndon Johnson's Great Society—was also driven by public demands. Income and education levels had risen dramatically after the Second World War, and Americans wanted more and better services from government. When the states were slow to respond, Americans pressured federal officials to act.[40] Public opinion is also behind the current rollback in federal authority. The Republican takeover of Congress in 1995 was in large part a result of Americans' increased dissatisfaction with the performance of the federal government.[41]

The public's role in defining the boundaries between federal and state power would come as no surprise to the Framers of the Constitution. For them, federalism was a pragmatic issue, one to be decided by the nation's needs rather than inflexible rules. And indeed, each succeeding generation of Americans has seen fit to devise a balance of federal and state power that would serve their interests.

SUMMARY

Perhaps the foremost characteristic of the American political system is its division of authority between a national government and the states. The first U.S. government, established by the Articles of Confederation, was essentially a union of the states.

In establishing the basis for a stronger national government, the U.S. Constitution also made provision for safeguarding state interests. The Great Compromise—whereby each state was equally represented in the Senate, as the smaller states demanded, and membership in the House of Representatives was apportioned by population, as the larger states insisted—was the breakthrough that enabled the delegates to the constitutional convention of 1787 to reach agreement. However, this agreement on the structure of Congress has been less historically significant than the Philadelphia convention's pragmatic decision to create a federal system in which sovereignty was vested in both national and state governments. The Constitution enumerates the general powers of the national government and grants it implied powers through the "necessary and proper" clause. Other powers are reserved to the states by the Tenth Amendment.

From 1789 to 1865, the nation's survival was at issue. The states found it convenient at times to argue that their sovereignty took precedence over national authority. In the end, it took the Civil War to cement the idea that the United States was a union of people, not of states. From 1865 to 1937, federalism reflected the doctrine that certain policy areas were the exclusive responsibility of the national government, while others belonged exclusively to the states. This constitutional position permitted the laissez-faire doctrine that big business was largely beyond governmental control. Federalism in a form recognizable today began to emerge in the late 1930s.

In the areas of commerce, taxation, spending, civil rights, and civil liberties, among others, the federal government now has an important role, one that is the inevitable consequence of the increasing complexity of American society and the interdependence of its people. National, state, and local officials now work closely together to solve the country's problems, a situation that is described as cooperative federalism. Grants-in-aid from Washington to the states and localities have been the chief instrument of national influence. States and localities have received billions in federal assistance; in accepting that money, they have also accepted both federal restrictions on its use and the national policy priorities that underlie the granting of the money.

In the past few years, the relationship between the nation and the states has again become a priority issue. Power is shifting downward to the states, and a new balance in the ever-evolving system of U.S. federalism is taking place. This change, as has been true throughout U.S. history, has sprung from the demands of the American people.

MAJOR CONCEPTS

block grants
categorical grants
commerce clause
confederacy
cooperative federalism
devolution
dual federalism
enumerated powers (expressed
    powers)

federalism
fiscal federalism
implied powers
"necessary and proper" clause (elastic
    clause)
reserved powers
sovereignty
supremacy clause
unitary system

SUGGESTED READINGS

Beer, Samuel H. *To Make a Nation: The Rediscovery of American Federalism*. Cambridge, Mass.: The Belknap Press of Harvard University Press, 1993. An innovative interpretive framework for understanding the impact of federalism and nationalism on the nation's development.

Elkins, Stanley, and Eric McKitrick. *The Age of Federalism: The Early American Republic, 1788–1800*. New York: Oxford University Press, 1993. An award-winning book on the earliest period of American federalism.

Federalist Papers. Many editions, including a one-volume paperback version edited by Isaac Kramnick (New York: Penguin, 1987). A series of essays written by Alexander Hamilton, James Madison, and John Jay under the pseudonym "Publius." The essays, published in a New York newspaper in 1787–1788, explained the Constitution and supported its ratification.

Ferrand, Max. *The Records of the Federal Convention of 1787*. New Haven, Conn.: Yale University Press, 1966. A four-volume work that includes all the important records of the Philadelphia convention.

Maidment, Richard A. *The Judicial Response to the New Deal: The U.S. Supreme Court and Economic Regulation*. New York: Manchester University Press, 1992. An analysis of a major turning point in the constitutional interpretation of federalism.

Ostrom, Vincent. *The Meaning of American Federalism: Constituting a Self-Governing Society.* San Francisco: Institute for Contemporary Studies, 1991. An insightful assessment of federalism by a leading scholar in the field.

Peterson, Paul A. *The Price of Federalism.* Washington, D.C.: Brookings Institution, 1995. A careful analysis of how federalism works, including its costs and benefits.

Ross, William G. *A Muted Fury: Populists, Progressives, and Labor Unions Confront the Courts, 1890–1937.* Princeton, N.J.: Princeton University Press, 1993. A valuable study of the political conflict surrounding the judiciary's laissez-faire doctrine in the 1890–1937 period.

Storing, Herbert. *What the Anti-Federalists Were For.* Chicago: University of Chicago Press, 1981. An analysis of Anti-Federalist thought and its origins.

Thompson, Tommy. *Power to the People: An American State at Work.* New York: HarperCollins, 1996. An argument for state-centered federalism by one of its leading practitioners, the governor of Wisconsin.

R E A D I N G   2

Deficits and Devolution
R. KENT WEAVER

The emergence of devolution as a major component of the agenda of House Republicans in the 104th Congress [1995–96] had complex—and mutually reinforcing—roots. In the terminology of John Kingdom, devolution represented a conjunction of the problem, politics, and policy streams. Ideological mistrust of the federal government, suspicion that many programs did not work or (notably in the case of AFDC) were counterproductive, and anger over the hundreds of social policy funding streams were reinforced by a belief that governments closer to the people are more responsive to popular sentiment and more likely to constrain the growth of those programs. In short, transferring programmatic authority to the states through block grants made sense to conservatives as part of a project of *structural* retrenchment (i.e., not just cutting projected expenditures, but also transforming programs in ways that were likely to weaken the political power of their constituencies in Washington, D.C. and make it much more likely that they would stay smaller in the future).

Deficit reduction also figured directly in the devolution agenda. Giving states increased discretion was used to deflect criticism of budget cuts. States could make up for reduced funding, it was argued, if they had to deal with less red tape and could direct funds to where they were needed most in their states. Having the states make those decisions could at least partially insulate the new Republican majority from any backlash. Replacing open-ended entitlements with capped block grants also allowed escalating savings over time. . . .

It was the conjunction of these political, policy, and problem streams, bringing deficits and devolution together, and that the fact that they appeared to reinforce one another, that made them such an important element of the [Republicans'] *Contract with America*. Rather than having to make difficult trade-offs that would divide the party and alienate constituents, the contract's devolution agenda appeared to make those trade-offs disappear or shift responsibility for them to someone else.

There were, of course, serious limits to the conjunction of deficits and devolution, even at early stages of the process. The Republicans decided not to include Medicaid reform in the *Contract with America* despite the fact that it is by far the biggest grant program, both because they wanted to avoid measures that were likely to alienate voters and because of uncertainty over the fate of the Clinton administration's health care proposal. The strong pressure from social conservatives for anti-illegitimacy and time-limit mandates in family assistance, and work mandates in both family assistance and Food Stamps also complicated devolution initiatives for those programs.

More generally, Republican devolution initiatives were limited by the existing structure of the welfare state. Devolution was proposed primarily in programs where the federal government was already working in partnership with the states rather than by "denationalizing" programs where the federal government had previously acted alone. There were a few exceptions (notably Food Stamps and SSI for disabled children), but even in these cases, the states were already playing an important role in implementing the programs, or the programs were closely related to other programs where the states played the predominant role. The core social insurance programs of the federal government—Social Security and Medicare—remained untouched by the initial deficit-reduction and devolution initiatives contained in the contract, in large measure because (1) the political costs of proposing major structural changes was seen as too high, and (2) without the ability to use devolution to diffuse responsibility for spending cuts, the political costs of proposing deficit-reduction in these programs was intolerable. . . .

Deficit reduction also changed the incentives and behavior of key actors. Belief that deep spending cuts were inevitable clearly increased the interest of Republican governors in winning as much discretion as possible over as many pots of funds as possible in order to compensate at least in part for a decline in the size of overall transfers from the federal government; Republican congressional leaders, seeking allies outside for their program of tough budget cuts, tried to accommodate the governors wherever they could. As Representative Steve Gunderson (R-WI) put it, "We couldn't give them more money, so we had to give them something else." That something else was more flexibility in using federal funds and in shifting those funds among programs. Moreover, having the endorsement of the Republican governors helped to shield Republican leaders in the Congress from charges that they were planning to make the poor worse off. Republican legislators repeatedly defended themselves in congressional debates by asking which governors the Democrats were accusing of plotting to hurt the poor with their new-found autonomy. The response by Democrats and liberal advocacy groups, that it was not gubernatorial malevolence they feared but a silent but inexorable competitive "race to the bottom" between states seeking to avoid becoming a magnet for dependent individuals, is difficult to sell to a public that wants to believe that its elected officials have real choice over public policies.

Insofar as governors were willing to accept reduced funding in exchange for more autonomy—and taking more of the long-term heat for any cutbacks in services—the Republican devolution and deficit-reduction agendas reinforced one another. . . .

At first glance, the experience of the 104th Congress appears to suggest the possibility of a dramatically increased role for the nation's governors as actors on the national political stage. Certainly Republican governors were major participants in the reformulation of contract proposals after November 1994, and the National Governors' Association welfare/Medicaid package helped to set the congressional domestic policy agenda and pave the way for enactment of welfare reform in 1996.

These experiences, however, benefitted from an unusual conjunction of events. Immediately after the 1994 election, most Republican politicians believed that the long-delayed electoral realignment ushering in an era of Republican dominance was finally nearing its culmination. There was thus an unusually strong perception on the part of Republican state and federal politicians that (1) their political fates were intertwined and mutually reinforcing, (2) completing the electoral realignment depended upon enacting real policy change in the Congress, and (3) given the shift in party control of the Congress in 1994, cuts in federal expenditures were inevitable, and the only questions were over their scope, shape, and management. All of these perceptions gave Republican politicians in the Congress and the statehouses powerful incentives to cooperate with each other, and to appear to be cooperative. These incentives were especially strong for several of the key Republican governors who had political ambitions in the national arena.

By early 1996, each of these perceptions appeared less certain than they had at the end of 1994. The bruising budget battles of November 1995 through January 1996 left congressional Republicans divided and less popular with the public. The unpopularity of Speaker Newt Gingrich led many Republican legislators to try to distance themselves from him as they prepared for their upcoming races for reelection. The fact that no budget agreement was reached when the Republican revolution had maximum momentum in 1995 made it seem much less inevitable that Republican cooperation could bring about such cutbacks in the election year of 1996. The experience of Medicaid formula fights in 1995 and the failed effort in early 1996 to substitute a bipartisan NGA initiative on Medicaid for the partisan Republican governors' initiative of the previous year also reinforced awareness of differing state and partisan interests.

The experience of 1995 and 1996, in short, probably does not presage a permanently enhanced role for the governors in national politics. It suggests instead that the form (bipartisan or partisan) and the scope of gubernatorial participation depends very much on an opportunity structure defined primarily by Washington-based politicians. The latter hold the keys to the inner sanctums of Washington policymaking. It is national politicians who decide whether the governors (or some subset of them) will be treated as equal partners in policymaking or as just another interest group, and they make that decision based largely on their own changing interests.

SOURCE: R. Kent Weaver, "Deficits and Devolution in the 104th Congress," *Publius* 26 (Summer 1996): 45–85. Reprinted by permission.
R. Kent Weaver is senior fellow in governmental studies at the Brookings Institution.

CHAPTER THREE

Constitutional Democracy

In framing a government which is to be administered by men over men, the great difficulty lies in this: you must first enable the government to control the governed; and in the next place oblige it to control itself.

JAMES MADISON[1]

WHO'S IN charge here? The Senate majority leader, Trent Lott, said that his legislative chamber with its enlarged Republican majority would play the pivotal role in national policy. The newly reelected Speaker of the House Newt Gingrich took a somewhat different view. He said that his chamber's Republican majority would continue to pursue its agenda, particularly in regard to achieving a balanced federal budget.

For his part, Democratic President Bill Clinton promised to work with the Republican majorities in the House and Senate but claimed he would not be hostage to their agenda. Saying that the American people had re-elected him in 1996 to bring about "responsible change," Clinton threatened to veto any Republican initiative that conflicted with his sense of the nation's best interests.

These varying claims to national leadership can be traced to the work, two centuries ago, of the writers of the Constitution. They sought a government that could satisfy two different and somewhat competing goals. It would have to protect liberty and, at the same time, allow the majority to rule. The first objective was **limited government**—a government that is subject to strict limits on its lawful uses of power. The second objective was **self-government**—a government that is subject to the will of the people as expressed through the preferences of a majority. These objectives are not wholly compatible. Self-government requires that the voters' preferences find their way into public policy in a substantial and timely way. However, liberty requires restraints on the majority as a way of protecting the rights and interests of the minority.

The Framers resolved this conflict through an elaborate system of checks and balances, which allows the majority's will to work through representative institutions but provides for substantial checks on this power. One of these checks is a division of power between the executive and legislative branches, such that neither can act in most cases without the support or acquiescence of the other. Another check is separate elections and terms of office for the president, House, and Senate.

The situation is different elsewhere. In most democracies, all national elected officials are chosen at the same time and for the same term of office, run on a common platform, and operate in a political system where executive and legislative power are combined in a single institution. The connection between election outcomes and policy action is accordingly more direct and predictable than in the United States.

This chapter describes how the principles of self- and limited government are embodied in the Constitution and explains the tension between them. The chapter also indicates how these principles have been modified in practice in the course of American history, before closing with a brief analysis of the contemporary situation. The major ideas that are discussed in the chapter are these:

* *Limited government and democratic government in America had roots in the colonial period.*

* *The Constitution provides for limited government mainly by defining lawful powers and by dividing those powers among competing institutions.*

* *The Constitution provides for self-government mainly through direct and indirect systems of popular election of representatives.*

* *The idea of popular government—in which the majority's desires have a more direct and immediate impact on public policy—has gained strength since the nation's beginning.*

THE ROOTS OF LIMITED GOVERNMENT

Early Americans' admiration for limited government was based partly on their English heritage. Although other European nations of the eighteenth century implicitly acknowledged the divine right of kings, England was an exception. British courts had developed a system of precedent known as "common law," which guaranteed trial by jury and due process of law as safeguards of life, liberty, and particularly property. These rights were defended by the courts and usually respected by the king and Parliament.

The English tradition of limited government was reflected in the American colonial governments. In each colony there was a right to trial by jury.

There was also freedom of expression, although of a limited kind. Religious freedom, for example, was not granted by all colonies.

The Revolutionary War was partly a rebellion against England's failure to respect its own tradition of limited government in the colonies. Many of the colonial charters had conferred upon Americans "the rights of Englishmen," but English kings and ministers showed progressively less respect for this guarantee as time went on. Americans were forced to garrison English soldiers in their homes, and Parliament in 1765 levied a stamp tax on colonial newspapers and business documents, which would have disrupted commerce and public communication. As the colonists were not represented in the British Parliament that had imposed the tax, they refused to pay it. The pamphleteer James Otis declared that the Stamp Act violated the fundamental rights of the colonists as "British subjects and men."

Although Parliament repealed the Stamp Act, it imposed other taxes, including one on tea entering the colonies that was intended mainly to display its authority. The colonists viewed the tea tax as a petty insult, and in the "Boston Tea Party" of December 1773 a small band of patriots disguised as Indians boarded an English ship in Boston Harbor and dumped its cargo of tea overboard. Within three years, sporadic acts of defiance had turned into a full-scale revolution. In a pamphlet called *Common Sense*, Thomas Paine claimed that all of Europe—England, too—was rife with political oppression and that America was humanity's last hope of liberty.

This grand belief was codified in the Declaration of Independence, prepared by Thomas Jefferson and adopted by Congress on July 4, 1776. The Declaration was rooted in the ideas of the English philosopher John Locke (1632–1704) who advanced the liberal principle that people have **inalienable** (or **natural**) **rights,** including those of life, liberty, and property, which belonged to people in their natural state before governments were created. When people agreed to come together (or, in Locke's term, entered into a "social contract") in order to have the protection that only organized government could provide, they retained these natural rights. No government could legitimately deny citizens their rights, and, if it did, they could rebel against it.[2] Even two centuries later, the words of the Declaration of Independence are an eloquent testimony to the Lockean vision of human freedom:

> We hold these truths to be self-evident, that all men are created equal, that they are endowed by their Creator with certain unalienable rights, that among these are life, liberty and the pursuit of happiness.

That to secure these rights, governments are instituted among men, deriving their just powers from the consent of the governed.

That whenever any form of government becomes destructive of these ends, it is the right of the people to alter or to abolish it, and to institute new government. . . .

CONSTITUTIONAL RESTRAINTS ON POLITICAL POWER

The U.S. Constitution was written eleven years after the Declaration of Independence, with a different purpose. The Declaration was a call to revolution. The Constitution would create a framework for government. Nevertheless, a concern for liberty was no less fundamental to the delegates at the constitutional convention in 1787 than it had been to leaders of the Revolution.

The challenge facing the Framers of the Constitution was how to control the coercive force of government. Government's unique characteristic is that it alone can legally arrest, imprison, and even kill people who break its rules.[3] Force is not the only basis of effective government, but govern-

John Locke *(left)* was an English philosopher who contended that every individual has a right to personal liberty. Thomas Jefferson *(right)* admired Locke's views and used some of his phrases almost word for word in writing the Declaration of Independence. *(Left:* National Portrait Gallery, London; *right:* The White House Historical Association; photograph by the National Geographic Society)

ment must have a final recourse to coercion if its authority is to prevail. Otherwise, persons could break the law with impunity, and society would degenerate to anarchy. The dilemma is that government itself can destroy civilized society by using its force to brutalize its opponents. "It is a melancholy reflection," James Madison wrote to Thomas Jefferson shortly after the Constitution's ratification, "that liberty should be equally exposed to danger whether the government has too much or too little power."[4]

This is a portion of Thomas Jefferson's handwritten draft of the Declaration of Independence, a formal expression of America's governing ideals. (Library of Congress)

The men who wrote the Constitution sought to establish a government strong enough to enforce national interests, including defense and commerce among the states (see Chapter 2), but not so strong as to destroy liberty. Limited government was built into the Constitution through both grants and restrictions of political power.

Grants and Denials of Power

The Framers chose to limit the national government in part by confining its scope to constitutional **grants of power.** For example, as we saw in Chapter 2, Congress's lawmaking authority is constitutionally confined to seventeen specified powers. Authority not granted to the government by the Constitution is in theory denied to it. In a period when other governments held broad discretionary powers, this was a remarkable restriction.

The Framers also used **denials of power** as a means to limit government, prohibiting certain practices that European rulers had routinely used to intimidate their political opponents. The French king, for example, could imprison a subject indefinitely without charge or trial. The U.S. Constitution prohibits such action: individuals have the right to be brought before a court under a writ of habeas corpus for a judgment as to the legality of their confinement. The Constitution also forbids Congress and the states from passing *ex post facto* laws, under which citizens can be prosecuted for an act that was not illegal at the time it was committed.

Using Power to Offset Power

Although the Framers believed that grants and denials of power could act as controls on government, they had no illusion that written words alone would restrain power. As a consequence, they sought to check power with power. The idea was to divide the authority of government, so that no single institution could exercise great power without the agreement of other institutions.[5]

The idea that a separation of powers was necessary to the preservation of liberty had been proposed decades earlier by the French theorist Montesquieu. His argument was widely accepted in America, and when the states drafted new constitutions after the start of the Revolutionary War, they built their governments around the concept of a separation of powers. Pennsylvania was an exception, and its experience only seemed to prove the necessity of separated powers. Unrestrained by an independent judiciary or executive, Pennsylvania's all-powerful legislature systematically deprived minority groups of their basic rights and freedoms: Quakers were disenfranchised for their religious beliefs, conscientious objectors to the Revolutionary War were prosecuted, and the right of trial by jury was eliminated.

In *Federalist* No. 10, Madison asked why governments often act according to the interests of overbearing majorities rather than according to principles of justice. He attributed the cause to "the mischiefs of faction." People, he argued, are divided into opposing religious, geographical, ethnic, economic, and other factions. These divisions are natural and desirable, in that free people have a right to their personal opinions and interests. Yet factions can themselves be a source of oppressive government. If a faction gains full power, it will use government to advance itself at the expense of all others. (*Federalist* No. 10 is widely regarded as the finest political essay ever written by an American. It is reprinted in part at the end of this chapter.)

Out of this concern came the Framers' special contribution to the doctrine of the separation of powers. They did not believe that it would be enough, as Montesquieu had suggested, to divide the government's author-

Gilbert Stuart, *Portrait of President James Madison.* Madison
is often called "the father of the Constitution" because he
was instrumental in its writing and in its ratification
(through his contributions to the *Federalist Papers*).
(Bowdoin College Museum of Art, Brunswick, Maine)

ity strictly along institutional lines, granting all legislative power to the legislature, all judicial power to the courts, and all executive power to the presidency. This *total* separation would make it too easy for a single faction to exploit a particular kind of political power. A faction that controlled the legislature, for example, could enact laws ruinous to other interests. A better system of divided government would be one in which political power could be applied forcibly only when institutions agreed on its use. This would require a system of separated but *overlapping* powers. Since no one faction could easily gain control over all institutions, factions would have to work together, a process that would require each to moderate its demands and thus would serve many interests rather than one or a few.[6]

Separated Institutions Sharing Power: Checks and Balances

The Framers' concept of divided powers has been described by political scientist Richard Neustadt as the principle of **separated institutions sharing power.**[7] The separate branches are interlocked in such a way that an elaborate system of **checks and balances** is created (see Figure 3-1). No institution can act decisively without the support or acquiescence of the other institutions. Legislative, executive, and judicial powers in the American system are divided in such a way that they overlap; each of the three branches of government checks the others' powers and balances those powers with powers of its own.

SHARED LEGISLATIVE POWERS   Under the Constitution, Congress has legislative authority, but that power is partly shared with the other branches and thus checked by them. The president can veto acts of Congress, recommend legislation, and call special sessions of Congress. The president also has the power to execute—and thereby to interpret—the laws made by Congress.

The Supreme Court has the power to interpret acts of Congress that are disputed in legal cases. By tradition, the Court also has the power of judicial review; it can declare laws of Congress void when it finds that they are not in accord with the Constitution.

Within Congress, there is a further check on legislative power. Legislation requires a majority in each house of Congress; thus the Senate and the House of Representatives can block each other's actions.

SHARED EXECUTIVE POWERS   Executive power is vested in the president but is constrained by legislative and judicial checks. The president's power to make treaties and appoint high-ranking officials, for example, is subject to Senate approval. In practical terms, Congress's greatest checks on

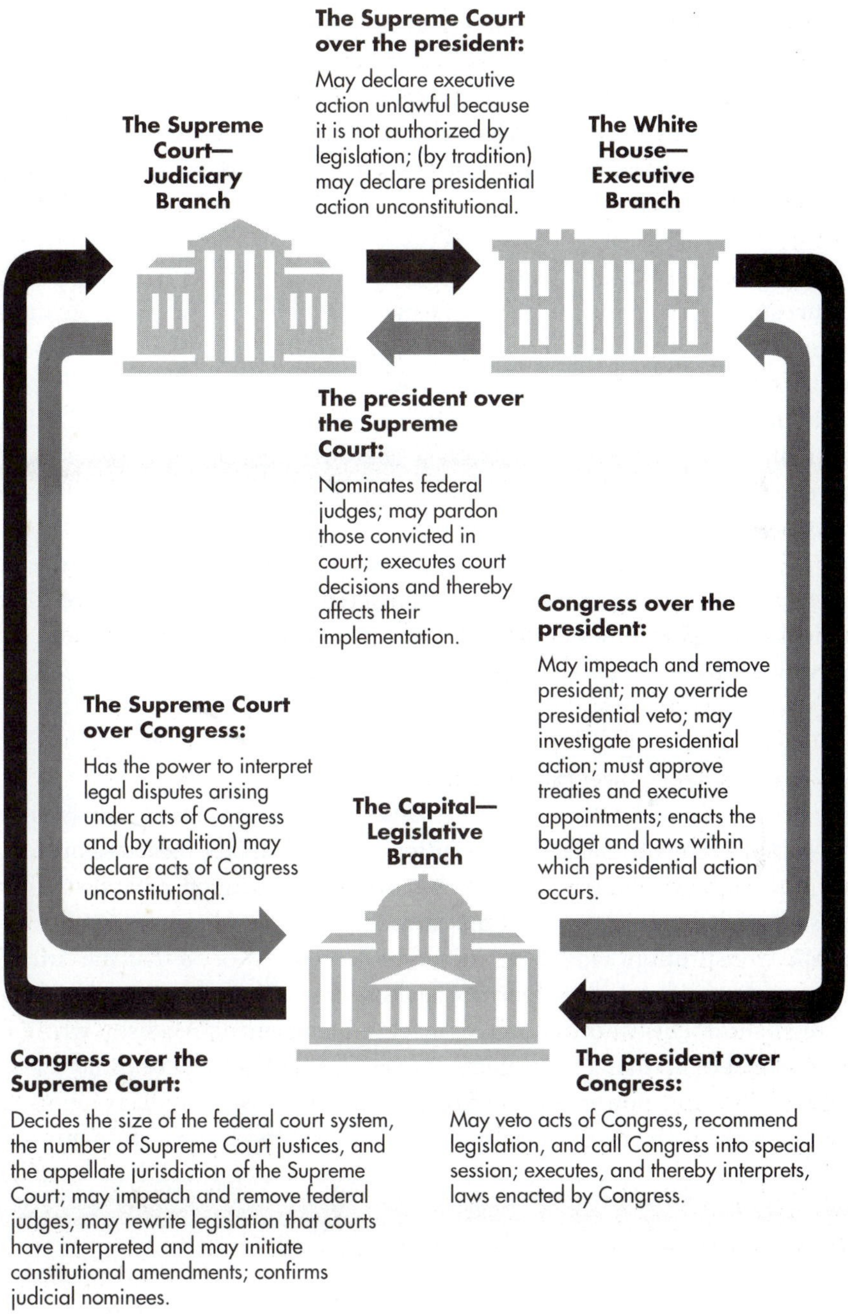

The Supreme Court over the president:

May declare executive action unlawful because it is not authorized by legislation; (by tradition) may declare presidential action unconstitutional.

The Supreme Court— Judiciary Branch

The White House— Executive Branch

The president over the Supreme Court:

Nominates federal judges; may pardon those convicted in court; executes court decisions and thereby affects their implementation.

Congress over the president:

May impeach and remove president; may override presidential veto; may investigate presidential action; must approve treaties and executive appointments; enacts the budget and laws within which presidential action occurs.

The Supreme Court over Congress:

Has the power to interpret legal disputes arising under acts of Congress and (by tradition) may declare acts of Congress unconstitutional.

The Capital— Legislative Branch

Congress over the Supreme Court:

Decides the size of the federal court system, the number of Supreme Court justices, and the appellate jurisdiction of the Supreme Court; may impeach and remove federal judges; may rewrite legislation that courts have interpreted and may initiate constitutional amendments; confirms judicial nominees.

The president over Congress:

May veto acts of Congress, recommend legislation, and call Congress into special session; executes, and thereby interprets, laws enacted by Congress.

FIGURE 3-1 THE SYSTEM OF CHECKS AND BALANCES

executive action are its lawmaking and appropriations powers. The executive branch cannot act without laws that authorize its activities or without the money that pays for these programs.

The judiciary's major check on the presidency is its power to declare an action unlawful because it is not authorized by the legislation that the executive claims to be implementing.

SHARED JUDICIAL POWERS   Judicial power rests with the Supreme Court and with lower federal courts, which are subject to checks by the other branches of the federal government. Congress is empowered to establish the size of the federal court system; to restrict the Supreme Court's appellate jurisdiction in some circumstances; and to impeach and remove federal judges from office. More important, Congress can rewrite legislation that the courts have misinterpreted and can initiate amendments when it disagrees with the courts' rulings on constitutional issues.

The president has the power to appoint federal judges with the consent of the Senate and to pardon persons convicted in the courts. The president is also responsible for executing court decisions, a function that provides opportunities to influence the way rulings are implemented.

Federalism as a Further Check on Government Power

Theorists such as Locke and Montesquieu had not proposed a division of power between national and local authorities as a further means of protecting liberty. Nevertheless, the Framers came to look upon federalism (discussed in Chapter 2) as part of the system of checks and balances established by the Constitution. Hamilton argued in *Federalist* No. 28 that the American people could shift their loyalties back and forth between the national and state governments in order to keep each under control. Madison wrote in *Federalist* No. 51 that a federal system was a superior form of limited government because power was divided between two distinct governments, as well as among their separate branches. "The different governments will control each other," he said, "at the same time that each will be controlled by itself."

The Bill of Rights

Although the delegates to the Philadelphia convention discussed the possibility of placing a list of individual rights (such as freedom of speech and the right to a fair trial) in the Constitution, they ultimately decided that such a

Limits on Government in the U.S. Constitution

Grants of power: Powers granted to the national government by the Constitution. Powers not granted it are denied it unless they are necessary and proper to the carrying out of granted powers.

Denials of power: Powers expressly denied to the national and state governments by the Constitution.

Separated institutions sharing power: The division of the national government's power among three branches, each of which is to act as a check on the powers of the other two.

Bill of Rights: The first ten amendments to the Constitution, which specify rights of citizens that the national government must respect.

Federalism: The division of political authority between the national government and the states, enabling the people to appeal to one authority if their rights and interests are not respected by the other authority.

Judicial review: The power of the courts to declare governmental action null and void when it is found to violate the Constitution.

list was unnecessary because of the doctrine of expressed powers: government could not lawfully assume powers, such as the abridgment of human rights, that were not authorized by the Constitution. Moreover, the delegates concluded that a bill of rights was undesirable because government might feel free to disregard any right that was inadvertently left off the list or that emerged at some future time.

These considerations did not allay the fears of Americans who believed that no safeguard against tyrannical government should be omitted. "A bill of rights," Jefferson argued, "is what the people are entitled to against every government on earth, general or particular, and what no just government should refuse or rest on inference." A bill of rights was included in the constitution Jefferson wrote for Virginia at the outbreak of the Revolutionary War, and all but four states had followed Virginia's example.

Opposition to the absence of a bill of rights in the federal constitution led the Federalists finally to support its addition. Madison himself introduced a series of amendments during the First Congress, ten of which were subsequently ratified by the states. These amendments, traditionally called the *Bill of Rights*, include such rights as free expression and due process for persons accused of crimes. (These rights, termed "civil liberties," are the subject of Chapter 4.)

The Bill of Rights is a precise expression of the concept of limited government. In consenting to be governed, the people agree to accept the authority of government in certain areas but not in others; the people's constitutional rights cannot lawfully be denied by governing officials.

CHECKS AND BALANCES IN PRACTICE

The writers of the Constitution both empowered and limited government. But who was to decide whether the government was operating within its constitutional powers? The Framers did not specifically entrust this power to a particular branch of government, although they did grant the Supreme Court the authority to decide on "all cases arising under this Constitution."

Most delegates to the Philadelphia convention apparently assumed that the Supreme Court would have the power of **judicial review:** the power of the courts to decide whether a governmental institution has acted within its constitutional powers and, if not, to declare its action null and void. There was precedent for judicial review in several states and a form of it had existed during the colonial period. It is also noteworthy that the power of the courts to declare laws null and void was discussed and accepted at the ratifying conventions of at least eight of the thirteen states.[8] Still, because the Constitution did not explicitly provide for judicial review, it was a principle that had to be established in practice.

Interpreting the Constitution: Marbury v. Madison

The opportunity arose with an incident that occurred after the election of 1800, in which John Adams lost his bid for a second presidential term after a bitter campaign against Jefferson. Between November 1800, when Jefferson was elected, and March 1801, when he was inaugurated, the Federalist-controlled Congress created fifty-nine additional lower-court judgeships, enabling Adams to appoint loyal Federalists to those positions before he left office. However, Adams's term expired before the secretary of state could deliver the judicial commissions to all the appointees. Without this formal authorization, an appointee could not take office. Knowing this, Jefferson told his secretary of state, James Madison, not to deliver them. William Marbury was one of those who did not receive his commission, and he asked the Supreme Court to issue a writ of *mandamus* (a court order that directs an official to take a specific action) requiring Madison to deliver it.

Marbury v. *Madison* (1803) became the foundation for judicial review by the federal courts. Chief Justice John Marshall wrote the *Marbury* opinion, which declared that Marbury had a legal right to his commission. The opinion also said, however, that the Supreme Court could not issue him a writ of *mandamus* because it lacked the constitutional authority to do so. Congress had granted the Court the power to issue such writs in the Judiciary Act of 1789, but Marshall pointed out that the Constitution prohibits any extension of the Supreme Court's original jurisdiction except through an amendment to the Constitution. That being the case, Marshall stated, the portion of the Judiciary Act that provided the authorization was constitutionally invalid.[9]

Marshall's decision was ingenious since it asserted the power of judicial review without creating the possibility of its rejection by either the executive or the legislative branch. In declaring that Marbury had a right to his commission, the Court in effect said that President Jefferson had failed in his constitutional duty to execute the laws faithfully. But since it did not order Jefferson to deliver the commission, he had no opportunity to refuse to comply with the Court's judgment. At the same time, the Court admonished Congress for passing legislation that exceeded its constitutional authority. And in the process of invalidating an act of Congress on constitutional grounds, the Court asserted its power of judicial review—that is, the power to determine the rightful limits of the constitutional powers of another branch of government.

Judicial Review in Protection of Liberty

John Marshall served as chief justice for more than thirty years after *Marbury*, and his Court did not again invalidate an act of Congress. Nevertheless, *Marbury* had asserted the principle that the lawful powers of government are subject to judicial scrutiny. *Marbury* became a precedent for later Court rulings that clearly established the Supreme Court's position as the chief authority on the Constitution's grants of power and thus a critical actor in the preservation of limited government. The judiciaries of many other countries lack this authority. The British high court, for example, can-

John Marshall forcefully expressed his nationalist views in
important Supreme Court decisions during his thirty-four
years as chief justice. (Boston Athenaeum Collection)

not invalidate an act of Parliament (see box: How the United States Compares).

Judicial review has been an important element in our system of limited
government. Judicial review was essential if the Court was to be the constitutional equal of the two other branches and thus to have legitimate authority
to act against them when necessary. Neither elected branch has much to gain
and might have much to lose by being rebuffed by the Supreme Court.
Congress and the president have sometimes refrained from actions of questionable constitutionality simply because they knew that the Supreme Court
could rule against them, thereby damaging their prestige and undermining
the legitimacy of their actions.[10]

Ironically perhaps, judicial review's major contribution to the protection
of liberty has come in its application not to actions of Congress or the president but to those of the states. The states have the major responsibility for
law enforcement and other policies where the interests of the majority and
the rights of the individual most directly clash. Moreover, as Madison foresaw in *Federalist* No. 10, the smaller the unit of government, the more likely

a single faction will gain full political power and use it to the disadvantage of others. The clearest example occurred shortly after Reconstruction, when the South's white majority systematically stripped African Americans of their rights. In comparison with the states, periods of repression by the national government have been relatively infrequent, moderate, and brief.[11]

HOW THE UNITED STATES COMPARES

Checks and Balances

All democracies place constitutional limits on the power of government. The concept of rule by law, for example, is characteristic of democratic governments but not of authoritarian regimes. Democracies differ, however, in the extent to which political power is restrained through constitutional mechanisms. The United States is an extreme case in that its government rests on an elaborate system of constitutional checks and balances. The system employs a separation of powers among the executive, legislative, and judicial branches. It also includes judicial review, the power of the courts to invalidate actions of the legislature or executive. These constitutional restrictions on power are not part of the governing structure of all democracies.

Country	Separation of Powers?	Judicial Review?
Belgium	No	No
Canada	No	Yes
France	Yes	No
Germany	No	Yes
Great Britain	No	No
Israel	No	Yes
Italy	No	Yes
Japan	No	Yes
Mexico	In theory only	Yes
United States	Yes	Yes

For a long period, as the next chapter explains, the Bill of Rights did not apply to state and local governments. Since the 1920s, however, the Supreme Court has struck down hundreds of local and state laws in cases that involved issues of individual rights and liberties, such as infringements of free expression, fair trial, and equal protection under the laws. The authors of the Bill of Rights would no doubt be amazed by the range of protections it now encompasses, but they probably would not be surprised that it has become a prime instrument in the protection of individual rights. The Bill of Rights was added to the Constitution to transform what were regarded as inalienable rights into legal rights and thereby, as Justice Robert Jackson noted, "to place them beyond the reach of majorities and officials and to establish them as legal principles to be applied by the courts."[12]

The Separation of Powers

Of all features of the U.S. constitutional system, none has been more important to the control of power than its allocation among separate branches. Throughout most of the country's history, each branch has jealously guarded its authority from the others, a system that has served to check the power of all three branches.

Of course, each branch of the national government has significantly broadened its authority since the Constitution was written 200 years ago. Congress's taxing and commerce powers, the president's executive and national security powers, and the judiciary's power over civil rights and social policy are far greater than anything the Framers could have anticipated in 1787. Such developments might be interpreted as contrary to the Framers' plan to limit government by enumerating the powers granted to it. Yet the writers of the Constitution were well aware that government would necessarily evolve in response to social change. The Framers used broad language when they listed the constitutional powers of the national government and added the "necessary and proper" clause so that their concept of a government with elastic powers would not be misunderstood (see Chapter 2). In the final analysis, however, the Framers recognized that restraints on government rest not with grants and denials of power but with competition for power. "Ambition must be made to counteract ambition," said James Madison in *Federalist* No. 51.

In the American experience, determined action by one branch of government has ordinarily constrained another branch's attempts to overreach its authority. Few events more clearly illustrate this restraint than the Watergate affair, which first came to public attention when five burglars with links to President Richard Nixon's reelection campaign were apprehended inside the National Democratic Party headquarters. Nixon called the incident "bizarre," but the break-in was actually part of an orchestrated campaign of "dirty tricks" designed to ensure Nixon's reelection. Funded by illegal contributions and conducted through the CIA, IRS, FBI, Secret Service, and Nixon's own operatives (called the White House "plumbers"), the dirty-tricks campaign extended to wiretaps, tax audits, and burglaries of Nixon's political opponents (the "enemies list"), who included journalists and antiwar activists in addition to Democrats.

Although the Nixon White House managed for a time to obstruct justice (in one ploy, the president's assistants asked the CIA to tell the FBI to stop the Watergate investigation on fictitious "national security" grounds), the facts of Nixon's dirty-tricks campaign gradually became known. The investigation was helped along, ironically, by Nixon's own words. During Senate hearings, a White House assistant revealed that Nixon had tape-recorded all his telephone calls and personal conversations in the Oval Office. At first Nixon refused to release transcripts of the tapes, but he then made public what he claimed were "all the relevant" ones. The House Judiciary Committee demanded additional tapes, as did the special prosecutor who had been appointed to investigate criminal aspects of the Watergate affair. In late July the Supreme Court of the United States (which included four justices appointed by Nixon) unanimously ordered the president to supply sixty-four additional tapes, which provided incriminating evidence against the president. Two weeks later, on August 9, 1974, Richard Nixon resigned from office, the first president in U.S. history to do so.

REPRESENTATION IN THE CONSTITUTION

"We the People" is the opening line of the Constitution. It expresses the idea that, in the United States, the people will have the power to govern themselves. In a sense, there is no contradiction between this idea and the Constitution's provisions for limited government, since individual liberty is part of the process of self-government. In another sense, the contradiction is clear: restrictions on the power of the majority are a denial of its right to govern society as it chooses.

The Framers believed that the majority's power should be controlled.[13] In their judgment, a great risk of popular government was **tyranny of the majority.** Inflamed by an issue of the moment, the majority could become an irrational mob without any regard for the interests of others. To the Framers, the record of democracies left much to be desired. There were even examples from the nation's brief history since the Revolution. In 1786, debtors had gained control of Rhode Island's legislature and made paper money a legal means of paying debts, even though existing contracts called for payment in gold. Creditors were then hunted down and held captive in public places so that debtors could come and pay off their debts with worthless paper money. A Boston newspaper wrote that Rhode Island should be renamed *Rogue* Island.

Democracy versus Republic

No form of self-government could eliminate completely the threat to liberty of majority tyranny, but the Framers believed that the danger would be greatly diminished by properly structured institutions.[14] Madison summarized the Framers' intent when he said in *Federalist* No. 10 that the Constitution was "a republican remedy" for the excesses historically associated with "democratic" rule. Today the terms **democracy, republic,** and **representative democracy** are used interchangeably to refer to a system of government in which ultimate political power rests with the majority through its capacity to choose representatives in free and open elections. To the writers of the Constitution, however, "democracy" and "republic" had different meanings. When the Framers complained about the risks of democracy, they were referring to "pure democracy," in which popular opinion was translated directly into public policy. In their use of the term "republic," the Framers were referring to representative government in which elected officials met in representative institutions to decide policy through extended debate and deliberation.[15]

The Framers' concept of a proper system of representation was similar to an idea put forth by the English theorist Edmund Burke (1729–1797). In his *Letter to the Sheriffs of Bristol*, Burke argued that representatives should act as public **trustees:** they are obliged to promote the interest of those who elected them, but the nature of this interest is for the representatives, not the voters, to decide. Burke was concerned about the ease with which society could degenerate into selfishness, and he thought it unwise for representatives to surrender their judgment to popular whim.

Limited Popular Rule

The Constitution provided that all power would be exercised through representative institutions. There was no provision for any form of direct popular participation in the making of policy decisions. In view of the fact that the United States was much too large to be governed directly by the people in popular assemblies, a representative system was necessary. Moreover, the separation of powers meant that the majority's will, again by necessity, would be filtered through an institutional structure. The Framers went beyond what was necessary, however, and substantially restricted the public's ability to control their representatives (see Table 3-1).

The House of Representatives was the only institution that would be based on direct popular election—its members would be elected for two-year terms of office through vote of the people. Frequent and direct election of House members was intended to make government sensitive to the concerns of popular majorities.

U.S. senators would be appointed by the legislatures of the states they represented. Because state legislators were popularly elected, the people would be choosing their senators indirectly. Every two years, a third of the senators would be appointed to six-year terms. The Senate was expected to check and balance the House, which, by virtue of the more frequent and direct election of its members, would presumably be more responsive to popular opinion.

TABLE 3-1 METHODS OF CHOOSING NATIONAL LEADERS
Fearing the concentration of political power, the Framers devised alternative methods of selection and terms of service for national officials.

Office	Method of Selection	Terms of Service
President	Electoral College	4 years
U.S. senator	State legislature	6 years ($\frac{1}{3}$ of senators' terms expire every 2 years)
U.S. representative	Popular election	2 years
Federal judge	Nominated by president, approved by Senate	Indefinite (subject to "good behavior")

Presidential selection was an issue of considerable debate at the Philadelphia convention. Direct election of the president was twice proposed and twice rejected because it linked executive power directly to popular majorities. The Framers finally chose to have the president selected by the votes of electors (the so-called Electoral College). Each state would have as many electors as it had members in Congress and could select them by any method it chose. The president would serve a four-year term and be eligible for reelection.

The Framers decided that federal judges and justices would be appointed rather than elected. They would be nominated by the president and confirmed through approval by the Senate. They would "hold their offices during good behavior." In effect, they would be allowed to hold office for life unless they committed a crime. The judiciary would be more of a "guardian" institution than a "representative" one.[16]

These differing methods of selecting national officeholders would not prevent a determined majority from achieving unbridled power, but control could not be attained easily or quickly. Unlike the House of Representatives, institutions such as the Senate, presidency, and judiciary would not yield to an impassioned majority in a single election. The delay would reduce the probability that government would degenerate into mob rule driven by momentary whims.

MODIFYING THE FRAMERS' WORK: TOWARD A MORE DEMOCRATIC SOCIETY

The Framers' conception of self-government was at odds with the one held by many Americans in 1787. The promise of self-government was one of the reasons that ordinary people had made great sacrifices during the American Revolution. This democratic spirit was reflected in the constitutions of the states. Every state but South Carolina held annual legislative elections, and several states also chose their governors through annual election by the people.

In this context, the Constitution's provisions for popular rule were rather thin. Richard Henry Lee of Virginia criticized even the House of Representatives, which he said had "very little democracy in it" because each of its members would represent a large population and area.[17] And it was not long after ratification of the Constitution that Americans sought a stronger voice in their own governing. The search has continued throughout the country's history: in no other constitutional area have Americans shown a greater willingness to experiment with new arrangements.[18]

The Era of Jeffersonian Democracy

Thomas Jefferson, who otherwise admired the Constitution, was among the prominent Americans who questioned its provisions for self-government. To Jefferson, America was the hope of ordinary people everywhere for liberation from elite rule, and he reasoned that the American people might someday rebel against the small governing role assigned them by the Constitution.[19]

Ironically, it was Jefferson who may have spared the nation a bloody revolution over the issue of popular sovereignty. Under John Adams, the second president, the national government increasingly favored the nation's wealthy interests. Adams publicly suggested that the Constitution was designed for a governing elite, while Alexander Hamilton urged him to use force if necessary to suppress popular dissent.[20] Jefferson asked whether Adams, with the aid of a strong army, planned soon to deprive ordinary Americans of their freedoms altogether. Jefferson challenged Adams in the next presidential election and, upon defeating him, hailed the victory as the "Revolution of 1800."

Although Jefferson was a champion of the common people, he had no clear vision of how a popular government might work in practice. He believed that congressional majorities were the proper expression of popular majorities and accordingly was reluctant to use his presidency as the instrument of the people.[21] Jefferson also had no illusions about a largely illiterate population's readiness for a significant governing role and feared the ruinous consequences of inciting the masses to contest the moneyed class. Jeffersonian democracy was thus mainly a revolution of the spirit; Jefferson taught Americans to look upon the national government as belonging to all, not just to the privileged few.[22]

The Era of Jacksonian Democracy

Not until Andrew Jackson became president in 1828 did the country have a powerful leader who was willing and able to involve the public more fully in government. Jackson carried out the constitutional revolution that Jeffersonian democracy had foreshadowed.

Jackson recognized that the president was the only official who could legitimately claim to represent the people as a whole. Unlike the president, members of Congress were elected from separate states and districts rather than from the entire country. Yet the president's claim to popular leadership was diminished by the existence of the Electoral College. Jackson persuaded the states to choose their presidential electors on the basis of popular voting. Jackson's reform, which is still in effect today, basically places the selection of a president in the voters' hands. The winner of the popular vote in each state is awarded its electoral votes; hence the candidate who wins most of the popular votes in the states is also most likely to receive a majority of their electoral votes. Since Jackson's time, only twice has the loser of the popular vote won the presidency (Rutherford B. Hayes in 1876 and Benjamin Harrison in 1888).

Jackson also sought to put an end to the domination of wealthy families who controlled most high public offices, both elective and appointive. He persuaded states to abolish property ownership as a requirement for voting and promoted the rotation of public office (which his opponents derided as a mere "spoils system") as a means of keeping appointive officials in close touch with the people.

Jacksonian democracy also brought with it the development of parties built on "grassroots" organization—that is, based on participation at the local level by ordinary citizens. The party's strength derived from its popular base, not, as had previously been the case, its network of elites. By the time he won a second term in 1832, Jackson's Democratic party had enlisted the participation of thousands of citizens. The election of 1832 also marked the introduction of the party nominating convention in presidential politics. Presidential nominations had earlier been controlled by party leaders in Congress and the state legislatures.

The development of grassroots political parties in the 1830s gave the people a powerful means of collective influence. Until then, each voter could only influence the selection of his single representative. With the advent of grassroots parties, a majority of individuals throughout the nation, united by affiliation with a political party, could choose a majority of representatives who shared the same policy goals. Majority opinion could thereby be more readily translated into public policy. So fundamental was the emergence of the grassroots party to the influence of the people that the historian James MacGregor Burns has called it America's "second constitution."[23]

The Progressive Era

The Progressive era of the early 1900s brought another wave of democratic reforms. After the 1840s, the parties had gradually drifted toward localism and favoritism. In the cities especially, they were taken over by powerful party bosses with an appetite for patronage. By the 1880s, some party bosses were in league with the robber barons to block government from regulating business trusts (see Chapter 2).[24] Progressive reformers sought to weaken the power of corporations and party bosses and to give the public a more direct voice in politics.

Grassroots parties resulted in increased citizen participation in nineteenth-century elections. This painting depicts the fanfare surrounding Grover Cleveland's 1892 election campaign. (Chicago Historical Society)

As with other reform movements, the Progressives were driven by political considerations in addition to a desire for honest government. The Progressives were mostly small-town Republicans who were also Protestant and from older immigrant groups. The party machines they sought to weaken were mostly Democratic and located in the cities. And the machines were dominated by Catholics from newer immigrant groups, particularly the Irish and Italians.

The Progressives rejected the Burkean idea (discussed earlier in this chapter) of representatives as trustees; they embraced instead the idea of representatives as **delegates**—officeholders who are obligated to respond directly to the expressed opinions of the people whom they represent.

MORE POWER TO THE PEOPLE   Two Progressive reforms gave voting majorities the power to decide policy at the state and local levels. One device was the *initiative*, which allows citizens through petition to place legislative measures on the ballot. A related measure was the *referendum*, which permits legislative bodies to submit proposals to the voters for approval or rejection (see box: States in the Nation).

STATES IN THE NATION

Direct Democracy: The Initiative and Referendum

The Progressive movement's reforms included the initiative and referendum. Not all states adopted these devices or have them today. The initiative and referendum are common in the Midwest and West, where the Progressive movement was strong. They are less prevalent in the Northeast, where the party machines were strong, and in the South, where political elites opposed reforms that would have enabled African Americans and poor whites to exercise more power.

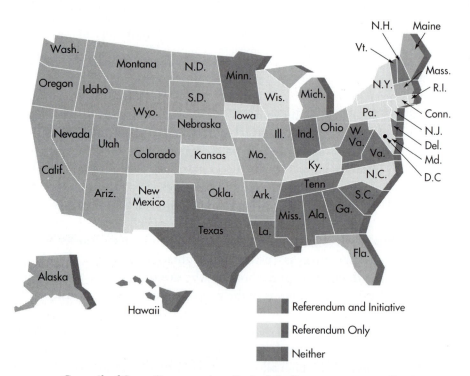

SOURCE: Council of State Governments, *Book of the States, 1992–1993* (Lexington, Ky: Council of State Governments, 1992), 329, 340–41.

In terms of national politics, a significant Progressive reform was the direct election of U.S. senators, who, before the Seventeenth Amendment was ratified in 1913, had been chosen by state legislatures and were widely perceived as agents of big business (the Senate was nicknamed the "millionaires' club"). Senators who stood to lose their seats in a direct popular vote had blocked earlier attempts to amend the Senate election procedure. Eventually, however, the Senate was persuaded to support an amendment by pressure from the Progressives and by the public outcry at revelations that corporate bribes had influenced the selection of several senators.

Another significant Progressive reform was the *primary election*, which gave rank-and-file voters the opportunity to select party nominees. Nearly all states in the early 1900s adopted the primary election as a means of choosing nominees for at least some federal and state offices. Before this change, nominees were chosen by party leaders.

BEARD'S ECONOMIC THEORY OF THE CONSTITUTION   The Progressive view that the original Constitution gave the majority too little power inspired

---

How the National Political System Was Made More Responsive to Popular Majorities

Earlier Situation	*Subsequent Development*
Separation of powers, as a means of dividing authority and blunting passionate majorities	Political parties, as a means of uniting authorities and linking them with popular majorities
Indirect election of all national officials except House members, as a means of buffering officials from popular influence	Direct election of U.S. senators and popular voting for president (linked to electoral votes), as a means of increasing popular control of officials
Nomination of candidates for public office through political party organizations	Primary elections, as a means of selecting party nominees

attacks on the Framers' motives, most notable of which is the historian Charles S. Beard's *An Economic Interpretation of the Constitution.*[25] Arguing that the Constitution grew out of wealthy Americans' fear of debtor rebellions, Beard claimed that its elaborate systems of power and representation were devices for keeping power in the hands of the rich. As evidence, Beard cited the Constitution's protections of property and referred to James Madison's secret notes on the Philadelphia convention, which showed that the delegates had placed a high priority on property interests.

Other historians challenged Beard's thesis, and he later acknowledged that he had not taken the Framers' full array of motives into account. Their concept of separation of powers, for example, was a time-honored governing principle that had previously been incorporated into state constitutions. Nevertheless, the Framers' system of representation was premised on a fear of unrestricted popular majorities and allowed the states to restrict suffrage. The Constitution required only that a state not impose stricter qualifications for voting in elections for the U.S. House of Representatives than were applied to elections for the larger house of the state legislature. The states allowed only propertied white males to vote, and it is likely that most of the Framers supported this limitation on suffrage.

But it would be inaccurate to conclude that the Framers were opposed to a government by the people. They were intent on establishing a government that was subject to popular influence and yet would offer protection against a tyrannical majority. The Constitution was an attempt to strike a balance between representative government, which makes government more responsive to the will of the majority, and limited government, which restricts the power of the government and hence the majority. Today, such a government is called a **constitutional democracy.** It is democratic in its provisions for majority influence through popular elections, and constitutional in its requirement that this power be exercised in accordance to law and with due respect for individual rights.

THE MODERN ERA: THE TERM-LIMITATION REFORM MOVEMENT

The debate over representation that began with the writing of the Constitution continues to the present day. An example is the debate over *term limitations,* or legal restrictions on the number of years that elected officials can remain in office.[26]

Voters in Oklahoma were the first to act on term limitations, deciding by a more than 2-to-1 margin in 1990 to restrict state legislators to twelve years of service. California and Colorado voters followed suit in the same year. In the 1992 and 1994 elections, citizens in twenty-one states and the District of Columbia voted on term limitations; in all these locations but one, term limits were adopted.

In 1995, however, the Supreme Court in *United States* v. *Thornton* dealt a serious setback to term-limitation advocates. The U.S. Constitution specifies age, citizenship, and residency requirements for House and Senate office, and the Court held that additional limits on the holders of these federal offices would require a constitutional amendment.[27] State and local offices are unaffected by the decision.

The term-limitation movement in many ways resembles the reform efforts of the past: it is based on the public's dissatisfaction with government, a belief that entrenched politicians are part of the problem, and a sense that the solution to these problems is to connect public officials more closely to the people they serve. The public's confidence in Congress, for example, has declined precipitously since the 1960s. This attitude is the culmination of a series of scandals, from Watergate on, that rocked government and of chronic policy problems, such as rising budget deficits, that public officials seemed unwilling or unable to address adequately. At the same time, the American people have been subject to countless claims that incumbents have increasingly received large campaign contributions from interest groups that stand to benefit from keeping them in office. These developments have convinced many Americans that they have lost control of their representatives and that term limitations could restore that control (see Figure 3-2).

As was true of the reforms of the Jeffersonian, Jacksonian, and Progressive eras, the term-limitation movement has had its opponents. They have argued that the measure would force strong leaders from office along with the weak ones and would give power to the experienced lobbyists and bureaucrats with whom the newly elected representatives would have to contend. The term-limitation issue, like similar reforms of the past, has also been a partisan one. Many of its strongest advocates were Republican leaders, who saw the reform as a way to break the Democrats' hold on Congress and state legislatures. This motivation vanished with the GOP's big victory in the 1994 midterm elections, and a bill that would have established term limits for Congress was defeated in 1995 in the Republican-controlled House of Representatives. Partisan considerations are *always* a part of institutional debates. The rules under which political power is won and lost usually give some sort of advantage to one side or the other, with the result that the rules themselves are a source of partisan conflict.

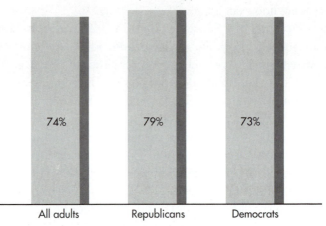

In a recent poll the question was asked: Do you think there should be a limit to the number of years members of Congress should serve, or do you think they should serve as long as the voters keep reelecting them?

Percent in Each Group Who Supported Term Limits

All adults	Republicans	Democrats
74%	79%	73%

FIGURE 3-2 THE PUBLIC'S VIEW OF TERM LIMITATIONS
A majority of Americans, regardless of party, favor term limitations for members of Congress. Source: Gallup Poll, April 23–25, 1996.

CONSTITUTIONAL DEMOCRACY TODAY

The United States today has a hybrid system of democracy that combines original countermajoritarian elements with newer majoritarian aspects.

In certain respects, the U.S. political system is a model of popular rule. The United States conducts elections for its larger legislative chamber (the House of Representatives) and its chief executive more frequently than any other democracy. In addition, it is the only country that relies extensively on primary elections instead of party organizations for the selection of party nominees. The principle of popular election to office, which the writers of the Constitution regarded as a prerequisite of popular sovereignty but also one to be used sparingly, has been extended further in the United States than anywhere else.

In other respects, however, the U.S. system is less democratic than many others. Popular majorities must work against the barriers to influence—the elaborate system of divided powers, staggered terms of office, and separate constituencies—that were devised by the Framers. In fact, the link between an electoral majority and a governing majority is far less direct in the American system than in European systems. In Great Britain, Germany, Sweden, and other European parliamentary democracies, elections usually reward the winning party with full control of legislative and executive power, leaving no doubt that its policy agenda should prevail. The will of the majority is expressed through the platform of the victorious party. The situation is different in the United States. Since World War II, the president and a majority in one or both houses of Congress more often have been from different parties. Even when they are of the same party, their separate constituencies and election cycles often place them at odds with each other over policy (see Chapters 11 and 12).

SUMMARY

The Constitution was designed to provide for a limited government in which political power would be confined to its proper uses. Liberty has been a basic value of America's political tradition and was a reason for the colonies' revolt against British rule. The Framers wanted to ensure that the government they were creating would not itself be a threat to freedom. To this end, they confined the national government to expressly granted powers and also denied it certain specific powers. Other prohibitions on government were later added to the Constitution in the form of stated guarantees of individual liberties—the Bill of Rights. The most significant constitutional provision for limited government, however, was a separation of powers among the three branches. The powers given to each branch enable it to act as a check on the exercise of power by the others, an arrangement which, during the nation's history, has in fact served as a barrier to abuses of power.

The Constitution, however, made no mention of how the powers and limits of government were to be judged in practice. In its historic ruling in *Marbury* v. *Madison*, the Supreme Court assumed the authority to review the constitutionality of legislative and executive actions and to declare them unconstitutional and thus invalid.

The Framers of the Constitution respected the idea of self-government but distrusted popular majorities. They designed a government that they felt would temper popular opinion and slow its momentum, so that the public's "true interest" (which includes a regard for the rights and interests of the minority) would guide public policy. Different methods were established to select members of the House of Representatives and of the Senate, the president, and federal judges as a means of separating political power from momentary and unreflective majorities.

Since the adoption of the Constitution, however, the public has gradually assumed more direct control of its representatives, particularly through measures affecting the ways in which officeholders are chosen. Political parties, presidential voting (linked to the Electoral College), direct election of senators, and primary elections are among the devices aimed at strengthening the majority's influence.

These developments are rooted in the idea, deeply held by ordinary Americans, that the people must have substantial direct control of their government if it is to serve their real interests.

MAJOR CONCEPTS

checks and balances
constitutional democracy
delegates
democracy
denials of power
grants of power
inalienable (natural) rights
judicial review

limited government
representative democracy
republic
self-government
separated institutions sharing power
trustees
tyranny of the majority

SUGGESTED READINGS

Beard, Charles S. *An Economic Interpretation of the Constitution.* New York: Macmillan, 1941. Argues that the Founders had selfish economic interests uppermost in mind when they wrote the Constitution.

Benjamin, Gerald, and Michael J. Malbin, eds. *Limiting Legislative Terms.* Washington, D.C.: Congressional Quarterly Press, 1992. A series of essays on the pros and cons of term limitations.

Bianco, William T. *Trust: Representatives and Constituents.* Ann Arbor: University of Michigan Press, 1994. Examines the relationship between representatives and constituents.

Ericson, David F. *The Shaping of American Liberalism: The Debates over Ratification, Nullification, and Slavery.* Chicago: University of Chicago Press, 1993. An analysis upholding the argument that issues of liberty have consistently been dominant in American ideology.

Finegold, Kenneth. *Experts and Politicians: Reform Challenges to Machine Politics in New York, Cleveland, and Chicago.* Princeton, N.J.: Princeton University Press, 1995. A careful study of the successes and failures of party-reform efforts in three major cities during the Progressive era.

Mayhew, David. *Divided We Govern.* New Haven, Conn.: Yale University Press, 1991. An evaluation of the causes and consequences of the tendency toward divided control of U.S. government.

Sandel, Michael J. *Democracy's Discontent: America in Search of a Public Philosophy.* Cambridge, Mass.: Harvard University Press, 1996. An argument for a community-oriented conception of democracy.

Simmons, A. John. *The Lockean Theory of Rights.* Princeton, N.J.: Princeton University Press, 1994. A careful analysis of John Locke's views on individual rights.
Tocqueville, Alexis de. *Democracy in America,* vols. 1 and 2, ed. J. P. Mayer. New York: Doubleday/Anchor, 1969. A classic analysis (originally published 1835–1840) of American democracy by an insightful French observer.

READING 3

The Mischiefs of Faction

JAMES MADISON

Among the numerous advantages promised by a well-constructed Union, none deserves to be more accurately developed than its tendency to break and control the violence of faction. . . .

By a faction I understand a number of citizens, whether amounting to a majority or minority of the whole, who are united and actuated by some common impulse of passion, or of interest, adverse to the rights of other citizens, or to the permanent and aggregate interests of the community.

There are two methods of curing the mischiefs of faction: the one, by removing its causes; the other, by controlling its effects.

There are again two methods of removing the causes of faction: the one, by destroying the liberty which is essential to its existence; the other, by giving to every citizen the same opinions, the same passions, and the same interests.

It could never be more truly said than of the first remedy that it was worse than the disease. Liberty is to faction what air is to fire, an ailment without which it instantly expires. But it could not be a less folly to abolish liberty, which is essential to political life, because it nourishes faction than it would be to wish the annihilation of air, which is essential to animal life, because it imparts to fire its destructive agency.

The second expedient is as impracticable as the first would be unwise. As long as the reason of man continues fallible, and he is at liberty to exercise it, different opinions will be formed. As long as the connection subsists between his reason and his self-love, his opinions and his passions will have a reciprocal influence on each other; and the former will be objects to which the latter will attach themselves. The diversity in the faculties of men, from which the rights of property originate, is not less an insuperable obstacle to a uniformity of interest. The protection of these faculties is the first object of government. From the protection of different and unequal faculties of acquiring property, the possession of different degrees and kinds of property immediately results; and from the influence of these on the sentiments and views of the respective proprietors ensues a division of the society into different interests and parties.

The latent causes of faction are thus sown in the nature of man; and we see them everywhere brought into different degrees of activity, according to the different circumstances of civil society. A zeal for different opinions concerning religion, concerning government, and many other points, as well of speculation as of practice; an attachment to different leaders ambitiously contending for pre-eminence and power; or to persons of other descriptions whose fortunes have been interesting to the human passions, have, in turn, divided mankind into parties, inflamed them with mutual animosity, and rendered them much more disposed to vex and oppress each other than to cooperate for their common good. So strong is this propensity of mankind to fall into mutual animosities that where no substantial occasion presents itself the most frivolous and fanciful distinctions have been sufficient to kindle their unfriendly passions and excite their most violent conflicts. But the most common and durable source of factions has been the various and unequal distribution of property. Those who hold and those who are without property have ever formed distinct interests in society. . . .

It is in vain to say that enlightened statesmen will be able to adjust these clashing interests and render them all subservient to the public good. Enlightened statesmen will not always be at the helm. Nor, in many cases, can such an adjustment be made at all without taking into view indirect and remote considerations, which will rarely prevail over the immediate interest which one party may find in disregarding the rights of another or the good of the whole.

The inference to which we are brought is that the *causes* of faction cannot be removed and that relief is only to be sought in the means of controlling its *effects*.

If a faction consists of less than a majority, relief is supplied by the republican principle, which enables the majority to defeat its sinister views by regular vote. . . . When a majority is included in a faction, the form of popular government, on the other hand, enables it to sacrifice to its ruling passion or interest both the public good and the rights of other citizens. To secure the public good and private rights against the danger of such a faction,

and at the same time to preserve the spirit and the form of popular government, is then the great object to which our inquiries are directed.

By what means is this object attainable? Evidently by one of two only.
Either the existence of the same passion or interest in a majority at the same
time must be prevented, or the majority, having such coexistent passion or
interest, must be rendered, by their number and local situation, unable to
concert and carry into effect schemes of oppression. If the impulse and the
opportunity be suffered to coincide, we well know that neither moral nor
religious motives can be relied on as an adequate control. They are not
found to be such on the injustice and violence of individuals, and lose their
efficacy in proportion to the number combined together, that is, in proportion as their efficacy becomes needful.

From this view of the subject it may be concluded that a pure democracy, by which I mean a society consisting of a small number of citizens, who
assemble and administer the government in person, can admit of no cure for
the mischiefs of faction. A common passion or interest will, in almost every
case, be felt by a majority of the whole, a communication and concert results from the form of government itself; and there is nothing to check the
inducements to sacrifice the weaker party or an obnoxious individual. Hence
it is that such democracies have ever been spectacles of turbulence and contention; have ever been found incompatible with personal security or the
rights of property; and have in general been as short in their lives as they
have been violent in their deaths. . . .

A republic, by which I mean a government in which the scheme of representation takes place, opens a different prospect and promises the cure for
which we are seeking. Let us examine the points in which it varies from pure
democracy, and we shall comprehend both the nature of the cure and the
efficacy which it must derive from the Union.

The two great points of difference between a democracy and a republic are: first, the delegation of the government, in the latter, to a small number of citizens elected by the rest; secondly, the greater number of citizens
and greater sphere of country over which the latter may be extended.

The effect of the first difference is, on the one hand, to refine and en-
large the public views by passing them through the medium of a chosen body
of citizens, whose wisdom may best discern the true interest of their country and whose patriotism and love of justice will be least likely to sacrifice it

to temporary or partial considerations. Under such a regulation it may well happen that the public voice, pronounced by the representatives of the people, will be more consonant to the public good than if pronounced by the people themselves, convened for the purpose. . . .

The other point of difference is the greater number of citizens and extent of territory which may be brought within the compass of republican than of democratic government; and it is this circumstance principally which renders factious combinations less to be dreaded in the former than in the latter. The smaller the society, the fewer probably will be the distinct parties and interests composing it; the fewer the distinct parties and interests, the more frequently will a majority be found of the same party; and the smaller the number of individuals composing a majority, and the smaller the compass within which they are placed, the more easily will they concert and execute their plans of oppression. Extend the sphere and you take in a greater variety of parties and interests; you make it less probable that a majority of the whole will have a common motive to invade the rights of other citizens; or if such a common motive exists, it will be more difficult for all who feel it to discover their own strength and to act in unison with each other. . . .

Hence, it clearly appears that the same advantage which a republic has over a democracy in controlling the effects of faction is enjoyed by a large over a small republic—is enjoyed by the Union over the States composing it.

SOURCE: James Madison, *Federalist* No. 10.
James Madison, the fourth president of the United States, has been called the "Father of the Constitution."

CHAPTER FOUR

Civil Liberties

A bill of rights is what the people are entitled to against every government on earth, general or particular, and what no just government should refuse, or rest on inference.

THOMAS JEFFERSON[1]

 OBERT AND Sarisse Creighton and their three children were asleep when FBI agents broke into their home in the middle of the night. Brandishing guns, the officers searched the house for a relative of the Creightons who was suspected of bank robbery. When asked to show a search warrant, they said, "You watch too much TV." The suspect was not there, and the officers abruptly left. The Creightons sued the FBI agent in charge, Russell Anderson, for violating their constitutional right against unlawful search.

The Creightons won a temporary victory when the Eighth U.S. Court of Appeals, noting that individuals are constitutionally protected against warrantless searches unless officers have good reason ("probable cause") for a search and unless they have good reason ("exigent circumstances") for conducting that search without a warrant, concluded that the FBI's Anderson should have sought a warrant from a judge, who would have decided whether a search of the Creightons' home was justified.

The Supreme Court of the United States overturned the lower court's ruling. The Court's majority opinion said: "We have recognized that it is inevitable that law enforcement officials will in some cases reasonably but mistakenly conclude that probable cause is present, and we have indicated that in such cases those officials . . . should not be held personally liable." Justice John Paul Stevens sharply dissented. He accused the Court's majority of showing "remarkably little fidelity" to the Constitution.[2] Civil liberties groups also claimed that the Court's decision gave police an open invitation to invade people's homes on the slightest pretext. However, the Court's decision was praised by law enforcement officials, who contended that a ruling in the Creightons' favor would have made police hesitant to pursue suspects for fear of a lawsuit if a search failed to produce the person sought.

As this case illustrates, issues of individual rights are complex and political. No right is absolute. For example, the Fourth Amendment protects Americans not from all searches but from "unreasonable searches." The public would be unsafe if police could never search for evidence of a crime. Yet the public would also not be secure if police could frisk people at will or break into their homes whenever they pleased. The challenge to a civil society is to establish a proper balance between the need for public safety and the need for individual freedom.

This chapter discusses **civil liberties:** specific individual rights which are constitutionally protected against infringement by government. As we saw in Chapter 3, the Constitution's failure to enumerate individual freedoms led to demands for the **Bill of Rights.** Enacted in 1791, these first ten amendments to the Constitution specify certain rights of life, liberty, and property which the national government is obliged to respect. A later amendment, the Fourteenth, became the basis for extending these protections of individual rights to actions by state and local governments.

Issues of individual rights have become increasingly complex and important. The writers of the Constitution could not possibly have foreseen the United States of the late twentieth century, with its huge national government, enormous corporations, urban crowding, and the rest. These developments are potential threats to personal freedom, and the judiciary in recent decades has seen fit to expand the rights to which individuals are entitled. However, these rights are constantly being balanced against competing individual rights and society's collective interests, and it is at this juncture that issues of civil liberties arise. Should an admitted murderer be entitled to recant a confession? Should prayer be allowed in the public schools? Should extremist groups be allowed to voice their messages of prejudice and hate? Such questions are among the subjects of this chapter, which focuses on the following major points:

* *Freedom of expression is the most basic of democratic rights, but, like all rights, it is not unlimited. Individual rights are constantly being weighed against the demands of majorities and the collective needs of society.*

* *"Due process of law" refers to legal protections (primarily procedural safeguards) that are designed to ensure that individual rights are respected by government.*

 ★ *During the last half-century, the civil liberties of individual Americans have been substantially broadened in law and given greater judicial protection from action by all levels of government. Of special significance has been the Supreme Court's use of the Fourteenth Amendment to protect these individual rights from action by state and local governments.*

FREEDOM OF EXPRESSION

Freedom of political expression is the most basic of democratic rights.[3] Unless citizens can openly express their political opinions, they cannot properly influence their government or act to protect their other rights.

It is for such reasons that the First Amendment provides the foundation for **freedom of expression**—the right of individual Americans to hold and communicate views of their choosing. For many reasons, such as a psychological need to conform to social pressure or a fear of harassment, Americans do not always choose to express themselves freely. Nevertheless, the First Amendment prohibits laws that would abridge the freedoms of conscience, speech, press, assembly, and petition.

Freedom of expression, like other rights, is not absolute. It does not entitle individuals to say or do whatever they want, to whomever they want. Free expression can be denied, for example, if it endangers national security, wrongly damages the reputations of others, or deprives others of their basic freedoms. An individual's private thoughts are completely free, but words and actions may not be. The Supreme Court has ruled, for example, that abortion protesters can be arrested if they violate laws or court orders that bar them from protesting within a certain distance of abortion clinics or from physically interfering with a woman's attempt to enter a clinic.[4]

In recent decades, free expression has received broad protection from the courts. Today, under most circumstances, Americans can freely verbalize their political views without fear of governmental interference. In earlier times, Americans were less free to express their political views.

The Early Period: The Uncertain Status of the Right of Free Expression

The first legislative attempt by the U.S. government to restrict free expression was the Sedition Act of 1798, which made it a crime to print false or malicious newspaper stories about the president or other national officials.

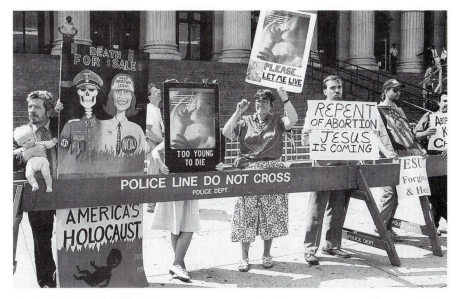

Exercising their right of free expression, antiabortion protestors gather outside a government building. (Robert Brenner/PhotoEdit)

Thomas Jefferson called the Sedition Act an "alarming infraction" of the Constitution and, upon replacing John Adams as president in 1801, pardoned those who had been convicted under it. As the Supreme Court did not review the sedition cases, however, the judiciary's position on free expression remained an open question. The Court also did not rule on free speech during the Civil War era, when the government severely restricted individual rights.

In 1919 the Court finally ruled on a case challenging the national government's authority to restrict free expression. Two years earlier, Congress had passed the Espionage Act, which prohibited forms of dissent deemed to be harmful to the nation's effort in World War I. Nearly 2,000 Americans were convicted for such activities as interfering with draft registration and distributing antiwar leaflets. The Supreme Court upheld one of these convictions in *Schenck* v. *United States* (1919), ruling unanimously that the Espionage Act of 1917 was constitutional. In the opinion written by Justice Oliver Wendell Holmes, the Court said that Congress could restrict speech that was "of such a nature as to create a clear and present danger" to the nation's security. This **clear-and-present-danger test** also expressed the converse: government had to allow political speech that did not pose any such danger.[5]

The Modern Period: Protecting Free Expression

Until the twentieth century, the tension between national security interests and free expression was not a pressing dilemma for the United States. The country's great size and ocean barriers provided protection from potential enemies, minimizing concerns of internal subversion. World War I, however, intruded upon America's isolation, and World War II brought it to an abrupt end. Since then, Americans' rights of free expression have been defined largely in the context of national security concerns.

FREE SPEECH   During the cold war that developed after World War II, many Americans perceived the Soviet Union as bent on destroying the United States through internal subversion and global expansion. In this period, the Supreme Court allowed government to put substantial limits on free expression, In 1951, for example, the Court upheld the convictions of eleven members of the U.S. Communist party who had been prosecuted under a law that made it illegal to advocate the forceful overthrow of the U.S. government.[6]

By the late 1950s, however, fear of internal communist subversion was subsiding, and the Supreme Court expanded the scope of permissible speech.[7] The Court implicitly embraced a legal doctrine first outlined by Justice Harlan Fiske Stone in 1938. Stone argued that First Amendment rights of free expression are the basis of Americans' liberty and ought to have a "preferred position" in the law. If government can control what people know and say, it can manipulate their opinions and thereby deprive them of the right to decide for themselves how they will be governed. Therefore government should be broadly prohibited from restricting free expression.[8]

This philosophy has led the Supreme Court to rule that government officials must show that national security is directly and substantially imperiled before they can lawfully prohibit citizens from speaking out. For example, during the Vietnam era, despite the largest sustained protest movement in America's history, not a single individual was convicted solely for voicing objections to the government's war policy. (Some dissenters were found guilty on other grounds, such as inciting riots and assaulting police.)

The Supreme Court's protection of "symbolic speech" has been less substantial than its protection of verbal speech. For example, the Court in 1968 upheld the conviction of a Vietnam protester who had burned his draft registration card. The Court said that government can prohibit action that threatens a legitimate public interest as long as the main purpose of the policy is not to restrict free expression. The Court concluded that the federal law prohibiting the destruction of draft cards was designed primarily to protect the military's need for soldiers, not to prevent people from criticizing government policy.[9]

The Supreme Court, however, has not granted the government broad power to restrict "symbolic speech." In 1989, for example, the Court ruled that the burning of the American flag is a protected form of free expression. The ruling came in the case of Gregory Lee Johnson, a member of the Communist Youth Brigade. Johnson had set fire to a U.S. flag outside the hall in Dallas where the 1984 Republican National Convention was being held. The Supreme Court rejected the state of Texas's argument that flag burning is, in every instance, an imminent danger to public safety. A year later the Court struck down a new federal statute that made it a federal crime to burn or deface the flag.[10] "If there is a bedrock principle underlying the First Amendment," the Court ruled in the *Johnson* case, "it is that the Government may not prohibit the expression of an idea simply because society finds the idea itself offensive or disagreeable."[11]

Civil rights attorney William Kunstler (*right*), with defendant Gregory Lee Johnson (*second from right*), addresses reporters outside the Supreme Court building. Kunstler defended Johnson in the celebrated case that ultimately established flag burning as a constitutionally protected form of political expression. (Bob Daugherty/AP/Wide World Photos)

PRESS FREEDOM AND PRIOR RESTRAINT   Freedom of the press has also received strong judicial support in recent decades. In *New York Times Co.* v. *United States* (1971) the Court ruled that the *Times*'s publication of the "Pentagon Papers" (secret government documents revealing official deception about the success of the Vietnam war policy) could not be blocked by the Department of Justice, which claimed that publication would hurt the war effort. The documents had been illegally obtained by antiwar activists, who had turned them over to the *Times* for publication. The Court ruled that "any system of prior restraints" on the press is unconstitutional unless the government can fully justify the restriction.[12]

The unacceptability of **prior restraint**—government prohibition of speech or publication before the fact—is basic to the current doctrine of free expression. The Supreme Court has said that any attempt by government to prevent expression carries "a 'heavy presumption' against its constitutionality."[13] News organizations and individuals are legally responsible after the fact for what they report or say (for example, they can be sued by an individual whose reputation is wrongly damaged by their words), but generally government cannot stop them in advance from expressing their views. An exception is coverage of military operations. During the Persian Gulf war, U.S. journalists in Saudi Arabia had to work within limits placed on them by military authorities. The courts have also upheld the government's authority to ban uncensored publications by certain past and present government employees, such as CIA agents, who have taken part in classified national security activities.

Free Expression and State Governments

In 1790 Congress rejected a proposed amendment to the Constitution which would have applied the Bill of Rights to the states. Thus the freedoms guaranteed in the Bill of Rights were initially protected only from action by the national government, a constitutional arrangement that the Supreme Court upheld in 1833.[14] A century later, however, the Court began to protect individual rights from infringement by state governments. The vehicle for this change was the due-process clause of the Fourteenth Amendment to the Constitution.

THE FOURTEENTH AMENDMENT AND SELECTIVE INCORPORATION Ratified in 1868, the Fourteenth Amendment forbids a state to deprive any person of life, liberty, or property without due process of law. It was not until 1925 in *Gitlow* v. *New York*, however, that the Supreme Court decided that the Fourteenth Amendment applied to state action in the area of freedom of expression. Although the Court upheld Benjamin Gitlow's conviction for violating a New York law that prohibited advocacy of the violent overthrow of the U.S. government, the Court indicated that the states were not completely free to limit expression:

> For present purposes we may and do assume that freedom of speech and of the press—which are protected by the First Amendment from abridgement by Congress—are among the fundamental personal rights and "liberties" protected by the due process clause of the Fourteenth Amendment from impairment by the states.[15]

There is no indication that Congress, when it passed the Fourteenth Amendment after the Civil War, meant it to protect First Amendment rights from state action. The Supreme Court justified this new interpretation by reference to **selective incorporation**—the absorption of certain provisions of the Bill of Rights, particularly freedom of speech and press, into the Fourteenth Amendment so that these rights would be protected from infringement by the states.

Having developed a new interpretation of the Fourteenth Amendment, the Supreme Court proceeded during the next decade to overturn state laws that restricted expression in the areas of speech, press, religion, and assembly and petition (see Table 4-1).[16] The most famous of these judgments is *Near* v. *Minnesota* (1931). Jay Near was the publisher of a Minneapolis weekly newspaper that regularly made scurrilous attacks on blacks, Jews, Catholics, and labor union leaders. His paper was closed down on authority of a state law that banned "malicious, scandalous, or defamatory" publications. Near appealed the shutdown, and the Supreme Court ruled in his favor, saying that the Minnesota law was "the essence of censorship."[17]

LIMITING THE AUTHORITY OF STATES TO RESTRICT EXPRESSION
Since the 1930s, the Supreme Court has broadly protected freedom of expression from action by the states and by local governments, which derive their authority from the states. The Court has held that the states cannot restrict free expression except when such expression is almost certain to result in imminent lawlessness. A leading free-speech case was *Brandenburg* v. *Ohio* (1969). The appellant was a Ku Klux Klan member who, in a speech delivered at a Klan rally, said that "revenge" might have to be taken if the national government "continues to suppress the white Caucasian race." He was convicted of advocating force under an Ohio law prohibiting "crimi-

TABLE 4-1   SELECTIVE INCORPORATION OF RIGHTS OF
FREE EXPRESSION
In the 1920s and 1930s, the Supreme Court selectively incorporated
the free-expression provisions of the First Amendment into the
Fourteenth Amendment so that these rights would be protected from
infringement by the states.

Supreme Court Case	Year	Constitutional Right at Issue
Gitlow v. New York	1925	First Amendment's applicability to free speech
Fiske v. Kansas	1927	Free speech
Near v. Minnesota	1931	Free press
Hamilton v. Regents, U. of California	1934	Religious freedom
DeJonge v. Oregon	1937	Freedom of assembly and of petition

nal syndicalism," but the Supreme Court reversed the conviction, saying the First Amendment prohibits a state from suppressing speech that advocates the unlawful use of force "except where such advocacy is directed to inciting or producing imminent lawless action, and is likely to produce such action."[18]

In a key case involving freedom of assembly, the U.S. Supreme Court in 1977 upheld a lower-court ruling against local ordinances of Skokie, Illinois, which had been invoked to prevent a parade by the American Nazi party.[19] Skokie had a large Jewish population, including many survivors of Nazi Germany's concentration camps. The Supreme Court held that the right of free expression takes precedence over the mere *possibility* that exercising the right may have undesirable consequences. Before government can lawfully prevent a speech or rally, it must offer persuasive evidence that an evil will almost certainly result from the event and must also demonstrate the lack of alternative ways (such as assigning police officers to control the crowd) to prevent the evil from happening.

The Court has broadly held that "hate speech" cannot be silenced. This ruling came in a unanimous 1992 opinion that struck down a St. Paul, Minnesota, ordinance making it a crime to engage in speech likely to arouse "anger or alarm" on the basis of "race, color, creed, religion or gender." The Court said the First Amendment prohibits government from "silencing speech on the basis of its content."[20] This protection of violent *speech* does not, however, extend to violent *crimes*, such as assault, that are motivated by racial or other forms of prejudice. A Wisconsin law that provided for increased sentences for these crimes was challenged as a violation of the First Amendment. In a unanimous 1993 opinion, the Court said that the law was aimed at "conduct unprotected by the First Amendment" rather than the defendant's speech.[21]

The Supreme Court has recognized that freedom of speech and assembly may conflict with the routines of daily life. Accordingly, individuals do not have the right to hold a public rally at any time or place of their choosing. The Court has held that officials can regulate the time, place, and conditions of public assembly, provided that these regulations are reasonable and do not discriminate on the basis of who is speaking.[22] In general, the Supreme Court's position is that the First Amendment makes any government effort to regulate the *content* of a message highly suspect. In the flag-burning case, Texas was regulating the content of the message—contempt for the flag and the principles it represents. Texas could not have been regulating the act itself, for the state's own method of disposing of worn-out flags is also to burn them. But a content-neutral regulation (no public rally can be held in the middle of a busy intersection at rush hour) is acceptable as long as it is reasonable and nondiscriminatory.

Libel and Slander

The right of free expression is not a legal license to avoid responsibility for the consequences of what is said or written. If false information that greatly harms a person's reputation is published (libel) or spoken (slander), the injured party can sue for damages. The ease of winning such suits has obvious implications for free expression. Individuals and organizations are less likely to express themselves openly if they stand a good chance of subsequently losing a libel or slander suit.

Libel is the more important issue for the political process because it affects the news media's ability to criticize public officials. A leading decision in this area is *New York Times Co.* v. *Sullivan* (1964), in which the Court overruled an Alabama state court that had found the *Times* guilty of libel for printing an advertisement accusing Alabama officials of physically assaulting black civil rights demonstrators. The Court ruled that libel of a public official requires proof of "actual malice," which was defined as a knowing or reckless disregard for the truth.[23] It is *very* difficult to prove that a publication acted with reckless or deliberate disregard for the truth. In fact, no federal official has won a libel judgment against a news organization in the three decades since the *Sullivan* ruling. (The press has less protection against a libel judgment when its target is a "private" person rather than a "public" official. The courts regard the communication of information about private individuals as less basic to the democratic process than information about public officials, and hence the press accordingly must take greater care in ascertaining the validity of claims about an ordinary citizen.)

The *Sullivan* decision notwithstanding, the strongest protection against a libel judgment is truthfulness. The Court has held that expressions of opinion deserve "full constitutional protection" against the charge of libel as long as they do not contain "a provably false factual connotation."[24]

Obscenity

In 1990 the director of a Cincinnati museum, Dennis Barrie, was arrested on an obscenity charge for holding an exhibit that included homoerotic art by the photographer Robert Mapplethorpe. Although Barrie was acquitted in a jury trial, his arrest provoked a controversy that extended to Congress. Conservative Senator Jesse Helms (R-N.C.) attempted unsuccessfully to withdraw appropriations for the National Endowment for the Arts (NEA), which had partially underwritten the Mapplethorpe exhibit.

Obscenity is a form of expression that is not protected by the First Amendment. However, the Supreme Court has found it difficult to define which publicly disseminated sexual materials are obscene and which are not. The Court has struggled to develop a standard that gives predictability to the law without endangering First Amendment rights.

"Contemporary community standards" is one measure the Court applies. The Court has said that what might offend residents of "Mississippi might be found tolerable in Las Vegas" and that such community differences ought to be taken into account in obscenity judgments.[25] However, the Court has also concluded that material cannot be judged obscene simply because the "average" local resident might object to it. Apparently "community standards" are to be judged in the context of a "reasonable person"—someone with a broad enough outlook to evaluate the material on its overall merit rather than its most objectionable feature. To be judged obscene, sexual content must be of a particularly offensive type—still a rather vague criterion.[26]

The Supreme Court has distinguished between obscene materials in public places and in the home. A unanimous ruling in 1969 held that what adults read and watch in the privacy of their homes cannot be made a crime.[27]

Museum visitors examine Robert Mapplethorpe's photographs in the Cincinnati exhibit that was the focus of a controversy over the definition of obscenity. (Michael Keating-Cincinnati Enquirer/Gamma-Liaison)

The Court created an exception to this rule in 1990 by upholding an Ohio law making it a crime to possess pornographic photographs of children.[28] The Court reasoned that purchase and distribution contributed to the spread of the crime of abusing minors through pornography.

The shielding of children from the effects of sexually explicit material has also affected cable television policy. In 1996, the Supreme Court held that, although cable operators are not required to scramble the signal of channels that provide "adult" programming, they must do so for individual subscribers who request that the signal be scrambled. Cable operators can also choose not to carry a commercial channel that offers adult programming, just as they can refuse to carry other commercial channels. However, cable operators are not permitted to censor "public-access channels" (those made available free to community groups) since the purpose of these channels is to facilitate the expression of views that might not otherwise be heard on television. If cable operators have authority to restrict this form of expression on grounds it is sexually offensive, some of them, the Court said, would "erroneously exclude" content that "should be broadcast."[29] In other words, the Court in its cable television decision tried to find an acceptable balance between society's interest in promoting free expression and its interest in curtailing obscenity.

FREEDOM OF RELIGION

Free religious expression is the precursor of free political expression, at least within the English tradition of limited government. England's Glorious, or Bloodless, Revolution of 1689 centered on the issue of religion and resulted in the Act of Toleration, which gave Protestant sects the right to worship freely and publicly. The English philosopher John Locke (1632–1704) extended this principle, arguing that legitimate government could not inhibit free expression, religious or otherwise. The First Amendment reflects this tradition, providing for freedom of religion along with freedom of speech, press, assembly, and petition.

In regard to religion, the First Amendment reads: "Congress shall make no law respecting an establishment of religion, or prohibiting the free exercise thereof." The prohibition of laws aimed at "establishment of religion" (the establishment clause) and its "free exercise" (the free-exercise clause) applies to states through the Fourteenth Amendment.

The Establishment Clause

The **establishment clause** has been interpreted by the courts to mean that government may not favor one religion over another or support religion over no religion. (This position contrasts with that of a country such as England, where Anglicanism is the official, or "established," state religion, though no religion is prohibited.) The Supreme Court's interpretation of the establishment clause has been described as maintaining a "wall of separation" between church and state.[30] However, the Court has taken a pragmatic approach, allowing government under some circumstances to assist religion.

The Court has developed a three-point test to determine whether a law providing aid to religion is constitutional: first, the main purpose of the aid must be secular, not religious; second, the main effect of the assistance must not be to promote one religion or religion per se; and third, the aid must not *excessively* involve the government in religion.[31] These restrictions do not, for example, allow substantial government grants to religious schools (for example, government cannot pay for teachers' salaries[32]) but do permit lesser contributions under some circumstances (for example, government has been allowed to provide secular text and exam materials, such as math books and SAT examinations[33]).

In 1962, the Court held that the establishment clause prohibits the reciting of prayers in public schools.[34] A year later the Court struck down Bible readings in public schools.[35] Religion is a strong force in American life, and the Supreme Court's position on school prayer has evoked strong opposition, particularly from Protestant fundamentalists. An Alabama law attempted to circumvent the prayer ruling by permitting public schools to set aside one minute each day for silent prayer or meditation. In 1985 the Court declared the law unconstitutional, ruling that "government must pursue a course of complete neutrality toward religion."[36] Nevertheless, the Court's majority concluded that the law would have been acceptable if it had merely set aside "a moment of silence." Presidents Reagan's and Bush's five appointees to the Court raised hopes among advocates of school prayer of a change of precedent, but the Court in 1992 reaffirmed the ban on state-sponsored prayer by extending it to include graduation ceremonies.[37]

The Free-Exercise Clause

The First and Fourteenth amendments also prohibit governmental interference with the "free exercise" of religion. The idea underlying the **free-exercise clause** is clear: Americans are free to hold any religious belief they choose.

Although people are free to believe what they want, they are not always free to act on their religious beliefs. The courts have allowed government interference when it is the secondary result of an overriding social goal. An example is the legal protection of sick children whose parents refuse to permit medical treatment on religious grounds. A court may order that such children be given medical assistance because the social good of saving their lives overrides their parents' free-exercise rights.

In some circumstances exceptions to certain laws have been permitted on free-exercise grounds. The Supreme Court ruled in 1972 that Wisconsin could not compel Amish parents to send their children to school beyond the eighth grade because this policy violates a centuries-old Amish religious practice of having children leave school and begin work at an early age.[38] In upholding free exercise in such cases, the Court may be said to have violated the establishment clause by granting preferred treatment to people who hold a particular religious belief. The Court has recognized the potential conflict between the free-exercise and establishment clauses and, as in other such situations, has tried to strike a reasonable balance between the competing claims.

When the free-exercise and establishment clauses cannot be balanced, the Supreme Court has been forced to make a choice. In 1987 the Court overturned a Louisiana law requiring that creationism (the Bible's account of how the world was created) be taught along with the theory of evolution in public school science courses. Creationism, the Court concluded, is a religious doctrine, not a scientific theory; thus its inclusion in public school curricula violates the establishment clause by promoting a religious belief. Creationists viewed the decision as a violation of their right to the free exercise of religion; they argued that their children were being forced to study a theory that contradicts the biblical account of human origins.

THE RIGHT OF PRIVACY

Until the 1960s, Americans' constitutional rights were confined largely to those enumerated in the Bill of Rights. This situation prevailed despite the Ninth Amendment, which reads: "The enumeration in the Constitution, of certain rights, shall not be construed to deny or disparage others retained by the people."

In 1965, however, the Supreme Court added to the list of individual rights, declaring that Americans have "a right of privacy." This judgment arose from the case of *Griswold* v. *Connecticut*, which challenged a state law prohibiting the use of birth control devices, even by married couples. The Supreme Court invalidated the statute, concluding that a state had no business interfering with a married couple's decision regarding contraception. The Court did not base its decision on the Ninth Amendment but reasoned instead that the freedoms in the Bill of Rights imply an underlying right of privacy.[39]

The right of privacy was the basis for the Supreme Court's ruling in *Roe* v. *Wade* (1973), which gave women full freedom to choose abortion during the first three months of pregnancy.[40] In overturning a Texas law prohibiting abortion except to save the life of the mother, the Supreme Court said that the right of privacy is "broad enough to encompass a woman's decision whether or not to terminate her pregnancy."

After *Roe*, antiabortion activists sought to reverse or weaken the Court's ruling. Attempts to pass a constitutional amendment that would ban abortions were unsuccessful, but abortion foes succeeded in a campaign to prohibit the use of government funds to pay for abortions for poor women.

Abortion rights activists demonstrate outside the Supreme Court, while the justices inside hear arguments on Pennsylvania's controversial abortion law. By a 5–4 vote, the Court narrowly reaffirmed the principle that a woman has the right to choose an abortion during the early months of pregnancy. (Greg Gibson/AP/Wide World Photos)

Then, in *Webster* v. *Reproductive Health Services* (1989), the Supreme Court upheld a Missouri law that prohibits abortions in public hospitals and by public employees.[41] The ruling was in part a consequence of the efforts of antiabortion groups to influence Supreme Court appointments during the Reagan presidency. The Missouri law was upheld by a 5–4 majority, and all three Reagan appointees on the Court (Justices O'Connor, Scalia, and Kennedy) voted with the majority.

The *Webster* decision was followed in 1992 by a judgment in the Pennsylvania abortion case *Planned Parenthood* v. *Casey*. Pennsylvania's law placed a 24-hour waiting period on women who sought an abortion, required doctors to counsel women on abortion and alternatives to abortion, required a minor to have a parent's consent or a judge's approval before having an abortion, and required a married woman to notify her husband before obtaining an abortion. Antiabortion advocates saw the Pennsylvania law as an opportunity for the Supreme Court to overturn the *Roe* precedent. However, in a decision that surprised many observers, the Court by a 5–4 margin reaffirmed the "essential holding" of *Roe* v. *Wade:* that a woman, because of the constitutional guarantee of privacy, has a right to abortion during the early months of pregnancy. The Court also ruled, however, that states can regulate abortion as long as they do not impose an "undue burden" on women seeking abortion. The Court concluded that the 24-hour waiting period, physician counseling, and the informed-consent requirement for minors were not undue burdens and were therefore permissible. The spousal-notification requirement, however, was judged to place a "substantial obstacle" in the path of women seeking abortion and was thereby declared unconstitutional.[42]

Abortion will certainly be a leading controversy for years to come. The American public is divided on the issue (see Figure 4-1), and there are a great many deeply committed activists on both sides.[43] The Supreme Court is itself divided, although the possibility that *Roe* v. *Wade* will be overturned decreased with Bill Clinton's election in 1992. His initial nominees to the Court, Ruth Bader Ginsberg and Stephen Breyer, are proponents of a woman's right to abortion. Ginsberg's appointment was particularly critical. She replaced Byron White, one of the four dissenting judges in the Pennsylvania case.

As with other rights, the right of choice of abortion is not only, or even primarily, played out in the courts. Abortion opponents have waged sit-ins and demonstrations outside clinics in an effort to stop the practice. Some of

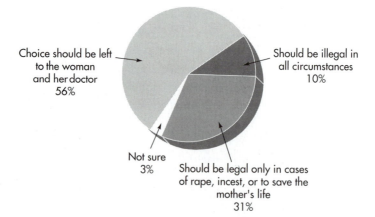

Choice should be left
to the woman
and her doctor
56%

Should be illegal in
all circumstances
10%

Not sure
3%

Should be legal only in cases
of rape, incest, or to save the
mother's life
31%

FIGURE 4-1 OPINIONS ON THE ABORTION ISSUE
Americans are divided over abortion. Respondents were asked which position best represents their view on abortion. Source: NBC News/Wall Street Journal poll, March 1996.

these protests have erupted in violent acts toward women and staff who tried to enter the clinics. In 1994, Congress made it unlawful to block the entrance to abortion clinics or otherwise prevent people from entering. The Freedom of Access to Clinic Entrances Act has been effective in reducing the violence outside abortion clinics but has not eliminated it, nor did it prevent gunmen in Massachusetts and Florida from killing abortion workers. Responsible voices within the antiabortion movement condemned the senseless murders, but few believe it could never happen again.

RIGHTS OF PERSONS ACCUSED OF CRIMES

Justice Felix Frankfurter once wrote that "the history of liberty has largely been the history of the observance of procedural guarantees."[44] No system of justice is foolproof; innocent people have been convicted and punished even in the best systems. But the scrupulous application of procedural safeguards, such as a defendant's right to legal counsel, greatly increases the likelihood that real justice will result.

Procedural Due Process

"Due process" refers to legal protections that have been established to preserve the rights of individuals. The most significant form of these protections is **procedural due process;** the term refers primarily to procedures that authorities must follow before a person can legitimately be punished for an offense.

The U.S. Constitution provides for several procedures designed to protect a person from wrongful arrest, conviction, and punishment. According to Article I, section 9, any person taken into police custody is entitled to seek a writ of habeas corpus, which requires law enforcement officials to bring him or her into court and explain the legal reason for the detention. The Fifth and Fourteenth amendments provide generally that no person can be deprived of life, liberty, or property without due process of law. And specific procedural protections for the accused are spelled out in the Fourth, Fifth, Sixth, and Eighth amendments:

- *The Fourth Amendment* forbids the police to conduct searches and seizures unless they have probable cause to believe that a crime has been committed.

- *The Fifth Amendment* protects against double jeopardy (being prosecuted twice for the same offense), self-incrimination (being compelled to testify against oneself), and indictment for a crime except through grand jury proceedings.
- *The Sixth Amendment* provides the right to have legal counsel, to confront witnesses, to receive a speedy trial, and to have a trial by jury in criminal proceedings.
- *The Eighth Amendment* protects against excessive bail or fines and prohibits the infliction of cruel and unusual punishment on those convicted of crimes.

These procedural protections have always been subject to interpretation. The Sixth Amendment, for example, provides the right to have legal counsel. But what if a person cannot afford a lawyer? For most of the nation's history, poor people had almost no choice but to act as their own attorneys. Today, if a person is accused of a serious crime and cannot afford a lawyer, the government must provide one. This change came about not through a constitutional amendment but through Supreme Court rulings that gave new meaning in practice to the Sixth Amendment.

Selective Incorporation of Procedural Rights

For most of the nation's history, the procedural protections in the Bill of Rights applied only to the actions of the national government; states were not bound by them. There were limited exceptions, such as a 1932 Supreme Court ruling that a defendant charged in a state court with a crime carrying the death penalty had to be provided with an attorney.[45]

Not until the 1960s did the Court broadly require states to safeguard procedural rights. Changes in public education and communication made Americans more aware of their rights, and the civil rights movement dramatized the fact that minority group members and the poor had many fewer rights in practice than other Americans. In response, the Supreme Court in the 1960s "incorporated" Bill of Rights protections for the accused in state courts by ruling that these protections are covered by the Fourteenth Amendment's guarantee of due process of law (see Table 4-2).

This selective incorporation process began with *Mapp* v. *Ohio* (1961). Dollree Mapp's home had been entered by Cleveland police, who, though they failed to find the drugs they were looking for, happened to discover some pornographic material. Mapp's conviction for its possession was overturned

TABLE 4-2   SELECTIVE INCORPORATION OF RIGHTS OF
THE ACCUSED

In the 1960s, the Supreme Court selectively incorporated the fair-trial
provisions of the Fourth through Eighth Amendments into the
Fourteenth Amendment so that these rights would be protected from
infringement by the states.

Supreme Court Case	Year	Constitutional Right at Issue
Mapp v. *Ohio*	1961	Unreasonable search and seizure
Robinson v. *California*	1962	Cruel and unusual punishment
Gideon v. *Wainwright*	1963	Right to counsel
Malloy v. *Hogan*	1964	Self-incrimination
Pointer v. *Texas*	1965	Right to confront witnesses
Miranda v. *Arizona*	1966	Self-incrimination
Klopfer v. *North Carolina*	1967	Speedy trial
Duncan v. *Louisiana*	1968	Jury trial in criminal cases
Benton v. *Maryland*	1968	Double jeopardy

by the Supreme Court on the grounds that she had been subjected to un-reasonable search and seizure.[46] The Court ruled that illegally obtained evidence could not be used in state courts.

Two years later, the Supreme Court's decision in *Gideon* v. *Wainwright* (1963) required the states to furnish attorneys for poor defendants in all felony cases. Clarence Gideon, an indigent drifter, had been convicted and sentenced to prison in Florida for breaking into a poolroom. He successfully appealed on the grounds that he had been denied due process because he could not afford to pay an attorney.[47]

During the 1960s the Court also ruled that defendants in state criminal proceedings cannot be compelled to testify against themselves;[48] have the rights to remain silent and to have legal counsel when arrested;[49] have the right to confront witnesses who testify against them;[50] must be granted a speedy trial;[51] have the right to a jury trial;[52] and cannot be subjected to double jeopardy.[53] The best known of these cases is *Miranda* v. *Arizona* (1966), as a result of which police are required to inform suspects of their rights at the time of arrest. Ernesto Miranda had confessed during police interrogation to kidnapping and raping a young woman. His confession led to his conviction, but the Supreme Court overturned it on the grounds that he had not been informed of his rights to remain silent and to have legal counsel present during interrogation. Using other evidence of Miranda's crime, the state of Arizona then retried and convicted him again. He was paroled from prison in 1972 and four years later was stabbed to death in a bar fight. Ironically, Miranda's assailant was read his "Miranda rights" when police arrested him. By now the wording has become familiar: "You have the right to remain silent. . . . Anything you say can and will be used against you in a court of law. . . . You have the right to an attorney."

Weakening the Exclusionary Rule

As the Supreme Court expanded defendants' rights during the 1960s, many law enforcement officials, politicians, and private citizens accused the Court of "coddling criminals." When Richard Nixon won the presidency after promising to restore "law and order" in the country, there were widespread expectations of a tougher policy on issues of crime. Although Nixon appointed four new justices to the Supreme Court, its positions on the rights of the accused did not immediately change.

Since the 1980s, a shift in the Court's philosophy has been evident. The greatest change can be seen in the application of the **exclusionary rule,** which bars the use in trials of evidence obtained in violation of the Fourth Amendment's protection against "unreasonable searches and seizures." The rule was formulated in a 1914 Supreme Court decision,[54] and its application was further expanded in federal cases. The *Mapp* decision extended the exclusionary rule to state trial proceedings as well. Subsequent decisions of the Supreme Court broadened its application to the point where almost any type of illegally obtained evidence was considered inadmissible in a criminal trial.

In the 1980s, the Supreme Court reversed the trend by placing restrictions on the rule's application, concluding that illegally obtained evidence can be admitted in trials if the procedural errors are small, inadvertent, or ultimately inconsequential. In a key 1984 decision, for example, the Court ruled that illegally obtained evidence can be used against a defendant if the prosecution can prove that it would have discovered the evidence anyway.[55]

Recent Supreme Court decisions have further weakened the exclusionary rule. In the 1960s, the Court developed the principle that police had to have a solid basis ("probable cause") for believing that an individual was involved in a specific crime before they could engage in search and seizure activity. This principle has been downgraded. In 1990, for example, the

Supreme Court held that roadside checkpoints where police systematically stop drivers to check them for signs of intoxication do not violate their right to protection against unreasonable search.[56]

A more definitive statement of the Court's new position is *Whren* v. *United States* (1996), which unanimously upheld the conviction of an individual who had been found with packets of drugs in the front seat of his car after being stopped for a minor traffic infraction. The police had no evidence (no "probable cause") to believe that drugs were actually in the car but suspected the driver was involved with drugs and used the traffic infraction as a pretext to stop and check him. The Supreme Court accepted defense arguments that the police had no clear evidence on which to base their suspicion; that the traffic infraction was not the real reason the individual was stopped; and that police usually do not stop a person for the infraction in question (turning a corner without signaling). But the Court concluded that the officers' motive was irrelevant, as long as an officer in some situations might reasonably stop a car for the infraction that occurred. Thus the stop

The Supreme Court in recent years has relaxed the restrictions on search and seizure by police. For example, it is legal for police forces to set up roadblocks to apprehend drunk drivers as long as they proceed systematically—stopping every fourth vehicle, say, rather than examining drivers on the basis of arbitrary criteria such as age or appearance. (Dan Chidester)

and search of the driver was deemed to meet the Fourth Amendment's reasonableness standard.[57]

The Supreme Court has also recently restricted habeas corpus appeals to federal courts by individuals who have been convicted of crimes in state courts. (Habeas corpus gives defendants access to federal courts in order to argue that their rights under the Constitution were violated when they were convicted in a state court.) A 1960s Supreme Court precedent had assured prisoners of the right to have their petitions heard in federal court unless they had "deliberately bypassed" the opportunity to make the appeal in state courts.[58]

This precedent was overturned in 1992, when the Court held that inmates can lose the right to a federal court hearing even if, through a lawyer's mistake, they have first failed to present their appeal properly in state courts.[59] Another significant habeas corpus defeat for inmates occurred in 1993 when the Supreme Court held that federal courts cannot overturn a state conviction on the basis of constitutional error unless the prisoner can demonstrate that the error contributed to the conviction.[60] Previously, the burden of proof was on the state: it had to prove that the error did not affect the case's outcome. Then, in *Felker* v. *Turpin* (1996), the Court upheld a recent federal law that severely restricts federal habeas corpus appeals by state prison inmates who have already filed one.[61]

The new limits are applauded by those who believe that multiple habeas corpus appeals clog the federal courts and delay the hearing of other cases of greater merit. On the other hand, civil libertarians argue that no procedure that can protect the innocent from wrongful conviction is too big a burden to place on the courts.[62]

However, no one claims that recent decisions mark a return to the lower procedural standards that prevailed before the 1960s. Many of the vital precedents set in that decade remain in effect, including the most important one of all: the principle that procedural protections guaranteed to the accused by the Bill of Rights must be observed by the states as well as by the federal government.

In addition, the Supreme Court in the last decade has extended procedural rights in some areas. Among the key rulings are that African Americans are denied their rights in some instances when prosecuting attorneys use peremptory challenges (that is, rejections without explanation) to exclude black potential jurors, so that the trial is conducted with an all-white jury;[63] that police must immediately halt an interrogation if the accused asks for a lawyer;[64] and that patients' discussions with psychotherapists and other mental health professionals do not have to be disclosed in judicial proceedings.[65]

STATES IN THE NATION

The Death Penalty

All but a dozen states permit the death penalty as a punishment for crime, but they vary greatly in its application. About ten states with the death penalty have not executed a single prisoner since 1976, when the Supreme Court reinstated the death penalty as a constitutionally permissible form of punishment. Other states have executed only a few prisoners during this period. On the other hand, a few states, most of which are located in the South, have applied the death penalty frequently. The state of Texas alone accounted for a third of the 257 executions that took place between 1976 and 1994.

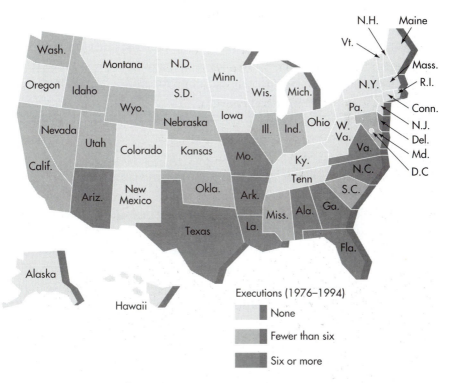

Executions (1976–1994)

None

Fewer than six

Six or more

SOURCE: U.S. Bureau of Justice Statistics.

How the United States Compares

Law and Order

Individual rights are a cornerstone of the American governing system and receive strong protection from the courts. The government's ability to restrict free expression is severely limited, and the individual's right to a fair trial is protected through elaborate due-process guarantees.

According to Amnesty International, a watchdog group that monitors human rights achievements and violations around the world, the United States has a good record in terms of its constitutional protection of civil liberties.

Although human rights groups admire America's elaborate procedural protections for those accused of crime, they are critical of its sentencing and incarceration policies. The United States is a world leader in terms of the number of people it places behind bars and in the length of sentences for various categories of crime. Defenders of U.S. policy say that although overall crime rates are about the same here as elsewhere, there is more violent crime in America. Critics reply that although the murder rate is high in the

Crime and Punishment

The theory and practice of procedural guarantees are often two quite different things, as Adrienne Cureton discovered on January 2, 1995. She is a plain-clothes police officer who, with a uniformed partner, was called to the scene of a domestic dispute. When a struggle ensued, her partner radioed for help. When the officers arrived, Cureton and her partner had already handcuffed the homeowner. The officers barged in and mistook Cureton, an African American, for the other person involved in the dispute. They grabbed her by the collar, dragged her by the hair onto the porch, and clubbed her repeatedly with flashlights, despite her screams that she was a police officer.[66]

There are no reliable estimates of how often Americans' rights are violated in practice, but infringements of one sort or another are a daily occurrence in every major city. Minorities and poor people are the usual victims.

United States, it is also true that more than half of those in prison were convicted of nonviolent offenses, such as drug use or a crime against property. Whatever the reasons, the United States is second only to Russia in the proportion of its people who are in prisons.

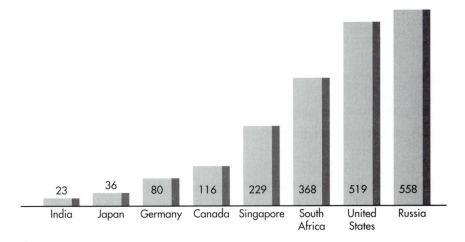

India	Japan	Germany	Canada	Singapore	South Africa	United States	Russia
23	36	80	116	229	368	519	558

SOURCE: Locking People Up around the World," *U.S. News & World Report*, September 19, 1994, p. 17.

Another issue of justice in America is whether adherence to proper legal procedures produces reasonable outcomes. The Eighth Amendment prohibits "cruel and unusual punishment" for those convicted of crime, but judgments in this area are relatively subjective. Although the Supreme Court has ordered officials to relieve inmate overcrowding and to improve prison facilities in a few instances, it has concluded that inmates cannot sue over prison conditions unless prison officials show "deliberate indifference" to conditions.[67] The severity of a sentence can also be an Eighth Amendment issue. A divided Supreme Court in 1991 upheld a Michigan law that mandated life imprisonment without parole for a nonviolent first-offense conviction for possession of as little as 1.5 pounds of cocaine.[68] In general, the Court has shied away from decisions about what constitutes cruel and unusual punishment, preferring to leave them in the hands of legislative bodies.

This philosophy is evident in the Supreme Court's stand on capital punishment. Although the Court in the 1970s temporarily halted the use of capital punishment on grounds it was being applied arbitrarily (race, gender, and income substantially affect the likelihood that a defendant will receive the death penalty), the Court has since upheld the death penalty's constitutionality and has rarely granted reprieves in cases of alleged discrimination. The Court has developed some guidelines that states are required to follow when a sentence of death is a possible outcome in a criminal case, but the states otherwise have considerable latitude in the area of capital punishment (see box: States in the Nation).

In recent years, legislators in the United States have taken a tougher stance on crime. Congress and most states have mandated stiffer sentences, and the number of federal and state prisoners has more than doubled in the past decade. The U.S. prison population is the second largest in the world on a per capita basis (see box: How the United States Compares).

These actions reflect growing public concern with crime. Polls indicate that Americans would like to see police get a lot tougher on crime, apparently even to the extent of infringing on constitutional rights. A Time/CNN survey, for instance, indicated that half of adult Americans would allow police to stop and frisk a person for weapons if he or she merely looked suspicious (see Figure 4-2).

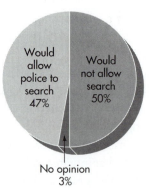

FIGURE 4-2   OPINIONS ON POLICE SEARCHES
WITHOUT PROBABLE CAUSE
Americans are nearly as likely to say that they would allow police to search anyone who merely looked like a criminal as to say that they would prohibit such a search. Source: Time/CNN survey by Yankelovich Partners, Inc., January 17–18, 1994.

THE COURTS AND A FREE SOCIETY

A free and democratic nation has a vital stake in maintaining individual freedoms. The United States was founded on the belief that individuals have an innate right to personal liberty—to speak their minds, to worship as they choose, to be free of police intimidation. The greatest threat to individual rights in a democratic society is a popular majority backed by elected leaders determined to carry out its will. Majorities have frequently preferred policies that would diminish the freedom of those who hold minority views, have unconventional lifestyles, or simply "look different."

Greater support for individual rights exists among the political elite. Those who are most active politically, including officeholders and journalists, are more likely to express strong support for free expression and fair-trial rights. They are also better positioned than the ordinary citizen to express their beliefs. But they are not always willing to act on them. Often, the exercise of rights involves society's least savory characters—its murderers, rapists, drug dealers, and hate peddlers. Miscreants are hardly the type of people who engender public support at any level.

The courts are not isolated from the public mood. They inevitably balance society's demand for safety and order against the rights of the individual. Nevertheless, the judicial branch can normally be expected to grant more consideration to the rights of the individual, however unpopular his or her views or actions, than will the general public or elected officials. How far the courts will go in protecting a person's rights depends on the facts of the case, the existing status of the law, prevailing social needs, and the personal views of the judges. Nevertheless, the courts regard the protection of individual rights as one of their most significant responsibilities, a perspective that is owed in no small measure to the Bill of Rights. It transformed the inalienable rights of life, liberty, and property into legal rights, thus putting them under judicial protection.[69]

Nevertheless, the judiciary alone cannot provide adequate protection for individual rights. A civil society also rests on enlightened representatives and a tolerant citizenry. If, for example, politicians and the public encourage police to infringe on the rights of vaguely threatening minorities or nonconformists, the judiciary's protection of persons accused of crimes will not ensure justice. It may be said that the test of a truly civil society is not its treatment of popular ideas and of its best citizens but its willingness to tolerate ideas that the majority detests and to respect equally the rights of its least popular citizens.

SUMMARY

In their search for personal liberty, Americans added the Bill of Rights to the Constitution shortly after its ratification. These amendments guarantee certain political, procedural, and property rights against infringement by the national government. Freedom of expression is the most basic of democratic rights. People are not free unless they can freely express their views. Nevertheless, free expression may conflict with the nation's security needs during times of war and insurrection. The courts at times have allowed government to limit expression substantially for purposes of national security. In recent decades, however, the courts have protected a very wide range of free expression in the areas of speech, press, and religion.

The guarantees embodied in the Bill of Rights originally applied only to the national government. Under the principle of selective incorporation of these guarantees into the Fourteenth Amendment, the courts extended them to state governments, though the process was slow and uneven. In the 1920s and 1930s, First Amendment guarantees of freedom of expression were given protection from infringement by the states. The states, however, continued to have wide discretion in criminal proceedings until the early 1960s, when most of the fair-trial rights in the Bill of Rights were given federal protection.

"Due process of law" refers to legal protections that have been established to preserve individual rights. The most significant form of these protections consists of procedures or methods (for example, the right of an accused person to have an attorney present during police interrogation) designed to ensure that an individual's rights are upheld. A major controversy in this area is the breadth of the exclusionary rule, which bars the use in trials of illegally obtained evidence. The right of privacy, particularly as it applies to the abortion issue, is also a source of controversy.

Civil liberties are not absolute but must be balanced against other considerations (such as national security or public safety) and against one another when different rights come into conflict. The judicial branch of government, particularly the Supreme Court, has taken on much of the responsibility for protecting and interpreting individual rights. The Court's positions have changed with time and conditions, but the Court has generally been more protective of and sensitive to civil liberties than have elected officials or popular majorities.

MAJOR CONCEPTS

Bill of Rights
civil liberties
clear-and-present-danger test
establishment clause
exclusionary rule

free-exercise clause
freedom of expression
prior restraint
procedural due process
selective incorporation

SUGGESTED READINGS

Blanchard, Margaret A. *Revolutionary Sparks: Freedom of Expression in Modern America*. New York: Oxford University Press, 1992. A historical study of twentieth-century freedom of expression.

Bodenhamer, David J. *Fair Trial: Rights of the Accused in American History*. New York: Oxford University Press, 1991. A comprehensive historical survey of the rights of the accused.

Daniels, Cynthia R. *At Women's Expense: State Power and the Politics of Fetal Rights*. Cambridge, Mass.: Harvard University Press, 1993. A look at the issue of fetal rights that goes beyond the issue of abortion alone.

Graber, Mark A. *Rethinking Abortion: Equal Choice, the Constitution, and Reproductive Politics*. Princeton, N.J.: Princeton University Press, 1996. Argues that constitutional principles require that all U.S. women be afforded the same abortion rights.

Haiman, Franklyn S. *Speech and Law in a Free Society*. Chicago: University of Chicago Press, 1981. An assessment of the primacy of speech in a free society.

Lewis, Anthony. *Gideon's Trumpet*. New York: Random House, 1964. The riveting story of Clarence Gideon and the effect of his case on the right to legal counsel.

Murphy, Paul L. *The Shaping of the First Amendment: 1791 to the Present*. New York: Oxford University Press, 1991. A description of the development and application of First Amendment principles in American history.

Nagel, Robert F. *Judicial Power and American Character*. New York: Oxford University Press, 1996. Concludes that the real protection for legal rights resides in political action rather than judicial decisions.

Segers, Mary, and Ted G. Jelen. *A Wall of Seperation? Debating the Public Role of Religion*. Lanham, Md.: Rowman & Littlefield, 1997. An assessment of the relationship between church and state as a constitutional issue and in practice.

Uviller, Richard H. *Virtual Justice: The Flawed Prosecution of Crime in America*. New Haven, Conn.: Yale University Press, 1996. A critical analysis of the U.S. criminal justice system.

Reading 4

Flag Burning and Free Expression
Texas v. Johnson (1989)

In 1984, Gregory Lee Johnson, a member of the Communist Youth Brigade, set fire to a U.S. flag outside the hall in Dallas where the Republican National Convention was being held. The purpose of the event was to protest Reagan administration policies. While the flag burned, the protesters chanted, "America, the red, white, and blue, we spit on you." No one was physically injured or threatened with bodily harm by the demonstrators, but some witnesses claimed to have been deeply offended by the flag burning. Of the approximately 100 demonstrators, Johnson alone was accused of a crime; he was charged with violating a Texas law prohibiting the desecration of a venerated object. He was tried and convicted in a Texas court, which sentenced him to a year in prison and a $2000 fine. His conviction was overturned by Texas's highest court as a violation of his First Amendment rights, and the state of Texas appealed that decision to the Supreme Court of the United States.

Justice Brennan, joined by Justices Marshall, Blackmun, Scalia, and Kennedy, wrote the majority opinion, saying in part:

> Johnson was convicted of flag desecration for burning the flag rather than for uttering insulting words. This fact somewhat complicates our consideration of his conviction under the First Amendment. We must first determine whether Johnson's burning of the flag constituted expressive conduct, permitting him to invoke the First Amendment in challenging his conviction. . . .
>
> The First Amendment literally forbids the abridgement only of "speech," but we have long recognized that its protection does not end at the spoken or written word. . . .
>
> In deciding whether particular conduct possesses sufficient communicative elements to bring the First Amendment into play, we have asked whether "[a]n intent to convey a particularized message was present, and [whether] the likelihood was great that the message would be understood by those who

viewed it." . . . Hence, we have recognized the expressive nature of students' wearing of black armbands to protest American military involvement in Vietnam; . . . of a sit-in by blacks in a "whites only" area to protest segregation, . . . of the wearing of American military uniforms in a dramatic presentation criticizing American involvement in Vietnam, . . . and of picketing about a wide variety of causes. . . .

Especially pertinent to this case are our decisions recognizing the communicative nature of conduct relating to flags. Attaching a peace sign to the flag, . . . saluting the flag, and displaying a red flag, we have held, all may find shelter under the First Amendment. . . . That we have had little difficulty identifying an expressive element in conduct relating to flags should not be surprising. The very purpose of a national flag is to serve as a symbol of our country; it is, one might say, "the one visible manifestation of two hundred years of nationhood." . . . Texas claims that its interest in preventing breaches of the peace justifies Johnson's conviction for flag desecration. However, no disturbance of the peace actually occurred or threatened to occur because of Johnson's burning of the flag. . . .

The State's position, therefore, amounts to a claim that an audience that takes serious offense at particular expression is necessarily likely to disturb the peace and that the expression may be prohibited on this basis. Our precedents do not countenance such a presumption. On the contrary, they recognize that a principal "function of free speech under our system of government is to invite dispute. It may indeed best serve its high purpose when it induces a condition of unrest, creates dissatisfaction with conditions as they are, or even stirs people to anger." . . .

Nor does Johnson's expressive conduct fall within that small class of "fighting words" that are "likely to provoke the average person to retaliation, and thereby cause a breach of the peace." . . . No reasonable onlooker would have regarded Johnson's generalized expression of dissatisfaction with the policies of the Federal Government as a direct personal insult or an invitation to exchange fisticuffs. . . .

We thus conclude that the State's interest in maintaining order is not implicated on these facts. . . .

It remains to consider whether the State's interest in preserving the flag as a symbol of nationhood and national unity justifies Johnson's conviction. . . .

Johnson's political expression was restricted because of the content of the message he conveyed. We must therefore subject the State's asserted interest in preserving the special symbolic character of the flag to "the most exacting scrutiny." . . .

Texas argues that its interest in preserving the flag as a symbol of nationhood and national unity survives this close analysis. . . . According to Texas, if one physically treats the flag in a way that would tend to cast doubt on either the idea that nationhood and national unity are the flag's referents or that national unity actually exists, the message conveyed thereby is a harmful one and therefore may be prohibited.

If there is a bedrock principle underlying the First Amendment, it is that the Government may not prohibit the expression of an idea simply because society finds the idea itself offensive or disagreeable. . . .

To conclude that the Government may permit designated symbols to be used to communicate only a limited set of messages would be to enter territory having no discernible or defensible boundaries. Could the Government, on this theory, prohibit the burning of state flags? Of copies of the Presidential seal? Of the Constitution? In evaluating these choices under the First Amendment, how would we decide which symbols were sufficiently special to warrant this unique status? To do so, we would be forced to consult our own political preferences, and impose them on the citizenry, in the very way that the First Amendment forbids us to do. . . .

There is, moreover, no indication—either in the text of the Constitution or in our cases interpreting it—that a separate juridical category exists for the American flag alone. Indeed, we would not be surprised to learn that the persons who framed our Constitution and wrote the Amendment that we now construe were not known for their reverence for the Union Jack. The First Amendment does not guarantee that other concepts virtually sacred to our Nation as a whole—such as the principle that discrimination on the basis of race is odious and destructive—will go unquestioned in the marketplace of ideas. . . . We decline, therefore, to create for the flag an exception to the joust of principles protected by the First Amendment. . . .

The way to preserve the flag's special role is not to punish those who feel differently about these matters. It is to persuade them that they are wrong. . . . We can imagine no more appropriate response to burning a flag than waving one's own, no better way to counter a flag-burner's message than by saluting the flag that burns, no surer means of preserving the dignity even of the flag that burned than by—as one witness here did—according its remains a respectful burial. We do not consecrate the flag by punishing its desecration, for in doing so we dilute the freedom that this cherished emblem represents.

Chief Justice Rehnquist, joined by Justices White and O'Connor, dissented from the majority opinion, saying in part:

> For more than 200 years, the American flag has occupied a unique position as the symbol of our Nation, a uniqueness that justifies a governmental prohibition against flag burning in the way respondent Johnson did here. . . .

> No other American symbol has been as universally honored as the flag. In 1931, Congress declared "The Star Spangled Banner" to be our national anthem. In 1949, Congress declared June 14th to be Flag Day. In 1987, John Philip Sousa's "The Stars and Stripes Forever" was designated as the national march. Congress has also established "The Pledge of Allegiance to the Flag" and the manner of its deliverance. . . .

> The American flag, then, throughout more than 200 years of our history, has come to be the visible symbol embodying our Nation. It does not represent the views of any particular political party, and it does not represent any particular political philosophy. The flag is not simply another "idea" or "point of view" competing for recognition in the marketplace of ideas. . . .

> Uncritical extension of constitutional protection to the burning of the flag risks the frustration of the very purpose for which organized governments are instituted. The Court decides that the American flag is just another symbol, about which not only must opinions pro and con be tolerated, but for which the most minimal public respect may not be enjoined. The government may conscript men into the Armed Forces where they must fight and perhaps die for the flag, but the government may not prohibit the public burning of the banner under which they fight. I would uphold the Texas statute as applied in this case.

SOURCE: *Texas* v. *Johnson*, 491 U.S. 397 (1989).

CHAPTER FIVE

Equal Rights

I have a dream that one day this nation will rise up and live out the true meaning
of its creed: "We hold these truths to be self-evident: that all men are created
equal."

MARTIN LUTHER KING, JR.[1]

HE PRODUCERS of ABC television's *Prime Time Live* put hidden
cameras on two young men, equally well dressed, and sent them
on different routes to do the same things—search for an apartment, shop
for a car, look at albums in a record store. The cameras recorded the reactions the two men received. One was greeted with smiles and was invited to
buy, sometimes at favorable prices. The other man was treated with suspicious looks, was sometimes made to wait, and was sometimes asked to pay
more. Why the difference? The explanation was simple: the young man who
was routinely well received was white; the young man who was treated badly
was an African American.

The Urban Institute conducted a similar but more elaborate experiment.
It was based on pairs of specially trained white and black male college students who were the same in all respects—education, work experience, speech
patterns, physical builds—except for their race. The students responded individually to nearly 500 classified job advertisements in Chicago and Washington, D.C. The black applicants got fewer interviews, had shorter interviews, and were given fewer job offers than the white applicants. An Urban
Institute spokesperson said, "The level of reverse discrimination [favoring
blacks over whites] that we found was limited, was certainly far lower than
many might have been led to fear, and was swamped by the extent of discrimination against black job applicants."[2]

These two experiments suggest why some Americans are still struggling
for equal rights. In theory, Americans are equal in their rights, but in practice, they are not equal today, nor have they ever been. African Americans,
women, Hispanic Americans, the disabled, Jews, Native Americans,

Catholics, Asian Americans, homosexuals, and members of nearly every other minority group have been victims of discrimination in fact and in law. The nation's creed—"all men are created equal"—has encouraged minorities to believe that they deserve equal justice and has given weight to their claims for fair treatment. But inequality is built into almost every aspect of our society. To take but one example: African Americans with a correctable heart problem are three times less likely to receive the necessary surgery than are whites with the same problem.[3]

This chapter focuses on **equal rights,** or **civil rights**—terms that refer to the right of every person to equal protection under the law and equal access to society's opportunities and public facilities. We saw in Chapter 4 that "civil liberties" refer to *individual* rights, such as freedom of speech, that are protected from infringement by government. "Equal rights" or "civil rights" have to do with whether individual members of differing *groups*—racial, sexual, and the like—are treated equally by government and, in some areas, by private parties. To oversimplify, civil liberties deal with issues of personal freedom, and civil rights involve issues of equality.

Although the law refers to the rights of individuals first and to those of groups in a secondary and derivative way, this chapter concentrates on groups because the history of civil rights has been largely one of group claims to equality. The chapter emphasizes the following main points:

* *Disadvantaged groups have had to struggle for equal rights.*
* *Americans have attained substantial equality under the law. They have, in legal terms, equal protection of the laws, equal access to accommodations and housing, and an equal right to vote.*
* *Legal equality for all Americans has not resulted in* de facto *equality. African Americans, women, Hispanic Americans, and other traditionally disadvantaged groups are given a disproportionately small share of America's opportunities and benefits.*

THE STRUGGLE FOR EQUALITY

Equality has always been the least fully developed of America's founding concepts. Not even Thomas Jefferson, who had a deep admiration for the "common man," believed that broad meaning could be given to the claim of the Declaration of Independence that "all men are created equal." To Jefferson, "equality" had a restricted, though significant, meaning: people are of equal moral worth and as such deserve equal treatment under the law.[4] Even then, Jefferson made a distinction between free men, who were entitled to legal equality, and slaves, who were not.

The history of America shows that disadvantaged groups have rarely achieved an additional degree of legal equality without a struggle. Equality has rarely been bestowed by the more powerful upon the less powerful, as is evident by a brief look at the efforts of African Americans, women, Native Americans, Hispanic Americans, Asian Americans, and other groups to achieve fuller equality.

African Americans

Of all America's problems, none has been as persistent as the white race's unwillingness to yield a fair share of society's benefits to members of the black race. The ancestors of most African Americans came to this country as slaves, after having been captured in Africa, shipped in chains across the Atlantic, and sold in markets in Charleston and other southern seaports.

It took a civil war to bring slavery to an end, but the battle did not end institutionalized racism. When Reconstruction ended in 1877 with the withdrawal of federal troops from the South, whites in the region gradually reestablished racial segregation by enacting laws that prohibited black citizens from using the same public facilities as whites.[5] In *Plessy* v. *Ferguson* (1896), the Supreme Court endorsed these laws, ruling that "separate" facilities for the two races did not violate the Constitution as long as the facilities were "equal." "If one race be inferior to the other socially," the Court asserted, "the Constitution of the United States cannot put them on the same plane."[6] The *Plessy* decision became a justification for the separate and *unequal* treatment of African Americans. Black children, for example, were forced into separate schools that had few teachers and had to get by with worn-out books that had been used previously in white schools.

Black leaders challenged these discriminatory state and local policies through legal action, but not until the late 1930s did the Supreme Court begin to respond favorably to their demands. The Court began modestly by ruling that where no public facilities existed for African Americans, they must be allowed to use those reserved for whites.[7]

THE *BROWN* DECISION Substantial relief for African Americans was finally achieved in 1954 with *Brown* v. *Board of Education of Topeka*, arguably the most significant ruling in Supreme Court history. The case involved Linda Carol Brown, a black child in Topeka, Kansas, who was denied admission to an all-white elementary school that she passed every day on her way to her all-black school, which was twelve blocks farther away.[8] In its decision, the Court fully reversed its "separate but equal" doctrine by declaring that racial segregation of public schools "generates [among black children] a feeling of inferiority as to their status in the community that may affect their hearts and minds in a way unlikely ever to be undone. . . . Separate educational facilities are inherently unequal."[9]

As a 1954 Gallup Poll indicated, a sizable majority of southern whites opposed the *Brown* decision, and billboards were erected along southern roadways calling for the impeachment of Chief Justice Earl Warren. For their part, northern whites were neither strongly for nor strongly against school desegregation. A Gallup Poll revealed that only a slim majority of whites outside the South agreed with the *Brown* decision.

THE BLACK CIVIL RIGHTS MOVEMENT   After *Brown*, the struggle of African Americans for their rights became a political movement. Perhaps no single event turned national public opinion so dramatically against segregation as a 1963 march led by Dr. Martin Luther King, Jr., in Birmingham, Alabama. An advocate of nonviolent protest, King had been leading peaceful demonstrations for nearly eight years before that fateful day in Birmingham.[10] As the nation watched in disbelief on television, police officers led by Birmingham's sheriff, Eugene "Bull" Connor, attacked King and his followers with dogs, cattle prods, and firehoses.

The modern civil rights movement peaked with the triumphant March on Washington for Jobs and Freedom on August 2, 1963, which attracted 250,000 demonstrators, one of the largest gatherings in the history of the nation's capital. "I have a dream," the Reverend King told the gathering, "that my four little children will one day live in a nation where they will not be judged by the color of their skin but by the content of their character."

A year later, after a prolonged fight in Congress that included every legislative obstacle that racial conservatives could muster, the Civil Rights Act of 1964 was enacted. The tide was turning against racial inequality. President Lyndon Johnson, who had been a decisive force in the battle to pass the Civil Rights Act, called for new legislation that would end racial barriers to voting.[11] Congress's answer was the 1965 Voting Rights Act.

Although the most significant progress in history toward the legal equality of all Americans occurred during the 1960s, Dr. King's dream of a color-blind society has remained elusive.[12] By some indicators, the status of African Americans has actually deteriorated since Martin Luther King was assassinated in 1968. According to U.S. Department of Labor statistics, the unemployment rate for African Americans in the late 1960s was about 50 per-

Two police dogs attack a black civil rights activist *(center left of picture)* during the 1963 Birmingham demonstrations. Such images of hatred and violence shook many white Americans out of their complacency regarding race relations. (Charles Moore/Black Star)

cent higher than the rate for whites; by 1995 it was roughly 100 percent higher. During the same period, the gap in the incomes of black and white Americans has widened, not narrowed. The income of the average African American is now about 60 percent of the average white person's (see box: States in the Nation).

Even the legal rights of African Americans do not, in practice, match the promise of the civil rights movement.[13] Studies have found, for example, that African Americans accused of crime are more likely to be convicted and to receive stiffer sentences than white Americans on trial for comparable offenses. Or consider the Florida study that observed traffic on a stretch of interstate highway and found that African Americans, although constituting less than a sixth of the drivers, accounted for more than two-thirds of those stopped by the highway patrol and, once pulled over, were detained twice as long on average as white drivers.[14] It is hardly surprising that many African Americans believe that the nation has two standards of justice, an inferior one for blacks and a higher one for whites.

S T A T E S I N T H E N A T I O N

Income Inequality, Blacks versus Whites

African Americans in every state have substantially lower incomes than the white Americans who reside there. New Hampshire has the least income inequality (on average, blacks' income is 78.4 percent of whites' income) while Mississippi has the greatest income inequality (on average, blacks' income is only 42.6 percent of whites' income). In general, income inequality is greatest in the former slave states of the South.

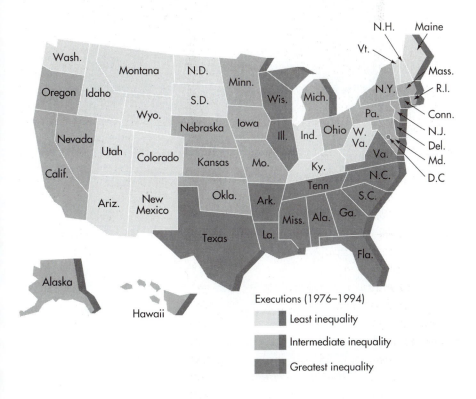

Executions (1976–1994)

- Least inequality
- Intermediate inequality
- Greatest inequality

SOURCE: U.S. Bureau of the Census.

A particularly ugly indicator of racism in America was a rash of fires in black churches in 1996; dozens of predominantly black churches in the South were torched. The Reverend Jesse Jackson, a prominent black leader, blamed the fires on a "cultural conspiracy" that treats black Americans as somehow less deserving of equal treatment and respect.[15]

African Americans have made progress since the 1960s in winning election to public office.[16] Although the percentage of black elected officials is still far below the proportion of African Americans in the population, it has risen sharply over recent decades. As of 1997, there were more than 30 black members of Congress and 200 black mayors—including the mayors of some of the largest cities, such as Atlanta and Detroit.

In 1992 Carol Mosely-Braun (D-Ill.) became the first African American woman elected to the U.S. Senate. She is shown here with First Lady Hillary Rodham Clinton during "Youth America Day" activities at the White House. (Brad Markel/Gamma-Liaison)

Women

The United States carried over from English common law a political disregard for women, forbidding them to vote, hold public office, and serve on juries. Upon marriage, a woman essentially lost her identity as an individual and could not own and dispose of property without her husband's consent. Even the wife's body was not fully hers. A wife's adultery was ruled by the Supreme Court to be a violation of the husband's property rights![17]

The first women's rights convention in America was held in 1848 in Seneca Falls, New York, after Lucretia Mott and Elizabeth Cady Stanton had been barred from the main floor of an antislavery convention. Thereafter, however, the struggle for women's rights became closely aligned with the abolitionist movement, but the passage of the post–Civil War constitutional amendments proved to be a setback for the women's movement. The Fifteenth Amendment, for example, said that the right to vote could not be abridged on account of race or color but said nothing about sex.[18] After decades of struggle, the Nineteenth Amendment was finally adopted in 1920, forbidding denial of the right to vote "by the United States or by any state on account of sex."

WOMEN'S LEGAL AND POLITICAL GAINS   Ratification of the Nineteenth Amendment encouraged leaders of the women's movement to propose in 1923 a constitutional amendment that would guarantee equal rights for women. Congress rejected that proposal and several subsequent ones. In 1973, however, Congress approved an Equal Rights Amendment (ERA) and submitted it to the states for ratification or rejection. The ERA failed by three states to get the three-fourths majority required for ratification.[19]

Although the ERA did not become part of the Constitution, it helped bring women's rights to the forefront at a time when developments in Congress and the courts were contributing significantly to the legal equality of the sexes.[20] Among the congressional initiatives that have helped women are the Equal Pay Act of 1963, which prohibits sex discrimination in salary and wages by some categories of employers; the Civil Rights Act of 1964, which prohibits sex discrimination in programs that receive federal funding; Title IX of the Education Amendment of 1972, which prohibits sex discrimination in education; the Equal Credit Act of 1974, as amended in 1976, which prohibits sex discrimination in the granting of financial credit; and the Civil Rights Act of 1991 and the Family Leave Act of 1993 (discussed later in the chapter).

Women have made clear gains in the area of appointive and elective offices.[21] In 1981 President Reagan appointed the first woman to serve on the Supreme Court, Sandra Day O'Connor. When the Democratic party in 1984 chose Geraldine Ferraro as its vice-presidential nominee, it was the first time a woman ran on the national ticket of a major political party. The election of California's Dianne Feinstein and Barbara Boxer in 1992 marked the first time that women occupied both U.S. Senate seats from a state.

Despite such signs of progress, women are still a long way from political equality with men.[22] Women occupy only 10 percent of congressional seats and only 20 percent of statewide and city council offices (see box: How the United States Compares). Moreover, women in office are more likely than their male counterparts to believe there are significant obstacles to political advancement.[23]

Although women are underrepresented in political office, their vote is becoming increasingly powerful. Until the 1970s, there was almost no difference in the voting patterns of men and women. Today, there is a substantial **gender gap:** women are considerably more likely than men to cast their votes for Democratic candidates (see Figure 5-1). In the 1996 presidential race, the difference was a record 16 percent. The gender gap reflects women's more liberal attitudes on social and economic issues, including government assistance for the poor, minorities, children, and the elderly (see Chapter 6).[24] The gender gap increases when a woman is running on the Democratic ticket.[25]

JOB-RELATED ISSUES: FAMILY LEAVE, COMPARABLE WORTH, AND SEX-UAL HARASSMENT   In recent decades, increasing numbers of women have sought employment outside the home. Government statistics indicate that three in five women worked outside the home in 1995 compared with only one in eight in 1950. Women have made gains in many traditionally male-dominated fields. For example, women now make up a third of the new lawyers who enter the job market each year. The change in women's status is also reflected in education statistics. In 1972, more white, black, and Hispanic men than women enrolled in college. By 1991, the reverse was true: more women than men of each race were enrolled.

The increase in the number of women in the workplace has created demands for the expansion of programs such as day care centers and parental leave. In 1993, Congress passed the Family and Medical Leave Act, which provides up to twelve weeks of unpaid leave for employees, male or female, to care for a new baby or a seriously ill family member. Upon return from

HOW THE UNITED STATES COMPARES

Women's Inequality

The one form of inequality common to all nations is that of gender: nowhere are women equal to men in law or in fact. But there are large differences between countries. A study by the Population Crisis Committee ranked the United States third overall in women's equality, behind only Sweden and Finland. The rankings were based on five areas—jobs, education, social relations, marriage and family, and health—where U.S. women had an 82.5 percent rating compared with men.

The inequality of women is also underlined by their lack of representation in public office. There is no country in which women comprise as many as half the members of the national legislature. The Scandinavian countries rank highest in terms of the percentage of female lawmakers. Other northern European countries have lower levels, but the levels are higher than that of the United States. Until the 1992 election, only 6 percent of U.S. House members were women. In 1992, as a consequence of reapportionment and the retirement of an unusually large number of incumbents, the number of women in the House nearly doubled and has since stayed at about the 10 percent level. The accompanying figure, estimated from several sources, indicates the approximate percentage of seats held by women in the largest chamber of each country's national legislature.

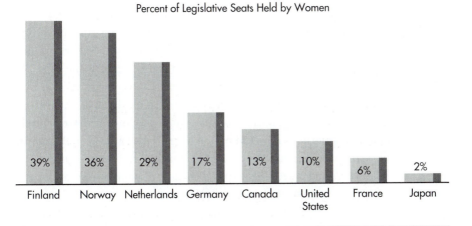

Percent of Legislative Seats Held by Women

Finland	Norway	Netherlands	Germany	Canada	United States	France	Japan
39%	36%	29%	17%	13%	10%	6%	2%

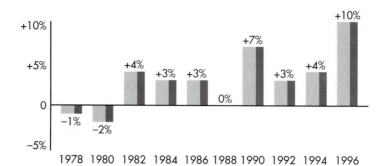

FIGURE 5-1 THE GENDER GAP IN CONGRESSIONAL VOTING
Women are now more likely than men to vote Democratic, as shown by the net difference between the women's vote and the men's vote for Democratic candidates in U.S. House races. Source: National Election Studies, 1978–1994; Emily's List, exit poll, 1996.

leave, employees must ordinarily be restored to their original or equivalent positions with equivalent pay, benefits, and other employment terms.

Nevertheless, women are less than equal to men when it comes to job opportunities and benefits. Women increasingly occupy managerial positions, but they are less likely to receive promotions than men and rarely get the top corporate jobs. The term "glass ceiling" refers to the invisible but nonetheless real barrier to advancement that talented women encounter after having reached the middle-management level.

Women also hold a disproportionate number of the poorer-paying jobs in society. On average, full-time women employees earn only about three-fourths as much as full-time men employees (see Figure 5-2). This situation has led to demands by women for equal pay for work that is of similar difficulty and responsibility and that requires similar levels of education and training—a concept called **comparable worth.** A comparable-worth policy would eliminate salary inequities resulting from the fact that some jobs (for example, secretaries) have traditionally been dominated by women and thus pay less than male-dominated jobs (for example, truck drivers). Advocates of comparable worth gained an early victory when the Supreme Court held in 1981 that female guards at a prison had to be paid the same as male guards even if their work assignments differed.[26] In general, however, proponents of comparable worth have had only limited success in persuading public and private employers to accept their view.[27] Opponents have argued that market forces alone should decide the wages and salaries that individuals receive.[28]

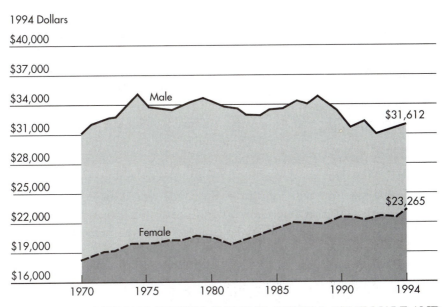

1994 Dollars

FIGURE 5-2 MEDIAN ANNUAL INCOME OF FULL-TIME MALE AND FEMALE WORKERS
Women's income has increased relative to men's income during the past quarter-century but is still substantially lower. Source: U.S. Bureau of the Census, 1995.

Workplace discrimination against women includes sexual harassment. Lewd comments and unwelcome advances are a part of everyday life for many working women, and the courts have taken an increasingly firm stand against firms that tolerate such behavior. The legal standard for what constitutes sexual harassment is known as the "reasonable woman" standard. The question in each case is whether a reasonable woman would be offended by a supervisor's or co-worker's request for sexual favors, a display of sex-related pictures or objects, sexual language, or physical contact.

Native Americans

When white settlers began arriving in America in large numbers during the seventeenth century, nearly 10 million Native Americans were living in the territory that would become the United States. By 1900, the Native American population had plummeted to less than 1 million. Diseases brought by white settlers had taken a toll on the various Indian tribes, but so had wars and massacres. "The only good Indian is a dead Indian" is not simply a hackneyed expression from cowboy movies. It was part of a strategy of westward expansion, as settlers and U.S. troops alike mercilessly drove the eastern Indians from their ancestral lands to the Great Plains, and then took those lands as well.

Today Native Americans number more than 1 million, about half of whom live on or close to reservations set aside for them by the federal government. Native Americans are less than half as likely to attend college as other Americans, their life expectancy is more than ten years lower than the national average, and their infant mortality rate is more than three times higher than that of white Americans.

The civil rights movement of the 1960s at first did not include Native Americans, but they benefited from the legislative climate it created. In 1968 Congress enacted the Indian Bill of Rights, which gives Native Americans on reservations constitutional guarantees that are similar to those held by other Americans.

Hispanic Americans

The fastest-growing minority in the United States is that of Hispanic Americans, people with Spanish-speaking backgrounds. The 1990 census counted 22.4 million Hispanics living in the United States, an increase of 53 percent over the 1980 census; and it is projected that Hispanics will replace African Americans as the nation's largest racial or ethnic minority group soon after the year 2000. They have emigrated to the United States primarily from Mexico and the Caribbean islands, mainly Cuba and Puerto Rico. About half of all Hispanics in the United States were born in Mexico or claim a Mexican ancestry. Hispanics are concentrated in their states of entry; thus Florida, New York, and New Jersey have large numbers of Caribbean Hispanics, while California, Texas, Arizona, and New Mexico have many immigrants from Mexico. More than half the population of Los Angeles is of Hispanic—mostly Mexican—descent.

The term "Hispanic" can be misleading if it is construed to mean a group of people who all think alike (see Table 5-1). Hispanics cover a wide political spectrum, from the conservative Republican-leaning Cuban Americans of southern Florida to the liberal Democratic-leaning Puerto Ricans of the Northeast. Hispanic Americans share a common language, Spanish, but they are not monolithic in their politics.[29]

ILLEGAL ALIENS Hispanic Americans have benefited from laws and court rulings aimed primarily at protecting other groups. Thus, although the Civil Rights Act of 1964 was largely a response to the condition of black

TABLE 5-1   HISPANICS' PARTY IDENTIFICATION, BY
NATIONAL ORIGIN
Hispanics share a common language and ancestry but differ substantially
in their political leanings.

Party Identification	Puerto Rican Americans	Mexican Americans	Cuban Americans
Democratic	64%	60%	19%
Independent	22	24	17
Republican	14	16	64
	100%	100%	100%

SOURCE: *Latino National Political Survey*, reported in Rudolfo O. de la Garza, Angelo Falcon, F. Chris Garcia, and John A. Garcia, "Hispanic Americans in the Mainstream of U.S. Politics," *The Public Perspective*, July/August 1992, p. 19.

people, its provisions against discrimination apply broadly to other groups as well.

Hispanics face some distinctive problems. The fact that many do not speak English led to a 1968 amendment to the 1964 Civil Rights Act that funds public school programs offering English instruction in the language of children for whom English is a second language. In addition, many Hispanics are illegal aliens and do not have the full rights of citizens. In *De Canas* v. *Bica* (1976), for example, the Supreme Court upheld a state law barring illegal aliens from employment.[30]

In 1986 Congress passed the landmark Immigration Reform and Control Act, commonly known as the Simpson–Mizzoli Act, which primarily affected Hispanics. The legislation offered citizenship to illegal aliens who could prove they had lived continuously in the United States for five years. Roughly 2 million Hispanics received their citizenship in this way. The act also mandated fines on employers who hired aliens without work permits; it was expected that the resulting lack of job opportunities would eliminate a main incentive for aliens to enter the country illegally.

The issue of illegal aliens was also addressed through California's controversial Proposition 187. Placed on the state's ballot in 1994 through a citizen petition, Proposition 187 received the votes of a majority of Californians even though a majority of the state's Mexican Americans voted against it. The initiative aimed to cut off public services to illegal immigrants, the great majority of whom are Mexicans. They would no longer receive state-funded food stamps, welfare, and medical care except in life-threatening circumstances, and they would no longer be eligible for public schooling at any level. Supporters of the initiative claimed it would save the state from bankruptcy (for example, 10 percent of California's primary and secondary school students are illegal aliens, and their education costs the state more than $1 billion annually).[31] To many of the state's Mexican Americans, the initiative was a thinly disguised attempt to keep additional people from Mexico out of the state. The implementation of Proposition 187 was delayed pending a definitive court decision on the constitutionality of a provision denying a public education to children of illegal immigrants.

GROWING POLITICAL POWER Hispanic Americans are an important political force in some states and communities, and their influence is likely to increase substantially in the future. Hispanics are projected to become the largest single population group in California in the next century. Like other immigrant groups, their political involvement can be expected to increase as they become more deeply rooted in the society and economy. At present, nearly half of all Hispanic adults are not registered to vote, which limits the group's political power.

Hispanic Americans are growing in political and cultural influence as their numbers increase in California and other states. (Alon Reininger/Woodfin Camp & Associates)

More than 4,000 Hispanic Americans nationwide hold public office. In 1974 Arizona and New Mexico elected governors of Spanish-speaking background. New Mexico elected its second Hispanic governor in 1982. About twenty Hispanic Americans currently serve in the House of Representatives.

Asian Americans

Chinese and Japanese laborers were the first Asians to come to the United States in large numbers. They were brought into western states during the late 1800s to work in mines and to build railroads. When the need for this labor declined, Congress in 1892 ordered a temporary halt to Chinese immigration. Over the next three decades, informal agreements kept all but a few Asians out of the country. In 1921 the United States ended its traditional policy of unlimited immigration and established immigration quotas based on country of origin. Western European countries were given large quotas and Asian countries tiny ones. About 150 Japanese a year were allowed to immigrate until 1930, when Congress excluded them entirely.[32]

This discrimination against Asians did not change substantially until 1965, when Congress enacted legislation that adjusted the immigration quotas to favor those who had previously been disadvantaged. This change in the law was a product of the 1960s civil rights movement, which, as we have indicated, sensitized national leaders to all forms of discrimination. About half a million people now emigrate to the United States each year, and a majority come from Asian and Latin American countries. By the year 2000, Asian Americans will number about 12 million, or between 4 and 5 percent of the total U.S. population. Most Asian Americans live on the West Coast, particularly in California.

The rights of Asian Americans have been expanded primarily by court rulings and legislation, such as the Civil Rights Act of 1964, that were responses to the problems of other minorities. In a few instances, however, the rights of minorities have been defined by actions of Asian Americans. For example, in *Lau* v. *Nichols* (1974), a case involving Chinese Americans, the Supreme Court ruled that public schools with a large proportion of children for whom English is a second language must offer English instruction in the children's first language.[33]

Asian Americans are an upwardly mobile group. The values of most Asian cultures include a commitment to hard work, which, in the American context, has included an emphasis on academic achievement. For example, Asians make up a disproportionate share of the students at California's leading public universities, which base admission primarily on high school grades

Asian American children study U.S. history in a middle-school classroom. Many Asian American families emphasize academic achievement as a means of upward mobility. (Anthony Suau/Gamma-Liaison)

and standardized test scores. However, Asian Americans are still underrepresented in certain areas of the workplace. According to U.S. government figures, Asian Americans account for about 5 percent of professionals and technicians, nearly the same as their percentage of the population. Yet they hold less than 2 percent of managerial jobs; past and present discrimination has kept them from obtaining a larger share of top business positions.

Other Groups and Their Rights

Although civil rights efforts have been directed mainly at women and racial and ethnic minorities, other groups are also involved.

One such group are the nearly 15 million Americans (5 percent of the population) who have a physical disability so severe that they are unable to perform some critical function, such as hearing, seeing, or walking. A major goal for the disabled is equal access to society's opportunities, which was facilitated by the 1990 Americans with Disabilities Act. It extends to the disabled the same employment and other protections enjoyed by other disadvantaged groups. In addition, the Education for All Handicapped Children

Act of 1975 mandates that all children, however severe their disability, receive a free, appropriate education. Before the legislation, 1 million handicapped children were getting no education and another 3 million were receiving an inappropriate one (as in the case of a blind child who is not taught Braille).[34]

The government has also acted to protect the elderly from discrimination. The Age Discrimination Act of 1975 and the Age Discrimination in Employment Act of 1967 outlaw discrimination against older workers in hiring for jobs in which age is not clearly a crucial factor in job performance. More recently, mandatory retirement ages for most jobs have been eliminated by law. Forced retirement for reasons of age is permissible only if justified by the nature of a particular job or the performance of a particular employee.

A group that until very recently had not received substantial legal protection is homosexuals. In *Bowers* v. *Hardwick* (1986), the Supreme Court upheld a state law banning sexual acts between consenting homosexual adults, ruling that the constitutional right of privacy does not extend to such acts. Gay rights also were dealt a setback when President Clinton's proposal to permit homosexuals to serve in the military was strongly opposed in Congress. The compromise policy that resulted is called "don't ask, don't tell." According to this informal policy, homosexuals in the military cannot be compelled to admit their sexual preference but can be dismissed from the armed services if they engage in verbal or behavioral displays of homosexuality.

However, gays gained a significant legal victory when the Supreme Court in *Romer* v. *Evans* (1996) struck down a Colorado constitutional amendment that nullified all existing and any new legal protections for homosexuals. In a 6–3 ruling, the Court said the Colorado law violated the Constitution's guarantee of equal protection since it subjects individuals to employment and other forms of discrimination simply because of their sexual preference. The Court concluded that the law had no reasonable purpose but was motivated instead by "animus" (hostility) toward homosexuals.[35]

EQUALITY UNDER THE LAW

The catchphrase of nearly any group's claim to a more equal standing in American society has been "equality under the law." The importance that people attach to legal equality is understandable. Once secure in their legal rights, people are in a stronger position to seek equality in other arenas, such as the economic sector. Once encoded in law, a claim to equality can also force officials to take positive action on behalf of a disadvantaged group.[36] Americans' claims to legal equality are contained in a great many laws, a few of which are particularly noteworthy.

Equal Protection: The Fourteenth Amendment

The Fourteenth Amendment, which was ratified in 1868, declares in part that no state shall "deny to any person within its jurisdiction the equal protection of the laws." Through this **equal-protection clause,** the courts have protected such groups as African Americans and women from discrimination by state and local governments.

The Fourteenth Amendment's equal-protection clause does not require government to treat all groups or classes of people the same way in all circumstances. In fact, laws routinely treat people unequally. By law, for example, twenty-one-year-olds can drink alcohol but twenty-year-olds cannot. The judiciary allows such inequalities because they are held to be "reasonably" related to a legitimate government interest. In applying this **reasonable-basis test,** the courts give the benefit of doubt to government. It need only show that a particular law has a sound rationale. For example, the courts have held that the goal of reducing fatalities from alcohol-related accidents involving young drivers is a valid reason for imposing a twenty-one-year minimum drinking age requirement. (The *Romer* decision discussed earlier provides an example of a law that failed the reasonable-basis test. The Supreme Court concluded that Colorado's law affecting gays had "no legitimate government purpose.")

The reasonable-basis test does not apply, however, to racial or ethnic classifications, particularly when these categories serve to discriminate against minority group members. Any law that posits a racial or ethnic classification is subject to the **strict-scrutiny test,** under which such a law is unconstitutional in the absence of an overwhelmingly convincing argument that it is necessary. The strict-scrutiny test has virtually eliminated race and ethnicity as permissible classifications when the effect is to put members of a minority group at a disadvantage. The Supreme Court's position is that race and national origin are **suspect classifications**—that such classifications have invidious discrimination as their purpose and therefore any law containing such a classification is in all likelihood unconstitutional.

The strict-scrutiny test emerged after the 1954 *Brown* ruling and became a basis for invalidating laws that discriminated against black people. As other groups, especially women, began to organize and press for their rights in the late 1960s and early 1970s, the Supreme Court gave early signs that it might expand the scope of suspect classifications to include gender.[37] In the end, however, the Court announced in *Craig* v. *Boren* (1976) that sex classifications were permissible if they served "important governmental objectives" and were "substantially" related to the achievement of those objectives.[38] The Court thus placed sex distinctions in an "intermediate" (or "almost suspect") category, to be scrutinized more closely than some other classifications (for example, income levels) but, unlike racial classifications, justifiable in some instances. In *Rostker* v. *Goldberg* (1980), for example, the policy of male-only registration for the military draft was upheld on grounds that the exclusion of women from combat duty serves a legitimate and important purpose.[39]

The inexactness of the intermediate-scrutiny test has led some scholars to question its validity as a legal principle. Nevertheless, when evaluating claims of sex discrimination, the judiciary applies a stricter level of scrutiny than is required by the reasonable-basis test. Rather than giving government broad leeway to treat men and women differently, the Supreme Court has recently invalidated most of the laws it has reviewed that contain sex classifications. A leading case is *United States* v. *Virginia* (1996), in which the Supreme Court determined that the male-only admissions policy at Virginia Military Institute (VMI), a 157-year-old state-supported college, was unconstitutional. The state had developed an alternative program for women at another college, but the Court concluded it was no substitute for the unique educational and other opportunities that resulted from attending VMI. (The VMI decision also had the effect of ending the all-male admissions policy of the Citadel, a state-supported military college in South Carolina.)[40]

Equal Access: The Civil Rights Acts of 1964 and 1968

The Fourteenth Amendment applies only to action by government. It does not prohibit discrimination by private parties. As a result, for a long period in the nation's history, owners could legally bar black people from restaurants, hotels, and other accommodations, and employers could freely discriminate in their job practices. Since the 1960s private firms have had much less freedom to discriminate for reasons of race, sex, ethnicity, or religion.

ACCOMMODATIONS AND JOBS   The Civil Rights Act of 1964, which is based on the commerce power of Congress under the Constitution, entitles all persons to equal access to restaurants, bars, theaters, hotels, gasoline stations, and similar establishments serving the general public. The legislation also bars discrimination in the hiring, promotion, and wages of employees of medium-sized and large firms. A few forms of job discrimination are still lawful under the Civil Rights Act of 1964. For example, an owner-operator of a small business can discriminate in hiring his or her co-workers, and a religious school can take the religion of a prospective teacher into account.

The Civil Rights Act of 1964 has nearly eliminated the most overt forms of discrimination in the area of public accommodations. Some restaurants and hotels may provide better service to white customers, but outright refusal to serve African Americans or other minority group members is rare. Such a refusal is a violation of the law and could easily be proved in many instances. It is harder to prove discrimination in job decisions; accordingly, the act has been less effective in rooting out employment discrimination—a subject that will be discussed in detail later in the chapter.

Deacon John Hodge stands at the charred remains of Rising Star Baptist Church in Greensboro, Alabama. His church is one of several dozen predominately black churches that were torched by arsonists in 1996 alone. The burnings are an ugly reminder that racism—"America's curse," in the words of the sociologist Gunner Myrdal—is still the nation's most conspicuous shortcoming.
(Karim-Shamsi-Basha/SABA)

HOUSING   In 1968, Congress passed civil rights legislation designed to prohibit discrimination in housing. A building owner ordinarily cannot refuse to sell or rent housing because of a person's race, religion, ethnicity, or sex. An exception is allowed for owners of small multifamily dwellings who reside on the premises.

Despite legal prohibitions on discrimination, housing in America remains highly segregated. Less than a third of all African Americans live in a neighborhood that is mostly white. One reason is the fact that the annual income of most black families is substantially below that of most white families. Another reason is banking practices. At one time, banks contributed to housing segregation by refusing to grant mortgage loans in certain neighborhoods, thus driving down their housing prices and leading to an influx of African Americans and an exodus of whites. This banking practice, known as "redlining," is prohibited by the 1968 Civil Rights Act. However, a recent study by the Federal Reserve Bank makes it clear that race is still a factor in the lending practices of many banks. Their rejection rate on mortgage loans for African Americans, Hispanics, and Asian Americans is substantially higher than for white Americans, even within the same income categories.[41]

Equal Ballots: The Voting Rights Act of 1965, as Amended

Free elections are perhaps the foremost symbol of American democracy, yet the right to vote has only recently become a reality for many citizens, particularly African Americans.

The Nineteenth Amendment, which in 1920 gave women the right to vote, effectively ended resistance to women's suffrage; paradoxically, resistance to black suffrage was intensified by the Fifteenth Amendment, which in 1870 gave black persons the right to vote. Southern whites invented a series of devices, including whites-only primaries, poll taxes, and rigged literacy tests to keep African Americans from registering and voting.[42] For example, almost no votes were cast by African Americans between 1920 and 1946 in North Carolina.[43]

Barriers to black participation in elections began to crumble in the mid-1940s, when the Supreme Court declared that whites-only primary elections were unconstitutional.[44] Two decades later, through the Twenty-fourth Amendment, poll taxes were outlawed.

The major step toward equal voting rights for African Americans was passage of the Voting Rights Act of 1965, which forbids discrimination in voting and registration. Black voting rose sharply after enactment of the legislation, which empowers federal agents to register voters and to oversee participation in elections. The Voting Rights Act, as interpreted by the courts, also eliminated literacy tests: local officials can no longer deny registration and voting for reasons of illiteracy. In fact, in communities where a language other than English is widely spoken, officials are now required by law to provide ballot materials in that language.

Congress renewed the Voting Rights Act in 1970, 1975, and 1982. The 1982 extension is noteworthy because it renews the act for twenty years and requires states and localities to clear with federal officials any electoral change that has the effect, intended or not, of reducing the voting power of a minority group. When congressional district boundaries were redrawn after the 1990 census, the 1982 extension became the basis for the creation of districts that included a majority of Hispanic or African American voters. The result was the election of an unprecedented number of minority group members to Congress in 1992; Hispanic and African American representatives increased from ten and twenty-five to seventeen and thirty-eight, respectively.

In two 1996 decisions, however, the Supreme Court declared unconstitutional the redistricting of four congressional districts in Texas and North Carolina because race had been the "dominant" factor in their creation. The states were directed to redraw the districts. A year earlier, the Court had invalidated a Georgia redistricting plan, holding that the state's Eleventh Congressional District violated the rights of white voters under the Fourteenth Amendment's equal-protection clause. The Georgia district stretched from Savannah to Atlanta and had all sorts of twists and turns designed to exclude white residential areas. However, these rulings have not necessarily settled the issue of racial redistricting. The 1996 cases were each decided by a 5–4 majority, and three of the justices in the majority indicated that there might be instances in which race, along with other factors, could be taken into account in redistricting decisions. But the Court's majority made it clear that race could not be the *deciding* factor in redistricting arrangements.[45]

EQUALITY OF RESULT

America's disadvantaged groups have made significant progress toward equal rights, particularly during the past few decades. Through acts of Congress and rulings of the Supreme Court, most forms of government-sponsored discrimination—from racially segregated public schools to gender-based pension plans—have been banned.

However, civil rights problems involve deeply rooted conditions, habits, and prejudices and affect whole categories of people. For these reasons, a new civil rights policy rarely produces a sudden and dramatic change in society. Despite their greater equality in law, America's traditionally disadvantaged groups are still substantially unequal in their daily lives. Consider the issue of income disparity (see Figure 5-3). The average Asian American's income is about 95 percent of the average white person's income. But the average falls to 60 percent for African Americans and 55 percent for Hispanic Americans.

Such figures reflect *de facto* **discrimination**, which is discrimination that is a consequence of social, economic, and cultural biases and conditions. This type of discrimination is different from *de jure* **discrimination**, which is discrimination based on law, as in the case of segregation in southern public schools during the pre-*Brown* period. *De facto* discrimination is difficult to root out because it is embedded not in the law but in the very structure of society. **Equality of result** is the aim of policies intended to reduce or eliminate *de facto* discriminatory effects so that members of disadvantaged groups may obtain the same benefits as members of advantaged groups. Such policies are inherently more controversial because many Americans believe that government's responsibility extends no further than the removal of legal bar-

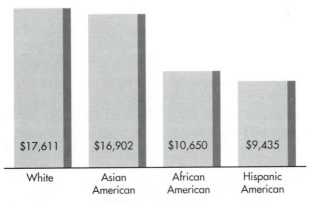

| $17,611 | $16,902 | $10,650 | $9,435 |
| White | Asian American | African American | Hispanic American |

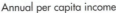

Annual per capita income

FIGURE 5-3 U.S. PER CAPITA INCOME, BY RACE AND ETHNICITY
The average income of white Americans is substantially higher than that of most other Americans. Source: U.S. Bureau of the Census, 1995.

riers to equality. Nevertheless, a few policies—notably affirmative action and busing—have been implemented to achieve equality of result.

Workplace Integration: Affirmative Action

The difficulty of making newly acquired legal rights a part of everyday reality is evident in the fact that, with passage of the 1964 Civil Rights Act, which prohibited discrimination in employment, women and minorities did not suddenly find it easier to obtain jobs for which they were qualified. Many employers maintained a deliberate though unwritten preference for white male employees, while other employers adhered to established employment procedures that continued to keep women and minorities at a disadvantage; membership in many union locals, for example, was handed down from father to son. Moreover, the Civil Rights Act placed the burden of proof on the woman or minority group member who had been denied a particular job, and discrimination was costly and often difficult to prove in court. In addition, a victory in court affected only the individual in question; such case-by-case settlements were no remedy for a situation in which established

Affirmative action is a response to employment practices that have discriminated against women and minorities. Opponents claim that affirmative action is itself discriminatory. (Richard Kalvar/Magnum)

hiring practices kept millions of women and minority group members from competing on an equal basis for job opportunities.

A broader remedy was obviously required, and the result was the emergence during the late 1960s of affirmative action programs. **Affirmative action** is a deliberate effort to provide full and equal opportunities in employment, education, and other areas for women, minorities, and individuals belonging to other traditionally disadvantaged groups. Affirmative action requires corporations, universities, and other organizations to establish programs designed to ensure that all applicants are treated fairly. Affirmative action also places the burden of proof on the providers of opportunities; to some extent, they must be able to demonstrate that any disproportionate granting of opportunities to white males is not the result of discriminatory practices.

OPINIONS ON AFFIRMATIVE ACTION   Few issues in recent years have provoked more controversy than has affirmative action.[46] Although most Americans say they believe that minorities and women deserve a truly equal chance at jobs and other opportunities, they also say they worry that aggressive affirmative action programs will discriminate against more qualified males, an outcome that is called *reverse discrimination*. In fact, by a 2-TO-1 margin in a 1996 *Newsweek* poll, more adults said that reverse discrimination against whites is a bigger problem than racial discrimination against blacks.[47]

Opposition to affirmative action has intensified in recent years. Although the policy once had majority support in polls, it no longer does (see Figure 5-4). In a 1995 Gallup Poll, 50 percent of Americans supported affirmative action for women and 40 percent supported it for racial minorities. Even fewer thought that affirmative action was still needed as a means of helping women and minorities overcome the effects of discrimination. When the issue of quotas (the setting aside of specific numbers of jobs or school admissions for women and minorities) was included, support for affirmative action dropped below 15 percent. Opposition to affirmative action was more pronounced among white Americans, men, and Republicans than among minorities, women, and Democrats.

Some restrictions on affirmative action are likely in the near future, inasmuch as even many of its supporters believe that it is now heightening white resistance to other civil rights measures and that it is diminishing the accomplishments of women and minorities who would have gotten ahead even if the policy had not existed. It is unlikely, however, that affirmative action will be eliminated entirely. Objective indicators show that women and minorities, as groups, are still at a substantial disadvantage to white males in terms of job hiring, pay, and promotion. Moreover, many educational insti-

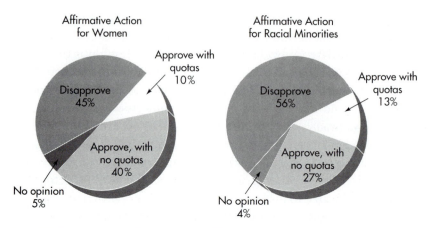

FIGURE 5-4 OPINIONS ON AFFIRMATIVE ACTION
Americans only weakly support affirmative action, particularly when it applies
to racial minorities or involves the use of quotas. Source: Gallup Poll, February
24–26, 1995.

tutions and corporations have discovered that they benefit from the inclusion of women and racial minorities and find that affirmative action procedures are helpful in their efforts to achieve greater diversity.

AFFIRMATIVE ACTION IN THE LAW   Most issues that pit individuals
against each other in a struggle over society's benefits eventually end up in
the courts, and affirmative action is no exception. The policy was first tested
before the Supreme Court in *University of California Regents* v. *Bakke* (1978).
Alan Bakke, a white man, had twice been denied admission to a University
of California medical school, even though his admission test scores were
higher than those of several minority group students who had been accepted. Bakke sued, claiming the school had a "quota" system for minorities that discriminated against white males. The Court ruled in Bakke's favor
but did not invalidate affirmative action per se. The Court said only that rigid
racial quotas were an impermissible form of affirmative action in determining medical school admissions.[48]

Bakke was followed by two rulings in favor of affirmative action programs, one of which—*Fullilove* v. *Klutnick* (1980)—upheld a quota system that
required 10 percent of federal public works funds to be set aside for minority-
owned firms.[49]

In the 1980s, the appointment of new, more conservative justices to the
Supreme Court narrowed the scope of affirmative action policy. The Court

held, for example, that preferential treatment of minorities could normally be justified only in cases where discrimination had been severe and that affirmative action could be applied only in a way that did not infringe on the rights of white employees to keep their jobs (thus restricting the use of race as a basis for determining which employees would be terminated in the case of job layoffs).[50]

In a key 1995 decision, *Adarand v. Pena*, the Supreme Court sharply curtailed the federal government's affirmative action authority. The case arose when Adarand Constructors filed suit over a federal contract that was awarded to a Hispanic-owned company even though Adarand had submitted a lower bid. The Court in a 5–4 ruling said that the government had to prove that a preference program for minorities was a response to specific past acts of discrimination, not just discrimination in a historic sense. This decision essentially reversed earlier precedents that allowed the federal government to give a preference to minority applicants. The Court said that Washington cannot set aside contracts for minority applicants unless, through costly and conclusive studies, it can demonstrate past discrimination particular to a situation; and even then, it must devise a program "narrowly tailored" to the problem that is being remedied.[51] In other words, the government cannot issue general requirements (such as a 10 percent set-aside) as a means of remedying past discrimination.

Even supporters of affirmative action concluded that the *Adarand* decision likely marked the end of the era of extensive racial and gender preferences. By holding that affirmative action must be narrowly tailored and based on specific past acts of discrimination, the Court substantially restricted the authority of federal authorities to mandate broad affirmative action remedies. Earlier, the Court had restricted the authority of state and local governments to institute such requirements.

Another blow to affirmative action proponents is the California Civil Rights Initiative, which bans in California any public employment, education, or contracting program that is based on race or sex. Known as Proposition 209, the initiative was enacted by California voters in 1996 by a 54–46 percent margin. The measure received close national attention as a possible indicator of public attitudes on affirmative action.

Proponents of affirmative action have succeeded, however, in shifting some of the burden of proof about discrimination from employees to employers. After the Supreme Court in the 1980s allowed business firms more latitude in defending their hiring practices,[52] Congress responded with the Civil Rights Act of 1991, which requires larger firms in some instances to prove why their overwhelmingly male or white work force is the result of business necessity (such as the nature of the work or the locally available labor pool), not the result of systematic discrimination against women or minorities.

Social Integration: Busing

In 1944 the Swedish sociologist Gunnar Myrdal gained fame for his book *An American Dilemma*, whose title referred to deep-rooted racism in a country that proclaimed itself to be the epitome of an equal society.[53] Since then, legal obstacles to the mixing of the races have been nearly eliminated. Public opinion has also changed significantly in the past half-century. In the early 1940s a majority of white Americans believed that black children should not be allowed to go to school with white children; today only 5 percent of white Americans express this belief.

However, the majority of black people still live largely apart from white people. The reality of American life today is racial segregation. More than two-thirds of African Americans live in neighborhoods that are all or mostly black; more than two-thirds of black children go to schools that are mostly black; and one-third attend schools that are more than 90 percent black.[54]

THE *SWANN* DECISION   In 1971 the Supreme Court took the controversial step of requiring the busing of children in some circumstances. Affirming a lower-court decision, the Supreme Court held in *Swann v. Charlotte–Mecklenburg County Board of Education* that the busing of children from one neighborhood to another was a permissible way for courts to compel the integration of public schools in instances where past years of official segregation had created residential patterns that had the effect of keeping the races in separate schools.[55]

Few policies of recent times provoked as much controversy as the introduction of forced busing. There were angry demonstrations lasting weeks in Charlotte. When busing was ordered in Detroit and Boston, the protests turned violent. A 1972 University of Michigan survey indicated that more than 80 percent of white Americans disapproved of forced busing, and the proportion has not changed significantly since then.

THE COURSE AND IMPACT OF BUSING   In large part because busing has been unpopular with the public, the policy has never been strongly supported by elected officials. For example, Congress on several occasions in the 1970s came close to forbidding the use of federal funds to assist busing in any way.

Despite the controversy surrounding it, busing remains a part of national policy. Thousands of children throughout the nation are bused out of their neighborhoods for purposes of school integration. Busing has provided equality of result for some black children, but its effectiveness has been undercut by restrictions on it. In part because of the adverse reactions to busing, the Supreme Court has limited across-district busing to situations in which it can be shown that school district boundaries were purposely drawn so as to segregate the races.[56] Since school districts in most states coincide with community boundaries, the effect of this position has been to insulate most suburban schools from integration plans. As a result, the burden of busing has fallen most heavily on poorer whites and African Americans in the inner cities.

In a key 1995 decision, *Missouri v. Jenkins*, the Supreme Court ruled that judges cannot order other taxpayers to finance improvements in inner-city schools in order to attract suburban white students to these schools. Kansas City had established magnet schools for this purpose, and the state of Missouri had objected to funding them. The case was decided by a 5–4 vote, and the dissenting justices argued that the ruling essentially overturned the precedent of allowing far-reaching measures to counteract the effects of historic discrimination.[57] Since the Court's decision, more than a dozen major cities have begun to halt racially based school busing.

PERSISTENT DISCRIMINATION: SUPERFICIAL DIFFERENCES, DEEP DIVISIONS

Discrimination has been called America's curse. In a country that is otherwise bountiful and generous, superficial differences—sex, skin color, country of origin—are sources of deep divisions and stark contrasts. To cite but one example: a black child born in the United States has more than twice the chance of dying before reaching his or her first birthday than a white child. The difference in the infant mortality rates of whites and African Americans reflects differences in their nutrition, medical care, and education—in other words, differences in their access to the most basic resources of a modern society.

Discrimination, today as in the past, is at the root of these differences. America's professed commitment to equality for all has a decidedly narrow focus—on equality under the law but not on the opportunity to share fully in all that American society has to offer. No greater challenge faces America as it approaches the twenty-first century than the rooting out of discrimination based on race, sex, and ethnicity.[58]

SUMMARY

During the past few decades, the United States has undergone a revolution in the legal status of its traditionally disadvantaged groups, including African Americans, women, Native Americans, Hispanic Americans, and Asian Americans. Such groups are now provided equal protection under the law in areas such as education, employment, and voting. Discrimination by race, sex, and ethnicity has not been eliminated from American life but is no longer substantially backed by the force of law.

Traditionally disadvantaged Americans have achieved fuller equality primarily as a result of their struggle for greater rights. The Supreme Court has been an important instrument of change for minority groups. Its ruling in *Brown* v. *Board of Education* (1954), which declared racial segregation in public schools to be an unconstitutional violation of the Fourteenth Amendment's equal-protection clause, was a major breakthrough in equal rights. Through its busing, affirmative action, and other rulings, the Court has also mandated the active promotion of integration and equal opportunities.

However, because civil rights policy involves large issues of social values and the distribution of society's resources, questions of civil rights are politically explosive. For this reason, legislatures and executives as well as the courts have been deeply involved in such issues, siding at times with established groups and sometimes backing the claims of underprivileged groups. Thus Congress, with the support of President Lyndon Johnson, enacted the landmark Civil Rights Act of 1964; but Congress and recent presidents have been ambivalent about or hostile to busing for the purpose of integrating public schools.

In recent years affirmative action programs, designed to achieve equality of result for African Americans, women, Hispanic Americans, and other disadvantaged groups, have been a civil rights battleground. Affirmative action has had the strong support of civil rights groups and has won the qualified endorsement of the Supreme Court but has been opposed by those who claim that it unfairly discriminates against white males. Busing is another issue that has provoked deep divisions within American society.

MAJOR CONCEPTS

affirmative action
comparable worth
de facto discrimination
de jure discrimination
equal-protection clause
equal rights (civil rights)

equality of result
gender gap
reasonable-basis test
strict-scrutiny test
suspect classifications

SUGGESTED READINGS

Armor, David. *Forced Justice: School Desegregation and the Law.* New York: Oxford University Press, 1995. An evaluation that concludes the federal courts have overstretched their legal mandate by requiring school integration rather than simply school desegregation.

Bergmann, Barbara A. *In Defense of Affirmative Action.* New York: Basic Books, 1997. An economist's analysis of affirmative action that concludes that policy is necessary for women and broadly beneficial to society.

de la Garza, Rudolfo O., Louis DeSipio, F. Chris Garcia, John Garcia, and Angelo Falcon. *Latino Voices: Mexican, Puerto Rican, and Cuban Perspectives on American Politics.* Boulder, Colo.: Westview Press, 1992. A study of the opinions and behaviors of Hispanic Americans.

Hochschild, Jennifer L. *Facing Up to the American Dream: Race, Class, and the Soul of the Nation.* Princeton, N.J.: Princeton University Press, 1995. A careful assessment of what is required of American society if its ideal of equal opportunity is to be realized.

Kinder, Donald R., and Lynn M. Sanders. *Divided by Color: Racial Politics and Democratic Ideals.* Chicago: University of Chicago Press, 1996. An analysis of the factors that shape people's opinions on race and related issues.

McClain, Charles J. *In Search of Equality: The Chinese Struggle against Discrimination in Nineteenth-Century America.* Berkeley: University of California Press, 1994. A careful study of how Chinese in nineteenth-century California used the legal system to fight racism and injustice.

Nagel, Joane. *American Indian Ethnic Renewal: Red Power and the Resurgence of Identity and Culture.* New York: Oxford University Press, 1996. Explores the meaning of activism for Native Americans' ethnic identification.

Rinehart, Sue Tolleson. *Gender Consciousness and Politics.* New York: Routledge, 1992. An insightful evaluation of the impact of women's heightened political consciousness.

Skrentny, John David. *The Ironies of Affirmative Action: Politics, Culture, and Justice in America.* Chicago: University of Chicago Press, 1996. An empirical analysis of affirmative action and its impact.

Stavans, Hans. *The Hispanic Condition: Reflections on Culture and Identity in America.* New York: HarperPerennial, 1996. An analysis of the behavioral and cultural differences and similarities among the major Hispanic groups.

Witt, Linda, Karen M. Paget, and Glenna Matthews. *Running as a Woman: Gender and Power in American Politics.* New York: Free Press, 1994. A careful analysis of the way women campaign and how the process differs from the way men campaign.

READING 5

College Admission and Equal Protection
United States *v.* Virginia *(1996)*

In 1996, the Supreme Court ruled that the males-only admissions policy at Virginia Military Institute (VMI) was unconstitutional. VMI was the only single-sex school among Virginia's public colleges and universities. Its mission is to provide "citizen soldiers" and it has a long history of producing high-ranking military officers, business executives, and public officials. The stature of VMI's alumni is reflected in the fact that it has the largest per-student endowment of any undergraduate institution in the nation.

In response to an earlier adverse court ruling, Virginia had established an alternative program for women (Virginia Women's Institute for Leadership) at a private liberal arts college, Mary Baldwin College. The Supreme Court concluded that the alternative program did not offer benefits comparable to those received by VMI students. Virginia was thereby judged to have failed in its constitutional obligation to provide women the equal protection of its laws, and VMI was ordered to admit women to its program.

Justice Ginsberg delivered the opinion of the Court, in which Justices Stevens, O'Connor, Kennedy, Souter, and Breyer joined. Chief Justice Rehnquist voted with the majority but filed a concurring opinion. Justice Scalia dissented. Justice Thomas, whose son was enrolled in VMI, did not participate in the Court's deliberation or vote on the case.

The majority opinion included the following statements (those in quotes are from other cases cited by the Court's majority in support of its position):

1. Parties who seek to defend gender-based government action must demonstrate an "exceedingly persuasive justification" for that action. Neither federal nor state government acts compatibly with equal protection when a law or official policy denies to women, simply because they are women, full citizenship stature—equal opportunity to aspire, achieve, participate in and contribute to society based on their individual talents and capacities. To meet the burden of justification, a State must show "at least that the [challenged]

classification serves 'important governmental objectives and that the discriminatory means employed' are 'substantially related to the achievement of those objectives.' " The justification must be genuine, not hypothesized or invented *post hoc* in response to litigation. And it must not rely on overbroad generalizations about the different talents, capacities, or preferences of males and females. The heightened review standard applicable to sex based classifications does not make sex a proscribed classification, but it does mean that categorization by sex may not be used to create or perpetuate the legal, social, and economic inferiority of women.

2. Virginia's categorical exclusion of women from the educational opportunities VMI provides denies equal protection to women.

(a) Virginia contends that single sex education yields important educational benefits and that provision of an option for such education fosters diversity in educational approaches. Benign justifications proffered in defense of categorical exclusions, however, must describe actual state purposes, not rationalizations for actions in fact differently grounded. Virginia has not shown that VMI was established, or has been maintained, with a view to diversifying, by its categorical exclusion of women, educational opportunities within the State. A purpose genuinely to advance an array of educational options is not served by VMI's historic and constant plan to afford a unique educational benefit only to males. However well this plan serves Virginia's sons, it makes no provision whatever for her daughters.

(b) Virginia also argues that VMI's adversative method of training provides educational benefits that cannot be made available, unmodified, to women, and that alterations to accommodate women would necessarily be so drastic as to destroy VMI's program. It is uncontested that women's admission to VMI would require accommodations, primarily in arranging housing assignments and physical training programs for female cadets. It is also undisputed, however, that neither the goal of producing citizen soldiers, VMI's *raison d'être*, nor VMI's implementing methodology is inherently unsuitable to women. The District Court made "findings" on "gender based developmental differences" that restate the opinions of Virginia's expert witnesses about typically male or typically female "tendencies." Courts, however, must take "a hard look" at generalizations or tendencies of the kind Virginia pressed, for state actors controlling gates to opportunity have no warrant to exclude qualified individuals based on "fixed notions concerning the roles and abilities of males and females." The notion that admission of women would downgrade VMI's stature, destroy the adversative system and, with it, even the school, is a judgment hardly proved, a prediction hardly different from other "self fulfilling prophec[ies] once routinely used to deny rights or opportunities. Women's successful entry into the federal military academies, and their participation in the Nation's military forces, indicate that Virginia's fears for VMI's future may not be solidly grounded. The State's justification for excluding all women from "citizen soldier" training for which some are qualified, in any event, does not rank as "exceedingly persuasive."

3. The remedy proffered by Virginia—maintain VMI as a male only college and create VWIL as a separate program for women—does not cure the constitutional violation.

(a) A remedial decree must closely fit the constitutional violation; it must be shaped to place persons unconstitutionally denied an opportunity or advantage in the position they would have occupied in the absence of discrimination. The constitutional violation in this case is the categorical exclusion of women, in disregard of their individual merit, from an extraordinary educational opportunity afforded men. Virginia chose to leave untouched VMI's exclusionary policy, and proposed for women only a separate program, different in kind from VMI and unequal in tangible and intangible facilities. VWIL affords women no opportunity to experience the rigorous military training for which VMI is famed. Kept away from the pressures, hazards, and psychological bonding characteristic of VMI's adversative training, VWIL students will not know the feeling of tremendous accomplishment commonly experienced by VMI's successful cadets. Virginia maintains that methodological differences are justified by the important differences between men and women in learning and developmental needs, but generalizations about "the way women are," estimates of what is appropriate for *most women*, no longer justify denying opportunity to women whose talent and capacity place them outside the average description. In myriad respects other than military training, VWIL does not qualify as VMI's equal. The VWIL program is a pale shadow of VMI in terms of the range of curricular choices and faculty stature, funding, prestige, alumni support and influence. Virginia has not shown substantial equality in the separate educational opportunities the State supports at VWIL and VMI.

(b) The Fourth Circuit failed to inquire whether the proposed remedy placed women denied the VMI advantage in the position they would have occupied in the absence of discrimination and considered instead whether the State could provide, with fidelity to equal protection, separate and unequal educational programs for men and women. In declaring the substantially different and significantly unequal VWIL program satisfactory, the appeals court displaced the exacting standard developed by this Court with a deferential standard, and added an inquiry of its own invention, the "substantive comparability" test. The Fourth Circuit plainly erred in exposing Virginia's VWIL plan to such a deferential analysis, for "all gender based classifications today" warrant "heightened scrutiny." Women seeking and fit for a VMI quality education cannot be offered anything less, under the State's obligation to afford them genuinely equal protection.

SOURCE: *United States* v. *Virginia et al.*, 94–1941 (1996).

CHAPTER SIX

Public Opinion and Political Socialization

To speak with precision of public opinion is a task not unlike coming to grips with the Holy Ghost.

V. O. KEY, JR.[1]

W HEN THE Dayton peace accord was signed in late 1995, most Americans were ill equipped to pass judgment on what was happening. They had been hearing about the war in Bosnia for several years, but polls indicated they had only a sketchy idea of the nature of the conflict. And most Americans said they opposed the use of U.S. troops as a means of resolving it. A majority had supported the limited use of U.S. warplanes against Serb forces, particularly in the immediate aftermath of horrific events, such as the Serb mortar attack on a Sarajevo marketplace that killed 37 innocent men, women, and children. But Americans were opposed to a larger role. Asked in a November 1995 Washington Post poll whether they would support sending U.S. troops to Bosnia, only 38 percent said they were in favor, while 56 percent were opposed.

Yet the Dayton accord called for a 60,000-troop NATO peacekeeing force, a third of whom would be Americans. It was not expected that the NATO troops would engage in large-scale military operations, but they would be heavily armed and had authority to use lethal force if threatened with harm.

Six days after the accord was signed, President Clinton went on national television to ask Americans to support the Bosnian deployment. He appealed to their conscience, saying that intervention was necessary to stop the slaughter that had already left as many as 250,000 dead, most of them Bosnian Muslims. Polls taken immediately after the speech indicated that public support for the deployment rose slightly. Yet a majority continued to oppose the use of U.S. combat troops in Bosnia. Nevertheless, a month later, as the first of the U.S. combat units were airlifted into Bosnia, there were no mass protests against the president's policy. Americans accepted the deployment, hoping only that the casualties would ultimately be few in number.

The unfolding of the Bosnian intervention is a revealing example of the influence of public opinion on government. Public opinion rarely compels officials to take a particular action. Clinton was not forced by public opinion to forgo the commitment of U.S. troops in Bosnia, nor did public opinion erupt into widespread resistance when he did. If Clinton made an obvious concession to public opinion, it was in his promise that all U.S. troops would be withdrawn in a year's time. Yet a year later even this concession was modified: rather than withdrawing all the troops, Clinton decided that a substantial number would stay in Bosnia for much, if not all, of 1997.

Public opinion has an important place in democratic societies because of the idea that democratic government springs from the will of the people. However, public opinion is a far more elusive phenomenon than conventional wisdom suggests. It is widely assumed that there is a conclusive pub-

U.S. soldiers were deployed to Bosnia in early 1996 as part of a multinational force. Their mission was to promote peace by acting as a buffer between the warring sides. Their deployment occurred despite lukewarm public support for the action. (Stoddart/Katz/SABA)

lic opinion on major issues, but in fact, as the Bosnian situation illustrates, public opinion is seldom fixed when it comes to questions of how to resolve policy problems. Political leaders typically have leeway in deciding a course of action. They may be held accountable by the public for the results, but the action itself is often theirs to choose.

This chapter discusses public opinion and its influence on the U.S. political system. A major theme is that public opinion is a powerful and yet inexact force in American politics. The policies of the U.S. government cannot be understood apart from public opinion; at the same time, public opinion is not a precise determinant of public policy. The main points made in this chapter are the following:

* *Public opinion consists of those views held by ordinary citizens that are publicly expressed.*
* *The process by which individuals acquire their political opinions is called political socialization. This process begins during childhood and continues into adulthood.*
* *Americans' political opinions are shaped by several frames of reference, the most important of which are political culture, ideology, group attachments, and partisanship.*
* *Public opinion has an important influence on government but works primarily to channel and impose limits on the choices made by officials.*

THE NATURE OF PUBLIC OPINION

Public opinion is a relatively new concept in the history of political ideas. Not until democracy arose in the eighteenth century did the need arise to obtain some idea of what the people were thinking on political issues. If democracy is truly to be a government of and for the people, then the public's opinions must be a central concern.

Defining Public Opinion

Today, "public opinion" is a widely used term. It is typically applied in ways which suggest that the people have a common set of concerns. In fact, however, it is not very meaningful to lump all citizens together as if they constituted a single coherent public.[2] There is, to be sure, an occasional issue of such power and breadth that it captures the attention of nearly all citizens. The large majority of issues, however, attract the attention of some citizens but not others. The tendency is so pervasive that opinion analysts have described America as a nation of *many* publics.[3]

There are a great many issues where there is literally no majority opinion. Agricultural conservation programs are a matter of intense concern to farmers but of little interest to city dwellers. In such situations, a form of *pluralist* democracy usually prevails: government responds to the views of the intense minority. In still other cases, *elitist* opinion prevails. On the question of U.S. relations with Madagascar, for example, there is little likelihood of a popular constituency that knows or cares what the federal government does. In such instances, the policy opinions of an elite group of business and policy leaders ordinarily prevail. *Majority* opinion, to the degree it governs policy, is normally confined to those few, broad issues that elicit widespread attention and concern, such as social security and employment. Although this situation may suggest a limited role for popular majorities, such issues, although few in number, typically have the most impact on society as a whole.

Hence, in defining "public opinion" we cannot assume that all citizens, or even a majority, are actively interested and have a preference about all aspects of political life. We will define **public opinion** as those opinions held by ordinary citizens that they are willing to express openly.[4] This expression need not be verbal. It could also take the form, for example, of a protest demonstration or a vote for one candidate rather than another. The crucial point is that a person's private thoughts on an issue become public opinion when expressed publicly.

How Informed Is Public Opinion?

A major limitation on the role of public opinion is the citizenry's relatively low level of political information. Some citizens pay close attention to politics, but most do not, and some people pay hardly any attention at all. As a result, most people are poorly informed about politics. Fewer than half of adult Americans can readily recall both U.S. senators from their state.

Most citizens would "flunk" a current affairs test. In 1993, a Times-Mirror survey asked a cross section of Americans five questions on people and events that were prominent in the news (the correct answers are in parentheses):

Who is the president of Russia? (Boris Yeltsin)

Do you happen to know the name of the country that is threatening to withdraw from the nuclear nonproliferation treaty? (North Korea)

Who is Boutros Boutros-Ghali? (Secretary General of the U.N.)

Do you happen to know the name of the ethnic group that has conquered much of Bosnia and has surrounded the city of Sarajevo? (Serbs)

Do you happen to know the name of the group with whom the Israelis recently reached a peace accord? (Palestinians)

Only 6 percent of the respondents answered all five questions correctly, and 9 percent knew four answers; 37 percent could answer none of the questions, and 21 percent answered only one question correctly. In other words, a majority of citizens knew little or nothing when asked relatively simple questions about world developments. (Citizens in six other countries were asked the same five questions; the results are summarized in the box: How the United States Compares.)

The public's lack of information restricts the role it can play in policy disputes. Public opinion can direct government toward certain goals, but it rarely provides a detailed guide to the way these goals are to be accomplished. The choice of one course of action over another requires knowledge of the likely consequences of the various alternatives. The average citizen rarely possesses such knowledge.

Measuring Public Opinion

Woodrow Wilson once said he had spent nearly all of his adult life in government and yet had never seen a "government." What Wilson was saying, in effect, was that government is a system of relationships. A government is not a building or a person; it is not tangible in the way that an automobile or a bottle of soda is. So it is with public opinion. No one has ever seen a "public opinion," and thus it cannot be measured directly. It must be assessed indirectly.

A time-honored method of interpreting public opinion is election returns. The vote is routinely interpreted by the press and politicians as an indicator of the public's mood—whether liberal or conservative, angry or satisfied, quiet or intense. Letters to the editor in newspapers and the size of crowds at mass demonstrations are other means to judge what the public feels on an issue. Yet another device is the activity of lobbyists who bring the concerns of their constituents to government's attention.

All these indicators of public opinion are important and deserve the attention of those in power. These indicators, however, have shortcomings as a guide to what is on the minds of the people. Elections offer the peo-

HOW THE UNITED STATES COMPARES

Citizens' Awareness of Public Affairs

Americans' knowledge of public affairs is relatively low. Even the simplest facts sometimes elude the average citizen's grasp. A 1994 Gallup Poll found, for example, that a third of Americans were unable to name the vice-president of the United States.

Low levels of public information are characteristic of most countries, but Americans rank lower than citizens of other western democracies by some indicators. In a seven-country survey conducted by the Times-Mirror Center for the People and the Press, Americans ranked next to last in terms of their ability to respond correctly to five questions about world leaders and events. Americans did their best on a question that asked them to name the president of Russia: 50 percent said Boris Yeltsin, but this was far lower than the 94 percent of Germans who named Yeltsin. In light of America's leading role in the world, its citizens might be expected to be uniquely well informed about international affairs. However, they are less knowledgeable in this area than Europeans, who live in closer proximity to other countries and who thus may be more attentive to world politics.

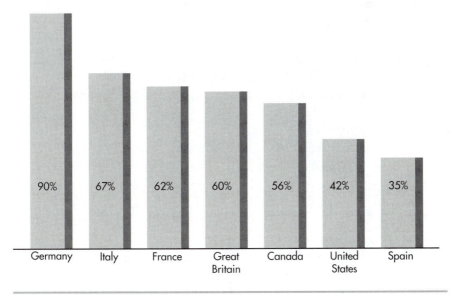

Germany	Italy	France	Great Britain	Canada	United States	Spain
90%	67%	62%	60%	56%	42%	35%

ple only a yes-or-no choice between candidates, and different voters will make the same choice for quite different reasons. The winning candidate may claim that the public has based its choice on a particular issue or inclination, but election returns almost always mask a much more complex reality.

As for letter writers and demonstrators, they are not at all representative of the general population. Less than 1 percent of Americans participate each year in a mass demonstration, and fewer than 10 percent write to the president or a member of Congress. Studies have found that the views of letter writers and demonstrators are more intense and more extreme than those of other citizens.[5]

Public Opinion Polls In an earlier day, such things as elections and letters to the editor were the only means by which public officials could gauge

Public opinion includes contradictory elements. According to surveys, for example, most Americans say they want lower taxes but also say they want more public services. At a Boston rally, this demonstrator expresses his anger with President Clinton's tax-increase legislation while also demanding that government provide free health care. (Joel Stettenheim/SABA)

what the public was thinking. Today, they can also rely on polls or surveys, which provide a more systematic and in some respects more reliable method of estimating public sentiment.

In a **public opinion poll** a relatively small number of individuals—the **sample**—are interviewed in order to estimate the opinions of a whole **population,** such as the students of a college, the residents of a city, or the citizens of a country. If a sufficient number of individuals are chosen at random, their views will tend to be representative—that is, roughly the same as the views held by the population as a whole.

The accuracy of a poll is usually expressed in terms of **sampling error,** which is a function of sample size. The larger the sample, the smaller the sampling error (see Table 6-1). Many people assume that a poll of the United States, with its 250 million people, must have a much larger sample to achieve the same level of accuracy as, say, a poll of Massachusetts or Arizona. In fact, the mathematics of polling are such that sample size is the critical factor.[6] Thus a sample of 1,000 people will have nearly the same level of accuracy whether the population is that of a city, a state, or the nation. A jar

TABLE 6-1   APPROXIMATE SAMPLING ERROR
BY NUMBER OF OPINION-POLL RESPONDENTS
The larger a poll's sample, the smaller the error in
estimating the opinions of the population from which
the sample is taken.

Approximate Number of Respondents	Approximate Sampling Error
200	±7%
275	±6
375	±5
600	±4
1,075	±3
2,400	±2
9,600	±1

Note: Figures are based on a 95 percent confidence level. This means that for a given sample size (e.g., 600), the chances are 19 in 20 (95 percent) that the sample will produce results that are within the sampling error (e.g., ±4 percent) of the results that would have been obtained if the whole population had been interviewed.

filled with marbles can illustrate the point. If half of them were blue and half were red, it would be predicted that the random selection of 1,000 marbles would yield about a 50–50 distribution by color, whether the jar held a million marbles, 10 million, or 250 million.

A properly drawn sample of 1,000 individuals has a sampling error of plus or minus 3 percent, which is to say that the proportions of the various opinions expressed by the people in the sample are likely to be within 3 percent of those of the whole population. For example, if 55 percent of a sample of 1,000 respondents say that they intend to vote for the Republican candidate for president, then the chances are high that 52 to 58 percent (55 percent plus or minus 3 percent) of the whole population plan to vote for the Republican.

The impressive record of the Gallup Poll in predicting the outcomes of presidential elections indicates that the theoretical accuracy of polls can be matched in practice. For example, the Gallup Poll predicted a 52–41 percent victory for Bill Clinton over Bob Dole in 1996. The actual margin was 49–41. The Gallup Organization has erred badly only once: it stopped polling several weeks before the 1948 election and missed a late trend that carried Harry Truman to victory over Thomas E. Dewey.

Sources of Polling Error Mathematical estimations of poll accuracy require a **probability sample**—a sample in which each individual in the population has a known probability of being selected at random for inclusion. In practice, pollsters can only approximate this ideal. Because pollsters rarely have a list of all individuals in a population from which to draw a random sample, they usually base their sample on telephones or locations. Random-digit telephone sampling is the most commonly used technique. Pollsters use computers to pick random telephone numbers, which are then dialed by interviewers to reach respondents. Because the computer is as likely to pick one telephone number as any other and because 95 percent of U.S. homes have a telephone, a sample selected in this way is usually assumed to be representative of the population.[7]

Some polls are not based on probability sampling. For example, news reporters sometimes conduct "people-in-the-street" interviews to obtain individual responses to political questions. Although a reporter may imply that the views of those interviewed are representative of the general public's, the fallacy of this reasoning should be readily apparent. The sample will be biased by where and when the reporter chooses to conduct the interviews. For example, interviews conducted on a downtown street at the noon hour will include a disproportionate number of business employees who are taking their lunch breaks. Housewives, teachers, factory workers, not to mention farmers, are among the many groups that would be underrepresented in such a sample.

Polls can also be misleading if they include poorly worded or leading questions or ask people about remote topics. Despite such drawbacks, the poll or survey is the most relied-upon method of measuring public opinion. More than 100 organizations are in the business of conducting public opinion polls. Some, like the Gallup Organization, conduct polls that are then released to the news media by syndication. Most large news organizations also have their own in-house polls; one of the foremost of these is the CBS News/New York Times poll, which conducts about fifteen surveys annually for use in the *Times* and on CBS's newscasts. Finally, there are polling firms that specialize in conducting surveys for candidates and officeholders.

POLITICAL SOCIALIZATION: HOW AMERICANS LEARN THEIR POLITICS

Analysts have long been interested in the process by which public opinion is formed. The learning process by which people acquire their opinions, beliefs, and values is called **political socialization.** For most Americans, the process starts in the family with exposure to the political views of the parents. The schools later contribute to the process, as do the mass media, friends, and other influences. Political socialization is thus a lifelong process.

The Process of Political Socialization

The process of political socialization in the United States has several major characteristics. First, although socialization continues throughout life, most people's political outlook is substantially influenced by their childhood learning. The *primacy tendency* refers to the fact that what is learned first is often lodged most firmly in one's mind.[8] Most people do not reflect deeply on how they acquired their political preferences. Basic ideas about race, gender, and political party, for example, are often formed uncritically in childhood, much in the way that belief in a particular religion, typically the religion of one's parents, is acquired.

A second characteristic of political socialization is that it is cumulative. The *structuring tendency* refers to the tendency of earlier learning to structure later learning.[9] This tendency is less a function of age itself than of an accumulated attachment to particular ideas or values. Of course, the fact that the United States is a diverse and mobile society makes a basic change in a person's political views possible, especially when previous and current experiences are at odds with one another. However, individuals have psychological defense mechanisms that protect their ingrained beliefs; when faced with situations that might challenge their original views, they can readily muster reasons for clinging to them.

Dramatic political transformation is uncommon and, when it has occurred on a large scale, it has nearly always been preceded by an extraordinary event that has shaken people out of their complacency. In such instances, it is usually younger adults who are more responsive. Their beliefs are less firmly rooted in past experiences and are therefore more easily changed. The *age-cohort tendency* holds that a significant break in the pattern of political socialization is almost always concentrated among younger citizens. Democratic President Franklin Roosevelt's New Deal initiatives, which sought to alleviate the economic hardship of the Great Depression, resulted in a substantial increase in Democratic loyalists among first-time voters but not among older ones.

The Agents of Political Socialization

As we have noted, the socialization process takes place through a variety of influences, including family, schools, peers, the mass media, and political leaders and events. It is helpful to consider briefly some ways in which these so-called *agents of socialization* affect people's opinions. Although these agents will be discussed separately, it should be kept in mind that, by and large, their influences overlap. Many of the same political values that people acquire at home and in school, for example, are emphasized regularly by the mass media and political leaders.[10]

THE FAMILY   The family is a powerful agent of socialization because children begin with no political attitudes of their own and tend to accept uncritically those of their parents.[11] By the time the child is a teenager and is less likely to listen to a parent, many of the beliefs and values that will stay with the child throughout life are already in place.

Some of these orientations are overtly political. Many adults are Republicans or Democrats today largely because they accepted their parents' party loyalty.[12] They now can give all sorts of reasons for preferring their party to the other. But the reasons come later in life; the loyalty comes first, during childhood. The family also contributes to basic orientations that, while not directly political, have political significance. For example, the American family tends to be more egalitarian than families in other nations, and American children often have a voice in family decisions. Such basic American values as equality, individualism, and personal freedom have their roots in patterns of family interaction.[13] Of course, a critical event, such as the Great Depression or the Vietnam war, may intervene to disrupt family influences.

SCHOOLS The school, like the family, has its major impact on children's basic political beliefs and values rather than on specific issues of policy. Teachers at the elementary level extol the exploits of national heroes and the superiority of the country's economic and political systems.[14] While students in the middle and high school grades may encounter a more critical perspective in the classroom, they are more likely to receive a fabled version of the country's history and politics (see Chapter 1). U.S. schools are probably more instrumental in building support for the nation than the schools in other democracies. The Pledge of Allegiance, which is recited daily in many U.S. schools, has no equivalent in European countries.

Students in a North Carolina school reciting the Pledge of Allegiance. Such childhood socialization experiences can have a profound impact on an individual's basic political beliefs. (Charles Gupton/The Stock Montage)

There was a time when the schools contributed greatly to Americans' sense of social equality. Most American children, regardless of family income, attended public schools and studied a fairly standard curriculum. Today, because of the increase in private school enrollment and the sharp contrast between suburban and inner-city districts, the school plays a lesser role in maintaining a sense of equality.

PEERS Members of peer groups—friends, neighbors, and co-workers—tend to have similar political views. Belonging to a peer group usually reinforces what a person already believes. One reason is that most people trust the views of their friends and associates. Another is that they may be reluctant to deviate too far from what their peers think. In her book *The Spiral of Silence*, Elisabeth Noelle-Neumann contends that individuals fear social isolation and hence are reluctant to speak out against a dominant opinion.[15]

THE MASS MEDIA The mass media are another powerful socializing agent. The media's influence, although diffuse and difficult to measure, is nonetheless substantial. While experts disagree, for example, on the extent to which violence on television contributes to violence in American society, few hold it entirely blameless.

The media's socializing influence is also felt through its news coverage. Studies indicate that the way in which news stories are "framed" affects people's political perceptions.[16] For example, the press in recent years has increasingly framed political leaders in the context of their tactics and mistakes (rather than their policy goals and accomplishments), with the result that the public thinks less highly of its leaders than at an earlier time.[17] (The media's influence is examined more fully in Chapter 10.)

POLITICAL LEADERS AND INSTITUTIONS People look to political leaders and institutions, particularly the presidency and the political party, as guides to opinion. The level of public approval of a nuclear arms limitation agreement with the USSR rose in 1987 after President Ronald Reagan endorsed the idea. In broader terms, political leaders play a significant role in shaping political debate and opinion through the symbols and slogans they use.[18]

Their ability to mold opinion, however, has substantial limits. When Republicans took control of Congress in 1995, for example, the budget-balancing goal of their Contract with America had broad public support. By 1996, after a year of bitter partisan debate and growing concern over Republican plans to restrict spending on programs affecting the elderly, poor, and children, the Republican plan was perceived as too radical by most Americans. Republican lawmakers tried to sell the public on their plan but failed to convince a majority that it was an acceptable solution to the nation's budgetary problems. (Chapters 8, 11, and 12 discuss further the impact of political leaders and institutions on public opinion).

FRAMES OF REFERENCE: HOW AMERICANS THINK POLITICALLY

What are the frames of reference that guide the political thinking of Americans? The question is important in at least two respects. First, the way in which citizens think politically provides clues about the way in which public opinion is likely to affect government. The government in a democratic system is expected to more often act in accordance with public opinion than against it.

A second reason it is important to understand how the people think politically is that a shared frame of reference can bring citizens together in the pursuit of a common goal. The opinions of millions of Americans would mean almost nothing if each of these opinions was different from all the others. If enough people think the same way, however, they may be able to exert political power.

The subject of how Americans think politically fills entire books; here we will outline four of the major frames of reference through which Americans evaluate political alternatives. The first tends to unite Americans; the other three give rise to differences of opinion among them.

Cultural Thinking: Common Ideas

As we indicated in Chapter I, Americans are unusual in their commitment to a common set of ideals that define the nature of the American political experience. Such principles as individualism, equality, and self-government have always meant somewhat different things to different people but nonetheless are a source of opinion consensus.[19] For example, government programs aimed at redistributing wealth from the rich to the poor are common in western Europe but are less appealing to Americans, who have a deeper commitment to individualism.

There are limits, of course, to the degree to which Americans' basic beliefs shape their policy opinions. For nearly two centuries African Americans were inferior by law to white Americans, despite the American creed that "all men are created equal." Such inconsistencies speak to the all-too-human capacity to voice one idea and live another.

Nevertheless, Americans' political ideals are a powerful influence on public opinion. They affect the way in which disputes are argued and affect what people regard as reasonable and desirable. Americans' ideals serve to define the boundaries of acceptable political action and opinion.

Ideological Thinking: The Outlook for Some

Commentators on public opinion in the United States often use such ideological words as "liberal" and "conservative" in describing how ordinary citizens think about political issues. When Republicans triumphed in the 1994 midterm elections, for example, analysts spoke of "a conservative tide" that was supposedly sweeping the country. Conservatism is an example of an **ideology,** a consistent pattern of opinion on particular issues that stems from a basic underlying belief or beliefs. An ideology is a relatively sophisticated pattern of thought. It requires that individuals have general beliefs that they can apply when responding to emerging issues. Their political opinions are thus highly structured and consistent; they form in predictable ways around basic beliefs.

Most Americans do not have a well-defined ideology. Their opinions are somewhat inconsistent and do not spring from a broad framework of belief. Studies indicate that only a minority of citizens—no more than a third and perhaps as few as a tenth—readily understand and apply an ideological frame of reference when evaluating political issues.[20]

Nevertheless, analysts sometimes find it useful to apply ideological terms when describing people's views. The traditional approach is to categorize individuals as liberals, moderates, or conservatives, depending on the level of their support for or opposition to activist government. However, this measure is not entirely satisfactory. For example, whereas conservatism is associated with opposition to government activism in the economic realm, it accepts the use of government as a means of strengthening traditional social values.

As a consequence, recent surveys have sought to measure ideological tendencies in the mass public by asking two questions of respondents: whether they support or oppose an activist role for government in determining the distribution of economic benefits in society and whether they support or oppose activist government as a means of promoting a particular set of social values. The support–oppose responses to the two questions have been the

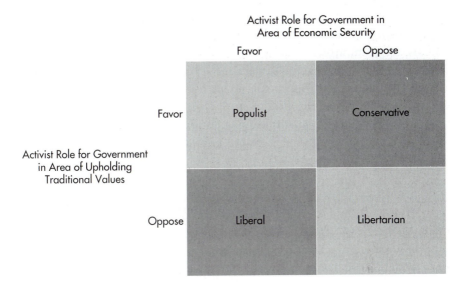

FIGURE 6-1 TYPES OF IDEOLOGIES

Americans can be classified as liberals, conservatives, populists, or libertarians, depending on their attitudes toward the government's role in the areas of economic security and social values.

basis for establishing four ideological types: conservatives, liberals, populists, and libertarians (see Figure 6-1).

Conservatives are defined as individuals who emphasize the marketplace as the means of distributing economic benefits but look to government to uphold traditional social values. In contrast, **liberals** favor activist government as an instrument of economic redistribution but reject the notion that government should favor a particular set of social values. True liberals and conservatives could be expected to differ, for instance, on the issues of homosexual rights (a social values question) and government-guaranteed health care (an economic distribution question). Liberals would view homosexuality as a private issue and believe that government should see to it that everyone has access to adequate medical care. Conservatives would oppose government-mandated access to health care and favor government policies that actively discourage homosexual lifestyles. **Populists** are defined as individuals who share with conservatives a concern for traditional values but, like liberals, favor an active role for government in providing economic security. **Libertarians** are opposed to government intervention in both the economic and social spheres.[21]

In sum, libertarians are the most committed to individual freedom, and populists are the most committed to government activism. Conservatives and liberals are committed to individual freedom in one area (the economic sphere for conservatives, the social sphere for liberals) but to government activism in the other (the social sphere for conservatives, the economic sphere for liberals). Of these ideological types, conservatives are the largest group. A 1996 Gallup Poll, for example, estimated that 35 percent of Americans are conservatives, 20 percent are libertarian, 20 percent are populist, and 13 percent are liberal.[22]

Group Thinking: The Outlook of Many

For most Americans, groups are a more important frame of reference than is ideology. Many people see politics through the lens of a group to which they belong or with which they identify. These individuals nearly always pay closer attention to issues that affect their group's interests than to more remote issues. Farmers, for example, are more likely to follow agricultural issues than they are labor–management issues.

Because of the country's great size, settlement by various immigrant groups, and economic pluralism, Americans are a very diverse people. Later chapters will examine group tendencies more fully, but it is useful here to mention a few of the major group orientations.

RELIGION Religious differences have always been a source of solidarity within a group and conflict with outsiders. At an earlier time, religion was a bitterly divisive force, as newly arrived Catholic and Jewish immigrants encountered widespread hostility and discrimination from entrenched Protestant groups. Today, Catholics, Protestants, and Jews share similar opinions on most policy issues.

Nevertheless, some important religious differences remain. The most powerful religious force in contemporary American politics is the so-called religious right, which consists primarily of individuals who see themselves as born-again Christians and view the Bible as the infallible truth. Their views on such issues as homosexual rights, abortion, and school prayer differ significantly from those of the population as a whole. A Time/CNN survey found, for example, that born-again Christians are 37 percent more likely than other Americans to agree that "the Supreme Court and the Congress have gone too far in keeping religious and moral values like prayer out of our laws, schools, and many areas of our lives."

CLASS Economic class has less influence on political opinion in the United States than in Europe, but it is nevertheless related to opinions on certain economic issues. For example, lower-income Americans are more supportive of social welfare programs, business regulation, and progressive taxation than are those in higher-income categories. An obstacle to class-based politics in the United States is that people with similar incomes but different occupations do not share the same opinions. Support for collective bargaining, for example, is substantially higher among factory workers than among small farmers, service workers, and those in the skilled crafts. The interplay of class and opinion will be examined more closely in Chapter 9, which discusses interest groups.

REGION Region has declined as a basis of political opinions. The increased mobility of the U.S. population has resulted in the relocation of millions of Americans from the Northeast and Midwest to the South and West. Their beliefs on issues such as social welfare tend to be more liberal than those of people who are native to these regions. Nevertheless, regional differences are still evident in the areas of social welfare, civil rights, and national defense. Conservative opinions on these issues are more prevalent in the southern and mountain states than elsewhere (see box: States in the Nation).

RACE Race, as we saw in Chapter 5, is a significant source of opinion differences. Whites and African Americans differ on issues of integration: black people are more in favor of affirmative action, busing, and other measures designed to promote racial equality and integration. Racial groups also differ on many pocketbook issues, largely as a result of the differences in their economic situations: African Americans are more supportive of social welfare programs and government-backed job and training programs. The crime issue is another area where opinion differences are pronounced and predictable: African Americans are less trusting of police and the judicial system. A recent Gallup Poll indicated, for example, that 68 percent of African Americans believe that the U.S. justice system is racially biased.

GENDER Although male–female differences of opinion are small on most issues, gender does affect opinion on some questions. Perhaps surprisingly, these issues are not primarily those that touch directly on gender or sexual equality. Men and women have generally similar views on issues such as abortion rights and affirmative action.

STATES IN THE NATION

Conservatives and Liberals

Nearly half of Americans describe themselves as moderates. Of the rest, the large majority are conservatives. According to a 1996 poll, liberals outnumber conservatives only in Massachusetts, Vermont, and the District of Columbia. The concentration of conservatives is especially high in the southern, plains, and mountain states.

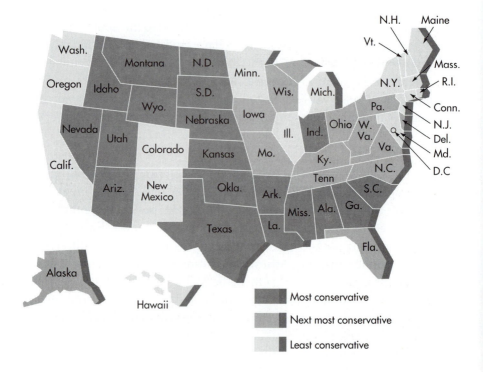

SOURCE: CNN exit polls, 1996. Classification based on the difference in the proportions of self-identified conservatives and liberals in each state.

There are two areas, however, where men's and women's opinions diverge significantly: social welfare and the use of force by the state.[23] Women are more supportive of government spending on social welfare (such as for education and poverty programs) and more opposed to state-sponsored force (for example, military power as an instrument of foreign policy). Some analysts have suggested that such differences reflect women's heightened sense of compassion and community responsibility. Men are said to believe more strongly in self-reliance and accountability. In any case, women tend to hold less conservative views than men (see Figure 6-2). This difference is a basis for the *gender gap* (the tendency of women to vote more strongly Democratic than men), which was discussed in Chapter 5. (The politics of gender is discussed further in Chapters 9 and 17.)

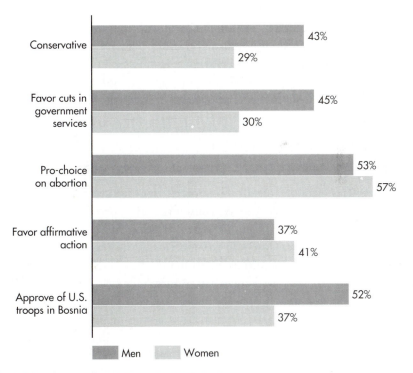

FIGURE 6-2 GENDER AND OPINION

Compared with men, women are less conservative, more supportive of social welfare services, and more opposed to the use of military force. Sources (polls, from top to bottom): National Election Studies (NES), 1994; NES, 1994; NBC/Wall Street Journal, 1996; ABC/Washington Post, 1995; Time/CNN, 1996.

AGE   Another division of growing importance is the "age gap." Young and old have always had somewhat divergent opinions as a consequence of differences in their ages and socialization experiences, but their disagreements are becoming greater. In her book *Young v. Old*, the political scientist Susan MacManus notes that the elderly tend to oppose increases in public school funding while supporting increases in social security and Medicare (government-assisted medical care for retirees). In states with large numbers of retirees, such as Florida and Arizona, proposed increases in local school budgets are regularly voted down and, more than any other group, the elderly helped defeat Republican lawmakers' plan in 1995–96 to cut Medicare spending as a means of balancing the federal budget. Such acts are at least somewhat at odds with the interests of younger adults, who may have children in the public schools and who, through payroll deductions, pay the taxes that fund the social security and Medicare programs.[24]

MacManus predicts that issues of age will increasingly dominate American politics and that the elderly have the political clout to prevail. They vote at a much higher rate than young people, are better organized politically (through groups such as the powerful American Association of Retired Persons), and are increasing in number as a result of lengthened life spans (the so-called graying of America). (The politics of age is also discussed in Chapters 9 and 17.)

Partisan Thinking: The Line That Divides

In the everyday play of politics, no source of opinion more clearly divides Americans than that of their partisanship. Figure 6-3 provides examples, but they indicate only a few of the differences. On nearly every major issue of economic, social, and foreign policy, Republicans and Democrats have views that are at least somewhat different. In many cases, such as spending programs for the poor, the differences are substantial.

The term **party identification** refers to a person's ingrained sense of loyalty to a political party. Party identification is not formal membership in a party but rather an emotional attachment to a party—the feeling that "I am a Democrat" or "I am a Republican." Scholars and pollsters have typically measured party identification with a question of the following type: "Generally speaking, do you think of yourself as a Republican, a Democrat, an independent, or what?" About 65 percent of adults call themselves Democrats or Republicans. Of the 35 percent who prefer the label "independent," most say they lean slightly toward one party or the other.

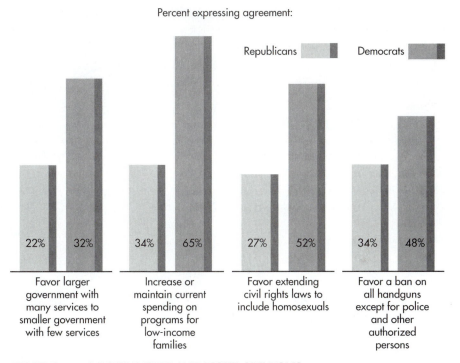

Percent expressing agreement:

FIGURE 6-3 PARTISANSHIP AND ISSUE OPINIONS
Republicans and Democrats differ significantly in their opinions on many policy
issues. Source: In order of questions: *Los Angeles Times* survey, January 19–22, 1995; Gallup
surveys, December 2–5, 1994; September 6–7, 1994; December 17–19, 1993.

Early studies of party identification concluded that partisan attitudes
were highly stable and seldom changed over the course of adult life.[25] Subsequent studies have shown that party loyalties are more fluid than originally
believed; they can be influenced by the issues and candidates of the moment.[26] Nevertheless, most adults do not switch their party loyalties easily,
and a substantial proportion never waver from an initial commitment to a
party, which can often be traced to childhood influences. Partisanship affects
opinions in the same way as do other psychological commitments. Just as
nationality colors people's views of their country, partisanship tints people's
political views.

For most people, partisanship is not simply a "blind" faith in the party
of their choice. Some Republicans and Democrats know very little about
their party's traditions, policies, or group commitments and unthinkingly

Party loyalties are embedded in government's response to social and economic conditions. The loyalty of African Americans to the Democratic party is largely a consequence of its leadership on civil rights and social welfare issues. (Robert Fox/Impact Visuals)

embrace the candidates and issues of their party. Party loyalties, however, are not randomly distributed across the population but are embedded in social and economic conditions. The fact that most African Americans are Democrats and most business executives are Republicans is not mere coincidence; their partisanship is rooted in their different life circumstances and the policy traditions of the Democratic and Republican parties.

Partisanship is obviously a strong force in American politics, but its influence is declining. In recent decades, the proportion of voters who identify with the Democratic or Republican party has declined and the proportion of independents has increased (see Figure 6-4). As a result, elections are more volatile than in the past. People are less likely to vote on the basis of a longstanding party loyalty and more likely to base their choice on the issues and candidates of the moment. This and other issues of partisanship are examined in depth at various points in this book, particularly in Chapters 7, 8, 11, and 12.

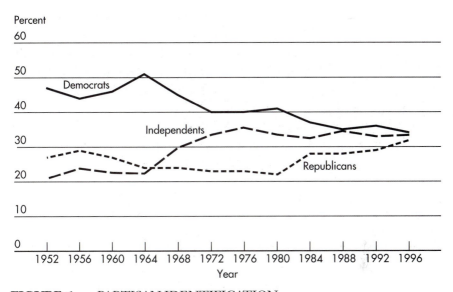

FIGURE 6-4 PARTISAN IDENTIFICATION
Party loyalties weakened in the late 1960s, and the proportion of independents increased. Source: National Election Studies, 1952–1992; Gallup, 1996.

THE INFLUENCE OF PUBLIC OPINION ON POLICY

Yet unanswered in the discussion is the central question about public opinion: What impact does it have on government?

The fundamental principle of democracy is that the *majority* ought to prevail on public issues. It is difficult, however, to put this principle into practice. In any society of appreciable size, it is simply not possible for the people directly to formulate public policies and programs. However, democracy can be said to exist when officials take the majority's views into account when making policy decisions and when the people have recourse to free and fair elections when they believe their opinions are being ignored.[27]

Some analysts argue that the majority's views do not count for enough; the *elites*, it is claimed, are so entrenched and remote that they pay little attention to the preferences of ordinary citizens.[28] The most comprehensive study ever conducted of the relationship between public opinion and policy, however, concluded otherwise. In a study spanning fifty years of trends, Benjamin Page and Robert Shapiro found a substantial relationship between changes in public opinion and subsequent changes in public policy, particularly on highly visible issues. More often than not, policy changed in response to opinion rather than the reverse. In addition, the more important the issue, the more likely that policy adapted to changes in public opinion. Page and Shapiro concluded that U.S. officials are reasonably responsive to majority opinion.[29]

Not all scholars have interpreted the evidence on public opinion and policy so favorably,[30] but there is little question that the public's views do have an impact. Public opinion is rarely powerful enough to force officials into a specific course of action, but public opinion does serve as a guiding force in public policy. There are many actions, for example, that officials dare *not* take for fear of public retribution. No politician who wants to stay in office is likely to say, for example, that social security for the elderly should be abolished. And there are many actions that politicians willingly take in order to appeal to public opinion. In 1994, for example, Congress passed a $30-billion crime bill that authorized the building of more prisons, the placement of more police on the streets, and tough mandatory sentences for certain crimes. The legislation was enacted at a time when crime ranked first in the polls as America's major problem and despite predictions from criminal justice experts that it would not significantly deter crime.

Such examples, however, do not provide an answer to the question of whether government is *sufficiently* responsive to public opinion. This question, as was discussed in Chapter 3, is in part a normative one, the answer to which rests on assumptions about the proper relationship between people's everyday opinions and what government does. The question is also complicated by the fact that politics includes a battle over the control of public opinion. People's views are neither fixed nor simply a product of personal circumstances. Public opinion is dynamic and can be changed, activated, and crystallized through political action.

In fact, one of the best indicators of the power of public opinion is the effort of political leaders to harness it in support of their goals. In American politics, popular demand for a policy is a powerful argument for it. For this reason and others, great effort is made to organize and represent public opinion through elections (Chapter 7), political parties (Chapter 8), interest groups (Chapter 9), the news media (Chapter 10), and political institutions (Chapters 11 to 14). Later chapters will also examine the direct impact of public opinion in particular policy areas: the economy (Chapter 15), social welfare (Chapter 16), and foreign affairs (Chapter 17).

SUMMARY

Public opinion can be defined as those opinions held by ordinary citizens which government takes into account in making its decisions. Public officials have many ways of assessing public opinion, such as the outcomes of elections, but have increasingly come to rely on public opinion polls. There are many possible sources of error in polls, and surveys sometimes present a misleading image of the public's views. However, a properly conducted poll can provide an accurate indication of what the public is thinking and can dissuade political leaders from thinking that the views of the most vocal citizens (such as demonstrators and letter writers) are also the views of the broader public.

The process by which individuals acquire their political opinions is called political socialization. During childhood the family and schools are important sources of basic political attitudes, such as beliefs about the parties and the nature of the U.S. political and economic systems. Many of the basic orientations that Americans acquire during childhood remain with them in adulthood; but socialization is a continuing process. Major shifts in opinion during adulthood are usually the consequence of changing political conditions; for example, the Great Depression of the 1930s was the catalyst for wholesale changes in Americans' opinions on the government's economic role. There are also short-term fluctuations in opinion that result from new political issues, problems, and events. Individuals' opinions in these cases are affected by prior beliefs, peers, political leaders, and the news media. Events themselves are also a significant short-term influence on opinions.

The frames of reference that guide Americans' opinions include cultural beliefs, such as individualism, which result in a range of acceptable and unacceptable policy alternatives. Opinions can also stem from ideology, although most citizens do not have a strong and consistent ideological attachment. In addition, individuals develop opinions as a result of group orientations, notably religion, income, occupation, region, race, gender, or age. Partisanship is perhaps the major source of political opinions; Republicans and Democrats differ in their voting behavior and views on many policy issues. However, party loyalty has declined in importance in recent decades as a frame of reference for people's opinions.

Public opinion has a significant influence on government but seldom determines exactly what government will do in a particular instance. Public opinion constrains the policy choices of officials. Some policy actions are beyond the range of possibility because the public will not accept change in existing policy or will not seriously consider policy that seems clearly at odds with basic American values. Evidence indicates that officials are reasonably attentive to public opinion on highly visible and controversial issues of public policy.

MAJOR CONCEPTS

conservatives	populists
ideology	probability sample
liberals	public opinion
libertarians	public opinion poll
party identification	sample
political socialization	sampling error
population	

SUGGESTED READINGS

Brace, Paul, and Barbara Hinckley. *Follow the Leader: Opinion Polls and Modern Presidents.* New York: Basic Books, 1992. An analysis concluding that presidents follow public opinion closely, even too closely, in the making of decisions.

Dionne, E. J. *They Only Look Dead: Why Progressives Will Dominate the Next Political Era.* New York: Simon & Schuster, 1996. A claim by one of the nation's top journalists of the pending revival of liberalism.

Dunn, Charles W., and J. David Woodard. *The Conservative Tradition in America.* Lanham, Md.: Rowman & Littlefield, 1996. A study of the philosophical and political roots of conservatism from its origins to the present.

Frum, David. *What's Right: The New Conservative Majority and the Remaking of America.* New York: Basic Books, 1996. A claim by a conservative commentator that the nation and its policies are moving to the right.

Jennings, M. Kent, and Richard Niemi. *Generations and Politics: A Panel Study of Young Adults and Their Parents.* Princeton, N.J.: Princeton University Press, 1981. A careful study of the relationship over time between the political beliefs of parents and their children.

Just, Marion R., Ann N. Crigler, Dean E. Alger, Timothy E. Cook, Montague Kern, and Darrell M. West. *Crosstalk: Citizens, Candidates, and the Media in a Presidential Campaign.* Chicago: University of Chicago Press, 1996. An exhaustive study of the factors that shape campaign information and how citizens use this information.

MacManus, Susan A. *Young v. Old: Generational Combat in the 21st Century.* Boulder, Colo.: Westview Press, 1996. A study of the emerging conflict in the political self-interest of younger and older Americans.

Noelle-Neumann, Elisabeth. *The Spiral of Silence,* 2d ed. Chicago: University of Chicago Press, 1993. An intriguing theory of how public opinion is formed and muted.

Popkin, Samuel L. *The Reasoning Voter: Communication and Persuasion in Presidential Campaigns.* Chicago: University of Chicago Press, 1991. An analysis of how citizens form reasonable opinions despite their low level of information about politics.

Traugott, Michael W., and Paul J. Lavrakas. *The Voter's Guide to Election Polls.* Chatham, N.J.: Chatham House, 1996. A clear guide to survey methods and analysis with an emphasis on election polling.

R E A D I N G   6

Democracy, Information, and the Rational Public

BENJAMIN I. PAGE AND ROBERT Y.
SHAPIRO

The suggestion that ordinary citizens are simply too ignorant to know their own or their country's interests lies at the heart of many objections to majoritarian democracy. The authors of the Federalist Papers, for example, worried not merely that public opinion vacillated but that it erred. John Stuart Mill, considered a father of democratic theory, nonetheless advocated a severely limited suffrage and favored public rather than secret ballots, extra votes for the prosperous and the educated, "merit" appointment rather than election of most officials, no pledges by representatives to their constituents, and very limited functions for the elected body—all on the grounds that common people, especially the working class, were not competent to rule and were likely to demand class legislation.

In more recent times, . . . Walter Lippmann issued scathing denunciations of the public's capabilities, maintaining that reality differs sharply from the "stereotypes" or "pictures" in people's heads. Joseph Schumpeter declared that individuals' opinions are not "definite" or "independent" or "rational" and that on most political matters individual volition, command of fact, and method of inference are defective.

Early survey research seemed to bear out these low estimates of public capacity. Surveys indicated that most Americans knew little about politics, cared little, and apparently made their voting decisions on the basis of demographic characteristics or party loyalties, which scholars (perhaps too quickly) took to indicate lack of rational deliberation. Converse's demonstration of weak ideological structure and unstable individual survey responses seemed, for a while, to close the case.

The result was a wholesale revision of democratic theory. Schumpeter's weak procedural definition of democracy, in which elite leadership competes for voters' acquiescence but does not necessarily respond to their policy preferences, influenced more than a generation of scholars. Dahl cast doubt on the desirability of "populistic" democracy. Berelson et al. speculated that citizens' passivity might function as a useful buffer for system stability. Most of the leaders of the political science and sociology professions rejected majoritarian democracy, embracing some form of pluralistic or "polyarchical" system in which organized interest groups play an important part and in which participation by, and responsiveness to, the general public is limited.

We agree with Walker, Kariel, Pateman, Barber, and others that this revisionism mistakenly blamed the citizen victims, ignoring system-level influences upon peoples' behavior (apathy about elections, for example, may result from legal restrictions, repression, or lack of attractive candidates and parties rather than from defects of the citizenry); that it abandoned a worthy normative ideal and turned democratic theory into little more than a conservative ratifier of the status quo; and that it neglected the possibility that broader participation could promote political education and human development.

In particular, we believe that the revisionists misinterpreted survey research results and gave up too quickly on the public. This should have been clear even before research contrasting the 1960s with the 1950s cast a more favorable light on citizens' capacities by showing that people displayed more interest, knowledge, and ideological thinking when the political environment was more lively. The original findings that most Americans did not live up to "classical democratic theory"—a construct of dubious provenance, which called for citizens to have unrealistically and unnecessarily high levels of political knowledge and sophistication—never really had much relevance to the desirability or feasibility of majoritarian democracy.

People probably do not need large amounts of information to make rational voting choices. Cues from like-minded citizens and groups (including cues related to demographic characteristics and party labels) may be sufficient, in an environment where accurate information is available, to permit voters to act as if they had all the available information.

Much the same reasoning applies to our own topic, policy preferences. (We have had nothing new to say about voting, though we suspect that similar principles apply.) Using their underlying beliefs and values, together with cues from leaders and like-minded citizens they trust, people can come up with reasonable opinions (i.e., opinions consonant with their basic beliefs and values) about a wide variety of issues. . . .

Our research has led us to a view of collective public opinion that justifies the use of terms like "reasonable," "responsible," and "rational." Without claiming that we have any unique knowledge of what people's true interests are, we are convinced by the general stability, differentiation, and coherent patterning of collective policy preferences, and by their responsiveness to new situations and new information, that characterizations of public opinion as ignorant fall very wide of the mark. We do not know who is better able to judge the public interest than the public itself. Any alternative invites minority tyranny. . . .

It is simply not the case that the collective policy preferences of the U.S. public are nonexistent, unknowable, capricious, inconsistent, or ignorant. Instead, they are real, meaningful, well measured by polls, differentiated, coherent, and stable. They react understandably and predictably to events and new information. The classic justifications for ignoring public opinion do not hold up.

Moreover, the information system works well enough so that public opinion does not merely respond sensibly to available information; it has generally reacted directly and responsibly to objective realities. Collective deliberation does occur, and substantial political education takes place.

Thus our research provides little reason for anyone to fear or oppose majoritarian democracy in the United States. There is no need to sneer at politicians who "read the Gallup polls," so long as they do so correctly. In our view, in fact, government should pay more attention to what the public wants. More democratic responsiveness, rather than less, would be all to the good, and institutional changes to that end (reducing the role of money in politics, easing voter registration, strengthening political competition, broadening electoral accountability) should be encouraged.

At the same time, we have suggested that political education—in the broad sense of providing useful political experience and information and moral guidance to the citizenry—is not what it could be; that concealment of (or failure to provide) relevant information sometimes permits government to pursue unpopular policies, outside of public view; and that the public's policy preferences may sometimes be manipulated by deceptive leaders and by flows of information subject to various biases or distortions.

There is some truth to the epigram of V. O. Key, Jr., that "(t)he voice of the people is but an echo." The public has a remarkable collective capacity for reasonable political thought, even in the face of misleading or downright false counsel from its leaders. But information inputs do matter; they can have substantial effects on policy preferences, bending them away from citizens' true interests or conceptions of the common good.

A chief focus for improvement, we believe, should be the political information system. The public deserves better political education, more opportunities for participation, and access to better information about public policy. Thomas Jefferson expressed the point neatly, in a famous passage from his letter of September 28, 1820, to William C. Jarvis:

> I know of no safe depository of the ultimate powers of the society but the people themselves, and if we think them not enlightened enough to exercise their control with a wholesome discretion, the remedy is not to take it from them but to inform their discretion by education.

SOURCE: Benjamin I. Page and Robert Y. Shapiro, *The Rational Public: Fifty Years of Trends in Americans' Policy Preferences* (Chicago: University of Chicago Press, 1992). Reprinted by permission.
Benjamin I. Page is Gordon Scott Fulcher Professor of Decision Making at Northwestern University; Robert Y. Shapiro is professor of political science at Columbia University.

CHAPTER SEVEN

Voting and Participation

We are concerned in public affairs, but immersed in our private ones.

WALTER LIPPMANN[1]

IT WAS THE year of the angry voter. President Bill Clinton's ambitious health care reform proposal had gone down to defeat in Congress after yearlong partisan wrangling and without so much as a vote being taken on the floor of either the House or the Senate. Promised reforms of lobbying and campaign spending also never materialized. In a blistering editorial, *The New York Times* described the 103d Congress as the least productive and most fractious in memory.[2]

Americans were thoroughly disenchanted with Washington politics as they prepared to vote in the midterm congressional elections. Polls indicated that confidence in Congress had fallen to a record low: fewer than 20 percent of Americans said they trusted the institution to represent their interests. On election day, the voters' anger produced a Republican victory of historic proportions. A net loss of fifty-two Democratic seats placed the House of Representatives in Republican hands for the first time since 1954. The Democrats also lost control of the Senate, which they had held for all but six years since 1954. Newt Gingrich, the House Republican leader, called the election "an American revolution," saying it was a final repudiation of Democratic liberalism.

Although the Republicans' sweeping victory was the outstanding feature of the 1994 elections, there was another feature worth noting: only 38 percent of the adult population voted. Despite the public's expression of anger at their elected representatives and despite a concerted get-out-the-vote campaign by the political parties, the media, and public service groups, more than 125 million Americans of voting age did not cast a ballot on election day. Had they voted, the outcome might have been very different. A CNN/USA Today poll indicated that nonvoters preferred Democratic candidates by nearly a 10-percent margin.

Voting is a form of **political participation**—a sharing in activities designed to influence public policy and leadership. Political participation involves other activities in addition to voting, such as joining political parties and interest groups, writing to elected officials, demonstrating for political causes, and giving money to political candidates.

Democratic societies are distinguished by their emphasis on citizen participation. The concept of self-government rests on the idea that ordinary people have a right, even an obligation, to involve themselves in the affairs of state. A political system that claims to represent the public's interest is not necessarily a truly democratic system; citizens must also be given meaningful opportunities to participate in the process. From this perspective, the extent of political participation—how much and by whom—is a measure of how fully democratic a society is.[3]

The question of participation also extends to the reasons people are politically involved or not involved. It is one thing if political participation is like attendance at a rock concert, which is mostly a matter of individual taste and proximity, and quite another if participation is like attendance at an elite prep school, which is mostly a matter of social privilege. A democratic political system implies that society will not place substantial barriers in the way of those who want to participate. As we will see in this chapter, differences in the extent of political participation among Americans are explained by both individual and systemic factors, although the latter are more influential in the United States than in most other western democracies. One result is that the participation rate in U.S. elections is less than that of other countries, particularly among citizens of lower income and less education. The major points made in this chapter are the following:

- ★ *Voter turnout in U.S. elections is low in comparison with that of other democratic nations, which is due to differences in registration requirements, the frequency of elections, and the nature of political parties.*
- ★ *Although most Americans do not participate actively in politics in areas other than voting, they are more active in these areas than citizens of other democracies.*
- ★ *Most Americans make a sharp distinction between their personal lives and national life, which reduces their incentive to participate politically.*

VOTER PARTICIPATION

At the nation's founding, **suffrage**—the right to vote—was restricted to property-owning males. Thomas Paine ridiculed this policy in *Common Sense*. Noting that a man whose only item of property was a jackass would lose his right to vote if the jackass died, Paine asked, "Now tell me, which was the voter, the man or the jackass?" It was not until the 1820s that a majority of states extended suffrage to propertyless white males, a change made possible by their insistence on the vote and by the realization on the part of the wealthy that the nation's abundant opportunities offered a natural defense against attacks on property rights by the voting poor.

Women did not secure the vote until 1920, with the ratification of the Nineteenth Amendment. By then, men had run out of excuses for denying women the vote. Senator Wendell Phillips expressed the pro-suffrage view: "One of two things is true: either woman is like man—and if she is, then a ballot based on brains belongs to her as well as to him. Or she is different, and then man does not know how to vote for her as she herself does."[4]

African Americans had to wait nearly fifty years longer than women to be granted full suffrage. They seemed to have won the right to vote with passage of the Fifteenth Amendment after the Civil War, but they were effectively disenfranchised in the South by a number of electoral tricks, including poll taxes, literacy tests, and whites-only primary elections. The poll tax

After a hard-fought, decades-long campaign, American women finally won the right to vote in 1920. (Culver Pictures)

was a fee of several dollars that had to be paid before one could register to vote. Since most blacks in the South were too poor to pay the poll tax, it barred them from voting. Not until the ratification of the Twenty-fourth Amendment in 1964 was the poll tax outlawed in national elections. Supreme Court decisions and the Voting Rights Act of 1965 swept away other legal barriers to fuller participation by African Americans.

Today virtually any American—rich or poor, man or woman, black or white—who is determined to vote can legally and actually do so. Americans attach great importance to the power of their votes. They claim that voting is their greatest source of influence over political leadership and their strongest protection against an uncaring or corrupt government.[5] In view of this attitude and the historical struggle of various groups to gain voting rights, the surprising fact is that many Americans are not active voters, a tendency that sets them apart from citizens of most other western democracies.

Factors in Voter Turnout: The United States in Comparative Perspective

Voter turnout is the proportion of persons of voting age who actually vote in a given election. Since the 1960s the turnout level in presidential elections has not reached 60 percent (see Figure 7-1). In 1996, the level fell to 49 percent, the first time since 1924 that fewer than half of adults cast a vote for president.

Turnout is even lower in the midterm congressional elections that take place between presidential elections. Midterm election turnout has not reached 50 percent since 1920, nor made it past the 40 percent mark since 1970. After a recent midterm election, the cartoonist Rigby showed an election clerk eagerly asking a stray cat that had wandered into a polling place, "Are you registered?"[6]

Nonvoting is far more prevalent in the United States than in nearly all other democracies (see box: How the United States Compares). In recent decades, turnout in major national elections has averaged less than 60 percent in the United States, compared with more than 90 percent in Belgium, more than 80 percent in France and Denmark, and more than 70 percent in Great Britain and Germany.[7] The disparity in turnout between the United States and other nations is not as great as these official voting rates indicate, however. Some nations calculate turnout solely on the basis of eligible adults, while the United States bases its figures on all adults, including noncitizens and other ineligible groups. Nevertheless, even when such statistical dis-

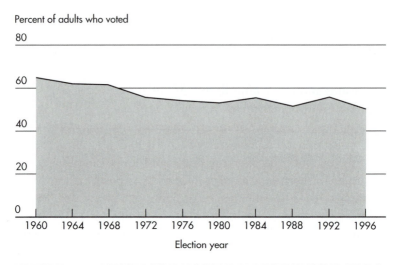

Percent of adults who voted

FIGURE 7-1 VOTER TURNOUT IN PRESIDENTIAL ELEC-
TIONS, 1960–1996
Voter turnout has declined substantially since the 1960s.   Source: U.S.
Bureau of the Census, 1960–1968; Federal Election Commission, 1972–1996.

parities are corrected, turnout in U.S. elections remains low in comparison
with that of nearly every other western democracy.

Voting does not require vast amounts of time. It takes most people
longer to go to a video store and select a movie than it takes to go to the
neighborhood polling place and cast a ballot. Thus the explanation for the
relatively low turnout rate of Americans must entail other considerations:
registration requirements, the frequency of elections, and the lack of clear-
cut differences between the political parties.

REGISTRATION REQUIREMENTS   Before Americans are allowed to
vote, they must be registered—that is, their names must appear on an official list of eligible voters. **Registration** began around 1900 as a way of preventing voters from casting more than one ballot during an election.

Although other democracies also require registration, they place this responsibility on government. In European nations, public officials have the
duty to enroll citizens on registration lists. The United States—in keeping
with its individualistic culture—is the only democracy in which registration
is the individual's responsibility.[8] In addition, registration laws have traditionally been established by the state governments, and some states make it
relatively difficult for citizens to qualify. Registration periods and locations

HOW THE UNITED STATES COMPARES

Voter Turnout

The United States ranks near the bottom among the world's democracies in the percentage of eligible citizens who participate in national elections. One reason for the low voter turnout is that individual Americans are responsible for registering to vote, whereas in most other democracies, voters are automatically registered by government officials. In addition, unlike some other democracies, the United States does not encourage voting by holding elections on the weekend or imposing penalties, such as fines, on those who do not participate.

Another factor affecting the turnout rate in the United States is the absence of a major labor or socialist party, which would serve to bring lower-income citizens to the polls. In democracies where such parties exist, the turnout difference between upper- and lower-income groups is relatively small. In the United States, however, lower-income persons are much less likely to vote than higher-income persons.

Country	Voter Turnout	Personal Registration?	Social Democrat, Socialist, or Labor Party?
Belgium	92%	No	Yes
Italy	86	No	Yes
France	85	Yes	Yes
Denmark	83	No	Yes
Austria	82	No	Yes
Germany	78	No	Yes
Great Britain	78	No	Yes
Canada	69	No	No
Japan	67	No	Yes
United States	55	Yes	No

SOURCE: Foreign embassies, except data on United States, which is based on Federal Elections Commission information.

are usually not highly publicized, and many citizens simply do not know when or where to register. Eligibility can also be a problem. In most states, a citizen must establish legal residency by living in the same place for a minimum period, usually thirty days but sometimes as long as fifty days, before becoming eligible to register.

States with a tradition of lenient registration laws generally have a higher turnout than other states. Maine, Minnesota, and Oregon allow people to register at their polling place on election day, and these states rank high in voter turnout. Those states that have erected the most barriers are in the South, where restrictive registration was originally intended to prevent black people from voting. These historical differences continue to be reflected in state voter turnout levels (see box: States in the Nation).

In 1993, in an effort to increase registration levels nationwide, Congress enacted a voting registration law known as "motor voter." Its supporters predicted that the legislation, so named because it requires states to permit people to register to vote when applying for a driver's license (it also requires states to provide registration through the mail and at certain state welfare offices), would add as many as 50 million new voters to registration rolls by the end of the century. The prediction seems optimistic, since state agencies cannot compel applicants to register. Congressional Republicans made their support of the legislation contingent upon this nonmandatory provision. They had blocked the bill for several years, fearing that it would help the Democrats by adding mainly lower-income Americans to the registration rolls. For the same reason, Republican governors in several states, including California and South Carolina, delayed putting the law into effect. Partisan concerns have always played a role in shaping registration laws, but in this case they appear miscalculated. Early registrations under the motor-voter law have been about evenly divided between the Republican and Democratic parties.

By the time of the 1996 presidential election, roughly 20 million people had been registered as part of the motor-voter law.[9] Yet the increase did not result in a higher turnout rate; the number of voters actually declined in 1996. Clearly, registration is only one of the factors underlying America's low turnout rate.

FREQUENCY OF ELECTIONS   Another factor that reduces voter turnout is the frequency with which Americans are asked to vote. No other democracy has elections for the lower chamber of its national legislature (the equivalent of the U.S. House of Representatives) as often as every two years or elects its chief executive as often as every four years. In addition, elections of state and local officials in the United States are often scheduled separately

S T A T E S   I N   T H E   N A T I O N

State-by-State Voter Turnout in Presidential Elections

Southern states have a tradition of more restrictive registration laws, and even today they tend to have lower rates of voter turnout. States with large recent immigrant populations, such as California and New York, also have lower turnout. Categories are based on turnout average in recent presidential elections.

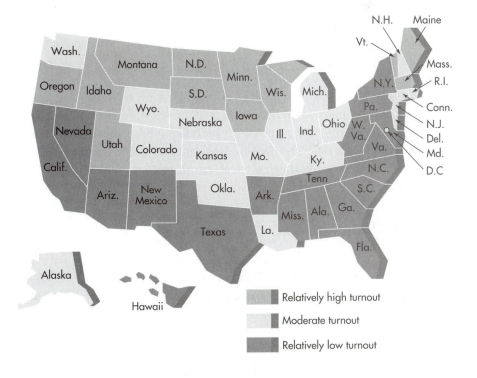

from national races. Two-thirds of the states elect their governors in non-presidential election years, and 60 percent of U.S. cities hold elections of municipal officials in odd-numbered years.

The frequency of U.S. elections reduces turnout by increasing the effort required to participate in all of them.[10] Most European nations have less frequent elections, and the responsibility of voting is thus less burdensome. Many European nations also schedule their elections on Sundays or declare election day to be a national holiday, thus making it more convenient for working people to vote. In the United States, elections are traditionally held on Tuesdays, and most people must vote before or after work.

The contrast with European practice is especially marked in the case of primary elections. The United States is the only democratic nation in which party nominees are commonly chosen by voters through primary elections rather than by party leaders. Consequently, Americans are asked to vote twice to fill a single office. Many voters skip the primaries, preferring to vote just once, in the general election. In contested statewide and presidential primaries, the average voter turnout is about 30 percent, substantially lower than the turnout in general elections.

PARTY DIFFERENCES   A final explanation for low voter turnout has to do with voters' perception that there is not much difference between the Republican and Democratic parties.[11] This belief is not entirely unfounded. Each party depends on citizens of all economic and social backgrounds for support; consequently, neither party can afford to take an extreme position that would alienate a sizable segment of the electorate. For example, both parties share a commitment to the private-enterprise system and to a basic social security system (see Chapter 8).

Parties in Europe divide more sharply over policies. In European elections, the choice between a conservative party and a socialist party may mean a choice between private and government ownership of major industries. Turnout is higher when political parties represent clear-cut alternatives, particularly when religious or class divisions are involved.[12] European parties, particularly those on the left, are also more closely tied to other organizations, such as labor unions, which assist in the mobilization of the electorate.[13]

Why Some Americans Vote and Others Do Not

Even though turnout is lower in the United States than in other democracies, some Americans do vote in all or nearly all elections. But other Americans seldom or never vote. What accounts for such *individual* differences?

The factors that account for differences in public opinion (see Chapter 6) are not in all cases related to turnout differences. The turnout rates of men and women, for example, are nearly the same.[14] Race was once a very significant predictor of turnout but has become less important. African Americans still have a substantially lower turnout rate than whites, but the difference, which is about 10 percent in presidential elections, is far less than the 40 percent that existed before legal barriers to African American participation were lowered in the 1960s.

Large differences in voter turnout are associated with citizens' sense of civic involvement, age, education, and economic class.

FEELINGS OF CIVIC DUTY, ALIENATION, AND APATHY   Regular voters are characterized by a strong sense of **civic duty**—that is, they regard participation in elections as one of the responsibilities of citizenship. A sense of civic duty is an attitude that most individuals acquire during their political socialization in childhood and adolescence. When parents vote regularly and take an interest in politics, their children are likely to grow up believing that voting is an obligation of citizenship.

Many citizens do not have a strong sense of civic duty, and some of them display almost no interest in politics. **Apathy** is a general lack of interest in or concern with politics. Just as some people would not attend the Super Bowl even if it were free and being played across the street, some people would not bother to vote even if a ballot were delivered to their door. As with civic duty, a sense of apathy is often the consequence of childhood socialization. When parents disparage voting and other forms of political participation, their children are likely to hold a similar view when they reach voting age.

However, voter turnout is also affected by the degree to which people believe that their participation will make a difference.[15] The level of turnout tends to increase when citizens have a high degree of trust in government and to fall when they are politically disillusioned.[16] Turnout in U.S. presidential elections dropped by 10 percentage points between 1958 and 1980, a period in which Americans' trust in Washington declined sharply under the onslaught of the Vietnam war, the Watergate scandal, economic stagnation, and other national problems. Trust in government has remained at a relatively low level ever since and so, too, has the level of voter turnout.

Alienation is a sense of personal powerlessness that includes the notion that government does not care about the opinions of people like oneself.[17] It might be thought foolish for people to withdraw from politics when they believe government is inept and uncaring. Yet for some individuals, the vote

is as much an affirmation of citizenship as it is an opportunity to influence
the direction of government. Most people know that their single vote is unlikely to affect the outcome of an election. When disgusted with government,
they may choose simply to retreat from politics.

AGE   When viewers tuned in MTV at various times during the most
recent presidential campaign, they might have thought at first that they had
selected the wrong channel. Rather than a video of their favorite rock star,
they saw the presidential candidates urging young people to vote.

The candidates had targeted the right audience. Young adults are much
less likely to vote than middle-aged citizens. Even senior citizens, despite the
infirmities of old age, have a far higher turnout rate than voters under the
age of thirty. Young people are less likely to have the political concern that
can accompany such lifestyle characteristics as homeownership, a permanent
career, and a family.[18] In fact, citizens under the age of thirty have a lower
turnout rate than any other demographic group of comparable size.

Young people have the lowest rate of voter turnout of any group. To increase their
participation level, party and civic activists have developed novel approaches to
registration, as in the case of this registration booth at a Hollywood Palace rock
concert. (David Butow/Black Star)

EDUCATION   What does your college education mean?[19] One thing it means is that you have a much higher probability of becoming an active citizen. The difference is striking. Persons with a college education are about 40 percent more likely to vote than persons with a grade school education. Researchers have concluded that education generates a greater interest in politics, a higher level of political information, a greater confidence that one can make a difference politically, and peer pressure to participate—all of which are related to the tendency to vote.[20] Education, in fact, is the single best predictor of voter turnout.

ECONOMIC CLASS   Turnout is also strongly related to economic status. Americans at the bottom of the economic ladder are much less likely to vote than those at the top.[21] In presidential elections, for example, the turnout rate of low-income citizens is only about half that of high-income citizens (see Figure 7-2).

In contrast, low-income citizens in Europe have a turnout rate only slightly lower than that of high-income citizens. Europe's political traditions and institutions—its strong socialist and labor parties, its politically oriented trade unions, and its class-based ideologies—encourage lower-class

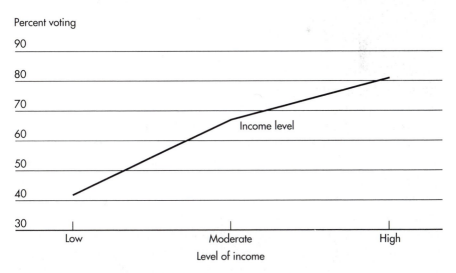

FIGURE 7-2   VOTER TURNOUT AND INCOME
Lower-income Americans are much less likely to vote than higher-income Americans, which is different from the situation in European democracies, where income level has only a marginal impact on turnout level.   Source: U.S. Bureau of the Census.

participation in ways that the U.S. political system does not.[22] For example, the United States does not have, and has never had, a major socialist or labor party. The interests of lower-income Americans have been addressed primarily through the Democratic party, but, like the Republican party, it focuses primarily on the interests of middle-class voters.

The Impact of the Vote

Through their votes, the people choose the representatives who will govern in their name. But what is the relationship between the vote and the actions of government? What influence does the vote have on public policy? Fuller answers to these questions will be provided later in the book (see Chapters 8, 11, and 12), but it is useful to consider at least a partial response at this point.

Elections do *not* ordinarily produce a popular mandate for the policies advocated by the winning candidate. A mandate requires voters to consciously choose between candidates on the basis of the promises they make during the campaign. A difficulty with this interpretation of election results is that voters are not usually well informed about candidates' policy positions. In U.S. House campaigns, fewer than half the voters can recall on their own the names of the two major-party nominees in their district and even fewer can identify these candidates' positions on major issues.[23] In presidential races, the voters are better informed, but most of them cannot readily recall more than a few of the differences in the candidates' platforms.

Several influences combine to limit the voters' awareness of issues. The candidates do not always make their positions altogether clear, either because they fear that taking a firm stand will lose them votes or because they do not have specific policies in mind. Many candidates have dodged the abortion issue in recent years by expressing personal opposition to it while at the same time promising to uphold a woman's right to choose as long as the courts permit it. Additionally, the news media concentrate their election coverage not on issues but on the strategic aspects of the candidates' pursuit of office. By covering campaigns as if they were horse races, the media deemphasize substantive issues of policy, thereby making it more difficult for the voters to discover where the candidates stand. Finally, voters can hardly be aware of issues if they are personally inattentive to politics. Most citizens do not follow campaigns closely and do not necessarily gain knowledge of even highly publicized issues.[24]

There are, to be sure, some voters who are highly informed on the issues and cast their ballots on this basis. **Prospective voting** describes this forward-looking type of voting. Prospective voting occurs when voters know the issue positions of the candidates and choose the candidate whose proposals best match their own issue preferences.

A more prevalent form of voting is **retrospective voting,** which is the situation in which voters support the incumbent party or candidate when they are pleased with the performance and reverse their position when they are displeased. George Bush's fate in 1988 and 1992 illustrates the importance that voters attach to past governmental performance. The nation's economy in 1988 was in the midst of the longest sustained upturn in a half-century, and opinion polls showed that a majority of Americans believed that the Republican party was more likely than the Democrats to keep the country prosperous. These conditions, more than any promise of future action or any personality traits of Bush, were the key to his victory. He had the support of more than 85 percent of the voters who had backed Reagan four years earlier.

In 1992, however, the U.S. economy was in its longest recession since World War II, and Bush was in political trouble. Three-fourths of the American public expressed concern about his handling of the economy, and their dissatisfaction was reflected in the outcome of the election. Bush lost by a substantial margin to Bill Clinton, who, despite widespread reservations about his personal character, represented the prospect of change.

As in these cases, economic conditions are usually the key factor in the electorate's retrospective judgments. When voters' confidence in the in-party's handling of the economy has been high, its nominee has usually won the presidential election. Conversely, its nominee has usually lost when the voters are dissatisfied with the state of the economy.[25] Congressional elections are affected to a lesser extent by national conditions, since these races often hinge on local issues and incumbents' superior funding and name recognition (see Chapter 11). Nevertheless, House and Senate elections can be affected by the public's view of the federal government's performance. Voters' disenchantment with Washington politics was the catalyst for the Republicans' sweeping victory in the 1994 midterm congressional elections.

Retrospective voting is a somewhat weaker form of public control than prospective voting, because it occurs after the fact: government has already acted, and nothing can change what has already taken place. Nevertheless, retrospective voting can be an effective form of popular control over policy because it forces public officials to anticipate the voters' likely response in the next election. The fear that they might be voted out of office by an electorate upset with their policies is a powerful constraint on elected representatives.[26]

CONVENTIONAL FORMS OF PARTICIPATION OTHER THAN VOTING

In one sense, voting is an unrivaled form of citizen participation and influence. Free and open elections are the defining characteristic of democratic government, and hence voting is regarded as the most basic duty of citizens.[27] Voting is also the only form of citizen participation engaged in by a majority of adults in every democratic country.[28]

In another sense, however, voting is a restricted form of participation.[29] Citizens have the opportunity to vote only at a particular time and place, and only on those predetermined items listed on a ballot. Voting takes up less than an hour a year for most citizens, and there is no guarantee that candidates will be able to keep the promises they make during the campaign. There are other forms of participation that offer a greater opportunity for personal influence or involvement. These may be divided into campaign activities, community activities, lobbying group activities, and attentiveness to the news.

Campaign Activities

A citizen may engage in such campaign-related activities as working for a candidate or a party, attending election rallies or meetings, contributing money, and wearing a candidate's campaign button. The more demanding of these activities, such as doing volunteer work for a candidate or a party, require a lot more time and effort than voting. These activities are also less imbued with notions of civic duty than is voting.[30] Not surprisingly, the proportion of citizens who engage in these activities is relatively small. For example, about one in twenty adult Americans say they worked for a party or a candidate within the past year.

Nevertheless, campaign participation is higher in the United States than in Europe. A five-country comparative study found that Americans ranked ahead of citizens of Germany, Austria, the Netherlands, and Great Britain in such activities as volunteering to work for a party or a candidate during an election campaign.[31]

One reason Americans, even though they vote at a lower rate than Europeans, are more likely than Europeans to work in a campaign is that they have more opportunities to do so.[32] Elections take place more often in the United States, and citizens can become involved in an election campaign by volunteering to work for either a party or a candidate (see Chapter 8). In Europe, campaigns are organized through the parties, and participation op-

Parents vote on a resolution at a PTA meeting in Denver. Citizen participation in community groups such as the PTA is much higher than participation in party politics. (Chris Takagli/Impact Visuals)

portunities for those who are not party members are restricted. Moreover, the United States is a federal system, which results in campaigns for national, state, and local offices. A citizen who wishes to participate is almost certain to find an opportunity at one level of office or another. Most of the governments of Europe are unitary in form (see Chapter 2), which means that there are fewer elective offices and thus fewer campaigns in which to participate.

Community Activities

Many Americans participate in public affairs not through campaigns and political parties but through local organizations such as parent–teacher associations, neighborhood groups, Rotary clubs, church-affiliated groups, and hospital auxiliaries (see Table 7-1). Apart from their other purposes, these organizations also serve as a means to influence the public life of the community.

The actual number of citizens who fully participate in community affairs is difficult to estimate, but the number is surely in the tens of millions.

TABLE 7-1   GROUP PARTICIPATION IN FIVE NATIONS
The United States has been described as a "nation of joiners." The
tendency is reflected in a higher group participation rate in the United
States than in other western democracies.

Percent Belonging to:	United States	Great Britain	France	Germany	Italy
No group	18%	46%	61%	33%	59%
One–three groups	63	45	35	60	41
Four or more groups	19	9	4	7	—
	100%	100%	100%	100%	100%

SOURCE: World Values Surveys, 1990–1993.

The United States has a tradition of community participation that goes back to colonial days. Moreover, compared with local communities in Europe, those in the United States have more authority over policy issues, which is an added incentive to participation. Due to increased mobility and other factors, Americans may be less tied to their local communities than in the past and therefore less involved in community action. Nevertheless, a third of Americans claim that they frequently or sometimes participate in a group effort to solve a community problem, compared with about 15 percent in most European countries.[33]

Lobbying Group Activities

Increasingly, Americans are also involved in public affairs through membership in lobbying groups. This form of participation seldom consists of more than the contribution of annual dues that enable a national organization to pressure government officials or otherwise attempt to influence public policy. Examples of these groups are the National Organization for Women, Common Cause, the Christian Moral Government Fund, the American Civil Liberties Union, and the National Conservative Political Action Committee. Chapter 9 discusses lobbying groups more fully.

Following Politics in the News

Campaign work and community participation are active forms of political involvement. There is also a passive form of participation: following politics by reading newspapers and newsmagazines and by listening to news reports on television or radio. It can safely be said that no act of political participation takes up more of people's time than does news consumption. The news is important to citizen participation: if people are to participate effectively and intelligently in politics, they must be aware of what is taking place in their communities, in their nation, and in the world.

News about politics is within easy reach of nearly all Americans. More than 95 percent of U.S. homes have a television set, and about 50 percent of Americans receive a daily newspaper. However, the regular audience for news is much smaller than these figures suggest. The mere fact of having a television or getting a daily paper does not mean that a person pays attention to the news these media provide. If the regular audience for politics is defined as those who read a newspaper's political sections or watch television newscasts on a regular basis, then about a third of Americans can be classified as closely attentive to the news. Another third follow the news intermittently, catching an occasional newscast or scanning a paper's news sections somewhat often. The final third pay no appreciable attention to the news either on television news or in a newspaper.

Television is the medium through which most Americans get most of their news (see Figure 7-3). In recent decades, citizens who say television is their main source of news have substantially outnumbered those who rely mainly on a newspaper. Radio and magazines account for even smaller proportions. The figures are somewhat misleading in that people are asked where they get "most" of their news, not how much news they actually get. People who say they get "most" of their news from television do not necessarily watch the news a lot. They may not read a newspaper at all, so that

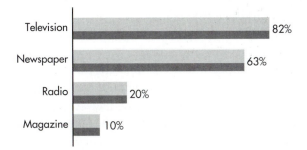

FIGURE 7-3 AMERICANS' MAJOR NEWS SOURCES
When Americans are asked where they get most of their news, they mention television most often.   Source: Pew Research Center, 1995. Respondents were asked to identify their top *two* sources.

even a little exposure to television news makes it their leading news source. Since almost every American home has a television set but only half receive a daily newspaper, television has the edge.[34]

The news audience has shrunk considerably in size in recent years. Newspapers have lost audience to television newscasts, which in turn have lost audience to television entertainment programs. Before cable television was widely available, many television viewers had no alternative to a newscast during the dinner hour. With cable, viewers always have a wide variety of choices, and many viewers, as many as 40 percent by some estimates, choose to ignore the news unless a sensational event occurs, such as the Oklahoma City bombing in 1995 that killed more than 100 people. To be sure, cable has also fostered a core of news "junkies" who immerse themselves in the Cable News Network (CNN), C-SPAN, and other news and public affairs programming. The more significant effect of cable, however, has been to contribute to a substantial decrease in the size of the news audience.

Young Americans in particular are ignoring the news. A survey by the Times Mirror Center for the People and the Press found that Americans under thirty years of age know less and care less about politics than any generation of the last half-century and pay less attention to newspapers. They are inclined toward television use generally but do not pay much attention to television news. Many young people apparently cannot be bothered with news in any form.[35]

UNCONVENTIONAL ACTIVISM: SOCIAL MOVEMENTS AND PROTEST POLITICS

Before mass elections became prevalent, the public often resorted to rioting as a way of expressing dissatisfaction with government. The advent of elections allowed the masses to communicate their views in an institutionalized and less disruptive way. Elections are double-edged, however. Although they are commonly viewed as a means by which the people control the government, *elections are also a means by which the government controls the people.*[36] Because representatives have been freely chosen by popular vote, they can claim that their policies reflect the will of the majority and therefore ought to be obeyed. It is a claim that most citizens accept.

Voting in elections is also limited to the options listed on the ballot. America's voters effectively have only two choices: they can back the Democratic or Republican party. No other party has much chance of victory, and any citizen who is dissatisfied with the major parties realistically has no way to express a policy preference through the ballot.

Social movements are an alternative method of influence. **Social movements,** or **political movements,** as they are sometimes called, refer to broad efforts to achieve change by citizens who feel that government is not properly responsive to their interests.[37] Their efforts are sometimes channeled through traditional forms of participation, such as political lobbying, but citizens can also take to the streets in protest against government.

Social movements do not always succeed, but they sometimes enable otherwise politically weak groups to force government to resp nd to their desires. For example, the timing and scope of the landmark 1964 Civil Rights Act and 1965 Voting Rights Act can be explained only as a response by Congress to the pressure created by the civil rights movement. The movement was in great part nonviolent, but it existed outside established channels—civil disobedience was one of its techniques—and it challenged existing power structures.

Protest politics in America goes back to the Boston Tea Party and earlier, but it has taken on new forms in recent years. Protest was traditionally

Students at a California state university demonstrate against Proposition 209. The initiative proposed to end all racial, ethnic, and gender preferences in the awarding of university admissions, jobs, and government contracts in the state. The initiative passed by a 54–46 percent vote margin in 1996. (Kim Kulish/Saba)

a desperate act that began, often spontaneously, when a group lost hope of succeeding through more conventional methods. Today, however, protest is usually a calculated act—a means of bringing added attention and impetus to a cause.[38] These tactical protests often involve a great deal of planning, including, in some instances, the busing of thousands of people to Washington for a rally staged for television. Civil rights, environmental, agricultural, gay rights, and pro- and antiabortion groups are among those that have staged tactical protests in Washington in recent years.

Most citizens, however, believe that the proper way to express disagreement over public policy is through voting, not through protesting, despite the First Amendment's guarantee of the right "peaceably to assemble." In a 1972 University of Michigan survey, only 15 percent of those interviewed expressed approval of the Vietnam war protests. Public opinion about demonstrations against the Gulf war was also negative, although less so than for protests against the Vietnam war, perhaps because U.S. involvement in the Gulf was shorter and more successful. A Gallup Poll in early 1991 indicated that by a 2-to-1 margin Americans believed it was "a bad thing for Americans to be demonstrating against the war when U.S. troops are fighting overseas." This view was particularly pronounced among women, older persons, Republicans, and persons with lower education levels (see Table 7-2).

Citizens who participate in social movements tend to be younger than nonparticipants, which is a reversal of the situation with voting. In fact, age is the best predictor of protest activity.[39] Participants in social movements also tend to emphasize nonmaterial values more than do nonparticipants. Social movements often develop in response to real or perceived injustices and thus attract idealists.[40]

PARTICIPATION AND THE POTENTIAL FOR INFLUENCE

Although Americans claim that political participation is important, most of them do not practice what they preach. As we have seen, most citizens take little interest in participation except to vote, and a significant minority cannot be persuaded to do even that. Americans are obviously not completely apathetic: many millions of them give their time, effort, and money to political causes, and roughly 100 million go to the polls in presidential elections.

Yet sustained political activism does not engage a large proportion of the public. Moreover, many of those who do participate are drawn to politics by a habitual sense of civic duty rather than by an intense concern with current

TABLE 7-2   OPINIONS ABOUT PEACE DEMONSTRATIONS
DURING THE GULF WAR, 1991
Most Americans believed that protests against the war were "a bad thing."

| | *Are Current Demonstrations . . . ?* | | |
	A Bad Thing	*Not a Bad Thing*	*No Opinion*
All respondents	63%	34%	3%
Male	58	40	2
Female	67	28	5
18–29 years	57	40	3
30–49 years	58	39	3
50 years and over	72	23	5
College grads	47	47	6
Some college	59	37	4
High school grads	68	30	2
Not high school grads	76	20	4
Republicans	71	26	3
Democrats	61	35	4
Independents	57	40	3

SOURCE: Gallup Poll, January 23–26, 1991.

issues. The emphasis that American culture places on individualism tends to discourage a sense of urgency about political participation. "In the United States, the country of individualism *par excellence*," William Watts and Lloyd Free write, "there is a sharp distinction in people's minds between their own personal lives and national life."[41] Although wars and severe recessions can lead the American public to rely on government, most people under most conditions expect to solve their own problems. This is not to say that Americans have a disdain for collective action. In their communities particularly, citizens frequently take part in collective efforts to support a local hospital, improve the neighborhood, and the like. But most Americans do not see their material well-being as greatly dependent on their active involvement in politics.

This tendency contributes to a class bias in American politics. For one thing, it helps maintain a relatively sharp distinction between that which is properly public (political) and that which is properly private (economic). The private component, which includes most economic relationships, is largely beyond the realm of political debate and action. Americans, says political scientist Robert Lane, have a preference for market justice rather than political justice.[42] They prefer to see benefits distributed primarily through the economic marketplace rather than through the policies of government. The nation's health care system is an example. Unlike the systems of Europe, which provide government-paid coverage for everyone, access to medical care in the United States is to some degree based on a person's ability to pay for it. There are about 38 million Americans who do not have access to adequate health care because they cannot afford health insurance.

America's individualistic culture also contributes to a class bias by its effect on the participation level of lower-income groups. As we have seen, citizens of lower economic status are substantially less involved politically than those of higher status. The difference is much greater in the United States than in other western democracies. These countries assist the participation of poorer citizens by placing the burden of registering voters on government and by fostering class-based political organizations. By comparison, the poor in the United States have to arrange their own registration and have a choice only between major political parties that are attuned primarily to the middle and upper classes. The experiences of democratic countries make it clear that the poor, who have fewer personal skills and resources to take part in politics on their own, need supportive structures to foster their participation. "The rich have the capacity to participate with or without assistance," Benjamin Ginsberg writes. "When assistance is given it is primarily the poor who benefit."[43]

The relatively high participation rate of the country's middle-class citizens, who constitute the bulk of the population in any case, tends to direct public policies to their benefit. Representatives are typically more responsive to the demands of participants than to those of nonparticipants,[44] although it must be kept in mind that participants do not always promote only their own interests. It would be a mistake, however, to conclude that large numbers of people regularly support policies that impose great costs on themselves.

In sum, the pattern of individual political participation in the United States parallels the distribution of influence that prevails in the private sector. However, the issue of individual participation is only one piece of the larger puzzle of who rules America and for what purposes. Subsequent chapters will provide additional pieces.

SUMMARY

Political participation is an involvement in activities designed to influence public policy and leadership. A main issue of democratic government is the question of who participates in politics and how fully they participate.

Voting is the most widespread form of active political participation among Americans. Yet voter turnout is significantly lower in the United States than in other democratic nations. The requirement that Americans must personally register in order to establish their eligibility to vote is one reason for lower turnout among Americans; other democracies place the burden of registration on government officials rather than on the individual citizen. The fact that the United States holds frequent elections also discourages some citizens from voting regularly. Finally, the major American political parties, unlike many of those in Europe, do not clearly represent the interests of opposing economic classes; thus the policy stakes in American elections are correspondingly lower. Some Americans do not vote because they think that policy will not change greatly regardless of which party gains power.

Prospective voting is one way that people can exert influence on policy through their participation. It is the most demanding approach to voting: voters must develop their own policy preferences and then educate themselves about the candidates' positions. Most voters are not well-enough informed about the issues to respond in this way. Retrospective voting demands less from voters: they need only decide whether the government has been performing well or poorly in terms of the goals and values they hold. The evidence suggests that the electorate is, in fact, reasonably sensitive to past governmental performance, particularly in relation to economic prosperity.

Only a minority of citizens engage in the more demanding forms of political activity, such as work on community affairs or on behalf of a candidate during a political campaign. The proportion of Americans who engage in these more demanding forms of activity exceeds the proportion of Europeans who do so. Nevertheless, only about one in every four Americans will take an active part in a political organization at some point in their lives. Most political activists are individuals of higher income and education; they have the skills and material resources to participate effectively and tend to take greater interest in politics. More than in any other western democracy, political participation in the United States is related to economic status.

Social movements are broad efforts to achieve change by citizens who feel that government is not properly responsive to their interests. These efforts sometimes take place outside established channels: demonstrations, picket lines, and marches are common means of protest. Protesters are younger and more idealistic on average than other citizens, but they are a very small proportion of the population. In addition, protest activities do not have much public support, despite the country's tradition of free expression.

Overall, Americans are only moderately involved in politics. They are concerned with political affairs but mostly immersed in their private pursuits, a reflection in part of the culture's emphasis on individualism. The lower level of participation among low-income citizens has particular significance in that it works to reduce their influence on public policy and leadership.

MAJOR CONCEPTS

alienation	registration
apathy	retrospective voting
civic duty	social (political) movements
political participation	suffrage
prospective voting	voter turnout

SUGGESTED READINGS

Entman, Robert. *Democracy without Citizens: Media and the Decay of American Politics.* New York: Oxford University Press, 1989. A critical evaluation of citizen involvement in the context of news about politics and public affairs.

Key, V. O., Jr. *The Responsible Electorate.* Cambridge, Mass.: Belknap Press of Harvard University Press, 1966. The classic analysis of voting as a response to government's performance.

Neuman, W. Russell, Marion R. Just, and Ann N. Crigler. *Common Knowledge: News and the Construction of Meaning.* Chicago: University of Chicago Press, 1992. An assessment of how citizens interpret and use the news they receive.

Nie, Norman H., Jane Junn, and Kenneth Stehlik-Barry. *Education and Democratic Citizenship in America.* Chicago: University of Chicago Press, 1996. A provocative study of the relationship between education and political participation.

Piven, Frances Fox, and Richard A. Cloward. *Why Americans Don't Vote.* New York: Pantheon, 1988. An analysis of nonvoting which focuses on registration requirements and calls for simplified procedures.

Rimmerman, Craig A. *The New Citizenship: Unconventional Politics, Activism, and Service.* Boulder, Colorado: Westview Press, 1997. A provocative assessment of citizenship in the modern age.

Rosenstone, Steven J., and John Mark Hansen. *Mobilization, Participation, and Democracy in America.* New York: Macmillan, 1993. A careful analysis of participation in America based mainly on national surveys.

Tate, Katherine. *From Protest to Politics: The New Black Voters in American Elections,* enlarged ed. Cambridge, Mass.: Harvard University Press, 1994. A study of the transformation of a social movement into a conventional form of political participation.

Verba, Sidney, Kay Schlozman, and Henry Brady. *Voice and Equity*. Cambridge, Mass.: Harvard University Press, 1995. A careful study of political attitudes and participation.

Woliver, Laura R. *From Outrage to Action: The Politics of Grass-Roots Dissent*. Urbana: University of Illinois Press, 1993. A valuable case study of the impact of grass-roots protest.

Reading 7

Participation and Equality
SIDNEY VERBA, KAY LEHMAN
SCHLOZMAN, AND HENRY E. BRADY

[M]eaningful democratic participation requires that the voices of citizens in politics be clear, loud, and equal: clear so that public officials know what citizens want and need, loud so that officials have an incentive to pay attention to what they hear, and equal so that the democratic ideal of equal responsiveness to the preferences and interests of all is not violated. Our analysis of voluntary activity in American politics suggests that the public's voice is often loud, sometimes clear, but rarely equal.

Americans who wish to take part in politics have many participatory options available. They can attempt to affect government policy directly by communicating their wishes or indirectly by influencing who holds public office. They can get involved on the local, state, or national level. They can act on their own or with others. They can engage in forms of activity that require inputs of time or forms that require inputs of money.

Participation in America can be loud. If they are active beyond voting, activists can multiply the volume of their activity by participating in several different ways or by increasing their investment of time or money—attending more than one demonstration, making several contacts with public officials, devoting substantial time to an electoral campaign or community effort, or writing bigger checks.

The voices of activists can be clear. Although the vote is singularly ill-suited for conveying precise instructions to policymakers, citizens engage in many kinds of participation that permit them to send clear messages to governing officials. Collectively, those messages encompass a dazzling number of issues and contradictory preferences. Nevertheless, the individual who chooses to become involved in any of a number of information-rich activities has the opportunity to speak in detail.

The participatory system also appears to be open. Significant legal barriers to the equal participation of all citizens were lowered during the 1960s.

Although non-citizens are not permitted to vote, of course, we found little evidence that legal impediments impede political action. Furthermore, although there is anecdotal and case study evidence to the contrary, we did not find evidence of abstention resulting from fear. When asked, those who refrain from politics cited many reasons for their inactivity, but few indicated that they thought political participation would get them into trouble.

Beyond the absence of barriers created by law or intimidation, the system appears to be open to citizens who become excited about one issue or another. Those whose life circumstances create a stake in some policy or whose values and beliefs lead to engagement on some issue can and do become active on that subject. Activity may depend in large part on resources, generalized political engagement, and recruitment—the participatory factors at the heart of our Civic Voluntarism Model—but the citizen who becomes aroused will often speak up beyond what those factors would predict.

In short, participation in America is lively and varied. Public opinion studies have documented an increase in the number of citizens who believe that the government is out of touch and unresponsive. Still, citizens seem not to have given up on participation. Moreover, . . . active citizens do not deem their participation to be ineffectual: among activists, substantial majorities reported that they received satisfactory replies to their contacts, that the protest they attended made a difference, or that their campaign work swayed at least some votes. Clearly, a survey like ours does not permit us to judge whether activists overstate the efficacy of their participation and, if so, by how much. Many of them may be deluding themselves or seeking to please the interviewer. Nonetheless, for many of the activities we consider, it is entirely plausible to believe that taking part made a difference, especially when we compare these activities to casting a ballot—the political act on which political scientists have focused most often when discussing the ineffectiveness of the individual citizen. Besides, even if citizens overestimate their clout, it is important that they miscalculate on the high rather than the low side. Although citizens may believe that, in general, they have little voice, they do not report feelings of impotence with respect to their own activity. It is often argued that a benign consequence of participation is to bolster the legitimacy of the regime. The way in which the participants surveyed interpret their own experiences as activists substantiates this claim.

As expressed through political participation, the voices of citizens may be loud and clear, but they are decidedly not equal. The voices of certain people—and people with certain politically relevant characteristics—are more resonant in participatory input. The consequences of unequal participation for what is communicated through political activity are complex and have formed one of the main themes of this volume. Whether participatory inequalities imply distortion in the messages sent to policymakers depends upon both the politically relevant characteristic and the mode of political activity we are considering. We have seen that, in terms of their policy preferences, those who take part are not very different from those who do not. However, when it comes to economic circumstances, needs for government assistance, or participatory agendas—the actual issues that animate activity—the discrepancies are much more substantial. In addition, we have seen the variation across activities in the extent of participatory distortion. Voters are relatively representative of the public. In terms of other forms of participation—acts that can be multiplied in their volume and that have the capacity to communicate more information—distortion in participatory input is more substantial. It is especially pronounced for political contributions. Indeed, when we investigated the extent of participatory distortion for a series of politically relevant characteristics, in each case we found it to be markedly greater for contributions than for other forms of activity.

Because the extent of participatory distortion depends upon the particular political act and the particular politically relevant characteristic in question, it is impossible to assess in the aggregate how biased is the set of messages communicated through citizen participation. The political battles over how votes should be counted make clear that the principle of political equality is not simple even when it comes to voting. However, the matter becomes many times more complicated when we move beyond the aggregation of votes to the aggregation of participatory acts that involve differing volume and various metrics—letters sent, dollars donated, or hours devoted. The complexities increase exponentially when we add consideration of the myriad politically relevant characteristics—preferences on a range of issues, actual circumstances and needs, even demographic characteristics—about which information is conveyed through participation. In short, across the totality of political input it is impossible to specify what one person, one vote would look like.

Nonetheless, whatever the difficulties of establishing a benchmark for aggregate participatory equality, we must recognize a systematic bias in representation through participation. Over and over, our data showed that participatory input is tilted in the direction of the more advantaged groups in society—especially in terms of economic and educational position, but in terms of race and ethnicity as well. The voices of the well-educated and the well-heeled—and, therefore, of those with other politically relevant characteristics that are associated with economic and educational privilege—sound more loudly.

SOURCE: Sidney Verba, Kay Lehman Schlozman, and Henry E. Brady, *Voice and Equality: Civic Voluntarism in American Politics* (Cambridge, Mass.: Harvard University Press, 1995). Reprinted by permission.
Sidney Verba, Kay Lehman Schlozman, and Henry E. Brady are professors of political science at Harvard University, Boston College, and the University of California at Berkeley, respectively.

CHAPTER EIGHT

Political Parties, Candidates, and Campaigns

> Political parties created democracy and . . . modern democracy is unthinkable save in terms of the parties.
>
> E. E. SCHATTSCHNEIDER[1]

 ALFWAY ACROSS the country and two weeks apart, they faced off, each offering their own plan for a better America.

The Republicans met first, in San Diego. Their 1996 platform included a 15-percent across-the-board cut in personal income taxes, a constitutional ban on abortions, a balanced federal budget, parental choice of schools, business deregulation, and the assignment of a broad range of federal programs to state and local governments. The Republicans chose former Senate majority leader Bob Dole as their presidential nominee and named Jack Kemp, a former U.S. representative and cabinet secretary, as his running mate.

The Democrats met in Chicago, the same city where twenty-eight years earlier a Democratic national convention had been torn apart by the dispute over Vietnam war policy. This time, however, the Democrats were fully united. Bill Clinton's nomination was uncontested, the first time since Franklin Roosevelt in 1936 that an incumbent Democratic president seeking reelection had not faced opposition within his own party. The Democrats also unanimously chose Al Gore to run again for the vice-presidency. The Democrats' lengthy platform included tax benefits for low- and middle-income families, restrictions on handguns, protection of social security, reproductive freedom for women, and pledges to strengthen the nation's environmental, educational, and health systems.

The political party, as its nominees and platform illustrate, is the one institution that aims to develop broad policy and leadership choices and then presents them to the voting public to accept or reject. This process is what gives the citizens an opportunity, through elections, to influence how they will be governed. "It is the competition of political organizations that provides the people with an opportunity to make a choice," the political scientist E. E. Schattschneider once wrote. "Without this opportunity popular sovereignty amounts to nothing."[2]

A **political party** is an ongoing coalition of interests joined together in an effort to get its candidates for public office elected under a common label.[3] As such, a party is actually three election parties in one. There is, first, the *party in the electorate*, which consists of the voters who identify with it and support its candidates. This component of the party was discussed in Chapter 6 and is also addressed briefly in this chapter. The main subjects of this chapter, however, are the other two components: the *party as organization*, staffed and led by party activists, and the *party as candidates*, which consists of those individuals who run for public office under its label.[4]

A theme of this chapter is that party organizations are alive and well in America but are also secondary to candidates as the driving force in contemporary campaigns. **Party-centered politics** is an important dimension of U.S. elections, but much of what goes on in the campaign is better described by the term **candidate-centered politics.** For the most part, candidates for the presidency and Congress raise their own funds, form their own campaign organizations, and choose for themselves the issues on which they will run. Parties still play an important, indeed an indispensable, role in these elections, but their campaign role is secondary to that of the candidates.

This chapter will explain this development and also explore the history of U.S. parties, the patterns of party politics, and the conduct of modern campaigns. The following points are emphasized in this chapter:

* *Political competition in the United States has centered on two parties, a pattern that is explained by the nature of America's electoral system, political institutions, and political culture.*

* *To win an electoral majority, candidates of the two major parties must appeal to a diverse set of interests; this necessity normally leads them to advocate moderate and somewhat overlapping policies.*

* *U.S. party organizations are decentralized and fragmented. The national organization is a loose collection of state organizations, which in turn are loose associations of autonomous local organizations.*

* *The ability of America's party organizations to control nominations and election to office is weak, which in turn enhances the candidates' role. Congressional and presidential contenders largely organize and run their own campaigns.*

PARTY COMPETITION AND MAJORITY RULE: THE HISTORY OF U.S. PARTIES

Political parties give direction and strength to the people's votes. Through their numbers, citizens have the potential for great influence, but that potential cannot be realized unless they have the capacity to act together. Parties give them that capacity. When Americans go to the polls, they have a choice between the Republican and Democratic parties. This **party competition** narrows their options to two and in the process enables people with different opinions to render a common judgment. In electing a party, the voters choose its candidates, its philosophy, and its policies over those of the opposing party.

The history of democratic government is virtually synonymous with the history of parties. When the countries of eastern Europe gained their freedom a few years ago, one of their first steps toward democracy was the legalization of parties. When the United States was founded two centuries ago, the formation of parties was also a first step toward the erection of its democracy. The reason is simple: it is the competition between parties that gives popular majorities a chance to determine how they will be governed.

The First Parties

America's early leaders mistrusted parties. George Washington in his Farewell Address warned the nation of the "baneful effects" of parties, and James Madison likened parties to special interests. However, Madison's initial misgivings about parties gradually gave way to a grudging admiration; he recognized that they provided a way for like-minded people to jointly promote their vision of how the new nation should be governed.

America's parties originated in the rivalry within George Washington's administration between Thomas Jefferson, a supporter of states' rights and small landholders, and Alexander Hamilton, who promoted a strong national government and commercial interests (see Chapter 2). When Hamilton's ideas prevailed in Congress, Jefferson and his followers formed a political party, the Republicans, as a means of advancing their goals (see Figure 8-1).

Hamilton responded by organizing his supporters into a formal party—the Federalists—and in the process created America's first competitive party system. However, Federalist policies fueled Jefferson's claim that his opponents were bent on establishing a government for the rich and wellborn. After John Adams's defeat by Jefferson in the election of 1800, the Federalists were finished as a political force of any consequence.

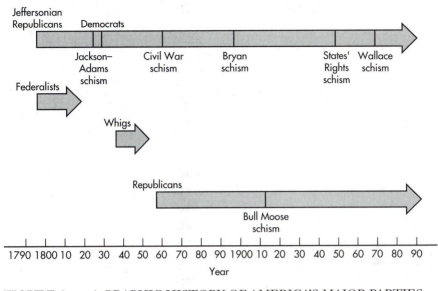

FIGURE 8-1 A GRAPHIC HISTORY OF AMERICA'S MAJOR PARTIES

During the so-called Era of Good Feeling, when James Monroe ran unopposed in 1820 for a second presidential term, it appeared as if the nation might exist without parties. Yet by the end of Monroe's second term, policy differences had split the Republicans. The dominant faction, led by Andrew Jackson, retained Jefferson's commitment to the interests of small farmers, tradesmen, and shopkeepers. To better reflect its base among ordinary citizens, this faction called itself Democratic Republicans, later shortened to Democrats. Thus the Republican party of Jefferson is the forerunner of today's Democratic party rather than today's Republican party.

Andrew Jackson and Grassroots Parties

For all its shortcomings, competition between parties is the only system that can regularly mobilize collective influence on behalf of the many who are individually powerless against those few who have extraordinary wealth and prestige.[5]

This realization led Jackson during the 1820s to develop a "grassroots" party. Whereas Jefferson's party had been well organized only at the leadership level, Jackson sought a party that was built from the bottom up. Jackson's Democratic party consisted of committees and clubs at the national, state, and local levels, with membership open to all eligible voters. These organizational activities, along with more liberal suffrage laws, contributed to a nearly fourfold rise in voter turnout during the 1830s.[6] At the peak of Jacksonian democracy, Alexis de Tocqueville wrote: "The People reign in the American political world as the Deity does in the universe."[7] Although Tocqueville exaggerated the people's true power, he caught the spirit of popular government that was behind the development of grassroots parties under Andrew Jackson.

In this period, a new opposition party, the Whigs, emerged to challenge the Democrats. The Whigs were a residual party of sorts. Its followers were united not by a coherent philosophy of their own but by their opposition for one reason or another to the philosophy and policies of the Jacksonian Democrats.

Competition between the Whigs and the Democrats was relatively short-lived. During the 1850s the slavery issue began to tear both parties apart. In 1860 the Democratic party's northern faction nominated for president Stephen A. Douglas, who held that the question of whether a new territory permitted slavery was for a majority of its voters to decide, while the southern faction nominated John C. Breckinridge, who called for the legalization of slavery in all territories. The Democratic vote in the fall election was split sharply along regional lines between these two candidates—with the result that the Republican nominee, Abraham Lincoln, was able to win the presidency with only 40 percent of the popular vote. The Republicans had eclipsed the Whigs and become America's other major party. However, the U.S. party system essentially collapsed in 1860, for the only time in the nation's history.[8] The issues of slavery and union were too powerful to be settled peaceably through political compromise and competition between political parties.

Republicans versus Democrats: Realignments and the Enduring Party System

After the Civil War, the nation settled into the pattern of competition between the Republican and Democratic parties that has prevailed ever since. The durability of these two parties is due not to their ideological consistency but to their remarkable ability to adapt during periods of crisis. By abandoning at these crucial times their old ways of doing things, the Republican and Democratic parties have essentially remade themselves—with new bases of support, new policies, and new public philosophies.

These periods of great political change are known as "realignments." A party **realignment** involves four basic elements:

1. The disruption of the existing political order because of the emergence of one or more unusually powerful and divisive issues
2. An election contest in which the voters shift their support strongly in favor of one party
3. A major change in policy through the action of the stronger party
4. An enduring change in the party coalitions, which works to the lasting advantage of the dominant party

Realignments are rare. They do not occur simply because one party wrests control of government from the other. They involve deep and lasting changes in the party system that affect not just the most recent election but later ones as well.

The Civil War realignment, for example, brought about a thorough change in the party system. The Republicans replaced the Democrats as the nation's majority party. The Republicans were the dominant party in the larger and more populous North; the Democratic party was left with a stronghold in what became known as "the Solid South." For the next three decades, the Republicans held the presidency except during Grover Cleveland's two terms of office.

Abraham Lincoln said that this portrait of him by Mathew
Brady, which he used in his campaign literature,
contributed to his election to the presidency as a
Republican in 1860. (Library of Congress)

The 1896 election resulted in a further realignment of the Republican–Democratic party system. Three years earlier, an economic panic following a bank collapse had resulted in a severe depression. The Democrat Cleveland was president when the panic broke out, and that circumstance worked to the advantage of the Republicans. During the four decades between the 1890s realignment and the next one in the 1930s, the Republicans held the presidency except for Woodrow Wilson's two terms and had a majority in Congress for all but six years.

The Great Depression of the 1930s triggered a thoroughgoing realignment of the American party system. The Republican Herbert Hoover was president when the stock market crashed in 1929, and many Americans blamed Hoover, his party, and its business allies for the economic catastrophe that followed. The Democrats became the country's majority party, and their political and policy agenda favored a significant social and economic role for the national government. Franklin D. Roosevelt's presidency was

The new order begins: Franklin D. Roosevelt rides to his inauguration with outgoing president Herbert Hoover after the realigning election of 1932. (UPI/Bettmann Newsphotos)

characterized by unprecedented policy initiatives in the areas of business regulation and social welfare (see Chapters 2, 15, and 16). His election in 1932 began a thirty-six-year period of Democratic presidencies that was interrupted only by Dwight D. Eisenhower's two terms in the 1950s. In this period, the Democrats also dominated Congress, losing control only in 1947–1948 and 1953–1954.

The reason realignments have such a substantial effect on future elections is that they affect voters' *party identification* (see Chapter 6). Young voters in particular are likely to identify with the newly ascendant party, and they tend to maintain that identity, giving the party a solid base of support for years to come. In the 1930s, for example, the Democratic party's image as the party of the common people, jobs, and social security was vastly more appealing to young voters than the Republican party's image as the party of business and wealthy interests. First-time voters in the 1930s came to identify by a 2-to-1 margin with the Democratic party, which established it as the nation's majority party and enabled it to dominate national politics for the next three decades.[9]

A New Realignment?

A party realignment inevitably loses strength over time, because the issues that gave rise to it cannot remain dominant indefinitely. By the late 1960s, when the Democratic party was divided over the Vietnam war and civil rights, it was apparent that the era of New Deal politics was over.[10]

A realignment affecting part of the nation was soon evident. The South, which had been solidly Democratic at all levels, was becoming staunchly Republican in presidential elections and increasingly competitive at the state and local levels. As the Democratic party became increasingly identified as the party of civil rights and social change, it had less and less appeal to conservative white southerners.[11]

Yet Republican inroads were otherwise moderate or temporary. The Republicans gained the presidency in 1972 and held it through 1992, except for Jimmy Carter's term of office. However, the GOP lost the presidency again in 1992, just as it had failed to hold onto the U.S. Senate after capturing it in 1980. And throughout this period, the Democrats controlled the U.S. House of Representatives. Indeed, by winning the presidency in 1992, the Democrats temporarily controlled all three nationally elected institutions.

In 1994, however, the Republicans won an electoral victory that had earmarks of a realignment. The GOP picked up 52 House seats and, in the process, took control of the House of Representatives for the first time in four decades. The Republicans also gained a majority in the Senate. The election was so one-sided that no Republican governor or member of Congress lost a bid for reelection.

The 1994 Republican victory also had another characteristic of a realigning election. The victory was built on deep public dissatisfaction. Voters believed that their representatives in Washington were indifferent to their needs and controlled by powerful special interests. Voters were also concerned about disruptive social changes, including a perception of rising crime and declining moral values. The Democrats were an inviting target for voters who believed "big government" was wasting their hard-earned tax dollars and fostering moral and economic irresponsibility through its welfare programs.

Yet by 1996 the public had serious doubts about the GOP's political "revolution." Protection for workers, the elderly, children, and the poor seemed at risk. Polls indicated that most Americans still liked the GOP's basic idea of smaller, less intrusive government but did not like the way Republican lawmakers were attempting to implement it. The 1996 election was a setback for the GOP: it picked up two Senate seats but failed to win the presidency and lost nine House seats. A lasting realignment favorable to the Republican party could be taking place but, if so, it is unlike past ones—slower, more fitful, and less encompassing.

The Dealignment Thesis

An alternative explanation for what has been happening in American elections is put forth by advocates of the dealignment thesis. They suggest that the U.S. electoral system, rather than undergoing a realignment favorable to one party, has been in the process of **dealignment,** a partial but enduring movement of voters away from partisan loyalties.[12] The process is characterized by an electorate that wavers in its support of the parties, sometimes favoring one party and sometimes the other.

Parties, in fact, have a weaker hold on the voters than in the past. As we noted in Chapter 6, the number of voters who describe themselves as independents has increased significantly in recent decades. Moreover, people who today identify with a party are more likely to say it is only a weak attachment. These changes are reflected in increased **split-ticket voting,** where the voter selects candidates of both parties for different offices when casting a ballot. A few decades ago, the large majority of voters engaged in **straight-ticket voting,** supporting candidates of one party only.

The decline of partisanship began during the 1960s and 1970s when divisive issues arose and disrupted existing loyalties. The civil rights issue, for example, was unsettling not only to many southern Democrats but also to some white northern Democrats, particularly blue-collar workers from newer immigrant groups who felt that African Americans were making progress at their expense.[13] Vietnam, abortion, social welfare, and a host of other issues also divided followers of each party. Americans' trust in their elected representatives declined, as did their faith in parties.

Party loyalties have been weak ever since, and some analysts see little likelihood of a dramatic reversal. For one thing, voters of today are better educated and more likely to believe they can judge the candidates for themselves, on the basis of what they hear through the media rather than on the basis of party labels. Moreover, people today are protected by programs like social security and Medicare from the economic hardships that in the past fueled party realignments. Finally, Americans today want higher incomes and lower taxes, but they also want a cleaner environment, services for the elderly, and better schools. As a result, they are less likely to be drawn fully to either the Republican argument for a less active government or the Democratic argument for a more active one.[14]

If advocates of the dealignment thesis are correct, neither party in the foreseeable future will enjoy the prolonged success of the type the Democratic party had from the 1930s on. The predicted scenario is one of shifting support, with the Republicans prevailing at some times and the Democrats at other times.

ELECTORAL AND PARTY SYSTEMS

The United States has traditionally had a **two-party system:** Federalists versus Jeffersonian Republicans, Whigs versus Democrats, Republicans versus Democrats. These have not been the only American parties, but they have been the only ones with a realistic chance of acquiring political control. A two-party system, however, is the exception rather than the rule (see box: How the United States Compares). Most democracies have a **multiparty system,** in which three or more parties have the capacity to gain control of government separately or in coalition. Why the difference? Why three or more major parties in most democracies but only two in the United States?

The Single-Member-District System of Election

A chief reason for the persistence of America's two-party system is the fact that the nation chooses its officials through plurality voting in **single-member districts.**[15] Each constituency elects a single candidate to a par-

HOW THE UNITED STATES COMPARES

Party Systems

Electoral competition in the United States centers on the Republican and Democratic parties. By comparison, most democracies have a multiparty system, in which three or more parties receive substantial support from voters. The difference is significant. In a two-party system, the parties tend to have overlapping coalitions and programs, because each party must appeal to the middle-of-the-road voters who provide the margin of victory. In multiparty systems, particularly those with four or more strong parties, the parties tend to separate themselves, as each tries to secure the enduring loyalty of voters who have a particular viewpoint.

Whether a country has a two-party or a multiparty system depends on several factors, but particularly the nature of its electoral system. The United States has a single-member plurality district system that is biased against smaller parties; even if they have some support in a great many races, they win nothing unless one of their candidates places first in an electoral district. By comparison, in proportional representation systems, each party gets legislative seats in proportion to its share of the total vote. All the countries in the chart that have four or more parties also have a proportional representation system of election.

NUMBER OF COMPETITIVE PARTIES		
Two	*Three*	*Four or More*
New Zealand	Canada	Belgium
United States	Great Britain	Denmark
		France
		Germany
		Italy
		Netherlands
		Sweden

ticular office, such as U.S. senator or representative; only the party that gets the most votes (a plurality) in a district wins the office. This system discourages minor parties. Assume, for example, that a minor party received exactly 20 percent of the vote in each of the nation's 435 congressional races. Even though one in five voters nationwide backed the minor party, it would not win any seats in Congress because none of its candidates placed first in any of the 435 single-member-district races. The winning candidate in each case would be the major-party candidate who received the larger proportion of the remaining 80 percent of the vote.

By comparison, most European democracies use some form of **proportional representation,** in which seats in the legislature are allocated according to a party's share of the popular vote. This type of electoral system provides smaller parties an incentive to organize and compete for power. In the 1994 German elections, the Green and Free Democratic parties each won slightly more than 5 percent of the national vote and each received about 5 percent of the seats in the Bundestag, the German parliament. If these par-

Germany's electoral system allocates legislative seats on the basis both of single-district voting and of the overall proportion of votes a party receives. This system requires that the German voter cast two ballots in legislative races: one to choose among the candidates in the particular district and one to choose among the parties. Shown here is a ballot from a German election. The left-hand column lists the candidates for the legislative seat in a district, and the right-hand column lists the parties. (Note the relatively large number of parties on the ballot.)
(Photoreporters, Inc.)

ties had been competing under the rules of the American electoral system, they would not have won any seats and would have had no chance of exercising a share of legislative power.

Policies and Coalitions in the Two-Party System

The overriding goal of a major American party is to gain power by getting its candidates elected to office. Because there are only two major parties, however, the Republicans or Democrats can win consistently only by attracting majority support. In Europe's multiparty systems, a party can hope for a share of power if it has the firm backing of a minority faction. Not so in the United States. If either party confines its support to a narrow segment of society, it forfeits its chance of gaining control of government.

SEEKING THE CENTER, USUALLY This situation encourages both parties to stay near the center of the political spectrum and to avoid the minority position on deeply divisive issues. American parties, Clinton Rossiter said, are "creatures of compromise."[16] The two parties typically try to develop stands that have broad appeal or at least will not alienate significant blocs of voters. Any time a party makes a pronounced shift toward either extreme, the middle is left open for the opposing party. Barry Goldwater, the Republican presidential nominee in 1964, proposed the elimination of mandatory social security and said he would consider the tactical use of small nuclear weapons in such wars as the Vietnam conflict—extreme positions that cost him many votes.

Nonetheless, the Republican and Democratic parties do offer somewhat different alternatives and, at times, a clear choice. When Roosevelt was elected president in 1932, Johnson in 1964, and Reagan in 1980, the parties were relatively far apart in their priorities and programs. Roosevelt's New Deal, for example, was an extreme alternative within the American political tradition and caused a decisive split along party lines. A lesson of these periods is that the center of the American political spectrum can be moved. Candidates risk a crushing defeat by straying too far from established ideas during normal times, but they may do so with some chance of victory during turbulent times.

Another lesson of such periods is that public opinion is the critical element in partisan change. Critics who say that the Democratic and Republican parties fail to offer the voters a real choice ignore the parties' tendency to tailor their appeals to majority opinion.[17] When the public's mood shifts, the parties usually also shift. The Republicans' Contract with America in 1994, for example, was a response to public discontent with the federal government's taxing and spending policies. When the Republicans won in 1994, many Democratic officeholders also embraced cutbacks in federal power, thus shifting the entire party system toward the right. President Clinton, a Democrat, summed up the change in his 1996 State of the Union address when he said: "The era of big government is over."

PARTY COALITIONS The groups and interests that support a party are collectively referred to as the **party coalition.** In multiparty systems, each party is supported by a relatively narrow range of interests. European parties tend to divide along class lines, with the center and right parties drawing most of their votes from the middle and upper classes and the left parties drawing theirs from the working class. By comparison, America's two-party system requires each party to accommodate a wide range of interests in order to gain the voting plurality necessary to win elections.[18] The Republican and Democratic coalitions are therefore very broad. Each includes a substantial proportion of voters of nearly every ethnic, religious, regional, and economic grouping.

Although the Republican and Democratic coalitions overlap, they are hardly identical (see Table 8-1). Each party likes to appear to be all things

---

TABLE 8-1 COMPONENTS OF THE REPUBLICAN AND
DEMOCRATIC COALITIONS
Both parties include voters of all backgrounds, although their coalitions are
based more heavily on certain groups.

Democratic Coalition	*Republican Coalition*
Blacks (+40%)	Whites (+5%)
Hispanics (+20%)	White men (+7%)
Women (+4%)	White southerners (+8%)
Income under $15,000 (+14%)	Incomes over $75,000 (+10%)
Union households (+11%)	Employed (+2%)
Jews (+18%)	
Catholics (+3%)	

SOURCE: National Election Studies. Figures are estimates based on percent deviation of group's vote from overall two-party vote in 1976–1996 presidential elections.

to all Americans, but in fact each builds its coalition through a process of both unification and division. If a party did not stand for something—if it never took sides—it would lose all support.

Since the 1930s, the major policy differences between the Republicans and the Democrats have involved the national government's role in solving social and economic problems. Each party has supported government action to promote economic security and social equality, but the Democrats have consistently favored a greater degree of governmental involvement. To some extent, the national Democratic party's coalition reflects this tradition: it draws support disproportionately from society's "underdogs"—blacks, union members, the poor, city dwellers, Jews, and other "minorities."[19] Of course, many formerly underprivileged groups that are now part of the middle class have remained loyal to the Democratic party, which also includes a significant proportion of the nation's better-educated and higher-income voters.

In contrast, the Republican coalition consists mainly of white, middle-class Protestants. However, the GOP has recently made inroads among such traditionally Democratic groups as Catholics, Hispanics, and blue-collar workers. The GOP's biggest gains have been among fundamentalist Christians. The party's positions on abortion, school prayer, and other social issues have drawn them to the GOP; in all recent presidential elections, the Republican nominee has garnered at least two-thirds of the votes of fundamentalist Christians.

These differences in the party coalitions are sharpest in presidential elections. At the state and local levels, the parties in some cases define themselves differently than they do in national polities. Democratic candidates in the South, for example, tend to be more conservative than Democratic candidates elsewhere. As a result, the Democratic party, which in the 1960s lost its hold on the South in presidential voting, still controls most of the region's state legislatures (see box: States in the Nation).

Minor Parties

Although the U.S. electoral system discourages the formation of third parties, the nation has always had minor parties—more than a thousand during the nation's history.[20] Most of them have been short-lived, and only a few have had a lasting impact. Only one minor party, the Republican party, has ever achieved majority status.

Minor parties in the United States have formed largely to advocate positions that their followers believe are not being adequately represented by either of the two major parties. When a minor party gains a large following,

The religious right is a major force within the Republican party. The Rev. Pat Robertson (*right of center, front row*) and the Rev. Jerry Falwell (*center of second row*) are shown here at the 1992 Republican National Convention. Rush Limbaugh and Marilyn Quayle, the wife of Vice-President Dan Quayle, are among those seated near Robertson and Falwell. (Joe Traver/Gamma-Liaison)

which has happened a few times in history, the major parties are inevitably transformed by its influence. They are forced to pay attention to the problems that are driving people to look outside the two-party system for leadership. Strong support for a minor party has typically encouraged the major parties to try to capture its supporters.

Minor parties may be formed in response to the emergence of a single controversial issue, out of a commitment to a certain ideology, or as a result of a rift within one of the major parties.

SINGLE-ISSUE PARTIES   Some minor parties form around a single issue of overriding concern to their supporters, such as the present-day Right-to-Life party, which was formed to oppose the legalization of abortion. Some single-issue parties have seen their policy goals enacted into law. The Prohibition party contributed to the ratification in 1919 of the Eigh-

STATES IN THE NATION

Party Control of State Government

The strength of the major parties varies substantially among states. An indicator of party dominance is whether one party controls all elected institutions: the governor's seat and the two legislative chambers (except in Nebraska, which has a unicameral, nonpartisan legislature). As of 1997, the Democratic party had a slight edge, controlling twenty states to the Republican party's eighteen states.

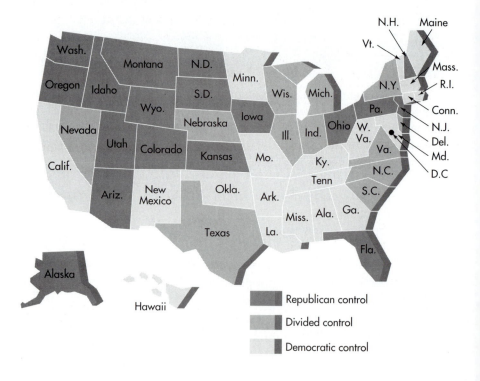

Republican control

Divided control

Democratic control

teenth Amendment, which prohibited the manufacture, sale, and transportation of alcoholic beverages (but was repealed in 1933). Single-issue parties usually disband when their issue is favorably resolved or fades in importance.[21]

IDEOLOGICAL PARTIES Other minor parties are characterized by their ideological commitment, or belief in a broad and radical philosophical position, such as redistribution of economic resources. Modern-day ideological parties include the Citizens party, the Socialist Workers party, and the Libertarian party, each of which operates on the fringe of American politics.

One of the strongest ideological parties in the nation's history was the Populist party. Its candidate in the 1892 presidential election, James B. Weaver, gained 8.5 percent of the national vote and won twenty-two electoral votes in six western states. The party began as an agrarian protest movement in response to an economic depression and the anger of small farmers over low commodity prices, tight credit, and the high rates charged by railroad monopolies to transport farm goods. The Populists' ideological platform called for government ownership of the railroads, a graduated income tax, low tariffs on imports, and elimination of the gold standard. The Populist party in 1896 endorsed the Democratic presidential nominee, William Jennings Bryan, but its support probably hurt the Democrats nationally. Large numbers of eastern Democrats abandoned their party's nominee in fear of the western Populists' radical ideas.[22]

FACTIONAL PARTIES The Republican and Democratic parties are relatively adept at managing internal divisions. Although each party's support is diverse, the differences among its varying interests can normally be reconciled. However, there have been times when factional conflict within the major parties has led to the formation of minor parties.

The most successful of these factional parties at the polls was Theodore Roosevelt's Bull Moose party. In 1908 Roosevelt, after having served eight years as president, declined to seek a third term and handpicked William Howard Taft for the Republican nomination. When Taft as president showed neither Roosevelt's enthusiasm for a strong presidency nor his commitment to the goals of the Progressive movement, Roosevelt unsuccessfully challenged Taft for the 1912 Republican nomination. Roosevelt led a Progressive walkout to form the Bull Moose party (a reference to Roosevelt's claim that he was "as strong as a bull moose"). Roosevelt won 27 percent of the vote to Taft's 25 percent, but the split within Republican ranks enabled the Democratic nominee, Woodrow Wilson, to win the presidency.

The States' Rights party in 1948 and the American Independent party in 1968 are other examples of strong factional parties. Each of these parties was formed by southern Democrats who were angered by northern Democrats' support of racial desegregation.

Deep divisions within a party give rise to factionalism and can lead eventually to a change in its coalition. The conflict over civil rights that began within the Democratic party during the Truman years continued for the next quarter-century, which initially led many southern whites to support Republican presidential candidates and later to shift their party loyalty to the Republican party.

INDEPENDENT CANDIDATES Campaigns have increasingly been shaped by money and media, a development that has enabled candidates to seek high-level office without a party's backing. The most successful independent candidacy was Texas billionaire Ross Perot's 1992 presidential bid, which gained 19 percent of the vote (second only to Roosevelt's 1912 percentage among candidates who were not major-party nominees). Perot's campaign was based on middle-class discontent with the major parties, was conducted almost entirely on television, and was funded by more than $60 million of his own money. Perot's money was a critical factor; in 1980, when the public mood was similar, Congressman John Anderson ran a poorly funded independent campaign that netted only 7 percent of the presidential vote. Perot ran again in 1996 but as the nominee of the Reform party, which he founded. This time, Perot accepted public funds for his campaign, which limited his spending to roughly $30 million (see Chapter 12). He ran a media-based campaign that attracted 8 percent of the vote. Whether the Reform party will be a force in future elections is unclear.

PARTY ORGANIZATIONS

The Democratic and Republican parties have organizational units at the national, state, and local levels. These **party organizations** engage in a variety of activities, but their main purpose is the contesting of elections.

A century ago, party organizations were in control of nominations and elections. The party organizations still perform all the activities they formerly engaged in. They recruit candidates, raise money, develop policy positions, and canvass for votes. But they do not control these activities to the degree they once did.[23] For the most part, these activities are now dominated by the candidates themselves.[24]

The Weakening of Party Organizations

Nomination refers to the selection of the individual who will run as the party's candidate in the general election. Until the early twentieth century, nominations were entirely the responsibility of party organizations. To be nominated, an individual had to be loyal to the party organization, a requirement that included a willingness to share with it the spoils of office—government jobs and contracts. The situation allowed party organizations to acquire campaign workers and funds but also enabled unscrupulous party leaders to extort money from those seeking political favors. Reform-minded Progressives argued for *party democracy*, claiming that party organizations should operate according to the same principle that governs elections: power should rest with ordinary voters rather than the party bosses (see Chapter 3).

The most serious assault of the Progressives on the party organizations was the introduction of the **primary election** (or **direct primary**) as a method of choosing nominees. In place of party-designated nominees, the primary system placed nomination in the hands of voters. Today all states have primary elections for contested nominations for U.S. Senate and House seats, and nearly forty states use primaries to select their delegates to the presidential nominating conventions (see Chapter 12).

Primaries are the severest impediment imaginable to the strength of the party organizations. If primaries did not exist, candidates would have to work through party organizations in order to gain nomination, and they could be denied renomination if disloyal to the party's goals. Because of primaries, however, candidates have the option of seeking office on their own, and, once elected (with or without the party's help), they can build an independent electoral base that effectively places them beyond the party's direct control.

Party organizations also lost influence over elections because of a decline in patronage. When a party won control of government a century ago, it also gained control of public jobs, which were doled out to loyal party workers. However, as government jobs in the early twentieth century shifted from patronage to the merit system (see Chapter 13), the party organizations lost control of many of these positions. Today, because of the expanded size of government, thousands of patronage jobs still exist. These government employees help staff the party organizations along with volunteers, but most of them are more indebted to an individual politician than to a party organization. The people who work for members of Congress, for example, are all patronage employees, but they owe their jobs and their loyalty to their senator or representative, not their party.

In the process of taking control of nominations, candidates have also acquired control of most campaign money. At the turn of the century, when party machines were at their peak, most campaign funds passed through the hands of party leaders. Today, 90 percent of the money spent on congressional and presidential campaigns goes to the candidates without first passing through the parties.

In Europe, where there are no primary elections, the situation is much different. Parties control their nominations and, because of this, also control campaign money and workers. Popular leaders in Europe are given fairly wide latitude by their party, but it is the parties, not the candidates, who are at the center of elections.

The Structure and Role of Party Organizations

Although the influence of party organizations has declined, parties are not about to die out. Political leaders and activists need a stable organization through which they can work together, and the parties serve that purpose. Moreover, certain activities, such as voter registration drives and get-out-the-vote efforts on election day, benefit all of a party's candidates and are therefore more efficiently conducted through the party organization. Indeed, parties have staged a comeback of sorts.[25] National and state party organizations in particular have developed the capacity to assist candidates with polling, research, and media production, which are costly but essential ingredients of a successful modern campaign.

Structurally, U.S. parties are loose associations of national, state, and local organizations (see Figure 8-2). The national party organizations cannot dictate the decisions of the state organizations, which in turn do not control the activities of local organizations. However, there is communication between the levels, which have a common interest in strengthening the party's position.[26]

LOCAL PARTY ORGANIZATIONS   In a sense, U.S. parties are organized from the bottom up, not the top down. There are about 500,000 elective offices in the United States, of which fewer than 500 are contested statewide and only two—the presidency and vice-presidency—are contested nationally. All the rest are local offices; not surprisingly, at least 95 percent of party activists work within local organizations.

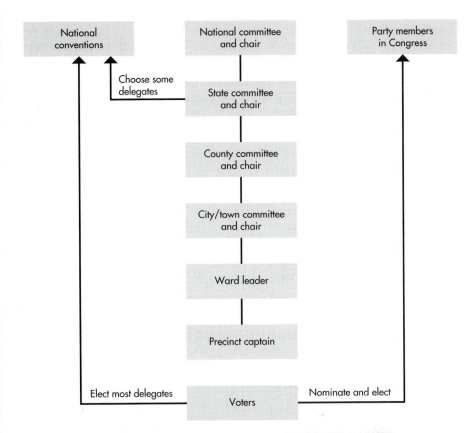

FIGURE 8-2 ORGANIZATION OF THE POLITICAL PARTY
U.S. parties today are loosely structured alliances of national, state, and local organizations.

It is difficult to generalize about local parties because they vary greatly in their structure and activities. Today only a few local parties, including the Democratic organizations in Albany, Philadelphia, and Chicago, bear any resemblance to the old-time machines. But local parties tend to be strongest in urban areas and in the Northeast and Midwest, where parties traditionally have been more highly organized. In any case, local parties tend to specialize in elections that coincide with local electoral boundaries. Campaigns for mayor, city council, state legislature, county offices, and the like motivate most local parties to a greater degree than do statewide and national contests.

In most urban areas, the party organizations do not have enough workers to staff even a majority of precincts on an ongoing basis. However, they do become active during campaigns, when they open campaign headquarters, conduct voter registration drives, send mailings or deliver leaflets to voters, and help get out the vote. The importance of these activities should not be underestimated. Most local campaigns are not well funded, and the party's backing of a candidate can make a vital difference.

In suburbs and towns, the party's role is less substantial. The parties exist organizationally but typically have little money and few workers; hence they cannot operate effectively as electoral organizations. The individual candidates must carry nearly the entire burden.

STATE PARTY ORGANIZATIONS   At the state level, each party is headed by a central committee made up of members of local party organizations and local and state officeholders. These state central committees do not meet regularly, and they provide only general policy guidance for the state organizations. Day-to-day operations and policy are directed by a chairperson, who is a full-time, paid employee of the state party. The central committee appoints the chairperson, but it often accepts the individual recommended by the party's leading politician, usually the governor or a U.S. senator.

In recent decades the state parties have expanded their budgets and staffs considerably and, therefore, have been able to play a more active electoral role.[27] In contrast, thirty years ago about half of the state party organizations had no permanent staff at all. The increase in state party staff is largely due to improvements in communication technology, such as computer-assisted direct mail, which have made it easier for political organizations of all kinds, parties included, to raise funds. Having acquired the ability to pay for permanent staffs, state parties have used them to expand their activities, which range from polling to issues research to campaign management. (These activities are discussed in greater detail later in this chapter.)

State party organizations concentrate on statewide races, including those for governor and U.S. senator,[28] and also focus on races for the state legislature. They play only a small role in campaigns for national or local offices, and in most states they do not endorse candidates in statewide primary contests.

NATIONAL PARTY ORGANIZATIONS   The national party organizations are structured much like those at the state level: they have a national committee, a national party chairperson, and a support staff. The national headquarters for the Republican and Democratic parties are located in Washington, D.C. Although in theory the national parties are run by their committees, neither the Democratic National Committee (DNC) nor the Republican National Committee (RNC) has great power. The RNC (with more than 150 members) and the DNC (with more than 300 members) are too cumbersome to act as deliberative bodies. The national committees are convened only periodically, to ratify decisions made by a smaller core of party leaders. The national party's day-to-day operations are directed by a national chairperson chosen by the national committee.

The national party administers the quadrennial presidential nominating convention. This is a major responsibility, but it carries no political power. Influence at the national conventions rests with the delegates, who are chosen in the states they represent, although the national party organizations are legally empowered to tell state organizations how to choose and certify their national convention delegates.[29] When it comes to electoral activity, the national party organizations concentrate on campaigns for national office—the Senate, House, and presidential races. Both the RNC and DNC raise campaign funds and distribute them directly to candidates.

Even more important than the DNC and RNC to the funding of elections are the Democratic and Republican campaign committees in the House and Senate: the Democratic Congressional Campaign Committee (DCCC), National Republican Congressional Committee (NRCC), Democratic Senatorial Campaign Committee (DSCC), and National Republican Senatorial Committee (NRSC). These committees account for more than 75 percent of the party funds provided to congressional candidates.[30] This money is not, as might be assumed, provided only to incumbents or even to all incumbents. The House and Senate committees target their funds on close races, whether or not an incumbent is involved. Their goal is to win for their party as many House or Senate races as possible.

THE CANDIDATE-CENTERED CAMPAIGN

Although competition between the Republican and Democratic parties provides the backdrop to today's campaigns, the campaigns themselves are largely controlled by the candidates. Each candidate has a personal organization, created especially for the campaign and disbanded once it is over.

Running for Office

Today's candidates tend to be self-starters. Some candidates still rise through the ranks of the party or are drafted because no other qualified person is willing to run. But most candidates seek high office because they aspire to a career in politics. They are entrepreneurs who play what the political consultant Joe Napolitan called "the election game."[31] The game begins with money, lots of it.

SEEKING FUNDS: "THE MONEY CHASE"   Campaigns for high office are expensive, and the costs keep rising. In 1980, about $250 million was spent on all Senate and House campaigns combined. The figure had jumped to $425 million by 1990 and topped $600 million in 1996.

Because of the high cost of campaigns, candidates are forced to spend much of their time raising funds, which come primarily from individual contributors, interest groups (through PACs, discussed in Chapter 9), and political parties. The "money chase" is relentless.[32] It has been estimated that a U.S. senator must raise $10,000 a week on average throughout the entire six-year term in order to raise the $3 million or so that it takes to run a competitive Senate campaign in most states. A Senate campaign in a large state can cost several times that amount. In 1994, Michael Huffington spent $27.9 million of his own money in a losing effort in California. House campaigns

U.S. Senate candidate Michael Huffington and his wife at a campaign gathering on election day. Huffington spent about $25 million of his own money on the campaign and lost by less than 1 percent to incumbent Senator Dianne Feinstein. (David Butow/Black Star)

are less costly, but expenditures of $500,000 or more are commonplace.[33] As for presidential elections, even the nominating race is expensive. It is generally thought that a candidate needs at least $20 million to have a realistic chance of gaining nomination. (In presidential races, but not congressional ones, candidates in the general election are eligible to receive federal funds, a topic discussed in Chapter 12.)

As might be expected, incumbents have a distinct advantage in fundraising. They have contributor lists from past campaigns and have acquired the public visibility and political clout that donors like. In recent House and Senate races, incumbents have outspent their challengers by roughly 2-to-1.[34]

CREATING ORGANIZATION: "HIRED GUNS"   The "old politics" emphasized party rallies and door-to-door canvassing, which required organizations built around campaign volunteers. The "new politics" is based on the mass media and requires a much different kind of organizational structure. The key operatives are campaign consultants, pollsters, media producers, and fund-raising specialists. They are "hired guns" who charge hefty fees for their services. The "new king-makers" is how the writer David Chagall characterized these "pros."[35]

Some of them are specialists in campaign management. Inexperienced candidates often think that campaigns are simple to run and entrust the job to an amateur, who is often a relative or friend. They soon discover that their campaign is headed nowhere. At this point, if they have the money, they hire a seasoned professional. Over the years, some of these operatives, like Joe Napolitan, Ed Rollins, Stu Spencer, and Roger Ailes, have developed almost legendary reputations.

Fund-raising specialists are also part of the new politics. Direct mail operators have developed contributor lists for every state and nearly every type of candidacy, and they flood the mail with computer-generated letters. There are also numerous specialty mailing lists, such as EMILY's List (*early mail is like yeast*, "it makes the dough rise"). EMILY's List was started in the 1980s to provide seed money for liberal women candidates. Effective fund-raisers also know how to tap into the networks of large contributors and interest groups who give to election campaigns (see Chapter 9).

Polling is another essential component of the modern campaign. Although candidates make use of the public polls conducted by Gallup, the news media, and other organizations, they also hire their own pollsters.[36] They also rely on focus groups, which are small groups of voters assembled to talk at length about the issues and candidates and, in some instances, to evaluate proposed themes and materials, such as televised political ads. Polls and focus groups enable candidates to identify messages that are likely to resonate with the voters. At one point in the 1996 presidential race, for example, Bob Dole shifted from attacks on Bill Clinton's character to issues of taxes and economic growth after his polls and focus groups indicated that voters were more concerned about their disposable income than the president's personal history.

Media consultants are another staple of the modern campaign. These experts are adept at producing televised political advertising and creating the "photo-ops" and other staged events that attract news coverage. They also "teach" the candidates how to use the media properly. Inexperienced candidates soon discover that they cannot "just be themselves" when talking with journalists or participating in a televised debate. They have to conform to the demands of the media, such as the preference of television journalists for "sound bites"—short, pithy statements that add zest and zing to a news story.[37]

DEVISING STRATEGY: "PACKAGING THE CANDIDATE"   In the old days, candidates were nearly prepackaged. They were labeled as Democrats or Republicans, which was about all the guidance most voters wanted or needed. Party labels are still meaningful, but today's campaigns are also based on media "images."

Often depicted as hollow deceptions, images are more typically rooted in factual arguments.[38] They are constructed by placing aspects of the candidate's partisanship, policy positions, record, and personality in the context of the voters' "ideal" candidate. The voters want a representative who is honest, able, straightforward, resolute, and responsive to their interests, but there are limits on the claims a candidate can reasonably make. It would be difficult, for example, for Democratic incumbents who have been long-time advocates of welfare spending to convincingly portray themselves as fiscal conservatives. Instead, they would base their images as responsive legislators on other issues. In any case, officeseekers try to create a favorable portrayal of their candidacy that is also plausible. In a way, this type of packaging is as old as politics itself. Andrew Jackson's self-portrayal as "the champion of the people" is an image that any modern candidate could appreciate. What is new is the need to fit the image to the requirements of a media campaign. It must conform to a world of sound bites, thirty-second ads, and televised debates.

Most candidates also try to pin an image on their opponent. It is, predictably, a negative image. Studies indicate that attack messages are based heavily on factual statements about an opponent's personal and political record.[39] There is also evidence that, message for message, negative appeals have more impact than positive ones. Unfortunately, one effect of negative campaigning is to depress voter turnout. By driving up an opponent's "negatives," a candidate can drive down the proportion of the opponent's potential supporters who actually vote on election day.[40]

GOING PUBLIC: "AIR WARS" AND "SPIN"   The battleground of the modern campaign is the mass media. Televised advertising in particular enables candidates to communicate directly, and on their own terms, with the voters. Candidates spend heavily on the production and airing of televised ads, which account for more than half the expenditures in every presidential campaign and most congressional races.

"Air wars" is the term that the political scientist Darrell West applies to candidates' use of televised ads. Candidates increasingly play off each other's ads, seeking to gain the strategic advantage.[41] Modern production techniques enable well-funded candidates to get new ads on the air within a few hours' time, which allows them to rebut attacks and exploit fastbreaking developments. "Rapid-response" was the term used by the Clinton campaign in 1992 and 1996 for its capacity to counter Republican charges. For example, when Bush ads in the 1992 campaign accused Clinton of having raised taxes when governor of Arkansas, Clinton aired an immediate rebuttal based on his interpretation on his tax record.[42]

The media campaign also takes place through news vehicles, but coverage varies depending on the race and location. Many House candidates are nearly ignored by their local news media. The New York City media market, for example, includes more than a score of House districts in New York, New Jersey, Pennsylvania, and Connecticut, and candidates in these districts get little or no coverage from the New York media. The presidential campaign, in contrast, gets daily coverage from both national and local media. Between these extremes are Senate races and House races in less populated areas; they always get some news coverage and, if hotly contested, may get heavy coverage.

Candidates try to put a positive "spin" on their news coverage. They also try to campaign in ways that will lessen the negative "spin" they have come to expect from journalists. The news is mostly critical in tone, and a candidate's blunder or misstatement can result in a torrent of bad news.[43] As a result, candidates increasingly rely on scripted statements rather than spontaneous remarks when dealing with the press.

The media campaign also includes debates and talk-show appearances. Debates are particularly important since they often attract a large and attentive audience. But they are also risky encounters since they provide a chance to directly compare the candidates. A weak or bumbled performance can seriously damage a candidate's chances in a close race. To reduce the risks, candidates often spend the day or two before a debate "rehearsing" their presentation.

USING THE PARTY: THE "SERVICE ROLE"   The political parties have adapted to the demands of the new politics; at the state and national levels particularly, the parties make a significant contribution to the candidates' efforts.

The GOP took the lead in this development. In the late 1970s, Republican leaders saw that a revamped national party organization had a role to play in technology-based campaigns. The RNC developed campaign-management "colleges" and "seminars" for candidates and their staffs, compiled massive amounts of computer-based electoral data, sent field representatives to assist state and local party leaders in modernizing their operations, and established a media production division. The range of services the RNC provides is substantial. For example, the RNC tapes and catalogues C-SPAN's televised coverage of congressional debate and can instantly retrieve the statement of any speaker on any issue. Republican challengers use this material to create attack ads directed at Democratic incumbents, while Republican incumbents use it to show themselves acting forcefully on issues of concern to their constituents.

The DNC in the early 1980s followed the Republicans' example, but its later start and less affluent followers have kept the Democrats behind. Modern campaigns, as David Adamany notes, are based on a "cash economy," and Democrats are relatively cash-poor.[44] The Republican model has also filtered down to the state party committees, which, in varying degrees, provide the types of media, data-research, and educational services that the national committees offer.

Party organizations also furnish candidates with what is known as "soft money." Federal law limits the amount a candidate can accept from a single individual ($1,000 is the maximum) or interest group ($5,000 is the maximum). The parties can also give only a small amount to a candidate. This funding is termed "hard money" since it goes directly to the candidate. However, federal law has a "loophole" that allows contributors to give unlimited amounts to parties. But, of course, this "soft money" in the end actually helps particular candidates since it funds campaign activities. In 1996, for example, $250 million in soft money from around the country poured into party coffers; it was used to fund advertising, registration, and get-out-the-vote drives.

In their dealings with candidates, the national and state parties have more of a **service relationship** than a power relationship.[45] The parties may acquire some additional loyalty from officeholders as a result of the contributions they make to their campaigns. Nevertheless, the parties offer help to virtually any candidate with a chance of victory. Without the ability to control the nominating process, the party has little choice but to embrace all candidates who run under its banner. At a minimum, this approach increases the likelihood that the party will gain a congressional majority and thus acquire control of the committees and top leadership positions in the House or Senate (see Chapter 11).

PARTIES, CANDIDATES, AND THE PUBLIC'S INFLUENCE

Candidate-centered campaigns have some distinct advantages. First, they lend flexibility and infuse new blood into electoral politics. When political conditions and issues change, self-directed candidates quickly adjust, bringing new ideas into the political arena. Strong party organizations are rigid by comparison. Until recently, for example, the British Labour party was controlled by old-line activists who refused to concede that changes in the British economy called for changes in the party's trade unionist and economic policies. The result was a series of humiliating defeats to the Conservative party.

Second, candidate-centered campaigns encourage national officeholders to be responsive to local interests. In building personal followings among their state and district constituents, members of Congress respond to local needs. Nearly every significant domestic program enacted by Congress is adjusted to accommodate the interests of states and localities that would otherwise be hurt by the policy. Members of Congress are not obliged to support the legislative position of their party's majority, and they often extract favors for their constituents as the price of their support. Where strong national parties exist, national interests take precedence over local concerns. In both France and Britain, for example, the pleas of representatives of underdeveloped regions typically go unheeded by their party's majority.

In other respects, however, candidate-centered campaigns have some real disadvantages. Often, they degenerate into mere personality contests and are fertile ground for powerful special interests, which contribute much of the money that underwrites them. Candidate-centered campaigns also blur the connection between electing and governing. If national policy goes awry, the individual member of Congress can always blame the problem on others in Congress or on the president.[46] By comparison, lawmakers in a party-centered system cannot easily evade responsibility for what the government has done; in such systems, public dissatisfaction with the performance of government often leads to the majority party's defeat in the next election.

The problem of accountability in the U.S. system is apparent from surveys that have asked Americans about the performance of Congress and its individual members (see Figure 8-3). In recent years, many citizens have had a low opinion of the work of Congress as a whole and yet have believed that their own congressional representative was doing a relatively good job. This paradoxical attitude prevails in so many districts that the net result in most elections is a Congress whose membership is not greatly changed from the previous one (see Chapter 11).

Candidate-centered campaigns also make it difficult for voters to act in unison. Candidates of the same party in different constituencies stand for different things, which deprives the national electorate of an opportunity to elect a lawmaking majority pledged to a common platform. Of course, U.S.

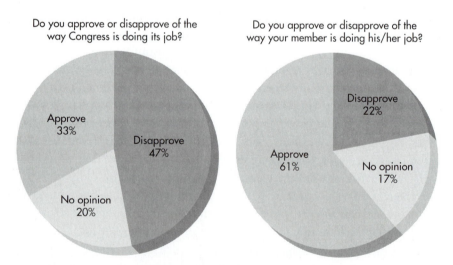

Do you approve or disapprove of the way Congress is doing its job?

Approve 33%
Disapprove 47%
No opinion 20%

Do you approve or disapprove of the way your member is doing his/her job?

Disapprove 22%
Approve 61%
No opinion 17%

FIGURE 8-3 THE PUBLIC'S RATING OF CONGRESS AND OF THEIR OWN MEMBERS OF CONGRESS, 1996
Americans have a higher regard for their own congressional representative than for Congress as a whole. Source: CBS News/New York Times poll, October 17–20, 1996.

elections produce lawmaking majorities, and it is safe to assume that most elected officials of a particular party share certain ideas even when they run and win on their own.[47] But this is a far cry from a system in which voters in all districts choose among candidates who are committed to sharply defined party platforms.

In sum, candidate-centered campaigns strengthen the relationship between the voters and their individual representative while, at the same time, weakening the relationship between the full electorate and their representative institutions. Whether this arrangement serves the public's interest is debatable. It is clear, however, that Americans do not want truly strong parties. Parties survived the shift to candidate-centered campaigns and will persist, but their heyday has passed. (Congressional and presidential campaigns are discussed further in Chapters 11 and 12, respectively.)

SUMMARY

Political parties serve to link the public with its elected leaders. In the United States this linkage is provided by a two-party system; only the Republican and Democratic parties have any chance of winning control of government. The fact that the United States has only two major parties is explained by several factors: an electoral system—characterized by single-member districts—that makes it difficult for third parties to compete for power; each party's willingness to accept differing political views; and a political culture that stresses compromise and negotiation rather than ideological rigidity.

Because the United States has only two major parties, each of which seeks to gain majority support, their candidates normally tend to avoid controversial or extreme political positions. Candidates typically pursue moderate and somewhat overlapping policies. Nonetheless, the Democratic and Republican candidates sometimes do offer sharply contrasting policy alternatives, particularly in times of political unrest.

America's parties are decentralized, fragmented organizations. The national party organization does not control the policies and activities of the state organizations, and they in turn do not control the local organizations. Traditionally the local organizations have controlled most of the party's work force because most elections are contested at the local level. Local parties, however, vary markedly in their vitality. Whatever their level, America's party organizations are relatively weak. They lack control over nominations and elections. Candidates can bypass the party organization and win nomination through primary elections. Individual candidates also control most of the organizational structure and money necessary to win elections. Recently the state and national party organizations have expanded their capacity to provide candidates with modern campaign services. Nevertheless, party organizations at all levels have few ways of controlling the candidates who run under their banner. They assist candidates with campaign technology, workers, and funds but cannot compel candidates' loyalty to organizational goals.

American political campaigns, particularly those for higher-level office, are candidate-centered. Most candidates are self-starters who become adept at "the election game." They spend much of their time raising campaign funds, and they build their personal organizations around "hired guns": pollsters, media producers, and election consultants. Strategy and image-making are key components of the modern campaign, as is televised political advertising, which accounts for roughly half of all spending in presidential and congressional races.

Because America's parties cannot control their candidates or coordinate their policies at all levels, they are unable to present the voters with a coherent, detailed platform for governing. The national electorate as a whole is thus denied a clear choice among policy alternatives and has difficulty exerting a decisive and predictable influence through elections.

MAJOR CONCEPTS

candidate-centered politics
dealignment
multiparty system
nomination
party-centered politics
party coalition
party competition
party organizations
political party

primary election (direct primary)
proportional representation
realignment
service relationship
single-member districts
split-ticket voting
straight-ticket voting
two-party system

SUGGESTED READINGS

Aldrich, John H. *Why Parties? The Origin and Transformation of Political Parties in America*. Chicago: University of Chicago Press, 1995. An insightful analysis of what parties are and how they emerge and develop.

Burnham, Walter Dean. *Critical Elections and the Mainsprings of American Politics*. New York: Norton, 1970. The classic analysis of how long-term stability in the electoral process is punctuated periodically by major change.

Keith, Bruce E., David B. Magleby, Candice J. Nelson, Elizabeth Orr, Mark C. Westlye, and Raymond E. Wolfinger. *The Myth of the Independent Voter*. Berkeley: University of California Press, 1992. An analysis which asserts that independent voters are actually not very "independent" in their voting patterns.

King, Anthony. *Running Scared: The Victory of Campaigning over Governing in America*. New York: Free Press, 1997. An analysis of why America's leaders have succumbed to the pressure of the permanent campaign.

Lijphardt, Arend. *Electoral Systems and Party Systems: A Study of Twenty-Seven Democracies, 1945–1990*. New York: Oxford University Press, 1994. A comprehensive study of the relationship between electoral systems and party systems.

Pomper, Gerald M. *Passions and Interests: Political Party Concepts of American Democracy*. Lawrence: University of Kansas Press, 1992. A broad theoretical analysis of American political parties.

Rosenstone, Steven J., Roy L. Behr, and Edward H. Lazarus. *Third Parties in America*, 2d ed. Princeton, N.J.: Princeton University Press, 1996. An analysis of America's third parties and their impact on the two-party system.

Sabato, Larry, and Glenn Simpson. *Dirty Little Secrets: The Persistence of Corruption in American Politics*. New York: Times Books, 1996. Argues that money is the main problem in elections and that strict reforms are needed.

West, Darrell M. *Air Wars: Television Advertising in Election Campaigns, 1952–1992*. Washington, D.C.: Congressional Quarterly Press, 1993. A thorough study of the role of televised advertising in election campaigns.

READING 8

The Politics of Ambition
ALAN EHRENHALT

A political career in America in the 1990s . . . is not easy, lucrative, or a particularly good route to status in life. This places increased importance on one other motive for entering politics: sheer enjoyment. You pretty much have to like the work.

You also have to be good at it. Almost as important as the question of what sorts of people want a political career is the question of what sorts of people possess the skills to do it well. Here too there is no reason to assume that the answers are the ones that would have applied earlier in this century, or even earlier in the postwar years.

The skills that work in American politics at this point in history are those of entrepreneurship. At all levels of the political system, from local boards and councils up to and including the presidency, it is unusual for parties to nominate people. People nominate themselves. That is, they offer themselves as candidates, raise money, organize campaigns, create their own publicity, and make decisions in their own behalf. If they are not willing to do that work for themselves, they are not (except in a very few parts of the country) going to find any political party structure to do it for them.

At one time in American politics, parties represented the only real professionalism that existed. A century ago, when defenders of "good government" complained that public life was being usurped by professional politicians, they did not mean candidates. They meant bosses—the people who chose the candidates. Legislators came and went, in Congress as they did at lesser levels. The institutions of professionalism were the party machines: New York's Tammany Hall, the Republican organization of Pennsylvania, the Cook County Democratic Central Committee. The leaders of these machines were the lifelong political practitioners who reaped the rewards of power and graft that the system offered.

Today's professional politicians are less imposing figures, even to those who do not like them. Their influence as individuals is modest, and their opportunities for graft are few. In most cases they do not control anyone's election but their own. Their ties to any political party are limited. They are solo practitioners. It is a different brand of professionalism altogether.

There is no need to dwell on the evidence of party decline; it is all around us. At the national level, it is true, there were some interesting signs of party renewal in the 1980s, centered in the congressional campaign committees. Both the Democratic and the Republican parties in Washington play a far greater role in recruiting and helping candidates than they did two decades ago. But that does not contradict the fundamental point that in the states and cities across America, where elections are fought and won, parties make little difference. Candidates for all sorts of offices are perfectly capable of going on about their business without them. And it is not just parties that have lost their role of anointing political candidates. Other community institutions that used to perform that task have also lost their authority in recent years. . . .

Who sent us the political leaders we have? There is a simple answer to that question. They sent themselves. And they got where they are through a combination of ambition, talent, and the willingness to devote whatever time was necessary to seek and hold office.

In the age of the entrepreneurial candidate, character traits that used to be helpful turn out to be counterproductive. When Alfred E. Smith entered politics in Manhattan in the early years of this century, the one crucial trait he had to exhibit to win nomination was loyalty—uncomplaining devotion to the organization and leaders who placed him in the state assembly. If his loyalty to Tammany Hall had been less than total, he would not have been rewarded with a seat in the legislature, and if his loyalty had declined when he assumed office, he would have been dumped. But the people who have represented Smith's old territory in Congress or in the New York legislature in recent years have not been there because of loyalty. There has been no organization, even in the old machine strongholds, worth a pledge of allegiance. The quality that nourishes political careers today, in Manhattan as elsewhere, is independence.

Most candidates who succeeded on the basis of loyalty did not have to be especially articulate. Political organizations required spokesmen, but they did not require that all their officeholders be capable of playing a visible public role. A genial young man blessed with the support of the party organization did not need to express himself vigorously on the issues of the moment.

That is no longer true. A candidate for virtually any office has to know how to talk. Voters may not make their choices very often on the basis of public policy, but they do not like to vote for candidates who seem uncomfortable expressing themselves. More than in the old days, campaigns for all offices are exercises in communication: in town meetings, in door-to-door canvassing, on television, in direct-mail literature that the candidate has to write himself. Even if it does not matter a great deal what the candidate says, it makes an enormous difference how he looks and sounds saying it. The politics of the 1990s, unlike the politics of earlier generations, is an enterprise in which the inarticulate have no place to hide. When candidates are left to themselves to orchestrate campaigns and do their own communicating with the voters, it is only natural that the glib will survive and the tongue-tied will be drawn toward other lines of work. . . .

Money and television are important. It has been true for the past twenty years that TV commercials can sway election results, local as well as national. And even in the smaller media markets, commercials are expensive to produce and to put on the air. Television has pushed up the cost of campaigns for an entire range of offices to disturbing levels. It is very difficult now to win an open seat in Congress without raising and spending half a million dollars. Usually it takes more. A contested state Senate campaign, even in a medium-sized state, often costs $100,000. And it is clear to anybody who follows politics where most of this money comes from. It comes from people and interests with a stake in the policy decisions of the institution whose seats are up for grabs.

But who gets it? How did Jim Jontz, running for Congress in 1986 as a Democrat in Indiana's Fifth District, a thirty-three-year-old full-time legislator with no significant resources of his own, manage to raise and spend nearly $500,000 to get himself elected in an impossibly Republican constituency? One can argue, of course, that Jontz was simply an instrument—a tool of the labor unions and liberal pressure groups who found his politics appealing and provided most of the money. But to say that is to misconstrue the role of these groups—and their business-oriented counterparts on the Republican side—in the American political system.

Special interests reward politicians. They buy access to politicians. They

seek to influence votes, and frequently they do. But they do not generate careers. They do not pluck people off college campuses or out of entry-level
private jobs and lure them into politics. The candidates who raise the large
amounts that campaigns now require are people who launched political careers on the basis of their own values, ambitions, and interests. They throw
themselves into politics full-time, and they learn where the money is, just as
they learn to campaign door to door, address a town meeting, or put together
a piece of direct mail. These are the skills that make them successful.

In a similar sense it is not quite true that television wins elections. The
ability to look and sound good on television wins elections. It is true that,
in a number of well-publicized campaigns every year, people without any
such natural ability are made presentable through the efforts of consultants
whom they had the personal resources to hire, but those campaigns are exceptions. The vast majority of candidates who win elections through television are people whose commitment to politics over the course of their adult
lives put them in a position to afford it and to understand how to use it.

No matter how much importance we want to place on the roles of
money and media in the campaign process, we are driven back to questions
about which sorts of people are succeeding in that process. Political office
today flows to those who want it enough to spend their time and energy mas-
tering its pursuit.

SOURCE: Alan Ehrenhalt, *The United States of Ambition: Politicians, Power, and the Pursuit of Office* (New York: Times Books, 1992). Reprinted by permission.
Alan Ehrenhalt is executive editor of Governing magazine and was previously political editor of Congressional Quarterly.

CHAPTER NINE

Interest Groups

The flaw in the pluralist heaven is that the heavenly chorus sings with a strong upper-class bias.

E. E. SCHATTSCHNEIDER[1]

HEY LAUNCHED their attack within hours of the announcement that congressional Republicans had included Medicare in their balanced-budget proposal. The GOP lawmakers planned a $1.1 trillion reduction in federal spending over seven years, including a $270 billion cut in health care for the elderly. Senior-citizen groups assailed the plan and quickly organized a mass demonstration outside the Capitol building. The next step was an orchestrated campaign of thousands of angry calls, letters, telegrams, and faxes from retirees to their congressional representatives.

President Clinton sided with the seniors' lobby, promising to veto the Republican bill, which led to a showdown between Congress and the White House that forced a temporary shutdown of the federal government. In January 1996, after a six-week battle and with their poll ratings dropping almost daily, Republican lawmakers shelved their balanced-budget proposal.

The campaign against the Republicans' Medicare initiative suggests why interest groups are both admired and feared. On the one hand, groups have a legitimate right to express their views on public policy issues. It is entirely appropriate for senior citizens or any other group—whether farmers, consumers, business firms, or college students—to actively promote their interests through collective action.

In fact, the *pluralist* theory of American politics (see Chapter 1) holds that society's interests are most effectively represented through the efforts of groups. An extreme statement of this view is Arthur F. Bentley's claim in 1908 that society is "nothing other than the complex of groups that compose it."[2] Although modern pluralists make far less sweeping claims, they do contend that the group process, on balance, is open to a great range of interests, nearly all of which benefit from organized activity in one significant way or another.

Yet groups can wield too much power. If a group gets its way at an unreasonable cost to the rest of society, the public interest is harmed. When the Republican budget package was prepared in Congress, polls indicated that most Americans wanted a balanced federal budget and were willing to bear a fair share of the costs. Did the senior-citizen lobby, in pursuit of its own narrow interest, derail a sound budgetary proposal? Or did the Re-

Environmental activists protest against ocean dumping from a sailboat in New York harbor. Greenpeace U.S.A. is one of the country's most visible and influential interest groups. (Jim Sulley/The Image Works)

publican package, which also included tax cuts for upper-income Americans, place on the elderly too much of the burden of a balanced budget?

Opinions on these questions would differ widely, but there is no doubt that the special interest in some cases wrongly prevails over the general interest. Indeed, most observers are of the opinion that groups have achieved too much influence over public policy in recent decades. Some analysts describe the situation as the triumph of **single-issue politics:** separate groups organized around nearly every conceivable policy issue, with each group pressing its demands and influence to the utmost, at whatever cost to the broader society.

An **interest group** can be defined as a set of individuals who organize to promote a shared political interest. Also called a "faction" or "pressure group" or "special interest," an interest group is characterized by its formalized organization and by its pursuit of policy goals that stem from its members' shared interest. Thus a bridge club or an amateur softball team is not an interest group because it does not seek to influence the political process. Organizations such as Common Cause, the National Organization for Women, the World Wildlife Fund, the National Rifle Association, and the Anti-Defamation League of B'nai B'rith are interest groups because, despite their differences, they all meet the definition's two criteria: each is an organized entity and each seeks to further its members' interests through political action.

Interest groups promote public policies, encourage the political participation of their members, support candidates for public office, and work to influence policymakers. Interest groups are thus similar to political parties in certain respects, but the two types of organizations differ in important ways. Major political parties address a broad range of issues so as to appeal to diverse blocs of voters. Parties exist to contest elections. They change their policy positions as the voters' preferences change; for the party, winning is almost everything. In comparison, interest groups focus on specific issues of immediate concern to their members; farm groups, for example, concentrate on agricultural policy. A group may involve itself in elections, but its purpose is to influence public policy.

This chapter examines the degree to which various interests in American society are represented by organized groups, the process by which interest groups exert influence, and the costs and benefits of group politics in regard to the public good. The main points made in the chapter are the following:

⋆ *Although nearly all interests in American society are organized to some degree, those associated with economic activity, particularly business enterprises, are by far the most thoroughly organized.*

* *Lobbying and electioneering are the traditional means by which groups communicate with and influence political leaders.*
* *When public policy is decided solely by group demands, the group process does not serve the collective interest, regardless of the number of separate interests that benefit from the process.*

THE INTEREST-GROUP SYSTEM

In the 1830s the Frenchman Alexis de Tocqueville wrote that the "principle of association" was nowhere more evident than in America.[3] Organized groups have always flourished in the United States. The country's tradition of free association has made it easy for Americans to join together for political purposes, and their diverse interests have given them reason to seek influence through specialized groups. Few nations have as many separate economic, ethnic, religious, social, and geographic interests as the United States (see box: How the United States Compares).

The extraordinary number of groups in the United States does not suggest, however, that these various interests are all fully organized. Some groups are inherently more attractive to potential members than others and thus find it easier to build large or loyal followings.[4] Organizations also differ in their access to financial resources and thus in their capacity for political action.

Therefore, a first consideration in regard to group politics in America is the issue of how thoroughly various interests are organized. Group politics is the politics of organization. Interests that are highly organized stand a good chance of having their views heard by policymakers. Poorly organized interests run the risk of being ignored.

Economic Groups

No interests are more fully or effectively organized than those that have economic activity as their primary purpose. An indication of their advantage is the fact that their Washington lobbyists outnumber those of other groups by more than 2 to 1.

Economic groups include corporations, labor unions, farm groups, and professional associations. They exist primarily for economic purposes: to make profits, provide jobs, improve pay, or protect an occupation. For the sake of discussion, such organizations will be called **economic groups,** although it is important to recognize that their political goals can include poli-

HOW THE UNITED STATES COMPARES

Groups: "A Nation of Joiners"

"A nation of joiners" is how the Frenchman Alexis de Tocqueville described the United States during his visit to this country in the 1830s.

Even today, Americans are more actively involved in groups and community causes than are Europeans. The American tradition of group activity is only one reason. Another is the structure of the U.S. political system. Because of federalism and the separation of powers, the American system offers numerous points at which groups can try to influence public policy. If unsuccessful with legislators, groups can turn to executives or the courts. If thwarted at the national level, groups can turn to state and local governments. By comparison, the governments of most other democratic nations are not organized in ways that facilitate group access and influence. France's unitary government, for example, concentrates power at the national level.

Such differences are reflected in citizens' participation rates. Americans are more likely to contribute to group activity than, for example, the French or the Germans, as the accompanying figure indicates.

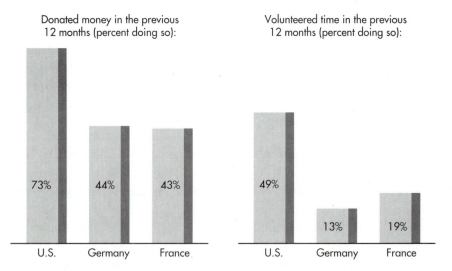

Donated money in the previous 12 months (percent doing so):

U.S.	Germany	France
73%	44%	43%

Volunteered time in the previous 12 months (percent doing so):

U.S.	Germany	France
49%	13%	19%

SOURCE: Helmut I. Anheier, Lester M. Salamon, and Edith Archambault, "Participating Citizens: U.S.–Europe Comparisons in Volunteer Action," *The Public Perspective* vol. 5, no. 3 (March/April 1994): 17.

cies that transcend the narrow economic interests of their members. Thus the AFL-CIO concentrates on labor objectives, but it also takes positions on broader issues of foreign and domestic policy.

One reason for the abundance of economic groups is their access to financial resources. Political activity does not come cheap. If a group is to make its views known, it normally must have a headquarters, an expert staff, and communication facilities. Economic groups can obtain the requisite money and expertise from their economic activities. Corporations have the greatest natural advantage. They do not have to charge membership dues or conduct fund-raisers to get money to support their lobbying. Their political money comes from the goods and services they produce and sell.

Some economic groups do depend on dues for their support, but they can offer prospective members a powerful incentive to join: **private (individual) goods**, which are the benefits that a group can grant directly to the individual member. For example, workers in the state of Michigan cannot hold automobile assembly jobs unless they belong to the United Auto Workers (UAW). Economic groups are highly organized in part because they serve the individual economic needs of potential members. The predominance of economic interests was predicted in *Federalist* No. 10, in which James Madison declared that property is "the most common and durable source of factions." Stated differently, nothing seems to matter quite so much to people as their pocketbooks and livelihoods.

BUSINESS GROUPS   Writing in 1929, E. Pendleton Herring noted, "Of the many organized groups maintaining offices in [Washington], there are no interests more fully, more comprehensively, and more efficiently represented than those of American industry."[5] Although corporations do not dominate the group system to the same degree as they did in the past, Herring's general conclusion still holds: more than half of all groups formally registered to lobby Congress are business organizations. Nearly all large corporations and many smaller ones are politically active. They concentrate their activities on policies that directly affect business interests, such as tax and regulatory decisions.

Business firms are also represented through associations. Some of these associations, such as the U.S. Chamber of Commerce, which represents more than 180,000 medium-sized and small businesses, seek to advance the general interests of business and to articulate a business perspective on broad policy issues.[6] Other business associations, such as the American Petroleum Institute, are confined to a single industry. Because each trade association represents a single industry, it can promote the interests of member corporations even when these interests conflict with those of business generally. Thus, while the Chamber of Commerce promotes a free trade policy, some trade associations seek protective tariffs because their member firms want barriers against foreign competition.[7]

LABOR GROUPS   Since the 1930s, organized labor has been politically active on a large scale. Its goal has been to promote policies that benefit workers in general and union members in particular. Although some independent unions, such as the United Mine Workers, lobby actively, the dominant labor group is the AFL-CIO, which maintains its national headquarters in Washington, D.C. The AFL-CIO has more than 12 million members in its 100 affiliated unions, which include the International Brotherhood of Electrical Workers, the Sheet Metal Workers, the Communication Workers of America, and, as of 1987, the giant International Brotherhood of Teamsters.

At one time a third of the U.S. work force was unionized, but only about one-seventh of all workers currently belong to unions. Skilled and unskilled laborers have been the core of organized labor, but their numbers are decreasing while professionals, technicians, and service workers are increasing in number. Professionals have shown little interest in union organization, perhaps because they identify with management or see themselves as economically secure. Service workers and technicians are also more difficult for unions to organize than traditional laborers because they work closely with managers and, often, in small offices.

However, unions have made important inroads in recent decades in their efforts to organize public employees. Teachers, postal workers, police, firefighters, and social workers are among the public-employee groups that have become increasingly unionized. Today, the nation's largest unions are those that represent service and public employees rather than skilled and unskilled laborers (see Table 9-1).

AGRICULTURAL GROUPS   Farm organizations represent another large economic lobby. The American Farm Bureau Federation is the largest of the farm groups, with roughly 3 million members. The National Farmers Union, the National Grange, and the National Farmers Organization are smaller farm lobbies. Agricultural groups do not always agree on policy issues. For instance, the Farm Bureau sides with agribusiness and owners of large farms, while the Farmers Union promotes the interests of smaller, "family" farms.

There are also numerous specialty farm associations, including the As-

TABLE 9-1   THE LARGEST LABOR UNIONS, 1950s AND 1990s
The largest labor unions today represent service and public employees; in the past, the largest unions represented skilled and unskilled workers.

1950s	*1990s*
1. United Auto Workers	1. National Education Association
2. United Steel Workers	2. International Brotherhood of
3. International Brotherhood of	Teamsters
Teamsters	3. American Federation of State,
4. United Brotherhood of	County, & Municipal Employees
Carpenters & Joiners	4. United Food and Commercial
5. International Association of	Workers International
Machinists	5. Service Employees International

SOURCE: U.S. Department of Labor.

sociation of Wheat Growers and the Associated Milk Producers. Each association acts as a separate lobby to try to obtain policies beneficial to its members' narrow agricultural interests.

PROFESSIONAL GROUPS   Most professions have lobbying associations. Perhaps the most powerful of these groups is the American Medical Association (AMA), which, with more than 250,000 members, represents about half of the nation's physicians. The AMA has consistently opposed any government policy that would substantially limit physicians' autonomy. Other professional groups are the American Bar Association and the American Association of University Professors, each of which maintains a lobbying office in Washington.

Citizens' Groups

Although economic interests are the best organized groups, they do not have a monopoly on group activity. There are a great number and variety of other organized interests, which we shall refer to collectively as **citizens' (noneconomic) groups.** The members of groups in this category are drawn together not by the promise of direct economic gain but by **purposive incentives**— opportunities to promote a cause in which they believe.[8] Whether a group's goal is to protect the environment, reduce the threat of nuclear war, return prayer to the public schools, feed the poor at home or abroad, or whatever, there are citizens who are willing to participate simply because they believe the policy goal is a worthy cause.[9]

In comparison with economic groups, citizens' groups have a harder time gathering the resources necessary for organized political activity. These groups do not generate profits or fees that can be used for lobbying. Moreover, the incentives they offer to prospective members are not exclusive. Unlike the private, or individual, goods offered by many economic groups (such as the jobs that firms and unions provide), citizens' groups typically offer **collective (public) goods** as an incentive to potential members. Collective goods are, by definition, benefits that must be shared; they cannot be allotted on an individual basis. The air we breath and the national forests we visit are examples of collective goods; they are available to one and all, those who pay dues to a clean-air group or a wilderness group and those who do not.

This characteristic of collective goods creates what is called the **free-rider problem,** which refers to the fact that individuals will receive the benefit even if they have not contributed to the group's finances. In a purely economic sense, it is not rational for individuals to pay dues to such a group since they can obtain the benefit without paying for it.[10] Moreover, the dues paid by any single member are too small to affect the group's success one way or another. Why pay dues to a clean-air group when any improvement in air quality from its lobbying efforts is available to everyone and when one's contribution is too small to make a real difference? Although many people do join such groups anyway,[11] there is no doubt that the free-rider problem is a reason why citizens' groups are less highly organized than economic ones.

Citizens' groups try to surmount the free-rider problem by creating individual benefits, akin to those offered by economic groups, to make membership more attractive.[12] Organizational newsletters and social activities are among the individual benefits that citizens' groups offer as a lure to membership. Computer-assisted direct mail has also helped citizens' groups attract members. Group organizers buy mailing lists and flood the mails with computer-typed "personal" letters asking recipients to pay a small annual membership fee. For some individuals, a fee of $25 to $50 annually represents no great sacrifice and offers the personal satisfaction of supporting a cause in which they believe. Until the computer era, citizens' groups had great difficulty in identifying and contacting potential members, which is a reason why the number of such groups was so much smaller in the past than is true today. On the whole, however, the organizational advantages rest with economic groups. In nearly all respects, they have the edge on citizens' groups (see Table 9-2).

Most citizens' groups are of three general types: public interest groups, single-issue groups, and ideological groups.

Public Interest Groups Public interest groups are those that claim to represent the broad interests of society as a whole. Despite their label, public interest groups are not led by people elected by the public at large, and the issues they target are ones of their own choosing, not the public's. Nevertheless, there is a basis for distinguishing such groups from economic groups: the latter seek direct material benefits for their members, while the former seek benefits that are less tangible and more broadly shared. For example, the National Association of Manufacturers, an economic group,

TABLE 9-2 ADVANTAGES AND DISADVANTAGES HELD BY ECONOMIC AND CITIZENS' GROUPS
Compared with economic groups, citizens' groups have fewer advantages and more disadvantages.

Economic Groups	*Citizens' Groups*
Advantages Economic activity provides the organization with resources necessary for political action. Individuals are encouraged to join the group because of economic benefits they individually receive (e.g., wages).	*Advantages* Members are likely to support leaders' political efforts because they joined the group in order to influence policy.
Disadvantages Persons within the group may not support leaders' political efforts because they did not join the group for political reasons.	*Disadvantages* The group has to raise funds, especially for its political activities. Potential members may choose not to join the group because they get collective benefits even if they do not join (the free-rider problem).

seeks policies favorable to large corporations, while the League of Women Voters, a public interest group, seeks policies—such as simplified voter registration—that can benefit the public in general.

The League of Women Voters has existed for many decades, but more than half of the currently active public interest groups have been formed since 1960. One of the more visible of these newer organizations is Common Cause, which has more than 200,000 members; Common Cause describes itself as "a national citizens' lobby" and concentrates on political reform in such areas as campaign finance.

SINGLE-ISSUE GROUPS   A single-issue group is organized to influence policy in just one area. Notable current examples are the various right-to-life and pro-choice groups that have formed around the issue of abortion. The number of single-issue groups has risen sharply in the past two decades, and they now lobby on almost every conceivable issue, from nuclear arms to day care centers to drug abuse.

Environmental groups are sometimes classified as public interest groups, but they may also be considered single-issue organizations in that most of them seek to influence public policy in a specific area, such as pollution reduction, wilderness preservation, or wildlife protection. The Sierra Club is one of the oldest of such groups; it was formed in the 1890s to promote the preservation of scenic areas. Between 1960 and 1970, membership in environmental groups tripled in response to increased public concern about the quality of the environment.[13] Since then, membership in environmental groups has continued to grow. Greenpeace USA, founded in 1978, has rapidly become one of the largest and best-known environmental groups in the country.

IDEOLOGICAL GROUPS   Single-issue groups have a narrowly focused policy agenda. Other groups take a broader view, usually from the perspective of a general philosophical or moral stance. These groups have been labeled ideological groups. An example is the Christian Coalition, which was organized to restore "Christian values" to American life and politics.[14] Americans for Democratic Action (ADA) is another example; the ADA supports liberal positions on a wide range of social, economic, and foreign policy issues. Ideological groups on both the left and right have increased substantially in numbers since the 1960s.

Groups such as the National Organization for Women (NOW) and the National Association for the Advancement of Colored People (NAACP) can

Ralph Reed of the Christian Coalition, an interest group, is a leading conservative activist and theoretician. (Donna Binder/Impact Visuals)

also be classified as ideological groups. Their aim is to promote the broad interests of a particular demographic segment of society.

A Special Category of Interest Group: Governments

While the vast majority of organized interests in the United States represent private concerns, a growing number of interest groups represent governments, both foreign and subnational.

The U.S. government's policies affect the economic development, political stability, and security of nations throughout the world. Arms sales, foreign aid, immigration, and trade practices have a great impact on foreign nations. For this reason, most foreign nations supplement the political efforts made through their embassies with the services of paid lobbying agents in Washington.[15]

States, cities, and other governmental units within the United States also lobby heavily in Washington. While most major cities across the United States and two-thirds of the states have their own Washington lobbyist, these entities also work together through such groups as the Council of State Governments, the National Governors Conference, the National Association of Counties, the National League of Cities, and the U.S. Conference of Mayors.

INSIDE LOBBYING: SEEKING INFLUENCE THROUGH OFFICIAL CONTACTS

Modern government provides a supportive environment in which interest groups can seek to achieve their policy goals. First, government today is involved in so many issue areas—business regulation, income maintenance, urban renewal, cancer research, and energy development, to name only a few—that hardly any interest in society could fail to benefit significantly from having influence over federal policies.

Second, modern government is oriented toward action. Officials are inclined to look for policy solutions to problems rather than to let problems linger. For example, when severe flooding along the Mississippi and Missouri rivers caused a steep decline in farm production and income in these parts of the country in 1993, Washington did not leave farmers to sink or swim on their own but quickly mobilized to assist them through government programs.

Groups seek support through **lobbying,** a term that refers broadly to efforts of groups to influence public policy through contact with public officials. According to Norman Ornstein and Shirley Elder, the two main lobbying strategies may be labeled as "inside lobbying" and "outside lobbying."[16] Each strategy involves communication between public officials and group lobbyists, but the strategies differ in what is communicated, who does the communicating, and who receives the communication.

Inside lobbying is based on group efforts to develop and maintain close ("inside") contacts with policymakers. Inside lobbying is designed to give a group direct access to officials in order to influence their decisions. Access is a critical first step.[17] Unless a group can get the attention of officials, it has no chance of persuading them to support its position.

Inside lobbying once depended significantly on tangible inducements, sometimes including indirect or even outright bribes. This type of lobbying survives, but modern lobbying generally involves more subtle and sophisticated methods than providing money or personal favors to officials. It focuses on supplying officials with information and indications of group strength that will persuade them to adopt the group's perspective.[18]

For the most part, inside lobbying is directed at policymakers who are inclined to support the group rather than those who have opposed it in the past. This tendency reflects both the difficulty of persuading opponents to change long-held views and the advantage of having trusted allies who will actively support the group's position in policy deliberations. Thus union lobbyists work mainly with pro-labor officials, just as corporate lobbyists work mainly with policymakers who support business interests.

Money is the essential ingredient of inside lobbying efforts. The American Petroleum Institute, for example, with its abundant financial resources, can afford a downtown Washington office staffed by lobbyists, petroleum experts, and public relations specialists who help the oil companies to maintain access to and influence with legislative and executive leaders.[19] Many groups spend $1 million or more annually on lobbying. Other groups survive with much less, but it is hard to run a first-rate lobbying campaign on less than $100,000 a year. Given the costs of maintaining a Washington lobby, the domination by corporations and trade associations is understandable. They have the money to retain high-priced lobbyists, while many other interests do not.

The targets of inside lobbying are officials of all branches—the legislative, executive, and judicial.

Lobbying Congress

The benefits of a close relationship with members of Congress are substantial. With support in Congress, a group can obtain the legislative help it needs to achieve its policy goals. By the same token, members of Congress also gain from working closely with lobbyists. The volume of legislation facing Congress is enormous, and members rely on trusted lobbyists to identify bills that deserve their attention and support. When Republican lawmakers took control of Congress in 1995, they invited corporate lobbyists to participate directly in drafting legislation affecting business. Congressional Democrats complained loudly, but Republicans said they were merely getting help from those who best understood business's needs.

Lobbyists' effectiveness with members of Congress depends in part on their reputation for fair play. Lobbyists are expected to play it straight. Said one congressman: "If any [lobbyist] gives me false or misleading information, that's it—I'll never see him again."[20] Arm-twisting is another unacceptable practice. During the debate over the North American Free Trade Agreement (NAFTA) in 1993, the AFL-CIO threatened retaliation against congressional Democrats who supported the legislation. The backlash from

Lobbyists discuss pending legislation with members of the U.S. House of Representatives. Access to public officials and the capacity to provide them with useful information are crucial to effective inside lobbying. (Dennis Brack/Black Star)

these Democrats was so intense that the union backed down on its threat. The safe lobbying strategy is the aboveboard approach: provide information, rely on long-time allies among members of Congress, and push steadily but not too aggressively for legislative goals.

Lobbying Executive Agencies

As the scope of the federal government has expanded, lobbying of the executive branch has grown in importance. Bureaucrats make key administrative decisions and develop policy initiatives that the legislative branch later enacts into law. By working closely with government agencies, groups can influence policy at the implementation and initiation stages. In return, groups assist government agencies by providing information and lending support when their programs are reviewed by Congress and the president.[21]

Nowhere is the link between groups and the bureaucracy more evident than in the regulatory agencies that oversee the nation's business sectors. For example, the Federal Communications Commission (FCC), which regulates the nation's broadcasters, uses information provided by broadcast organizations to determine many of the policies governing their activities. The FCC is sometimes cited as an example of agency "capture." The capture theory suggests that regulatory agencies pass through a series of phases that constitute a "life cycle." Early in an agency's existence, it regulates an industry on the public's behalf, but as the agency matures, its vigor declines until at best it protects the status quo and at worst it falls captive to the very industry it is supposed to regulate.[22] In the 1950s, the commercial networks successfully lobbied the FCC in a campaign against the establishment of a strong public sector television system. For example, public stations were assigned UHF frequencies, while commercial stations held the more powerful VHF frequencies, which were also the only ones that most television sets of the 1950s were programmed to receive. Without the support of a large audience, public television was in a weak position to request additional funding from Congress. Without more funds, it had to struggle to develop the type of programming that would attract a larger audience. The consequences of this vicious circle linger today. Compared with Europe, where public broadcasting was established early and on a solid footing, the American system is very weak.

Research has shown that the capture theory describes only some agencies—and then only some of the time.[23] Agencies selectively cooperate with or oppose interest groups, depending on which strategy better suits agency purposes.[24] Agency officials are aware that they can lose support in Congress, which controls agency funding and program authorization, if they show too much favoritism toward an interest group.

Lobbying the Courts

Recent rulings by the courts in areas such as education and civil rights have made interest groups recognize that the judiciary, too, can help them reach their goals.[25] Interest groups have several judicial lobbying options, including efforts to influence the selection of federal judges. Right-to-life groups pressured the Reagan and Bush administrations to make opposition to abortion a prerequisite for nomination to the federal bench.

Groups typically try to influence public policy through the courts by filing lawsuits. For some organizations, such as the National Association for the Advancement of Colored People (NAACP) and the American Civil Liberties Union (ACLU), legal action is the primary means of lobbying government. The NAACP has emphasized legal action since its founding in 1909 because it recognizes that minorities often lack influence with elected officials. The NAACP financed the 1954 *Brown* case, in which the Supreme Court declared that racial segregation of public schools is unconstitutional. Had the NAACP tried to achieve the same result by lobbying state legislators in the South, it almost certainly would have failed.

As interest groups increasingly resort to legal action, they often find themselves facing one another in court. Such environmental litigation groups as the Sierra Club Legal Defense Fund, the Environmental Defense Fund, and the Natural Resources Defense Council have frequently sued larger oil, timber, and mining corporations.

Webs of Influence: Groups in the Policy Process

Lobbying efforts provide an incomplete picture of how groups obtain influence. It is also necessary to consider two policy processes, iron triangles and issue networks, in which many groups are enmeshed.

IRON TRIANGLES   An **iron triangle** consists of a small and informal but relatively stable set of bureaucrats, legislators, and lobbyists who seek to develop policies beneficial to a particular interest.[26] The three "corners" of one such triangle are the Department of Veterans Affairs (bureaucrats), the veterans' affairs committees of Congress (legislators), and veterans' groups such as the American Legion and the Veterans of Foreign Wars (lobbyists), which together determine many of the policies affecting veterans. Of course, the support of others, including the president and the majority in Congress, is needed to enact new programs. However, they often defer to the views voiced by the veterans' triangle, whose members best understand the policy needs of veterans.

A group in an iron triangle has an inside track to those legislators and bureaucrats who are in the best position to promote its cause. And because it can offer something of value to each of them in return, the relationship tends to be ironclad. The group provides lobbying support for the agency's programs and gives campaign contributions to its congressional allies. The American Dairy Association, for example, contributes hundreds of thousands of dollars each election year to the campaigns of members of the House and Senate Agriculture committees. Figure 9-1 summarizes the benefits that flow to each member of an iron triangle.

ISSUE NETWORKS   Iron triangles represent the pattern of influence only in certain policy areas and are less dominant than in the past. A more common pattern of influence today is the **issue network,** which is an in-

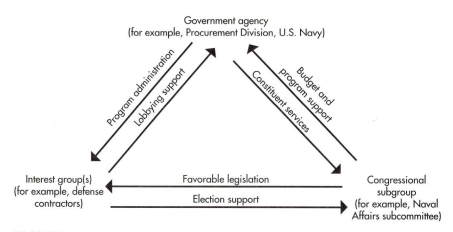

FIGURE 9-1 HOW AN IRON TRIANGLE BENEFITS ITS PARTICI-
PANTS
An iron triangle works to the advantage of each of its participants—an interest
group, a congressional subgroup, and a government agency.

formal grouping of officials, lobbyists, and policy specialists (the "network")
who are brought together by their shared interest and expertise in a particular policy area (the "issue").

Issue networks are a result of the increasing complexity and intercon-
nectedness of policy problems. The complexity of modern issues often makes
it essential that a participant have specialized knowledge of the issue at hand
in order to join in the debate. Thus, unlike iron triangles, where one's position is everything, an issue network is built around policy expertise. On any
given issue, the participants might come from a variety of executive agencies, congressional committees, interest groups, and institutions, such as
universities or "think tanks." And, unlike iron triangles, issue networks are
less stable and less clearly defined. As the issue develops, new participants
may join the debate and old ones drop out. Once the issue is resolved, the
network disbands.[27]

An example of an issue network is the set of participants who would come
together if Congress proposed a significant change in the requirements for
operating nuclear power plants. In earlier times this issue might have been
settled by an iron triangle consisting of the Nuclear Regulatory Commission, the nuclear power industry, and the energy committees in Congress.
Today, the issue network that would form would also include energy policy
specialists and representatives of environmental groups, consumer advocacy
groups, oil companies, and labor unions, to name just a few. Unlike an iron

triangle, which is dominated by like-minded groups, an issue network can involve opposing groups.

OUTSIDE LOBBYING: SEEKING INFLUENCE THROUGH PUBLIC PRESSURE

Although an interest group may rely solely on Washington lobbying, this approach is not likely to be successful unless it can demonstrate that its concerns reflect those of a vital constituency. Accordingly, groups make use of constituency connections when it is advantageous to do so. They engage in **outside lobbying,** which involves bringing public ("outside") pressure to bear on policymakers.[28] The "outside" approach typically takes the form of either *constituency advocacy* or *electoral action* (see Table 9-3).

Constituency Advocacy: Grassroots Lobbying

Some groups depend heavily on **grassroots lobbying**—that is, pressure designed to convince government officials that a group's policy position has broad public support. To mobilize constituents, groups can mount adver-

---

TABLE 9-3   TACTICS USED IN INSIDE AND OUTSIDE
LOBBYING STRATEGIES
Inside lobbying and outside lobbying are based on different tactics.

Inside Lobbying	Outside Lobbying
Developing contacts with legislators and executives	Encouraging group members to write or phone their representatives in Congress
Providing information and policy proposals to key officials	Seeking favorable coverage by news media
Forming coalitions with other groups	Encouraging members to support particular candidates in elections
	Targeting group resources on key election races
	Making PAC contributions to candidates

tising and public relations campaigns through the media. They can also encourage their members to write or call their elected representatives, or even see their representatives personally.

No group illustrates this better than the American Association of Retired Persons (AARP). With more than 30 million members and a staff of 1,600 employees, AARP has been a powerful lobby on issues affecting the elderly. Pressure from the AARP is a major reason that social security and Medicare are politically explosive issues whenever proposals to reduce the federal budget are discussed. AARP members are so responsive to policies affecting them that they generate more mail to Congress than any other group.[29]

As with other forms of lobbying, the precise impact of a grassroots campaign is usually difficult to assess. Some members of Congress downplay its influence, but all congressional offices monitor letters and phone calls from constituents as a way of tracking their views. Most members receive hundreds of letters and phone calls each week from constituents, not counting fax messages, computer-generated mail, and organized grassroots postcard campaigns.

Electoral Action: Votes and PAC Money

"Reward your friends and punish your enemies" is a political adage that loosely describes how interest groups view election campaigns. As part of an "outside" strategy, organized groups work to elect their supporters and defeat their opponents. The possibility of electoral opposition from a powerful group can keep an officeholder from openly obstructing its goals. For example, opposition from the 3-million-member National Rifle Association (NRA) is a major reason the United States has lagged behind other western societies in its handgun control laws, although polls show that most Americans favor such laws.

The principal way in which interest groups try to gain influence through elections is by contributing money to candidates' campaigns. As one lobbyist said, "Talking to politicians is fine, but with a little money they hear you better."[30] Money does not literally "buy" votes in Congress, but it does buy access. Members of Congress listen to the groups that underwrite their campaigns.

The vehicle for group contributions is the **political action committee (PAC)**.[31] A group cannot give organizational funds (such as corporate profits or union dues) to candidates; but through its PAC, a group can raise money for election campaigns by soliciting voluntary contributions from members or employees. A PAC is legally limited in the amount it can contribute to the campaign of a candidate for federal office. As of 1997, the ceiling was $10,000 per candidate—$5,000 in the primary campaign and $5,000

Former White House Press Secretary James Brady, who was shot and partially paralyzed during the 1981 assassination attempt on President Reagan, celebrates a hard-fought victory over the National Rifle Association, a powerful gun lobby. Despite the NRA's opposition, the Senate had just passed a bill requiring a five-day waiting period for handgun purchases. (Wide World Photos)

in the general election campaign; there was no legal limit on the number of candidates a PAC could support. These financial limits do not apply to candidates for state and local office. Their campaigns are regulated by state laws, and many states allow PACs to make unlimited campaign contributions (see box: States in the Nation).

PACs mushroomed in the 1970s as a result of favorable changes in campaign finance laws (see Figure 9-2). There are now more than 4,000 PACs, and PAC contributions account for roughly a third of total contributions to congressional campaigns. Because PAC money can be raised earlier and more quickly than money from individual contributors, PACs have become a critical factor in getting congressional campaigns off the ground. Their role is less significant in presidential campaigns, which are larger in scale and publicly funded in part and therefore less dependent on PAC contributions.

PACs target most of their support to congressional incumbents. PACs are well aware of the fact that incumbents are likely to win and thus to remain in a position to make policy. One PAC director, expressing a common view, said "We always stick with the incumbent when we agree with them both."[32] In House and Senate elections, PACs typically contribute more than five times as much money to incumbents as to their challengers (see Chapter 11).

STATES IN THE NATION

Limits on PAC Spending in State Elections

Elections for state office are regulated by the states, which in some cases limit PAC contributions. Of the states that permit contributions of more than $2,000, only New York and Nevada allow contributions in excess of $10,000.

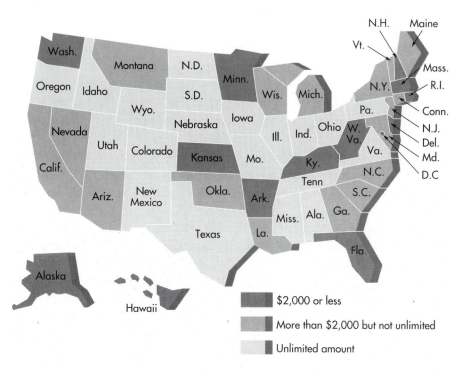

$2,000 or less

More than $2,000 but not unlimited

Unlimited amount

SOURCE: Federal Elections Commission.

Number of PACs

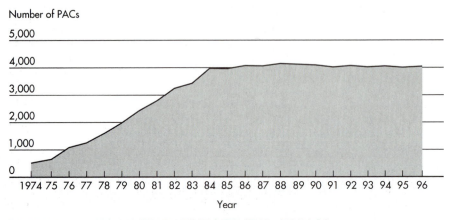

FIGURE 9-2 GROWTH IN THE NUMBER OF PACS, 1974–1996
The number of PACs began to increase sharply after campaign finance reforms
were enacted in the early 1970s. Source: Federal Elections Commission.

The tendency of PACs to back incumbents has to some extent blurred longstanding partisan divisions in campaign funding. Business interests are the most pragmatic. Although they generally favor Republican candidates and strongly supported them in 1994 when it became clear the GOP would sweep the congressional elections, business groups are usually reluctant to anger Democratic incumbents. The result is that Democratic candidates, particularly in House races, have received substantial support over the years from business-related PACs.[33] Other PACs, especially those organized to promote a particular public policy or ideology, are less pragmatic. The Christian Moral Government Fund, for example, backs only candidates who take conservative stands on issues such as school prayer and abortion.

More than 40 percent of all PACs are associated with corporations (see Table 9-4). Examples include the Ford Motor Company Civic Action Fund, the Sun Oil Company Political Action Committee (Sunpac), and the Coca-Cola PAC. The next largest group of PACs consists of those linked to citizens' groups (that is, public interest, single-issue, and ideological groups), such as the liberal People for the American Way and the conservative NCPAC (National Conservative Political Action Committee). Ranking third are PACs tied to trade and professional associations, such as AMPAC (American Medical Association) and R-PAC (National Association of Realtors). Labor unions were once the major source of group contributions, but they now rank fourth.

TABLE 9-4   NUMBER AND PERCENTAGE OF POLITICAL
ACTION COMMITTEES (PACS) IN FIVE CATEGORIES
Most PACs represent business interests: corporations and trade associations
make up 65% of the total.

Category	Number	Percentage
Corporate	1,803	45%
Citizens'	1,020	26
Trade/membership association	815	20
Labor	334	8
Agriculture	44	1
All categories	4,016	100%

SOURCE: Federal Election Commission figures, 1995.

PACs are admired by those who believe that a campaign finance system based on pooled contributions by individuals is superior to one in which candidates rely on a few wealthy donors.[34] The advocates of PACs also claim that groups have a right to be heard, which includes the right to express themselves with money.

Critics argue, however, that PACs give interest groups altogether too much influence over public officials.[35] The opposition to PACs has increased in the last few years, as citizens have come to associate the influence of interest groups with what they see as costly government programs. Although members of Congress deny that they are unduly influenced by PAC contributions, there has been a growing sentiment within Congress to place restrictions on PACs. Agreement on the changes, however, has been difficult to achieve because of differences between Democrats and Republicans in the way they would reform the process and also because many incumbents are unwilling to support any change that would significantly alter the advantage they have under the present system.

THE GROUP SYSTEM:
INDISPENSABLE BUT BIASED

As we noted in the introduction to this chapter, pluralist theory holds that organized groups provide for the representation of society's many and diverse interests. On one level, this claim is beyond dispute. Without groups to carry the message, most of society's interests would find it difficult to gain government's attention and support. Yet the issue of representation is also a question of whether all interests in society have a fair chance to succeed, and here the pluralist argument is less compelling.

The Contribution of Groups to Self-Government: Pluralism

Group activity is an essential part of self-government. A major obstacle to popular sovereignty is the many difficulties that public officials encounter in trying to discover what the people want from government. To determine their wishes, lawmakers consult public opinion polls, meet with constituents, and assess the meaning of recent elections. Organized groups are an additional means of determining popular sentiment, as they provide policymakers with a better picture of the policy concerns of various interests in society.[36] On any given issue, the policy positions that are likely to be expressed most clearly and intensely are those held by organized interests.

Moreover, government does not exist simply to serve majority interests. The fact that most people are not retirees or labor union members or farmers or college students or Hispanics does not mean that the special needs and concerns of such "minorities" are undeserving of attention. And what better instrument exists for promoting the interests of such "minorities" than organizations formed around them? Groups are not antithetical to the democratic process: they are basic to it.

Some pluralists even question whether such terms as "the common good" and "the collective interest" are very useful. If people disagree on society's goals and priorities, as they nearly always do, how can it be said that people have a "common" or "collective" concern? As an alternative, pluralist theory would substitute the sum of people's varied (that is, plural) interests as a rough approximation of society's collective interest. The logic of this proposition is that, because society has so many interests, the common good is ultimately served by a process that enables a great many interests to gain favorable policies. Thus if manufacturing interests prevail on one issue, environmentalists on another, farmers on a third, minorities on a fourth, and so on until a wide range of particular interests are served, the collective interest of society will have been promoted.[37]

Finally, interest groups often take up issues that are neglected by the party system. Party leaders typically shy from issues, such as affirmative action and abortion, on which the party's voters disagree. Such issues would get less notice if not for the groups that promote them. And when groups succeed in drawing attention to these issues, the parties are nearly compelled also to address them. In this sense, as the political scientist Jack L. Walker, Jr., noted, the party and group systems "are complementary and together constitute a much more responsive and adaptive system than either would be if they somehow operated on their own."[38]

Flaws in Pluralism: Interest-Group Liberalism and Economic Bias

Although pluralist theory offers some compelling arguments, it also has questionable aspects. In a direct attack on pluralism, Theodore Lowi argues that there is no concept of society's collective interest in a system that allows special interests to determine for themselves which policy benefits they receive, regardless of how many interests are served.[39] When each group makes its own choice, the basis of decision in each case is not majority (collective) rule but minority (special-interest) rule.

It is seldom safe to assume that what a popular majority favors is what a special-interest group wants. Consider the case of the federal law that re-

Sometimes the interests of a group clearly diverge from majority opinion, as when the National Association of Auto Dealers lobbied successfully against legislation that would have required auto dealers to inform customers about any defects in used cars. (R. Sidney/The Image Works)

quired auto dealers to list the known defects of used cars on window stickers. The law was repealed after an extensive lobbying campaign financed by contributions of more than $1 million by the National Association of Automobile Dealers to the reelection campaigns of nearly 200 members of the U.S. House of Representatives.[40] Although an overwhelming majority of the general public would surely have favored retention of the law, the car dealers' view prevailed.

Lowi uses the term **interest-group liberalism** to describe the tendency of officials to support the policy demands of the interest group or groups that have a special stake in a policy. Interest-group liberalism constitutes a partial abdication by government of its authority over policy. In practical terms, it is the group, as much as the government, that decides policy. The adverse effects include a weakening of majoritarian institutions and an inefficient use of society's resources: groups get what they want, whether or not their priorities match those of society as a whole.

Another flaw in the pluralist argument resides in its claim that the group system is representative. Pluralists recognize that better-organized interests have more influence but argue that the group process is relatively open and that few interests are at a serious disadvantage. These claims contain an element of truth but are far from the complete truth.

As we have seen, organization is a political resource that is distributed unequally across society. Economic interests, particularly corporations, are the most highly organized, and some analysts argue that group politics works chiefly to the advantage of business.[41] This generalization is less valid today. In fact, many of the public interest groups formed in the past three decades were deliberately created to check and balance the influence of existing groups, particularly corporate lobbies.[42]

Big government has also brought the group political system into closer balance. Groups form not only to influence policy but also in response to policy. When new programs were created in the 1960s for the benefit of less advantaged interests in society, these interests mobilized to protect their newly acquired benefits. The National Welfare Rights Organization was formed during the 1960s after new welfare programs were established.[43] Many of the newer interest groups have had a significant impact in areas such as civil rights, the environment, social welfare programs for the elderly and the poor, public morality, and business regulation. Moreover, policy today is less often decided by the actions of one or a few groups. The group system is thus not closed and rigid; it is open to new interests and new patterns of influence.

Nevertheless, interests differ significantly in their level of organization.

Well over half of all lobbying groups in Washington are still business-related. The interest-group system is biased toward America's economically oriented groups, particularly its corporations.

The group system is also slanted toward upper-middle-class interests.[44] Studies indicate that individuals of higher socioeconomic status are disproportionately represented among group members and even more so among group leaders. These tendencies are predictable. Educated and affluent Americans have the skills and money that give organizational form to special-interest politics. Less advantaged Americans lack the money, information, contacts, and communication skills to participate even when they desire to do so. The poor, minorities, women, and the young are greatly underrepresented in the group-politics system. A lack of organization does not ensure an interest's failure, just as the existence of organization does not guarantee success. However, organized interests are obviously in a better position to make their views known.

The business and class bias of the group system is especially significant because the most highly organized interests are, in a sense, those least in need of political clout. Corporations and affluent citizens already benefit from the distribution of society's material resources.

A Madisonian Dilemma

James Madison recognized the dilemma inherent in group activity. Although he worried that government would fall under the control of a dominant interest, whether of the majority or of the minority, he realized that a free society is obliged to permit the advocacy of self-interest. Unless people can promote the separate opinions that stem from differences in their talents, needs, values, and possessions, they do not have liberty.

Ironically, Madison's constitutional solution to the problem of factions has become part of the problem. The American system of checks and balances, with a separation of powers at its core, was designed primarily to prevent a majority faction from trampling on the interests of others. Indeed, throughout the nation's history, majorities have been frustrated in their efforts to gain full power by America's elaborate system of divided government.

This same system, however, makes it relatively easy for minority factions—or, as they are called today, special-interest groups—to protect the government benefits they receive. Benefits are hard to eliminate since concerted action by the executive and both houses of Congress is usually required. If a group has strong support in even a single institution, it can usually fend off attempts to terminate its benefits. This support is ordinarily easy to acquire, since the group can provide resources—money or votes—in return. Jonathan Rauch uses the term "demosclerosis" to describe the debilitating effect on government: its resources are increasingly absorbed by entrenched interests and it consequently undergoes a progressive loss in its ability to respond to new needs. Like the arteriosclerosis that slowly deprives the human body of the oxygen-laden blood it needs to survive, demosclerosis slowly robs government of its capacity.[45] Chapters 11 and 13 will discuss further the issue of interest-group power.

SUMMARY

A political interest group is a set of individuals organized to promote a shared political concern. Most interest groups owe their existence to factors other than politics. They form for economic reasons, such as the pursuit of profit, and maintain themselves by making profits (in the case of corporations) or by providing their members with private goods, such as jobs and wages. Such interest groups include corporations, trade associations, labor unions, farm organizations, and professional associations. Collectively, economic groups are by far the largest set of organized interests. The group system tends to favor interests that are already economically and socially advantaged.

Citizens' groups do not have the same organizational advantages as economic groups. They depend on voluntary contributions from potential members who may lack interest and resources, or who recognize that they will get the collective good from a group's activity even if they do not participate (the free-rider problem). These citizens' groups include public interest, single-issue, and ideological groups. Their numbers have increased dramatically since the 1960s despite their organizational problems.

Organized interests seek influence largely by lobbying public officials and contributing to election campaigns. Using an "inside strategy," lobbyists develop direct contacts with legislators, government bureaucrats, and members of the judiciary in order to persuade them to accept their group's perspective on policy. Groups also use an "outside strategy," seeking to mobilize public support for their goals. This strategy relies in part on grassroots lobbying—encouraging group members and the public to communicate their policy views to officials. "Outside" lobbying also includes efforts to elect officeholders who will support group aims. Through political action committees (PACs), organized groups now provide nearly a third of all contributions received by congressional candidates.

The policies that emerge from the group system bring benefits to many interests, and in some instances these benefits also serve the general interest. But when groups can essentially dictate policies, the common good is not served. The majority's interest is subordinated to group (minority) interests.

MAJOR CONCEPTS

citizens' (noneconomic) groups
collective (public) goods
economic groups
free-rider problem
grassroots lobbying
inside lobbying
interest group
interest-group liberalism

iron triangle
issue network
lobbying
outside lobbying
political action committee (PAC)
private (individual) goods
purposive incentives
single-issue politics

SUGGESTED READINGS

Browne, William P. *Cultivating Congress: Constituents, Issues, and Interests in Agriculture Policymaking.* Lawrence: University of Kansas Press, 1995. An analysis of the limits of "iron triangles" as a description of congressional policymaking.

Gatz, Thomas L. *Improper Influence: Campaign Finance Law, Political Interest Groups, and the Problem of Equality.* Ann Arbor: University of Michigan Press, 1996. An analysis of how PACs have changed the process of representation through groups.

Hansen, John Mark. *Gaining Access: Congress and the Farm Lobby, 1919–1981.* Chicago: University of Chicago Press, 1991. A case study of the farm lobby's influence on Congress.

Lowi, Theodore J. *The End of Liberalism,* 2d ed. New York: Norton, 1979. A thorough critique of interest groups' influence on American politics.

Olson, Mancur, Jr. *The Logic of Collective Action,* rev. ed. Cambridge, Mass.: Harvard University Press, 1971. A pioneering analysis of why some interests are more fully and easily organized than others.

Rauch, Jonathan. *Demosclerosis: The Silent Killer of American Government.* New York: Times Books, 1994. An attack on groups as the main cause of government's ineffectiveness in responding to society's emerging needs.

Rothenberg, Lawrence S. *Linking Citizens to Government: Interest Group Politics at Common Cause.* New York: Cambridge University Press, 1992. A careful case study of a leading lobbying group.

Sorauf, Frank J. *Inside Campaign Finance: Myths and Realities.* New Haven, Conn.: Yale University Press, 1992. An award-winning book that describes the structure of campaign finance, including the role of PACs.

Walker, Jack L., Jr. *Mobilizing Interest Groups in America: Patrons, Professions, and Social Movements.* Ann Arbor: University of Michigan Press, 1991. An insightful analysis of how interest groups form and how they flourish or fail.

Reading 9

The Paralyzing Effect of Group Politics
JONATHAN RAUCH

As the reality of demosclerosis [group-dominated policy] sinks in, it is bound to make many traditional liberals uncomfortable. American liberals tend to believe that government's problem-solving capacity is large and expandable. Programs solve problems; more problems require more programs. Many liberals have long assumed that government can do almost anything it puts its mind to, if only the right people are in charge.

Demosclerosis says otherwise. It posits, instead, a necessary trade-off between what government tries to do and what it *can* do. By creating programs that create lobbies that lock in programs, government can choke itself on its own output. And this problem can't be wished away. Programs, like medicines, can do good things, but if you don't take the inherent side effects into account you can wind up dead. Like a careful doctor meting out drugs carefully, government needs to stay constantly aware of the limits on how much it can do. Too often, liberals have failed to do that.

Some liberals will dismiss demosclerosis as conservative cant: just another attack on government (and on liberals). That would be unfortunate, a counterproductive act of denial. Another, more common, form of denial is "Yes, but never mind." A few weeks before Bill Clinton took office, I met with a Clinton adviser who advocated a fistful of targeted federal investment programs and industrial policies. Demosclerosis implies that it's almost impossible to insulate such programs from interest groups that capture the benefits and then hoard them. How, I asked, would you get around that problem? He said he had no firm answer, instead saying, "We *have* to make this kind of thing work."

That's "Yes, but never mind": "Yes, organized interests take over programs and engrave them in stone, but we'll keep on acting as though they didn't." Demosclerosis means that "Yes, but never mind" won't do. It means that liberals who want to start a new program or expand an old one ought, at least, to offer along with it a mechanism to protect it from calcification. I'm not sure that such an insulating mechanism is possible, but it might be. Maybe a program could be designed to end automatically if it didn't achieve specified goals in a specified period. (The problem, of course, would be seeing that the program actually died, given that organizations and political patrons would spring up to protect it.) Or maybe a program could measure its own performance and phase itself out. Given the difficulty, probably impossibility, of stopping lobbies and politicians from defending programs that are dear to them, I'm not hopeful that anyone will soon invent a reliable mechanism to keep programs flexible. But if one can be found, liberals, who care about making government work, are the best people to find it.

Until they do, their hope of using government in ever cleverer ways is fanciful and, ultimately, self-defeating. Visions of sharp-eyed government entrepreneurs making cutting-edge investments, or of agile officials fine-tuning innovative social programs, are mirages. That isn't to say that government needs to be dismantled. It is to say that government's effectiveness is naturally self-limiting, and that those who deny or defy government's natural limits are making its situation worse, not better.

Demosclerosis spells the end, not of liberalism, but of liberalism without limits. If politicians and the public pick their shots carefully, they can solve a handful of problems pretty well. But if they try to solve every problem at once—which is what they have done—they energize every possible lobby and every potential group, thus feeding the very process that destroys government's ability to adapt. My own frustration is that too few liberals are yet ready to understand this. They cling to a kind of unlimited governmentalism which, for example, undertakes to restore rural economies, revitalize inner cities, and shore up suburbs all at once.

In a sense, they're loving government to death, which really means they're loving liberalism to death, because liberalism relies on government to solve problems. When government fails, liberalism fails. And that is the story of the last twenty years.

Conservatives, who dislike government to begin with, will be happier than liberals with the government-limiting implications of demosclerosis. But they won't be all that happy. Demosclerosis, if it goes on unchecked, turns government into more and more of a rambling, ill-adapted shambles which often gets in the way but can't be gotten rid of. From a conservative point of view, demosclerotic government just sits there, like a big boulder in the middle of the road. If it fails to serve a liberal agenda, it is equally likely to block a conservative one. Liberals may not get new poverty programs that work, but conservatives also can't get rid of archaic banking regulations.

Conservatives would thus be foolish to think that demosclerosis is a victory for them. They, too, need to fight it. That means raising taxes and throwing coddled business lobbies out into the cold. It means saying no to financiers and insurance executives and manufacturers and Farm Bureau members and many other subsidized interests who are important parts of the conservative political base—and who don't at all mind subsidies and cozy deals that benefit themselves.

Most of all, it means cutting benefits to (among other people) the broad portion of the American middle class that votes for conservatives, grouses about "big government," and yet reaps a golden harvest of tax breaks and subsidies. The message for those people is: this means you. Government transfer payments are now a sum equivalent to a quarter of all wages and salaries earned by Americans—and that's before counting such massive tax breaks as the deduction for interest on mortgages. "As far as federal expenditures are concerned," writes Herbert Stein, a former chairman of the Council of Economic Advisers, "[the] welfare state for the not-poor is about five times as big as the welfare state for the poor." Tax breaks and regulatory protections are even more heavily skewed toward the not-poor. In 1991, notes former commerce secretary Peter G. Peterson, an average household whose income was over $100,000 collected almost twice as much in government entitlement and tax benefits as did a household earning less than $10,000. (If the government's goal is to equalize incomes, he says, "it would do a better job if it . . . simply scattered all the money by airplane over every population center, to be gathered at random by passersby.") No one is off the gravy train—certainly not conservatives.

Conservatives have talked a good game about "limiting spendthrift government," but the Reagan years showed clearly that they are more interested in talk than action. Real countermeasures against demosclerosis imply real attacks on real subsidies defended by real interest groups and enjoyed by real voters. So far, conservatives haven't had the stomach.

Can either side adjust? It's not easy, partly because their ideologies stymie each other. Conservatives hate to say no to their subsidized friends, or yes to tax increases, because they believe that liberals will just take the money and spend it on new benefits for big-city mayors and welfare bureaucrats. Liberals hate to say yes to program reductions because they believe that conservatives will just take the money and spend it on tax cuts for the rich. So neither side gets anywhere. Government stays too big for conservatives and too inflexible for liberals. It neither solves problems nor goes away.

SOURCE: Jonathan Rauch, *Demosclerosis: The Silent Killer of American Government* (New York: Times Books, 1995). Reprinted by permission.
Jonathan Rauch is a writer and a contributing editor of the National Journal.

CHAPTER TEN

The News Media

The press in America . . . determines what people will think and talk about—an authority that in other nations is reserved for tyrants, priests, parties and mandarins.

THEODORE H. WHITE[1]

I N THE night of June 12, 1994, Nicole Brown Simpson and a friend, Ronald Goldman, were brutally murdered outside her home in the fashionable Brentwood area of Los Angeles. When her ex-husband, the actor and former football star O. J. Simpson, was accused of the murders, every newspaper and television news program in the country gave the story prominent and repeated play. When replays of 911 calls revealed that O. J. Simpson had physically abused and intimidated his former wife after their 1992 divorce, a brief debate about the ravages of domestic violence ensued. The real story of the Simpson affair, however, was the question of his guilt or innocence. Underlying the mountain of news coverage was the dramatic question: Could O. J. Simpson's cultivated public image have masked a more violent personality, one capable of murder?

Not all developments receive such intensive news coverage. Between 1983 and 1993, the birthrate among unwed women rose by more than 70 percent. According to U.S. Census Bureau statistics, 6.3 million children (27 percent of all children under the age of 18) lived in 1993 with a single parent who had never married, an increase from 3.7 million in 1983. Most of these families are mired in poverty (the average income is less than $10,000), and the children in many cases receive no health care and have very little encouragement to perform well in school or stay out of trouble. The implications for society and public policy are enormous, yet this demographic trend is seldom mentioned in the news, let alone emblazoned in the headlines.

Although the news has been compared to a mirror held up to society, it is actually a highly selective portrayal of reality. The **news** is mainly an account of obtruding events, particularly those which are *timely* (new or unfolding developments rather than old or static ones), *dramatic* (striking developments rather than commonplace ones), and *compelling* (developments that arouse people's concerns and emotions as opposed to remote ones.)[2] These characteristics of the news have a number of origins, not the least of which is that the news is a business. News organizations seek to make a profit, which leads them to prefer news stories that will attract and hold an audience. Thus the Simpson story became headline news the instant the murders were discovered, and it remained newsworthy while the legal process surrounding the crime unfolded. The rising birthrate among unwed women is not considered particularly newsworthy, because it is a slow and steady process, dramatic only in its long-term implications. The columnist George Will notes that a development requires a defining event before it can become big news.[3] Without such an event, reporters have no peg on which to hang their stories.

News organizations and journalists, of either the print media (newspapers and magazines) or the broadcast media (radio and television), are referred to collectively as the **press** or the **news media.** The press is an increasingly important political actor. New technology, from television to cable to satellites, has dramatically increased the reach and speed of communication. In addition, the press has filled some of the void created by the decline in political parties and other political institutions.

Like political parties and interest groups, the press is a key link between the public and its leaders. On a daily basis, Americans connect to politics more through the news that is produced by the media than through the activities of parties or groups.

This chapter argues, however, that the news media are a very different kind of intermediary than either parties or groups and that problems arise when the press is expected to perform the same functions as these institutions. The chapter begins with a review of the news media's historical development and current tendencies in reporting; it concludes with an analysis of the roles the news media can and cannot perform adequately in the American political system. The main ideas presented in this chapter are the following:

* *The American press was initially tied to the nation's political party system (the partisan press) but gradually developed an independent position (the objective press).*

* *Although the United States has thousands of separate news organizations, they present a common version of the news which reflects journalists' shared view of what the news is.*

* *In fulfilling its responsibility to provide public information, the news media effectively perform three significant roles—those of signaler (the press brings relevant events and problems into public view), common carrier (the press serves as a channel through which political leaders can address the public), and watchdog (the press scrutinizes official behavior for evidence of deceitful, careless, or corrupt acts).*

* *The press cannot do the job of political institutions, even though it increasingly tries to do so.*

THE DEVELOPMENT OF THE NEWS MEDIA: FROM PARTISANSHIP TO OBJECTIVE JOURNALISM

Democracy requires a free flow of information. Communication enables a free people to keep in touch with one another, with their leaders, and with important events.

America's early leaders were quick to see the advantages of newspapers. At Alexander Hamilton's urging, the *Gazette of the United States* was founded by John Fenno to promote the policies of George Washington's administration. Hamilton was secretary of the treasury and supported Fenno's paper by granting it the Treasury Department's printing contracts. Thomas Jefferson, who was secretary of state and Hamilton's adversary, complained that the newspaper's content was "pure Toryism." Jefferson persuaded Philip Freneau to start the *National Gazette* as the opposition Democratic Republican party's publication and supported it by granting Freneau authority to print State Department documents.[4] Early newspapers were printed on hand presses, a process that limited production and kept the cost of each copy beyond the reach of ordinary citizens—most of whom were illiterate anyway. Leading papers such as the *Gazette of the United States* had fewer than 1,500 subscribers and could not have survived without party support. Not surprisingly, the "news" they printed was a form of party propaganda.[5] In this era of the **partisan press,** publishers openly took sides on partisan issues. President James K. Polk once persuaded a leading publisher to fire an editor who had attacked Polk's policies.[6]

From a Partisan Press to an "Objective" One

Technological changes helped bring about the decline of America's partisan press. After the invention of the telegraph in 1837, editors could receive timely information on developments in Washington and the state capital, and they had less reason to fill their pages with partisan harangues.[7] Another major innovation was the high-speed rotary press (invented in 1815), a breakthrough that enabled publishers to print their newspapers rapidly and cheaply and thus to increase their profit potential.[8] Increased circulation and revenues gradually freed newspapers from their dependence on government and parties.

By the late nineteenth century, several American newspapers were printing 100,000 or more copies a day and were getting rich from advertising revenues. The period marked the height in newspapers' power and the nadir in their sense of public responsibility.[9] A new style of reporting—"yellow journalism"—had emerged as a way of boosting circulation.[10] The "yellow"

Yellow journalism was characterized by its sensationalism. William Randolph Hearst's *New York Journal* whipped up public support for a war in Cuba with Spain through inflammatory reporting on the sinking of the battleship *Maine* in Havana Harbor in 1898. (Historical Pictures Service.)

press—so called because some of these newspapers were printed on cheap yellow paper—emphasized "a shrieking, gaudy, sensation-loving, devil-may-care kind of journalism which lured the reader by any possible means."[11] A circulation battle between William Randolph Hearst's *New York Journal* and Joseph Pulitzer's *New York World* is believed to have contributed to the outbreak of the Spanish-American War through sensational (and largely inaccurate) reports about the cruelty of Spanish rule in Cuba. A young Frederic Remington (who later became a noted painter and sculptor), working as a news artist for Hearst, planned to return home because Cuba appeared calm and safe; but Hearst cabled back, "Please remain. You furnish the pictures and I'll furnish the war."[12]

The excesses of yellow journalism led some publishers to consider how the news could be reported more responsibly. One step they took was to separate the newspaper's advertising department from its news department, thus reducing the influence of advertisers on news content. A second development was a new model of reporting called **objective journalism,** which was based on the reporting of "facts" rather than opinions and was "fair" in that it presented both sides of partisan debate.[13]

A chief advocate of this new form of journalism was Adolph Ochs of *The New York Times*. Ochs told his reporters that he "wanted as little partisanship as possible . . . as few judgments as possible."[14] The *Times's* approach to reporting appealed particularly to educated readers, and by the early twentieth century it had already acquired its reputation as the country's best newspaper. Objective reporting was also promoted through newly formed journalism schools. Among the first of these professional schools were those at Columbia University and the University of Missouri. The Columbia School of Journalism opened in 1912 with a grant of $2 million from Pulitzer.

Objective journalism is still a mainstay of daily news coverage. Although most newspapers have a partisan bias on their editorial pages, nearly all of them accord the Republican and Democratic parties nearly equal treatment on their news pages. From another perspective, however, the influence of objective journalism is waning. Newspapers increasingly rely on an **interpretive style of reporting,** in which the journalist's job is to analyze and explain developments rather than merely report them. As a result, newspaper coverage has become increasingly opinionated (see Figure 10-1). The older form of objective journalism (called *descriptive reporting*, because of its straightforward description of events) required that reporters stick to the "facts." The newer interpretive style allows them to speculate on what the facts mean. As we will see later in the chapter, interpretive reporting has

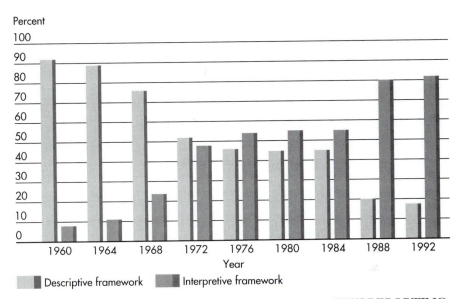

Percent

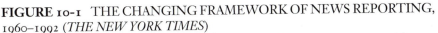

FIGURE 10-1 THE CHANGING FRAMEWORK OF NEWS REPORTING, 1960–1992 (*THE NEW YORK TIMES*)
In the 1960s the vast majority of news reports were descriptive in nature; today, the vast majority are interpretive in nature. Source: Thomas E. Patterson, *Out of Order* (New York: Vintage, 1994), 82.

greatly increased journalists' ability to shape the news to fit their own views, including their skeptical opinion of politicians' motives and accomplishments.

The Development of the Broadcast Media

RADIO AND TELEVISION: THE TRULY NATIONAL MEDIA   Until the early twentieth century, the print media were the only form of mass communication. Within a few decades, however, there were hundreds of radio stations throughout the nation. Radio represented a revolutionary change in communication. It allowed political leaders to bypass journalists and communicate directly with the people. Radio was also the first truly *national* mass medium. Newspapers had a local audience, whereas the newly formed radio networks (such as NBC) could reach millions of citizens across the country simultaneously.

Television followed radio, and by the late 1950s more than 90 percent of American homes had a television set. The political potential of television was evident as early as 1952, when 17 million homes tuned in to the national Republican and Democratic party conventions.[15] However, television newscasts of the 1950s were brief, lasting no more than fifteen minutes, and relied on news gathered by other organizations, particularly the Associated Press and other wire services. In the early 1960s, the three commercial networks—CBS, NBC, and ABC—expanded their evening newscasts to thirty minutes, and their audience ratings increased.[16] Simultaneously, they increased the size and funding of their news divisions, and television soon became the principal news medium of national politics.

Today, television provides a twenty-four-hour forum of political news and information. The advent of the Cable News Network (CNN) and C-SPAN in the late 1970s brought Americans round-the-clock public affairs communication. Television talk shows, such as *Larry King Live*, have broadened the range of choices available to politically interested viewers. A parallel development is the growth in the number of radio talk shows. Nearly

Franklin D. Roosevelt was the first president to make effective use of the radio to communicate directly with the American people. He broadcast a series of "fireside chats" that reached millions of listeners across the country. (Brown Brothers)

a fifth of the American public claims to listen regularly to a radio talk show, most of which are conservative in orientation. The undisputed king of the radio talk-show circuit is Rush Limbaugh, who is widely renowned for his blistering attacks on liberal politicians and policies.

Even more so than their newspaper counterparts, television journalists rely on an interpretive style of reporting. The reason is that television journalists use a narrative or storytelling mode in order to appeal to an audience accustomed to entertainment programming. "Facts" alone do not tell a story; they have to be interpreted in a way that makes them into a story. Reuven Frank, a network executive and pioneer in television journalism, once told his correspondents: "Every news story should . . . display the attributes of fiction, of drama. It should have structure and conflict, problem and denouement, rising action and falling action, a beginning, a middle and an end."[17]

GOVERNMENT LICENSING AND REGULATION OF BROADCASTERS

At first the government did not carefully regulate broadcasting. The result was chaos. Nearby stations often used the same or adjacent radio frequencies, interfering with each other's transmissions. Finally, in 1934, Congress passed the Communications Act, which requires that broadcasters be licensed and meet certain performance standards. The Federal Communications Commission (FCC) was established to administer the act and to develop regulations pertaining to such matters as signal strength, advertising rates and access, and political coverage.

The principle of scarcity justifies the licensing and regulation of broadcast media. Because the number of available broadcasting frequencies is limited, those few individuals who are granted a broadcasting license are expected to serve the public interest in addition to their own. In principle, licensing is a means of controlling broadcasting. If a station fails to comply with federal broadcast regulations, the FCC can withdraw its license. However, the FCC seldom even threatens revocation, for fear of being accused of infringing on freedom of the press. A broadcast station can apply for renewal of its license by postcard and is virtually guaranteed FCC approval, which covers seven years for radio and five for television.

Because broadcast frequencies are a scarce resource, licensees are required by law to be somewhat evenhanded during election campaigns. Section 315 of the Communications Act imposes on broadcasters an "equal-time" restriction, which means that they cannot sell or give airtime to a political candidate without granting equal opportunities to other candidates running for the same office. (Election debates are an exception; broadcasters can sponsor them and limit participation to nominees of the Republican and Democratic parties only.) During campaigns broadcasters are also required to make airtime available for purchase by candidates at the lowest rate charged to commercial advertisers.

FREEDOM AND CONFORMITY IN THE U.S. NEWS MEDIA

Some democracies impose significant legal restraints on the press. The media in Britain are barred from reporting on anything that the government has labeled an "official secret," and the nation's tough libel laws inhibit the press from publishing unsubstantiated allegations about an individual.

In the United States, as we saw in Chapter 4, the First Amendment gives the press substantial protection. The courts have held that government cannot block publication of a news story unless it can convincingly demonstrate in court that the information would jeopardize national security. U.S. libel laws also strongly protect the press. A public figure who is attacked through the media cannot collect libel damages unless it can be demonstrated that the news organization was false in its accusations and knowingly or recklessly careless in its search for the truth.

Moreover, the U.S. government provides the news media with substantial economic support. Newspapers and magazines have a special postal rate that helps them keep their circulation costs low, and broadcasters pay only a few dollars annually in license fees. Such policies have contributed to the development of a truly enormous news industry in the United States: 1,600 daily newspapers, 8,500 weeklies, 9,500 radio stations, 5 national television news networks, 850 local television stations, and 10,500 cable television systems.[18]

The audience reach of leading news organizations is substantial. Each weekday evening, more than 20 million Americans tune into a network newscast. *Time* and *Newsweek* magazines reach over 3 million readers each week. *U.S. News & World Report*'s weekly circulation exceeds 2 million copies. *The New York Times*, *The Wall Street Journal*, *USA Today*, and the *Los Angeles Times* have daily circulations exceeding 1 million readers. Another three-dozen newspapers have circulations in excess of 250,000 readers. The average daily circulation of America's newspapers is roughly 50 million; on

Sunday, newspaper circulation jumps to more than 60 million[19] (see box: States in the Nation).

In view of the great number and the freedom of news organizations in the United States, it might be expected that Americans would have a lot of choice in the news they receive. However, the opposite is true. Each day, newspapers and broadcast stations from coast to coast tend to highlight the same national news stories and to interpret them in similar ways. Any number of terms—pack journalism, groupthink, media concentration—have been used to describe the fact that news reporting is fairly homogeneous.

The basic reason the news is pretty much the same everywhere is that America's reporters, unlike their counterparts in some European democracies, do not take sides in partisan disputes. They do sometimes differ on which facts, events, and issues are more important than others, but these polite disagreements are a far cry from the disputes and diversity that characterized the nineteenth-century partisan press.

Of course, today's news organizations differ in the way they tell a given story. Broadcast news tends to be, in effect, headline news with pictures. A thirty-minute network news broadcast typically presents a dozen or so stories in the twenty-two minutes allotted to news content (the other eight minutes being devoted to commercials). Newspapers have the space to present news developments in greater depth; some, like *The New York Times* (which labels itself "the newspaper of record"), provide substantial detail. The reporting styles of news organizations also vary. Although most of them present the news in an understated way, others tend toward sensationalism. For example, when Jeffrey Dahmer, a convicted murderer who had cannibalized his victims, was himself murdered in a Wisconsin prison in 1994, the *New York Post* gave its whole front page to the headline: "Death of a Monster." *The New York Times*, in contrast, gave the story a standard-sized front-page headline, "Jeffrey Dahmer, Multiple Killer, Is Bludgeoned to Death in Prison." Such differences in approach, however, do not disguise the fact that most news organizations tell their audiences the same stories each day.

Domination of News Production

Another reason for the lack of diversity in national news reporting is that a small number of news organizations generate most of it. The quintessential case of concentrated news production is radio, with its "canned" network-provided news; almost no local radio station in the country produces its own national news reports.

States in the Nation

Newspaper Readership

Newspaper circulation is not particularly high in the United States. The dramatic exception is Washington, D.C., where 1.55 newspapers are sold for every resident. Virginia (0.40 papers per resident), New York (0.38), and Massachusetts (0.32) also rank fairly high. In other states, the average newspaper circulation deviates only slightly from the national average.

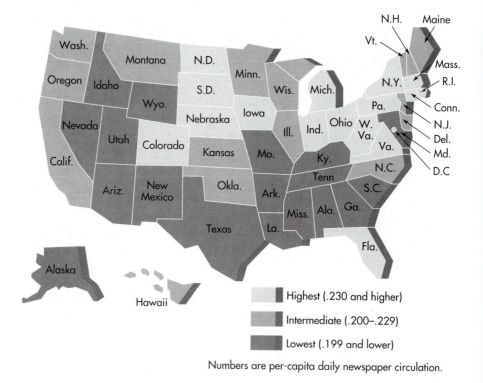

Highest (.230 and higher)

Intermediate (.200–.229)

Lowest (.199 and lower)

Numbers are per-capita daily newspaper circulation.

SOURCE: Editor and Publisher International Yearbook, 1992.

The Associated Press (AP) is the major producer of news stories. It has 300 full-time reporters stationed throughout the country and the world to gather news stories, which are relayed by satellite to subscribing newspapers and broadcast stations. More than 95 percent of the nation's dailies are serviced by AP, and some also subscribe to other wire services, such as Reuters and the New York Times.[20] Smaller dailies lack the resources to gather news outside their own localities and thus depend on wire service reports for most of their national and international coverage.

Television news production is similarly dominated by just a few organizations.[21] Six networks—ABC, CBS, NBC, PBS, Fox, and CNN—generate most of the news coverage of national and international politics. Local stations rely on video transmissions fed to them by the networks.

News Values and Imperatives

Competitive pressures also lead the producers of news to report the same stories. No major news organization wants to miss a story that the others are reporting.[22] The networks, wire services, and a few elite dailies, including *The New York Times, Washington Post, Wall Street Journal, Los Angeles Times,* and *Chicago Tribune,* establish a national standard of story selection. Whenever one of them highlights a story, others jump on the bandwagon. The chief trendsetter among news-gathering organizations is *The New York Times,* which has been described as "the bulletin board" for other major newspapers, newsmagazines, and television networks.[23]

The imperatives of the fast pace of daily journalism also tend to make the news homogeneous.[24] Journalists have the task each day of filling a newspaper or broadcast with stories. Their job is to produce an edition every twenty-four hours. Thus editors assign reporters to such beats as the White House and Congress, which can be relied on for a steady supply of news. On these beats the reporters of various news organizations see and hear the same things, exchange views on what is important, and, not surprisingly, produce similar news stories.

Finally, shared professional values guide journalists in their search for news.[25] Reporters are on the lookout for aspects of situations that lend themselves to interesting news stories—novel, colorful, and compelling developments. Long practice at storytelling leads journalists to develop a common understanding of what the news is. After the White House press corps has listened to a presidential speech, for example, nearly all of the journalists in attendance are in agreement on what was most newsworthy about the speech, often only a single statement within it.

THE NEWS MEDIA AS LINK: ROLES THE PRESS CAN AND CANNOT PERFORM

When the objective model of reporting came to dominate American news coverage, the relationship between the press and the public was fundamentally altered. The nineteenth-century partisan press gave its readers overt cues as to how to evaluate political issues and leaders. In the presidential election campaign of 1896, the *San Francisco Call* devoted 1,075 column-inches of photographs to the Republican ticket of McKinley–Hobart and only 11 inches to the Democrats, Bryan and Sewell.[26] Many European newspapers still function in this way, guiding their readers by applying partisan or ideological values to current events. The *Daily Telegraph*, for example, is an unofficial but fiercely loyal mouthpiece of Britain's Conservative party (see box: How the United States Compares).

In contrast, U.S. news organizations do not routinely and consistently take sides in partisan conflict. Their main task is to report and analyze events. The media are thus very different from political parties and interest groups, the other major links between the public and its leaders. The media are driven by the search for interesting and revealing stories; parties and interest groups exist to articulate political positions.

This distinction provides a basis for determining what roles the media can and cannot be expected to perform. The press is capable of fulfilling only those public responsibilities that are compatible with journalistic values: the signaler role, the common-carrier role, and the watchdog role. The media are less successful in their attempts to perform a fourth, politically oriented role: that of public representative.

The Signaler Role

As journalists see it, one of their responsibilities is to play the **signaler role,** alerting the public to important developments as soon as possible after they happen: a state visit to Washington by a foreign leader, a bill that has just been passed by Congress, a change in the nation's unemployment level, a terrorist bombing in a foreign capital.

The signaler role is one that the American media perform relatively well. The press is poised to converge on any fastbreaking major news event anywhere in the nation and nearly anywhere in the world. For instance, as the United States prepared to intervene forcefully in Haiti in 1994, dozens of U.S. journalists went to that trouble-ridden Caribbean nation to report from the scene. The NBC and CBS networks even sent their news anchors,

HOW THE UNITED STATES COMPARES

Partisan Neutrality as a News Value

In the nineteenth century, the United States had a partisan press. Journalists were partisan actors, and news was a blend of reporting and advocacy. This type of reporting gradually gave way to a model of journalism that emphasizes the "facts" and covers the two parties more or less equally.

European news organizations are less committed to partisan neutrality. Many European newspapers are aligned with a party, and although they focus on events, their coverage has a partisan component. In Great Britain, for example, the *Daily Telegraph* often serves as a voice of the Conservative party, while the *Guardian* favors the liberal side. Broadcasters in most European countries are politically neutral by law and practice, but there are exceptions, as in the case of the French and Italian broadcasters.

The difference between the U.S. and European media is evident in a five-country survey which asked journalists whether they agreed or disagreed with the statement: "Journalists should *not* try to influence the outcome of party conflict."

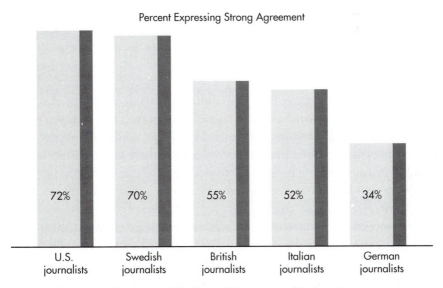

Percent Expressing Strong Agreement

U.S. journalists	Swedish journalists	British journalists	Italian journalists	German journalists
72%	70%	55%	52%	34%

SOURCE: Thomas E. Patterson, Media and Democracy Project, in progress.

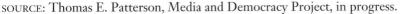

Through their signaler role, the news media alert the public to important developments in the nation and the world. Pictured here is CBS News anchorman Dan Rather, reporting live from Port Au Prince as U.S. military troops arrive in Haiti in 1994. (Haviv/SABA)

Tom Brokaw and Dan Rather, despite a possible risk to their personal safety.

The media are particularly well suited to signal developments from Washington. More than half of all reported national news emanates from the nation's capital, most of it from the White House and Congress. Altogether, more than 10,000 people in Washington work in the news business. The key players are the leading correspondents of the television networks and major newspapers, the heads of the Washington news bureaus, and a few top editors.[27]

The press, in its capacity as signaler, has the power to focus the public's attention. The term **agenda setting** has been used to describe the media's ability to influence what is on people's minds. By covering the same events, problems, issues, and leaders—simply by giving them space or time in the news—the media place them on the public agenda. The press, as Bernard Cohen notes, "may not be successful much of the time in telling people what to think, but it is stunningly successful in telling them what to think about."[28] This influence is most obvious in such situations as the Gulf war, an event that quickly received widespread attention. When the allies started their air raid on Baghdad, the broadcast networks began an unprecedented forty-two hours of continuous coverage. News of the war was almost inescapable.

The Common-Carrier Role

Journalists base many of their news stories on the words of public officials. The press thus plays what is labeled a **common-carrier role,** providing a channel through which political leaders can reach the public. The importance of this role to officials and citizens alike is obvious. Citizens cannot very well support or oppose a leader's plans and actions if they do not know about them. And leaders need news coverage if they are to get the public's attention.

Not surprisingly, political leaders make a great effort to get coverage. They hold news conferences, issue press releases, and stage events in an effort to garner the media's attention.[29] Indeed, national news is mainly about the actions of political leaders and institutions, as is reflected in the hundreds of reporters who station themselves regularly at the Capitol and White House.

Officials try to get the most favorable news coverage they can. For example, the White House Press Office and the White House Office of Communication try to shape information in a way favorable to the president. Sometimes they succeed in placing their "spin" (that is, the president's interpretation) on the media's coverage of events.

However, the press today is less deferential to political leaders than in the past. Even though the president and Congress can expect coverage, the press increasingly places its own "spin" on these stories. Because of their increased celebrity status, their heightened skepticism of politicians since Vietnam and Watergate, and the greater latitude afforded them by the interpretive style of reporting, journalists have become accustomed to not only covering what newsmakers say but having their own say as well. During the 1996 presidential campaign, as the Clinton White House was trying to focus coverage on the president's policy accomplishments and plans, the press was devoting much of its coverage to Whitewater and other developments that reflected unfavorably on the president.

In fact, the news today is as much journalist-centered as it is newsmaker-centered. For every minute that the presidential candidates spoke on the network newscasts during coverage of the 1996 campaign, for example, the journalists who were covering them talked for five minutes.[30] It was once the case that a candidate's "sound bite" (the length of time within a television story that the candidate speaks without interruption) was about forty-five seconds in length on average.[31] In recent campaigns, the average sound bite has been less than ten seconds, which is barely enough time for the candidate to utter a full sentence (see Figure 10-2).

The Watchdog Role

Traditionally the American press has accepted responsibility for protecting the public from deceitful, careless, incompetent, and corrupt officials.[32] In this **watchdog role** the press stands ready to expose any official who violates accepted legal, ethical, and performance standards.

The most notable exercise of the watchdog role in recent decades took place during the Watergate scandal. Bob Woodward and Carl Bernstein of the *Washington Post* spent months uncovering evidence that high-ranking officials in the Nixon White House were lying about their role in the burglary of the Democratic National Committee's headquarters and in the subsequent

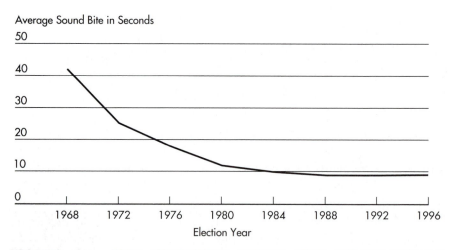

FIGURE 10-2 THE SHRINKING SOUND BITE OF TELEVISION ELECTION COVERAGE
The average length of time that presidential candidates are shown speaking without interruption on television newscasts has declined sharply in recent elections.
Source: Adapted from Daniel C. Hallin, "Sound Bite News: Television Coverage of Elections 1968–1988," *Journal of Communication* 42 (Spring 1992): 6. The 1992 and 1996 data were provided by the Center for Media and Public Affairs.

cover-up. Virtually all of the nation's media picked up on the *Post*'s revelations. Nixon was forced to resign, as was his attorney general, John Mitchell. The Watergate episode is a dramatic reminder that a vigilant press is one of society's best safeguards against abuses of political power.

There is an inherent tension between the watchdog role and the common-carrier role. The watchdog role demands that the journalist maintain a skeptical view of political leaders and keep them at a distance. The common-carrier role requires the journalist to maintain close ties with political leaders. In the period before Watergate, the common-carrier role was clearly the dominant orientation. It perhaps still is, but journalists have become increasingly critical of political leaders and institutions.

Some of this criticism revolves around scandals, such as the Iran-Contra affair (President Reagan) and the Whitewater affair (President Clinton). Most of the criticism, however, is leveled at the day-to-day conduct of politics. Journalists have become intent on publicizing the missteps of political leaders. Given the enormous size of the U.S. government, there is plenty to criticize if journalists want to focus on it. The media's preference for "bad news" can be seen, for example, in the fact that negative coverage of presi-

The president's views are always sought after by the press. Here, President Clinton addresses a phalanx of reporters armed with cameras, microphones, and recorders. (Jim Bourg/Reuters/Bettmann)

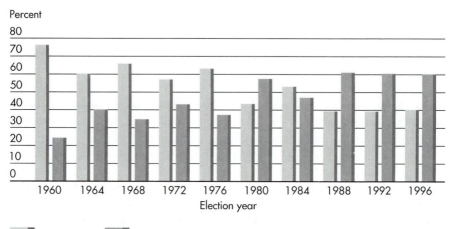

Percent

Good News Bad News

FIGURE 10-3 "BAD NEWS" COVERAGE OF PRESIDENTIAL CANDIDATES COMPARED TO "GOOD NEWS" COVERAGE, 1960–1996 In the 1960s, candidates received largely favorable news coverage; today, their coverage is mostly negative. Source: Thomas E. Patterson, *Out of Order* (New York: Vintage, 1994), 20, for 1960–1992 coverage; Center for Media and Public Affairs, for 1996.

dential candidates has risen steadily in recent decades and now exceeds their positive coverage (see Figure 10-3).

"Bad news" characterizes the coverage of Democrats and Republicans alike. Although surveys indicate that most journalists lean toward the Democratic party in their personal beliefs, studies have found partisan bias to be a relatively small factor in political coverage.[33] Other influences, including the norm of objectivity, counterbalance the effect of partisanship on journalists' news decisions. On the other hand, journalists' skeptical view of politicians is not offset by other factors. There is no rule that limits negativity, and thus the real bias of American journalists is a tendency to be critical of nearly everything and everybody.[34] Coverage of the Democratic-controlled Congress of 1993–1994 by the national media was nearly 70 percent negative; when the Congress shifted to Republican hands in 1995–1996, its coverage, too, was nearly 70 percent negative in tone.[35]

Critics argue that the press has gone too far in its search for bad news, claiming that it now faults nearly everything that politicians say and do, thereby undermining the public trust upon which effective leadership is built. Journalists claim they are merely doing their job—that the public is better served by a highly skeptical press than a compliant one.

The Public Representative Role

Traditionally, the **public representative role**—that of spokesperson for and advocate of the public—has belonged to political leaders, political institutions, and political organizations. Today, however, many reporters believe they also have a mandate to represent the public. "[Our] chief duty," newscaster Roger Mudd claims, "is to put before the nation its unfinished business."[36]

Although the press has to some degree always acted as a stand-in for the people, the desire of journalists to play the role of public advocate has increased significantly since the 1960s.[37] As journalists' status rose, they became more assertive, a tendency sharpened by the trend toward interpretive reporting. Vietnam and Watergate also contributed to the change; these events convinced many journalists that their judgments were superior to those of political leaders.

Nevertheless, there are at least two basic reasons for concluding that journalists are not nearly as well suited as political leaders to the role of public representative. First, the news media are not subject to the level of public accountability required of a public representative. Political institutions are made responsible to the public by a formal mechanism of accountability—elections. The vote gives officeholders a reason to act in the majority's interest, and it offers citizens an opportunity to boot from office anyone they feel has failed them. Thousands of elected officials have lost their jobs this way. The public has no comparable hold over the press. Journalists are neither chosen by the people nor removable by them. Irate citizens can stop watching a news program or buying a newspaper that angers them, but no major daily newspaper or television station has gone out of business as a result.

A second obstacle to journalists' attempts to play the role of public representative is that representation requires a point of view. Politics is essentially the mobilization of bias—that is, it involves the representation of particular values and interests. Political parties and interest groups, as we saw in Chapters 8 and 9, exist to represent particular interests in society. But what political interests do the media represent? CBS News executive Richard Salant once said that his reporters covered stories "from nobody's point of view."[38] What he was saying in effect was that journalists do not consistently represent the political concerns of any segment of society. They respond to news opportunities, not to political interests. Above all, they prize good stories.

The O. J. Simpson story is a prime example. His trial received more news coverage in 1994–1995 than any public policy issue, foreign or domestic.

Robert Shapiro, one of O. J. Simpson's lawyers, arrives at the Los Angeles courthouse. The Simpson trial was one of the most heavily covered news events in U.S. history. (Gilles Mingasson/Gamma-Liaison)

Judged by the media's priorities, Simpson's fate was more important than health care, unemployment, Haiti, drug abuse, education, and every other national problem. Murray Edelman said there is a "Gresham's law" of news prominence: "Dramatic incidents involving individuals in the limelight displace attention from the larger [issues]."

The restless search of the press for the riveting story works against its intention to provide citizens a clear understanding of their stake in policy choices. It is a difficult job to formulate society's problems in a way that allows citizens to understand and act upon them. The news media cannot do the job consistently well. The journalist Walter Lippmann put it plainly when he said:

> The press is no substitute for [political] institutions. It is like the beam of a searchlight that moves restlessly about, bringing one episode and then another out of darkness into vision. Men cannot do the work of the world by this light alone. They cannot govern society by episodes, incidents, and interruptions.[39]

ORGANIZING THE PUBLIC IN THE MEDIA AGE

Lippmann's point was not that news organizations are somehow inferior to political organizations but that each has a different role and responsibility in society. Democracy cannot operate effectively without a free press that acts effectively in its signaler, common-carrier, and watchdog roles. To keep in touch with one another and with the government, citizens must have access to timely and uncensored news about public affairs. In other words, the media must do their job well if democratic government is to succeed. However, the media cannot also be asked to do the job of political institutions. For reasons already noted, the task is beyond the media's capacity.

As previous chapters have emphasized, the problem of citizen influence is the problem of organizing the public so that people can act together effectively. The news media merely appear to solve this problem. The fact that millions of people each day receive the same news about their government does not mold them into an organized community. The news creates a pseudo-community: citizens feel they are part of a functioning whole until they try to act upon their news awareness. The futility of media-centered democracy was dramatized in the movie *Network* when its central character, a television anchorman, became enraged at the nation's political leadership and urged his viewers to go to their windows and yell, "I'm mad as hell and I'm not going to take it anymore!" Citizens heeded his instructions, but the main effect was to raise the network's ratings. It was not clear what officials in Washington were expected to do about several million people leaning out their windows and shouting a vague slogan at the top of their lungs. The film vividly illustrated the fact that the news can raise public consciousness as a prelude to organization, but the news itself cannot organize the public in any meaningful way. When public opinion on an issue is already formed, the media can serve as a channel for the expression of that opinion. But when society's choices are in their formative stage, the media are not an adequate guide to the actions that should be taken or the priority they should be given.

SUMMARY

In the nation's first century, the press was allied closely with the political parties and helped the parties mobilize public opinion. Gradually the press freed itself from this relationship and developed a form of reporting, known as objective journalism, that emphasizes the fair and accurate reporting of newsworthy developments. The foundation of modern American news rests on the presentation and evaluation of significant events, not on the advocacy of partisan ideas. The nation's news organizations do not differ greatly in their reporting; broadcast stations and newspapers throughout the country emphasize many of the same events, issues, and personalities, following the lead of the major broadcast networks, a few elite newspapers, and the wire services.

The press performs four basic roles in a free society. In their signaler role, journalists communicate information to the public about events and problems that they consider important, relevant, and therefore newsworthy. The press also serves as a common carrier, in that it provides political leaders with a channel for addressing the public. Third, the press acts as a public protector, or watchdog, by exposing deceitful, careless, or corrupt officials. The American media can and, to a significant degree, do perform these roles adequately.

The press is less well suited, however, to the other role it plays, that of public representative. This role requires a consistent political viewpoint and public accountability, neither of which the press possesses. The media cannot be a substitute for effective political institutions. The press's strength lies ultimately in its capacity to inform the public, not in its attempts to serve as their representative.

MAJOR CONCEPTS

agenda setting	partisan press
common-carrier role	press (news media)
interpretive style of reporting	public representative role
news	signaler role
objective journalism	watchdog role

SUGGESTED READINGS

Altheide, David L., and Robert P. Snow. *Media Worlds in the Postjournalism Era.* New York: Aldine de Gruyter, 1991. An analysis of the mass media and culture, including the conditions that lead journalists to present a version of reality that serves the media's own ends.

Bagdikian, Ben H. *The Media Monopoly,* 4th ed. Boston: Beacon, 1992. An examination of the growing power of the press, including tendencies toward monopolies of ownership and news production.

Fallows, James. *Breaking the News: How the Media Undermine American Democracy.* New York: Pantheon, 1996. A leading journalist's critique of his profession.

Iyengar, Shanto. *Is Anyone Responsible? How Television Frames Issues.* Chicago: University of Chicago Press, 1991. A careful study of how television's presentation of events affects the audience's response.

Lichter, S. Robert, and Richard E. Noyes. *Good Intentions Make Bad News: Why Americans Hate Campaign Journalism,* updated ed. Lanham, Md.: Rowman & Littlefield, 1997. A critical analysis of election coverage.

Maltese, John Anthony. *Spin Control: The White House Office of Communications and the Management of Presidential News.* Chapel Hill: University of North Carolina Press, 1994. An assessment of how presidents attempt to manage news coverage.

Patterson, Thomas E. *Out of Order.* New York: Vintage, 1994. An analysis of how election news coverage has changed in recent decades.

Sabato, Larry J. *Feeding Frenzy: How Attack Journalism Has Transformed American Politics.* New York: Free Press, 1991. An argument that recent tendencies in journalism are warping the democratic process.

Summers, Mark Wahlgren. *The Press Gang: Newspapers and Politics, 1863–1878.* Chapel Hill: University of North Carolina Press, 1994. A vivid portrayal of the press's transformation from partisan values to journalistic ones.

Walsh, Kenneth T. *Feeding the Beast: The White House versus the Press.* New York: Random House, 1996. A journalist's view of the relationship between the president and the press.

Reading 10

The Miscast Institution

THOMAS E. PATTERSON

The United States is the only democracy that organizes its national election campaign around the news media. Even if the media did not want the responsibility for organizing the campaign, it is theirs by virtue of an election system built upon entrepreneurial candidacies, floating voters, free-wheeling interest groups, and weak political parties.

It is an unworkable arrangement: the press is not equipped to give order and direction to a presidential campaign. And when we expect it to do so, we set ourselves up for yet another turbulent election.

The campaign is chaotic largely because the press is not a political institution and has no capacity for organizing the election in a coherent manner. The news can always be made better. Election coverage in 1992 was a marked improvement over 1988, and in a few respects the best coverage ever. The journalist Carl Bernstein, reflecting a widely shared opinion among members of the press, declared that 1992 coverage closely approximated "the ideal of what good reporting has always been: the best obtainable version of the truth."

Yet news and truth are not the same thing. The news is a highly refracted version of reality. The press magnifies certain aspects of politics and downplays others, which are often more central to issues of governing. During the last six weeks of the 1992 campaign, the economy got a lot of attention from the press, but it still received less coverage than campaign- trail controversies, including disputes over Clinton's draft record, Perot's on-again, off-again candidacy and spats with the press, and Bush's wild charges ("the Ozone Man," "bozos").

The attention that Clinton's trip to the Soviet Union while a graduate student at Oxford received in the closing weeks of the campaign was in itself revealing of the gap between news values and the nation's real concerns. When Bush questioned Clinton's trip on CNN's "Larry King Live," it exploded into the headlines in a way that policy issues seldom do. News of Clinton's Moscow visit overshadowed such October issues as developments on the North American Free Trade Agreement, CIA revelations on the U.S. government's role in the arming of Iraq, and a change in Clinton's health-care proposal.

The press's restless search for the riveting story works against its intention to provide the voters with a reliable picture of the campaign. It is a formidable job to present society's problems in ways that voters can understand and act upon. The news media cannot do the job consistently well. Walter Lippmann put it plainly when he said that a press-based politics "is not workable. And when you consider the nature of news, it is not even thinkable."

Lippmann's point was not that news organizations are somehow inferior to political organizations but that each has a different role and responsibility in society. Democracy cannot operate successfully without a free press that is acting effectively within its sphere. The problem arises when the press is expected to perform the job of political institutions as well. . . .

The belief that the press can substitute for political institutions is widespread. Many journalists, perhaps most of them, assume they can do it effectively. Scholars who study the media also accept the idea that the press can organize elections. Every four years, they suggest that the campaign could be made coherent if the media would only report it differently.

However, the press merely appears to have the capacity to organize the voters' alternatives in a coherent way. . . . The press is in the news business, not the business of politics, and because of this, its norms and imperatives are not those required for the effective organization of electoral coalitions and debate. Journalistic values and political values are at odds with each other.

The proper organization of electoral opinion requires an institution with certain characteristics. It must be capable of seeing the larger picture—of looking at the world as a whole and not in small pieces. It must have incentives that cause it to identify and organize those interests that are making demands for policy representation. And it must be accountable for its choices, so that the public can reward it when satisfied and force amendments when dissatisfied.

The press has none of these characteristics. The media has its special strengths, but they do not include these strengths.

The press is a very different kind of organization from the political party, whose role it acquired. A party is driven by the steady force of its traditions and constituent interests, which is why the Democratic leadership in 1952 chose Stevenson, a New Deal liberal, over Kefauver, a border-state populist. The press, in contrast, is "a restless beacon." Its concern is the new, the unusual, and the sensational. Its agenda shifts abruptly when a new development breaks.

The party has the incentive—the possibility of acquiring political power—to give order and voice to society's values. Its raison d'être is to articulate interests and to forge them into a winning coalition. The press has no such incentive and no such purpose. Its objective is the discovery and development of good stories. Television-news executive Richard Salant once said that his reporters covered stories from "nobody's point of view." What he was saying, in effect, was that journalists are driven by news opportunities, not by political values.

The press is also not politically accountable. The political party is made accountable by a formal mechanism—elections. The vote gives officeholders a reason to act in the majority's interest, and it offers citizens an opportunity to boot from office anyone they feel has failed them. Thousands of elected officials have lost their jobs this way. The public has no comparable hold on the press. Journalists are neither chosen by the people nor removable by them. . . .

Other democracies have recognized the inappropriateness of press-based elections. Although national voting in all Western democracies is media-centered in the sense that candidates depend primarily on mass communication to reach the voters, no other democracy has a system in which the press fills the role traditionally played by the political party. Journalists in other democracies actively participate in the campaign process, but their efforts take place within an electoral structure built around political institutions. In the United States, however, national elections are referendums in which the candidates stand alone before the electorate and have no choice but to filter their appeals through the lens of the news media.

SOURCE: Thomas E. Patterson, *Out of Order* (New York: Knopf, 1993). Reprinted by permission.
Thomas E. Patterson is the Bradlee Professor of Government and the Press at Howard University.

CHAPTER ELEVEN

Congress

There are really two Congresses, not just one. Often these two Congresses are widely separated; the tightly knit, complex world of Capitol Hill is a long way from the world of [the member's district or state]—not only in miles, but in perspective and outlook as well.

ROGER DAVIDSON AND WALTER OLESZEK[1]

I N 1993 CONGRESS enacted the North American Free Trade Agreement (NAFTA), which lowers trade barriers between the United States, Canada, and Mexico.

Initially, NAFTA appeared to be heading for defeat in Congress. Although the legislation had the support of the Clinton administration and most of the congressional leadership, its likely impact on the nation's economy was subject to dispute. Economic projections indicated that NAFTA was likely to benefit the nation as a whole but would also result in job and business losses in some areas. This prospect convinced a majority in Congress to withhold their support from the legislation; they did not want to vote for a bill that in the end might hurt the local economies of the states and districts they represented. Intense bargaining ensued between the legislations's supporters and those members of Congress who were willing to consider a vote for NAFTA in return for concessions that would protect their constituents. One such deal exempted citrus growers from a restrictive provision of the trade agreement, which was enough to persuade several Florida legislators to vote for it. In the end, the votes to assure NAFTA's passage were obtained, but at a cost to the free trade principle that underlay the legislation.

The story of the NAFTA vote illustrates the dual nature of Congress: it is both a lawmaking institution for the country and a representative assembly for states and districts.[2] Members of Congress have both an individual duty to serve the interests of their separate constituencies and a collective

Like all other members of Congress, Senator Dianne Feinstein of California tries to win reelection by serving the interests of her constituents. Here, Feinstein talks to the press about proposed military base closings in California. She pledged support for the California communities and workers adversely affected by cutbacks in defense spending. (Wide World Photos)

duty to protect the interests of the country as a whole. Attention to constituency interests is the common denominator of a national institution in which each member must please the voters back home in order to win reelection.[3]

This chapter examines Congress, beginning with congressional election and organization, and concluding with congressional policymaking. The following points are emphasized in this chapter:

* *Congressional elections tend to have a strong local orientation and to favor incumbents, who (particularly House members) have a substantial advantage in election campaigns.*

* *Although party leaders in Congress provide collective leadership, the work of Congress is done mainly through its committees and subcommittees, each of which has its separate leadership and policy jurisdiction.*

* *Congress lacks the direction and organization required for the development of comprehensive national policies, but it is well organized to handle policies*

of relatively narrow scope. At times, Congress takes the lead on broad national issues but ordinarily does not do so.

★ *Congress's policymaking role is based on three major functions: lawmaking, representation, and oversight.*

CONGRESS AS A CAREER: ELECTION TO CONGRESS

In the nation's first century, service in the Congress was not a career for most of its members. Before 1900 at least a third and sometimes as many as half of the seats in Congress changed hands at each election. Most members left voluntarily. Because travel was slow and arduous, serving in the nation's capital required them to spend months away from their families. And because the national government was not the center of power and politics that it is today, many politicians preferred to serve in state capitals.

The modern Congress is very different. Most of its members are professional politicians, and a seat in the U.S. Senate or House is as far as most of them can expect to go in politics. The pay (about $135,000 a year) is reasonably good, and the prestige of their office is substantial, particularly if they serve in the Senate. An extended stay in Congress is what most of its members aspire to attain.[4]

Incumbents have a good chance of being reelected (see Figure 11-1). They are not a sure bet to win again, but the odds are on their side.[5] In the last decade, the reelection rate of House incumbents seeking another term has exceeded 90 percent, as has the reelection rate of Senate incumbents.[6]

These figures overestimate somewhat an incumbent's chances of reelection. Some incumbents retire from Congress when faced with a campaign they fear they will lose. Moreover, incumbents must stand for reelection again and again if they intend to make Congress a career; a single loss will halt or interrupt this goal. Over the period of a few elections, a substantial number of congressional seats can change hands. The 1992 and 1994 congressional elections are an extreme example: the turnover in House membership in these two elections was a combined 188 seats, the highest total of any two consecutive elections since World War II.

On balance, however, incumbents have a clear edge over their opponents, as their margin of victory indicates. In recent elections, most House incumbents and nearly half of Senate incumbents seeking reelection have received 60 percent or more of the vote. Even when voters are convinced that

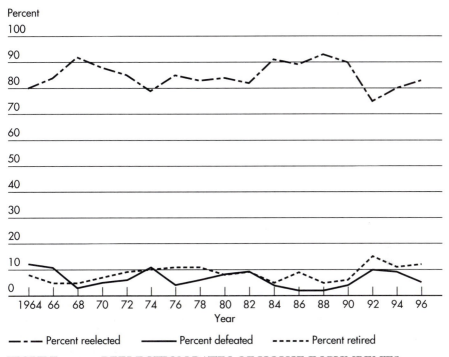

Percent

FIGURE 11-1 REELECTION RATES OF HOUSE INCUMBENTS
U.S. House incumbents have a very high rate of reelection, although the percentage has declined somewhat in the 1990s. Source: *Congressional Quarterly Weekly Report,* various dates.

Congress as an institution is performing badly, they reelect a large majority of its members. One reason is that many congressional districts and a few states are so lopsidedly Democratic or Republican that the candidate of the weaker party has no realistic chance of victory. All incumbents, however, gain important election advantages from the office they hold, a subject to which we now turn.

Using Incumbency to Stay in Congress

Incumbents promote their reelection prospects by responding to their **constituency**—the body of citizens eligible to vote in their state or district. Members of Congress pay close attention to constituency opinions when casting their votes on legislation,[7] and they work hard to get their share of **pork barrel projects** (a term referring to legislation that funds a special project for a particular locale, such as a new highway or hospital).

Constitutional Qualifications for Serving in Congress

Representatives: "No person shall be a Representative who shall not have attained to the age of twenty-five years, and been seven years a citizen of the United States, and who shall not, when elected, be an inhabitant of that State in which he shall be chosen" (Article I, section 2).

Senators: "No person shall be a Senator who shall not have attained to the age of thirty years, and been nine years a citizen of the United States, and who shall not, when elected, be an inhabitant of the State for which he shall be chosen" (Article I, section 3).

Members of Congress also boost their reelection chances by catering to their constituents' needs, a practice known as the **service strategy.** When constituents seek information about a government program, express an opinion about pending legislation, or want help in obtaining a federal benefit, their representative usually responds.[8] This assistance is made possible by the staff resources that are provided to members of Congress. Each House member receives an office allowance of $500,000 a year, which supports a personal staff of about twenty full-time staff members.[9] Senators have larger budgets depending on the population size of the state they represent. Senators' personal staffs average about forty employees.[10] Congressional staffers spend the bulk of their time not on legislative matters but on constituency relations, which includes publicity efforts, such as newsletters and press releases designed to enhance their legislator's image.[11] Each member of Congress is permitted several free mailings annually to constituent households, a privilege known as the *frank.*

Finally, incumbents have a decided advantage when it comes to raising campaign funds. The cost of running for Congress has risen sharply in recent decades as campaign techniques, such as televised advertising and polling, have become increasingly sophisticated and costly. Today, a successful Senate campaign usually costs several million dollars, and a successful House campaign can cost $300,000–$500,000 or more. A study by the *Congressional Quarterly* found that only 10 percent of incumbents said they had trouble raising enough money to conduct an effective campaign, compared with 70 percent of challengers.[12] Over half of House incumbents in recent elections have outspent their opponents by a ratio of 5 to 1 or more. Many challengers are able to raise only enough money for a token campaign.[13]

Incumbents obtain a fund-raising advantage from their past campaigns and constituent service, which enables them to create mailing lists of potential contributors. Individual contributions, most of which are $100 or less, account for about 50 percent of all campaign funds and are obtained mainly through direct mail solicitation. Incumbents also have an edge with interest groups. Through their political action committees (PACs, discussed in detail in Chapter 9), groups provide about 30 percent of campaign funds. Incumbents are well positioned to help groups achieve their legislative goals; in recent elections, incumbents have received six times as much money in PAC contributions as their opponents (see Figure 11-2).

The Pitfalls of Incumbency

Incumbency is not without its pitfalls. The potential problems are several: troublesome issues, personal misconduct, turnout variation, strong challengers, and, for some House members, redistricting.[14]

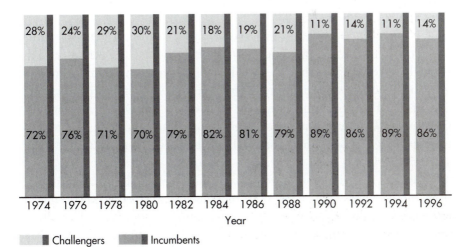

FIGURE 11-2 ALLOCATION OF PAC CONTRIBUTIONS BETWEEN INCUMBENTS AND CHALLENGERS IN CONGRESSIONAL RACES THAT INCLUDED AN INCUMBENT, 1972–1996
In allocating campaign contributions, PACs favor incumbent members of Congress over their challengers by a wide margin. Source: Federal Elections Commission.

TROUBLESOME ISSUES   Disruptive issues are a potential threat to incumbents. Although most elections are not waged against the backdrop of strong issues, those which are tend to produce the largest turnover in Congress. In the 1986–1990 period, when voters were relatively satisfied with national conditions, less than 5 percent of congressional incumbents lost their races. In the 1992–1994 period, when the public was angry over economic and social conditions and believed Congress was performing badly, the number of incumbents who were defeated exceeded 10 percent.

PERSONAL MISCONDUCT   Members of Congress can also fall prey to scandal. Life in Washington can be fast-paced, glamorous, and expensive, and some members of Congress get caught up in influence peddling, sexual promiscuity, and other forms of personal misconduct. These acts receive close attention from the news media and are a major threat to the reelection of incumbents. More than 60 percent of House incumbents who lost their bid for reelection in the 1988–1992 period were shadowed by ethical questions. "The first thing to being reelected is to stay away from scandal, even minor scandal," says the political scientist John Hibbing.[15] Even the top leaders are not immune, as evidenced by the experience of former House Ways and Means Committee Chairman Dan Rostenkowski. Accused of gross misuse of congressional funds, he lost his House seat in 1994, despite having won by 20 percentage points two years earlier and outspending his 1994 opponent by more than 10 to 1.

TURNOUT VARIATION: THE MIDTERM ELECTION PROBLEM   Historically, the party holding the presidency loses seats in the midterm congressional elections, particularly in the House of Representatives (see Figure 11-3). The 1994 midterm elections, when the Democrats had Bill Clinton in the White House and lost fifty-two House and eight Senate seats, produced higher losses than normal, but the president's party nearly always suffers a net loss.

The loss is attributable largely to a dropoff in turnout for midterm elections.[16] The voters who go the polls only during presidential election years tend to have weaker party loyalties and are therefore more responsive to the issues of the moment. In any given election, these issues tend to favor one party, which contributes to the success of its congressional candidates as well as its presidential nominee. Most of the party's congressional candidates who win narrowly owe their margin of victory to these voters. However, these voters stay home during midterm elections. Thus, unless these incumbents can make inroads among midterm voters who backed their opponent two

Number of Seats Lost

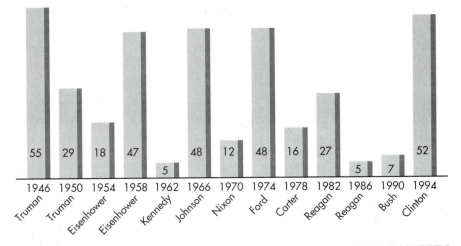

55	29	18	47	5	48	12	48	16	27	5	7	52
1946	1950	1954	1958	1962	1966	1970	1974	1978	1982	1986	1990	1994
Truman	Truman	Eisenhower	Eisenhower	Kennedy	Johnson	Nixon	Ford	Carter	Reagan	Reagan	Bush	Clinton

FIGURE 11-3   NET HOUSE SEATS LOST BY PRESIDENTIAL PARTY IN
MIDTERM ELECTIONS, 1946–1994
Historically, the party holding the White House has lost seats in the midterm
elections.

years earlier, they stand a good chance of losing. Since many of these voters are strong partisans, they are not easily swayed, and the typical result is
the midterm defeat of a significant number of these incumbents.

STRONG CHALLENGERS: A PROBLEM FOR SENATORS   Incumbents
are also vulnerable to strong challengers. Senators are particularly likely to
face formidable opponents: after the presidency, the Senate is the top rung
of the political ladder. Governors and House members are frequent challengers for Senate seats, and they have the electoral base, reputation, and
experience to compete effectively. Moreover, the U.S. Senate lures wealthy
challengers. Michael Huffington spent $25 million of his own money in
California's 1994 Senate race and nearly defeated incumbent Dianne Feinstein.

House incumbents have less reason to fear strong challengers. A House
seat is often not attractive enough to induce prominent local politicians, such
as mayors or state legislators, to risk their political careers in a challenge to
an incumbent.[17] This situation frequently leaves the field open to weak opponents with little or no governmental or political experience.[18]

REDISTRICTING: A PROBLEM FOR HOUSE MEMBERS   Every ten years, after each population census, the 435 seats in the House are reallocated among the states in proportion to their population. States that have gained population since the last census may acquire additional House seats, while those that have lost population may lose seats. This reallocation process is called **reapportionment.** (The Senate is not affected by population change, since each state has two senators regardless of its size.)

The responsibility for redrawing House election districts after a reapportionment—a process called **redistricting**—rests with the state governments. States are required by law to make their districts as nearly equal in population as possible.

Reapportionment and redistricting are a potential threat to House incumbents. Turnover in House elections is typically higher after a new census than in previous elections. The newly redrawn districts include voters who are unfamiliar with the incumbent, thereby diminishing an advantage that incumbents typically have over their challengers. Moreover, when a state loses congressional seats, there are fewer districts than there are incumbents, who may end up running against each other.

Competition and Representation

Although the obstacles to an incumbent's reelection can be substantial, the advantage in most congressional races clearly rests with the incumbent. As a result, Congress is not highly responsive to political change. The Republicans gained a decisive victory in 1994 on the strength of voters' anger at Washington, but a similar public mood in 1980 failed to translate into GOP control of the House of Representatives. In nearly every other western democracy, the conditions underlying the 1980 election would have produced a change in power. It is worth noting that national legislators in other democracies do not have the large personal staffs and the substantial travel and publicity budgets that members of Congress have. Elsewhere, incumbents tend to win or lose on the popularity of their political party, not on their capacity to generate public support through constituent service.

Safe incumbency weakens the public's influence on Congress. Democracy depends on periodic shifts in power between the parties to bring public policy into closer alignment with public opinion. Research indicates that changes in congressional voting patterns occur primarily around the replacement of defeated or retiring lawmakers with new members. Incumbents tend to hold relatively stable policy positions during their time in office.[19]

Safe incumbency is also a reason why Congress has relatively few women among its members. They now account for about 10 percent of the membership, which is twice that of a decade ago but less than that of many other national legislatures. Women have been no more successful than other challengers in dislodging congressional incumbents. In state and local elections, where incumbency is less important, women have made greater inroads.[20]

CONGRESSIONAL LEADERSHIP

The way in which Congress works is related to the way in which its members win election. Because of their independent power base in their state or district, members of Congress have substantial independence within the institution they serve. The Speaker of the House and the other top leaders in Congress are crucial to its operation, but, unlike their counterparts in European legislatures, they cannot demand the loyalty of the members they lead. Speaker Newt Gingrich's extraordinary success in pushing the Contract with America through the House in 1995 was based less on the formal

Newt Gingrich is generally regarded as the most powerful
Speaker of the House of Representatives in the post-war
era. His reputation and effectiveness, however, were
damaged when he admitted violating House ethics rules.
(Reuters/Win McNamee/Archive Photos)

powers of his office than on the galvanizing force of the ideas the contract contained. Gingrich is the most powerful congressional leader of recent times, and House Republicans in 1995 took steps to strengthen the power of the chamber's top party and committee leaders. But there is an inherent tension in Congress between the institution's need for strong leadership at the top and the individual members' need to exercise power on behalf of constituents. The result is an institution where power is widely dispersed.

Party Leadership in Congress

The House and Senate are organized along party lines. When members of Congress are sworn in at the start of a new two-year session, they automatically join either the Democratic or Republican caucus in their chamber. These caucuses select **party leaders** to represent the party's interests in the full chamber and to give direction to the body's deliberations.

THE HOUSE LEADERSHIP   The main party leaders in the House are the Speaker, majority leader, majority whip, minority leader, and minority whip. The Constitution provides only for the post of Speaker, who is to be chosen by a vote of the entire House. In practice, this means that the Speaker is selected by the majority party's members, since only they have enough votes to choose one of their own.

The Speaker is often said to be the second most powerful official in Washington, after the president. The Speaker has the right to speak first on legislation during House debate and has the power to recognize members—that is, give them permission to speak from the floor. Since the House places a time limit on floor debate, not everyone has a chance to speak on a bill, and the Speaker can sometimes influence legislation simply by exercising the power to decide who will speak and when.[21] The Speaker also chooses the chairperson and majority-party members of the powerful House Rules Committee, which controls the scheduling of bills for debate. Legislation the Speaker wants passed is likely to reach the floor under conditions favorable to its enactment; for example, the Speaker may ask the Rules Committee to delay sending a bill to the floor until there are enough votes for its passage. The Speaker has other ways of directing the work of the House. The Speaker assigns bills to committees, can place time limits on the reporting of bills out of committees, and assigns members to conference committees. (The importance of these powers over committee action will become apparent later in this chapter.)

The Speaker is assisted by the House majority leader and the House majority whip, who are elected by the majority party's members. The majority leader acts as the party's floor leader, organizing the debate on bills and working to line up legislative support. The whip has the important job of soliciting votes from party members and of informing them when critical votes are scheduled. As voting is getting under way on the House floor, the whip will sometimes position himself where he can easily be seen by party members and let them know where the leadership stands on the bill by giving a thumbs-up or thumbs-down signal.

The minority party has its own leaders in the House. The House minority leader heads the party's caucus and policy committee and plays the leading role in developing the party's legislative positions. The minority leader is assisted by a minority whip.

THE SENATE LEADERSHIP   In the Senate, the most important party leadership position is that of the majority leader, who heads the majority-party caucus. The majority leader's role is much like that of the Speaker of the House, in that he formulates the majority's legislative policies and strategies and seeks to develop influential relationships with his colleagues. Like the Speaker, the Senate majority leader chairs the party's policy committee and acts as the party's voice in the chamber.[22] The majority leader is assisted by the majority whip, who sees to it that members know when important votes are scheduled and ensures that the party's strongest advocates on a legislative measure are present for the debate. The Senate also has a minority leader and minority whip, whose roles are comparable to those performed by their counterparts in the House.

Unlike the Speaker of the House, the Senate majority leader is not the presiding officer of his chamber. The Constitution assigns this responsibility to the vice-president of the United States. However, since the vice-president is allowed to vote in the Senate only to break a tie, the vice-president seldom presides over Senate debates. The Senate has a president *pro tempore*, who, in the absence of the vice-president, has the right to preside over the Senate. President *pro tempore* is largely an honorary position that by tradition is usually held by the majority party's senior member. The presiding official has limited power, since each senator has the right to speak at any length on bills under consideration.

The Senate's tradition of unlimited debate derives from its relatively small size (only 100 members, compared with the House's 435 members). Moreover, senators like to view themselves as being equals and are thus less subject to leadership.[23] For such reasons, the Senate majority leader's position is weaker than that of the Speaker of the House. One former Senate

The U.S. Capitol in Washington, D.C., with the House wing in the foreground. The Senate meets in the wing at the right of the central rotunda (under the dome). The offices of the House and Senate party leaders—Speaker, vice-president, majority and minority leaders and whips—are located in the Capitol building. Other members of Congress have their offices in nearby buildings. (Vanessa Vick/Photo Researchers)

majority leader, Robert Byrd, jokingly called himself a "slave," saying that he served his fellow Democrats' needs without commanding their votes.[24]

The power of all party leaders, in the Senate and House alike, rests largely on the trust placed in them by the members of their party. They do not have strong formal powers, but they are expected to lead. If they are adept at promoting ideas and building coalitions, they will be able to exercise considerable power within their chamber.

Committee Chairpersons: The Seniority Principle

Party leaders are not the only important leaders in Congress. Most of the work of Congress takes place in the meetings of its thirty-nine standing (permanent) committees and their numerous subcommittees, each of which is headed by a chairperson. A committee chair schedules committee meetings, determines the order in which committee bills are considered, presides over committee discussions, directs the committee's majority staff, and can choose to lead the debate when a committee bill reaches the floor of the chamber for a vote by the full membership.

Committee chairs are always members of the majority party, and they nearly always have the most **seniority**—the most consecutive years of service on a particular committee. The seniority principle was instituted in the Senate in the mid-nineteenth century but was not formally applied in the House until the early twentieth century.

The seniority principle remained virtually absolute until the House Democratic majority decided in the early 1970s that committee chairs would henceforth be chosen by secret ballot. Abuses by some committee chairs led to the change. Virginia's Howard Smith, who chaired the House Rules Committee in the 1950s and 1960s and was opposed to racial change, would sometimes leave Washington for his Virginia farm when civil rights legislation reached his committee. Because the Rules Committee could not meet unless he called it into session, Smith's absence was sometimes enough to persuade the full committee to "table" a bill, or set it aside. A committee chair now has less power; for example, a majority of the committee members can vote to convene meetings in the chair's absence.

Although the seniority principle is no longer absolute, the congressional majorities usually abide by it.[25] Exceptions took place in 1995 when, at Speaker Gingrich's request, House Republicans bypassed some veteran members, most notably Representative Carlos Moorhead of California, who was the most senior Republican on both the Judiciary and Commerce committees. Gingrich wanted a more forceful individual than Moorhead as chair of these major committees.

The seniority system persists because it has several important advantages: it reduces the number of bitter power struggles that would occur if the chair were decided by open competition, provides experienced and knowledgeable committee leadership, and enables members to look forward to the reward of a position as chair after years of committee service. A drawback of the seniority system is that it places the committee chairs largely outside the power of the House or Senate's elected leaders.[26]

Congressional organization and leadership extend into subcommittees, which are smaller units within each committee formed to conduct specific aspects of the committee's business. Altogether there are about 200 subcommittees in the House and Senate, each with a chairperson who decides its order of business, presides over its meetings, and coordinates its staff. In both chambers, a subcommittee chair is often the most senior member on the panel, but seniority is not as important in these appointments as it is in the designation of committee chairs.

HOW THE UNITED STATES COMPARES

Unity and Fragmentation in National Legislatures

The U.S. House and Senate are separate and coequal chambers, each with its own legislative structure and rules. This type of legislative structure is not found in most democracies. Although many of them have a bicameral legislature like the U.S. Congress, nearly all power is vested in just one of the two chambers. In such a situation legislative power is more concentrated and easier to exercise.

However, legislative power depends heavily on party unity. All democratic legislatures are organized by party, but they differ greatly in the degree of control exercised by parties. At one extreme (for example, in Great Britain and Germany) a single legislative chamber dominates, one party has a majority in that chamber, and the members of the majority party display a high level of unity. Party control of the U.S. Congress is less pronounced. For one thing, Republicans may control one chamber while the Democrats control the other. For another, Congress is not characterized by strong party unity. Members often vote against their party's position on important legislation. This lack of a reliable party majority weakens Congress's ability to provide national leadership.

Country	Form of Legislature
Canada	One house dominant
France	One house dominant
Germany	One house dominant (except on regional issues)
Great Britain	One house dominant
Israel	One house only
Italy	Two equal houses
Japan	One house dominant
Mexico	Two equal houses
United States	Two equal houses

Oligarchy or Democracy: Which Principle Should Govern?

In 1995, House Republicans gave committee chairs the power to select the chairs of their subcommittees and to appoint all majority-party staff members, including those who work for the subcommittees. The changes were designed to give committee chairs more control over legislation.[27] The changes reversed House reforms of the 1970s that gave subcommittees and their chairs greater authority in order to make the House "more democratic" in its organization.[28]

The opposing forces embedded in the 1970s and 1995 reforms have played themselves out many times in the history of Congress. The institution is at once a place for conducting the nation's business and for promoting constituency interests. At times, the positions of senior leaders have been strengthened. At other times, the positions of less senior members have been enhanced. At all times, there has been an attempt to create a workable balance of the two. The result is an institution very different from European parliaments, where power is thoroughly concentrated at the top (an arrangement reflected even in the name for rank-and-file members—"backbenchers"). The distinguishing feature of congressional power is its dispersion across the membership, with some provision for added power at the top (see box: How the United States Compares).

THE COMMITTEE SYSTEM

As indicated earlier, most of the work in Congress is conducted through **standing committees,** which are permanent committees with responsibility for a particular area of public policy. At present there are nineteen standing committees in the House and sixteen in the Senate (see Table 11-1). Both the House and the Senate, for example, have a standing committee that specializes in foreign policy issues. Other important standing committees are those which deal with agriculture, commerce, the budget, the interior (natural resources and public lands), defense, government spending, labor, the judiciary, and taxation. House committees, which average about thirty-five to forty members each, are about twice the size of the Senate committees. Each standing committee has legislative authority in that it can draft and rewrite proposed legislation and can recommend to the full chamber the passage or defeat of the legislation it considers.

Each standing committee in Congress has its own staff, which, altogether, totals about 1,000 employees in the Senate and 1,300 in the House.

TABLE 11-1 THE STANDING COMMITTEES OF CONGRESS	
House of Representatives	*Senate*
Agriculture	Agriculture, Nutrition, and Forestry
Appropriations	Appropriations
Banking and Financial Services	Armed Services
Budget	Banking, Housing, and Urban
Commerce	Affairs
Economic and Educational	Budget
Opportunities	Commerce, Science, and
Government Reform and	Transportation
Oversight	Energy and Natural Resources
House Oversight	Environment and Public Works
International Relations	Finance
Judiciary	Foreign Relations
National Security	Governmental Affairs
Resources	Judiciary
Rules	Labor and Human Resources
Science	Rules and Administration
Small Business	Small Business
Standards of Official Conduct	Veterans' Affairs
Transportation and Infrastructure	
Veterans' Affairs	
Ways and Means	

Unlike the members' personal staffs, which concentrate on constituency relations, the committee staffs perform an almost entirely legislative function. They help draft legislation, prepare reports, organize hearings, and participate in altering bills within committee.

In addition to its standing committees, Congress also has a number of *select committees*, which are created to perform specific tasks and are disbanded after they have done so; *joint committees*, composed of members of both houses, which perform advisory or coordinating functions for the House and the Senate; and *conference committees*, which are joint committees formed temporarily to work out differences in House and Senate versions of a particular bill. The role of conference committees is discussed more fully later in the chapter.

Congress could not possibly handle its work load without the help of its standing committees and their staffs. About 10,000 bills are introduced during each two-year session of Congress; the sheer volume of this legislation would paralyze the institution if it did not have a division of labor. Yet the very existence of standing committees and their subcommittees helps to fragment Congress: each of these units is relatively secure in its power, jurisdiction, and membership.[29]

Committee Membership

Each committee includes Republicans and Democrats, but the majority party holds the majority of seats on each committee and subcommittee. The ratio of Democrats to Republicans on each committee is approximately the same as the ratio in the full House or Senate, but there is no fixed rule on this matter, and the majority party sets the proportions as it chooses (mindful that at the next election it could become the chamber's minority). Members of the House typically serve on only two committees. Senators often serve on four, although they can sit on only two major committees, such as Foreign Relations and Finance. There are also limits on subcommittee assignments; no House member, for example, can serve on more than five subcommittees.

Each standing committee has a fixed number of members, and a committee must have a vacancy before a new member can be appointed. These vacancies usually occur at the start of a new congressional session, when the committee positions of members who have retired or been defeated for reelection are reallocated. On nearly all committees, members retain their seats unless they decide to relinquish them or are forced to do so by changes in party ratios or committee size. The biggest change in committee memberships comes when a party loses control of the House or Senate; several Democrats had to relinquish committee assignments when the Republicans took control of Congress in 1995.

Each party has a special committee in the House and Senate which has responsibility for deciding who will fill vacancies on standing committees. Several factors influence these decisions, including the preferences of the legislators themselves. Most newly elected members of Congress receive a committee assignment that they have requested.[30] New members usually ask for assignment to a committee on which they can serve their constituents' interests and at the same time increase their reelection prospects.[31] For example, when Phil Gramm was first elected to the Senate from Texas, a state that depends heavily on the defense industry, he requested and received a position on the Armed Services Committee.

Members of Congress also prefer membership on one of the most important committees, such as Foreign Relations or Finance in the Senate and Ways and Means or Appropriations in the House. Such factors as members' intelligence, experience, party loyalty, ideology, region, length of congressional service, and work habits weigh heavily in the determination of appointments to these prestigious committees.[32]

Subcommittee assignments are handled differently. The members of each party on a committee decide who among them will serve on each of its subcommittees. The members' preferences, seniority, and personal backgrounds and the interests of their constituencies are key influences on subcommittee assignments.

Committee Jurisdiction

The 1946 Legislative Reorganization Act requires each bill introduced in Congress to be referred to the proper committee. An agricultural bill introduced in the Senate must be assigned to the Senate Agriculture Committee, a bill dealing with foreign affairs must be sent to the Senate Foreign Relations Committee, and so on. This requirement is a major source of each committee's power. Even if its members are known to oppose certain types of legislation, bills clearly within its **jurisdiction**—the policy area in which it is authorized to act—must be sent to it for deliberation.

Nevertheless, House and Senate leaders do have some discretion when they assign certain bills to committee. Although the House Commerce Committee has primary jurisdiction over commerce policy, for example, more than a dozen other House committees have some responsibility for commerce policy, so that the Speaker has a choice when some bills in this policy area are to be assigned.

House subcommittees have secure jurisdictions like those of the committees: bills must be referred to the appropriate subcommittees within two weeks of their arrival in committee. The Senate has a similar policy. Thus responsibility in Congress is thoroughly divided, with each subcommittee having formal authority over a small area of public policy.

The Role of Committees in the Passage of Legislation

At times, particularly when bills dealing with major issues are introduced, the full membership of Congress takes decisive action. On most bills, however, the full chamber merely votes to confirm or modify decisions made previously by committees and subcommittees.

COMMITTEE HEARINGS AND DECISIONS The power of committees is evident in the process by which bills become law (see Figure 11-4). A **bill** is a proposed legislative act. Many bills are prepared by executive agencies, interest groups, or other outside parties, but members of Congress also draft bills and only they can formally submit a bill for consideration by their chamber. Once a bill is introduced by a member of the House or Senate, it is given a number and a title and is then sent to the appropriate committee, which assigns it to one of its subcommittees. Most bills that reach a subcommittee are tabled on the grounds that they are not worthwhile. Only about 10 percent of the bills that committees consider reach the floor for a vote; the others are "killed" when committees decide that they do not warrant further consideration and table them. The full House or Senate can overrule these committee rejections but seldom does so.

If a bill seems to have merit, the subcommittee will schedule hearings on it. The subcommittee invites testimony on the proposed legislation by lobbyists, administrators, and experts, who inform members about the suggested policy, provide an indication of the support the bill has, and disclose possible weaknesses in the proposal. After the hearings, if the subcommittee still feels that the legislation is warranted, members recommend the bill to the full committee, which can hold additional hearings. In the House, both the full committee and a subcommittee can "mark up," or revise, a bill; in the Senate, markup is usually reserved for the full committee.

When a committee recommends passage, a bill has about a 90 percent chance of being approved by the full House or Senate, although these bills are frequently amended on the floor. In the House, the Rules Committee has the power to determine when the bill will be voted on, how long the debate on the bill will last, and whether the bill will receive a "closed rule" (no amendments will be permitted), an "open rule" (members can propose amendments relevant to any of the bill's sections), or something in between (for example, only certain sections of the bill will be subject to amendment). The Rules Committee has this scheduling power because the House is too large to operate effectively without strict rules for the handling of legislation by the full chamber.

The Senate has no Rules Committee, relying instead on the majority leader to schedule bills. All Senate bills are subject to unlimited debate unless a three-fifths majority of the full Senate votes for **cloture,** which limits debate to 100 hours. Cloture is a way of thwarting a Senate **filibuster,** a procedural tactic whereby a minority of senators prevent a bill from coming to a vote by holding the floor and talking until other senators give in and the

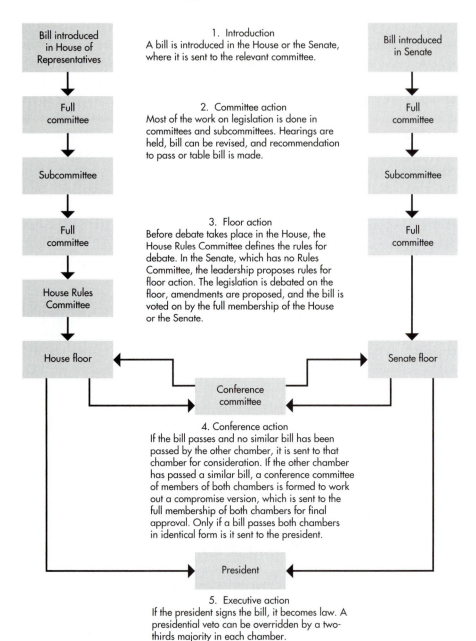

1. Introduction
A bill is introduced in the House or the Senate, where it is sent to the relevant committee.

Bill introduced in House of Representatives

Bill introduced in Senate

Full committee

Full committee

Subcommittee

Subcommittee

2. Committee action
Most of the work on legislation is done in committees and subcommittees. Hearings are held, bill can be revised, and recommendation to pass or table bill is made.

Full committee

Full committee

House Rules Committee

3. Floor action
Before debate takes place in the House, the House Rules Committee defines the rules for debate. In the Senate, which has no Rules Committee, the leadership proposes rules for floor action. The legislation is debated on the floor, amendments are proposed, and the bill is voted on by the full membership of the House or the Senate.

House floor

Senate floor

Conference committee

4. Conference action
If the bill passes and no similar bill has been passed by the other chamber, it is sent to that chamber for consideration. If the other chamber has passed a similar bill, a conference committee of members of both chambers is formed to work out a compromise version, which is sent to the full membership of both chambers for final approval. Only if a bill passes both chambers in identical form is it sent to the president.

President

5. Executive action
If the president signs the bill, it becomes law. A presidential veto can be overridden by a two-thirds majority in each chamber.

FIGURE 11-4　HOW A BILL BECOMES A LAW
Although the legislative process can be short-circuited in many ways, this diagram describes the most typical way in which a bill becomes law.

bill is withdrawn from consideration. The Senate also differs from the House in that its members can propose *any* amendment to *any* bill. Unlike House amendments, those in the Senate do not have to be germane to a bill's content. For example, a senator may propose an antiabortion amendment to a bill dealing with defense expenditures. Such amendments are called *riders* and are frequently introduced.

THE ROLE OF CONFERENCE COMMITTEES   To become **law,** a bill must be passed in identical form by both the House and the Senate. About 10 percent of all proposals that are approved by both chambers—the proportion is larger for major bills—differ in important respects in their House and Senate versions and are referred to a **conference committee** to resolve their differences. Each conference committee is formed temporarily to handle a particular bill; its members are usually appointed from the House and Senate standing committees that worked on the bill originally. The conference committee's job is to bargain over the differences in the House and Senate versions and to develop a compromise version. It then goes to the House and Senate floors, where it can be passed, defeated, or returned to conference, but not amended.

Legislation that is passed by the House and Senate is not assured of becoming law. The president also has a role. If the president exercises the *veto*, a refusal to sign a bill, it is sent back to its originating chamber with the president's reasons for the veto. Congress can override a veto by a two-thirds vote of each chamber; the bill then becomes law. If the president fails to sign a bill within ten days (Sundays excepted) and Congress has remained in session, the bill automatically becomes law anyway. If the president fails to sign a bill within ten days and Congress has adjourned for the term, the bill does not become law. This last situation is called a *pocket veto* and forces Congress in its next session to start from the beginning: the bill must again pass both chambers and is again subject to presidential veto.

COMMITTEES: POWERFUL, BUT NOT ALL POWERFUL   Although the power of committees and subcommittees should not be underestimated, statistics on their influence can be misleading. The fact that committee recommendations are followed about 90 percent of the time does not mean that committees hold 90 percent of the power in Congress. In making their decisions, committees take into account the fact that their positions can be reversed by the full chamber, just as subcommittees recognize that the full committee can overrule their actions.[33]

Nevertheless, committees and subcommittees remain the locus of congressional decision making. A century ago, Woodrow Wilson described Congress as a system of "little legislatures." His view is still relevant; Congress depends on subsets of members, in committees and subcommittees, to do most of its work and make most of its decisions.

CONGRESS'S POLICYMAKING ROLE

The Framers of the Constitution expected Congress to be the leading branch of the national government. It was to the legislature—the embodiment of representative government—that the people were expected to look for policy leadership. During most of the nineteenth century, Congress, not the president, was clearly the dominant national institution. Aside from a few strong leaders such as Jackson and Lincoln, presidents did not play a major legislative role (see Chapter 12). However, as national and international forces combined to place greater leadership and policy demands on the federal government, the president became a vital part of the national legislative process. Today Congress and the president substantially share the legislative effort, although their roles differ greatly.[34]

Congress's policymaking role revolves around its three legislative functions—lawmaking, representation, and oversight. In practice, the three functions overlap, but they are conceptually distinct.

The Lawmaking Function of Congress

Under the Constitution, Congress is granted the **lawmaking function**—the authority to make the laws necessary to carry out the powers granted to the national government. However, whether Congress takes the lead in the making of laws depends heavily on the type of policy at issue.

CONGRESS IN RESPONSE: FRAGMENTATION AS A POLICYMAKING LIMITATION   Some of the policy questions addressed by the national government transcend local boundaries. A sluggish economy, for example, affects Americans of all regions and of most occupational groups. Such issues normally call for a broad and well-coordinated policy response. Because of its divided chambers, weak leadership, and segmented committee structure, Congress finds it difficult to take the lead on these issues.

Congress normally depends on the president to initiate broad policy proposals, and for good reason: the presidency is strong in ways that Congress is not. First, whereas Congress's authority is fragmented, the presidency's authority is vested in a single individual.[35] As a result, the presidency is capable of a degree of policy planning and coordination that is far beyond the normal capacity of Congress. Second, whereas members of Congress see issues mainly from the perspective of their state or district, the president has a national outlook. The president cannot ignore state and local interests but must concentrate on national ones in order to retain power.

These differences are also reflected in news coverage of the two institutions. As a nationally elected official and sole head of the executive branch, the president ordinarily gets considerably more attention from the press than any member of Congress. In fact, during most periods, the president gets more news coverage than all Senate and House members combined,[36] a situation that contributed to Congress's decision to establish its own cable network, C-SPAN (Cable Satellite Public Affairs Network). Congressional debates and hearings are carried live on C-SPAN, and journalists are authorized to use the televised material for reporting purposes.

Presidential leadership means that Congress will pay attention to the White House, not that it will accept whatever the president proposes. The same factors that make it difficult for Congress to routinely initiate broad policy also make it difficult for presidents to routinely get Congress to accept their initiatives. Former senator Robert Dole compared Congress to a wet noodle: "If it doesn't want to move, it's not going to move."[37] Nevertheless, Congress often welcomes presidential initiatives as a starting point in its deliberations.

Organizational changes have improved Congress's ability to evaluate and modify presidential proposals. Of particular importance is the Congressional Budget Office (CBO), which was created as part of the Budget Impoundment and Control Act of 1974. Before this time, the president through the Office of Management and Budget (OMB) had a significant advantage in budgetary matters. Congress had no independent way to systematically assess the president's budgetary proposals or their projected impact. The CBO gives Congress this capacity. Its 200 employees provide Congress with general economic projections, overall estimates of government expenditures and revenues, and specific estimates of the costs of proposed programs. Since the CBO's inception, its calculations have often been at odds with those of the OMB. For example, the OMB's estimates of the cost of presidential initiatives are usually optimistic, and the CBO's figures have been a basis by which Congress has trimmed or rejected these proposals. (The budgetary process, and the CBO's role in it, are described more fully in Chapter 15. The OMB is discussed further in Chapters 12 and 14).

Congress also has three other agencies that lessen its dependence on the executive branch for information relevant to legislative decisions. The General Accounting Office (GAO), with roughly 5,000 employees, is the largest congressional agency. Formed in 1921, it has the primary responsibility of overseeing executive agencies' spending of money that has been appropriated by Congress.[38] Created in 1914, the Congressional Research Service (CRS) is the oldest congressional agency, has a staff of 1,000 employees, and operates as a nonpartisan reference agency. If a member of Congress wants information on a bill or other matter, the CRS will provide it. The Office of Technology Assessment (OTA), established in 1972 and having 200 employees, assesses technical policy proposals.

CONGRESS IN THE LEAD: FRAGMENTATION AS A POLICYMAKING STRENGTH Congress occasionally does take the lead on large issues. Except during Roosevelt's New Deal, Congress has been a chief source of major labor legislation. Environmental legislation, federal aid to education, and urban development are other areas in which Congress has played an initiating role.[39] The Republicans' Contract with America is yet another example of congressional policy leadership. The contract included broad fiscal, regulatory, and social initiatives. In 1996, for example, the Republican-controlled Congress led the way on legislation that fundamentally changed the nation's welfare system (see Chapter 16). Nevertheless, Congress does not routinely develop broad policy programs and carry them through to passage. "Congress remains organized," James Sundquist notes, "to deal with narrow problems but not with broad ones."[40]

As it happens, the great majority of the roughly 10,000 bills that Congress considers each session deal with narrow issues. The leading role in the disposition of these bills falls not on the president but on Congress and, in most cases, on a relatively small number of its members. The same fragmentation that makes it difficult for Congress to take the lead on a broad issue makes it easy for Congress to tackle scores of narrow issues simultaneously. Most of the legislation passed by Congress is "distributive"—that is, it distributes benefits to a particular group while spreading the costs among the general public. Veterans' benefits and business tax incentives are examples.[41]

Such legislation, because it directly benefits a constituent group, is the type of policy that members of Congress are most inclined to support. It is also the type of policy that Congress, through its committee system, is organizationally best suited to handle. Most committees parallel a major constituent interest, such as agriculture, commerce, and labor.

After their stunning victory in the 1994 elections, congressional Republicans launched an aggressive attempt to reduce the scope of the federal government, illustrating that, in some instances, Congress can take the lead on broad national issues. (Reuters/Bettmann Newsphotos)

The Representation Function of Congress

In the process of making laws, the members of Congress represent various interests within American society, giving them voice and attention in the national legislature. The proper approach to the **representation function** has been debated since the nation's founding. A recurrent issue has been whether the primary concern of a representative should be the interests of the nation as a whole or those of his or her own constituency. These interests overlap to some degree but rarely coincide. Policies that are of benefit to the full society are not always equally advantageous to particular localities and can even cause harm to some constituencies.

REPRESENTATION OF STATES AND DISTRICTS   The choice between national and local interests is not a simple one, even for a legislator who is inclined toward either orientation. To be fully effective, a member of Congress must be reelected time and again, a necessity that compels him or her

STATES IN THE NATION

Partisan Makeup of U.S. House Delegations

The U.S. Representatives from a given state are called its House delegation. They often work together on issues affecting their state, but party differences tend to divide them on other issues. Republican and Democratic members, even from the same state, tend to end up on opposite sides of most legislative issues. The House delegations differ considerably in their partisan makeup. Nearly half of them are more than 60 percent Republican while about a quarter are more than 60 percent Democratic. The other states have delegations that are more evenly split between the parties.

More than 60 percent Republican

40–60 percent split

More than 60 percent Democratic

to pay attention to local demands. Yet, as part of the nation's legislative body, no member can easily put aside his or her judgment as to the nation's needs. In making the choice, most members of Congress, it appears, tend toward a local orientation. They are particularly reluctant to oppose local sentiment on issues of intense concern. Support for gun control legislation, for example, has always been much lower among members of Congress from rural areas where sporting guns are part of the fabric of everyday life.

Nevertheless, representation of constituency interests has its limits. A representative's constituents have little interest in most issues that come before Congress and even less information about them. Whether the government should appropriate a few million dollars in foreign aid for Bolivia or should alter patent requirements for copying machines is not the sort of issue that local people are likely to know or care about. Moreover, members of Congress often have no choice but to go against the wishes of a significant portion of their constituency. The interests of small and large farmers in an agricultural state, for example, can differ considerably.

REPRESENTATION OF THE NATION THROUGH PARTIES   When a clear-cut and vital national interest is at stake, members of Congress can be expected to respond to that interest. The difficulty of using the common good as a routine basis for thinking about representation, however, is that Americans often disagree on what constitutes the common good and what government should do to further it.

In Congress, conflicts over national goals occur primarily along party lines. Republicans and Democrats have different perspectives on national issues because their parties differ philosophically and in their political base (see box: States in the Nation).[42] There are real and substantial differences between members of the two parties, such that they often end up on the opposite sides of broad national issues. Historically, nearly every major wave of national legislation has been driven by party ideology and enacted along party lines. Party is also the primary basis of ongoing conflict in Congress; on roll-call votes, a majority of Democrats often vote against a majority of Republicans (see Figure 11-5). The incidence of party-line voting has recently been very high; in the 1995–1996 term, for example, the average Senate and House Democrat voted with the Democratic majority more than 80 percent of the time, and the average Senate and House Republican voted with the Republican majority more than 80 percent of the time. Divisions along party lines are common in committee voting as well.[43]

Partisanship also affects the president's relationship with Congress. Presidents serve as legislative leaders not so much for the whole Congress

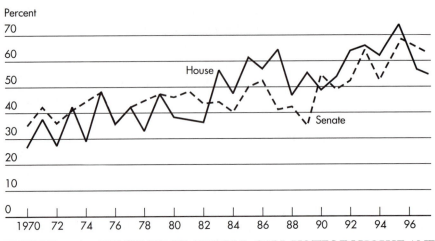

FIGURE 11-5 PERCENTAGE OF ROLL-CALL VOTES IN HOUSE AND SENATE IN WHICH A MAJORITY OF DEMOCRATS VOTED AGAINST A MAJORITY OF REPUBLICANS, 1970–1996
Democrats and Republicans in Congress are often on opposite sides of issues; party-line voting has increased in recent years. Source: *Congressional Quarterly Weekly Report*, various dates.

as for members of their own party. More than half the time, opposition and support for presidential initiatives divide along party lines (see Chapter 12).

In short, any accounting of representation in Congress that minimizes the influence of party is faulty. If constituency interests drive the thinking of many members of Congress, so also do partisan values. In fact, constituent and partisan influences are often difficult to separate in practice. In the case of conflicting interests within their constituency, members of Congress naturally side with those which align with their party. When local business and labor groups take opposing sides on issues before Congress, for example, Republican members tend to back business's position while Democratic members usually side with labor.

The Oversight Function of Congress

Although Congress enacts the nation's laws and appropriates the money to implement them, the administration of these laws is entrusted to the executive branch. Congress has the responsibility to see that the executive carries out the laws faithfully and spends the money properly, a supervisory activity that is referred to as the **oversight function** of Congress.[44]

Oversight is carried out largely through the committee system of Congress and is facilitated by the parallel structure of the committees and the executive bureaucracy: the House International Relations and Senate Foreign Relations committees oversee the work of the State Department, the House and Senate Agriculture committees look after the Department of Agriculture, and so on.

When an agency is suspected of serious abuses, a committee is likely to hold hearings. Except in cases involving "executive privilege" (the right to withhold confidential information affecting national security), executive-branch officials are compelled to testify at these hearings. If they refuse, they can be cited for contempt of Congress, which is a criminal offense. Congress's investigative power is not listed in the Constitution, but the judiciary has not challenged the power, and Congress has used it extensively. The Watergate, Iran-Contra, and Whitewater affairs prompted congressional investigations, which have also been used to focus attention on national problems, such as crime, poverty, and health care.

Most federal programs must have their funding renewed every year, a requirement that gives Congress crucial leverage in its ongoing oversight function. If an agency has acted improperly, Congress may reduce the agency's appropriation or tighten the restrictions on the way its funds can be spent. A major difficulty is that the House and Senate Appropriations committees must review nearly the entire federal budget, a task that limits the amount of attention they can give any particular program.

Oversight conducted after the bureaucracy has acted has an obvious drawback: if a program has been administered improperly, some damage has already been done. For this reason, Congress in recent years has developed ways of limiting the bureaucracy's discretion in advance. One method is to include detailed instructions in appropriations bills. Such instructions serve to limit bureaucrats' flexibility when they spend funds on programs and provide a firmer basis for holding them accountable if they disregard the intent of Congress. Another oversight device is the "sunset law," which fixes a date on which a program will end (or "fade into the sunset") unless it is renewed by Congress. Sunset provisions help to prevent a program from outliving its usefulness because, once its expiration date is reached, Congress can reestablish it only by passing a new law. The "legislative veto" is a more intrusive and controversial oversight tool. It requires that an executive agency have the approval of Congress before it can take a specified action. Legisla-

Exercising its oversight function, the Senate Banking Committee held hearings into the alleged involvement of President Clinton in the Whitewater scandal. Here Treasury Department official Roger Altman testifies before the committee. Altman resigned his position after he was accused by senators of both parties of withholding information from the committee. (Terry Ashe/Gamma-Liaison)

tive vetoes are under challenge as an unconstitutional infringement on executive authority, and their future is unclear.

Oversight is easier to mandate than to carry out. If congressional committees were to try to monitor all the bureaucracy's activities, they would have no time or energy to do anything else. Oversight normally is not pursued aggressively unless members of Congress are annoyed with an agency, have discovered that a legislative authorization is being grossly abused, or are reviewing a program for possible major changes.[45] (Congress's oversight function is discussed further in Chapter 13.)

CONGRESS: TOO MUCH PLURALISM?

The congressional debate in 1996 on the line-item veto revealed a lot about the institution. A line-item veto was needed, proponents said, because Congress lacked the discipline to say no to constituent and special interests. The spiraling national debt could be slowed by a curb on pork barrel spending, but Congress seemed unable to exercise this restraint on its own. Supporters of the veto were willing to surrender part of their institution's power of the purse to the president, who would be able to veto those provisions of an appropriations bill that seemed unnecessary or excessive without killing the entire bill. The discipline to bring pork barreling under control would come from outside the Congress rather than from within.

As the example illustrates, Congress is an institution torn between service to the nation and to the separate constituencies within it. Its members have responsibility for the nation's laws. Yet they depend for reelection on the voters of their states and districts and are highly responsive to constituency interests. This focus is facilitated by the committee system, which is organized around particular interests.

Pluralists argue that Congress should be responsive to constituent interests. The United States has in the presidency a majoritarian institution, and Congress is where the nation's diversity finds representation. From the pluralist perspective, Congress adds a necessary balance to the nation's politics. To its critics, on the other hand, Congress is so responsive to particular interests that it cannot ordinarily deal adequately with national policy needs. This criticism is quieted from time to time by a strong majoritarian thrust in Congress, as in the case of the Great Society programs of the 1960s or the more recent Contract with America. But these periods are atypical. Congress is ordinarily more responsive to a plurality of interests.

The fact is, Congress cannot at once be an institution that is highly responsive to overarching national problems and also highly responsive to local and particular concerns. In a real sense, the strengths of Congress are also its weaknesses. The features of Congress that make it responsive to constituent interests are the very same ones that make it difficult for Congress to act as a strong instrument of the majority. In a large and diverse nation, there is merit in an institution that is sensitive to the local and the particular. The enduring question is whether Congress leans too far in that direction.

SUMMARY

Members of Congress, once elected, are likely to be reelected. Members of Congress can use their office to publicize themselves, pursue a "service strategy" of responding to the needs of individual constituents, and secure pork barrel projects for their state or district. House members gain a greater advantage from these activities than do senators, whose larger constituencies make it harder for them to build close personal relations with voters and whose office is more likely to attract a strong challenger. Incumbency does have some disadvantages. Members of Congress must take positions on controversial issues, may blunder into a political scandal or indiscretion, must deal with changes in the electorate, or may face strong challengers; any of these conditions can reduce their reelection chances. By and large, however, the advantages of incumbency far outweigh the disadvantages, particularly for House members. Incumbents' advantages extend into their reelection campaigns. Their influential positions in Congress make it easier for them to raise campaign funds.

Congress is a fragmented institution. It has no single leader; the House and Senate have separate leaders, neither of whom can presume to speak for the other chamber. The principal party leaders of Congress are the Speaker of the House and the Senate majority leader. They share leadership power with committee and subcommittee chairpersons, who have influence on the policy decisions of their committee or subcommittee.

It is in the committees that most of the work of Congress is conducted. Each standing committee of the House and Senate has jurisdiction over congressional policy in a particular area (such as agriculture or foreign relations), as does each of its subcommittees. In most cases, the full House and Senate accept committee recommendations about passage of bills, although amendments to bills are quite common and committees are careful to take other members of Congress into account when making legislative decisions. Congress is a legislative system in which influence is widely dispersed, an arrangement that suits the power and reelection needs of its individual members.

The major function of Congress is to enact legislation. Yet the role it plays in developing legislation depends on the type of policy involved. Because of its divided chambers, weak leadership, and committee structure, as well as the concern of its members with state and district interests, Congress only occasionally takes the lead on broad national issues. Congress normally looks to the president for this leadership; nevertheless, presidential initiatives are passed by Congress only if they meet its members' expectations and usually only after a lengthy process of compromise and negotiation. Congress is more adept at handling legislation dealing with problems of narrow interest. Legislation of this sort is decided mainly in congressional committees, where interested legislators, bureaucrats, and groups concentrate their efforts on issues of mutual concern.

A second function of Congress is the representation of various interests. Members of Congress are highly sensitive to the state or district on which they depend for reelection. Members of Congress do respond to overriding national interests, but for most of them, local concerns generally come first. National and local representation often work through party representation, particularly on issues that divide the Democratic and Republican parties and their constituent groups.

Congress's third function is oversight, the supervision and investigation of the way the bureaucracy is implementing legislatively mandated programs. Although oversight is a difficult process, it is an important means of control over the actions of the executive branch.

MAJOR CONCEPTS

bill	party leaders
cloture	pork barrel projects
conference committee	reapportionment
constituency	redistricting
filibuster	representation function
jurisdiction	seniority
law	service strategy
lawmaking function	standing committees
oversight function	

SUGGESTED READINGS

Campbell, James E. *Cheap Seats: The Democratic Party's Advantage in U.S. House Elections.* Columbus: Ohio State University Press, 1997. A study of the relationship between turnout and outcomes in U.S. House races.

Herrnson, Paul S. *Congressional Elections: Campaigning at Home and in Washington.* Washington, D.C.: Congressional Quarterly Press, 1995. A thorough study of the changing nature of congressional campaigns.

Hibbing, John R., and Elizabeth Theiss-Morse. *Congress as Public Enemy: Public Attitudes toward American Political Institutions.* New York: Cambridge University Press, 1995. An analysis through survey and focus group data of Americans' attitudes toward Congress.

Hinckley, Barbara. *Less Than Meets the Eye: Foreign Policy Making and the Myth of the Assertive Congress.* Chicago: University of Chicago Press, 1994. An analysis of the limits of congressional attempts to influence foreign policy.

Krasno, Jonathan S. *Challenges, Competition, and Reelection: Comparing Senate and House Elections.* New Haven, Conn.: Yale University Press, 1995. A comparison of the competitiveness of House and Senate races that uses National Election Study (NES) data as evidence.

Sinclair, Barbara. *Legislators, Leaders, and Lawmaking: The U.S. House of Representatives in the Postreform Era.* Baltimore, Md.: Johns Hopkins University Press, 1995. A richly documented study of party leadership in Congress.

Swain, Carol M. *Black Faces, Black Interests: The Representation of African Americans in Congress.* Cambridge, Mass.: Harvard University Press, 1993. A critical assessment of the role of race in elections and representation.

Thomas, Sue. *How Women Legislate.* New York: Oxford University Press, 1994. A well-researched study that indicates women legislators pursue different policy agendas than men.

READING 11

Running for Congress
PAUL S. HERRNSON

In order to win a congressional election or even to be remotely competitive, candidates must compete in two campaigns: one for votes and one for resources. The campaign for votes is the campaign that generally comes to mind when people think about congressional elections. It requires a candidate to assemble an organization and to use that organization to target key groups of voters, select a message they will find compelling, deliver that message, and get the candidate's supporters to the polls on election day.

The other campaign, which is based largely in Washington, D.C., requires candidates to convince the party officials, political action committee (PAC) managers, political consultants, and political journalists who are the leaders of the nation's political community that their races will be competitive and worthy of support. Gaining the backing of these leaders is a critical step in attracting the money and campaign services that are available in the nation's capital and in other major urban centers. These resources enable the candidate to run a credible campaign back home. Without them, most congressional candidates would lose their bids for election. . . .

Candidates, not political parties, are the major focus of congressional campaigns, and candidates, not parties, bear the ultimate responsibility for election outcomes. These characteristics of congressional elections are striking when viewed from a comparative perspective. In most democracies, political parties are the principal contestants in election campaigns, and the campaigns tend to focus on national issues, ideology, and party programs and accomplishments. In the United States, parties do not actually run congressional campaigns nor do they become the major focus of elections. Instead, candidates run their own campaigns, and parties may contribute money or election services to them. A comparison of the terminology commonly used to describe elections in the United States and that used in Great Britain more than hints at the differences. In the United States, candidates are said to *run* for Congress, and they do so with or without party help. In

Great Britain, on the other hand, candidates are said to *stand* for election to Parliament, while their party runs most of the campaign. The difference in terminology only slightly oversimplifies reality.

Candidates are the most important actors in American congressional elections. Most of them are self-selected rather than recruited by party organizations. All of them must win the right to run under their party's label through a participatory primary, caucus, or convention. Only after they have secured their party's nomination are major-party candidates assured a place on the general election ballot. Independent and minor-party candidates can get on the ballot in other ways, usually by paying a registration fee or collecting several thousand signatures from district residents.

The nomination process in most other countries, on the other hand, usually begins with a small group of party activists pursuing the nomination through a "closed" process that allows only formal, dues-paying party members to participate. While the American system amplifies the input of caucus participants and primary voters, these other systems respond more to the input of local party activists and place more emphasis on peer review.

The need to win a party nomination forces congressional candidates to assemble their own campaign organizations, formulate their own election strategies, and conduct their own campaigns. The images and issues that they convey to voters in trying to win the nomination carry over to the general election. The efforts of individual candidates and their campaign organizations have a bigger impact on election outcomes than the activities of party organizations and other groups. . . .

Potential candidates survey the local political scene to determine whether conditions are ripe for a competitive election. Often they are not, and the result is that most congressional incumbents face weak challengers and many win by large margins. Between 1950 and 1990, House incumbents enjoyed reelection rates of better than 90 percent; the 1988 and 1990 elections returned to Congress 98.3 percent and 96 percent, respectively, of those who sought to keep their jobs. Most potential challengers find these success rates discouraging and choose to wait until a seat becomes vacant rather than run against an incumbent. Consequently, many House seats go uncontested, and a substantial portion fail to attract meaningful two-party competition.

Senate elections have been more competitive. Senate reelection rates ranged from 55.2 percent to 96.9 percent between 1946 and 1992. Between

1986 and 1990 only 5 percent of all Senate incumbents had no major-party opponent, and 58 percent of those involved in contested races won by 60 percent or more of the two-party vote. Fourteen percent of all senators seeking reelection during this six-year span were defeated. . . .

The desire of incumbents to retain their seats has changed Congress in ways that help discourage electoral competition. Most who are elected to Congress quickly come to terms with the fact that they will probably never hold a higher office because there are too few of these to go around. Like most people, they do everything in their power to hold on to their jobs. Congress has adapted to the career aspirations of its members by providing them with resources that can be used to increase their odds of reelection. Members use free mailings, WATS lines, district offices, and subsidized travel to gain visibility among their constituents. Federal "pork-barrel" projects also help incumbents gain popularity and visibility among voters. Congressional staffs help members write speeches, respond to constituent mail, resolve problems that constituents have with executive branch agencies, and follow the comings and goings in their bosses' districts. These "perks" of office give incumbents tremendous advantages over challengers. They also work to discourage those experienced politicians who could put forth a competitive challenge from taking on an entrenched incumbent.

The dynamics of campaign finance have similar effects. Incumbents have tremendous fund-raising advantages over challengers, especially among PACs. Many incumbents build up large war chests to discourage potential challengers from running against them. Those challengers who decide to contest a race against a member of the House or Senate typically find they are unable to raise the funds needed to mount a viable campaign.

Given that the cards tend to be so heavily stacked in favor of congressional incumbents, most electoral competition takes place in open seats, especially those that are not dominated by one party. Open-seat contests draw a larger than usual number of primary contestants. They also attract significantly more money and election assistance from party committees, PACs, and individuals than do challenger campaigns. Special elections are a form of open-seat contest that tend to be particularly competitive and unpredictable. They bring out even larger numbers of primary contenders than normal open-seat elections, especially when the seat that has become vacant was formerly held by a long-time incumbent.

The concentration of competition in open-seat elections and the decennial reapportionment and redistricting of House seats have combined to produce a ten-year, five-election cycle of political competition. Redistricting leads to the creation of many new House seats and the redrawing of the boundaries of numerous others. It encourages an increase in congressional retirements, leads more nonincumbents than usual to run for the House, and thereby increases competition in many House elections. Competition in the four election cycles that follow redistricting generally decreases as incumbents shore up their electoral support and work to discourage challenges by potentially strong opponents.

SOURCE: Paul S. Herrnson, *Congressional Elections: Campaigning at Home and in Washington* (Washington, D.C.: Congressional Quarterly Press, 1995). Reprinted by permission.
Paul S. Herrnson is a professor of government and politics at the University of Maryland.

CHAPTER TWELVE

The Presidency

[The president's] is the only voice in national affairs. Let him once win the admiration and confidence of the people, and no other single voice will easily overpower him.

Woodrow Wilson[1]

I N 1994 BILL Clinton demonstrated why the presidency has been described as "both the most dynamic and most dangerous of our political institutions."[2] Ignoring complaints from Congress that it had a legitimate voice in the decision, Clinton prepared to invade Haiti, whose military generals had taken power in a coup that unseated the nation's constitutionally elected president. The generals brutalized their opponents and caused a tide of refugees to depart for the United States in ramshackle boats. Many of those fleeing were lost at sea. When an embargo imposed by the United Nations failed to persuade the Haitian generals to leave office, Clinton readied an invasion force. Casualties were anticipated, and there were fears that the United States would get bogged down in the running of Haiti for years to come. Critics also questioned whether the United States had any business invading a country simply because it had one of the world's many brutal regimes.

Although the worst could have happened in Haiti, it did not. Within the hour that U.S. combat troops were scheduled to invade the island, the generals agreed to leave office. No lives were lost when the troops landed, and most of the U.S. forces in Haiti returned home within a few months. A potential disaster had become a policy success.

In pursuing his Haitian policy, Clinton exploited the leeway inherent in the president's constitutional authority. The writers of the Constitution knew what they wanted from a president—national leadership, statesmanship in foreign affairs, command in time of war or insurgency, enforcement of the laws—but could devise only general phrases to describe the president's constitutional authority. Compared with Article I, which enumerates Congress's specific powers, Article II of the Constitution contains relatively vague statements on the president's powers. This constitutional ambiguity, James W. Davis says, gives presidents "wide latitude in defining their presidential duties."[3]

Over the course of American history, each of the president's constitutional powers has been extended in practice beyond the Framers' intention. For example, the Constitution grants the president command of the nation's military, but only Congress can declare war. In *Federalist* No. 69 Alexander Hamilton wrote that a surprise attack on the United States was the only justification for war by presidential action. Nevertheless, the nation's presidents have sent troops into military action abroad more than 200 times. Of the twelve wars included in that figure, only five were declared by Congress.[4] Each of America's most recent wars—the Korean, Vietnam, and Persian Gulf wars—was undeclared.

The Constitution also empowers the president to act as diplomatic leader with the authority to receive ambassadors and the power to initiate diplomatic relations with other nations. The president is further empowered to appoint U.S. ambassadors and to negotiate treaties with other countries, subject to approval by the Senate. The Framers anticipated that Congress would have responsibility for developing foreign policy, while the president's job would be to oversee its implementation. However, the president has become the principal architect of U.S. foreign policy and has even acquired the power to make treatylike arrangements with other nations, in the form of executive agreements. In 1937 the Supreme Court ruled that such agreements, signed and approved only by the president, have the same legal status as treaties, which require approval by a two-thirds vote of the Senate.[5] Since World War II, presidents have negotiated more than 10,000 executive agreements, as compared with fewer than 1,000 treaties ratified by the Senate.[6]

The Constitution also vests "executive power" in the president. This includes the responsibility to execute the laws faithfully and to appoint major administrators, such as heads of the various departments of the executive branch. In *Federalist* No. 76 Hamilton indicated that the president's real authority as chief executive was to be found in this appointive capacity. Presidents have indeed exercised substantial power through their appointments, but they have found their administrative authority—the power to execute the laws—to be of even greater value, because it enables them to determine how laws will be interpreted and applied. President Ronald Reagan used his executive power to *prohibit* the use of federal funds by family-planning clinics that offered abortion counseling. President Bill Clinton exerted the same power to *permit* the use of federal funds for this purpose. The *same* act of Congress was the basis for each of these actions. The wording of the legislation was ambiguous enough to allow Reagan and Clinton to interpret it in opposite ways.

Finally, the Constitution provides the president with legislative authority, including use of the veto and the opportunity to recommend proposals to Congress. The Framers expected this authority to be used in a limited and largely negative way. George Washington acted as the Framers anticipated: he proposed only three legislative measures and vetoed only two acts of Congress. Modern presidents have a different, more activist view of their legislative role. They routinely submit legislative proposals to Congress and often veto legislation they find disagreeable.

The presidency is a more powerful office than the Framers envisioned for many reasons, but two features of the office in particular—*national election* and *singular authority*—have enabled presidents to make use of changing demands on government to claim the position of national leader. This chapter explores this development and then examines the presidential selection process and the staffing of the modern presidency, both of which contribute to the president's prominence in the American political system. The chapter concludes with an examination of presidents' policy role and the factors that contribute to the success and failure of their policy leadership. The main ideas of the chapter are these:

* *Changing national and world conditions have required the presidency to become a strong office; underlying this development is the public support that the president acquires from being the only nationally elected official.*

* *The modern presidential election campaign is a marathon affair in which self-selected candidates must plan for a strong start in the nominating contests and center their general election strategies on media and a baseline of party support.*

* *The modern presidency could not operate without a large staff of assistants, experts, and high-level managers, but the sheer size of this staff makes it impossible for the president to exercise complete control over it.*

* *The president's election by national vote and position as sole chief executive ensure that others will listen to the president's ideas; to succeed, however, the president must get others to back these ideas.*

FOUNDATIONS OF THE
MODERN PRESIDENCY

The first president forcefully to assert a claim to popular leadership was Andrew Jackson, who had been swept into office in 1828 on a tide of public support that broke the hold of the upper classes on the presidency. Jackson used his popular backing to challenge Congress's claim to national policy leadership, contending that he was "the people's tribune."

Jackson's view of the presidency, however, was not shared by most of his successors during the nineteenth century, because national conditions did not routinely call for strong presidential leadership. The prevailing conception of the presidency was the **Whig theory,** which held that the presidency was a limited or constrained office whose occupant was confined to the exercise of expressly granted constitutional authority. The president had no implicit powers for dealing with national problems but was primarily an administrator, charged with carrying out the expressed will of Congress. "My duty," said President James Buchanan, a Whig adherent, "is to execute the laws . . . and not my individual opinions."[7]

Theodore Roosevelt rejected the Whig tradition when he took office in 1901; he attacked the business trusts, pursued an aggressive foreign policy, and pressured Congress to adopt progressive domestic policies. Roosevelt embraced the **stewardship theory,** which calls for a strong, assertive presidential role that is confined only at points specifically prohibited by law, not by undefined inherent restrictions. As "steward of the people," Roosevelt said, he was obliged "to do anything that the needs of the Nation demanded unless such action was forbidden by the Constitution or by the laws."[8]

Roosevelt's image of a strong presidency was shared by Woodrow Wilson, but his other immediate successors reverted to the Whig notion of the limited presidency.[9] Herbert Hoover's restrained conception of the presidency prevented him from taking decisive action even during the economic devastation that followed the Wall Street crash of 1929. Hoover argued that he lacked the constitutional authority to establish public relief programs for jobless and penniless Americans.

Hoover's successor, Franklin D. Roosevelt, shared the stewardship theory of his distant cousin Theodore Roosevelt, and FDR's New Deal signaled the end of the limited presidency. Today the presidency is an inherently strong office.[10] The modern presidency becomes a more substantial office in the hands of a persuasive leader such as Lyndon Johnson or Ronald Reagan, but even a less forceful person such as Jimmy Carter or George Bush is now expected to act assertively. This expectation not only is the legacy of former strong presidents but also stems from changes that have occurred in the federal government's national and international policy responsibilities.

The Need for Presidential Leadership of an Activist Government

During most of the nineteenth century the United States did not need a strong president. The federal government's policymaking role was small, as was its bureaucracy. Moreover, the nation's major issues were of a sectional nature (especially the North–South split over slavery) and thus suited to action by Congress, which represented state and local interests. The U.S. government's role in world affairs was also small.

Today the situation has greatly changed. The federal government has such broad national and international responsibilities that strong leadership from presidents is essential.

FOREIGN POLICY LEADERSHIP   The president has always been the nation's foreign policy leader, but the role was initially a rather undemanding one. The United States avoided getting entangled in the turbulent politics of Europe, and though it was involved in foreign trade, its major preoccupation was its internal development. By the end of the nineteenth century, however, the nation was seeking to expand the world market for its goods, and the size and growing industrial power of the United States was attracting more attention from other nations. President Theodore Roosevelt advocated an American economic empire, looking south toward Latin America and west toward Hawaii, the Philippines, and China (the "Open Door" policy) for new markets. However, the United States' tradition of isolationism remained a powerful influence on national policy. The United States fought in World War I but immediately thereafter demobilized its armed forces. Over President Woodrow Wilson's objections, Congress then voted against the entry of the United States into the League of Nations.

World War II fundamentally changed the nation's international role and the president's role in foreign policy. In 1945 the United States emerged as a global superpower, a giant in world trade, and the recognized leader of the noncommunist world. The United States today has a military presence in nearly every part of the globe and an unprecedented interest in trade balances, energy supplies, and other international issues affecting the nation.[11]

The effects of these developments on America's political institutions have been largely one-sided.[12] Because of the president's constitutional authority

Harry S Truman's presidency was characterized by bold foreign policy initiatives. He authorized the use of nuclear weapons against Japan in 1945, created the Marshall Plan as the basis for the economic reconstruction of postwar Europe, and sent U.S. troops to fight in Korea in 1950. Truman is shown here greeting British Prime Minister Winston Churchill at a Washington airport in early 1952. (UPI/Bettmann Newsphotos)

as chief diplomat and military commander and the special demands of foreign policy leadership, the president, not Congress, has taken the lead in addressing the United States' increased responsibilities in the world. Foreign policy requires singleness of purpose and, at times, fast action. Congress—a large, divided, and often unwieldy institution—is poorly suited to such a response. In contrast, the president, as sole head of the executive branch, can act quickly and can speak authoritatively for the nation as a whole in its relations with other nations.

DOMESTIC POLICY LEADERSHIP   The change in the president's domestic leadership has also been substantial. Throughout most of the nineteenth century Congress jealously guarded its constitutional powers, making it clear that domestic policy was its business. James Bryce wrote in the 1880s that Congress paid no more attention to the president's views on legislation than it did to the editorial positions of prominent newspaper publishers.[13]

By the early twentieth century, however, the national government was taking on regulatory and policy responsibilities imposed by the nation's transition from an agrarian to an industrial society, and stronger presidential leadership was becoming necessary. In 1921 Congress conceded that it lacked the centralized authority to coordinate the growing national budget and enacted the Budget and Accounting Act, which provided for an executive budget.[14] Federal departments and agencies would no longer submit their annual budget requests directly to Congress. The president would oversee the initiation of the budget, developing the various agencies' requests into a comprehensive budgetary proposal, which would then be submitted to Congress as a starting point for its deliberations.

During the Great Depression of the 1930s, Franklin D. Roosevelt's New Deal responded to the public's demand for economic relief with a broad program that involved a level of policy planning and coordination that was beyond the capacity of Congress. In addition to initiating public works projects and social welfare programs aimed at providing immediate relief, the New Deal made the government a partner in nearly every aspect of the nation's economy. If economic regulation was to work, unified and continuous policy leadership was needed, and only the president could routinely provide it.

Presidential authority has continued to grow since Roosevelt's time. In response to pressures from the public, the national government's role in such areas as education, health, welfare, safety, and protection of the environment has expanded greatly, which in turn has created additional demands for presidential leadership.[15] Big government, with its emphasis on comprehensive planning and program coordination, has favored executive authority at the expense of legislative authority.

Executive authority was also strengthened when Americans looked increasingly to the national government for solutions to their common problems. Senators and representatives are chosen by voters within a single state or district, a limitation that diminishes the claim of any one of them to national leadership. The president, in contrast, is a nationally elected official and the sole chief executive. These features of the office enabled presidents, as the policy demands on the national government increased during the twentieth century, to assume powers and leadership that helped to transform the presidency into a permanently more powerful office.

CHOOSING THE PRESIDENT

As the president's policy and leadership responsibilities changed during the nation's history, so too did the process of electing presidents. The changes do not parallel each other exactly, but they are related politically and philosophically. As the presidency drew ever closer to the people, their role in selecting the president grew ever more important.[16] The United States in its history has had four systems of presidential selection, each more "democratic" than its predecessor (see Table 12-1).

TABLE 12-1   THE FOUR SYSTEMS OF PRESIDENTIAL SELECTION

Selection System	Period	Features
1. Original	1788–1828	Party nominees are chosen in congressional caucuses.
		Electoral College members act somewhat independently in their presidential voting.
2. Party convention	1832–1900	Party nominees are chosen in national party conventions by delegates selected by state and local party organizations.
		Electoral College members cast their ballots for the popular-vote winner in their respective states.
3. Party convention, primary	1904–1968	As in system 2, except that a *minority* of national convention delegates are chosen through primary elections (the majority still being chosen by party organizations).
4. Party primary, open caucus	1972–present	As in system 2, except that a *majority* of national convention delegates are chosen through primary elections.

Toward a More "Democratic" System of Presidential Election

The delegates to the constitutional convention of 1787 were steadfastly opposed to popular election of the president. They feared that popular election would make the office too centralized and too powerful, which would undermine the principles of federalism and separation of powers. The Framers devised a novel system, which came to be called the Electoral College. Under the Constitution, the president is chosen by a vote of electors who are appointed by the states; the candidate who receives the majority of electoral votes is elected president. Each state is entitled to as many electors as it has members of Congress.

In choosing the nation's first presidents, electors acted somewhat independently, exercising their own judgment in casting their votes. This pattern changed after the election in 1828 of Andrew Jackson, who believed the people's will had been denied four years earlier when he placed first in the popular voting but failed to gain an electoral majority. Jackson could not persuade Congress to support a constitutional amendment which would have eliminated the Electoral College but did obtain the next-best alternative: he persuaded the states to tie their electoral vote to the popular vote. Under Jackson's reform, which is still in effect today, each party in a state has a separate slate of electors who gain the right to cast a state's electoral votes if their party's candidate places first in the state's popular voting. Thus the popular vote for the candidates directly affects their electoral vote, and one candidate is likely to win both forms of the presidential vote. Since Jackson's time, only Rutherford B. Hayes (in 1876) and Benjamin Harrison (in 1888) have won the presidency after having lost the popular vote.

Jackson also championed the national convention as a means of nominating the party's presidential candidate (before this time, nominations were made by party caucuses in Congress and in state legislatures). The parties had their strength at the grassroots, among the people, and Jackson saw the convention process as a means of bringing the citizenry and the presidency closer together. Since Jackson's time, presidential nominees have been formally chosen at national party conventions.

The system of presidential selection that Jackson had created remained intact until the early twentieth century, when the Progressives initiated primary elections as a way of wresting control over presidential nominations from party bosses (see Chapter 3). However, most states either stayed with the older system of party selection or adopted nonbinding primaries. As a result, party leaders continued to control a majority of the convention delegates who selected the presidential nominees.

Through 1968, a strong showing in the primaries enabled a candidate to demonstrate popular support but did not guarantee nomination. In 1952, for example, Senator Estes Kefauver beat President Harry Truman in New Hampshire's opening primary and went on to win twelve of the thirteen primaries he entered; however, Kefauver was denied nomination by party leaders, who believed that his views were inconsistent with the party's traditions.

In 1968, the Democratic nomination went to Vice-President Hubert Humphrey, who had not entered a single primary and was closely identified with the Johnson administration's Vietnam war policy. After Humphrey narrowly lost the 1968 general election to Richard Nixon, reform-minded Democrats forced changes in the nominating process. The new rules gave rank-and-file party voters more control by requiring that states choose their delegates through either primary elections or **open party caucuses** (meetings open to any registered party voter who wants to attend). Although the Democrats initiated the change, the Republicans were also affected by it. Most states that adopted a presidential primary in order to comply with the Democrats' new rules also required Republicans to select their convention delegates through a primary.

Today it is the voters in state primaries and open caucuses who play the decisive role in the selection of the Democratic and Republican presidential nominees.[17] A state's delegates are awarded the candidates in accordance with how well they do in the state's primary or caucus. Thus, to win the majority of national convention delegates necessary for nomination, a candidate must place first in a lot of states and do at least reasonably well in most of the rest. (In recent presidential elections, about three-fourths of the states have chosen their delegates through a primary election while one-fourth have used a caucus system).

In sum, the presidential election system has changed from an elite-dominated process to one that is based on popular support. This arrangement has strengthened the president by providing the office with the reserve of power that popular election confers upon democratic leadership.

The Campaign for Nomination

The fact that the voters pick the nominees has made the nominating races more competitive than ever before.[18] The system is basically open to any politician with the energy and resources to run a major national campaign. Nominating campaigns, except those in which an incumbent president is seeking reelection, typically attract a half-dozen or more candidates. The most recent such contest, the 1996 Republican race, had nine contenders: four U.S. senators, a U.S. representative, a former governor, a former ambassador, a TV commentator, and a millionaire publisher.

A key to success in the nominating campaign is **momentum**—a solid showing in the early contests which leads to a buildup of public support in subsequent ones. If candidates start off strongly, the press will cover them more heavily, contributors will provide them more funding, and voters will give more thought to supporting them. For these reasons, presidential contenders now give extraordinary attention to the early contests, particularly the first caucuses in Iowa and the first primary in New Hampshire.[19]

Money has become a critical factor in the nominating races. This is so because many states have moved their primaries and caucuses to the early phase of the nominating period in an effort to increase their influence on the outcome. In the first month alone of the 1996 campaign, twenty-four state contests were scheduled. To compete effectively in so many contests in such a short period, candidates need money, lots of it. Dan Quayle and Jack Kemp were two of the potential challengers for the 1996 Republican nomination who decided not to run because of the money demands. By contrast, Bob Dole, Phil Gramm, and Lamar Alexander spent months on end in 1995 seeking the estimated $20 million that strategists believed would be necessary to run a strong campaign.

Candidates in primary elections are assisted by the Federal Election Campaign Act of 1974 (as amended in 1979). This act provides for federal "matching funds" to be given to any candidate who raises at least $5,000 in individual contributions of up to $250 in each of twenty states. Candidates who accept matching funds must agree to limit their expenditures to a set amount, which is adjusted each election year to account for inflation. In 1996 the spending limit for each candidate for the nominating phase of the campaign was roughly $30 million.

After the state primaries and caucuses have been held, the national party conventions occur. These were once tumultuous affairs during which lengthy, heated bargaining took place before a presidential nominee was chosen. An extreme case was the Democratic convention of 1924, at which delegates took 103 ballots and ended up nominating an unknown "dark horse," John W. Davis. Today's conventions are relatively tame; not since 1952 has a nomination gone past the first ballot. The leading candidate has usually acquired enough delegates in the primaries and caucuses to lock up the nomination before the convention even begins. Nevertheless, the party convention is a major event. It brings together the delegates elected in state cau-

Although the national conventions are not the tumultuous and decisive events they once were, they do offer the political parties a showcase for their candidates and platforms. Shown here is a scene from the 1996 Republican convention, which selected Bob Dole and Jack Kemp as the party's presidential and vice-presidential nominees. (Joe Traver/Gamma-Liaison)

cuses and primaries, who then vote to approve a party platform and to nominate the party's presidential and vice-presidential candidates.

By tradition, the choice of the vice-presidential nominee rests with the presidential nominee. Critics have argued that the vice-presidential nomination should be decided in open competition, since the vice-president stands a good chance of becoming president someday. The chief argument for keeping the existing system is that the president needs a trusted and like-minded vice-president.

The Campaign for Election

The winner in the November general election is almost certain to be either the Republican or the Democratic nominee. A minor-party or independent candidate, such as George Wallace in 1968, John Anderson in 1980, or Ross Perot in 1992 and 1996, can draw votes away from the major-party nominees but stands almost no chance of defeating them. A major-party nominee has the critical advantage of support from the party faithful. Although party loyalty has declined in recent decades (see Chapters 6, 7, and 8), two-thirds of the nation's voters still identify themselves as Democrats or Republicans, and most of them support their party's presidential candidate. Even Democrat George McGovern, who had the lowest level of party support among recent nominees, was backed in 1972 by 60 percent of his party's voters.

ELECTION STRATEGY   The candidates' strategies in the general election are shaped by many considerations, including the constitutional provision that each state shall have electoral votes equal in number to its representation in Congress. Each state thus gets two electoral votes for its Senate representation and a varying number of electoral votes depending on its House representation. Altogether, there are 538 electoral votes (including three for the District of Columbia, even though it has no voting representatives in Congress). To win the presidency, a candidate must receive at least 270 votes, an electoral majority.

The importance of the electoral votes is magnified by the existence of the *unit rule;* all the states except Maine and Nebraska grant all their electoral votes as a unit to the candidate who wins the state's popular vote. For this reason, candidates are particularly concerned with winning the most populous states, such as California (with 54 electoral votes), New York (33), Texas (32), Florida (25), Pennsylvania (23), Illinois (22), and Ohio (21). Victory in the eleven largest states alone would provide an electoral majority, and presidential candidates therefore spend most of their time campaigning in those states.[20] Because of the unit rule, a relatively small popular vote margin can produce a lopsided electoral vote margin. Clinton received 49 percent of the popular vote in 1996, compared with Dole's 41 percent and Perot's 9 percent, but Clinton won in states that gave him an overwhelming 379 electoral votes, compared with 159 for Dole and none for Perot (see box: States in the Nation).

MEDIA AND MONEY   The modern presidential campaign is a media campaign. At one time, candidates relied heavily on party organization and rallies to carry their messages to the voters, but now they depend on the media, particularly television.[21] Candidates strive to produce the pithy ten-second "sound bites" that the television networks prefer to highlight on the evening newscasts. They also rely on the power of the "new media," making frequent appearances on such programs as *Larry King Live.*

Television is the forum for the major confrontation of the fall cam-

STATES IN THE NATION

Electoral Votes and the 1996 Election

The larger a state's population is, the more electoral votes it has—and the more important it is to presidential candidates. Each state's electoral votes are shown on the map below, along with the states carried by candidates Bill Clinton and Robert Dole in the 1996 election. Because of the unit rule, the electoral vote outcome is usually one-sided. Clinton won 49 percent of the popular vote but received 70 percent of the electoral votes (379 out of 538 total votes) by placing first in thirty-one states and the District of Columbia.

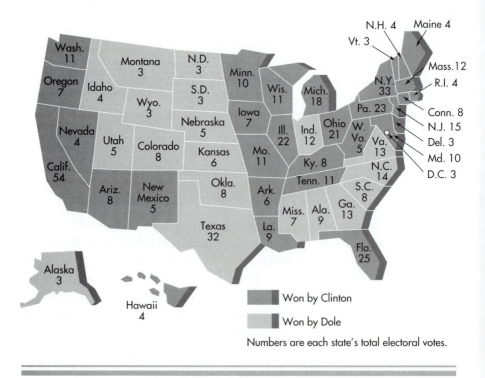

Won by Clinton

Won by Dole

Numbers are each state's total electoral votes.

paign—the presidential debates. The first televised debate took place in 1960 between Kennedy and Nixon, and an estimated 100 million people saw at least one of their four debates.[22] Televised debates resumed in 1976 and have become an apparently permanent fixture of presidential campaigns.

The television campaign includes political advertising. Televised commercials are by far the most expensive part of presidential campaign politics. Since 1976, political commercials on television have accounted for about half the candidates' expenditures in the general election campaign. Kathleen Hall Jamieson describes the role of advertising in the modern campaign as "packaging the presidency."[23] In 1996 Clinton and Dole each spent more than $30 million on advertising in the general election, and Perot spent more than $20 million. Perot relied heavily on "infomercials"— thirty-minute and hourlong commercials that emphasized substance over slogans.

The Republican and Democratic nominees are each eligible for a federal grant for their general election campaigns. The grant was set at $20 million in 1975 and is adjusted for inflation during each campaign. Clinton and Dole each received a grant of about $60 million in 1996 for their general election campaigns. The only string attached to this funding is that candidates who accept it can spend no additional funds on their campaigns (though their party can spend additional money on their behalf). Presidential candidates can refuse to accept public funding, in which case the amount they spend is limited only by their ability to raise money privately. However, all major-party nominees since 1976 have accepted public funding. Other candidates for the presidency qualify for federal funding if they receive at least 5 percent of the vote and do not spend more than $50,000 of their own money on the campaign. In 1992, Perot spent over $60 million of his own money and thus was ineligible for federal funding.

THE WINNERS   The Constitution specifies only that the president must be at least thirty-five years old, a natural-born U.S. citizen, and a U.S. resident for at least fourteen years. Yet the winners of all recent presidential elections, as it has been throughout the nation's history, have been white males. The great majority of presidents have also been well-to-do Anglo-Saxon Protestants. Only one Catholic (Kennedy) has been elected. Except for four Army generals, no man has won the presidency who has not first held high public office. Nearly a third of the nation's presidents had previously been vice-presidents, and most of the rest were former U.S. senators, state governors, or top federal executives. In recent times, the vice-presidency has been the inside track to the presidency. Five of the ten presidents between 1948 and 1996 were former vice-presidents (Truman, Nixon, Johnson, Ford, and Bush), and two other vice-presidents (Humphrey and Mondale) were presidential nominees.

STAFFING THE PRESIDENCY

When Americans go to the polls on election day, most of them have in mind the choice between two individuals, the Democratic and the Republican presidential nominees. In effect, however, they are choosing a lot more than a single executive leader. They are also picking a secretary of state, the director of the FBI, the chair of the Federal Reserve Board, and a host of other executives, all of whom are presidential appointees.

Presidential Appointees

Newly elected presidents gain important advantages from their appointment powers. First, their appointees are a source of policy information. Modern policymaking requires a detailed understanding of policy issues, and this knowledge is a source of considerable power in Washington. Second, these appointees extend the president's reach into the huge federal bureaucracy, exerting influence on the day-to-day workings of the agencies they head. Not surprisingly, presidents have tended to appoint individuals who share their political and policy goals.

THE EXECUTIVE OFFICE OF THE PRESIDENT   The key staff organization is the Executive Office of the President (EOP), which Congress created in 1939 to provide the president with the staff necessary to coordinate the activities of the executive branch.[24] The EOP has since become the command center of the presidency.[25] It currently consists of ten organizations (see Figure 12-1). They include the White House Office (WHO), which consists of the president's closest personal advisers; the Office of Management and Budget (OMB), which consists of experts who formulate and then administer the federal budget; the National Security Council (NSC), which advises the president on foreign and military affairs; and the Council of Economic Advisers (CEA), which advises the president on the national economy.[26] The Office of the Vice-President is also part of the EOP.

The Vice-President.   Although the vice-president works in the White House, no constitutional authority comes along with this office. Accordingly, the president decides the role the vice-president will play. Earlier presidents

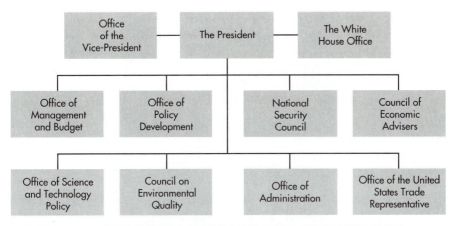

FIGURE 12-1 EXECUTIVE OFFICE OF THE PRESIDENT (EOP)
The EOP helps the president to manage the rest of the executive branch and promotes the president's policy and political goals.

often refused to assign any significant duties to their vice-president, which diminished the office's appeal. Nomination to the vice-presidency was refused by many leading politicians, including Daniel Webster and Henry Clay. Said Webster, "I do not propose to be buried until I am really dead."[27] Recent presidents, however, have assigned important duties to their vice-presidents. Bill Clinton, for instance, gave Al Gore broad responsibility for environmental policy and put him in charge of the National Performance Review, a 200-member task force that sought ways to streamline government. Among its recommendations was a 12 percent cut in federal employment over five years at an estimated savings of $108 billion.

The White House Office. Of the EOP's ten organizations, the White House Office serves the president most directly and personally. The WHO consists of the president's personal assistants, including close personal advisers, press agents, legislative and group liaison aides, and special assistants for domestic and international policy. They work in the White House, and the president can hire and fire them at will. The personal assistants do much of the legwork for the president and serve as a main source of advice. Because of their closeness and loyalty to the president, they are among the most powerful individuals in Washington.

Policy Experts. The president is also served by the policy experts in the EOP's other organizations, who include economists, legal analysts, national security specialists, and others. The president is advised on economic issues, for example, by the Council of Economic Advisers, headed by three econo-

At the start of his second term, President Clinton chose
Erskine Bowles to head his staff. The White House chief-
of-staff manages the president's time and coordinates the
work of White House assistants. Bowles replaced Leon
Panetta, a former member of Congress, who was widely
credited with helping Clinton to resuscitate his presidency
after a weak first year. (Reuters/Ira Schwarz/Archive Photos)

mists who are appointed by the president and assisted by an expert staff. The
CEA gathers information to develop indicators of the economy's strength and
applies economic theories to various policy alternatives. Modern policymaking cannot be conducted in the absence of such expert advice and knowledge.

THE PRESIDENT'S CABINET   The heads of the fourteen executive departments, such as the Department of Defense and the Department of Agriculture, constitute the president's **cabinet.** They are appointed by the president, subject to confirmation by the Senate. Although the cabinet once
served as the president's main advisory group, it has not played this role since
Herbert Hoover's administration. As national issues have become increasingly complex, the cabinet has become outmoded as a policymaking forum:
department heads are likely to understand issues only in their respective policy areas.[28] Cabinet meetings have been largely reduced to gatherings at
which only the most general matters are discussed.

Although the cabinet as a collective decision-making body is a thing of the past, the cabinet members, as individuals who head major departments, are important figures in any administration. The president chooses them for their prominence in politics, business, government, or the professions. Many of them also bring to their office a high level of policy expertise.[29] The secretary of state, for example, is normally a person with years of high-level experience in foreign affairs.

OTHER PRESIDENTIAL APPOINTEES In addition to cabinet secretaries, the president appoints the directors and top deputies of federal agencies, members of federal commissions, and heads of regulatory agencies. Altogether, the president appoints more than 5,000 executive officials. However, most of these appointees are selected at the agency level or are part-time workers. This still leaves nearly 700 appointees who serve the president more or less directly, which is a much larger number than any other democracy's chief executive appoints.[30]

The Problem of Control

Although the president's appointees are a valuable asset, they also pose a problem: because they are so numerous, the president has difficulty controlling them. Most appointees are not under the president's direct supervision and have considerable freedom to act on their own initiative—not necessarily in accord with the president's wishes. President Truman had a wall chart in the Oval Office listing more than 100 officials who reported directly to him and often told visitors, "I cannot even see all of these men, let alone actually study what they are doing."[31] Since Truman's time the number of bureaucratic agencies has more than doubled, compounding the problem of presidential control over subordinates.[32]

The nature of the control problem varies with the type of appointee. The advantages of having the advice of policy experts, for example, is offset somewhat by the fact that they often have little political experience and tend to exaggerate the importance of their particular policy interests. As a result, their proposals are sometimes impractical or politically unacceptable. On the other hand, top political appointees, while adept at politics, have a tendency to act too independently. WHO assistants tend naturally to skew information in a direction that supports the course of action they favor.[33] At times they even presume to undertake important actions without first obtaining clearance from the president or a chief assistant, leading others to question the president's authority or performance.[34] In 1996, for example, President

Clinton found himself embroiled in controversy when it became known that a low-ranking White House assistant, Craig Livinstone, had unlawfully requested hundreds of personnel files from the FBI, many of them on top Republicans who had served in the Reagan and Bush administrations. "File-gate," as the incident came to be called, resulted in congressional hearings and news stories that were highly critical of Clinton's administrative oversight.

The problem of presidential control is even more severe in the case of appointees who work outside the White House, in the departments and agencies. The loyalty of agency heads and cabinet secretaries is often split between a desire to help the president with his goals and an interest in boosting themselves or the agency they lead.[35] Lower-level appointees within the departments and agencies pose a different type of problem. The president rarely, if ever, sees them, and they are typically political novices (most have fewer than two years of government experience) and not very knowledgeable about policy. These appointees are often "captured" by the agency in which they work because they depend for advice on the agency's career bureaucrats (Chapter 13 examines further the relationship between presidential appointees and career bureaucrats.)

In sum, the modern presidency is a double-edged sword. Presidents today have greater responsibilities than their predecessors, and the increase in responsibilities expands their opportunities to exert power. At the same time, the range of these responsibilities is so broad that they must rely on staffers who may or may not act in the best interests of the president. The modern president's recurring problem is to find some way of making sure that aides serve the interests of the presidency above all others. The subject of presidential control of the executive branch will be discussed further in Chapter 13.

FACTORS IN PRESIDENTIAL LEADERSHIP

The president operates within a system of separate institutions that share power (see box: How the United States Compares). Significant presidential action normally depends on the approval of Congress, the cooperation of the bureaucracy, and sometimes the acceptance of the judiciary. Since other officials have their own priorities, presidents do not always get their way. Congress in particular—more than the courts or the bureaucracy—holds the key to presidential success. Without congressional authorization and funding, most presidential proposals are nothing but ideas, empty of action.

HOW THE UNITED STATES COMPARES

Systems of Executive Policy Leadership

The United States instituted a presidential system in 1789 as part of its constitutional checks and balances. This form of executive leadership was copied in Latin America but not in Europe. European democracies adopted parliamentary systems, in which executive leadership is provided by a prime minister, who is a member of the legislature. In recent years some European prime ministers have campaigned and governed as if they were a singular authority rather than the head of a collective institution. France in the 1960s created a separate chief executive office but retained its parliamentary form of legislature.

The policy leadership of a president can differ substantially from that of a prime minister. As a singular head of an independent branch of government, a president does not have to share executive authority but nevertheless depends on the willingness of the legislative branch to support his leadership. By comparison, a prime minister shares executive leadership with a cabinet, but once agreement within the cabinet is reached, he or she is almost assured of the legislative support necessary to carry out policy initiatives.

Presidential System	Presidential/ Parliamentary System	Parliamentary System
Mexico	Finland	Australia
United States	France	Belgium
Venezuela		Canada
		Germany
		Great Britain
		Italy
		Japan
		Netherlands
		Sweden

Theodore Roosevelt expressed a wish that he could "be the president and Congress, too," if only for a day, so that he would have the power to adopt as well as propose programs.

Given that presidents must elicit support from others if they are to succeed, what is the record of presidential success? One way to judge is to measure the extent to which Congress backs legislative initiatives developed by the White House. No president has come close to getting enactment of all the programs that he placed before Congress. The average success rate is just below 50 percent, but there has been wide variation.[36] Johnson saw 69 percent of his 1965 initiatives enacted, whereas Nixon attained only 20 percent in 1973. Moreover, presidents have had markedly less success on their more ambitious proposals than on lesser ones.[37]

Whether a president's initiatives are likely to succeed or fail depends on several factors, including the force of circumstance, the stage of the president's term, the president's support in Congress, and the level of public support for the president's leadership. Let us examine each of these factors.

The Force of Circumstance

During his first months in office and in the midst of the Great Depression, Franklin D. Roosevelt accomplished the most sweeping changes in domestic policy in the nation's history. Congress moved quickly to pass nearly every New Deal initiative he proposed. In 1964 and 1965 Lyndon Johnson pushed landmark civil rights and social welfare legislation through Congress on the strength of the civil rights movement, the legacy of the assassinated President Kennedy, and large Democratic majorities in the House and Senate. When Ronald Reagan assumed the presidency in 1981, high unemployment and inflation had greatly weakened the national economy and created a mood for significant change, which enabled Reagan to persuade Congress to support some of the most notable taxing and spending changes in history.

From presidencies such as these has come the popular impression that presidents single-handedly decide national policy. However, each of these periods of presidential dominance was marked by a special set of circumstances: a decisive election victory that gave added force to the president's leadership, a compelling national problem that convinced Congress and the public that bold presidential action was needed, and a president who was mindful of what was expected and who vigorously advocated policies consistent with those expectations.

When conditions are favorable, the power of the presidency appears awesome. The problem for most presidents is that conditions are not normally conducive to strong leadership. The political scientist Erwin Hargrove suggests that presidential influence depends largely on circumstance.[38] Some presidents serve in periods when resources are scarce or important problems are surfacing in American society but have not yet become critical. Such a situation, Hargrove contends, works against the president's efforts to accomplish significant policy change. In 1994, reflecting on the constraints of budget deficits and other factors beyond his control, Clinton said he had no choice but "to play the hand that history had dealt him."

The Stage of the President's Term

If conditions conducive to great accomplishments occur infrequently, it is nonetheless the case that nearly every president has favorable moments. Such moments tend to come during the first months in office. Most newly elected presidents enjoy a **honeymoon period** during which Congress, the press, and the public anticipate initiatives from the Oval Office and are more predisposed than usual to support these initiatives.

Not surprisingly, presidents have put forth more new programs in their first year in office than in any subsequent year. James Pfiffner uses the term "strategic presidency" to refer to a president's need to move quickly on priority items to take advantage of the policy momentum that is gained from the election.[39] Later in their terms, presidents tend to do less well in presenting initiatives and getting them enacted. They may run out of good ideas or, more likely, deplete their political resources—the momentum of their election is gone and sources of opposition have emerged. Furthermore, if they blunder or if conditions turn sour—and it is hard for any president to serve for any length of time without a serious setback of one kind or another—they will lose some of their credibility and public support. Even highly successful presidents like Johnson and Reagan tend to have weak records in their final years. Franklin Roosevelt began his presidency with a remarkable period of achievement—the celebrated "Hundred Days"—but during his last six years in office, few of his major domestic proposals were enacted.

An irony of the presidency, then, is that presidents are most powerful when they are least knowledgeable—during their first months in office. These months can, as a result, be times of risk as well as times of opportunity. An example is the Bay of Pigs fiasco during the first year of John Kennedy's presidency, in which a U.S.-backed invasion force of anticommunist Cubans was easily defeated by Fidel Castro's army.

The White House contains, on the first floor, the president's Oval Office, other offices, and ceremonial rooms. The First Family's living quarters are on the second floor. (Bruce Hoertel/Gamma-Liaison)

Relations with Congress

Although the presidency is not nearly as powerful as most Americans assume, the capacity of presidents to influence the agenda of national debate is unrivaled, reflecting their unique claim to represent the whole country. Whenever the president directs attention to a particular issue or program, the attention of others usually follows. But will those others follow the president's lead? As we have noted, a president's support varies with conditions, some of which clearly cannot be controlled. Yet presidents are not entirely at the mercy of circumstance. As sole chief executive, a president is an active participant in his fate and can increase the chance of success by striving to build support in Congress and with the American people.

SEEKING COOPERATION FROM CONGRESS   As the center of national attention, presidents can easily start to believe that their ideas should prevail over those of Congress. This line of reasoning invariably gets any president into trouble. Jimmy Carter had not held national office before he was elected in 1976, so he had no clear understanding of how Washington operates.[40] Soon after taking office, Carter deleted from his budget nineteen public works projects that he believed were a waste of taxpayers' money, ignoring the importance that members of Congress attach to obtaining federally funded projects for their constituents. Carter's action set the tone for a conflict-ridden relationship with Congress.

In order to get the help of members of Congress, the president must respond to their interests as they respond to his. The presidential scholar Fred Greenstein concludes that "whatever else his qualities, the president needs to be a working politician who can work with or otherwise win over the Washington community."[41]

The use of the presidential veto illustrates the point. Presidents can sometimes force Congress to accommodate their views through the use or threatened use of the veto. Congress can seldom muster the two-thirds majority in each chamber required to override a presidential veto, and so the threat of a veto can make Congress more responsive to the president's demands.[42] When a major civil rights bill was being debated in Congress in 1991, George Bush said flatly that he would veto any bill that imposed hiring "quotas" on employers; his ultimatum forced Congress to alter provisions of the bill. Yet the veto is more effective as a presidential restraint on Congress than as a device by which Congress can be forced to take positive action on the president's proposals. The presidential scholar Richard Neustadt argues that the veto is more a sign of presidential weakness than strength, because it usually comes into play when Congress has refused to go along with the president's ideas.[43]

In 1996, Congress enacted legislation that gives the president a line-item veto of spending bills. This veto power allows the president to void (subject to override by a two-thirds vote of the House and Senate) specific spending items without vetoing the entire bill. Critics claim that the line-item veto cedes too much of Congress's power of the purse to the president. They also claim that the line-item veto is unconstitutional (a definitive court ruling on this point is virtually certain within a few years). Advocates see the line-item veto as a way for the president to curb unnecessary pork barrel projects that often get attached to spending bills.

THE PRESIDENT'S PARTISAN SUPPORT IN CONGRESS   The fact that they represent separate state or district constituencies can place individual members of Congress at odds with one another as well as with the president, whose constituency is a national one. Representatives of urban and rural areas, wealthier and poorer constituencies, and different regions of the country often have very different views of the national interest. To obtain majority support in Congress, the president must find ways to overcome these differences.

No source of unity is more important to presidential success than partisanship. Presidents are more likely to succeed when their own party controls Congress (see Figure 12-2). Between 1954 and 1992, each Republican president—Eisenhower, Nixon, Ford, Reagan, and Bush—had to contend with a Democratic majority in one or both houses of Congress. Congress passed a smaller percentage of the initiatives proposed by each of these presidents than by any Democratic president of the period—Kennedy, Johnson, or Carter.[44] In his first two years in office, backed by Democratic majorities in the House and Senate, Clinton had a high proportion of his initiatives enacted into law. After Republicans took control of Congress in 1995, Clin-

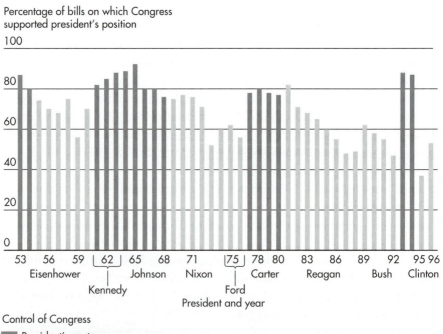

Percentage of bills on which Congress
supported president's position

Control of Congress
President's party
Other party (1 or both houses)

FIGURE 12-2 PERCENTAGE OF BILLS PASSED BY CONGRESS ON WHICH THE PRESIDENT ANNOUNCED A POSITION, 1953–1996
In most years, presidents have been supported by Congress on a majority of policy issues on which they have taken a stand. Presidents fare better when their party controls Congress. Source: *Congressional Quarterly Weekly Report*, December 21, 1996.

ton's legislative success rate sank to the lowest of any recent Democratic president.

COLLIDING WITH CONGRESS On rare occasions, presidents have pursued their goals so zealously that Congress has felt it had no choice but to take steps to curb their use of power.

The ultimate sanction of Congress is its constitutional power to impeach and remove the president from office. The House of Representatives decides whether the president should be impeached (placed on trial), and the Senate conducts the trial and then votes on the president's guilt, with a two-thirds vote required for removal from office. In 1868 Andrew Johnson was impeached and came within one Senate vote of being removed from office for his opposition to Congress's harsh Reconstruction policies after the Civil War. In 1974 Richard Nixon's resignation halted congressional proceedings on the Watergate affair that would almost certainly have ended in his impeachment and removal from office.

The gravity of impeachment action makes it an unsuitable basis for curbing presidential power except in rare instances. More often, Congress has responded to abuses of power with hearings or legislation designed to curb the practice. In 1974, for example, Congress passed a law forbidding the president from withholding appropriated funds. President Nixon had refused to release funds for programs he opposed, which meant in effect that the programs were nullified, even though they had been authorized and funded by Congress. The new legislation prohibits such action.

The Nixon presidency also contributed to the War Powers Act, which is perhaps Congress's most significant effort in history to curb presidential power. During the Vietnam war, presidents Johnson and Nixon repeatedly told Congress that victory was near, providing intelligence estimates of enemy casualties and capabilities to support their argument. This information contributed to the continued willingness of Congress to appropriate the funds necessary for the conduct of the war. However, congressional support changed abruptly in 1971 with *The New York Times*'s publication of secret government documents (the so-called Pentagon Papers) that revealed Johnson had misled Congress in order to pursue the war as he saw fit. To prevent future presidential wars, Congress in 1973 passed the War Powers Act. Nixon vetoed the measure, but Congress overrode his veto. The act stipulates that:

- Within 48 hours of committing combat troops, the president must inform Congress in writing of his reasons for doing so.

- Unless Congress acts to extend the period, hostilities involving American troops must end in sixty days, although the troops can remain for an additional thirty days if the president declares that extra time is needed for their safe withdrawal.

- Within the extra thirty days, Congress can demand the immediate withdrawal of the troops by passing a concurrent resolution, which is not subject to presidential veto.

- In every possible instance, the president must consult with Congress before dispatching troops into hostile situations or into areas where such situations are likely to arise.

Every president from Nixon to Clinton has claimed that the act infringes on his constitutional power as commander in chief, and each has refused to accept it fully. Nevertheless, since Vietnam, Congress has shown no willingness to give the president anything approaching a free hand in the use of military force.

U.S. troops move into Haiti in 1994 on the orders of President Bill Clinton, acting as commander in chief of the armed forces. Undertaking such short-term military actions without the formal consent of Congress is legal under the War Powers Act. (Stephen Ferry/Gamma-Liaison)

Thus the effect of executive efforts to circumvent congressional authority is heightened congressional opposition. Even if presidents gain in the short run by acting on their own, they undermine their capacity to lead in the long run by failing to keep in mind that Congress is a coequal branch of the American governing system.

Nurturing Public Support

Public support has a powerful effect on presidents' ability to achieve their policy goals.[45] Much of their power rests on a claim to national leadership, and the legitimacy of that claim is roughly proportional to public support of the president's performance. As long as the public is behind him, the president's leadership cannot easily be dismissed by other Washington officials. If public support sinks, they are less inclined to accept his leadership.[46]

Every recent president has had the public's confidence at the very start of the term of office. When asked in polls whether they "approve or disapprove of how the president is doing his job," a majority have expressed approval during the first months of the term. Sooner or later, however, all **presidential approval ratings** have slipped below this high point, and only Eisenhower, Kennedy, and Reagan left office with a final-year average higher than 50 percent (see Table 12-2).

EVENTS AND ISSUES The public's support for the president is affected by national and international conditions. Threats from abroad tend to produce a patriotic "rally 'round the flag" reaction that initially creates widespread support for the president. Every foreign policy crisis in the past four decades has fitted this pattern. Yet ongoing crises usually erode a president's support. Within a month after Iranian extremists invaded the U.S. embassy in Teheran in November 1979 and took fifty-nine Americans hostage, Carter's public approval rating jumped by 20 points.[47] As months passed without a resolution of the hostage situation, however, Carter's popularity began to sink and his hold on the presidency began to slip. He lost the November election, partly because the hostage crisis remained unresolved.

Pocketbook issues are most closely related to the president's ability to sustain a high level of public support. Research indicates that economic downswings sharply reduce the public's confidence in the president.[48] For example, Bush experienced a precipitous decline in popularity in late 1991,

TABLE 12-2 PERCENTAGE OF PUBLIC EXPRESSING
APPROVAL OF PRESIDENT'S PERFORMANCE, 1945–1993
Presidential approval ratings are typically higher at the beginning of the
term than at the end.

President	Years in Office	Average during Presidency	First-Year Average	Final-Year Average
Harry Truman	1945–1952	41%	63%	35%
Dwight Eisenhower	1953–1960	64	74	62
John Kennedy	1961–1963	70	76	62
Lyndon Johnson	1963–1968	55	78	40
Richard Nixon	1969–1974	49	63	24
Gerald Ford	1974–1976	46	75	48
Jimmy Carter	1977–1980	47	68	46
Ronald Reagan	1981–1988	53	58	57
George Bush	1989–1992	61	65	40
Bill Clinton	1993–	—	50	—

SOURCE: Averages compiled from Gallup polls.

which coincided with declining employment and productivity, and resulted ultimately in his defeat in the 1992 election. Apparently the best thing that a president can do to ensure his political success is to preside over a healthy economy.

THE TELEVISED PRESIDENCY   A major advantage that presidents enjoy in their efforts to nurture public support is their guaranteed access to the media, particularly television.[49] The television medium exalts personality, and the president is ordinarily the most compelling and familiar figure in the American political system. Only the president can expect the television networks to provide free airtime on demand, and in terms of the amount of news coverage received, the president towers over all members of Congress combined.

The political scientist Samuel Kernell calls it "going public" when the president bypasses inside bargaining with Congress and promotes "himself and his policies by appealing to the American public for support."[50] Such appeals are at least as old as Theodore Roosevelt's use of the presidency as a "bully pulpit" but have increased substantially in recent years.[51] As the president has moved from an administrative leader to a policy advocate and agenda setter, public support has become increasingly important to presidential success.[52] Television has made it easier for presidents to go public with their programs. Ronald Reagan was called the "Great Communicator" in part because of his ability to use television to generate public support for his initiatives.

However, the press is also adept at putting its own spin on events, and this spin is typically a negative one. The press is often very critical of politicians and of the process within which they operate. During Clinton's first year, for example, the press roundly criticized him for reneging on his campaign promises. This for a president who according to a Knight-Ridder summary had kept or was actively pursuing in Congress 75 percent of the promises he had made during his election campaign; included were major legislative battles already won, such as a tax increase on upper incomes, gun control, an end to the ban on abortion counseling in federally funded clinics, and budget-deficit reduction. The press's version of reality was based on broken promises on a couple of problems that would not go away. Clinton had backed away from a pledge to open the nation's shores to the Haitian boat people, and each tide of immigrants produced additional stories on his broken promise. In contrast, the promises he kept were in the news only a day or two and then not mentioned again. Kept promises are not nearly as newsworthy as broken ones. The media's interpretation of Clinton's presidency had a substantial impact. Every rise in the press criticism of Clinton was followed soon thereafter by a drop in his public approval rating.

THE ILLUSION OF PRESIDENTIAL GOVERNMENT   Presidents have no choice but to try to counter this type of press coverage with their own version of their accomplishments. A public relations effort can carry a president only so far, however. National conditions ultimately determine the level of public confidence in the president. Indeed, presidents run a risk by trying to build up their images through public relations. Through their frequent television appearances and claims of success, presidents contribute to the public's belief that the president is in charge of the national government, a perception that the political scientist Hugh Heclo calls "the illusion of presidential government."[53]

Because the public expects so much from its presidents, they get too much credit when things go well and too much blame when things go badly. Therein lies an irony of the presidential office. More than from any constitutional grant, more than from any statute, and more than from any crisis, presidential power derives from the president's position as the sole official who can claim to represent the whole American public. Yet because presidential power rests on a popular base, it erodes when public support declines. The irony is that the presidential office grows weaker as problems mount: just when the country could most use effective leadership, that leadership is often hardest to achieve.[54]

SUMMARY

The presidency has become a much stronger office than the Framers envisioned. The Constitution grants the president substantial military, diplomatic, legislative, and executive powers, and in each case the president's authority has increased measurably. Underlying this change is the president's position as the one leader chosen by the whole nation and as the sole head of the executive branch. These features of the office have enabled presidents to claim broad authority in response to the increased demands placed on the federal government by changing world and national conditions.

During the course of American history, the presidential selection process has been altered in ways that were intended to make it more responsive to the preferences of ordinary people. Today, they have a vote not only in the general election but in the selection of nominees. To gain nomination, a presidential hopeful must gain the support of the electorate in state primaries and open caucuses. Once nominated, the candidates receive federal funds for their general election campaigns, which are based on televised appeals.

Although the campaign tends to personalize the presidency, the responsibilities of the modern presidency far exceed any president's personal capacities. To meet their obligations, presidents have surrounded themselves with large staffs of advisers, policy experts, and managers. These staff members enable the president to extend control over the executive branch while providing the information necessary for policymaking. All recent presidents have discovered, however, that their control of staff resources is incomplete and that some things that others do on their behalf actually work against what they are trying to accomplish.

As sole chief executive and the nation's top elected leader, the president can always expect that his policy and leadership efforts will receive attention. However, other institutions, particularly Congress, have the authority to make this leadership effective. No president has come close to winning approval of all the programs he has placed before Congress, but the presidents' records of success have varied considerably. The factors in a president's success include the presence or absence of national conditions that require strong leadership from the White House and whether the president's party has a majority in Congress.

To retain an effective leadership position, the president depends on the backing of the American people. Recent presidents have made extensive use of the media to build support for their programs. Yet they have had difficulty maintaining that support throughout their terms of office. A major reason is that the public expects far more from its presidents than they can deliver.

MAJOR CONCEPTS

cabinet
honeymoon period
momentum
open party caucuses

presidential approval rating
stewardship theory
Whig theory

SUGGESTED READINGS

Burke, John P. *The Institutional Presidency.* Baltimore, Md.: Johns Hopkins University Press, 1992. A synthesis of what is known about the formal operations of White House personnel.

Haskell, John. *Fundamentally Flawed: Understanding and Reforming Presidential Primaries.* Lanham, Md.: Rowman & Littlefield, 1996. An analysis that argues the presidential nominating process is flawed and requires major reform.

Jones, Charles. *The Presidency in a Separated System.* Washington, D.C.: Brookings Institution, 1994. An insightful analysis of presidential power in a system of divided powers.

Light, Paul. *The President's Agenda: Domestic Policy Choice from Kennedy to Reagan*, rev. ed. Baltimore, Md.: Johns Hopkins University Press, 1991. An assessment of the process of presidential agenda setting, based on interviews with presidential staff members from Kennedy to Reagan.

Neustadt, Richard E. *Presidential Power and the Modern Presidents: The Politics of Leadership from Roosevelt to Reagan.* New York: Free Press, 1990. The classic analysis of the limitations on presidential power.

Patterson, Thomas E. *Out of Order.* New York: Vintage, 1994. A study of the news media's coverage of presidential campaigns.

Pfiffner, James P. *The Strategic Presidency: Hitting the Ground Running*, 2d ed. Chicago: Dorsey Press, 1996. An analysis of the way a newly elected president can convert electoral support into power in office.

Tulis, Jeffrey K. *The Rhetorical Presidency.* Princeton, N.J.: Princeton University Press, 1987. Argues that the modern presidency is split between its institutional and rhetorical aspects and that this division limits the president's effectiveness.

Walcott, Charles E., and Karen M. Hult. *Governing the White House: From Hoover through LBJ.* Lawrence: University Press of Kansas, 1995. An innovative study of how the organization of the White House affects presidential performance.

Warshaw, Shirley Anne. *Powersharing: White House–Cabinet Relations in the Modern Presidency.* Albany: State University of New York Press, 1995. A study of the cabinet's modern role.

Weko, Thomas J. *The Politicizing Presidency: The White House Personnel Office, 1948–1994.* Lawrence: University of Kansas Press, 1995. A careful study of the presidential appointment process and the institutionalization of the presidency.

READING 12

The Postmodern President
RICHARD ROSE

In two centuries, America has had three different Presidencies: a traditional President who had little to do; a modern President who had a lot to do at home and abroad; and a postmodern President who may have too much expected of him. As the world changes, our ideas must change, or we will become confused by applying the standards of one era to a different one. . . .

The traditional Presidency was designed two centuries ago to protect the American people against the abuses of an autocratic monarch and to guard against the emergence of an elected despot. For a century and a half, the White House was an office in a system of separated powers in which Congress and the Supreme Court each acted as a check on the Presidency and Congress was the leading branch. The traditional Presidency was not a driving force in government; with occasional exceptions, it was a dignified office of state.

The modern Presidency was created by Franklin D. Roosevelt's response to the depression of the 1930s. Although Roosevelt was not the first occupant of the Oval Office of the White House to believe in an active Presidency, he was the first to be an active leader in peacetime. To support his leadership, Roosevelt began the practice of appealing to the public for support through the new medium of radio broadcasting. Few Americans ever saw or heard the voice of Abraham Lincoln or Woodrow Wilson, but FDR's fireside chats made his voice familiar to every voter. America's involvement in World War II made President Roosevelt an international leader too. President Harry Truman placed America's world role on a permanent basis, deciding to drop the atomic bomb on Japan, and after 1945, committing American troops to the defense of places as far apart as Berlin and Korea. Because other nations were then devastated by war or had never been industrial powers, the modern President's eminence was at first a solitary eminence.

The military and economic eminence of America after 1945 resulted in American *hegemony* in the international system, that is, the United States was the dominant nation influencing what happened around the globe. The mobilization of American arms to contain the Soviet Union had a great impact because of America's vast population, double that of Japan and four times that of Britain, France, or Germany. The impact was enhanced by the development of new and increasingly sophisticated weapons systems. Whereas the Soviet Union is also a military superpower and Japan is also an economic superpower, only the United States has been both a military and economic superpower. American money stimulated the economies of Europe and Asia, and products such as IBM computers, Xerox machines, and Coca-Cola penetrated every corner of the earth. U.S. policies sought to secure mutual defense and worldwide economic growth: "For Americans it was the ideal outcome: one could do well by doing good."

The difference between the modern and the postmodern Presidency is that a postmodern President can no longer dominate the international system. President Carter and President Reagan have each appeared as helpless victims of forces abroad: oil-exporting nations, foreign armies, small bands of terrorists, and bankers and businessmen profiting from problems of the American economy. *Interdependence* characterizes an international system in which no nation is the hegemonic power. The President is the leader of a very influential nation, but other nations are influential too. In an interdependent world, what happens in the United States depends on what happens in other countries as well as what happens at home. For example, if America is to increase its exports, then other countries must increase their imports. The line between domestic and international politics is dissolving.

While the White House is accustomed to influencing foreign nations, the postmodern President must accept something less appealing: Other nations can now influence what the White House achieves. Whereas the Constitution made Congress and the Supreme Court the chief checks on the traditional and the modern President, the chief constraints on the postmodern President are found in other nations. The White House depends on the cooperation of the Kremlin to deter nuclear war and for agreement in arms-control negotiations. It makes a big difference to the White House whether the Soviet Union pursues a policy of *glasnost* or aggression. The White House looks to the Japanese government to act to reduce the American trade deficit, and it looks to the German central bank, the Bundesbank, to boost demand in Europe for American exports. . . .

Although America remains a world power, it is no longer the dominant power that it once was. The White House has not lost Britain or Germany or Japan, for these independent countries never belonged to the United States. Each remains an ally, but the terms of the relationship have changed. American support for other nations' development has met with such success that countries dependent on the United States shortly after World War II are now major players in the international system. As the United States becomes more integrated in the international system, it becomes more like other nations. America is no longer isolated geographically, as in the days of the traditional Presidency, or isolated by the preeminence of its power, as in the era of the modern Presidency.

In an interdependent world a President cannot always do what he wants, because policies cannot always be stamped *Made in America*.* A ruler with unchallenged authority could assume that to govern is to choose. A postmodern President must start from the assumption: *To govern is to cooperate*. A President has always needed to cooperate with Congress in order to succeed in a constitutional system that separates powers. What is novel is that a postmodern President must cooperate with foreign governments to achieve major economic and national security goals. Cooperation requires a mutuality of interests between nations. If this is lacking, then a postmodern President can face stalemate abroad, just as he can face stalemate in Congress. . . .

If a postmodern President does not adapt to changes in the international system, then he is doomed to fail at home as well as abroad. The rise of other nations to economic and military power presents greater challenges to the postmodern President, and lessens the capacity of America to influence international outcomes. Whereas a modern President had international influence consistent with his responsibilities, a postmodern President does not. Hence political commentators have shifted from worrying about the Imperial Presidency, deemed too powerful for the nation's good, to worrying about an imperiled Presidency, too weak for the nation's good.

The leading contemporary scholar of the Presidency, Richard E.

---

*Presidents are referred to as he, since every President has been a male, while countries as diverse as Britain, India, Israel, and Norway have had women as national leaders. To refer to Presidents by the phrase "he or she" would convey a misleading impression of gender equality.

Neustadt, has asked: "Is the Presidency possible?" His answer is not encouraging: "Weakness is what I see." The standard for presidential success that Neustadt offers is challenging but not impossible: A "minimally effective" President should match the achievements of President Truman; he adds that there is "nothing high-and-mighty about that." If Truman's achievement is taken as the standard for the Presidency, three-quarters of the country's leaders fall below this mark, in the judgment of historians. It is particularly worrisome that historians do not rate any occupant of the White House as having reached this standard since Truman left office in 1953.

It is right to worry about the capacity of the President, for the man in the White House is not an ordinary officeholder. The President is unique in his claim to political authority; he alone is elected by the nation as a whole. Lincoln's idea of government by the people is simply not practical. When America has a population of 240 million people, big decisions about the economy and foreign policy cannot be taken in a New England–style town meeting. Nor can 535 congressmen give clear and coherent direction to government, individually or collectively. The job of a congressman is to represent his or her district in Washington. The job of the President is to represent the whole of the nation in an uncertain and sometimes hostile world.

. . . To look back longingly to a world in which the President stood as a colossus is to default on our obligations to the future. We are much closer to the twenty-first century than we are to the days of George Washington, Franklin D. Roosevelt, or John F. Kennedy. . . . Reading history forward is a challenge to understand under what conditions and to what extent a postmodern President can succeed in an international system in which he is not the only leader who counts, because America is not the only nation that counts.

SOURCE: Richard Rose, *The Postmodern President*, 2d ed. (Chatham, N.J.: Chatham House, 1991). Reprinted by permission.
Richard Rose is professor and director of the Centre for the Study of Public Policy at the University of Strathclyde, Glasgow, Scotland.

CHAPTER THIRTEEN

The Bureaucracy

[No] industrial society could manage the daily operations of its public affairs
without bureaucratic organizations in which officials play a major policymaking
role.

NORMAN THOMAS[1]

 ARLY ON the morning of September 7, 1993, a truck pulled up to
the south lawn of the White House and unloaded pallets stacked
with federal regulations.[2] The mountainous display was the backdrop for a
presidential speech announcing the completion of the National Performance Review or, as it is commonly called, NPR. The federal regulations
piled atop the pallets symbolized bureaucratic red tape, and NPR was a
statement of the Clinton administration's efforts to make government more
responsive. "Our goal," said Clinton, "is to make the entire federal government both less expensive and more efficient, and to change the culture of
our national bureaucracy away from complacency and entitlement toward
initiative and empowerment. We intend to redesign, to reinvent, to rein-
vigorate the entire national government."[3]

The origins of the National Performance Review were plain enough. For
years, the federal bureaucracy had been derided as too big, too expensive,
and too intrusive. These charges gained weight as federal budget deficits increased and the public became increasingly dissatisfied with the performance of the government in Washington. Reform attempts in the 1970s and
1980s had some success but did not stem the tide of the federal deficit or
markedly improve the bureaucracy's performance. Clinton campaigned on
the issue of "reinventing government" and acted swiftly on the promise. During the transition phase, Vice President–elect Al Gore was placed in charge
of the National Performance Review. Once in office, Gore assembled more
than 200 career bureaucrats who knew firsthand how the bureaucracy operated and organized them into "reinventing teams" that would recommend
ways of improving government administration. The NPR's report included

384 specific recommendations, which were grouped into four broad imperatives: reducing red tape, putting customers first, empowering administrators, and downscaling to basics.

NPR is the latest in a long line of twentieth-century proposals to remake the federal bureaucracy. NPR is different in its particulars, but its claim to improve administration while saving money is consistent with the claims of earlier reform panels, including the Brownlow, Hoover, Volcker, and other management commissions. Whether NPR will actually achieve its goals in a major way is yet to be seen; most reform efforts have not lived up to their promise. Nevertheless, NPR addresses an enduring issue of American politics: the bureaucracy's efficiency, responsiveness, and accountability.

Modern government would be impossible without a bureaucracy. It is the government's enormous administrative capacity that makes it possible for the United States to have such ambitious programs as space exploration, social security, environmental protection, interstate highways, and universal postal service. Yet the bureaucracy is also a problem. Even those who work in federal agencies bemoan its rigidity and costliness. Both these elements, the need for bureaucracy and the problems associated with it, must be taken into account in any effort to understand the bureaucracy's place in modern American politics.

This chapter describes the nature of the federal bureaucracy and the politics that surrounds it. The discussion initially aims to clarify the bureaucracy's responsibilities, organizational structure, and management practices. But the chapter also shows that the bureaucracy is very much a part of the play of politics. Bureaucrats necessarily and naturally take an "agency point of view," seeking to promote their agency's objectives. The three constitutional branches of government impose a degree of accountability on the bureaucracy; but the sheer size and fragmented nature of the U.S. government confound the problem of control and make efforts to reform the bureaucracy a high priority. The main points discussed in this chapter are the following:

* *Modern government could not function without a large bureaucracy; through hierarchy, specialization, and rules, the bureaucratic form is the only practical way of organizing large-scale government programs.*
* *The bureaucracy is expected simultaneously to respond to the direction of partisan officials and to administer programs fairly and competently; these conflicting demands are addressed through a combination of personnel management systems—the patronage, merit, and executive leadership systems.*

★ *Bureaucrats naturally take an "agency point of view," which they promote through their expert knowledge, support from clientele groups, and backing by Congress or the president.*

★ *Although agencies are subject to scrutiny by the president, Congress, and the judiciary, bureaucrats are able to achieve power in their own right.*

THE FEDERAL BUREAUCRACY: FORM, PERSONNEL, AND ACTIVITIES

For many Americans, the word "bureaucracy" brings to mind waste, mindless rules, and rigidity. This image is not unfounded, but it is one-sided. Bureaucracy is also an effective method of organization. Although Americans tend to equate bureaucracy with government, bureaucracy is found wherever there is a need to manage large numbers of people and tasks. All large-scale, task-oriented organizations—public and private—are bureaucratic in form. General Motors is a bureaucracy. So, too, is every large university. Bureaucracy alone facilitates the coordination of a large work force.

In formal terms, **bureaucracy** is a system of organization and control that is based on three principles: hierarchical authority, job specialization, and formalized rules. **Hierarchical authority** refers to a chain of command, whereby the officials and units at the top of a bureaucracy have authority over those in the middle, who in turn control those at the bottom. In a system of **job specialization,** the responsibilities of each job position are explicitly defined and there is a precise division of labor within the organization. **Formalized rules** are the standardized procedures and established regulations by which a bureaucracy conducts its operations.

These features are the reason that bureaucracy, as a form of organization, is the most efficient means of getting people to work together on tasks of great magnitude and complexity. Hierarchy speeds action by reducing conflict over the power to make decisions: the higher an individual's position in the organization, the more decision-making power he or she has. Specialization yields efficiency because each individual is required to concentrate on a particular job: workers acquire specialized skills and knowledge. Formalized rules enable workers to make quick and consistent judgments because decisions are made on the basis of preestablished guidelines rather than by deliberation and personal inclination.

These organizational characteristics are also the cause of bureaucracy's pathologies. Administrators perform not as whole persons but as parts of an organizational entity. Their behavior is governed by position, specialty, and rule. At its worst, bureaucracy grinds on, heedless of the feelings and special needs of its members or their clients. Fixed rules come to dominate everything.[4]

If bureaucracy is an indispensable condition of large-scale organization, gross bureaucratic inefficiency and unresponsiveness are not, or at least that is the assumption underlying current efforts to reform the administration of government, a topic that will be examined later in this chapter.

The Federal Bureaucracy in Americans' Daily Lives

The U.S. federal bureaucracy has roughly 2.5 million employees, who have responsibility for administering thousands of programs. The president and Congress may get far more attention in the news, but it is the bureaucracy that has the more immediate impact on the daily lives of Americans. The federal bureaucracy performs a wide range of functions; for example, it delivers the daily mail, maintains national parks, administers social security, enforces environmental protection laws, develops the country's defense systems, provides foodstuffs for school-lunch programs, and regulates the stock markets.

Types of Administrative Organizations

The chief organizational feature of the U.S. federal bureaucracy is its division into areas of specialization. One agency handles veterans' affairs, another specializes in education, a third is responsible for agriculture, and so on. No two units are exactly alike. Nevertheless, most of them take one of five general forms: cabinet department, independent agency, regulatory agency, government corporation, or presidential commission.

CABINET DEPARTMENTS   The major administrative units are the fourteen **cabinet (executive) departments** (see Figure 13-1). Each is headed by a secretary (for example, the secretary of defense), who serves as a member of the president's cabinet and is responsible for establishing the department's general policy and overseeing its operations.

Cabinet departments vary greatly in their visibility, size, and importance. The Department of State is one of the oldest and most prestigious departments, but it is also one of the smallest, with approximately 25,000 employees. The Department of Defense has the largest work force, with more than 750,000 civilian employees (apart from the more than 1.5 million uniformed members of the armed services). The Department of Health and

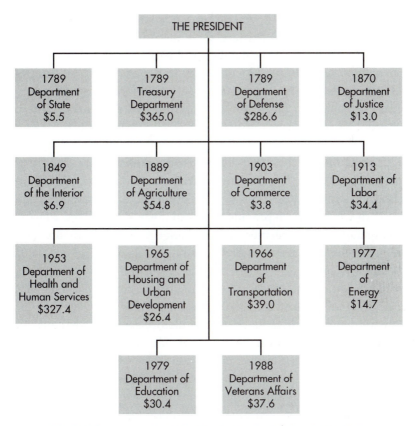

FIGURE 13-1 CABINET (EXECUTIVE) DEPART-
MENTS
Each executive department is responsible for a general policy area and is headed by a secretary, who serves as a member of the president's cabinet. Shown are each department's
year of origin (above the title) and annual budget in billions
of dollars (below the title). Source: U.S. Office of Management
and Budget, 1996.

Human Services has the largest budget; its activities account for about a third
of all federal spending, much of it for social security benefits.

INDEPENDENT AGENCIES   **Independent agencies** resemble the cabinet departments, but most of them have a narrower area of responsibility.
They include such organizations as the Central Intelligence Agency (CIA)
and the National Aeronautics and Space Administration (NASA). The heads
of these agencies are appointed by and report to the president but are not

members of the cabinet. In general, the independent agencies exist apart from cabinet departments because their placement within a department would pose symbolic or practical policy problems. NASA, for example, could conceivably be located in the Department of Defense, but this positioning would suggest that the space program is intended for military purposes and not also for civilian purposes, such as space exploration and satellite communication.

REGULATORY AGENCIES **Regulatory agencies** are created when Congress recognizes the importance of close and continuous regulation of an economic activity. Because such regulation requires more time and expertise than Congress can provide, the responsibility is delegated to a regulatory agency. The Securities and Exchange Commission (SEC), which oversees the stock and bond markets, is a regulatory agency. So is the Environmental Protection Agency (EPA), which works to monitor and control industrial pollution. Table 13-1 lists some of the regulatory agencies and other noncabinet units of the federal bureaucracy.

Beyond their executive functions, regulatory agencies have certain legislative and judicial functions. They issue regulations, implement them, and then judge whether individuals or organizations have followed them. For example, the SEC can impose fines on a corporation that violates the rules for the trading of stocks and can compel it to comply with the rules or face further penalties, including even the suspension of the sale of its stocks.

Some regulatory agencies, particularly the older ones such as the SEC, are "independent" by virtue of their relative freedom from ongoing political control. They are headed by a commission of several members who are nominated by the president and confirmed by the Senate but are not subject to removal by the president. Commissioners serve a fixed term, a legal stipulation intended to free their agencies from political interference. The newer regulatory agencies such as the EPA lack this autonomy; most are headed by a presidential nominee who can be removed at the president's discretion. (Regulatory agencies are discussed more fully in Chapter 15.)

GOVERNMENT CORPORATIONS **Government corporations** are similar to private corporations in that they charge clients for their services and are governed by a board of directors. However, government corporations receive federal funding to help defray operating expenses, and their directors are appointed by the president with Senate approval. The largest government corporation is the U.S. Postal Service, with roughly 800,000 employees. Other government corporations include the Federal Deposit

TABLE 13-1   SELECTED U.S. REGULATORY AGENCIES, INDEPENDENT AGENCIES, GOVERNMENT CORPORATIONS, AND PRESIDENTIAL COMMISSIONS

Central Intelligence Agency	National Foundation on the Arts and the Humanities
Commission on Civil Rights	National Labor Relations Board
Consumer Product Safety Commission	National Railroad Passenger Corporation (Amtrak)
Environmental Protection Agency	National Science Foundation
Equal Employment Opportunity Commission	National Transportation Safety Board
Export-Import Bank of the U.S.	Nuclear Regulatory Commission
Farm Credit Administration	Occupational Safety and Health Review Commission
Federal Communications Commission	Office of Personnel Management
Federal Deposit Insurance Corporation	Peace Corps
Federal Election Commission	Securities and Exchange Commission
Federal Emergency Management Agency	Selective Service System
Federal Maritime Commission	Small Business Administration
Federal Reserve System, Board of Governors of the	Tennessee Valley Authority
Federal Trade Commission	U.S. Arms Control and Disarmament Agency
General Services Administration	U.S. Information Agency
National Aeronautics and Space Administration	U.S. International Development Cooperation Agency
National Archives and Records Administration	U.S. International Trade Commission
	U.S. Postal Service

SOURCE: *The U.S. Government Manual.*

Insurance Corporation (FDIC), which insures savings accounts against bank failures, and the National Railroad Passenger Corporation (Amtrak), which provides passenger rail service.

PRESIDENTIAL COMMISSIONS   Some **presidential commissions** are permanent commissions that provide ongoing recommendations to the president in particular areas of responsibility. Two such commissions are the

Commission on Civil Rights and the Commission on Fine Arts. Other presidential commissions are temporary and disband after making recommendations on specific issues.

Federal Employment

The roughly 2.5 million civilian employees of the federal government include professionals who bring their expertise to the problems of governing a large and complex society, service workers who perform such tasks as the typing of correspondence and the delivery of mail, and middle and top managers who supervise the work of the various federal agencies.

More than 90 percent of federal employees are hired by merit criteria, which include educational attainment, employment experience, and performance on competitive tests (such as the civil service and foreign service examinations). The merit system is intended to protect the public from the inept or discriminatory administrative practices that can result if partisanship is the employment criterion. A 1990 Supreme Court ruling prohibits patronage in all personnel operations (hiring, firing, transfers, promotions, training, and so on) unless the government can demonstrate that party affiliation will improve performance in a particular position.[5] This can be demonstrated in some cases (for example, a staff assistant to the president) but not in the large majority of personnel operations, which are thereby off limits to partisan politics.

Although federal employees were once greatly underpaid in comparison with their counterparts in the private sector, they now receive somewhat competitive salaries, except at the top levels. The large majority of federal employees have a GS (Graded Service) job ranking. The rankings range from GS-1 (the lowest rank) to GS-18 (the highest). College graduates who enter the federal service usually start at the GS-5 level, which provides a salary of about $20,000 for a beginning employee. With a master's degree, the level is GS-9 at a $30,000 salary. Federal employees' salaries increase with rank and length of service. Public employees receive substantial fringe benefits, including full health insurance, liberal retirement plans, and generous vacation time and sick leave.

Public service has its drawbacks. Federal employees have few rights of collective action.[6] They can join labor unions, but their unions by law have limited authority: the government maintains full control of job assignments, compensation, and promotion. Moreover, the Taft-Hartley Act of 1947 prohibits strikes by federal employees and permits the firing of workers who do go on strike. There are also some limits on the partisan activities of civil servants. The Hatch Act of 1939 prohibited them from holding key positions in election campaigns. In 1993, Congress relaxed this prohibition but retained it for certain high-ranking career bureaucrats.

The Federal Bureaucracy's Policy Responsibilities

The Constitution mentions executive departments but does not grant them any powers. Their authority derives from grants of power to the three constitutional branches: Congress, the president, and the courts. Nevertheless, the bureaucracy is far more than an administrative extension of the three branches. It never merely follows orders. The primary function of administrative agencies is **policy implementation,** which is to say that they carry out the policy decisions of Congress, the president, and the courts.

Although implementation is sometimes described as "mere administration," it is a highly significant and creative function.[7] For example, many ideas for legislative programs are initiated by the bureaucracy. In the course of their work, administrators come up with policy ideas that are then brought to the attention of the president or members of Congress. Administrative agencies also develop public policy in the process of implementing it. The decisions of Congress, the president, and the courts typically need to be fleshed out by the bureaucracy. Most legislative acts specify general goals, which bureaucrats then develop into specific programs. Consider the Drug-Free Workplace Act, which directs all organizations that receive federal grants to take steps to keep drugs out of the workplace. The legislation provides that grantees will not lose their funds if drugs enter the workplace, if they have made "good-faith efforts" to keep drugs out. But what constitutes a "good-faith effort"? In large part, Congress left it to the administrators to devise the criteria for judging enforcement efforts, which in effect meant that they created the rules by which the Drug-Free Workplace Act would be applied. This development of policy—often through *rule making*—is perhaps the chief way that administrative agencies exercise real power. To an important degree, they decide how the law will operate in practice.

Agencies are also charged with the delivery of services—carrying the mail, processing welfare applications, approving government loans, and the like. Such activities are governed by rules, and in most instances the rules decide what gets done. But some services allow agency employees enough discretion that laws end up being applied arbitrarily, a situation that Michael Lipsky describes as "street-level bureaucracy."[8] For example, FBI agents more diligently pursue organized crime than white-collar crime.

In sum, administrators necessarily exercise discretion in carrying out their policy responsibilities. They initiate policy, develop it, evaluate it, apply

The U.S. Postal Service, the largest government corporation, moves more mail, and does so more cheaply and reliably than do the postal bureaucracies of most other industrialized nations. Yet the U.S. Postal Service, like most other federal agencies, has a poor public image. (Bob Daemmrich/Stock, Boston)

it, and determine whether others are complying with it. The bureaucracy does not simply administer policy; it also *makes* policy.

DEVELOPMENT OF THE FEDERAL BUREAUCRACY: POLITICS AND ADMINISTRATION

The organization and staffing of the bureaucracy have been administrative and political issues throughout the country's history. Agencies are responsible for carrying out programs that serve the society, and yet each agency was created and is maintained in response to partisan interests. Each agency thus confronts two simultaneous but conflicting demands: that it administer programs fairly and competently and that it respond to partisan claims.

Historically, this conflict has worked itself out in ways that have made the organization of the modern bureaucracy a blend of the political and the administrative. This dual line of development is clearly reflected in the mix of management systems that characterizes the bureaucracy today—the *patronage, merit,* and *executive leadership* systems.

Small Government and the Patronage System

The federal bureaucracy was originally small (3,000 employees in 1800, for instance). Under the U.S. Constitution, the states retained responsibility for nearly all domestic policy areas. The federal government's role was confined mainly to defense and foreign affairs, currency and interstate commerce, and the delivery of the mail. The nation's first six presidents, from George Washington through John Quincy Adams, believed that only distinguished men should be entrusted with the management of the national government. Nearly all top presidential appointees were men of education and political experience, and many of them were members of socially prominent families. They often remained in their jobs year after year.

The nation's seventh president, Andrew Jackson, did not share his predecessors' admiration for the elite. In Jackson's view, government would be more responsive to the people if it were administered by ordinary citizens of good sense. Jackson also believed that top administrators should remain in office for short periods, so that there would be a steady influx of fresh ideas.

Jackson's version of the **patronage system** was popular with the public, but critics labeled it a **spoils system**—a device for placing political cronies in government office as a reward for partisan service. Although Jackson was motivated as much by a concern for democratic government as by his desire to reward his campaign supporters, later presidents were often more interested in distributing the spoils of victory. Jackson's successors extended patronage to all levels of administration.[9]

Growth in Government and the Merit System

Because the government of the early nineteenth century was relatively small and limited in scope, it could be managed by employees who had little or no administrative training or experience. As the century advanced, however, the nature of the bureaucracy changed rapidly, as did the bureaucracy's person-nel needs.

An impetus for change was the Industrial Revolution, which was creat-ing a truly national economy and prompting economic groups to pressure Congress to protect and promote their interests. Farmers were one of the groups that looked to the federal government for market and price assistance; in response, Congress created the Department of Agriculture in 1889. Busi-ness and labor interests also pressed their claims, and in 1903 Congress es-tablished the Department of Commerce and Labor to "promote the mutual interest" of the nation's firms and workers. (The separate interests of busi-ness and labor proved stronger than their shared concerns, and so in 1913 Labor became a separate department.)[10]

Because of the increased need for continuous administration of govern-ment, an ever-larger bureaucracy was required (see Figure 13-2). By 1930 federal employment had reached 600,000, a sixfold increase over the level of the 1880s.[11] During the 1930s, as a result of President Franklin Roosevelt's New Deal, the federal work force increased enormously, to 1.2 million.

A large and active government requires skilled and experienced person-nel. In 1883 Congress passed the Pendleton Act, which established a **merit**

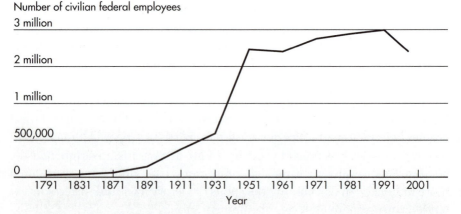

FIGURE 13-2   NUMBER OF PERSONS EMPLOYED BY THE FEDERAL GOVERNMENT, 1791–1996
The federal bureaucracy grew slowly until the 1930s, when an explosive growth began in the number of programs that required ongoing administration by the federal government. Source: *Historical Statistics of the United States and Statistical Abstract of the United States, 1986,* 322; 1991 and 1996 figures from U.S. Office of Personnel Man-agement.

(civil service) system whereby certain federal employees were hired through competitive examinations or by virtue of having special qualifications, such as an advanced degree in a particular field. The transition to a career civil service was gradual. Only 10 percent of federal positions in 1885 were filled on the basis of merit; by 1920, however, more than 70 percent were merit-based; and since 1950 the proportion of merit employees has not dipped below 80 percent.[12]

The Pendleton Act created a Civil Service Commission to establish job classifications, administer competitive examinations, and oversee merit employees. The commission was replaced by two independent agencies in 1978. The Merit Service Protection Board handles appeals of personnel actions, and the Office of Personnel Management (OPM) supervises the hiring and classification of federal employees.[13]

The administrative objective of the merit system is **neutral competence**.[14] A merit-based bureaucracy is "competent" in the sense that employees are hired and retained on the basis of their skills, and it is "neutral" in the sense that employees are not partisan appointees and thus are expected to do their work on behalf of everyone, not just those who support the incumbent administration.

Although the merit system contributes to the impartial and proficient administration of government programs, it has its own sources of bias and inefficiency. Career bureaucrats tend to place their agency's interests ahead of those of other agencies and typically oppose substantial efforts to trim their agency's activities. They are not partisans in the sense of Democratic or Republican politics, but they are partisans when it comes to protecting their own positions and agencies, as will be explained more fully later in the chapter.

Big Government and the Executive Leadership System

As problems with the merit system surfaced after the early years of this century, reformers looked to a strengthened presidency—an **executive leadership system**—as a means of coordinating the bureaucracy's activities to increase its efficiency and responsiveness.[15] The president was to provide the general leadership that would overcome agency fragmentation and provide a common direction. As we saw in Chapter 12, Congress in 1939 provided the president with some of the tools needed for improved coordination of the bureaucracy. The Office of Management and Budget (OMB) was created to give the president the authority to coordinate the annual budgetary process; agencies would be required to prepare their budget proposals under the direction of the president, who would then submit the overall budget to

Congress for its approval and modification. The president was also empowered to reorganize the bureaucracy, subject to congressional approval, in order to reduce duplication of activities and strengthen the chain of command from the president to the agencies. Finally, the president was authorized to develop the Executive Office of the President, which oversees the agencies' activities on the president's behalf, assisting in the development and implementation of policy programs.

Like the merit and patronage systems, the executive leadership system has brought problems as well as improvements to the administration of government. The executive leadership concept, if carried too far, can threaten the balance between executive power and legislative power on which the U.S. constitutional system is based, and it can make the president's priorities, not fairness, the criterion by which provision of services is determined. Richard Nixon abused the system, for example, by ordering the OMB to impound (that is, fail to spend) more than $40 billion in appropriated funds of programs he disliked. (The courts ruled that Nixon's action was an unlawful infringement on Congress's constitutional authority over spending. To prevent a recurrence of the problem, Congress in 1974 passed legislation that gives the president the authority to withhold funds for only 45 days unless Congress passes legislation to rescind the appropriation.)

The executive leadership system is not a panacea but, along with the patronage and merit systems, is a necessary component of any effective strategy for managing the modern federal bureaucracy.[16] The federal bureaucracy today embodies aspects of all three systems, a situation that reflects the tensions inherent in governmental administration. The bureaucracy is expected to carry out programs fairly, but it is also expected to respond to political forces and to principles of effective management. The first of these requirements is addressed primarily through the merit system, the second through the patronage system, and the third through the executive leadership system (see Table 13-2).

THE BUREAUCRACY'S
POWER IMPERATIVE

A common misperception is that the president, as the chief executive, has the sole claim on the bureaucracy's loyalty. In fact, each of the elected institutions has reason to claim proprietorship: the president as chief executive and Congress as the source of the authorization and funding of the bureaucracy's programs.

TABLE 13-2 STRENGTHS AND WEAKNESSES OF MAJOR SYSTEMS FOR MANAGING THE BUREAUCRACY		
System	*Strengths*	*Weaknesses*
Patronage	Makes the bureaucracy more responsive to election outcomes by allowing the president to appoint some executive officials.	Gives executive authority to individuals chosen primarily for their partisan loyalty rather than administrative experience or policy expertise; can result in bias in favor of interests that supported the president's election.
Merit	Provides for *competent* administration in that employees are hired on the basis of ability and allowed to remain on the job and thereby become proficient at their work, and provides for *neutral* administration in the sense that civil servants are not partisan appointees and thus are expected to do their work in an evenhanded way.	Can result in fragmented, unresponsive administration since career bureaucrats are secure in their jobs and tend to place the interests of their particular agency ahead of those of other agencies or the nation's interests as a whole.
Executive leadership	Provides for presidential leadership of the bureaucracy in order to make it more responsive and to give it greater coordination and direction (left alone, the bureaucracy tends toward fragmentation).	Can upset the balance between executive and legislative power and can make the president's priorities, not fairness or effective management, the basis for administrative action.

The U.S. system of separate institutions sharing power results in a natural tendency for each institution to guard its turf. In addition, the president and members of Congress differ in their constituencies and thus in the interests to which they are most responsive. For example, although the agricultural sector is just one of many concerns of the president, it is of vital interest to senators and representatives from farm states. Finally, because the president and Congress are elected separately, the White House and one or both houses of Congress may be in the hands of opposing parties. Since 1968, this source of executive–legislative conflict has been more often the rule than the exception.

If agencies are to operate successfully in this system, they must seek support where they can find it—if not from the president, then from Congress; if not today, then tomorrow. In other words, agencies must play politics.[17] Any agency that is content to sit idly by while new priorities for money and policy are determined is virtually certain to lose out to other agencies that are willing to fight for power.

The Agency Point of View

Administrators have little choice but to look out for their agency's interests, a perspective that is called the **agency point of view**.[18] This perspective comes naturally to most high-ranking civil servants. Their careers within the bureaucracy have taught them to do their part in making the organization effective. Many top bureaucrats are also personally committed to their agency's objectives as a result of having spent years working on its programs.[19] As one top administrator said when testifying before the House Appropriations Committee, "Mr. Chairman, you would not think it proper for me to be in charge of this work and not be enthusiastic about it . . . , would you? I have been in it for thirty years, and I believe in it."[20]

Professionalism also cements agency loyalties. As public policymaking has become more complex, high-level administrative positions have increasingly been filled by scientists, engineers, lawyers, educators, physicians, and other professionals (see box: How the United States Compares). Most of them take jobs in an agency whose programs are consistent with their professional values.

Studies confirm that bureaucrats believe in the importance of their agency's work. One study found that social welfare administrators are three times as likely as other civil servants to believe that social welfare programs should be given a high budget priority.[21]

HOW THE UNITED STATES COMPARES

Educational Backgrounds of Bureaucrats

To staff its bureaucracy, the U.S. government tends to hire persons with specialized educations to hold specialized jobs; this approach heightens the tendency of bureaucrats to take the agency point of view. By comparison, Great Britain tends to recruit its bureaucrats from the arts and humanities, on the assumption that general ability and intelligence are the best qualifications for detached professionalism. The continental European democracies also emphasize detached professionalism, but in the context of the supposedly impartial application of rules. As a consequence, high-ranking civil servants in Europe tend to have legal educations. The college majors of senior civil servants in the United States and other democracies reflect these tendencies.

College Major of Senior Civil Servants	Denmark	Germany	Great Britain	Italy	Netherlands	United States
Natural science/ engineering	16%	11%	11%	27%	25%	43%
Social science/ humanities	20	8	87	24	28	27
Law	60	65	—	49	45	24
Other	4	16	2	—	2	6

SOURCE: B. Guy Peters, *The Politics of Bureaucracy*, 3d ed. (New York: Longman, 1989), ch. 3. Table adapted from table 3.7, 102–103.

Sources of Bureaucratic Power

In promoting their agency's interests, bureaucrats rely on their specialized knowledge, the support of interests that benefit from the programs they run, and the backing of the president and Congress.

THE POWER OF EXPERTISE   Most of the policy problems that the federal government confronts do not lend themselves to simple solutions. Whether the issue is space travel or hunger in America, expert knowledge is essential to the development of effective public policy. Much of this expertise is held by bureaucrats. They spend their careers working in a particular policy area, and many of them have had scientific, technical, or other specialized training.[22]

By comparison, elected officials are generalists. To some degree, members of Congress do specialize through their committee work, but they rarely have the time or inclination to acquire a commanding knowledge of a particular issue. The president's understanding of policy issues is even more general. Not surprisingly, the president and members of Congress depend on the bureaucracy for policy advice and planning.

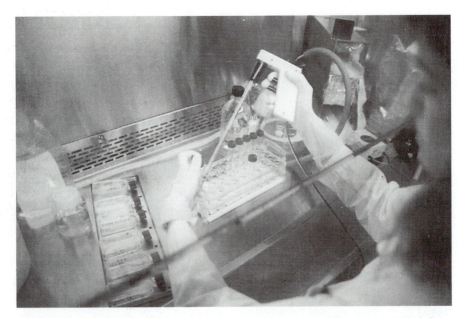

Research on AIDS conducted at the National Institutes of Health provided the expert knowledge that helped the agency to convince elected officials that AIDS-related policy measures were needed. (Shepard Sherbell/Picture Group)

All agencies acquire some power through their careerists' expertise.[23] No matter how simple a policy issue may appear at first, it invariably involves more than meets the eye. A recognition that the United States has a trade deficit with Japan, for example, can be the premise for policy change, but this recognition does not begin to address such basic issues as the form that the new policy might take, its probable cost and effectiveness, and its connection to other trade issues. Among the officials most likely to understand these issues are the bureaucrats in the Commerce Department and the Federal Trade Commission.

THE POWER OF CLIENTELE GROUPS   Most agencies have **clientele groups,** which are special interests that benefit directly from an agency's programs. Clientele groups place pressure on Congress and the president to retain the programs from which they benefit.[24] A result is that agency programs, once started, are difficult to terminate. "Government activities," as public administration expert Herbert Kaufman says, "tend to go on indefinitely."[25]

The importance of clientele groups was evident in 1995 when House Speaker Newt Gingrich threatened to "zero out" funding for the Corporation for Public Broadcasting. The threat produced an immediate response (some of it orchestrated by public broadcasting stations) from audience members and from groups such as the Childrens Television Workshop. They wrote, called, faxed, and cajoled members of Congress, saying that programs like *Sesame Street* and *All Things Considered* were irreplaceable by anything available from commercial broadcasting. Within a few weeks, Gingrich had relented somewhat, saying that a phase-out plan for ending the funding would be preferable to an abrupt cessation and that it might be prudent to retain funding for some activities, such as support of stations in rural areas not adequately served by commercial broadcasters.

In general, agencies lead and are led by the clientele groups that depend on the programs they administer.[26] Many agencies were created for the purpose of promoting particular interests in society. For example, the Department of Agriculture's career bureaucrats are dependable allies of farm interests year after year. The same cannot be said of the president, Congress as a whole, or either political party; they must balance farmers' demands against those of other interests.

THE POWER OF FRIENDS IN HIGH PLACES   Although members of Congress and the president sometimes appear to be at war with the bureaucracy, they need it as much as it needs them. An agency's resources—its programs, expertise, and group support—can assist elected officials in their efforts to achieve their goals. When George Bush came to the White House, he made the problem of drug-related crime a top priority, and he needed the help of Justice Department careerists to make his efforts successful. At a time when other agencies were feeling the pinch of a tight federal budget, the Justice Department's personnel increased by 20 percent during Bush's term of office.

Bureaucrats also seek favorable relations with members of Congress. Congressional support is vital because agencies' funding and programs are established through legislation. Agencies that offer benefits to major constituency interests are particularly likely to have close ties to Congress. In some policy areas, more or less permanent alliances—"iron triangles"— form among agencies, clientele groups, and congressional subcommittees.[27] In other policy areas, temporary "issue networks" form among bureaucrats, lobbyists, and members of Congress.[28] As we saw in Chapters 9 and 11, these alliances enable agencies and interest groups to promote the programs they want and provide members of Congress with electoral support.[29]

BUREAUCRATIC ACCOUNTABILITY

Bureaucratic politics raises the specter of a huge, permanent, and uncontrollable organizations run by entrenched unelected officials. Adapting the requirements of the bureaucracy to those of democracy has been a persistent challenge for public administration.[30] The issue is **accountability:** the capacity of the public to hold officials responsible for their actions. In the case of the bureaucracy, accountability works primarily through other institutions: the presidency, Congress, and the courts.

Accountability through the Presidency

The president can only broadly influence, not directly control, the bureaucracy.[31] "We can outlast any president" is a maxim of bureaucratic politics. In recent years, with the emphasis on scaling down the bureaucracy, the saying seems more wishful than truthful. Nevertheless, each agency has its clientele and its congressional supporters, as well as statutory authority for its existence and activities. No president can unilaterally eliminate an agency or its funding and programs. Nor can the president be indifferent to the opinions of career civil servants—not without losing their support and expertise in developing and implementing his own policy objectives.

To encourage the bureaucracy to follow his lead, the president has important management tools that have developed out of the "executive leadership" concept discussed previously. These tools include reorganization, presidential appointees, and the executive budget.

REORGANIZATION   The bureaucracy's extreme fragmentation—its hundreds of separate agencies—makes presidential coordination of its activities difficult. Agencies operate independently of each other, resulting in an undetermined amount of waste and duplication of effort. For example, more than 100 units are responsible for different pieces of education policy.

Although presidents have sometimes proposed large-scale reorganization plans, including elimination of whole departments, these efforts have usually failed because of opposition from the bureaucracy, interest groups, and Congress. Presidents have had more success with smaller changes, such as reducing the autonomy or number of employees of particular agencies. These changes serve to upgrade or downgrade programs but ordinarily have not greatly improved presidential control of the bureaucracy.[32]

PRESIDENTIAL APPOINTMENTS   Although there is almost no direct confrontation with a bureaucrat that a president cannot win, the president does not have time to deal personally with every troublesome careerist or make sure that the bureaucracy has complied with every presidential order. The president relies on political appointees in the agencies to ensure that directives are followed.

Regulatory agencies are the clearest illustration of the power of presidential appointments. Because these agencies have broad discretion over regulatory policy, a change in their leadership can have substantial effects. For example, President Reagan's appointee to head the Federal Trade Commission, James Miller III, was a strong-willed economist who shared Reagan's belief that consumer protection policy had gone too far and was adversely affecting business interests. In Miller's first year as head of the FTC, the commission dropped one-fourth of its pending cases against business firms. Overall, enforcement actions declined by about 50 percent during Miller's tenure compared with the previous period.[33]

However, as we noted in Chapter 12, there are limits to what a president can accomplish through appointments.[34] High-level presidential appointees number in the hundreds, and their turnover rate is high: the average appointee remains in the administration for less than two years before moving on to other employment.[35] No president can keep track of all appointees, much less instruct them in detail. In addition, some presidential

Madeleine Albright is the first woman to serve as secretary of state. Her policy authority, like that of other federal executives, derives from acts of Congress and from the president's constitutional powers. (Gamma Liaison Only)

appointees will have a vested interest in the agencies they head. In choosing political appointees, the president is lobbied by groups that depend on agency programs. Rather than antagonize these groups, the president will accept their recommendations in some cases.

THE EXECUTIVE BUDGET   Faced with the difficulty of controlling the bureaucracy, presidents have come to rely heavily on their personal bureaucracy, the Executive Office of the President (EOP).

In terms of presidential management, the key unit within the EOP is the Office of Management and Budget (OMB). Funding, programs, and regulations are the mainstays of every agency, and the OMB has substantial influence on each of these areas. No agency can issue a major regulation without the OMB's verification that the regulation's benefits outweigh its costs, and no agency can propose legislation to Congress without the OMB's approval. However, the OMB's greatest influence over agencies derives from its budgetary role. At the start of the annual budget cycle the OMB assigns each agency a budget limit in accord with the president's directives. The agency's tentative allocation requests are sent back to the OMB, which then conducts a final review of all requests before sending the full budget to Congress in the president's name.

In most cases, an agency's overall budget does not change much from year to year.[36] This fact indicates that a significant portion of the bureaucracy's activities persist regardless of who sits in the White House or Congress.

Accountability through Congress

Congress has powerful means of influencing the bureaucracy. All agencies depend on Congress for their existence, authority, programs, and funding.

The most substantial control that Congress exerts on the bureaucracy is through its power to authorize and fund programs. Without authorization or funding, a program simply does not exist, regardless of the priority an agency claims it deserves. Congress can also void an administrative decision through legislation that prohibits it or mandates an alternative course of action. However, Congress lacks the institutional capacity to work out complex policies down to the last detail.[37] The bureaucracy would grind to a halt if it had to get congressional approval for all of its policy decisions. Congress has no option in most cases but to give the bureaucracy a general heading and then let it proceed along that course.

Congress also exerts some control through its oversight function, which involves monitoring the bureaucracy's work to ensure compliance with legislative intent.[38] As we noted in Chapter 11, however, oversight is a difficult and relatively unrewarding task, and members of Congress ordinarily place less emphasis on oversight than on their other major duties. Only when an agency has clearly stepped out of line is Congress likely to take decisive corrective action by holding hearings to ask tough questions and to warn of legislative punishment.

A dramatic example is environmental regulation during Reagan's presidency. Regulatory activity dropped sharply when Reagan took office. Then in 1983, the news media disclosed that the Environmental Protection Agency (EPA) had privately arranged lenient settlements for firms that had committed serious violations of toxic-waste disposal regulations. The ensuing congressional investigation resulted in the resignation, dismissal, or conviction in court of more than a half-dozen top EPA officials. EPA director Anne Burford was cited for contempt of Congress for her refusal to cooperate with the investigation. Because of congressional pressure, the EPA's toxic-waste inspection level more than tripled soon thereafter, and when Congress re-

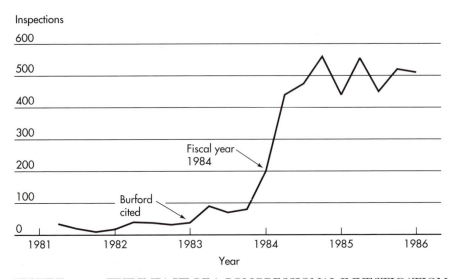

FIGURE 13-3 THE IMPACT OF A CONGRESSIONAL INVESTIGATION
A congressional investigation led to a contempt citation for EPA Director Anne
Burford and an increase in the agency's toxic-waste inspections. Source: Adapted
from B. Dan Wood and Richard W. Waterman, "Political Control of the Bureaucracy,"
American Political Science Review 85 (September 1991): 821, figure 7.

stored the EPA's budget, it rose again (see Figure 13-3). Within two years,
the EPA's inspection rate was nearly six times higher (from about 325 inspections a year to 2,000). In their study of this case, B. Dan Wood and
Richard W. Waterman concluded: "Thus, for the EPA policy in which Congress was most directly involved, legislative influence was clearly manifest
through the powers of oversight and appropriations."[39]

Of course, an awareness by bureaucrats that misbehavior can trigger a
response from Congress helps to keep them in line.[40] Nevertheless, oversight cannot correct mistakes or abuses that have already occurred. Recognizing this limit on oversight, Congress has devised ways to constrain the
bureaucracy *before* it acts. The simplest method is to draft laws that contain
very specific provisions which limit bureaucrats' options when they implement policy. Another restrictive device is the "sunset law," which establishes
a specific date when a law will expire unless it is reenacted by Congress. Advocates of sunset laws see them as a means to counter the bureaucracy's re-
luctance to give up programs that have outlived their usefulness. Since members of Congress usually want their policies to last far into the future,
however, most legislation does not include a sunset provision.

Accountability through the Courts

The judiciary's influence on agencies is less direct than that of the elected branches, but the courts, too, can and do act to ensure the bureaucracy's compliance with Congress's requirements. Legally, the bureaucracy derives its authority from acts of Congress, and an injured party can bring suit against an agency on the grounds that it has failed to carry out the law properly. Judges can then order an agency to change its application of the law.[41]

However, the courts have tended to support administrators if their actions seem at all consistent with the laws they are administering. The Supreme Court has held that agencies can choose rule-making procedures that meet the minimal threshold set down by Congress, that agencies can apply any reasonable interpretation of statutes unless Congress has specifically stated something to the contrary, and that agencies in many instances have wide discretion in deciding whether to enforce statutes.[42] These positions reflect the need for flexibility in administration; the bureaucracy and the courts would both grind to a halt if judges routinely chose to substitute their interpretations of the law for those of administrators. The judiciary cannot conduct a decision-by-decision oversight of the bureaucracy. The judiciary has promoted bureaucratic accountability primarily by encouraging administrators to act responsibly in their dealings with the public and by protecting individuals and groups from the bureaucracy's worst abuses.

Accountability within the Bureaucracy Itself

A recognition of the difficulty of ensuring adequate accountability of the bureaucracy through the presidency, Congress, and the courts has led to the development of mechanisms of accountability within the bureaucracy itself. Two measures, whistle-blowing and demographic representativeness, are particularly noteworthy.

WHISTLE-BLOWING   Although the bureaucratic corruption that is rampant in some countries is relatively uncommon in the United States, a certain amount of waste, fraud, and abuse is inevitable in a bureaucracy as big as that of the federal government. **Whistle-blowing,** the act of reporting instances of corruption or mismanagement by other bureaucrats, is a potentially effective internal check.[43] Whistle-blowing, however, has not been highly successful. A survey conducted by a Senate subcommittee indicated that most federal employees will not report instances of mismanagement because they fear reprisals from their superiors. In 1995, Alan Diehl, the U.S.

Karen Pitts (*left*) and Jacqueline Brever have sued the Rocky Flats plutonium plant
near Denver, claiming that they were threatened and forced out of their jobs
because managers feared that the two technicians would "blow the whistle" to the
FBI about improper handling of toxic and nuclear materials at the facility.
(Matthew Wald/New York Times)

Air Force's top civilian safety official, was asssigned to a lesser position after
releasing a report indicating that Air Force investigators had routinely mis-
represented the causes of military air crashes in order to save the Air Force
and its top officers the embarrassment that would have occurred if the actual causes had been revealed.[44]

To encourage federal employees to come forward when they see instances of mismanagement, Congress enacted the Whistle Blower Protection Act to protect them from retaliation. Federal law also provides whistle-
blowers with financial rewards in some cases.

DEMOGRAPHIC REPRESENTATIVENESS   Although the bureaucracy
is an unrepresentative institution in the sense that its officials are not elected
by the people, it can be representative in the demographic sense. If bu-

reaucrats were a demographic microcosm of the general public, they presumably would treat the various groups and interests in society more fairly.[45]

At present the bureaucracy is not demographically representative at its top levels (see Table 13-3). About 75 percent of managerial and professional positions are held by white males. Women and minorities hold proportionally few high-ranking posts. However, the employment status of women and minorities has improved somewhat in recent years, and top officials in the bureaucracy include a greater proportion of women and minorities than is found in Congress, the judiciary, the diplomatic corps, or among high-ranking military officers. Moreover, if all levels of the federal bureaucracy are considered, it comes reasonably close to being representative of the nation's population.

Demographic representativeness is only a partial answer to the problem of bureaucratic accountability. A fully representative civil service would still be required to play agency politics. The careerists in, say, defense agencies and welfare agencies are not very different in their demographic backgrounds, but they differ markedly in their opinions about policy. Each group believes that the goals of its agency should take priority. The inevitability of agency politics is the most significant of all political facts about the U.S. federal bureaucracy.[46]

TABLE 13-3   FEDERAL JOB RANKINGS (GS) OF VARIOUS DEMOGRAPHIC GROUPS

Women and minority group members are underrepresented in the top jobs of the federal bureaucracy.

Grade Level*	Women's Share		Blacks' Share		Hispanics' Share	
	1976	1994	1982	1994	1982	1994
GS 1–4 (lowest ranks)	78%	75%	23%	29%	5%	7%
GS 5–8	60	70	19	24	4	6
GS 9–12	20	39	10	13	4	5
GS 13–15 (highest ranks)	5	19	5	7	2	3

*In general, the higher-numbered grades are managerial and professional positions, and the lower-numbered grades are clerical and manual labor positions.

SOURCE: Office of Personnel Management.

REINVENTING GOVERNMENT

There have been numerous attempts during the twentieth century to enhance the bureaucracy's efficiency, responsiveness, and accountability. Another wave of this reform effort is under way, and it seeks to improve the administration of government by the reduction of its size, cost, and lines of authority.

This effort is based in part on the notion that the bureaucracy would be more effective and responsive if made smaller. In *Reinventing Government*, David Osborne and Ted Gaebler argue that the bureaucracy of today was created in response to earlier problems, particularly those spawned by the Industrial Revolution and a rampant spoils system. They claim that the information age requires a different kind of administrative structure, one that is more flexible and less hierarchical. Instead of the provision of goods and services, the bureaucracy ought to be in the business of creating incentives that will encourage individuals to make their own way and ought to foster competition among and between agencies and private firms. This requires a less centralized form of administration that is oriented toward consumers and results. Osborne and Gaebler would empower lower-level employees to make decisions that previously were made at the top of the bureaucracy.[47]

This concept informed the Clinton administration's National Performance Review and is embedded in some laws and administrative practices. An example is a recent law that requires agencies to monitor their performance by standards such as efficiency, responsiveness, and outcomes. These standards have long been considered gauges of administrative effectiveness but have often been overlooked as bureaucrats went about their customary ways of doing business. The law seeks to overcome this inertia by *requiring* agencies to actively monitor their performance.

The downsizing of the federal bureaucracy is also being driven by political forces. Chronic budget deficits and the public's dissatisfaction with Washington have helped create political momentum to reduce the scope of the federal government through both program reductions and the devolution of power to states and localities (see Chapter 2; see also box: States in the Nation). The momentum intensified with the Republican takeover of Congress in 1995 (see Chapter 11). If a balanced-budget amendment should become part of the Constitution, the change will be even more dramatic.

The new era will be one of smaller government, not small government. There are limits to how far the federal government can be trimmed. Some activities can be delegated to states and localities, and others can be priva-

STATES IN THE NATION

The Size of State Bureaucracies

Although the federal bureaucracy is often criticized as being "too big," it is actually smaller on a per capita basis than even the smallest of the state bureaucracies. There are 0.9 federal employees for every 100 Americans. California, with 1.0 state employees for every 100 residents, has the smallest state bureaucracy on a per capita basis. Hawaii, with 4.4 state employees per 100 residents, has the largest.

1.5 or fewer employees/100 residents

1.6–1.9 employees/100 residents

2.0 or more employees/100 residents

SOURCE: U.S. Bureau of the Census.

tized, but many, if not most, of Washington's programs cannot be reassigned. National defense, social security, and Medicare are but three examples, and they alone account for the bulk of federal spending (see Chapters 16 and 17).

Some analysts question the logic and presumed consequences of the changes that are taking place. They have asked, for example, whether the principles of decentralized management and market-oriented programs are as sound as their advocates claim. The delegation of control to lower-level administrators weakens the hierarchical connection between elected and administrative officials. A reason for hierarchy was to ensure that decisions made at the bottom of the bureaucracy were faithful to the laws made by Congress. Free to act on their own, lower-level administrators, as they did under the spoils system, might favor certain people and interests over others.[48] There is also the issue of the identity of the "customers" in a market-oriented administration.[49] Who are the Security and Exchange Commission's customers—firms, brokerage houses, or shareholders? Won't some agencies inevitably favor their more powerful customers at the expense of the less powerful ones?

A second objection to the changes taking place is that government may be "hollowed out" in the sense that it may not have the financial and human resources to adequately perform the missions it retains.[50] Even many of those who are the strongest advocates of scaling down the federal government worry about this possibility in particular areas. For example, the House Republicans' Contract with America, which otherwise called for deep cuts in federal programs, proposed an increase in defense spending out of a belief that earlier cutbacks had reduced military readiness to an unacceptable level.

Thus, although the current wave of administrative reform is unique in its specific elements, it involves longstanding questions about the bureaucracy. How can it be made more responsive, and yet act fairly? How can it be made more efficient, and yet accomplish what Americans require of it? How can it be made more creative, and yet be held accountable? There are, as history makes clear, no easy or final answers to these questions.

SUMMARY

Bureaucracy is a method of organizing people and work; it is based on the principles of hierarchical authority, job specialization, and formalized rules. As a form of organization, bureaucracy is the most efficient means of getting people to work together on tasks of great magnitude and complexity. It is also a form of organization that is prone to waste and rigidity, which is why efforts are being made to "reinvent" it.

The United States could not be governed without a large federal bureaucracy. The day-to-day work of the federal government, from mail delivery to provision of social security to international diplomacy, is done by the bureaucracy. Federal employees work in roughly 400 major agencies, including cabinet departments, independent agencies, regulatory agencies, government corporations, and presidential commissions. Yet the bureaucracy is more than simply an administrative giant. Administrators exercise considerable discretion in their policy decisions. In the process of implementing policy, they make important policy and political choices.

Each agency of the federal government was created in response to political demands on national officials. Because of its origins in political demands, the administration of government is necessarily political. An inherent conflict results from two simultaneous but incompatible demands on the bureaucracy: that it respond to the demands of partisan officials but also that it administer programs fairly and competently. These tensions are evident in the three concurrent personnel management systems under which the bureaucracy operates: patronage, merit, and executive leadership.

Administrators are actively engaged in politics and policymaking. The fragmentation of power and the pluralism of the American political system result in a policy process that is continually subject to conflict and contention. There is no clear policy or leadership mandate in the American system, and hence government agencies must compete for the power required to administer their programs effectively. Accordingly, civil servants tend to have an agency point of view: they seek to advance their agency's programs and to repel attempts by others to weaken their position. In promoting their agency, civil servants rely on their policy expertise, the backing of their clientele groups, and support from the president and Congress.

Because administrators are not elected by the people they serve yet wield substantial independent power, the bureaucracy's accountability is a major issue. The major checks on the bureaucracy are provided by the president, Congress, and the courts. The president has some power to reorganize the bureaucracy and the authority to appoint the political head of each agency. The president also has management tools (such as the executive budget) that can be used to limit administrators' discretion. Congress has influence on bureaucratic agencies through its authorization and funding powers and through various devices (including sunset laws and oversight hearings) that hold administrators accountable for their actions. The judiciary's role in ensuring the bureaucracy's accountability is smaller than that of the elected branches, but the courts do have the authority to force agencies to act in accordance with legislative intent, established procedures, and constitutionally guaranteed rights. Nevertheless, administrators are not fully accountable. They exercise substantial independent power, a situation that is not easily reconciled with democratic values.

Efforts are currently under way to scale down the federal bureaucracy. This reduction includes cuts in budgets, staff, and organizational units, and also involves changes in the way the bureaucracy does its work. This process is a response to both political forces and new management theories.

MAJOR CONCEPTS

accountability	independent agencies
agency point of view	job specialization
bureaucracy	merit (civil service) system
cabinet (executive) departments	neutral competence
clientele groups	patronage system
demographic representativeness	policy implementation
executive leadership system	presidential commissions
formalized rules	regulatory agencies
government corporations	spoils system
hierarchical authority	whistle-blowing

SUGGESTED READINGS

Aberbach, Joel D. *Keeping a Watchful Eye*. Washington, D.C.: Brookings Institution, 1990. A careful assessment of congressional oversight of the bureaucracy.

Barzlay, Michael. *Breaking through Bureaucracy: A New Vision for Managing in Government*. Berkeley: University of California Press, 1992. A provocative critique which argues that government must become more customer-centered.

Brehm, John, and Scott Gates. *Working, Shirking, and Sabotage: Bureaucratic Response to a Democratic Public*. Ann Arbor: University of Michigan Press, 1996. A generally favorable assessment of the bureaucracy's responsiveness to the public it serves.

Gore, Albert. *Creating a Government That Works Better and Costs Less: The Report of the National Performance Review*. Washington, D.C.: U.S. Superintendent of Documents, 1993. The report of Vice-President Gore's task force on streamlining government.

Ingraham, Patricia, and David Rosenbloom. *The Promise and Paradox of Civil Service Reform*. Pittsburgh, Pa.: University of Pittsburgh Press, 1992. An insightful analysis of the civil service reform issue.

Johnson, Cathy Marie. *The Dynamics of Conflict between Bureaucrats and Legislators*. Armonk, N.Y.: Sharpe, 1992. An analysis that indicates policy differences are an important source of conflict between bureaucrats and Congress.

Light, Paul C. *Thickening Government: Federal Hierarchy and the Diffusion of Accountability.* Washington, D.C.: Brookings Institution, 1995. An illuminating study of the impact of bureaucratic hierarchy on accountability.

Osborne, David, and Ted Gaebler. *Reinventing Government: How the Entrepreneurial Spirit Is Transforming the Public Sector.* New York: Addison-Wesley, 1992. The book that Washington policymakers regard as the guide to transforming the bureaucracy.

West, William F. *Controlling the Bureaucracy: Institutional Constraints in Theory and Practice.* Armonk, N.Y.: Sharpe, 1995. An assessment of bureaucratic control through administrative due process and presidential and congressional action.

Wood, B. Dan, and Richard W. Waterman. *Bureaucratic Dynamics: The Role of Bureaucracy in a Democracy.* Boulder, Colo.: Westview Press, 1994. A penetrating analysis of bureaucratic agencies and their power relationships with the president, Congress, and constituent groups.

READING 13

Reinventing Government
DAVID OSBORNE AND TED GAEBLER

It is hard to imagine today, but one-hundred years ago the word *bureaucracy* meant something positive. It connoted a rational, efficient method of organization—something to take the place of the arbitrary exercise of power by authoritarian regimes. Bureaucracies brought the same logic to government work that the assembly line brought to the factory. With their hierarchical authority and functional specialization, they made possible the efficient undertaking of large, complex tasks. Max Weber, the great German sociologist, described them using words no modern American would dream of applying:

> *The decisive reason for the advance of bureaucratic organization has always been its purely technical superiority over any other form of organization. . . .*
>
> *Precision, speed, unambiguity, . . . reduction of friction and of material and personal costs—these are raised to the optimum point in the strictly bureaucratic administration. . . .*

During times of intense crisis—the Depression and two world wars—the bureaucratic model worked superbly. In crisis, when goals were clear and widely shared, when tasks were relatively straightforward, and when virtually everyone was willing to pitch in for the cause, the top-down, command-and-control mentality got things done. The results spoke for themselves, and most Americans fell in step. By the 1950s, as William H. Whyte wrote, we had become a nation of "organization men."

But the bureaucratic model developed in conditions very different from those we experience today. It developed in a slower-paced society, when change proceeded at a leisurely gait. It developed in an age of hierarchy, when only those at the top of the pyramid had enough information to make informed decisions. It developed in a society of people who worked with their hands, not their minds. It developed in a time of mass markets, when most

Americans had similar wants and needs. And it developed when we had strong geographic communities—tightly knit neighborhoods and towns.

Today all that has been swept away. We live in an era of breathtaking change. We live in a global marketplace, which puts enormous competitive pressure on our economic institutions. We live in an information society, in which people get access to information almost as fast as their leaders do. We live in a knowledge-based economy, in which educated workers bridle at commands and demand autonomy. We live in an age of niche markets, in which customers have become accustomed to high quality and extensive choice.

In this environment, bureaucratic institutions developed during the industrial era—public *and* private—increasingly fail us.

Today's environment demands institutions that are extremely flexible and adaptable. It demands institutions that deliver high-quality goods and services, squeezing ever more bang out of every buck. It demands institutions that are responsive to their customers, offering choices of nonstandardized services; that lead by persuasion and incentives rather than commands; that give their employees a sense of meaning and control, even ownership. It demands institutions that *empower* citizens rather than simply *serving* them.

Bureaucratic institutions still work in some circumstances. If the environment is stable, the task is relatively simple, every customer wants the same service, and the quality of performance is not critical, a traditional public bureaucracy can do the job. Social security still works. Local government agencies that provide libraries and parks and recreational facilities still work, to a degree.

But most government institutions perform increasingly complex tasks, in competitive, rapidly changing environments, with customers who want quality and choice. These new realities have made life very difficult for our public institutions—for our public education system, for our public health care programs, for our public housing authorities, for virtually every large, bureaucratic program created by American governments before 1970. It was no accident that during the 1970s we lost a war, lost faith in our national leaders, endured repeated economic problems, and experienced a tax revolt. In the years since, the clash between old and new has only intensified. The result has been a period of enormous stress in American government. . . .

Unfortunately, we do not know how to get what we want. Most of our leaders assume that the only way to cut spending is to eliminate programs, agencies, and employees. Ronald Reagan talked as if we could simply go into the bureaucracy with a scalpel and cut out pockets of waste, fraud, and abuse.

But waste in government does not come tied up in neat packages. It is marbled throughout our bureaucracies. It is embedded in the very way we do business. It is employees on idle, working at half speed—or barely working at all. It is people working hard at tasks that aren't worth doing, following regulations that should never have been written, filling out forms that should never have been printed. It is the *$100 billion* a year that Bob Stone estimates the Department of Defense wastes with its foolish overregulation.

Waste in government is staggering, but we cannot get at it by wading through budgets and cutting line items. As one observer put it, our governments are like fat people who must lose weight. They need to eat less and exercise more; instead, when money is tight they cut off a few fingers and toes.

To melt the fat, we must change the basic incentives that drive our governments. We must turn bureaucratic institutions into entrepreneurial institutions, ready to kill off obsolete initiatives, willing to do more with less, eager to absorb new ideas.

The lessons are there: our more entrepreneurial governments have shown us the way. Yet few of our leaders are listening. Too busy climbing the rungs to their next office, they don't have time to stop and look anew. So they remain trapped in old ways of looking at our problems, blind to solutions that lie right in front of them. This is perhaps our greatest stumbling block: the power of outdated ideas. As the great economist John Maynard Keynes once noted, the difficulty lies not so much in developing new ideas as in escaping from old ones.

The old ideas still embraced by most public leaders and political reporters assume that the important question is *how much* government we have—not *what kind* of government. Most of our leaders take the old model as a given, and either advocate more of it (liberal Democrats), or less of it (Reagan Republicans), or less of one program but more of another (moderates of both parties).

But our fundamental problem today is not too much government or too little government. We have debated that issue endlessly since the tax revolt of 1978, and it has not solved our problems. Our fundamental problem is that we have *the wrong kind of government*. We do not need more government or less government, we need *better* government. To be more precise, we need better *governance*.

Governance is the process by which we collectively solve our problems and meet our society's needs. Government is the instrument we use. The instrument is outdated, and the process of reinvention has begun.

SOURCE: David Osborne and Ted Gaebler, *Reinventing Government: How the Entrepreneurial Spirit Is Transforming the Public Sector* (Reading, Mass.: Addison-Wesley, 1992). Reprinted by permission.
David Osborne and Ted Gaebler are managing partners of the Reinventing Government Network. Osborne was chief author of the National Performance Review. Gaebler heads his own consulting firm.

CHAPTER FOURTEEN

The Judiciary

It is emphatically the province and duty of the judicial department to say what the law is. Those who apply the rule to particular cases, must of necessity expound and interpret that rule. If two laws conflict with each other, the courts must decide on the operation of each.

JOHN MARSHALL[1]

I N ITS 1992 ruling in the Pennsylvania abortion case, *Planned Parenthood* v. *Casey*, the Supreme Court by a 5–4 margin reaffirmed the principle that a woman can legally choose an abortion during the early months of pregnancy.[2] The decision fueled a controversy that had begun two decades earlier, when the Supreme Court in *Roe* v. *Wade* first defined abortion as a constitutional right.[3]

The *Roe* decision touched off a debate within the legal community. Some legalists supported the decision, arguing that the judiciary must act to protect basic rights, even ones, including abortion, that are not explicitly provided by the Constitution.[4] Other legalists claimed that the Court had overstepped its authority. From their perspective, the problem with the *Roe* decision was that it is not supported by any specific guarantee in the Constitution, involving the type of issue that is "political" rather than "legal" in nature, and should therefore be properly settled by elected officials, not judges.[5]

The *Roe* decision provoked even greater controversy among the general public. Opponents of abortion vowed through protests and other actions to reverse the precedent, and succeeded in part. The Supreme Court subsequently upheld a prohibition on the use of government funds to pay for abortions for poor women and, in *Planned Parenthood*, upheld waiting-period and spousal-consent restrictions on women who sought an abortion. Proponents of the right to abortion fought these restrictions and were concerned that the *Planned Parenthood* case might result in a complete overturn of the

Roe precedent. They vowed to take their cause to the streets if that should happen.

Throughout the controversy, Supreme Court appointments were a major battlefield for the contending sides, as each sought the appointment of justices who would support their position. Until the election of Bill Clinton in 1992, it appeared as if the antiabortion side would win out. Indeed, by the *Planned Parenthood* case, the Court majority in favor of the right of abortion had shrunk to 5–4, compared with 7–2 in the *Roe* case. However, Clinton's first two nominees to the Court expressed support for the right of abortion, apparently ensuring that the policy will not change significantly in the foreseeable future.

The abortion example illustrates three key points about court decisions. First, the judiciary is an extremely important policymaking body; some of its rulings, including its abortion decisions, are as consequential as nearly any law passed by Congress or any executive action taken by the president. Second, federal courts have considerable discretion in their rulings. The *Roe* and *Planned Parenthood* decisions were not based on any literal reading of the law: the justices invoked *their* interpretation of the Constitution's provisions for individual rights. Third, the judiciary is a political as well as legal institution, as illustrated by the conflict surrounding recent Supreme Court nominations. Once a law is established, it is expected to be administered in an evenhanded way; but the law itself is a product of contending political forces, is developed through a political process, has political content, and is applied by political appointees.

This chapter describes the federal judiciary and the work of its judges and justices. The main points made in this chapter are the following:

* *The federal judiciary includes the Supreme Court of the United States, which functions mainly as an appellate court; courts of appeals, which hear appeals; and district courts, which hold trials. Each state has a court system of its own, which for the most part is independent of supervision by the federal courts.*

* *Judicial decisions are constrained by applicable constitutional law, statutory law, and precedent. Nevertheless, political factors have a major influence on judicial appointments and decisions; judges are political officials as well as legal ones.*

* *The judiciary has become an increasingly powerful policymaking body in recent decades, which has raised questions regarding the judiciary's proper role in a democracy.*

THE FEDERAL JUDICIAL SYSTEM

The writers of the Constitution were determined that the judiciary would be a separate and powerful branch of the federal government but, for practical reasons, did not spell out the full structure of the federal court system. The Constitution simply establishes the Supreme Court of the United States and grants Congress the authority to establish lower federal courts of its choosing.

Federal judges are nominated by the president, and if confirmed by the U.S. Senate, they are appointed by the president to the office. The Constitution states that judges "shall hold their offices during good behavior." However, the Constitution does not contain a precise definition of "good behavior," and no Supreme Court justice and only a very small number of lower-court judges have been removed from office through impeachment and conviction by Congress. In practice, federal judges and justices serve until they retire or die.

Unlike the offices of president, senator, and representative, the Constitution places no age, residency, or citizenship qualifications on federal judicial office. Nor does the Constitution require a judge to have legal training. Tradition alone dictates that federal judges have an educational or professional background in the law.

The Supreme Court of the United States

The Supreme Court of the United States is the nation's highest court. The chief justice of the United States presides over the Supreme Court and, like the eight associate justices, is selected by the president and is subject to Senate confirmation. The chief justice has the same voting power as the other justices but has usually exercised additional influence because of the position's leadership role.

The Constitution grants the Supreme Court both original and appellate jurisdiction. A court's **jurisdiction** is its authority to hear cases of a particular type. **Original jurisdiction** is the authority to be the first court to hear a case. The Supreme Court's original jurisdiction embraces legal disputes involving foreign diplomats and those in which the opposing parties are state governments. The Court in its entire history has convened as a court of original jurisdiction only a few hundred times and has rarely done so in recent years.

The Supreme Court does its most significant work as an appellate court. **Appellate jurisdiction** is the authority to review cases that have already been

The Supreme Court building is located across from the
Capitol in Washington, D.C. The courtroom, the justices'
offices, and the conference room are on the first floor.
Administrative staff offices and the Court's records and
reference materials occupy the other floors. (Dennis
Brack/Black Star)

heard in lower courts and are appealed to the higher court by the losing party;
such courts are called appeals courts or appellate courts. The Supreme
Court's appellate jurisdiction extends to cases arising under the Constitution, federal law and regulations, and treaties. The Court also hears appeals
involving admiralty or maritime issues and legal controversies that cross state
or national boundaries. Appellate courts, including the Supreme Court, do
not retry cases; rather, they determine whether a trial court acted in accord
with applicable law.

SELECTING CASES   The primary function of the judiciary is to interpret the law in such a way that rules made in the past (for example, the Constitution or legislation) can be applied reasonably in the present. This func-

tion gives the courts—all courts—a role in policymaking. Antitrust legislation, for example, is designed to prevent uncompetitive business practices, but like all such legislation, it is not self-enforcing. It is up to the courts to decide whether and how these laws apply to the case at hand.

As the nation's highest court, the Supreme Court is particularly important in establishing legal precedents that guide lower courts. A *precedent* is a judicial decision that serves as a rule for settling subsequent cases of a similar nature. Lower courts are expected to follow precedent—that is, to resolve cases of a like nature in ways consistent with upper-court rulings. However, for reasons that will be explained later, they do not always do so.

The Supreme Court's ability to set legal precedent is strengthened by its nearly complete discretion in choosing the cases it will hear. The large majority of cases reach the Supreme Court through a **writ of *certiorari*** in which the losing party in a lower-court case explains in writing why its case should be ruled upon by the Court. Four of the nine justices must agree to accept a particular case before it is granted a writ. Each year roughly 7,000 parties apply for *certiorari*, but the Court accepts only about 100 cases for a full hearing and written opinion that explains the basis for the Court's decision. The Court issues another 100 to 200 *per curiam* (unsigned) decisions, which are made summarily without a hearing and simply state the facts of the case and the Court's decision. The Court is most likely to grant *certiorari* when the U.S. government through the solicitor general (the high-ranking Justice Department official who serves as the government's lawyer in Supreme Court cases) requests it.[6]

The Court seldom accepts a routine case, even if the justices believe that a lower court has erred. The Supreme Court's job is not to correct every mistake of other courts but to resolve broad legal questions. As a result, the justices usually choose cases that involve substantial legal issues. This criterion is vague but essentially means that a case must center on an issue of significance not merely to the parties involved but to the nation. As a result, most of the cases heard by the Court raise major constitutional issues, or affect the lives of many Americans, or address issues that are being decided inconsistently by the lower courts, or are in conflict with a previous Supreme Court ruling.[7] The last of these situations is particularly likely to propel a case to the Supreme Court, which naturally takes a keen interest in lower-court judgments that depart from its rulings.

DECIDING CASES   Once the Supreme Court accepts a case, it sets a date on which the attorneys for the two sides will present their oral arguments. Strict time limits, usually thirty minutes per side, are placed on these arguments, because each side has already submitted written arguments to the justices.

The open hearing is far less important than the **judicial conference** that follows, which is attended only by the nine justices. The conference's proceedings are kept strictly confidential. This secrecy allows the justices to speak freely and tentatively about a case. The chief justice presides over the conference and ordinarily speaks first.[8] The other justices then speak in order of their seniority (length of service on the Court); this arrangement enhances the senior members' ability to influence the discussion. After the discussion, the justices vote on the case; the least senior justice usually votes first and the Chief Justice votes last.

ISSUING DECISIONS AND OPINIONS   After a case has been discussed and decided upon in conference, the Court prepares and issues its ruling, which consists of a decision and one or more opinions. The **decision** indicates which party the Court supports and by how large a margin. The **opinion** explains the reasons behind the decision. The opinion is the most important part of a Supreme Court ruling because it informs others of the justices' interpretations of laws. When a majority of the justices agree on the legal basis of a decision, the result is a **majority opinion.**

In some cases there is no majority opinion because a majority of the justices agree on the decision but cannot agree on the legal basis for it. The result is a **plurality opinion,** which presents the view held by most of the justices who side with the winning party. Another type of opinion is a **concurring opinion,** which is a separate view written by a justice who votes with the majority but disagrees with their reasoning.

Justices on the losing side can write a **dissenting opinion** to explain their reasons for disagreeing with the majority position. Sometimes these dissenting views become a later Court's majority position. In a 1942 dissenting opinion, Justice Hugo Black wrote that defendants in state felony trials should have legal counsel, even if they could not afford to pay for it. Two decades later, in *Gideon* v. *Wainwright* (1963), the Court adopted this position.[9]

Other Federal Courts

There are more than 100 federal courts but there is only one Supreme Court, and its position at the top of the country's judicial system gives the Supreme Court unparalleled importance. It is a mistake, however, to conclude that the Supreme Court is the only court of consequence. Judge Jerome

Types of Supreme Court Opinions

Majority opinion: A written opinion of the majority of the Court's justices stating the reasoning underlying their decision on a case.

Plurality opinion: A written opinion that in the absence of a majority opinion presents the reasoning of most of the justices who side with the winning party.

Concurring opinion: A written opinion of one or more justices who support the majority position but disagree with the majority's reasoning on a case. This opinion expresses the reasoning of the concurring justices.

Dissenting opinion: A written opinion of one or more justices who disagree with the majority's decision and opinion. This opinion provides the reasoning underlying the dissent.

Frank once wrote of the "upper-court myth," which is the view that appellate courts and in particular the Supreme Court are the only truly significant judicial arena and that lower courts just dutifully follow the rulings handed down by the appellate level.[10] The reality is very different, as the following discussion will explain.

U.S. DISTRICT COURTS   The lowest federal courts are the district courts (see Figure 14-1). There are more than ninety federal district courts altogether—at least one in every state and as many as four in some states. District-court judges, who number about 800 in all, are appointed by the president with the consent of the Senate. Federal cases usually originate in district courts, which are trial courts, where the parties argue their sides. District courts are the only courts in the federal system in which juries hear testimony. Most cases at this level are presented before a single judge.

Lower federal courts unquestionably rely on and follow Supreme Court decisions in their own rulings. This requirement was reiterated in a 1982 case, *Hutto v. Davis:* "Unless we wish anarchy to prevail within the federal judicial system, a precedent of this Court must be followed by the lower federal courts no matter how misguided the judges of those courts may think it to be."[11]

However, the idea that lower courts are guided strictly by Supreme Court rulings is part of the "upper-court myth." District-court judges may misunderstand the Supreme Court's position and deviate from it for that reason. In addition, the facts of a case before a district court are seldom exactly the same as those of a case settled by the Supreme Court. The lower-court judge must decide whether the facts are sufficiently different to require the application of a different legal principle. Finally, it is not unusual for the Supreme Court to take a very broad legal position that is general and ambiguous enough to allow lower courts to decide its exact meaning in practice. Trial-court judges then have a creative role in judicial decision making which rivals that of appellate-court judges.

Most federal cases end with the district court's decision; the losing party does not appeal the decision to a higher court. This is another indication of the highly significant role of district-court judges.

U.S. COURTS OF APPEALS   When cases are appealed from district courts, they go to a federal court of appeals. These appellate courts make up

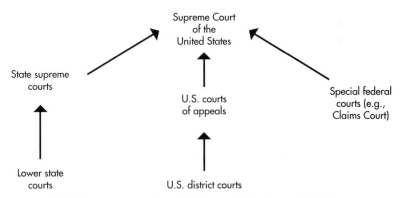

FIGURE 14-1   THE FEDERAL JUDICIAL SYSTEM
This simplified diagram shows the relationships among the various levels of federal courts and between state and federal courts. The losing party in a case can appeal a lower-court decision to the court at the next-highest level, as the arrows indicate. Decisions can be removed from state courts to federal courts only if they raise a constitutional question.

The Supreme Court is not the only federal court that "matters" in the American judicial system. Most federal cases originate in U.S. district courts, and most appealed cases are settled in U.S. courts of appeals, never reaching the Supreme Court. Shown here is testimony in a district court, the only level in the federal system in which juries decide the outcome of cases. (Billy E. Barnes/Stock, Boston)

the second level of the federal court system. Courts of appeals do not use juries. No new evidence is submitted in an appealed case; appellate courts base their decisions on a review of lower-court records. Appellate judges act as supervisors in the legal system, reviewing trial-court decisions and correcting what they consider to be legal errors. Facts (i.e., the circumstances of a case) found by district courts are presumed to be correct.

The United States has twelve general appeals courts, each of which serves a "circuit" that is comprised of between three and nine states, except the one that serves the District of Columbia only. There is also the U.S. Court of Appeals for the Federal Circuit, which specializes in appeals of cases involving patents and international trade. Between four and twenty-six judges sit on each court of appeals, but each case is usually heard by a panel of three judges. On rare occasions, all the judges of a court of appeals sit as a body (*en banc*) in order to resolve difficult controversies, typically ones that have resulted in conflicting decisions within the same circuit.

Courts of appeals offer the only real hope of reversal for many appellants, since fewer than 1 percent of the cases they hear are later reviewed by the Supreme Court.

SPECIAL U.S. COURTS   The federal judiciary includes a few specialty courts. Among them are the U.S. Claims Court, which hears cases in which the U.S. government has been sued for damages; the U.S. Court of International Trade, which handles cases involving appeals of U.S. Customs Office rulings; and the U.S. Court of Military Appeals, which hears appeals of military courts-martial. Some federal agencies and commissions also have adjudicative powers, and their decisions can be appealed to a federal court of appeals.

The State Courts

The American states are separate governments within a federal system. Each state is protected in its sovereignty by the Tenth Amendment, and each state has its own court system. Like the federal courts, state court systems have trial courts at the bottom level and appellate courts at the top.

Each state decides for itself the structure of its courts and the method of judicial appointment. In some states, judges are appointed by the governor, but judgeships are *elective offices* in most states. The common form involves competitive elections of either a partisan or nonpartisan nature, although some states use a system called the *merit plan* (also called the "Missouri Plan" because Missouri was the first state to use it) under which the governor selects a judge from a short list of acceptable candidates provided by a judicial selection commission. After a year or more on the bench, the judge selected must be approved by the voters in order to serve a longer term. Thereafter, the judge must face a periodic (usually every six years) "retention election" in which voters decide whether he or she will continue in the office (see box: States in the Nation).

Besides the upper-court myth, there exists a "federal court myth," which holds that the federal judiciary is the most significant part of the judicial system and that state courts play a subordinate role. This view is inaccurate as well. More than 95 percent of the nation's legal cases are decided in state courts. Most crimes (from shoplifting to murder) and most civil controversies (such as divorces and corporate disputes) are defined by state or local law. Moreover, nearly all cases that originate in state courts also end there; the federal courts never come into the picture since the case does not involve a federal issue.

STATES IN THE NATION

Principal Methods of Selecting State Judges

The states rely on a variety of methods for selecting their judicial officers, including the merit plan, partisan election, nonpartisan election, and political appointment. The states that appoint judges grant this power to the governor except in Virginia, Connecticut, and South Carolina, where the legislature makes the choice.

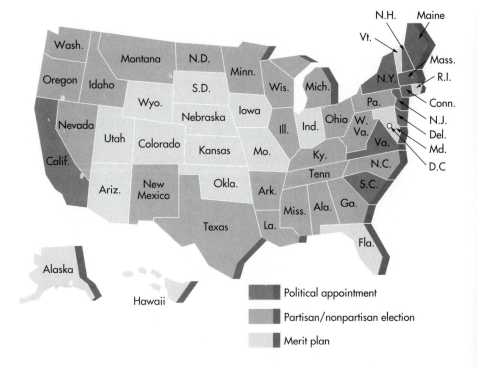

SOURCE: Council of State Governments.

In state criminal cases, after a person has been convicted and after all avenues of appeal in the state court system have been exhausted, the defendant can seek a writ of habeas corpus from a federal district court (see Chapter 4). The federal court often confines itself to the federal aspects of the matter, such as whether the defendant in a criminal case received the protections guaranteed by the U.S. Constitution. In addition, the federal court must accept the facts determined by the state court unless such findings are clearly in error. In short, legal and factual determinations of state courts can bind the federal courts—a clear contradiction of the federal court myth.

However, cases traditionally within the jurisdiction of the states can become federal cases through rulings of federal courts. In *Roe* v. *Wade* (1973), for example, the Supreme Court concluded that women had the right under the Constitution to choose an abortion, thus making abortion rights, which had been a state issue, also a federal one.[12] (This situation is called "diversity of citizenship" jurisdiction, meaning that both state and federal courts have some jurisdiction over the issue.)

FEDERAL COURT APPOINTEES

The quiet setting of the courtroom, the dignity of its proceedings, and the lack of fanfare with which a court delivers its decisions give the impression that the judiciary is about as far removed from the world of politics as a governmental institution can possibly be. The reality, however, is different. Federal judges and justices are political officials who exercise the authority of a separate and powerful branch of government. All federal jurists bring their political views with them to the courtroom and have regular opportunities to promote their political beliefs through the cases they decide. Accordingly, the process by which federal judges are appointed is a partisan one.

Selecting Supreme Court Justices and Federal Judges

The formal mechanism for appointments to the Supreme Court and the lower federal courts is the same: the president nominates and the Senate confirms or rejects. Beyond that basic similarity, however, there are significant differences.

SUPREME COURT NOMINEES   A Supreme Court appointment is a critical choice for a president. The cases that come before the Court tend to be controversial and have far-reaching implications. And since the Court is a small body, each justice's vote can be crucial to the decisions it makes. As most justices retain their positions for many years, presidents can influence judicial policy through their appointments long after they have left office. The careers of some Supreme Court justices provide dramatic testimony to the enduring effects of judicial appointments. Franklin D. Roosevelt appointed William O. Douglas to the Supreme Court in 1939, and for thirty years after Roosevelt's death in 1945, Douglas remained a strong liberal influence on the Court.

Presidents have employed a variety of approaches in their efforts to select a Supreme Court nominee who will reflect their political philosophy. A president may choose to depend chiefly on his own counsel, ask the Justice Department for advice, or seek the views of interested parties who share his general philosophy. Nominees must also be acceptable to others. Every nominee is closely scrutinized by the legal community, interested groups, and the media, and must also undergo an extensive background check by the FBI.[13]

Within the Senate, a key body is the Judiciary Committee, whose members have responsibility for conducting hearings on judicial nominees and recommending their confirmation or rejection by the full Senate. Nearly 20 percent of presidential nominees have been rejected by the Senate on grounds of judicial qualification, political views, personal ethics, or partisanship. Most of these rejections in the country's history occurred before 1900, and partisan politics was the main reason. Today a nominee with strong professional and ethical credentials is less likely to be blocked for partisan reasons alone.

Presidents often take into account the Senate's probable reaction when choosing a nominee. In selecting Ruth Bader Ginsberg and Stephen Breyer as his first nominees, President Clinton eschewed the choice of more controversial judges who might have been closer to his own views on issues before the Court. In general, though, the burden of proof rests with the Senate. To avoid the charge of unprincipled partisanship, the Senate has unofficially accepted the premise that it must build an overwhelming case against confirmation before denying the president's nominee a seat on the nation's highest court. This approach was evident in 1991 during confirmation hearings on Republican President George Bush's nomination of Clarence Thomas. Lacking confirming evidence of Anita Hill's charges of sexual harassment, the Democratic-controlled Senate voted to seat Thomas on the Supreme Court.

LOWER-COURT NOMINEES The president normally gives the deputy attorney general the task of screening potential nominees for lower-court judgeships.[14] **Senatorial courtesy** is also a consideration in these appointments: this tradition, which dates back to the 1840s, holds that a senator from the state in which a vacancy has arisen should be given a say in the nomination if the senator is of the same party as the president.[15] If not consulted, the senator involved can request that confirmation be denied, and other senators will normally grant the request as a "courtesy" to a fellow senator.[16] Not surprisingly, presidents have preferred to give senators a voice in judicial appointments.

Although the president does not become as personally involved in selecting lower-court nominees as in naming potential Supreme Court justices, lower-court appointments are collectively a significant factor in the impact of a president's administration. Recent presidents have appointed about 200 judges each term.

Justices and Judges as Political Officials

THE ROLE OF PARTISANSHIP   Presidents generally manage to appoint jurists who have a similar political philosophy. Although Supreme Court justices are free to make their own decisions, their legal positions can usually be inferred from their prior activities. A study by the judicial scholar Robert Scigliano found that about three of every four appointees have behaved on the Supreme Court approximately as presidents could have expected.[17] Of course, a president has no guarantee that a nominee will behave as expected. Justices Earl Warren and William Brennan proved more liberal than President Dwight D. Eisenhower would have liked. When he was asked whether he had made any mistakes as president, Eisenhower replied, "Yes, two, and they are both sitting on the Supreme Court."[18]

In nearly every instance, presidents have chosen members of their own party as Supreme Court nominees. Partisanship is also decisive in nominations to lower-court judgeships. All recent presidents except Gerald Ford have selected more than 90 percent of their district and appeals court nominees from among members of their own party.[19]

The fact that judges and justices are chosen through a partisan political process should not be interpreted to mean that they engage in blatant partisanship while on the bench. Judges and justices are officers of a separate branch and prize their judicial independence. All Republican appointees do not vote the same way on cases, nor do all Democrats. Nevertheless, the partisan backgrounds of judges are a significant influence on their decisions. A study of the voting records of appellate court judges, for example, found that Republican appointees tend to be more conservative than Democratic ap-

The justices of the U.S. Supreme Court pose for a photo. From left, they are: Antonin Scalia, Ruth Bader Ginsberg, John Paul Stevens, David Souter, Chief Justice William Rehnquist, Clarence Thomas, Sandra Day O'Connor, Stephen Breyer, and Anthony Kennedy. (Wide World Photos)

pointees in their civil rights and civil liberties decisions.[20] In Supreme Court cases, Democratic and Republican appointees have often been on opposite sides, although other divisions also occur.

OTHER CHARACTERISTICS OF JUDICIAL APPOINTEES   In recent years, increasing numbers of federal justices and judges have had prior judicial experience; the assumption is that such individuals are best qualified for appointment to the federal bench. Most recent appellate court appointees have been district or state judges or have worked in the office of the attorney general. Elective office (particularly a seat in the U.S. Senate) was once the typical route to the Supreme Court,[21] but now most justices have held an appellate court judgeship or high administrative office in the Justice Department before their appointment (see Table 14-1).

White males are greatly overrepresented on the federal bench, just as they dominate in Congress and at the top levels of the executive branch.[22] However, the number of women and minority-group judges increased substantially as a result of the appointments of President Clinton. Partisanship has been a significant factor in the appointment of women and minorities to the

TABLE 14-1   JUSTICES OF THE SUPREME COURT, 1996
Most recent appointees held an appellate-court position before being
nominated to the Supreme Court.

Justice	Year of Appointment	Nominating President	Position before Appointment
William Rehnquist*	1971	Nixon	Assistant attorney general, Department of Justice
John Paul Stevens	1975	Ford	Judge, U.S. Courts of Appeals
Sandra Day O'Connor	1981	Reagan	Judge, Arizona Courts of Appeals
Antonin Scalia	1986	Reagan	Judge, U.S. Courts of Appeals
Anthony Kennedy	1988	Reagan	Judge, U.S. Courts of Appeals
David Souter	1990	Bush	Judge, U.S. Courts of Appeals
Clarence Thomas	1991	Bush	Judge, U.S. Courts of Appeals
Ruth Bader Ginsberg	1993	Clinton	Judge, U.S. Courts of Appeals
Stephen Breyer	1994	Clinton	Judge, U.S. Courts of Appeals

*Appointed chief justice in 1986.

bench (see Table 14-2). Democratic presidents Carter and Clinton were more likely than Republican presidents Reagan and Bush to appoint such individuals, a reflection of the differences in the parties' coalitions (see Chapter 8).

The Supreme Court itself is also demographically unrepresentative. Until 1916, when Louis D. Brandeis was appointed to the Court, no Jewish justice had ever served. At least one Catholic, but at most times only one, has been on the Court almost continuously for nearly a century. Thurgood Marshall in 1967 became the first black justice, and Sandra Day O'Connor in 1981 became the first woman. Antonin Scalia in 1986 became the Court's first justice of Italian descent. No person of Hispanic or Asian descent has ever been a member of the Court.

TABLE 14-2 BACKGROUND CHARACTERISTICS OF
PRESIDENTS' JUDICIAL APPOINTEES
The judicial appointees of recent presidents have differed in their gender
and racial characteristics.

	Judicial Appointees of:			
	Carter	Reagan	Bush	Clinton
Men	84.5%	91.8%	82.8%	69%
Women	15.5	8.2	17.2	31
Whites	78.7%	93.9%	88.7%	69%
African Americans	14.3	2.1	6.3	22
Hispanics	6.2	3.4	4.6	8
Asians	0.8	0.5	0.4	1

SOURCES: Data on Carter, Reagan, and Bush presidencies provided by People for American Way; data on Clinton presidency (1993–94 only) provided by Department of Justice.

Judicial scholars disagree on the importance of the Court's demographic makeup. Henry J. Abraham dismisses concerns about it, claiming that the Court was never meant to be a representative body.[23] In contrast, Sheldon Goldman asserts that the judiciary's sensitivity to society's diverse interests depends to a degree on the social backgrounds that the justices bring with them to the Court.[24]

THE NATURE OF JUDICIAL DECISION MAKING

Federal judges and justices are political officials: they constitute one of three coequal branches of the national government (see box: How the United States Compares). Yet, unlike members of Congress or the president, judges serve in a legal institution and make their decisions in a legal context. As a consequence, their discretionary power is less than that of elected officials. Article III of the Constitution bars the federal judiciary from issuing decisions except on actual cases before it. As federal judge David Bazelon noted, a judge "can't wake up one morning and simply decide to give a helpful little push to a school system, a mental hospital, or the local housing agency."[25]

HOW THE UNITED STATES COMPARES

Judicial Power

U.S. courts are highly political by comparison with the courts of many other democracies. First, U.S. courts operate within a common-law tradition, which makes judge-made law (through precedent) a part of the legal code. Many democracies have a civil-law tradition, in which nearly all law is defined by legislative statutes. Second, because U.S. courts operate in a constitutional system of divided power, they are required to rule on conflicts between state and nation or between the executive and legislative branches, which thrusts them into the middle of political conflicts.

The power of U.S. courts is nowhere more evident than in the exercise of judicial review—the voiding of a legislative or executive action on the grounds that it is unconstitutional. In the so-called American system of judicial review, *any* judge can declare ordinary law invalid when it is deemed to conflict with constitutional law. By comparison, the so-called Austrian system restricts judicial review to a special constitutional court; judges in other courts are confined to the application of ordinary law only. Finally, some judicial systems have no provision for judicial review; for example, British courts even at the highest levels are not allowed to declare a parliamentary law void on the grounds that it is unconstitutional.

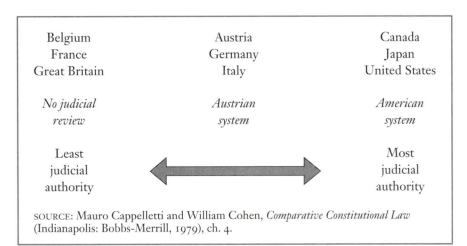

Belgium	Austria	Canada
France	Germany	Japan
Great Britain	Italy	United States
No judicial review	*Austrian system*	*American system*
Least judicial authority		Most judicial authority

SOURCE: Mauro Cappelletti and William Cohen, *Comparative Constitutional Law* (Indianapolis: Bobbs-Merrill, 1979), ch. 4.

The Legal Context of Judicial Decisions

The most substantial restriction on the courts is the law itself. Although a president or Congress can make almost any decision that is politically acceptable, the judiciary must justify its decision in terms of existing provisions of the law.[26] When asked by a friend to "do justice," Oliver Wendell Holmes, Jr., replied, "That is not my job. My job is to play the game according to the rules."[27] In playing according to the rules, judges engage in a creative legal process that requires them to identify the facts of the case, determine and sometimes formulate the relevant legal principles or rules, and then apply them to the case at hand.

THE CONSTRAINTS OF THE FACTS   A basic distinction in any legal case is between "the facts" and "the laws." The **facts** of a case, as determined by trial courts, are the relevant circumstances of a legal dispute or offense. In the case of a person accused of murder, for example, key facts would include evidence about the murder and whether police respected the alleged murderer's rights (for example, the right to have an attorney present during interrogation).

THE CONSTRAINTS OF THE LAW   In deciding cases, the judiciary is also constrained by existing laws. To use an obvious comparison, the laws governing a case of alleged murder differ from the laws that apply to an antitrust suit. As distinct from the facts of a case, the **laws** of a case are the constitutional provisions, legislative statutes, or judicial precedents that apply to the situation.

Interpretation of the Constitution.   The Constitution is the nation's highest law, but it is a sparsely worded document and for that reason is open to interpretation. For example, the Fourth Amendment of the Constitution protects individuals against "unreasonable searches and seizures," but the meaning of "unreasonable" is not spelled out. Nevertheless, judges respect the Constitution's purpose and intent. The question for a judge is what the Framers had in mind by a particular provision. For example, in deciding whether wire-tapping and other electronic means of surveillance are covered by the prohibition against unreasonable searches and seizures, the issue is what rights the amendment was designed to protect. Electronic surveillance was not invented until 150 years after the Fourth Amendment was ratified. But the Fourth Amendment was intended to protect individuals against the government's intrusion into their private lives; for this reason, the courts have concluded that government cannot indiscriminately tap a person's telephone.

Interpretation of Statutes. The power of the courts to decide whether a governmental institution has acted within its constitutional powers is called *judicial review* (see Chapter 3). Without this power, the judiciary would be unable to restrain a Congress or presidency that has gone out of control. Yet the process of judicial review pits a court's judgment against that of another institution and invokes the nation's highest law—the Constitution. The imposing nature of judicial review has led the judiciary, when possible, to prefer statutory rulings to constitutional ones.

As a practical matter, it is also true that most cases arising in the courts involve issues of statutory law rather than constitutional law. Statutory law includes legislation that has been enacted by Congress and administrative regulations that have been developed by the bureaucracy on the basis of statutory provisions. All federal courts are bound by federal statutes and administrative regulations, as well as treaties.

Interpretation of Precedent. The U.S. legal system developed from the English common-law tradition, which includes the principle that a court's decision on a case should be consistent with previous rulings. This princi-

---

Sources of Law That Constrain the Federal Judiciary's Decisions

U.S. Constitution: The federal courts are bound by the provisions of the U.S. Constitution. The sparseness of its wording, however, requires the Constitution to be applied in the light of particular circumstances. Thus judges are accorded a substantial degree of discretion in their constitutional judgments.

Statutory law: The Supreme Court is constrained by statutes and by administrative regulations derived from the provisions of statutes. Most laws, however, are somewhat vague in their provisions and often have unanticipated applications. As a result, judges have some freedom in deciding cases based on statutes.

Precedent: Federal courts tend to follow precedent (or *stare decisis*), which is a legal principle developed in earlier court decisions. Because times change and not all cases have a clear precedent, judges have some discretion in their evaluation of the way earlier cases apply to a current case.

ple is known as **precedent** and reflects the philosophy of *stare decisis* (Latin for "to stand by things that have been settled")—the doctrine that principles of law, once established, should be accepted as authoritative in all subsequent similar cases. Precedent is an important constraint on the courts. To persist in ignoring precedent would be to direct the law onto an unpredictable course, creating confusion and uncertainty among those who must make choices on the basis of their understanding of the law.[28]

Political Influences on Judicial Decisions

Although judicial rulings are justified by reference to laws, judges nearly always have some degree of discretion in their decisions. The Constitution is a sparsely worded document and must be adapted to new and changing situations; as a result, federal judges must interpret the Constitution in the context of the issue at hand. The judiciary also has no choice at times but to apply its own judgment to statutory law. Congress often cannot anticipate or reach agreement on all the specific applications of a legislative act and therefore uses general language to state the act's purpose. The judiciary must decide what this language means in the context of a specific case arising under the act. Precedent is even less precise as a guide to decision. Precedent is more a rule of thumb than a strict command; it must constantly be weighed against what Justice Oliver Wendell Holmes, Jr., described as the "felt necessities of the time."

In sum, judges have leeway in their decisions. As a consequence, their rulings reflect not only legal influences but political ones, which come from both outside and inside the judicial system.

"OUTSIDE" INFLUENCES ON COURT DECISIONS   The courts can make unpopular choices, but, in the long run, judicial decisions must be seen as fair if they are to be obeyed. In other words, the judiciary cannot ignore the expectations of the general public, interest groups, and elected representatives.

Judges are responsive to public opinion, although much less so than are elected officials. In some cases, for example, the Supreme Court has tailored its rulings in an effort to gain public support or dampen public resistance. In the *Brown* case, the justices, recognizing that school desegregation would be an explosive issue in the South, required only that desegregation take place "with all deliberate speed" rather than immediately or on a fixed timetable. The Supreme Court's apparent strategy has been to stay close enough to popular opinion so as to avoid seriously eroding public support for its decisions.[29]

The judicial branch is increasingly an arena in which interest groups contend for influence. Many of these disputes have pitted environmental groups against business firms. Shown here are demonstrators on both sides of the issue of whether protection of the spotted owl, an endangered species, should take precedence over the interests of the timber industry. (Joe Cempa/Black Star)

Groups make their opinions known to the judiciary through the lawsuits they file. The range of interests that use lawsuits as a policy tactic includes traditional advocacy groups such as the American Civil Liberties Union (ACLU) and newer ones such as the Christian Legal Society's Center for Law and Religious Freedom. Groups also participate in cases brought by others through *amicus curiae* ("friend of the court") briefs, which they file in support of one of the parties to a case.[30]

The influence of groups and the general public on the judiciary also takes place indirectly, through the elected branches of government. In response to public and group pressure, elected officials try to persuade the judiciary to hand down rulings favored by their constituents. Both Congress and the president have powerful means of influencing the federal judiciary.

Congress is constitutionally empowered to establish the Supreme Court's size and appellate jurisdiction, and Congress can rewrite legislation that it feels the Court has misinterpreted. Although Congress has seldom confronted the Court directly, it has often demonstrated displeasure with Supreme Court rulings, in the hope that the justices would respond favorably. For example, when the Court handed down its *Swann* decision permitting busing for the purpose of achieving racial integration in the schools, members of Congress threatened to pass legislation that would prevent the Court from hearing appeals of busing cases. Busing was never used to its full potential in part because of its unpopularity with many members of Congress.

The president is responsible for implementing court decisions and also affects the judiciary by pursuing or overlooking possible legal controversies, thereby influencing the cases that come before the courts. Under President Ronald Reagan, for instance, the Justice Department vigorously backed several suits challenging affirmative action programs and made no great attempt to push cases that would have expanded the application of such programs.

Presidents can also influence the federal courts through their judicial appointments.[31] When Democrat Bill Clinton took office in 1992, more than a hundred federal judgeships were vacant. President Bush had expected to win reelection and had not moved quickly to fill vacancies as they arose. By the time it was apparent that Bush might lose the election, the Democratic-controlled Congress was able to delay action on the appointments. This enabled Clinton to fill the positions with loyal Democrats who could be expected to partially offset the influence of the Republican judges appointed during the previous twelve years by presidents Reagan and Bush.

"INSIDE" INFLUENCES: THE JUSTICES' OWN POLITICAL BELIEFS

The judiciary symbolizes John Adams's characterization of the U.S. political system as "a government of laws, and not of men." The characterization has value as myth, but as the judicial scholar John Schmidhauser noted, "laws are made, enforced, and interpreted by men."[32] As an inevitable result, the decisions of the courts bear the indelible imprint of judges' political beliefs.[33]

This influence is most evident in the case of the Supreme Court. The justices are frequently divided in their opinions, and the divisions often reflect the justices' political backgrounds. During the 1996 Supreme Court term, for example, there were 41 nonunanimous decisions. In a majority of these cases, justices Antonin Scalia and Clarence Thomas, both Republicans when they were appointed to the Court, were opposed by justices Breyer and Ginsberg, both Democrats when they were appointed.[34]

Most Supreme Court justices hold relatively stable political views during their tenure. As a result, major shifts in the Supreme Court's position usually occur in conjunction with changes in its membership. When the Court in the 1980s moved away from the criminal justice rulings of the 1960s, it was largely because the more recently appointed justices believed that government should have more leeway in its efforts to fight crime.

JUDICIAL POWER AND DEMOCRATIC GOVERNMENT

The issue of judicial power is heightened by the fact that federal judges are not elected. The principle of self-government asserts that lawmaking majorities have the power to decide society's policies. Because the United States has a constitutional system that places checks on the will of the majority, there is obviously an important role in the system for a countermajoritarian institution such as the judiciary. Yet court decisions often reflect the political philosophy of the judges, who constitute a tiny political elite that wields significant power.[35] A critical question is how far unelected judges ought to go in substituting their policy judgments for those of officials who are elected by the people.

The Debate over the Proper Role of the Judiciary

The question of judicial power centers on the basic issue of **legitimacy**—the proper authority of the judiciary in a political system based in part on the principle of majority rule. The judiciary's policymaking significance and discretion have been sources of controversy throughout the country's history, but the controversies have perhaps never been livelier than during recent decades. The judiciary at times has acted almost legislatively by ordering broad social policies, such as busing and prison reform. In a recent year, for example, the prison systems in 42 states were operating under court orders that mandated improvements in health care or overcrowding. Through such actions the judiciary has restricted the policymaking authority of the states, has narrowed legislative discretion, and has made judicial action an effective alternative to election victory for certain interests.[36]

The judiciary has become more extensively involved in policymaking for many of the same reasons that Congress and the president have been thrust into new policy areas and become more deeply involved in old ones. Social and economic changes have required government to play a larger role in society, and this development has generated a seemingly endless series of new legal controversies.

Judicial action raises an important question. How far should the judiciary go in asserting its authority when that authority collides with or goes

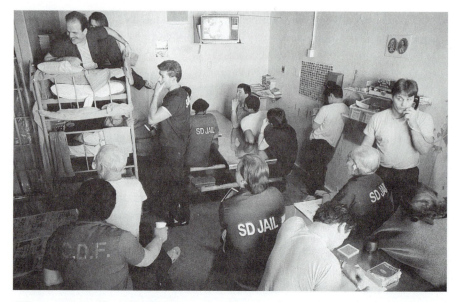

The question of how far the courts should go in placing their judgments ahead of those of elected officials is an ongoing controversy. For example, should the courts be allowed to order state and local officials to relieve overcrowding in jails? (Alon Reininger/Woodfin Camp & Associates)

beyond the action of elected institutions? There are two general schools of thought on this question: those of judicial restraint and judicial activism. Although these terms are somewhat imprecise and often misused, they are helpful in efforts to clarify opposing philosophical positions on the Court's proper role.[37]

THE DOCTRINE OF JUDICIAL RESTRAINT   The doctrine of **judicial restraint** holds that the judiciary should be highly respectful of precedent and should defer to the judgment of legislatures. The restraint doctrine emphasizes the consistency of law and rule through elected institutions. It holds that broad issues of the public good should be decided in nearly all cases by the majority through legislation enacted by elected officials. The judges' role is to discover the application of legislation and precedent to specific cases rather than to search for new principles that essentially change the meaning of the law.

Advocates of judicial restraint support their position with two major arguments. First, they contend that when the judiciary assumes policy functions that traditionally belong to elected institutions, it undermines the fundamental premise of self-government: the right of the majority to choose society's policies.[38] Second, judicial self-restraint is admired because it preserves the public support that is essential to the long-term authority of the courts. The judiciary must be concerned with **compliance**—with whether its decisions will be respected and obeyed. If the judiciary thwarts the majority's desires, public confidence in its legitimacy can be endangered, and other officials may act to undermine judicial decisions.[39]

Advocates of judicial restraint acknowledge that established law is never so precise as to provide exact answers to every question raised by every case and requires some degree of judicial discretion. And in rare circumstances, decisive judicial action may be both appropriate and necessary, as in the historic *Brown* v. *Board of Education* decision (1954). Although the Constitution does not provide an explicit basis for school desegregation, government-supported racial discrimination violates the principle of equal justice under the law.[40]

Yet many advocates of judicial restraint see no constitutional justification for many of the Supreme Court's civil rights decisions. In *Romer* v. *Evans* (1996), for example, the Court struck down an amendment to the Colorado constitution that was adopted by majority vote in a statewide referendum. The amendment had nullified existing civil rights protections for homosexuals in the state and had also barred the passage of new ones. In a blistering dissent, Justice Antonin Scalia, an advocate of judicial restraint, said the Court's decision to invalidate the Colorado amendment was "an act not of judicial judgment but of political will." Scalia said that the statewide referendum was "the most democratic of procedures" and that the decision of Colorado voters should have been upheld.[41]

THE DOCTRINE OF JUDICIAL ACTIVISM   In contrast to the judicial restraint position is the idea that the courts should take an expansive view of judicial power. Although advocates of this doctrine, which is known as **judicial activism,** acknowledge the principles of precedent and majority rule, they claim that the courts should not be overly deferential to existing legal principles or to the judgments of elected officials.

Until recently, the doctrine of judicial activism was associated almost entirely with liberal activists who contend that courts should resort to general principles of fairness when existing law is insufficient. Liberal judicial activists argue, for example, that fairness for African American children requires that in some circumstances children should be bused to achieve school integration. In areas where social justice depends substantially on protection of the rights of the individual, the judiciary is said to have a responsibility to act positively and decisively.[42]

Activists who emphasize the Court's obligation to protect civil rights and liberties find justification for their position in the U.S. Constitution's strong moral language and several of its provisions.[43] They view the Constitution as designed chiefly to protect people from unreasonable governmental interference in their lives—a goal that can be accomplished only by a judiciary that is willing to stand up to the lawmaking majority whenever the latter tries to restrict individual choice.

Judicial activism is not, however, confined to liberals. In the 1930s conservative activists on the Supreme Court struck down many of the early New Deal programs (see Chapter 2). Judicial activism from the right recently became an issue again when the Court overturned several precedents in the area of the rights of the accused. In 1990 Chief Justice William Rehnquist, in a rare action, asked Congress to restrict the right of people convicted in state courts to file habeas corpus appeals in federal courts. Congress rejected the proposal, and in 1991 a majority on the Rehnquist Court took action on its own to achieve the goal. In one ruling, the Court held that an inmate could not obtain a federal appeal simply because his or her lawyer had made a procedural mistake during the trial in a state court. Chief Justice Rehnquist wrote that precedent is not "an inexorable command."[44]

These examples illustrate the difficulty of applying the terms "judicial activism" and "judicial restraint" in consistent ways. In fact, some observers argue that all judges—conservatives, moderates, and liberals—are activists in the sense that their decisions are necessarily creative ones.

The Judiciary's Proper Role: A Question of Competing Values

The dispute between advocates of judicial activism and advocates of judicial restraint is a philosophical one that involves opposing values. The debate is important because it addresses the normative question of what role the judiciary ought to play in American democracy. Should unelected judges involve themselves deeply in policy by adopting a broad conception of their power, or should they give wide discretion to elective institutions? Should judges defer to precedent, or should they be willing to change course, even at the risk of sending the law down uncharted paths? These questions cannot be answered simply on the basis of whether one personally agrees or disagrees with a particular judicial decision. The answer necessarily depends on a judgment about the proper role of the judiciary in a governing system based on the often-conflicting concepts of majority rule and individual rights.

The United States is a constitutional democracy that recognizes both the power of the majority to rule and the claim of the minority to protection of its rights. The judiciary was not established as the nation's moral conscience and does not have a monopoly on the issue of minority interests and rights. Yet the judiciary was established as a coequal branch of government and was charged with the responsibility for protecting individual rights and minority interests. In short, the constitutional question of how far the courts should be allowed to go in substituting their judgment for that of elected institutions and established law is open to interpretation. The trade-off is significant on all issues: minority rights versus majority rule, states' rights versus federal power, legislative authority versus judicial authority. The question of whether judicial restraint or judicial activism is more desirable is one that every student of American government should ponder.

SUMMARY

At the lowest level of the federal judicial system are the district courts, where most federal cases begin. Above them are the federal courts of appeals, which review cases appealed from the lower courts. The U.S. Supreme Court is the nation's highest court. Each state has its own court system, consisting of trial courts at the bottom and one or two appellate levels at the top. Cases originating in state courts ordinarily cannot be appealed to the federal courts unless a federal issue is involved, and then the federal courts can choose to rule only on the federal aspects of the case. Federal judges at all levels are nominated by the president, and if confirmed by the Senate, they are appointed by the president to the office. Once on the federal bench, they serve until they die, retire, or are removed by impeachment and conviction.

The Supreme Court is unquestionably the most important court in the country. The legal principles it establishes are binding on lower courts, and its capacity to define the law is enhanced by the control it exercises over the cases it hears. However, it is inaccurate to assume that lower courts are inconsequential (the upper-court myth). Lower courts have considerable discretion, and the great majority of their decisions are not reviewed by a higher court. It is also inaccurate to assume that federal courts are far more significant than state courts (the federal court myth).

The courts have less discretionary authority than elected institutions. The judiciary's positions are constrained by the facts of a case and by the laws as defined through the Constitution, statutes and government regulations, and legal precedent. Yet existing legal guidelines are seldom so precise that judges have no choice in their decisions. As a result, political influences have a strong impact on the judiciary. It responds to national conditions, public opinion, interest groups, and elected officials, particularly the president and members of Congress. Another political influence on the judiciary is the personal beliefs of judges, who have individual preferences that are evident in the way they decide on issues that come before the courts. Not surprisingly, partisan politics plays a significant role in judicial appointments.

In recent decades the Supreme Court has issued broad rulings on individual rights, some of which have required governments to take positive action on behalf of minority interests. As the Court has crossed into areas traditionally left to law-making majorities, the legitimacy of its policies has been questioned. Advocates of judicial restraint claim that the justices' personal values are inadequate justification for exceeding the proper judicial role. They argue that the Constitution entrusts broad issues of the public good to elective institutions and that judicial activism ultimately undermines public respect for the judiciary. Judicial activists counter that the courts were established as an independent branch and should not hesitate to promote new principles when they see a need, even if this action puts them into conflict with elected officials.

MAJOR CONCEPTS

appellate jurisdiction
compliance
concurring opinion
decision
dissenting opinion
facts (of a court case)
judicial activism
judicial conference
judicial restraint
jurisdiction (of a court)

laws (of a court case)
legitimacy (of judicial power)
majority opinion
opinion (of a court)
original jurisdiction
plurality opinion
precedent
senatorial courtesy
writ of *certiorari*

SUGGESTED READINGS

Hughes, John C. *The Federal Courts, Politics, and the Rule of Law.* New York: Long-man, 1995. An analysis of the federal courts as a dynamic system.

Maltz, Earl M. *Rethinking Constitutional Law: Originalism, Interventionism, and the Politics of Judicial Review.* Lawrence: University of Kansas Press, 1994. A critical and timely analysis of constitutional interpretation in the modern age.

Nagel, Robert F. *Judicial Power and American Character: Censoring Ourselves in an Anxious Age.* New York: Oxford University Press, 1996. A questioning assessment of the judiciary's role in settling moral issues.

O'Brien, David M. *Storm Center,* 4th ed. New York: Norton, 1996. An analysis of the Supreme Court in the context of the controversy surrounding the role of the judiciary in the U.S. political system.

Perry, Michael J. *The Constitution and the Courts: Law or Politics?* New York: Oxford University Press, 1994. A sweeping assessment of the constitutional role of the Supreme Court by a proponent of judicial activism.

Salokar, Rebecca Mae. *The Solicitor General: The Politics of Law.* Philadelphia, Pa.: Temple University Press, 1992. A study of the important and increasingly political role of the nation's top trial lawyer.

Schwartz, Bernard. *Decision: How the Supreme Court Decides Cases.* New York: Oxford University Press, 1996. A behind-the-scenes look at Supreme Court justices' decisions.

Segal, Jeffrey A., and Harold J. Spaeth. *The Supreme Court and the Attitudinal Model.* New York: Cambridge University Press, 1993. A provocative analysis which claims that justices' personal beliefs are the main determinant of Supreme Court decisions.

Watson, George L., and John Alan Stookey. *Shaping America: The Politics of Supreme Court Appointments.* New York: Longman, 1995. An examination of the process by which Supreme Court justices are nominated and confirmed.

Yackle, Larry W. *Reclaiming the Federal Courts.* Cambridge, Mass.: Harvard University Press, 1994. An impassioned argument for judicial activism in the area of individual rights.

READING 14

Judicial Interpretation
WILLIAM J. BRENNAN, JR.

The Constitution is fundamentally a public text—the monumental charter of a government and a people—and a Justice of the Supreme Court must apply it to resolve public controversies. For, from our beginning, a most important consequence of the constitutionally created separation of powers has been the American habit, extraordinary to other democracies, of casting social, economic, philosophical and political questions in the form of lawsuits, in an attempt to secure ultimate resolution by the Supreme Court. . . . Not infrequently, these are the issues upon which contemporary society is most deeply divided. They arouse our deepest emotions. The main burden of my twenty-nine terms on the Supreme Court has thus been to wrestle with the Constitution in this heightened public context, to draw meaning from the text in order to resolve public controversies.

Two other aspects of my relation to this text warrant mention. First, constitutional interpretation for a federal judge is, for the most part, obligatory. When litigants approach the bar of court to adjudicate a constitutional dispute, they may justifiably demand an answer. Judges cannot avoid a definitive interpretation because they feel unable to, or would prefer not to, penetrate to the full meaning of the Constitution's provisions. Unlike literary critics, judges cannot merely savor the tensions or revel in the ambiguities inhering in the text—judges must resolve them.

Second, consequences flow from a Justice's interpretation in a direct and immediate way. A judicial decision respecting the incompatibility of Jim Crow with a constitutional guarantee of equality is not simply a contemplative exercise in defining the shape of a just society. It is an order—supported by the full coercive power of the State—that the present society change in a fundamental aspect. . . . More than the litigants may be affected. The course of vital social, economic and political currents may be directed.

These . . . defining characteristics of my relation to the constitutional text—its public nature, obligatory character, and consequentialist aspect—cannot help but influence the way I read that text. When Justices interpret the Constitution they speak for their community, not for themselves alone. The act of interpretation must be undertaken with full consciousness that it is, in a very real sense, the community's interpretation that is sought. Justices are not platonic guardians appointed to wield authority according to their personal moral predilections. Precisely because coercive force must attend any judicial decision to countermand the will of a contemporary majority, the Justices must render constitutional interpretations that are received as legitimate. The source of legitimacy is, of course, a wellspring of controversy in legal and political circles. At the core of the debate is what the late Yale Law School Professor Alexander Bickel labeled "the countermajoritarian difficulty." Our commitment to self-governance in a representative democracy must be reconciled with vesting in electorally unaccountable Justices the power to invalidate the expressed desires of representative bodies on the ground of inconsistency with higher law. . . .

There are those who find legitimacy in fidelity to what they call "the intentions of the Framers." In its most doctrinaire incarnation, this view demands that Justices discern exactly what the Framers thought about the question under consideration and simply follow that intention in resolving the case before them. It is a view that feigns self-effacing deference to the specific judgments of those who forged our original social compact. But in truth it is little more than arrogance cloaked as humility. It is arrogant to pretend that from our vantage we can gauge accurately the intent of the Framers on application of principle to specific, contemporary questions. All too often, sources of potential enlightenment such as records of the ratification debates provide sparse or ambiguous evidence of the original intention. Typically, all that can be gleaned is that the Framers themselves did not agree about the application or meaning of particular constitutional provisions, and hid their differences in cloaks of generality. Indeed, it is far from clear whose intention is relevant—that of the drafters, the congressional disputants, or the ratifiers in the state—or even whether the idea of an original intention is a coherent way of thinking about a jointly drafted document drawing its authority from a general assent of the states. And apart from the problematic nature of the sources, our distance of two centuries cannot but work as a prism refracting all we perceive. One cannot help but speculate that the chorus of lamentations calling for interpretation faithful to "original intention"—and proposing nullification of interpretations that fail this quick litmus test—must inevitably come from persons who have no familiarity with the historical record.

Perhaps most importantly, while proponents of this facile historicism justify it as a depoliticization of the judiciary, the political underpinnings of such a choice should not escape notice. A position that upholds constitutional claims only if they were within the specific contemplation of the Framers in effect establishes a presumption of resolving textual ambiguities against the claim of constitutional right. It is far from clear what justifies such a presumption against claims of right. Nothing intrinsic in the nature of interpretation—if there is such a thing as the "nature" of interpretation—commands such a passive approach to ambiguity. This is a choice no less political than any other; it expresses antipathy to claims of the minority rights against the majority. Those who would restrict claims of right to the values of 1789 specifically articulated in the Constitution turn a blind eye to social progress and eschew adaptation of overarching principles to changes of social circumstance.

Another, perhaps more sophisticated, response to the potential power of judicial interpretation stresses democratic theory: because ours is a government of the people's elected representatives, substantive value choices should by and large be left to them. This view emphasizes not the transcendent historical authority of the Framers but the predominant contemporary authority of the elected branches of government. . . .

The view that all matters of substantive policy should be resolved through the majoritarian process has appeal under some circumstances, but I think it ultimately will not do. Unabashed enshrinement of majority will would permit the imposition of a social caste system or wholesale confiscation of property so long as a majority of the authorized legislative body, fairly elected, approved. Our Constitution could not abide such a situation. It is the very purpose of a Constitution—and particularly of the Bill of Rights—to declare certain values transcendent, beyond the reach of temporary political majorities. The majoritarian process cannot be expected to rectify claims of minority right that arise as a response to the outcomes of that very majoritarian process. . . .

Faith in democracy is one thing, blind faith quite another. Those who drafted our Constitution understood the difference. One cannot read the text without admitting that it embodies substantive value choices; it places certain values beyond the power of any legislature. Obvious are the separation of powers; the privilege of the Writ of Habeas Corpus; prohibition of Bills of Attainder and *ex post facto* laws; prohibition of cruel and unusual punishments; the requirement of just compensation for official taking of property; the prohibition of laws tending to establish religion or enjoining the free exercise of religion; and, since the Civil War, the banishment of slavery and official race discrimination. With respect to at least such principles, we simply have not constituted ourselves as strict utilitarians. While the Constitution may be amended, such amendments require an immense effort by the People as a whole.

To remain faithful to the content of the Constitution, therefore, an approach to interpreting the text must account for the existence of these substantive value choices, and must accept the ambiguity inherent in the effort to apply them to modern circumstances. The Framers discerned fundamental principles through struggles against particular malefactions of the Crown; the struggle shapes the particular contours of the articulated principles. But our acceptance of the fundamental principles has not and should not bind us to those precise, at times anachronistic, contours. Successive generations of Americans have continued to respect these fundamental choices and adopt them as their own guide to evaluating quite different historical practices. . . .

We current Justices read the Constitution in the only way that we can: as Twentieth Century Americans. We look to the history of the time of framing and to the intervening history of interpretation. But the ultimate question must be, what do the words of the text mean in our time? For the genius of the Constitution rests not in any static meaning it might have had in a world that is dead and gone, but in the adaptability of its great principles to cope with current problems and current needs.

SOURCE: Address to the Text and Teaching Symposium, Georgetown University, October 12, 1985, Washington, D.C.
William J. Brennan, Jr., served for three decades as an associate justice of the Supreme Court of the United States.

CHAPTER FIFTEEN

Economic Policy

We the people of the United States, in order to . . . insure domestic tranquility . . .
PREAMBLE, U.S. CONSTITUTION

HE STOCK market had been on a dizzying ride upward. In 1995 stock prices rose by more than 30 percent, and they increased by another 15 percent in the first six months of 1996. Then, in midsummer, the market suddenly plummeted. Technology stocks had led the market's rise, and in the space of a week they lost nearly all their gains for the year. Would history repeat itself? Was the United States on the verge of another economic collapse like the stock market crash of October 1929 that sent the nation into the Great Depression?

In fact, Wall Street and the rest of America reacted calmly to declining stock prices in midsummer 1996, seeing it as merely an overdue "correction" in the market. Among the reasons for the calm reaction was the fact that substantial government programs were in place to help stabilize and stimulate the U.S. economy. When the Great Depression struck, no such programs existed. Moreover, the response to the 1929 crash guaranteed that the economic crisis would worsen. Businesses cut back on production, investors fled the stock market, depositors withdrew their bank savings, and consumers slowed their spending; all these actions accelerated the downward spiral. In 1996, however, government programs were in place to protect depositors' savings, to slow the drop in stock prices, and to steady the economy through adjustments in interest rates and spending programs.

This chapter examines the economic role of the government, focusing on its promotion and regulation of economic interests and its fiscal and monetary policies, which affect economic growth. Although the private decisions of firms and individuals are the main force in the American economic system, these decisions are made in the context of government policy. Washington seeks to regulate, promote, and maintain a strong national economy. The main ideas presented in the chapter are the following:

* *Through regulation, the U.S. government imposes restraints on business activity that are designed to promote economic efficiency and equity.*

* *Through promotion, the U.S. government helps private interests to achieve their economic goals.*

* *Through fiscal and monetary policy, the U.S. government seeks to maintain a stable and prosperous general economy.*

REGULATING THE ECONOMY

An **economy** is a system of production and consumption of goods and services, which are allocated through exchange. When a shopper gets groceries at a store and pays money in return, that transaction is one of the millions of economic exchanges that make up the economy. In *The Wealth of Nations* (1776), Adam Smith presented the case for the **laissez-faire doctrine,** which holds that private individuals and firms should be left alone to make their own production and distribution decisions. Smith reasoned that when there is a demand for a good (that is, when people desire a good and have the ability to buy it), private entrepreneurs will respond by producing the good and distributing it to places where demand exists. Smith argued that the desire for profit is the "invisible hand" that guides the system toward the greatest welfare for all.

Smith acknowledged that the doctrine of laissez-faire capitalism had a few limits. Certain areas of the economy, such as roadways and postal services, were natural monopolies and were better run by government than by private firms. In addition, by regulating banking, currency, and contracts, government could give stability to private transactions. Otherwise, Smith argued, the economy was best left in private hands.

In contrast, Karl Marx proposed a worker-controlled economy. In *Das Kapital* (*Capital,* 1867) Marx argued that a free market system is exploitative because producers, through their control of production and markets, can compel workers to labor at a wage below the value they add to production and can force consumers to pay higher prices for goods than are justified by the cost of production. To end this exploitation, Marx proposed a collective economy. When the workers owned the means of production, the economy would operate in the interest of all people.

Marx and Smith represent the extremes of economic theory. No country in the world has an economy that conforms fully to either the laissez-faire or the collectivist model. All national economies today are of "mixed" form in that they contain elements of both private and public control. However, the world's economies vary greatly in their mix. The United States tends toward private ownership, whereas China tends toward collective ownership. In between, but closer to the American economy, are certain European countries whose governments, on behalf of their people, own and operate a number of key industries, including steel, airlines, and oil.

Although the U.S. government itself owns only a few businesses (such as Amtrak), it plays a substantial economic role through **regulation** of privately owned businesses. U.S. firms are not free to act as they please but must operate within production and distribution bounds set by federal regulations. Regulatory policy is generally intended to promote either economic *efficiency* or *equity* (see Table 15-1).

Efficiency through Government Intervention[1]

Economic efficiency results when firms fulfill as many of society's needs as possible while using as few of its resources as possible. **Efficiency** refers to the relationship of inputs (the labor and material that go into making a product or service) to outputs (the product or service itself). The greater the output for a given input, the more efficient the production process.

TABLE 15-1 THE MAIN OBJECTIVES OF REGULATORY POLICY
The government intervenes in the economy to promote efficiency and equity.

Objective	Definition	Representative Actions by Government
Efficiency	Fulfillment of as many of society's needs as possible at the cost of as few of its resources as possible. The greater the output for a given input, the more efficient is the process.	Preventing restraint of trade; requiring producers to pay the costs of damage to the environment; reducing restrictions on business that cannot be justified on a cost-benefit basis.
Equity	When the outcome of an economic transaction is fair to each party.	Requiring firms to bargain in good faith with labor; protecting consumers in their purchases; protecting workers' safety and health.

Adam Smith and other classical economists believed that the free market was the optimal means of achieving efficiency. Producers would try to use as few resources as possible in order to keep their prices low so that they could compete successfully for customers. Efficient producers would be able to underprice inefficient ones, who would thereby be driven out of business.

PREVENTING RESTRAINT OF TRADE   The assumption that the market always determines price is flawed; the same incentive—the profit motive—that drives producers to respond to demand can drive them to corner the market on a good. If a producer gains a monopoly on a good or colludes with other producers to fix its price, consumers are forced to pay an artificially high price. Rather than selling at a low price in order to attract customers, the producer will charge as high a price as the market will bear.

Restraint of trade was prevalent in the United States in the late nineteenth century when large trusts came to dominate many areas of the economy, including the oil, steel, railroad, and sugar markets. Railroad companies, for example, had no competition on short routes and gouged their customers. In 1887, Congress took its first step toward regulating the trusts by enacting the Interstate Commerce Act. The legislation created the Interstate Commerce Commission (ICC), which was charged with regulating railroad practices and fares. Three years later, the Sherman Antitrust Act declared that any business combination or practice in restraint of trade was illegal. A pro-business Supreme Court made these legislative acts less effective than anticipated, and so the Mann-Elkins Act (1911) and the Clayton Act (1914) were passed to broaden the government's regulatory authority. The Federal Trade Commission (FTC) was established in 1914 to regulate trade practices.

Today the FTC is one of many federal agencies charged with regulating business competition. In a few cases, the government has prohibited mergers or required divestments in order to increase competition. The largest antitrust suit in the country's history was settled in 1984 when AT&T was forced to sell its regional Bell Telephone companies, which had enabled it to monopolize access to long-distance telephone service. AT&T must now compete for long-distance customers with MCI, Sprint, and other carriers.

In most cases, however, the government tolerates business concentration, even permitting the merger of competing firms, such as Time-Warner's merger with Turner Broadcasting in 1996. Although such mergers reduce competition, the government tolerates concentrated ownership in the oil, automobile, and other industries in which high capital costs make it diffi-

Although corporate mergers decrease competition, the government has generally tolerated mergers in business sectors in which high capital costs occur. Here, Ted Turner (*left*) and Gerald Levin (*right*) shake hands to mark the merger of the Turner Broadcasting System and Time-Warner, which created one of the world's largest news and entertainment conglomerates. (Gamma Liaison Only)

cult for smaller firms to compete successfully.[2] Government acceptance of corporate giants also reflects a realization that market competition no longer involves just domestic firms. For example, the "Big Three" U.S. automakers (General Motors, Ford, and Chrysler) face stiff competition from imports, particularly those from Japan and Germany.

The U.S. government's general policy toward corporate giants that act in restraint of trade has been to penalize them financially. In 1993, a number of air carriers (including American, Delta, United, Northwest, and US Air) were found to have engaged in price fixing and were ordered to award hundreds of millions of dollars in certificates to travelers who could prove they had flown on these carriers during the period in question. More than 4 million individuals, organizations, and businesses filed claims.

MAKING BUSINESS PAY FOR INDIRECT COSTS   Economic inefficiencies can result not only from restraint of trade but from the failure of businesses or consumers to pay the full costs of resources used in production. Classical economics assumes that market prices reflect all the costs of production, but this assumption is rarely warranted. Consider companies that dump their industrial wastes in a nearby river. The price of these companies' products does not reflect the water pollution, and hence customers do not pay all the costs that society has incurred in the making of the products. Economists label such unpaid costs **externalities.**

Until the 1960s, the federal government did not require firms to pay such costs. The impetus to begin doing so came not only from lawmakers but also from the scientific community and environmental groups. The Clean Air Act of 1963 and the Water Pollution Control Act of 1964 required industry to install antipollution devices to keep the discharge of air and water pollutants within specified limits. In 1970 Congress created the Environmental Pro-

The government has shifted some of the cost of cleaning up toxic-waste dumps and other kinds of pollution from the general public to the firms that discharge the pollutants.
(Fred Ward/Black Star)

tection Agency (EPA) to monitor compliance with federal regulations governing air and water quality and the disposal of toxic wastes.

Regulatory activity has had a dramatic impact on the quality of the environment. Pollution levels today are far below their levels of the 1960s when yellowish-gray fog hung over cities like Los Angeles and when rivers like the Potomac were open sewers. Environmental protection has gained broad public support. Although Americans are divided over the issue of whether government has gone too far in regulating business, they oppose the lifting of existing regulations in a wide range of areas, from automobile emission standards to industrial waste-water standards. Moreover, Americans have become environmentally informed and active.[3] Most of them recycle at least some of their garbage, and nearly two-thirds say they are either an active environmentalist or sympathetic to environmental concerns (see Figure 15-1).

CURBING OVERREGULATION   Although government intervention is intended to increase economic efficiency, the effect can be the opposite. Government regulation raises the cost of doing business. Firms have to expend work hours to monitor and implement government regulations, which in some instances (for example, pollution control) also require companies to

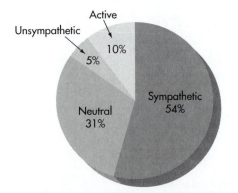

Respondents were asked: "Do you think of yourself as an active environmentalist, or as sympathetic to environmental concerns but not active, or neutral, or generally unsympathetic to environmental concerns?"

FIGURE 15-1   PUBLIC OPINION ON THE ISSUE OF ENVIRONMENTALISM
Most Americans regard themselves as either active environmentalists or as sympathetic to environmental concerns.
Source: Wirthlin Group survey, August 11–15, 1995.

buy and install expensive equipment. These costs are efficient to the degree that they produce commensurate benefits. As a result of regulation, for example, worker safety has improved greatly (for example, in the past decade or so, workplace deaths and injuries have declined by more than 20 percent).

Yet if government places needless or excessive regulatory burdens on firms, they waste resources in the process of complying. The result is higher-priced goods that are more expensive for consumers and less competitive in the domestic and global markets (see box: How the United States Compares). In other words, too much regulation is a source of inefficiency. An example is a provision of the Safe Drinking Water Act that required communities to reduce contaminants in their water supply from the current level, whatever that level happened to be. In most communities, the effect was to improve the quality of the water supply. But in Anchorage, Alaska, the result was an absurd remedy. The city's water supply was so clean already that officials had to ask local fish-processing plants to dump their wastes into the sewer system so that Anchorage would have impurities to remove from its water.[4]

Situations of this kind have led to regulatory reform.[5] In 1995, Congress enacted legislation to tighten the regulatory process by requiring cost-benefit analysis and risk assessment (the severity of the problem) to be taken into account in certain regulatory decisions. Other policy innovations of recent years include the Environmental Protection Agency's negotiated regulatory process, in which interested parties (for example, policymakers, firms, communities, and environmental groups) are brought together in advance of issuing a new regulation in order to negotiate its content.

DEREGULATION   Another response to regulatory excess is the policy of **deregulation**—the rescinding of regulations already in force for the purpose of improving efficiency. This process began in 1977 with passage of the Airlines Deregulation Act, which eliminated government-set air fares and, in some instances, government-mandated air routes. The change had the intended effect: air fares declined in price, and there was more competition between airlines on most routes.

Congress followed airline deregulation with partial deregulation of the trucking, banking, energy, and communications industries, among others. These industries had operated under federal regulations that substantially restricted their activities, including what they could charge for services. The free market would govern a wider range of their activities.

The free market principle has its limits, however, just as the regulatory principle can be carried too far. Deregulation has not been an unqualified success.[6] The savings and loan (S&L) industry is a prime example. S&Ls had

HOW THE UNITED STATES COMPARES

Global Economic Competitiveness

The United States ranks first in global economic competitiveness, according to a 1996 survey by the World Economic Forum, a private economic research organization in Switzerland.

The ranking is based on eight different factors: domestic economy, internationalization, government, management, finance, infrastructure, science and technology, and people. The United States was strongest on its domestic economy, technology, management, and finance, where it ranked at the top. Its weakest point was the people factor, where it was downgraded on education programs and welfare services (for example, the United States, unlike other advanced industrialized countries, does not have government-provided health care).

The United States is ranked substantially higher than its major economic rivals, Japan and Germany. They trailed by roughly 30 percentage points on the competitiveness index. Singapore and Hong Kong were closest to the United States on the index, but even they trailed by more than 10 points.

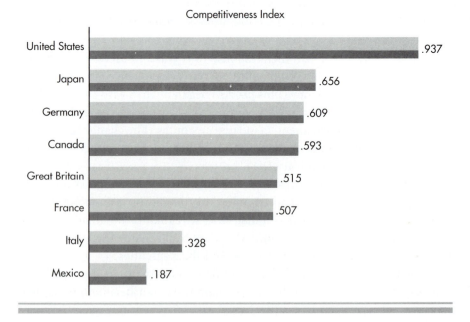

Competitiveness Index

United States	.937
Japan	.656
Germany	.609
Canada	.593
Great Britain	.515
France	.507
Italy	.328
Mexico	.187

been hit hard by the high inflation of the 1970s, and they hoped to restore their financial base through high-yield investments. Since existing regulations prevented them from pursuing riskier investments, the S&L industry successfully lobbied Congress for a change. When deregulation lifted restrictions on how S&Ls could invest depositors' savings, many of them began to engage in highly speculative ventures, such as commercial real estate.

By 1989 the S&L industry was in crisis. Bad management, poor investments, and outright fraud had resulted in an industrywide loss of billions of dollars. In order to save what was left of the industry, President Bush and Congress developed a bailout plan that will eventually cost the taxpayers more than $100 billion.

The savings and loan crisis demonstrates that the issue of business regulation is not a simple question of whether or not to regulate. On the one hand, too much regulation can burden firms with bureaucratic red tape, costly implementation procedures, and limited options. On the other hand, too little regulation can give firms the leeway to exploit the public unfairly or recklessly. Either too little or too much regulation can result in economic inefficiency. The challenge for policymakers is to strike the proper balance between regulatory measures and free market mechanisms.

Equity through Government Intervention

As we noted earlier, the government intervenes in the economy to bring equity as well as efficiency to the marketplace. **Equity** occurs when an economic transaction is fair to each party.[7] While efficiency refers to the relationship of inputs to outputs, equity refers to *outcomes:* whether they are reasonable and mutually acceptable. A transaction can be considered fair if each party enters into it freely and is not unknowingly at a disadvantage (for example, if the seller knows a product is defective, equity requires that the buyer also know of the defect).

An early equity measure was the creation of the Food and Drug Administration (FDA) in 1907. Because consumers are often unable to tell whether foods and drugs are safe to use, the FDA works to keep adulterated foods and dangerous or ineffective drugs off the market. In the 1930s, financial reforms were among the equity measures enacted under the New Deal. The Securities and Exchange Act of 1934 and the Banking Act of 1934 were designed in part to protect investors and savers from dishonest or imprudent brokers and bankers. The New Deal also provided greater equity for organized labor, which previously had been in a weak position in its dealings with management. Under the terms of the 1935 National Labor Relations Act (also called the Wagner Act), employers could no longer refuse to negotiate pay and working conditions with employees' unions. The Fair Labor Standards Act of 1938 established minimum wages, maximum working hours, and constraints on the use of child labor.

The 1960s and 1970s produced the greatest number of equity reforms. From 1965 to 1977, ten federal agencies, such as the Consumer Product Safety Commission, were established to protect consumers, workers, and the public from harmful effects of business activity. Among the products declared to be unsafe in the 1960s and 1970s were the insecticide DDT, cigarettes, the Chevrolet Corvair, phosphates, Firestone radial tires, and leaded gasoline.[8] The rule eliminating lead in gasoline, for example, has given society a major benefit; the average level of lead in children's blood has decreased by 75 percent since the measure went into effect.[9]

The Politics of Regulatory Policy

Economic regulation has come in waves, as changes in national conditions have produced intermittent bursts of social consciousness.

THE REFORMS OF THE PROGRESSIVE AND NEW DEAL ERAS The first wave of regulation came during the Progressive era, when reformers sought to break the power of the trusts by placing constraints on unfair business practices. The second wave came in the New Deal era, when reformers sought to stimulate economic recovery through regulatory policies that were designed as much to save business as to restrain it.

Health warnings on cigarette packages are an example of
government regulation aimed at achieving equity by
providing consumers with relevant product information.
(George W. Gardner/Stock, Boston)

Although business fought Progressive and New Deal reforms, long-term opposition was lessened by the fact that most of the resulting regulation applied to a particular industry rather than to firms of all types. This pattern made it possible for an affected industry to gain influence with those officials who were responsible for regulating its activities. By cultivating close ties to the Federal Communications Commission (FCC), for example, the networks managed to gain policies that protected their near monopoly on broadcasting and gave them high and sustained profits. Although not all industries have had as much leverage with their regulators as broadcasting, it is generally true that industries have not been greatly hampered by the older form of regulation and in many cases have substantially benefited from it.

THE ERA OF NEW SOCIAL REGULATION   The third wave of regulatory reform, in the 1960s and 1970s, differed from the Progressive and New Deal phases in both its policies and its politics. The third wave has been called the era of "new social regulation" because of the social goals it addressed in three major policy areas: environmental protection, consumer protection, and worker safety.

Most of the regulatory agencies established during the third wave have much broader policy mandates than those created earlier. They are responsible not just for a single industry but for firms of all types, and their policy scope covers a wide range of activities. The Environmental Protection Agency (EPA), for example, is charged with regulating environmental pollution of almost any kind by almost any firm.

Because newer agencies such as the EPA have a wide-ranging clientele, no one firm or industry can easily influence agency policy to a great extent. There is also strong group competition in some of the newer regulatory spheres; for example, business lobbies must compete with environmental groups such as the Sierra Club and Greenpeace for influence with the EPA.[10] The firms regulated by the older agencies, in contrast, do not face significant competition in their lobbying activities; broadcasters, for example, are largely unopposed in their efforts to influence the Federal Communications Commission.

HOW THE GOVERNMENT PROMOTES VARIOUS ECONOMIC INTERESTS

The U.S. government has always made important contributions to the nation's economy. The Constitution was written in part to provide for a national government strong enough to promote a sound economy. The Constitution stipulated that the government was to regulate commerce, create a strong currency, develop uniform commercial standards, and provide a stable credit system. The fledgling government also immediately demonstrated its concern for economic interests. Congress in 1789 gave a boost to the nation's shipping industry by placing a tariff on imported goods carried by foreign ships. Since providing that first boost, the U.S. government has awarded thousands of direct benefits to economic interests.

In Chapters 11 and 13 we described how congressional and bureaucratic politics results in the promotion of group interests. Here we will briefly examine a few illustrations of the scope of government's contribution to the interests of business, labor, and agriculture.

Promoting Business

American business is not opposed to government regulation *per se*. It objects only to regulatory policies that are adverse to its interests. We have noted that, at various times and in differing ways, many federal regulatory agencies have primarily served the interests of the industries they are intended to regulate. A primary example is broadcasting, which operates on public airwaves and pays almost nothing for the privilege.[11]

Tax breaks are another way that government promotes business. Firms receive tax credits for capital investments and get tax deductions for capital depreciation. Over the past forty years the burden of federal taxation has shifted dramatically, from corporations to individuals. A few decades ago, the revenues raised from taxes on corporate income were roughly the same as the revenues raised from taxes on individual income. Today, individual taxpayers carry the heavier burden by a more than 5-to-1 ratio. Some analysts do not regard the change as overly significant, arguing that higher corporate taxes would be passed along to the public anyway in the form of higher prices for goods and services.

Government also promotes business through loans and loan guarantees. In 1979 the Chrysler Corporation was about to go bankrupt. Instead, Washington guaranteed $1.5 billion in loans for Chrysler: the federal government would repay the lenders if Chrysler defaulted. Although this loan guarantee was controversial, the measure was remarkable only in the amount of money involved. The federal government guarantees thousands of business loans and also makes direct loans to businesses.

The most significant contribution that government makes to business is the traditional services it provides, such as education, transportation, and defense. Colleges and universities, which are funded primarily by governments, furnish business with most of its professional and technical work force and with much of the basic research that goes into product development. The nation's public roadways, waterways, and airports are other government benefits without which business could not thrive. There is an entire industry—defense contracting—that exists almost entirely on government money. In short, America's business has no better promoter than government.

Promoting Labor

Laissez-faire philosophy dominated government's approach to labor well into the twentieth century. The governing principle, developed by the courts in the early nineteenth century, held that workers had limited rights of collective action. Union activity was regarded as interference with the natural supply of labor and the free setting of wages. The extent of hostility toward labor is evident in the use of federal troops during the late 1800s to break up strikes.

The 1930s brought significant changes. The key legislation was the National Labor Relations Act of 1935, which guaranteed workers the right to bargain collectively and prohibited business from discriminating against union employees and from unreasonably interfering with union activities. The Taft-Hartley Act of 1947 took away some of labor's gains, including compulsory union membership for workers whose workplace is unionized. Under the provisions of Taft-Hartley, each state can decide for itself whether all workers in work units that are unionized must become union members (union shop) or whether a worker can choose not to join the union (open shop). Despite such modifications, the National Labor Relations Act has remained a cornerstone of labor's power. The legislation not only required that business bargain with organized labor but also established the National Labor Relations Board (NLRB), an independent regulatory commission that is empowered to enforce compliance with labor law by both business and labor. Government has also aided labor over the years by legislating minimum wages and maximum work hours, unemployment benefits, safer and more healthful working conditions, and nondiscriminatory hiring practices.

Although government support for labor extends beyond these examples, it is not nearly as extensive as its assistance to business. America's individualistic culture has hindered the formulation of public policies that are as favorable to labor as those in European countries.

Promoting Agriculture

Until well into the twentieth century, most Americans still lived on farms and in small rural communities. Agriculture was America's dominant business and was assisted by government's land policies. The Homestead Act of 1862, for example, opened government-owned lands to settlement, creating spectacular "land rushes" by offering 160 free acres of government land to each family that staked a claim, built a house, and farmed the land for five years.

Farm programs today provide assistance to small farmers and commercial enterprises (agribusinesses) and cost the federal government billions of dollars annually. One goal of this spending is to stabilize farmers' income, which can fluctuate greatly from one year to the next, depending on market and growing conditions. Midwestern floods in 1993, for example, caused extensive damage to farms along the Mississippi and Missouri rivers. The federal government responded with several billion dollars in emergency assistance to afflicted farmers. Income stabilization policy, however, is not limited to emergency aid. There are a variety of federal programs in place that aim to stabilize farmers' income. Price support programs, for example, are designed to keep the prices of farm products relatively high even when the market is weak.

In 1996, Congress enacted the Federal Agricultural Improvement and Reform Act (FAIR), which phases out nearly all price support policies. Within a few years, commodity prices will be determined almost solely by markets. The phase-out is a result of efforts to reduce the federal budget deficit and also of the realization that the expanding global market for U.S. agricultural goods has reduced the need for government subsidies.

MAINTAINING A STABLE ECONOMY

Until the 1930s, the federal government adhered to the prevailing free market theory and made no attempt to maintain the stability of the economy as a whole. The economy was regarded as largely self-regulating. The U.S. economy was fairly prosperous but periodically experienced economic depression that resulted in widespread joblessness and financial loss.

The greatest economic catastrophe in the nation's history—the Great Depression of the 1930s—finally brought an end to traditional economics. Franklin D. Roosevelt's emergency spending and job programs, designed to stimulate the economy and put Americans back to work, heralded the change. Roosevelt's efforts were controversial at the time, but today government is expected to have ongoing policies that will maintain high economic production, employment, and growth, and will control prices and interest rates.

Fiscal policy and *monetary policy* are the economic instruments which the government utilizes most heavily to promote these goals. Each mechanism is complex and is based on several schools of thought. Accordingly, the following discussion attempts merely to outline some of the basic components of fiscal and monetary policy.

Fiscal Policy

The government's efforts to maintain a stable economy are made mainly through its taxing and spending decisions, which together are referred to as its **fiscal policy** (see Table 15-2).

The annual federal budget is the foundation of fiscal policy. George Washington wrote his budget on a single sheet of paper, but the federal budget today is thousands of pages long and takes eighteen months to prepare and enact. The budget is a massive policy statement that allocates federal expenditures among thousands of government programs and provides for the revenues—taxes, social insurance receipts, and borrowed funds—to pay for these expenditures (see Figure 15-2). From one perspective, the budget is the national government's allocation of costs and benefits. Every federal program benefits some interest, whether it be farmers who get price supports, defense firms that obtain military contracts, or retirees who receive monthly social security checks (see box: States in the Nation). Not surprisingly, the process of enacting the annual federal budget is a highly political one. Agencies and groups have an obvious stake in promoting their interests.

TABLE 15-2 FISCAL POLICY: A SUMMARY	
Taxing and spending levels can be adjusted in order to affect economic conditions.	
Problem	*Fiscal Policy Actions*
Low productivity and high unemployment	Demand side: increase spending Supply side: cut business taxes
Excess production and high inflation	Decrease spending Increase taxes

WHERE IT COMES FROM . . .

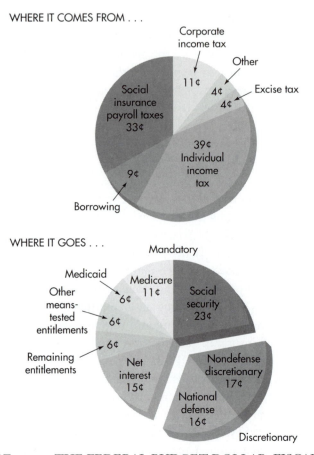

FIGURE 15-2 THE FEDERAL BUDGET DOLLAR, FISCAL YEAR 1997
Source: Office of Management and Budget.

From another standpoint, that of fiscal policy, the budget is a device for stimulating or dampening economic growth. Changes in overall levels of spending and taxing are means of keeping the economy's normal ups and downs from becoming extreme.

Fiscal policy has its origins in the economic theories of John Maynard Keynes. In *The General Theory of Employment, Interest, and Money* (1936), Keynes noted that employers become overly cautious during a depression and will not expand production, even as wages drop. Challenging the traditional idea that government should draw back during depressions, Keynes claimed that severe economic downturns can be shortened only by increased government spending. By placing additional money in the hands of con-

S T A T E S   I N   T H E   N A T I O N

Federal Fiscal Decisions and State Economies

Fiscal policy is rooted in federal spending and tax decisions, which differentially affect the states. Some states (the "winners") get an economic boost from the fact that their per capita federal taxes are low relative to the per capita direct payments (wages, benefits, etc.) that individuals who live in the state receive from the federal government. Other states are "losers" by this standard. And some states (the "in-betweens") get neither an exceptional economic boost nor burden. In general, the states that fare best by this indicator are those whose work force includes a high proportion of federal civilian employees or military personnel.

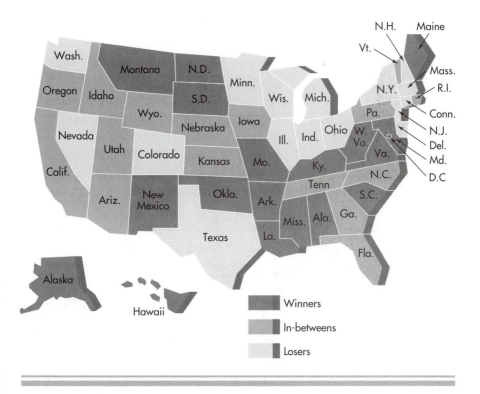

sumers and investors, government can stimulate production, employment, and spending and thus promote recovery.[12]

DEMAND-SIDE STIMULATION AND THE DEFICIT PROBLEM
Keynes's theory focused on government's efforts to stimulate consumer spending. This **demand-side economics** emphasizes the consumer "demand" component of the supply–demand equation. When the economy is sluggish, the government can increase its spending, thus placing more money in consumers' hands. With additional money to spend, consumers buy more goods and services. This increased demand, in turn, fosters production and employment. In this way, government spending contributes to economic recovery.

The use of fiscal policy as a means of economic stimulation has been greatly diminished by the unprecedented size of the national debt.[13] By 1995 it was approaching $5 trillion, up from less than $1 trillion in 1980 (see Figure 15-3). As a consequence, an enormous amount of money is required each year to pay the interest on the national debt. The interest payments today are larger than the entire federal budget as recently as 1969. They are now

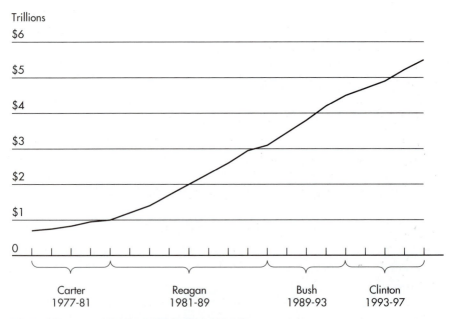

FIGURE 15-3 THE NATIONAL DEBT, 1977–1997
The national debt was relatively small until the the 1980s, when it increased rapidly. Source: Office of Management and Budget.

the third largest item in the federal budget; the only costlier programs are defense and social security.

This growing drain on the government's resources has made it very difficult for policymakers to increase the level of spending in order to boost the economy. In the early 1990s, the U.S. economy was in its longest downturn since World War II, but the government's fiscal condition ruled out any significant new spending programs. It must be noted, however, that federal spending is a *constant* economic stimulus. Every day, the federal government spends about $4 billion, which is more than the typical large corporation pumps into the economy during an entire year.

SUPPLY-SIDE STIMULATION   A fiscal policy alternative to demand-side stimulation is **supply-side economics,** which emphasizes the business (supply) component of the supply–demand equation.[14] Supply-side theory was a cornerstone of President Reagan's economic program. He believed that economic growth would flow as easily from stimulation of the business sector as from stimulation of consumer demand. "Reaganomics" included substantial tax breaks for businesses and upper-income individuals.

Reagan contended that increased prosperity for wealthy Americans would "trickle down" to those at the bottom as production increased and more jobs were created. However, the benefits of the economic growth of the 1980s were confined largely to higher-income Americans. The real income of the poorest 20 percent of families dropped by more than 10 percent during the decade, while the real income of the richest 20 percent rose by roughly 30 percent. Meanwhile, taxes for the poorest 20 percent increased by 3 percent, while taxes for the highest 20 percent decreased by 5 percent.[15]

Despite the discouragements of recent years, supply-side economics has its applications. Under some conditions, business tax cuts and incentives encourage firms to expand production, thus creating jobs and enlarging supply, each of which can stimulate consumer demand.

CONTROLLING INFLATION   High unemployment and low production are only two of the economic problems that government is called upon to solve. Another is inflation, which is an increase in the average level of prices of goods and services. Before the late 1960s, inflation was a minor irritant: prices rose by less than 4 percent annually. But inflation rose sharply during the last years of the Vietnam war and remained high throughout the 1970s, reaching a postwar record rate of 13 percent in 1979. Since then, inflation has moderated and concern about it has lessened.

Senate Budget Committee Chairman Pete Domenici (R-N.M.) points to a chart during a congressional hearing. The massive federal debt has restricted the use of government spending as a tool of fiscal policy. (Wide World Photos)

To fight inflation, government can apply remedies opposite to those used to fight unemployment and low productivity. Inflation normally occurs when jobs are plentiful and people have extra money to spend. Demand is high in such periods, and prices are pulled up in what is known as "demand-pull" inflation. By reducing its spending or by raising personal income taxes, government takes money from consumers, thus reducing demand and dampening prices. (The main policy tool for addressing inflation is monetary policy, which is discussed later in the chapter.)

THE FISCAL POLICY PROCESS   The president and Congress jointly determine fiscal policy, mainly through the annual budgetary process.

The process begins in the executive branch when, in consultation with the bureaucratic agencies, the president through the Office of Management and Budget (OMB) compiles a proposed federal budget. Hundreds of agencies and thousands of programs are covered by the budget, and the OMB decides on a preliminary basis how much each will receive (see Chapters 11, 12, and 13). The OMB usually has the role of restraining the agencies, since they tend naturally to want more resources while the OMB has the job of tailoring the budget to the president's priorities. As it happens, however, the proposed budget of most agencies is only "incrementally" different from that of the previous year, since most programs are ongoing and cannot possibly be reviewed from top to bottom every year.[16] The OMB also must bring spending proposals into line with the government's projected revenues from taxes and borrowed funds.

The president's budget is delivered in January to Congress (see Figure 15-4). The presidential budget is only a proposal, since Congress alone has the constitutional power to enact taxing and spending decisions. In reviewing and altering the president's proposals, Congress relies heavily on the Congressional Budget Office (CBO), which, as was discussed in Chapter 11, is the legislative equivalent of the OMB.

Most of the work in Congress on the budget is done through the House and Senate Budget and Appropriations committees. The Budget committees are responsible for preparing recommendations on the total amount of federal spending and its allocation among the major functions of government, such as defense. These guidelines are then submitted to the full Congress for its action. This phase is scheduled for completion by April 15.

The timetable for completion of the next budgetary phase is June 30, although Congress routinely goes beyond this date. This phase is centered in the Appropriations committees, which develop proposals on how to allocate the overall expenditure limits among the various agencies and programs. These allocations, of course, are subject to change and approval by the full House and Senate.

Once the budget has been passed by both the House and Senate and is signed by the president, it takes effect on October 1, which is the start of the federal government's fiscal year. If agreement on the budget has not been reached by October 1, temporary funding is required in order to maintain

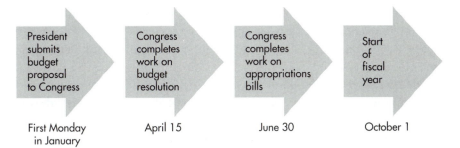

| President submits budget proposal to Congress | Congress completes work on budget resolution | Congress completes work on appropriations bills | Start of fiscal year |
| First Monday in January | April 15 | June 30 | October 1 |

FIGURE 15-4 SIMPLIFIED MODEL OF THE ANNUAL FISCAL POLICY (BUDGETARY) PROCESS
Congress has about six months in which to modify the president's proposed budget.

government operations. In late 1995, President Clinton and the Republican Congress deadlocked to such an extent on budgetary issues that they could not even agree on temporary funding. Their standoff twice forced a brief shutdown of nonessential government activities.

THE POLITICS OF FISCAL POLICY   Although the Republican and Democratic parties are both committed to maintaining a strong economy, their approach to fiscal policy differs. The Democratic coalition includes more lower-income and working-class Americans, who are usually the first and hardest hit by rising unemployment. For this reason, the Democratic party is more supportive of policy action (such as higher unemployment benefits and public jobs programs) aimed at alleviating the problem of joblessness. On the other hand, the Republican party is more likely to be concerned with inflation, which hurts those with money by reducing its value. Inflation also raises the cost of doing business, since firms must pay higher interest rates for the money they borrow. As a consequence, the Republican party is more inclined to hold down or trim government spending in order to reduce inflationary pressures.

For similar reasons, tax policy also divides the parties. Democrats have favored a progressive tax system, where the rate goes up substantially as income rises. Republicans have preferred to keep income taxes on wealthier individuals at a relatively low level, contending that this policy encourages the savings and investment that foster economic growth.

THE ELECTORAL CONNECTION   We noted in Chapter 12 that the issues that affect Americans' pocketbooks have the most influence on their presidential voting decisions, which makes fiscal policy largely an issue of *majoritarian* politics. As Seymour Martin Lipset writes, "Voters are disposed to credit or blame incumbent administrations for the state of the economy."[17]

An economic slowdown is a main concern of officials at election time. Officeholders get less credit when the economy is healthy than blame when it goes bad. A stagnant economy can result in a drop of several percentage points in the vote obtained by the party holding the presidency.[18] Like other presidents before him, George Bush faced the political consequences of poor economic conditions. The unemployment level rose steadily during 1991 and passed 7 percent at the beginning of 1992. The rise was accompanied by a steady decline in Bush's public support and contributed to his defeat in the November election.

It is difficult for incumbents to get the economy to respond to their efforts. If government could easily control the economy, it would always be

Economic prosperity is a key factor in determining a president's chances of being returned to office. One reason that Bill Clinton, shown here campaigning in West Virginia, was reelected by a comfortable margin in 1996 was that many voters perceived themselves as being better off economically than they had been before he came to office. (Dirck Halstead/Gamma-Liaison)

strong. In reality, however, the economy has natural ups and downs that so far have defied the mastery of economists and politicians.

Monetary Policy

We noted earlier that fiscal policy is not the only instrument of economic management available to government; another is **monetary policy,** which is based on manipulation of the amount of money in circulation (see Table 15-3). Monetarists such as the economist Milton Friedman hold that control of the money supply is the key to sustaining a healthy economy.[19] Too much money in circulation contributes to inflation because too many dollars are chasing too few goods, which drives up prices. Too little money in circulation results in a slackening economy and rising unemployment, because consumers lack the ready cash and easy credit required to push spending levels up. Monetarists believe in tightening or loosening the money supply as a way of slowing or invigorating the economy.

TABLE 15-3 MONETARY POLICY: A SUMMARY
The money supply can be adjusted in order to affect economic conditions.

Problem	Monetary Policy Action by Federal Reserve
Low productivity and high unemployment (require an increase in the money supply)	Buys securities Lowers interest rate on loans to member banks Lowers cash reserve that member banks must deposit in Federal Reserve System
Excess productivity and high inflation (require a decrease in the money supply)	Sells securities Raises interest rate on loans to member banks Raises cash reserve that member banks must deposit in Federal Reserve System

THE FEDERAL RESERVE SYSTEM Control over the money supply rests not with the president or Congress but with the Federal Reserve System (known as "the Fed"), which was created by the Federal Reserve Act of 1913. The Fed is directed by a board of governors whose seven members serve for fourteen years, except for the chair and vice-chair, who serve for four years. All members are appointed by the president with the approval of the Senate. The Fed regulates the activities of all national banks and those state banks which choose to become members of the Federal Reserve System—about 6,000 banks in all.

The Fed decides how much money to add or to subtract from the economy, seeking a balance that will permit steady growth without causing an unacceptable level of inflation. The most visible way that the Fed affects the money supply is by lowering or raising the interest rates charged on money borrowed from the Federal Reserve by its member banks. When the Fed raises the interest rate, banks also tend to raise the rate they charge for new loans, which discourages borrowing and thus reduces the amount of money entering the economy. Conversely, by lowering the interest rate, the Fed encourages firms and individuals to borrow from banks, which increases the money supply.

The Fed's interest-rate decisions are closely watched by the financial markets, political leaders, and the media. Any increase or decrease is a sign that the Fed has concluded that the economy is growing too quickly or too slowly.

The Fed also affects the money supply by selling and buying government securities in the open market. By offering securities at an attractive price, the Fed encourages investors to exchange their cash for securities, thus taking money out of the economy. On the other hand, when the Fed buys securities that people hold, it puts cash into their hands, thus expanding the money supply.

The third and final way the Fed affects the money supply is by raising or lowering the cash reserve that member banks are required to deposit with the Federal Reserve. This reserve is a proportion of each member's total deposits. By increasing the reserve rate, the Fed takes money from member banks and thus takes it out of circulation. When the Fed lowers the reserve rate, banks have more money available and can make more loans to consumers and investors.

Economists debate the relative effectiveness of monetary policy and fiscal policy, but monetary policy has one obvious advantage: it can be implemented more quickly. The Fed can adjust interest and reserve rates on short notice, thus providing the economy a psychological boost to go along with the financial effect of a change in the money supply. In contrast, changes in fiscal policy usually take much longer to implement; Congress is normally a slow-acting institution, and new taxing and spending programs ordinarily require a substantial preparation period before they can put into effect.

THE ISSUE OF THE FED'S ACCOUNTABILITY Washington's budgetary woes and the greater flexibility of monetary policy have positioned the Fed as the institution with primary responsibility for keeping the U.S. economy on a steady course. The situation raises an issue of accountability: Should the Fed, an unelected body, have this much power?

The Fed's policies are not always popular with elected officials. In 1994, for example, the Fed embarked on a series of interest-rate hikes to contain economic growth. In defending the action, the Fed's chairman, Alan Greenspan, argued that it was designed to head off an upward spiral of wages and prices. Yet the Fed acted before signs of inflation were clearly present in the economy, bringing criticism from congressional Democrats and Clinton administration officials, who complained that the Fed was blunting the nation's economic recovery. Unemployment exceeded the 6 percent level, and the Fed's critics said that unseen inflationary pressures should not drive economic policy when millions of Americans were still looking for work. House Democratic leader Richard Gephardt complained that the Fed was placing the interests of bankers and financiers ahead of those of ordinary Americans.[20]

The issue of the Fed's accountability remains unsettled. Because the Fed has nearly unrestricted powers to set interest rates and affect the money supply, it is unrealistic to expect it to watch idly when the economy sputters. But should the Fed routinely place its judgment ahead of that of elected officials? The Fed is a very powerful institution, yet it operates behind closed doors and its decisions are not subject to review.

The Fed is a preeminent example of *elitist* politics at work. Congress at some future point may decide that an independent Fed can no longer be tolerated and may bring monetary policy more directly under the control of elected institutions. Whether this happens may hinge on the Fed's willingness to exercise power sparingly and in the broad interests of society. (The economic role of the government in issues of social welfare and national security is discussed in the next two chapters.)

SUMMARY

Although private enterprise is the main force in the American economic system, the federal government plays a significant role through the policies it selects to regulate, promote, and stimulate the economy.

Regulatory policy is designed to achieve efficiency and equity, which require government to intervene, for example, to maintain competitive trade practices (an efficiency goal) and to protect vulnerable parties in economic transactions (an equity goal). Many of the regulatory decisions of the federal government, particularly those of older agencies, are made largely in the context of group politics; business lobbies have an especially strong influence on the regulatory policies that affect them. In general, newer regulatory agencies have policy responsibilities that are broader in scope and apply to a larger number of firms than those of the older agencies. As a result, the policy decisions of newer agencies are more often made in the context of party politics. Republican administrations are less vigorous in their regulation of business than are Democratic administrations.

Business is the major beneficiary of the federal government's efforts to promote economic interests. A large number of programs, including those to provide loans and research grants, are designed to assist businesses, which are also protected from failure through such measures as tariffs and favorable tax laws. Labor, for its part, gets government assistance through laws concerning such matters as worker safety, the minimum wage, and collective bargaining; yet America's individualistic culture tends to put labor at a disadvantage, keeping it less powerful than business in its dealings with the government. Agriculture is another economic sector that depends substantially on government's help, particularly in the form of income stabilization programs, such as those that provide subsidies and price supports.

Through its fiscal and monetary policies, Washington attempts to maintain a strong and stable economy—one that is characterized by high productivity, high employment, and low inflation. Fiscal policy is based on government decisions in regard to spending and taxing, which are aimed at either stimulating a weak economy or dampening an overheated (inflationary) economy. Fiscal policy is worked out through Congress and the president and is consequently responsive to political pressures. However, since it is difficult to raise taxes or cut programs, the government's ability to apply fiscal policy as an economic remedy is limited. Monetary policy is based on the money supply and works through the Federal Reserve System, which is headed by a board whose members hold office for fixed terms. The Fed is a relatively independent body, a fact that has given rise to questions as to whether it should have such a large role in national economic policy.

MAJOR CONCEPTS

demand-side economics
deregulation
economy
efficiency
equity
externalities

fiscal policy
laissez-faire doctrine
monetary policy
regulation
supply-side economics

SUGGESTED READINGS

Eisner, Marc Allen. *Regulatory Politics in Transition.* Baltimore, Md.: Johns Hopkins University Press, 1993. A thorough assessment of the changing nature of regulatory policy.

Friedman, Milton, and Walter Heller. *Monetary vs. Fiscal Policy.* New York: Norton, 1969. Opposing arguments by a leading monetarist and a leading Keynesian.

Fukuyama, Francis. *Trust: The Social Virtue and the Creation of Prosperity.* New York: Free Press, 1995. A claim that personal trust rather than public policy is the foundation of economic prosperity.

Harris, Richard A., and Sidney M. Milkis. *The Politics of Regulatory Change: A Tale of Two Agencies,* 2d ed. New York: Oxford University Press, 1996. An analysis of the Reagan, Bush, and Clinton administrations' approaches to regulatory policy.

Kettl, Donald F. *Deficit Politics: Public Budgeting in Its Institutional and Historical Context.* New York: Macmillan, 1992. Analysis of budgetary politics that aims to explain why the United States suffers repeated annual deficits.

Peterson, Peter G. *Facing Up: How to Rescue the Economy from Crushing Debt and Restore the American Dream.* New York: Simon & Schuster, 1993. A blueprint for economic revitalization by a former Commerce Department official.

Streeter, Thomas. *Selling the Air: A Critique of the Policy of Commercial Broadcasting in the United States.* Chicago: University of Chicago Press, 1996. An analysis of the impact of government regulation on the broadcasting market.

Wildavsky, Aaron. *The New Politics of the Budgetary Process,* 2d ed. New York: HarperCollins, 1992. An overview of the federal budgetary process, including new developments related to the deficit.

Young, H. Peyton. *Equity: In Theory and Practice.* Princeton, N.J.: Princeton University Press, 1995. A systematic assessment of what economic equity entails in theory and actual situations.

READING 15

Long-Term Goals for the Economy
ALICE M. RIVLIN

What should Americans expect from their economy? How should they assess whether it is performing well or badly? Most questions about the health of the economy relate to the short-run ups and downs of the business cycle. If the economy is recovering from recession, people are generally optimistic. They are likely to return incumbent politicians to office. If unemployment is rising, or prices are soaring, people are gloomier and readier for a political change.

Preoccupation with the immediate, however, obscures the longer-term trends that determine how the economy will be performing in the future and whether the next generation will live better than this one. . . .

There is no obvious single measure of how well the economy is performing in the long run, and there is lots of room for argument about what aspects are important and how to measure them. At a minimum, Americans ought to want three things from their economy: the average standard of living should be rising; the improving level of living should be shared by all groups; and the rising standard should be sustainable. All three elements of this definition are important. . . .

A rising standard of living makes many choices less agonizing and contentious. A family whose income is rising does not always have to give up something when a new need arises. A society with increasing resources can afford both greater private well-being and improved public services. As incomes rise, constant tax rates generate higher revenues. It is possible to have better schools, roads, and other public services without actually raising tax rates. (Although, of course, demands for public services may still outrun the available public resources.) A society with rising income can assist the less fortunate without forcing the more fortunate to accept cuts in their income.

To be sure, just as money does not always buy happiness for individuals or families, rising incomes do not always lead to harmonious politics. Public choices remain difficult and contentious, even in affluent countries. One reason may be that rich countries, like rich people, have a huge set of choices about what goods and services to provide and how to pay for them, including options to borrow now and pay later. Poor countries have fewer options. They have to defend their borders and provide basic services. They have a hard time obtaining credit from international lenders. Moreover, according to one theory, rising incomes intensify political struggles because they escalate the competition for goods that are physically scarce (such as seashore property) or socially scarce (such as political power or access to the "best" universities).

Nevertheless, just as most people prefer more income to less, most would rather live in a society in which average incomes are rising, winners outnumber losers, and new initiatives do not have to be paid for by reducing some ongoing activity, public or private. . . .

Increases in the average standard of living do not indicate satisfactory economic performance if those increases are confined to the favored few or even the favored many. A rising average does not constitute success if substantial groups of people are being left out and falling further behind the rest of the population. The situation is especially worrisome if the people being left out of the general prosperity are clearly identifiable both to themselves and to others because of race, sex, ethnic origin, or some other visible characteristic. If those who lose out are disproportionately concentrated in identifiable groups, they are bound to feel resentment and to allege favoritism and discrimination. Moreover, separation of the disadvantaged groups from the rest of the society is likely to be self-reinforcing. If people with specific characteristics are perceived as less successful, this fact is likely to undermine their confidence, discourage them from investing in education, and perpetuate stereotypes that lead to both increased discrimination and further lack of success.

Broad sharing of prosperity in America, like average rising income and sustainability, has international as well as domestic importance. U.S. efforts to encourage other countries to assist their poor and minorities and to promote freer market systems are undermined if the U.S. market system is visibly failing identifiable groups at home.

Individuals often increase their immediate standard of living in ways that reduce it later—by piling up credit card debts that have to be repaid out of future income, for example. Nations can be shortsighted too, so it is important to make certain that increases in the national standard of living are not achieved by creating serious problems for the future.

Economic growth accompanied by high inflation, for example, is neither desirable nor sustainable. Inflation distorts the economy. It encourages people to put their money in real estate and art objects rather than in investments that enhance future productivity. It favors debtors over creditors and discourages savers.

Nations, like individuals, can borrow beyond their capacity to repay, default on obligations, and damage their creditworthiness. They can borrow to finance consumption or ill-conceived investments and end up with burdensome interest charges and repayment obligations that reduce their future standard of living.

Economic activity that fails to replace the capital it uses is also unsustainable. Accounting principles that apply to companies require recognition that capital assets wear out and must be replaced. However, public capital such as roads, bridges, schools, and government buildings is often allowed to wear out or fall into disrepair without people recognizing that the future national standard of living will be reduced by such shortsighted policies. The decay is often gradual and the cost spread widely. Deteriorating roads, for example, cause accidents, delays, excess fuel consumption, and repair bills paid by owners of cars and trucks, not the government. For taxpayers and vehicle users together, building a highway to a high standard of durability and keeping it in repair can be much less costly in the long run than building it cheaply and repairing it sooner.

Economic growth can also be unsustainable if it damages the environment in ways that lower the standard of living in the future. Shortsighted agricultural development in vast areas of the United States in the nineteenth and early twentieth centuries depleted the soil and created the dust bowl. Deforestation in the Himalayas is producing fuel shortages, soil erosion, and flooding that threaten the livelihood of people in wide areas. The burning of tropical forests in the Amazon basin exposes poor soil that cannot support farming or ranching for long periods, as well as contributing to the buildup of greenhouse gases and destroying the treasures of the forests themselves. Development that pollutes lakes, rivers, and oceans or leads to buildup of toxic waste or mountains of trash and garbage cannot be sustained for long.

Most of the attention to sustainability and economic development in recent years has been focused on the environment and on less developed countries. Where people live at the margin of subsistence, there is great potential for famine and other disasters as a result of shortsighted practices. Moreover, the loss of millions of species from rapid destruction of tropical rain forests, extinction of wild animals in Africa, and the squandering of other irreplaceable assets of developing countries has aroused concern around the world for the common heritage of the planet.

Taking a longer view of economic processes, however, is no less important to the developed countries. Life in the United States could be far less attractive, healthy, and safe if economic growth destroys the natural beauty of the country, poisons the atmosphere, and pollutes the lakes and streams. Moreover, the United States cannot be effective in convincing developing countries to reform their practices if it fails to adhere to sustainable policies itself. American credibility in urging conservation of tropical forests is greatly undermined by our own rapid destruction of the ancient forests of the Pacific Northwest. Similarly, it is hard to preach responsible fiscal policy to developing countries when the United States is running huge deficits in its federal budget.

SOURCE: Alice M. Rivlin, *Reviving the American Dream: Congress, the States and the Federal Government* (Washington, D.C.: Brookings Institution, 1992). Reprinted by permission.
Alice M. Rivlin is a member of the Federal Reserve Board. She was previously director of the Office of Management and Budget (OMB) and director of the Congressional Budget Office (CBO).

CHAPTER SIXTEEN

Social Welfare Policy

We the people of the United States, in order to . . . promote the general
welfare . . .

PREAMBLE, U.S. CONSTITUTION

J OHN JONES is a fictitious retired businessman who has a company pension that pays him $1,500 a month. He also receives more than $1,000 a month in interest and dividends on his savings, bonds, and stocks. John's financial obligations are few. He is a widower, and the youngest of his three children graduated from college years ago.

Jane Smith is a fictitious recent divorcee with two children, aged eight and three. Jane was married the summer after she graduated from high school and had never worked outside the home before her husband deserted her. Without special job skills and with a small child at home, the only work that she could take is a part-time job paying $5 an hour. Jane's net financial assets total less than $500.

John and Jane seem very different, but they do have one thing in common: each gets a monthly social welfare check from government. Who, John or Mary, receives the larger government check? Who has fewer strings attached to continuing receipt of the check? Who incurs no stigma from receipt of the check? The answer to all of these questions is the same: John.

John is a social security recipient and gets about $900 each month from the government. He applied for social security upon retiring at age sixty-five, and the monthly checks have come regularly ever since. If John moves to another state, or even to another country, his monthly check will follow. Jane, who lives in New Jersey, gets less than $400 a month from the government through the Temporary Assistance for Needy Families (TANF) program. To get this money Jane had to provide proof of her divorce, low income, and lack of assets, and she is required to report regularly on whether her economic status has changed. If her income should rise above the poverty level, she would lose her monthly support. If Jane should move, say, to Florida, she would have to reapply for support and there would be a waiting period during which she would get no support. Moreover, by moving, she would take a 25 percent cut in her monthly benefit, because the state of Florida gives less to TANF recipients than does New Jersey. Finally, Jane carries the mark of a "welfare case" supported by the taxpaying public. John bears no such stigma. He "earned" his monthly check by paying social security taxes during his years of employment.

The U.S. welfare system reflects the country's individualistic culture, tinged with an element of egalitarian compassion. Economic security is not a right of citizenship. In European nations a different welfare philosophy prevails. Of course, citizens of these countries are encouraged to work and benefit economically from doing so; but they are considered to be more or less entitled to a minimum standard of living, at government expense if necessary. In contrast, Americans expect individuals to care for themselves and believe that welfare payments to able-bodied individuals discourage personal effort and create welfare dependency. Yet Americans also believe in helping those who are demonstrably unable to work or who need assistance while training for work.

Another influence on U.S. welfare policy is the country's federal system of government. Welfare was traditionally a responsibility of state and local governments; only since the 1930s has the federal government also played a significant role. Some welfare programs are jointly run by the federal and state governments, and they tend to be the most controversial ones. These programs are funded at different levels from one state to the next but operate within guidelines set down by the national government. Contentious issues of control, cost, and adequacy have been a persistent feature of these programs.

This chapter examines the social problems that federal welfare programs are designed to alleviate and describes how these programs operate. A goal of this chapter is to provide an informed basis for understanding issues of social welfare and to show why disagreements in this area are so substantial. Social welfare policy involves hard choices that almost inevitably require trade-offs between federal and state power and between the values of individual self-reliance and egalitarian compassion. The main points of the chapter are these:

* *Poverty is a large and persistent problem in America, affecting deeply about one in seven Americans, including many of the country's most vulnerable groups—children, female-headed families, and minorities.*

★ *Welfare policy has been a partisan issue, with Democrats taking the lead on government programs to alleviate economic insecurity and Republicans acting to slow down or reverse these initiatives.*

★ *Social welfare programs are designed to reward and foster self-reliance or, when this is not possible, to provide benefits only to those individuals who are truly in need.*

★ *As a result of America's individualistic culture, public support for social insurance programs (such as social security) is far higher than for public assistance programs (such as TANF).*

★ *A prevailing principle in the United States is equality of opportunity, which in terms of public policy is most evident in the area of education.*

POVERTY IN AMERICA: THE NATURE OF THE PROBLEM

In the broadest sense, social welfare policy encompasses all efforts by government to improve the social conditions of any and all citizens. In a narrower sense, which is the way the term will be used in most of this chapter, social welfare policy refers to those efforts by government to help individuals meet their basic human needs, including food, clothing, and shelter.

The Poor: Who and How Many?

America's social welfare needs are substantial. Although Americans are far better off economically than most of the world's peoples, poverty is a significant and persistent problem in the United States. In fact, the United States has the highest percentage of people living in poverty of any industrialized nation and by far the highest percentage of child poverty among these nations (see box: How the United States Compares).

The U.S. government defines the **poverty line** as the annual cost of a thrifty food budget for an urban family of four, multiplied by three to include the cost of housing, clothing, and other expenses. Families whose incomes fall below that line are officially considered poor. In 1997 the poverty line was set at an annual income of roughly $15,500 for a family of four. About one in seven Americans, more than 35 million people, including 15 million children, live at or below the poverty line. If they could join hands, they could form a line that stretched from New York to Tokyo and back again.

Sheer hard work does not guarantee that a family will rise above the

How the United States Compares

Children Living in Poverty

The United States has the highest child poverty rate among industrialized nations. One in five American children live in poverty; in most other industrialized nations, fewer than one in ten do so.

One reason for the difference is that income in the United States is less evenly distributed. As a consequence, the United States has the highest percentage of both rich and poor children in the industrialized world. In addition, the United States spends less on government assistance for the poor. Without government help, for example, the child poverty rate in the United States and France would be about equal—25 percent. Through its governmental programs, France reduces the rate to less than 7 percent. Through its welfare programs, the United States cuts the rate only slightly.

Child poverty in the United States is made worse by the relatively large number of single-parent families, although Sweden, which has a similarly large number, has one of the world's lowest rates of child poverty.

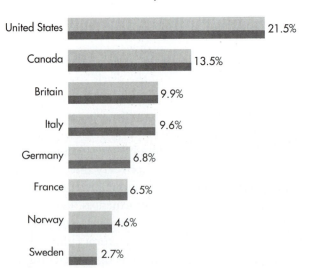

Child Poverty Rate

United States 21.5%
Canada 13.5%
Britain 9.9%
Italy 9.6%
Germany 6.8%
France 6.5%
Norway 4.6%
Sweden 2.7%

SOURCE: Luxembourg Income Study. Adapted From *The State of America's Children Yearbook* (Washington, D.C.: Children's Defense Fund, 1996).

poverty line. A family of four with one employed adult who works forty hours a week at the minimum wage level (about $5 an hour) has an annual income of $10,000, which is well below the poverty line. Many Americans—mostly household workers, service workers, unskilled laborers, and farm workers— are in this position. Many newly created jobs are in fast-food restaurants and other service businesses, which typically pay their employees relatively low wages. The U.S. Bureau of the Census estimates that nearly one in five Americans who work full time do not earn enough to lift their family above the poverty line.

America's poor include individuals of all ages, races, religions, and re- gions, but poverty is substantially more prevalent among some groups.[1] Children are one of the largest groups of poor Americans. They constitute nearly 40 percent of the total, and one in every five children live in poverty. Most poor children live in single-parent families, usually with the mother. In fact, as can be seen from Figure 16-1, a high proportion of Americans re- siding in families headed by divorced, separated, or unmarried women live below the poverty line. These families are at a disadvantage because most women earn less than men for comparable work, especially in nonprofes- sional fields. Women without higher education or a special skill often can- not find a job that pays enough to justify the child care expenses they incur due to their work. In recent years single-parent, female-headed families

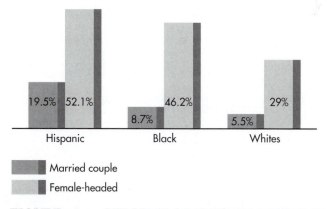

Married couple
Female-headed

FIGURE 16-1 PERCENT OF FAMILIES LIVING IN POVERTY, BY FAMILY COMPOSITION AND RACE/ETHNICITY
Poverty is far more prevalent among female-headed house- holds and African American and Hispanic households.
Source: U.S. Bureau of the Census, 1995.

have been five times as likely as two-income families to fall below the poverty line. Poverty in America is mainly a women's problem, a situation referred to as "the feminization of poverty."

Poverty is also widespread among minority group members. About 10 percent of whites live below the official poverty line, compared with about 30 percent of African Americans and Hispanics.

Poverty is geographically concentrated. Although it is often portrayed as an urban problem, it is somewhat more prevalent in rural areas. About one in six rural residents—as compared with one in eight urban residents—live in families with incomes below the poverty line. The urban figure is misleading, however, in that the poverty rate is very high in inner-city areas, where minority group members are concentrated. Suburbs are the safe haven from poverty. Because suburbanites are removed from it, many of them have no sense of the impoverished condition of what Michael Harrington called "the other America."[2] Edwin Meese, when he was serving as President Reagan's policy adviser, claimed there were no homeless people in the United States except for the bums who preferred to live on the streets. There are, in fact, hundreds of thousands of homeless people in America, some of

Of the millions of Americans who live below the poverty line, nearly half are female heads of household and their children, a situation referred to as "the feminization of poverty." (Alan Weiner/Gamma-Liaison)

whom are women and children. One estimate is that, of every 1,000 homeless people, 120 are adults with children, 100 are single women, and 100 are children without an accompanying adult.[3]

Welfare: Dependency or Misfortune?

Many Americans hold to the idea that welfare support creates a vicious cycle of dependency. In his controversial book *Losing Ground*, Charles Murray argued that welfare programs are the foundation for a permanent underclass of unproductive Americans, who prefer to live on welfare and whose children receive little educational encouragement at home and grow up in environments where crime, delinquency, drug abuse, and teenage pregnancy are commonplace.[4]

Many Americans are caught in the vicious circle described by Murray, and their numbers increase yearly. They are the toughest challenge for policymakers because almost nothing about their lives equips them to escape from poverty and its attendant ills. Their chances of committing a violent crime before reaching adulthood, for example, are nearly 20 times greater than that of others their age.[5]

Yet most people are poor as a result of transitory circumstances rather than chronic dependency.[6] A long-term study of American families by researchers at the University of Michigan found that the poor are usually only poor for a while, staying on the welfare rolls for three years or less, and that they are poor for temporary reasons—loss of a job, birth of a child, desertion by the father, and so on.[7] When the U.S. economy goes into a long tailspin, the impact devastates many families. In the recessionary period of 1990–1992, more than 4 million Americans fell into poverty as a result of job loss or unemployment.

THE POLITICS AND POLICIES OF SOCIAL WELFARE

Welfare policy has generally been debated along partisan lines, a reflection of differences in the coalitions and philosophies of the Republican and Democratic parties. With its ties to labor, the poor, and minorities, the Democratic party has initiated nearly all major federal welfare programs. The key House of Representatives vote on the Social Security Act of 1935, for example, found 85 percent of Democrats supporting it and 99 percent of Republicans against it.[8]

Republicans gradually came to accept the idea that the federal government has a role in social welfare but argued that the role should be kept as small as practicable. Thus, in the 1960s, Republican opposition to President Lyndon Johnson's Great Society was substantial. His programs included federal initiatives in health care, education, public housing, nutrition, and other areas traditionally dominated by state and local government.[9] More than 70 percent of congressional Republicans voted against the 1965 Medicare and Medicaid programs, which provide government-paid medical assistance for the elderly and the poor. In the 1980s, in the face of opposition from congressional Democrats, Republican President Reagan made social welfare spending the prime target of his efforts to cut the domestic budget. Compared with the decade beginning in the late 1960s, when welfare spending per poor person nearly tripled, the 1980s saw a 20 percent decline in actual dollars spent on each welfare recipient.

Although the Republican and Democratic parties have been at odds on the issue of social welfare, they have also had reason to work together. Social welfare is an ongoing issue because it is a pressing problem that requires action; there are millions of Americans who need help from government if they are to meet their basic subsistence needs. This help has taken various forms—job training efforts, special education programs, income redistribution measures, and individual-benefit policies.

JOB TRAINING　The government's social welfare effort has included attempts to provide jobs and job training. Employment policy and welfare policy have been loosely linked since the Great Depression, when Franklin Roosevelt combined public jobs programs with social security legislation. At one point during the Depression, a fifth of the nation's entire work force was employed in public jobs.

Americans strongly favor work over welfare as a means of public assistance. Work is believed to foster initiative and responsibility, while welfare is thought to create dependency and irresponsibility. In a Los Angeles Times poll, respondents were asked what action government should take to help the poor. Only 6 percent said that the government should provide money or services, whereas 20 percent preferred public works jobs and 72 percent favored job training. Most Americans even claim they would be willing to delay savings from welfare cutbacks to fund job training programs for welfare recipients (see Figure 16-2).

The history of work and job training programs, however, is an uneven one. For example, an ambitious program that began in the early 1970s under

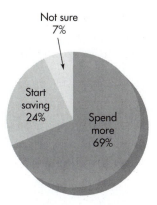

Not sure
7%

Start
saving
24%

Spend
more
69%

Respondents were asked:

Should welfare reform start
saving taxpayers money
immediately, or is it more
important to train welfare
recipients for jobs, which
means the government
would spend more money
in the short run?

FIGURE 16-2 OPINIONS ON JOB TRAINING FOR
WELFARE RECIPIENTS
Most Americans favor job training as the solution to the
nation's welfare problem. Source: Time/CNN survey by
Yankelovich Partners, December 7–8, 1994.

Republican President Richard Nixon, and which at its peak provided employment for 4 million people, was terminated a decade later amid charges
that it was too costly and had failed to place people in permanent jobs, as
opposed to subsidized temporary positions.

In his 1992 presidential campaign, Bill Clinton promised "to end welfare as we know it," claiming that a work-based welfare system alone could
break the cycle of poverty in which increasing numbers of welfare recipients
were trapped. It was not until the Republicans gained control of Congress,
however, that welfare reform became a reality. In 1996, the Republican-
controlled Congress passed a sweeping welfare reform act known as the Personal Responsibility and Work Opportunity Act.

The historic bill ended a six-decades federal guarantee of cash assistance
to needy families, replacing it with a system of cash grants to the states, which
have responsibility for caring for welfare recipients and getting them into
jobs. The legislation's goal is to reduce long-term welfare dependency by limiting the time that recipients can receive welfare and by providing the states
with incentives to prepare recipients for work. States may not let recipients
receive federal welfare assistance for more than five years (although a fifth
of recipients can be exempted from this requirement), and within two years
on welfare, a recipient must find work or face the loss of benefits. States receive federal funds with which to provide benefits, community service jobs,

President Clinton signs into law the 1996 welfare reform bill that ended the
61-year-old federal guarantee of aid to the poor. The new legislation limits
federal welfare assistance to a period of five years. (Stephen
Jaffe/Reuters/Archive Photos)

and job training, but unless they meet the program's goals (for example, half
of their welfare recipients must be moved from welfare to work by the year
2002), they will have their federal assistance reduced. In other words, the
welfare reform act includes incentives to encourage both states and welfare
recipients to create situations that will lead to employment.

SPECIAL EDUCATION: HEAD START   The social welfare effort also
includes special education programs, most notably Head Start. It provides
preschool education for poor children in order to give them a better chance
to succeed when they begin school. Head Start was established in the 1960s
as part of President Lyndon Johnson's War on Poverty, which was designed
to alleviate the problems of America's poor through initiatives in such areas
as nutrition, job training, health care, and housing. Funding in some of
these areas was cut sharply in the 1980s. Head Start's budget dropped to a

level which allowed only 10 percent of eligible children to participate. As evidence mounted of poverty's devastating impact on children's development, President Bush and the Democratic Congress concluded that Head Start was the kind of social investment that the country could hardly afford not to make, and it became one of the few domestic programs to receive a substantial funding increase during the Bush administration. Additional funding was provided when Bill Clinton took office. Nevertheless, less than half of the eligible children are enrolled in Head Start, and many who complete the program do not sustain their advantage because their home situation provides no support for educational achievement.

INCOME AND TAX MEASURES   The income of the average American family exceeds $35,000, which is substantial enough to provide a reasonable standard of living. Of course, the average income is just that—an average. It hides other averages—for example, the average white family has an income that is more than $15,000 higher than the average black family's income—and it hides wide disparities in the income of those individuals at the top and the bottom of the income ladder.

In fact, the United States has substantial income inequality (see Figure 16-3). The top 20 percent of Americans receive half of the total income, while the other 80 percent get the other half. The bottom 20 percent receive less

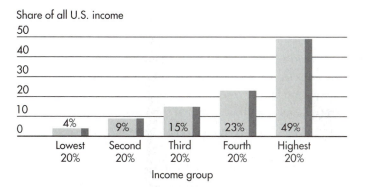

FIGURE 16-3   INCOME INEQUALITY
The United States has the highest degree of income inequality of any industrialized democracy. Citizens in the top fifth get nearly half of all income; those in the bottom fifth get less than one-twentieth of all income. Source: U.S. Bureau of the Census, 1996.

than 5 percent of the total income, and most of them live in poverty. In contrast, Americans at the top of the income ladder live very well. The upper 5 percent have about as much total yearly income as the bottom 50 percent. This 10-to-1 ratio is greater than that found in other industrialized democracies, and the gap between rich and poor in the United States has widened in recent decades.

Income taxes in the United States have not been the instrument of redistribution that they are in other democracies. The top tax rate in the United States is 39.5 percent and does not apply until income reaches the $250,000 level. An upper tax rate of 50 percent or more is common in Europe, and there are fewer loopholes, such as the deduction of home mortgage interest, that provide tax breaks for the more well-to-do. In terms of the actual rate of taxes paid, middle-income and moderately high-income Americans are in about the same situation. The higher marginal tax rate on the higher-income people is offset by their additional deductions and the existence of nonprogressive taxes such as the social security tax. (This tax is a flat rate which begins with the first dollar earned each year and stops completely after about $60,000 in earnings.)

Although well-to-do Americans pay relatively low taxes, the fact that they make a lot of money means, in absolute terms, that they contribute a sizable share of tax revenues. The top 10 percent of taxpayers in terms of income pay about half of the personal income taxes received by the federal government. Some of this tax revenue is redistributed downward to lower-income groups through social welfare programs.

The United States also has a policy designed to reallocate income directly to lower-income persons. This policy is the Earned Income Tax Credit (EITC). Low-income families with at least one child are eligible for EITC. About 10 million American families receive EITC payments; the maximum payment to any one family is about $3,500. Eligibility for payment is determined when persons file their personal income taxes. Those with family incomes below a specified level receive the payment, which phases out as income rises.

EITC involves what is called a **transfer payment,** or a government benefit that is given directly to an individual. All spending to promote the general welfare is designed to help individuals, but much of it—such as federal funds for public school construction and hospital equipment—is not in the form of transfer payments. Many federal programs, however, do provide benefits directly to individuals, such as social security payments to retired people. These individual-benefit programs are what most people have in mind when they speak of "social welfare."

INDIVIDUAL-BENEFIT PROGRAMS

Individual-benefit programs are designed to alleviate the personal hardships associated with such conditions as joblessness, poverty, and old age. For most of these programs, any individual who meets the established criteria of eligibility is entitled to the benefits. For this reason, such programs are termed **entitlement programs.** In this sense, they have the same force in law as taxes. Just as individuals are required by law to pay taxes to government on the income they earn, individuals are entitled by law to receive government benefits for which they qualify.

All told, individual-benefit programs are the major thrust of U.S. social welfare policy. The federal budget for such programs exceeds $800 billion, which is more money than is spent on any other government activity, including national defense.

At an earlier time in the nation's history, the federal government spent almost nothing on social welfare. Welfare policy was deemed to fall within the powers reserved to the states by the Tenth Amendment and to be adequately addressed by them, even though they did not offer substantial welfare services. Individuals were expected to fend for themselves, and those unable to do so were usually supported by relatives and friends. This approach reflected the idea of **negative government,** which holds that government governs best by staying out of people's lives, thus giving them as much freedom as possible to determine their own pursuits and encouraging them to become self-reliant.

The situation changed dramatically with the Great Depression. The unemployment level reached 25 percent, which prompted demands for help from the federal government. Franklin D. Roosevelt's New Deal brought economic relief in the form of public jobs and welfare programs, and helped to change opinions about the federal government's welfare role.[10] Americans came to look favorably upon Washington's help. This attitude reflected a faith in **positive government**—the idea that government intervention is necessary in order to enhance personal liberty and security when individuals are buffeted by economic and social forces beyond their control.

Since the 1930s the federal government's welfare role has increased immeasurably, and individuals now expect the federal government to provide benefits to ease the loss of income caused by retirement, disability, unemployment, and the like. Not all individual-benefit programs are alike, however, in their philosophy or level of public support. Individual-benefit programs fall into two general categories: *social insurance* and *public assistance.* Programs in the first category enjoy widespread public support and receive a higher level of funding; programs in the second category encounter substantial public opposition and receive less funding.

Social Insurance Programs

More than 40 million Americans receive benefits from social insurance programs—including social security, Medicare, unemployment insurance, and workers' compensation. The two major programs, social security and Medicare, cost the federal government more than $600 billion per year. Individuals who paid special payroll taxes when they were employed are eligible for benefits. This is why such programs are labeled **social insurance:** recipients get an insurance benefit under a program that they have helped to fund. This self-financing feature of social insurance programs accounts for their strong public support.

SOCIAL SECURITY   The leading social insurance program is social security for retirees.[11] The program began with passage of the Social Security Act of 1935 and is funded through payroll taxes on employees and employers. Franklin D. Roosevelt emphasized that retiring workers would receive an insurance benefit that they had earned through their payroll taxes, not a handout from the government. Today social security has Americans' full support. Public opinion polls indicate that upwards of 90 percent of Americans favor current or higher levels of social security benefits for the elderly. Social security is one of the few welfare programs run entirely by the federal government. Washington collects the payroll taxes that fund the program and sends monthly checks directly to the more than 35 million social security recipients, who, on average, receive more than $650 a month.

Although many people believe that an individual's social security benefits are financed by his or her past contributions, they are actually funded largely through payroll taxes on the current work force. The typical social security recipient gets far more money from the government than he or she has paid into the fund; thus it is necessary to use contributions from the current work force to finance the program. The average recipient takes less than eight years to recover his or her lifetime contributions plus interest and receives "free" benefits from that time forward. In the 1970s expenditures for social security began to exceed contributions as the number of retirees and the size of benefit payments increased. The program would have gone bankrupt in the late 1970s had the social security tax rate not been raised.[12]

Social security is likely to remain a lively political issue for years to come. Because of medical and other advances, Americans live longer than they once did, and this trend could create a social security crisis during the next century. Roughly 20 percent of the U.S. population—55 million people—will be over age sixty-five in the year 2030, and there may not be enough workers by then to fund the payout to retirees.

UNEMPLOYMENT INSURANCE   The 1935 Social Security Act provides for unemployment benefits for workers who have lost their jobs involuntarily. Unemployment insurance is a joint federal–state program. The federal government collects the payroll taxes that fund unemployment benefits, but states have the option of deciding whether the taxes will be paid by employers only or by both employees and employers (most states use the first option). Individual states also set the tax rate, conditions of eligibility, and benefit level, subject to minimum standards established by the federal government. Although unemployment benefits vary widely among states, they average about a third ($180 a week) of what an average worker makes while employed, and in most cases the benefits are terminated after twenty-six to thirty-nine weeks.

The unemployment program does not have the same high level of public support as social security. The situation reflects in part a common belief that the loss of a job, or the failure to find a new one right away, is somehow a personal failing. Unemployment statistics suggest otherwise. For example, U.S. Bureau of Labor statistics indicate that, of those who lost their jobs in 1994, only 16 percent had made the decision to quit working. The others became unemployed because of either a temporary layoff or the permanent elimination of a job position.

MEDICARE   After World War II, most European democracies instituted systems of government-paid health care, and President Harry Truman, a Democrat, proposed a similar program for Americans. The American Medical Association (AMA) called Truman's plan "un-American," lobbied hard against it, and threatened to mobilize local physicians to campaign against members of Congress who supported "socialized medicine." Truman's proposal never came to a vote in Congress. In 1961 President John F. Kennedy, also a Democrat, proposed a health care program restricted to social security recipients, but the AMA, the insurance industry, and conservative members of Congress succeeded in blocking the plan.[13]

The 1964 elections swept a tide of liberal Democrats into Congress, and the result was Medicare. Enacted in 1965, the program provides medical assistance to retirees and is funded primarily through payroll taxes. Medicare,

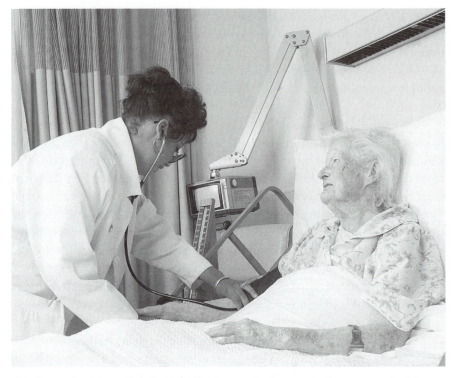

Medicare pays part of the hospitalization and other medical expenses of millions of elderly Americans. Rising medical costs threaten the solvency and scope of this popular federal program. (Larry Mulvehill/Photo Researchers)

too, is based on the insurance principle, and therefore it has gained nearly the same high level of public support as social security.

Medicare provides for care in a hospital or nursing home, but the recipient pays part of the initial cost and pays most of the expenses after 100 days. Medicare does not cover all physicians' fees, but enrollees in the program have the option of paying an insurance premium for fuller coverage of these fees. Enrollees who cannot afford the additional premium can apply to have the government pay it.

Public Assistance Programs

Unlike social insurance programs, **public assistance** programs are funded through general tax revenues and are available only to the financially needy. Eligibility for such entitlement programs is established by a **means test,** a demonstration that the applicant is poor enough to qualify for the benefit. In other words, applicants must prove that they are poor. Public assistance programs are commonly referred to as "welfare" and the recipients as "welfare cases." Opinion polls show that public assistance programs have less public support than do social insurance programs.

About 30 million Americans receive public assistance, typically through programs established by the federal government, administered mainly by the states, and funded jointly by the state and federal governments. Most Americans have the mistaken impression that public assistance programs account for the lion's share of federal welfare spending. In fact, the federal government spends more than twice as much on its two major social insurance programs, social security and Medicare, as it does on all public assistance programs combined.

SUPPLEMENTAL SECURITY INCOME (SSI) A major public assistance program is Supplemental Security Income (SSI), which originated as federal assistance to the blind and elderly poor as part of the Social Security Act of 1935. By the 1930s most states had begun or were considering such programs. Although the federal legislation was designed to replace their efforts, the states have retained a measure of control over benefits and eligibility and are required to provide some of the funding. Because SSI recipients (who now include the disabled in addition to the blind and elderly poor) have obvious reasons for their inability to provide for themselves, this public assistance program is not widely criticized. In 1996, however, Congress tightened SSI rules to exclude legal immigrants from the program.

AID TO NEEDY FAMILIES Perhaps the most controversial of the major public assistance programs was Aid for Families with Dependent Children (AFDC). Partly funded by the federal government but administered by the states, the AFDC program was created in the 1930s as survivors' insurance to assist children whose fathers had died prematurely. Relatively small and noncontroversial at inception, AFDC was the target of severe criticism by the 1970s. Although some attacks on it were based on false claims (for example, that most of the recipients were unwed teenage mothers when, in fact, less than 10 percent were in this category),[14] AFDC was widely unpopular because it was linked in people's minds to welfare dependency and irresponsibility. It was an entitlement program, which meant that any single parent (or, in some states, two parents) living in poverty could claim the benefit and keep it for as long as a dependent child was in the household. By 1995,

AFDC was supporting 14 million Americans at an annual cost of more than $20 billion.

In 1996, AFDC was terminated as part of the Personal Responsibility and Work Opportunity Act. Funding for AFDC was replaced by the Temporary Assistance for Needy Families block grant (TANF), which gives each state an annual cash grant that is to be used to design its own program for assisting needy families and getting welfare recipients into jobs. These programs must operate within tight federal guidelines, including:

- Americans' eligibility for federal cash assistance is limited to no more than five years in their lifetime.
- Within two years, the head of most families on welfare will have to find work or risk the loss of benefits.
- Unmarried teenage mothers are qualified for welfare benefits only if they remain in school and live with a parent or legal guardian.
- Single mothers will lose a portion of their benefits if they refuse to cooperate in identifying the father of their children.

Although states are allowed to make some exceptions to some of the rules (for example, an unmarried teenage mother who faces sexual abuse at home is permitted to live elsewhere), the rules govern in most cases. States are also empowered in some areas to impose more restrictive rules. For example, a state can deny increased benefits to a mother who is already receiving assistance and has another child.

Within the limits, states can design a program of their choosing, and wide differences are expected. Even AFDC benefits varied widely, ranging from less than $300 in most southern and southwestern states to more than $450 in most northeastern and some midwestern states. Since the TANF grants that states will initially receive are roughly proportional to the amounts they were spending on AFDC, these regional differences are certain to persist.

The new welfare program is such a radical departure from the past that its consequences are difficult to predict. Some observers believe it will be a disaster. The Urban Institute estimates that within a decade the bill will push more than 1 million children into poverty as their family's eligibility for assistance expires. Other observers see it as the long-awaited answer to welfare dependency. They point, for example, to a pilot program in Wisconsin that was reasonably successful in moving people off welfare without throwing them into poverty. The safest prediction, however, was offered by President Clinton. In signing the bill, he conceded that nobody knows for sure what will happen: "we all need a certain level of humility today." Perhaps the biggest challenge facing the states, in addition to ensuring that the poor do not wind up in the streets, is the development of welfare-to-work programs that actually do free families from welfare dependency.

FOOD STAMPS   The food stamp program, which took its present form in 1961, is fully funded by the federal government. The program provides an **in-kind benefit**—not cash, but food stamps that can be spent only on grocery items.

Food stamps are available only to people who qualify on the basis of low income. The program is intended to improve the nutrition of poor families by enabling them to purchase qualified items, mainly foodstuffs, with food stamps. Some critics say that food stamps stigmatize their users by making it obvious to onlookers in the checkout line that they are "welfare cases." More prevalent criticisms are that the program is too costly and that too many undeserving people receive food stamps.

The 1996 welfare reform bill eliminated food stamp eligibility for legal immigrants and also restricts to three months in any three-year period the eligibility of able-bodied adults with no dependent children.

SUBSIDIZED HOUSING   Low-income persons are also eligible for subsidized housing. Most of the federal spending in this area is on housing vouchers rather than the construction of low-income housing units. Under the voucher system, the individual receives a monthly rent-payment voucher, which is given in lieu of cash to the landlord, who then hands the voucher over to the government in exchange for cash. The welfare recipient is given a voucher (an in-kind benefit) rather than cash in order to ensure that the funds are actually used to obtain housing. About 5 million households annually receive a federal housing subsidy.

The U.S. government spends much less on public housing than on tax breaks for homeowners, most of whom are middle- and upper-income Americans. Homeowners are allowed tax deductions for their mortgage interest payments and their local property tax payments. The total of these tax concessions is three times as much as is spent by the federal government on housing for low-income families.

MEDICAID   When it enacted Medicare in 1965, Congress also established Medicaid, which provides health care for poor people who are already on welfare. It is considered a public assistance program, rather than a social

One of the many ironies of U.S. social welfare policy is that tax deductions on home mortgages for the middle and upper classes are government subsidies, just as are rent vouchers for the poor, but only the latter are stigmatized as "welfare handouts." (*Left*, Sally Weigand/Picture Cube; *right*, Glenn Kulbako/Picture Cube)

insurance program like Medicare, because it is based on need and funded by general tax revenues. Half of Medicaid funding is provided by the federal government and half by the states. More than 30 million Americans receive Medicaid assistance.

Medicaid is controversial because of its cost. As health care costs have spiraled, far ahead of the inflation rate, so have the costs of Medicaid. It absorbs about half of all public assistance dollars spent by the U.S. government and has forced state and local governments to cut other services to meet the costs of their share. "It's killing us," was how one local official described the impact of Medicaid on his community's budget.[15]

As is true of other public assistance programs, Medicaid has been criticized for supposedly serving too many people who could take care of themselves if they tried harder. The idea is contradicted, ironically, by the situation faced by many working Americans. There are nearly 40 million Americans who make too much money to qualify for Medicaid but who cannot afford health insurance. This situation encouraged President Clinton in 1993 to propose a comprehensive program that would entitle nearly all Americans to access to health care, at government expense if necessary. The proposal was defeated without coming to a vote in either the House or Senate.

EQUALITY OF OPPORTUNITY THROUGH EDUCATION: THE AMERICAN WAY

All democratic societies promote economic security, but they do so to different degrees. European democracies have instituted such programs as government-paid health care for all citizens, compensation for all unemployed workers, and retirement benefits for all elderly citizens. As we have seen, the United States provides these benefits only to some citizens in each category. For example, not all elderly Americans are entitled to social security benefits. If they paid social security taxes for a long enough period when they were employed, they (including their spouses) qualify for benefits. Otherwise, they do not, even if they are in dire economic need.

Such policy differences between Europe and the United States stem from cultural and historical differences. Democracy developed in Europe in reaction to centuries of aristocratic rule, the inequities of which brought the issue of human equality to the forefront. When strong labor and socialist parties then emerged as a consequence of industrialization, European democracies initiated sweeping social welfare programs that brought about greater economic equality. In contrast, American democracy emerged out of a tradition of limited government that emphasized personal freedom. Equality was a lesser issue, and class consciousness was weak. No major labor or socialist party emerged in America during industrialization to represent the working class, and there was no persistent and strong demand for welfare policies that would bring about an economic leveling.

Inequality and Public Opinion

These differing legacies are evident today in the opinions of Americans and Europeans toward liberty and equality. When asked in a Gallup study whether they placed a higher value on freedom or on equality, Americans chose freedom by 72 percent to 20 percent. Among Europeans, the margin was 49 percent to 35 percent.[16] On the basis of his study of political values, Karl Lamb concluded that most Americans "cannot really imagine a society that would provide substantial material equality."[17]

Americans' view of equality is best expressed by the term **equality of opportunity,** which is the idea that individuals should have an equal chance to succeed on their own. The concept embodies equality in its emphasis on giving everyone a fair chance to get ahead. Yet equality of opportunity also embodies liberty because it allows people to succeed or fail on their own as a result of what they do with their opportunities. The presumption is that people will end up differently—some rich, some poor. It is sometimes said that equality of opportunity offers individuals an equal chance to become unequal.

In practice, equality of opportunity works itself out primarily in the private sector, where Americans compete for jobs, promotions, and other advantages. However, a few public policies have the purpose of enhancing equality of opportunity. The most significant of these policies is public education.

Public Education: Leveling through the Schools

During the nation's first century, the question of a free public education to all children divided the landed wealthy from the advocates of broad-based democracy. The wealthy feared that an educated public would challenge their power. The democrats wanted to provide more people with the foundation for economic advantage. The democrats won out. Public schools sprang up in nearly every community and were open free of charge to children who could attend.

Today, as was discussed in Chapter 1, the United States invests more heavily in public education at all levels than any other country. The curriculum in American schools is also relatively standardized; unlike those countries that divide children even at the grade school level into different tracks that lead ultimately to different occupations, the United States aims to educate children in much the same way. Of course, public education is not a uniform experience for American children. The quality of education depends significantly on the wealth of the community in which a child resides since schools are funded primarily through local property taxes.

Nevertheless, the United States through its public schools educates a broad segment of the population. Arguably, no country in the world has made an equivalent effort to give children, whatever their parents' background, an equal opportunity in life through education. The spending level on public elementary and secondary schools averaged nearly $6,000 per pupil in 1995 (see box: States in the Nation), compared with an average of $2,500 per pupil in western Europe.

America's commitment to broad-based education extends to college; the United States is far and away the world leader in terms of the proportion of adults receiving a college education.[18]

STATES IN THE NATION

Per-Pupil Spending on Public Elementary and Secondary Schools

Each state spends more per pupil on public schools than does the typical country in western Europe. However, the states vary substantially in their school expenditures. The state of Utah spends the least—less than $4,000 per pupil each year. Alaska spends the most—nearly $10,000 per pupil each year.

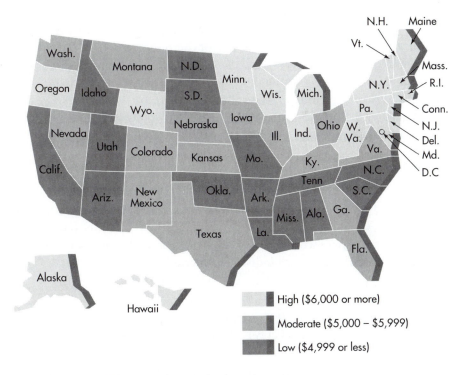

High ($6,000 or more)

Moderate ($5,000 – $5,999)

Low ($4,999 or less)

SOURCE: National Education Association, 1996.

The nation's education system preserves both the myth and reality of the American dream. The belief that success can be had by anyone who works for it could not be sustained if the education system were tailored for a privileged elite. And educational attainment is related to personal success, at least as measured by annual incomes. In fact, the gap in income between those with and without a college education is now greater than at any time in the country's history.

In part because the public schools have such a large role in creating an equal opportunity society, they have been heavily criticized in recent years. Violence in the schools is a major parental concern. So, too, is poor performance on standardized tests, such as the Scholastic Aptitude Test (SAT). American students are not even in the top ten internationally by their test scores in science or math.[19]

Disgruntled parents have demanded changes,[20] and these demands have led some communities to allow parents to choose the public school their children will attend. Under this policy, the schools compete for students, and those which attract the most students are rewarded with the largest budgets. A 1996 Gallup Poll indicated that Americans favor such a policy by more than a 2-to-1 margin. Advocates of the policy contend that it compels school administrators and teachers to do a better job and gives students the option of rejecting a school that is performing poorly. Opponents of the policy say that it creates a few well-funded schools and a lot of poorly funded ones, yielding no net gain in educational quality. Critics also claim that the policy discriminates against poor and minority group children, whose parents are less likely to be in a position to steer them toward the better schools.

The issue of school choice goes to the heart of the issue of equal opportunity. On the one hand, an elite-centered school system widens the gap between the country's richer and poorer groups. On the other hand, making students compete with one another for the best education can be justified in terms of the country's individualistic tradition.

CULTURE, POLITICS, AND SOCIAL WELFARE

Surveys have repeatedly indicated that a majority of Americans are convinced that most people on welfare could get along without it if they tried. Because public assistance programs have limited public support, there are constant political pressures to reduce welfare expenditures and to weed out undeserving recipients. The unwritten principle of social welfare in America, reflecting the country's individualistic culture, is that the individual must somehow earn any social welfare benefit or, barring that, demonstrate a convincing need for the benefit. The result is a welfare system that is both *inefficient*, in that much of the money spent on welfare never reaches the recipients, and *inequitable*, in that most of the money spent on social welfare never gets to the people who are most in need of help.

Inefficiency: The Welfare Web

The United States has by far the most intricate system of social welfare in the world. Scores of separate programs have been established to address different, often overlapping needs. A single individual in need of public assistance may qualify for many, none, or one of these programs, and the eligibility criteria are sometimes bizarre. Consider the case of Gary Myers, a security guard in Springfield, Missouri, who declared bankruptcy because he could not afford to pay $1,400 in hospital bills that his family had incurred. Had Myers made exactly $4 less than his $509 monthly wage, he would have qualified for government payment of his medical expenses. Because of the extra $4, however, Myers received nothing.

Beyond the question of the equity of such rules is the question of their efficiency. The unwritten principle that the individual must somehow earn or deserve a particular benefit makes the U.S. welfare system highly labor-intensive. Consider, for example, the 1996 welfare reform bill, which limits eligibility to families with incomes below a certain level and, in most instances, to families with a single parent living in the home. Because of this requirement, the eligibility of each applicant must be periodically checked by a caseworker (see Figure 16-4). This procedure makes such programs doubly expensive; in addition to payments to the recipients, there are the costs of paying caseworkers, supervisors, and support staffs, as well as processing the extensive paperwork involved.

The administrative costs of welfare are substantially lower in Europe since eligibility is either universal, as in the case of health care, or less stringently defined. There have been proposals to adopt a European-like system in the United States; President Nixon's attempt to establish a guaranteed annual income for every American family is an example. All of these proposals have failed to win broad support, mainly because they run counter to Americans' belief in individualism. Thus, it is not surprising that the 1996

FIGURE 16-4 THE CUMBERSOME ADMINISTRATIVE PROCESS BY WHICH WELFARE RECIPIENTS GET THEIR BENEFITS

welfare bill will create additional layers of welfare administration. Recipients' lifetime welfare histories will have to be maintained, and states will have to establish job placement and training programs that can move millions of people from welfare to work. Whether the change will be cost-effective will be determined by whether large numbers of welfare recipients actually find long-term employment. Whether the change fits the American way of welfare is more easily judged: it clearly does. The reform gives the poor an incentive to fend for themselves.

Inequity: The Middle-Class Advantage

Most Americans hold to the traditional belief in individualism and self-reliance, which they generalize to other people. Although they recognize a need for programs for the poor and disadvantaged, they tend to minimize both the number of such individuals and the extent of their need. The situation means that less-advantaged Americans cannot count on a great deal of political support from other sectors of society. Even the much-heralded War on Poverty of the 1960s was less a war than a skirmish. Weak middle-class support for the effort, reports that the programs were poorly administered and were not reaching the target audience, and the fiscal pressures of the Vietnam conflict combined to undermine the antipoverty effort. Congressional appropriations for the War on Poverty programs never totaled as much as $2 billion in a given year.

Social security and Medicare are another story entirely.[21] These two social insurance programs have broad public support even though together they cost the federal government more than twice what is spent on the major public assistance programs (see Figure 16-5). One major reason for the difference in public funding and approval for social security is that it benefits the

Social Insurance Expenditures

Public Assistance Expenditures

FIGURE 16-5 FEDERAL SPENDING FOR SOCIAL INSURANCE AND PUBLIC ASSISTANCE PROGRAMS
Social insurance spending far exceeds public assistance spending. Source: U.S. Social Security Administration, 1996.

majority. Most Americans are either actual or potential social security recipients. It is good politics for elected officials to appeal to the 40 million retired Americans who get a monthly social security check.

Social security recipients feel entitled to their benefits by virtue of their payroll-tax contributions. As indicated earlier, however, they receive far greater benefits than they have "earned" through their payroll taxes. So they are, in a sense, getting public assistance.

It is important to note, however, that the existence of social security substantially lessens the demand for other forms of public assistance. Monthly social security checks keep millions of Americans, mostly widows, out of poverty. About a fourth of social security recipients have no other significant source of income. Without social security, they would be completely dependent on public assistance programs.

Nevertheless, many social security recipients, while legally entitled to the benefits they receive, have no actual financial need for them. Only a third of social security recipients are in the lowest fifth of the population in income. Families in the top fifth of the income population receive more in federal social insurance benefits than is spent on TANF, food stamps, and housing subsidies combined.

The contradictions and difficulties of social welfare in America come together in the contrasting cases of social insurance and public assistance. Although the latter is targeted toward the truly needy, it is less acceptable politically and culturally and receives much less funding. The situation testifies to the strength of the traditional American values of individualism and self-reliance and to the power of money and votes.

What Does the Future of Welfare Reform Look Like?

Few analysts believe that the overhaul of the welfare system ended with passage of the 1996 welfare reform bill. Indeed, during negotiations with the White House and in Congress, the bill's sponsors dropped provisions that would have substantially revised the Medicaid and food stamp programs.

Social security is the one program that is not likely to be touched. Congressional Republicans and Democrats alike say no effort will be made to reduce spending on this entitlement. Small steps might be taken to slow the increase in social security spending, but even this would be politically difficult.

Medicare will also be around for decades to come. However, the program will run out of money in a few years, requiring changes in its funding. The political sensitivity of this issue was evident in late 1995 when congressional Republicans proposed to increase the share of Medicare costs to be paid by recipients, which President Clinton opposed. Senior-citizen groups sided with Clinton, forcing congressional Republicans into a showdown that strengthened Clinton's public support and led GOP lawmakers to withdraw their proposal. Given the political clout of the elderly, lawmakers may have to resolve the Medicare funding problem in the same way they handled the threatened insolvency of social security some years ago. Then, a nonpartisan commission was formed to develop a proposal that Congress could accept or reject in its entirety, thus reducing the direct pressure that the seniors' lobby could place on lawmakers.

Little else about the future of social welfare is clear. Social welfare, as we have seen, is the arena in which many of the conflicts of the American political system come together: individualism versus equality, Congress versus the president, national authority versus local authority, public sector versus private sector, Republicans versus Democrats, poorer versus richer, social insurance versus public assistance. The politics of welfare is a politics of contradictory values and competing interests, which ensures that it will be a contentious issue for years to come.

SUMMARY

The United States has a complex social welfare system of multiple programs addressing specific welfare needs. Each program applies only to those individuals who qualify for benefits by meeting the specific eligibility criteria. In general, these criteria are designed to reward and promote self-reliance or, when help is necessary, to ensure that laziness is not rewarded or fostered—in short, to limit benefits to those individuals who truly cannot help themselves. This approach to social welfare reflects Americans' traditional belief in individualism.

Poverty is a large and persistent problem in America. About one in seven people fall below the government-defined poverty line, and they include a disproportionate number of children, female-headed families, minority group members, and rural and inner-city dwellers. The ranks of the poor are increased by economic recessions and reduced through government welfare programs.

Welfare policy has been a partisan issue, with Democrats taking the lead on government programs to alleviate economic insecurity and Republicans acting to slow down or decentralize these initiatives. Changes in social welfare have usually occurred through presidential leadership in the context of majority support for the change. Welfare policy has been worked out through programs to provide jobs and job training, education programs, income measures, and, especially, transfer payments through individual-benefit programs.

Individual-benefit programs fall into two broad categories: social insurance and public assistance. The former includes such programs as social security for retired workers and Medicare for the elderly. Social insurance programs are funded by payroll taxes on potential recipients, who thus, in a sense, earn the benefits they later receive. Because of this arrangement, social insurance programs have broad public support. Public assistance programs, in contrast, are funded by general tax revenues and are targeted toward needy individuals and families. These programs are not controversial in principle: most Americans believe that government should assist the truly needy. However, because of a widespread belief that most welfare recipients could get along without assistance if they tried, these programs do not have universal public support, are only modestly funded, and are politically vulnerable.

The balance between economic equality and individualism tilts more heavily toward individualism in the United States than in other advanced industrialized democracies. Entitlement to social security, for example, is not a universal right of the elderly in the United States, whereas it is elsewhere. Compared to other democracies, however, the United States attempts to more equally educate its children, a policy consistent with its cultural emphasis on equality of opportunity.

Social welfare is a contentious issue. A major reason is that opposing sides disagree fundamentally on the nature of the problem. In one view, social welfare is too costly and assists too many people who could help themselves; another view holds that social welfare is not broad enough and that too many disadvantaged Americans live in poverty. In light of these irreconcilable differences, in combination with federalism and the widely shared view that welfare programs should target specific problems, the existing system of multiple programs, despite its administrative complexity and inefficiency, has been the only politically feasible alternative.

MAJOR CONCEPTS

entitlement programs

equality of opportunity

in-kind benefit

means test

negative government

positive government

poverty line

public assistance

social insurance

transfer payment

SUGGESTED READINGS

Chubb, John E., and Terry M. Moe. *Politics, Markets, and America's Schools*. Washington, D.C.: Brookings Institution, 1990. The authors recommend a new system of public education designed around parent–student choice and school competition.

Cook, Fay Lomax, and Edith J. Barrett. *Support for the American Welfare State: The Views of Congress and the Public*. New York: Columbia University Press, 1992. A thorough study of the views underlying welfare policy.

Gans, Herbert J. *The War against the Poor: The Underclass and Anti-Poverty Policy*. New York: Basic Books, 1996. A study of attitudes toward and policies affecting poverty.

Henig, Jeffrey R. *Rethinking School Choice: Limits of the Market Metaphor*. Princeton, N.J.: Princeton University Press, 1995. An argument against parental choice as the basis of public school enrollment.

Hochschild, Jennifer L. *Facing Up to the American Dream: Race, Class, and the Soul of the Nation*. Princeton, N.J.: Princeton University Press, 1996. An analysis of how whites and African Americans view their own and each other's opportunities.

Longman, Phillip. *The Return of Thrift: How the Collapse of the Middle Class Welfare State Will Reawaken Values in America*. New York: Free Press, 1996. Examines the relationship between the growth of middle-class welfare programs and changing American values.

Melnick, R. Shep. *Between the Lines: Interpreting Welfare Rights*. Washington, D.C.: Brookings Institution, 1994. An analysis of the intricate relationship between social welfare legislation and its interpretation in the courts.

Murray, Charles. *Losing Ground: American Social Policy, 1950–1980*. New York: Basic Books, 1984. An unfavorable assessment of the U.S. welfare system.

Rich, Michael J. *Federal Policymaking and the Poor: National Goals, Local Choices, and Distributional Outcomes*. Princeton, N.J.: Princeton University Press, 1993. A study of the impact of a federal poverty program.

Wilson, William Julius. *When Work Disappears: The World of the New Urban Poor*. New York: Knopf, 1996. An important analysis of jobs and poverty in the inner city.

READING 16

The New Poverty
B. GUY PETERS

The United States, along with other industrialized countries, is now facing a new type of inequality. The [old] form of inequality . . . was concentrated in the inner cities and among ethnic minorities, who often had relatively little experience in the labor force. This was the poverty of long-term unemployment and inadequate or nonexistent job skills reinforced by generations living on welfare. This new form of inequality, however, is affecting at least two different groups of people who might be expected to be able to support themselves adequately through the private economy. First, there are the many people who previously had been active participants in the labor force and who in some cases had been quite successful. As manufacturing jobs become less numerous, people with minimal education and no particular skills, who once could earn a middle-class income, find that this is increasingly impossible. Also, most corporations, in the name of enhancing competitiveness and productivity, have been eliminating middle management jobs, a trend made easier by the growth of office technology. Thus many people who believed they had a secure economic future now find themselves figuratively, if not literally, on the streets.

A second disadvantaged group emerging in the labor market are the working poor. For a significant segment of the population, the only work they can find is in jobs paying only the minimum wage and providing few if any benefits. Millions of people in the United States work full time and yet receive no health benefits, and the number grows almost daily. The benefits that have been so important for delaying the development of the public welfare state in the United States are now available to a decreasing share of the working population. The American dream is becoming increasingly only a dream for a large segment of the labor force, while for those still employed in full-time salaried jobs the good life continues unabated.

It also appears probable that the market will produce even greater inequality in the near future. An increasing share of the jobs being created in the American economy are part-time and/or temporary positions, with low wages and few benefits. One indication of this trend is that the largest single employer in the United States is now Manpower, Inc., a temporary employment agency, with 200,000 more employees than General Motors. As well as a gulf between the employed and the unemployed, the gap between the declining number of people with full-time, salaried positions and those with part-time and/or minimum wage positions is increasing. An individual can work a full 40-hour week at the official minimum wage ($4.25 per hour) and still be in poverty. In addition, the real value of the average wage paid in the American economy has been declining, from $275 per week in 1980 to $256 in 1991 in constant 1982 dollars, so that even those earning that wage will find their standard of living increasingly under threat.

Even if the jobs being generated are not very good, a job is generally better than unemployment. It appears, however, that the economy may not be the engine for producing jobs that it has been in the past, even if higher levels of economic growth should return. Employers appear more willing to work their existing employees longer hours than to add new workers, given the potential costs of benefits involved in new hiring. Further, employers may not want to make any commitment to training or socializing new employees and may prefer to have temporary employees meet any fluctuations in the demand for work. Finally, international competitiveness is a major force driving firms to be leaner and to shed labor in favor of technology. In sum, firms have few incentives to create new jobs even if they are becoming more profitable, but rather have a number of incentives to keep their labor costs as low as possible.

There appears to be a need to address the long-term changes in the economy through social programs, but neither the target populations nor the dynamics of inequality are those to which the political system is accustomed. The new targets of social programs often would have to be middle aged and formerly middle class. These new members of the poor, or at least the relatively deprived, believed that they had prepared themselves for a secure economic future, but have found themselves unemployed and dependent upon social welfare or private charity. The real problem is that these economic changes appear to be permanent, so that short-term programs to tide over the newly unemployed, and the new poor, may not really help them that much. Those newly poor who lack a sound basic education may never be able to adapt effectively to the economic changes, so that longer-term programs of assistance and support may be needed. Likewise, those who will be able to make the shift into a new information-age economy will also need financial support and substantial additional training, if they are to be successful.

Several types of social policy intervention will be required to address the problems arising from these shifts in the economy. One is short-term, or perhaps even medium-term, direct social assistance. The individuals affected and their families need to be able to live at or above the poverty level before any other types of programs can be effective. For the working poor who have little or no job skills, some forms of assistance may be required for the indefinite future, and may be supplied through existing programs such as Food Stamps, Medicare, and (less widely available) subsidized housing. For the newly poor with more education and job skills, the involvement of education and training programs will be required to prepare these individuals for new occupations. This may be just the beginning of long-term cycles of training and retraining, since the job market is projected to change much more rapidly in the future than it has in the past.

Several factors will complicate the provision of this range of services to the newly poor, just as has been true for the services delivered to the more typical impoverished populations. Even more than the other services, this range of services will involve coordination of a number of programs and organizations. In addition to social service agencies and agriculture (food stamps), the needed range of services would involve education and labor market organizations. One of the persistent problems of the social services has been the coordination of the services available to people. The Model Cities Program, for example, was designed in large part to ensure that residents of poor neighborhoods received the full range of services they should in an integrated manner. That program rarely worked as intended, and existing services for the poor often encounter coordination problems; there is little reason to believe that coordination would work better for this population.

Some of the same problems of family structure that afflict the traditional poor may also produce difficulties for the new poor. There might be no programs in effect like A.F.D.C. that tend to divide families, but the constraints of the market may produce strains on families now facing difficult economic times. These impacts may be felt even by families that are intact, i.e., with two parents. In particular, if parents can only earn a minimum wage, then often both must work full time to come close to making ends meet. Even for families who are earning the average wage in society, the declining purchasing power of that wage level may mean that both adults in a family will have to work. The United States has relatively little child care available, except that provided commercially, so that a good deal of income may be spent on child care.

In addition to the direct effects of inequality on social policies and the socioeconomic needs of members of society, there are a number of other, secondary, implications. These have a profound impact on public and private life in the United States, and the manner in which a number of other policies are conducted. Inequalities, other socioeconomic needs, and public policies at all levels of government reinforce each other to produce a cycle of poverty that tends to perpetuate inequality and poverty in the United States.

SOURCE: B. Guy Peters, "Social Policy," in Gillian Peele, Christopher J. Bailey, Bruce Cain, and B. Guy Peters, eds., *Developments in American Politics 2* (Chatham, N.J.: Chatham House, 1995). Reprinted by permission.
B. Guy Peters is Maurice Falk Professor of American Government at the University of Pittsburg.

CHAPTER SEVENTEEN

Foreign and Defense Policy

We the people of the United States, in order to . . . provide for the common defense . . .

PREAMBLE, U.S. CONSTITUTION

I N 1996, THE leaders of the world's seven most powerful industrial nations met in Lyons, France, for their third annual G-7 summit meeting. They devised a joint strategy for promoting global economic growth, including agreements on stabilizing currency exchange rates and accelerating debt forgiveness for poor countries. The G-7 leaders also tackled two issues thrust upon them by recent events. They expressed support for Russian President Boris Yeltsin, who was engaged in a tough reelection campaign. They also issued a forty-point plan for dealing with international terrorism, which was occasioned by a terrorist bombing in Saudi Arabia that killed and wounded scores of U.S. soldiers.[1]

The G-7 summit meeting sharply dramatized the changing nature of world politics and the role of the United States in it. America's once bitter enemy, Russia, was no longer a military threat. It was a struggling nation, trying with only some success to shed its authoritarian past. In fact, two of the countries at the summit, Germany and Japan, were closer to the position of rivals of the United States than was Russia. This rivalry, however, was economic in nature; Germany and Japan were America's strongest competitors in the global marketplace.

Yet the focus of the summit was cooperation rather than competition. The underlying assumption was that the world's most powerful nations could all gain if they set aside their differences and worked together to promote economic growth and limit political instability, such as that represented by international terrorism.

As the G-7 summit illustrates, national security is an issue of economic vitality as well as of military strength. The primary goal of U. S. foreign policy is the preservation of the American state. This objective requires military readiness in order to protect the territorial integrity and international interests of the United States. But the American state also represents a society of more than 250 million people, whose livelihood depends in significant part upon the nation's position in the international economy.[2] Through participation in global policies that foster economic growth, the United States can secure the jobs and trade that are essential to the maintenance of a high standard of living.

The national security policies of the United States embrace an extraordinary array of activities—so many, in fact, that they could not possibly be addressed adequately in an entire book, much less a single chapter. There are some 160 countries in the world, and the United States has relations of one kind or another—military, diplomatic, economic—with all of them. This chapter narrows the subject by focusing on a few main ideas:

* *Since World War II, the United States has acted in the role of world leader, which has substantially affected its military, diplomatic, and economic policies.*
* *The United States maintains a high degree of defense preparedness, which mandates a substantial level of defense spending and a worldwide deployment of U.S. conventional and strategic forces.*
* *Changes in the international marketplace have led to increased economic interdependence among nations, which has had a marked influence on the U.S. economy and on security planning; increasingly, national security has been defined in economic rather than military terms.*

THE ROOTS OF U.S. FOREIGN AND DEFENSE POLICY

For nearly half a century, U.S. defense policy was defined mostly by conflict with the Soviet Union. From the Berlin airlift in 1948 to the Vietnam escalation in 1965 to the Star Wars initiative in 1983, the United States seemed willing to pay any price to halt the global spread of communism. Then, in the late 1980s, the Soviet empire suddenly and dramatically began to fall apart. In December 1991, the Soviet Union itself ceased to exist. For decades, there had been two superpowers, the Soviet Union and the United States. Now there is only one.

With the end of the cold war, the United States has had to redefine its foreign and defense policies. The country is still at the center of world politics, but its challenges have changed: they are less military and more economic.[3] A strong domestic base, more than a mighty military arsenal, has become the key to global success.

Although the age of superpower conflict is over, the changes in foreign and defense policy that lie ahead will take shape within a context defined by that era. Decisions made in the past carry into the future, both informing and channeling new ones.

The United States as Global Superpower

Before World War II, the United States was an **isolationist** country, deliberately avoiding a large role in world affairs. A different America emerged from the war. It had more land, sea, and air power than any other country in the world, a huge military-industrial base, and several hundred overseas military bases. The United States had become an **internationalist** country, deeply involved in the affairs of other nations.

U.S. national security policy after World War II was built upon a concern with the power and intentions of the Soviet Union.[4] At the Yalta Conference in 1945, U.S. President Franklin Roosevelt and Soviet leader Josef

Great Britain's Winston Churchill, America's Franklin D. Roosevelt, and the Soviet Union's Josef Stalin meet at Yalta in 1945 to discuss the order of the postwar world. (Courtesy of the US Army)

Stalin had agreed that East European nations were entitled to self-determination within a Soviet zone of influence, but Stalin breached the agreement. After the war, Soviet occupation forces assisted the communist parties in eastern Europe in capturing state power, usually by coercive means. In the words of Britain's wartime prime minister, Winston Churchill, an "iron curtain" had fallen across Europe.

THE DOCTRINE OF CONTAINMENT   The Soviet Union's aggressive action led U.S. policymakers to assess Soviet aims.[5] Particularly noteworthy was the evaluation of George Kennan, a U.S. diplomat and expert on Soviet affairs. Kennan concluded that invasions from the west in World Wars I and II had made the Soviet Union (which had lost 25 million lives in World War II, compared with U.S. losses of 500,000) almost paranoid in its concern for regional security. Although Kennan believed that the USSR would some-day mature into a responsible world power, he contended that it was an immediate threat to neighboring countries and that the United States, although not directly endangered, would have to take the lead in discouraging Soviet aggression. He counseled a policy of "long-term, patient but firm, and vigilant containment."[6] Kennan's analysis contributed to the formulation of the doctrine of **containment,** which was based on the idea that the Soviet Union was an aggressor nation that had to be stopped from achieving its territorial ambitions.

Harry S Truman, who became president after Roosevelt's death in 1945, rejected Kennan's view that the USSR was motivated by a concern for *regional* security. Truman saw the Soviet Union as an aggressive ideological foe that was bent on *global* domination and that could be stopped only by the forceful use of U.S. power. Truman's view was based on assumptions derived from territorial concessions made to Germany's Adolf Hitler by Britain and France at a conference in Munich in 1938; rather than appeasing Hitler, these concessions convinced him that Germany could bully its way to further gains. The idea that appeasement only encourages further aggression was the *lesson of Munich*, and it became the dominant view of U.S. policymakers in the postwar period.

THE COLD WAR   Developments in the late 1940s embroiled the United States in a **cold war** with the Soviet Union. The term refers to the fact that the two countries were not directly engaged in actual combat (a "hot war") but were locked into a deep-seated hostility, which lasted forty-five years. From the United States' perspective, the cold war was an extension of containment policy and included support for governments threatened by communist takeovers. In June 1950, when the Soviet-backed North Koreans invaded South Korea, President Truman immediately committed U.S. troops to the conflict, which ended in stalemate and the loss of 35,000 American lives.

In order to contain the Soviet Union itself, the United States encircled it with a ring of military bases and built a powerful nuclear arsenal. In 1962 President John F. Kennedy took the country to the brink of war with the Soviet Union. U.S. intelligence sources had discovered that the Soviet Union was constructing nuclear missile sites in Cuba, which lies only 90 miles from Key West, Florida. Kennedy responded with a naval blockade of Cuba, threatening to attack any Soviet ship that tried to pass through the blockade. At the last moment, Soviet ships heading for Cuba turned around, and Premier Nikita Khrushchev ordered the dismantling of the missile sites. The Cuban missile crisis, however, provoked an arms race. The Soviets backed down over Cuba partly because they had a weak navy and an inferior nuclear force. Pledging not to be humiliated again, the Soviets began a twenty-year buildup of their naval and nuclear forces.

The Limits of American Power: The Vietnam War

For the United States, a major turning point in foreign policy was the Vietnam war. It was the most costly application of the containment doctrine: 58,000 American soldiers lost their lives.

Vietnam was part of France's colonial empire until the French army was defeated in 1954 by guerrilla forces, which were led by Ho Chi Minh, a nationalist with communist sympathies. The Geneva conference that ended the war resulted in a partitioning of Vietnam: the northern region was placed under Ho Chi Minh's leadership and the southern region under anticommunist leaders. The United States provided economic assistance to South Vietnam, anticipating that its government would develop the public support that would enable it to prevail in a Vietnam unification election that was scheduled for 1956. When it became apparent that Ho Chi Minh would easily win the election, the United States helped to get it canceled and began to increase its military assistance to the South Vietnamese army. By the time of President Kennedy's assassination in 1963, the United States had about 17,000 military advisers in South Vietnam. Lyndon Johnson sharply escalated the war in 1965 by committing U.S. combat units. By the late 1960s, 550,000 Americans were fighting in South Vietnam.

U.S. forces in Vietnam were technically superior in combat to the communist fighters, but they were fighting an enemy they could not easily iden-

In the jungle warfare of Vietnam, American soldiers had difficulty finding the enemy and adapting to guerrilla tactics. (UPI/Bettmann Newsphotos)

tify in a society they did not fully understand.[7] Vietnam was a guerrilla war, with no front lines and few set battles. As the conflict dragged on, American public opinion, most visibly among the young, turned against the war, which contributed to President Johnson's decision not to run for reelection in 1968. Public opinion forced Richard Nixon, who became president in 1969, to aim not for victory, but for a gradual disengagement that he called "peace with honor."

DÉTENTE   America's defeat in Vietnam forced U.S. policymakers to reconsider the country's international role. The *lesson of Vietnam* was that there were limits to the country's ability to assert its will in the world. Nixon claimed that the United States could no longer act as the "Lone Ranger" for the free world and sought to reduce tensions with communist countries.[8] This new philosophy was reflected by the Helsinki Accords of 1971, in which the United States accepted the territorial boundaries of eastern Europe that had been established at the end of World War II. Then Nixon took a historic journey to the People's Republic of China in 1972, the first official contact with that country since the communists took power in 1949.

Another indication of a change in policy was the Strategic Arms Limitation Talks (SALT), which began in 1969. The SALT talks presumed that the United States and the Soviet Union each had an interest in retaining enough nuclear weapons to deter the other from an attack but that neither side had an interest in mutual destruction. Along with the lowering of East–West trade barriers, these efforts marked the start of a new era of communication and cooperation, or **détente** (a French word meaning "a relaxing"), between the United States and the Soviet Union.[9]

DISINTEGRATION OF THE "EVIL EMPIRE" Although the period of détente during the 1970s marked a major shift in U.S.–Soviet relations, it did not last. The Soviet invasion of Afghanistan in 1979 convinced U.S. leaders that the USSR was still bent on expansion and threatened western interests in the oil-rich Middle East. Ronald Reagan, elected president in 1980, called for a renewed hard line toward the Soviet Union, which he described as the "evil empire."[10]

U.S. policymakers did not realize it at the time, but the Soviet Union was collapsing under its heavy defense expenditures, isolation from western technology and markets, and inefficient centralized command economy. In 1985 Mikhail Gorbachev became the Soviet leader and proclaimed a need to restructure the Soviet economy and society, an initiative known as *perestroika*. He also ordered the withdrawal of Soviet troops from Afghanistan (which had become his country's Vietnam) and sought to reduce tensions with the United States.

Gorbachev's efforts came too late to save the Soviet Union. In 1989, the withdrawal of Soviet troops from eastern Europe accelerated a pro-democracy movement that was already under way in the region. Poland initiated major reforms. Hungary dismantled the "iron curtain" that had blocked free travel to Austria. Then, in November, the Berlin Wall between East and West Germany—the most visible symbol of the separation of East and West—came down. On December 8, 1991, the leaders of the Russian, Belarus, and Ukrainian republics declared that the Soviet Union no longer existed.

A New World Order

The end of the cold war prompted President George Bush to call for a "new world order." His formulation abandoned the assumption that world affairs are a zero-sum game, in which for one nation to gain something, another nation has to lose. Bush contended that nations could move forward together.

The concept emphasized **multilateralism**—the idea that major nations should act together in response to problems and crises.[11]

Multilateralism characterized the U.S. response to Iraq's invasion of Kuwait in August 1990. President Bush worked through the United Nations, which passed resolutions demanding the unconditional withdrawal of Iraqi forces and placing a trade embargo on Iraqi oil. The military force arrayed against Iraq was also nominally a UN force, although it was led by a U.S. commander and consisted mostly of U.S. troops. Several countries, including Germany and Japan, supported the effort with money instead of troops.

The Gulf operation was militarily successful but did not resolve the regional conflicts or misguided leadership that had prompted Iraq's aggression. The termination of the UN operation was followed by ethnic and religious repression within Iraq and a renewal of Iraqi threats to Kuwait's sovereignty (in response to a particularly serious threat in 1994, U.S. troops were redeployed to the Gulf).

In 1992, as another application of multilateralism, U.S. troops were deployed as part of a UN force to Somalia, where thousands of people had died and thousands more had become refugees as a result of civil war and famine. The peace and humanitarian mission prevented additional deaths from starvation but turned sour when warring Somali clans turned against soldiers of the UN force. Thirty-six American soldiers were killed before U.S. troops were withdrawn, and a year later the UN mission was itself terminated. The anarchy and famine that had led to the UN mission still plagued Somalia when the last of the UN troops exited the country.

The war in Bosnia also prompted multilateral action. At first, the United Nations placed an arms embargo on Bosnia in an attempt to bring the fighting to a halt. However, the Bosnian Serbs continued their military attacks and used forced evacuations and mass executions to rid conquered areas of Bosnian Muslims and Croats. The UN then authorized limited air strikes against Serb positions by planes from the NATO countries (North Atlantic Treaty Organization, discussed below). When this strategy also failed, NATO planes, mainly from the United States, undertook a bombing campaign against the Serbs in September 1995. This action led directly to U.S.-negotiated peace talks in Dayton, Ohio, which finally brought the thirty-nine-month war to a halt. As part of the Dayton peace agreement, 60,000 troops from thirty-two countries, including 20,000 from the United States, were sent to Bosnia to maintain the peace. Whether the Dayton Accords will result in lasting peace and stability in Bosnia is yet to be determined, although many analysts are pessimistic about the prospects.

As these examples suggest, multilateralism has been only somewhat successful as a strategy for resolving international conflicts. With the deployment of enough resources, the world's major powers can intervene with some success in many parts of the developing world. However, these interventions are not always popular at home; public opinion in the United States, for example, turned strongly against the relief operation in Somalia after U.S. soldiers were killed there. Multilateral intervention also does not guarantee long-term success. Regional and internal conflicts typically stem from enduring ethnic, factional, or national hatreds, or from chronic problems such as famine and overcrowding. Even if these hatreds or problems can be momentarily eased, they are often too deep-seated to be permanently resolved. The preference of major nations for peaceful and low-cost solutions to regional and internal conflicts will continue to be tested by the hardship and animosity that afflict many of the world's people.

THE PROCESS OF FOREIGN AND MILITARY POLICYMAKING

National security is unlike other areas of government policy because it rests on relations with powers outside rather than within a country. Nations have sovereignty within their recognized territory; each nation is the ultimate governing authority over this territory and the people within it. In reality, of course, the world is not composed of equal sovereign states. Some are more powerful than others, and the strong will sometimes bully the weak. Nevertheless, there is no international body that is recognized by all nations as the final (sovereign) authority on disputes between them.

As a result, the chief instruments of national security policy—diplomacy, military force, economic exchange, and intelligence gathering—differ from those of domestic policy.

The Policymaking Instruments

Diplomacy is the process of negotiation between countries. In most cases, nations prefer to settle their differences by talking rather than by fighting. Through negotiation, countries can usually reach agreement on common (mutual) problems. By definition, acts of diplomacy involve two (*bilateral*) or more (*multilateral*) nations.

Military power is a second instrument of foreign policy, and it can be used *unilaterally*—that is, by a single nation acting alone. Most countries use military power as a defensive measure; they maintain forces, or enter into military alliances with other countries, in order to protect themselves from potential aggressors. Throughout the history of nations, however, there have always been a few countries that use military force more actively. The United States is such a nation. In the nineteenth century, it used force to take territory from the Indian tribes, Mexico, and Spain. Although the United States has not pursued territorial goals since then, it has otherwise made frequent use of its military power. Recent examples include the unilateral invasions of Grenada in 1983, Panama in 1989, and Haiti in 1994, and the multilateral war against Iraq in 1991 and bombing of Bosnian Serbs in 1995.

Economic exchange is a third instrument of world politics. This form of international relations usually takes one of two forms—trade or assistance. Trade among nations is the more important form. Nearly all countries aspire to a strong trading position so as to have access to outside products and markets for their products. Some countries, however, are so weak economically that they require assistance from more prosperous countries. This assistance is typically designed to help both the weaker and stronger partners.

A fourth instrument of world politics is intelligence gathering, which is the process of monitoring other countries' activities. For many reasons, but primarily because all nations pursue their individual self-interest, each nation keeps a watchful eye on the others.

The Policymaking Machinery

In the case of the United States, the lead actor in the application of these four instruments of foreign policy is the president. As we indicated in Chapter 12 and will discuss later in this chapter, the president shares power and responsibility for foreign and military policy with Congress, but the president has the stronger claim to leadership because of the constitutional roles of commander in chief, chief diplomat, and chief executive.

The president has an executive agency, the National Security Council (NSC), that provides advice on foreign and military issues. The NSC is chaired by the president; it includes the vice-president and the secretaries of state and defense as full members and the director of the Central Intelligence Agency (CIA) and the chairman of the Joint Chiefs of Staff as advisory members. Since State, Defense, and the CIA often have conflicting and self-centered views of national security, the NSC acts to keep the president in charge by providing a broader perspective. The NSC's staff of experts is directed by the president's national security adviser, who, with an office in

In a ceremony symbolizing America's role as world leader, President Clinton brings Israeli Prime Minister Yitzhak Rabin (*left*) and PLO Chairman Yasser Arafat together for a historic handshake after the signing of the Israeli–PLO peace accord in 1993. Rabin was later assassinated by an Israeli fanatic who opposed the accord. (Reuters/Bettmann)

the White House and access to defense, diplomatic, and intelligence sources, has become influential in the formulation of U.S. policy.

The complexity of international politics makes it impossible for the president or any government agency to fully control U.S. policy. Moreover, as a world power, the United States relies upon outside institutions, such as the United Nations, to pursue some of its policy objectives. The key organizational units in the foreign policy area can be categorized according to their primary functions—defense, intelligence, diplomacy, and trade.

DEFENSE ORGANIZATIONS   The Department of Defense (DOD), which has roughly 1.5 million uniformed personnel and 750,000 civilian employees, is in charge of the military security of the United States. DOD was created in 1947 when the three military services—the army, navy, and air force—were placed under the secretary of defense. Each service has its own secretary, but they report to the defense secretary, who represents all the services in relations with Congress and the president. Each service naturally regards its mission and budget as more important than those of the other services. The defense secretary helps reduce the adverse effects of these inter-service rivalries.

Of the country's military alliances, the North Atlantic Treaty Organization (NATO) is the most important. NATO was created as a "forward defense" against a possible Soviet invasion of western Europe. The NATO forces, which include troops of the United States, Canada, and most western European countries, conduct joint military exercises and engage in joint strategic and tactical military planning. The demise of the Soviet Union threatened NATO's survival. NATO's charter prohibits it from acting "out of area," so its operations extend only to Europe and North America. In 1991 NATO was restructured as a smaller, more flexible force that might deal with new risks, such as international terrorism and ethnic rivalries.

The Bosnian war created a rift within NATO over the use of military force in the European theater. Europe's NATO members, led by France, initially opposed U.S. proposals to use massive airpower to force the Bosnian Serbs to accept a permanent cease-fire. The Europeans favored a purely diplomatic solution and relented only after the Serbs repeatedly violated truce agreements.

NATO's latest plans include expanding its membership to include countries of eastern Europe, a move Russia opposes. Poland, Hungary, the Czech Republic, and other eastern European countries were once part of the Soviet military alliance (the Warsaw Pact countries), and Russia has said it would view any NATO expansion as a threat to its interests. NATO leaders see a European-wide alliance as the best guarantee of lasting peace on the continent.

INTELLIGENCE ORGANIZATIONS   Foreign and military policy require a high level of knowledge about what is happening in the world and what other countries are planning to do.[12] A large part of the responsibility for gathering such information falls on specialized federal agencies, including the Central Intelligence Agency; the National Security Agency, which specializes in electronic communications analysis; and intelligence agencies within the Departments of State and Defense. The CIA, which is the most prominent of the various agencies, gathers and assesses information on foreign affairs. Much of this effort consists of the routine monitoring of international developments. With the decline of the Soviet threat, the CIA is giving increased attention to drug trafficking, industrial espionage, and terrorism.

DIPLOMATIC ORGANIZATIONS   The U.S. Department of State conducts most of the country's day-to-day business with foreign countries through its embassies, headed by U.S. ambassadors. State's traditional duties include negotiating political agreements with other nations, protecting U.S. citizens and interests abroad, promoting U.S. economic interests, gathering foreign intelligence, and representing the United States abroad.

America's diplomatic efforts also take place through international organizations, such as the Organization of the American States (OAS) and the United Nations. The breakdown of the Soviet bloc in 1989 renewed the possibility that the world's great powers could work together to achieve common goals. Some analysts believe that the UN may now finally be able to play the prominent role in international affairs that was envisioned for it when it was chartered. International terrorism, famine, peacekeeping, and drug trafficking are among the problems that the UN has recently addressed.

ECONOMIC ORGANIZATIONS   The shift in emphasis in global affairs from military forces to economic markets has brought to the fore a new set of government agencies, those representing economic sectors. The Agriculture, Commerce, Labor, and Treasury departments are playing increasingly important roles in foreign affairs. In addition, some specialty agencies, such as the Federal Trade Commission and the Export-Import Bank of the United States, are involved in international trade and finance.

The United States also works through international institutions, such as the International Monetary Fund (IMF), the World Bank, and the World Trade Organization (WTO). These agencies tend to promote goals, such as economic development and free trade, that are consistent with U.S. policy goals. The IMF and the World Bank were established through the efforts of the United States for the purpose of assisting developing countries. The IMF provides short-term loans so that countries experiencing temporary trade deficits do not have to take drastic measures, such as the imposition of high tariffs, that would hurt them and the world economy in the long run. The World Bank makes long-term loans to poorer countries for capital investment projects, such as the construction of power plants and factories. The WTO is the formal organization through which nations administer and negotiate the general rules governing international trade.

THE MILITARY DIMENSION OF NATIONAL SECURITY POLICY

The dissolution of the Soviet Union has brought about the first significant scaling back of U.S. defense spending since the end of the Vietnam war (see Figure 17-1). Nevertheless, the United States spends far more on defense,

Billions of dollars

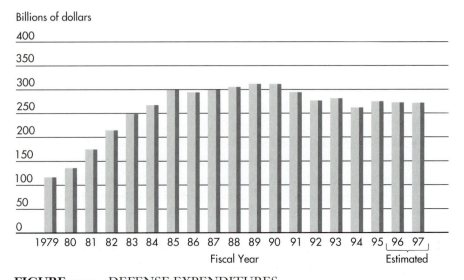

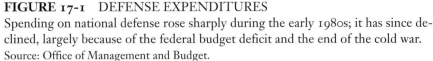

FIGURE 17-1 DEFENSE EXPENDITURES
Spending on national defense rose sharply during the early 1980s; it has since declined, largely because of the federal budget deficit and the end of the cold war.
Source: Office of Management and Budget.

in both relative and absolute terms, than its allies. On a per capita basis, U.S. military spending is more than twice that of other members of the NATO alliance (see box: How the United States Compares). The U.S. defense budget is second to none in the world, but so is the military power it buys. During the Gulf war, the world's fourth-largest army, Iraq's, was no match for the United States' superior military equipment and technology. The war lasted about six weeks, with fewer than 200 U.S. casualties, but left an estimated 50,000 to 100,000 Iraqi dead.

Defense Capability

The United States owes its status as the world's only superpower in part to the strength of its conventional forces. The United States Navy has a dozen aircraft carriers, nearly 100 attack submarines, and hundreds of other fighting and supply ships. The U.S. Air Force has thousands of high-performance aircraft. The U.S. Army has more than 500,000 troops on active duty, and they are amply supported by tanks, artillery pieces, armored personnel carriers, and attack helicopters.

HOW THE UNITED STATES COMPARES

The Burden of Military Spending

The United States bears a disproportionate share of the defense costs of the NATO alliance. The U.S. military establishment is huge and is deployed all over the world, and the taxpayers spend more than $250 billion per year to maintain it. These expenditures directly account for roughly 5 percent of the U.S. gross national product (GNP). By comparison, defense spending by Germany, Italy, and Canada accounts for 3 percent or less of their GNPs. The percentages for Britain and France are higher but not as high as for the United States. Japan, which is not part of NATO, spends only 1 percent of its GNP on defense. Japan's small military force is confined by World War II peace agreements to the country's islands and the adjoining waters.

The United States has pressured its allies to carry a larger share of the defense burden, but these countries have resisted, contending that the cost would be too high and that their security would not be substantially improved. A partial exception to this situation was the Persian Gulf war. U.S. troops and equipment accounted for the bulk of the military strength arrayed against Iraq, but the financial cost of the war effort was borne by other countries. Germany, Japan, Saudi Arabia, and Kuwait were among the countries that helped fund the war. In fact, other countries gave the United States $20 billion more than it spent on the war.

The chart below indicates the approximate per capita level of defense spending in the United States and countries with which it is closely aligned.

| $150 | $200 | $300 | $400 | $450 | $450 | $1200 |
| Japan | Italy | Canada | Germany | France | Great Britain | United States |

SOURCE: OECD and Defense Department statistics.

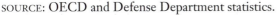

The main threat to the physical security of the United States during the cold war was not invasion but nuclear attack. The United States followed a policy of **deterrence,** based on the notion that the Soviet Union could be deterred from launching a nuclear attack by the knowledge that the United States would retaliate in kind.[13]

America's long-range nuclear weaponry is still deployed in what is called the "nuclear triad," which refers to the three ways in which nuclear weapons can be launched—land-based missiles, submarine-based missiles, and bombers. The triad provides a "second-strike capability"—the ability to absorb a first-strike nuclear attack and survive with enough nuclear power for massive retaliation (second strike). The United States also has tactical (battlefield) nuclear weapons in its arsenal. These are short-range, low-yield nuclear weapons that can be used against battlefield targets, such as enemy troop concentrations or artillery installations.

The Uses of Military Power

U.S. military forces have been trained for or called upon for six types of military action.

UNLIMITED NUCLEAR WARFARE   The idea of an all-out nuclear war was always too horrible to imagine, but the fear of nuclear holocaust has diminished greatly since the cold war ended. Following the lead of the United States, the president of the Russian republic, Boris Yeltsin, initiated deep, unilateral cuts in his country's nuclear arsenal. The United States reciprocated with unilateral cuts of its own. In the past, nuclear arms limitations had required protracted bilateral negotiations between the United States and the Soviet Union.

LIMITED NUCLEAR WARFARE   Some experts believe that, while the risk of an all-out nuclear attack on the United States has diminished, the possibility that a single nuclear weapon might be used against the United States may have increased. A major concern arising from the breakup of the Soviet Union has been control of its nuclear weapons, strategic and tactical. In addition, terrorist groups or "outlaw" regimes, such as Iraq, pose a serious threat because the technology and materials that are required to build nuclear weapons are more widely accessible than ever before. Accordingly, the United States, Russia, and other nuclear powers are cooperating to reduce the spread of nuclear weapons. One goal of the Persian Gulf conflict was the destruction of Iraq's nuclear program.

UNLIMITED CONVENTIONAL WARFARE   The end of the cold war has also reduced the prospect of an unlimited conventional war. A great part of U.S. military preparedness and strategy in the past half century was based on the scenario of an invasion of western Europe by the Soviet Union and its allies. Even if the cold war should begin anew, Russia or any other part of the former Soviet Union would require years to build its military capacity to the point where it could pose a credible threat to Europe.

LIMITED CONVENTIONAL WARFARE   The Persian Gulf war demonstrated that the United States possesses the might to win a limited conventional war against a well-organized and well-armed foe. Despite the size of Iraq's army and the combat readiness of its forces, the war turned out to be no contest, prompting George Bush to claim the United States had "kicked the Vietnam syndrome once and for all."

A problem of limited conventional wars is that they do not always produce satisfactory results. The military action is likely to be quick and decisive, but the political aspect tends to be troublesome. The Bush administration's decision to stop the Gulf war short of a march on Baghdad was a

A B-2 "Stealth" bomber sits on the runway of Whiteman Air Force Base in Missouri. The B-2 is one of the newest and most expensive weapons in America's arsenal. (P. Shambroom/Photo Researchers)

calculated one. Said one analyst: "The President was not prepared to pay the political price that increased American casualties would have involved or to take responsibility for putting Iraq back together after an unconditional surrender or to figure out how to contain the power of Iran and Syria once the Iraqi regime was destroyed."[14]

COUNTERINSURGENCY The Vietnam conflict was an **insurgency,** an uprising by irregular forces against an established government. In most Third World countries, insurgencies originate in the grievances of people who are struggling against the monopoly of economic and political power by a ruling elite. In the past, the insurgents often received support in the form of military equipment from the Soviet Union. Most insurgencies were therefore seen by the United States as a threat to its political and economic interests.

U.S. attempts to quell Third World insurgencies have declined somewhat since the Vietnam war, which reduced public support for U.S. military involvement in other countries. Throughout the 1980s, polls showed that a large majority of Americans were steadfastly opposed to sending American troops to quell insurgencies in Central America.

POLICE-TYPE ACTION With the end of the cold war, U.S. policymakers have begun to pay closer attention to other global problems, including drug trafficking, political instability, population movement, and terrorism. Each of these types of problems is on the rise. In the past two decades, for example, acts of international terrorism, which have included the bombing of commercial airliners, have doubled.[15]

The U.S. military has become increasingly involved with these problems. U.S. peacekeeping missions in Somalia, Bosnia, and Haiti are examples, as is the use of U.S. military advisers in drug-interdiction operations in Latin America. U.S. military personnel have also been used to stop "boatpeople" from Cuba, Haiti, and other Carribean islands from entering the United States illegally.

U.S. military commanders have not been particularly eager to expand their mission to include police-type actions, such as immigration control, that traditionally have been a civilian responsibility. But given the high cost of keeping a large defense force, the absence of a highly visible and dangerous enemy such as the former Soviet Union, and the increase in the types of problems that require police-type action, it is likely that the pressure to use U.S. troops in unconventional ways will continue.

The Politics of National Defense

All Americans would agree that the physical security of the United States is a paramount concern. The consensus breaks down, however, on specific issues. The Vietnam conflict created deep and lasting divisions of opinion over the proper uses of America's military capacity. In contrast, U.S. policy in the Persian Gulf crisis had majority support from start to end.

PUBLIC OPINION AND ELITE CONFLICT   Defense policy is a mix of *majoritarian* and *elite* politics. On issues of broad national concern, majority opinion is a vital component.[16] It was public opinion, for example, that ultimately forced U.S. policymakers to withdraw American troops from Vietnam and Somalia.

Debates over foreign and defense policy, however, typically take place among political elites.[17] Most citizens are too poorly informed to contribute significantly to these debates. Few Americans, for example, can name even half the countries in Africa, much less speak knowledgeably about their politics. This situation gives foreign policy experts and officials considerable freedom to decide policy. In some cases, partisan and institutional differences influence these decisions. Liberal Democratic elites are more likely than conservative Republicans, for example, to insist upon human rights guarantees as a condition for defense agreements with other countries.

THE MILITARY-INDUSTRIAL COMPLEX   Political disputes over defense policy are more than honest differences of opinion among people. They also involve billions of dollars in jobs and contracts. In fiscal year 1997, the U.S. defense budget exceeded $240 billion, or roughly 5 percent of the gross national product. A high level of defense spending has been justified by reference to the nation's security needs. However, an alternative explanation for high defense spending points to the insatiable demands of the U.S. armed services and defense firms. In his 1961 Farewell Address, President Dwight D. Eisenhower warned against the "unwarranted influence" and "misplaced power" of what he termed "the military-industrial complex."

The **military-industrial complex** has three components: the military establishment, the industries that manufacture weapons, and the members of Congress from states and districts that depend heavily on the arms industry. In other words, the military-industrial complex is an aggregation of interests that benefit from a high level of defense spending, regardless of whether these expenditures are justified from the standpoint of national security.

Many members of Congress are eager to approve arms contracts (or at least reluctant to oppose them) because of the economic impact such contracts have on constituents. The B-1 bomber, for example, was built with the help of 5,200 subcontractors located in forty-eight states and in all but a handful of congressional districts. A sharp reduction in defense spending would cause havoc in many local economies; nearly one in ten American jobs are directly or indirectly related to military spending.

Without doubt, some proportion of defense spending reflects the workings of the military-industrial complex.[18] The problem is that no one knows exactly what this proportion is, and the estimates vary widely.

THE ECONOMIC DIMENSION OF NATIONAL SECURITY POLICY

Economic considerations are a vital component of national security policy. In the simplest sense, economic strength is a prerequisite of military strength: a powerful defense establishment can only be maintained by a country that is economically well-off. However, in a broader and more important sense, economic prosperity enables a people to "secure" their way of life. As President Eisenhower said, it is folly to weaken at home what one is trying to strengthen abroad.

The cold war sometimes hid the essential truth of this observation. Global power, in addition to being a means by which nations achieved other goals, became an end in itself. The Soviet Union paid the highest price. In the end, its status as a military superpower was achieved at the expense of economic growth and development, and ultimately led to its collapse.[19] The United States also paid dearly for its superpower status. In a widely read book, *The Rise and Fall of the Great Powers*, Paul Kennedy concluded that the United States had succumbed to "imperial overstretch" by straining its resources to maintain its global military presence and, in the process, weakening substantially its domestic economic base.[20]

A Changing World Economy

Some aspects of U.S. superpower policy were economically beneficial. The clearest example is the European Recovery Plan, better known as the Marshall Plan. Proposed in 1947 and named after one of its chief architects, the widely respected General George Marshall, it was perhaps the boldest and most successful U.S. foreign policy initiative of the twentieth century. It called for $3 billion in immediate aid for the postwar rebuilding of Europe, with an additional $10 billion or so to follow. The Marshall Plan was unprecedented both in its scope (today, the equivalent cost would be more than $100 billion) and in its implications—for the first time, the United States had committed itself to a continuing major role in European affairs. Through the Marshall Plan, the countries of western Europe regained economic and political stability in a relatively short time.

Apart from enabling the countries of western Europe to better confront the perceived Soviet military and political threat, the Marshall Plan was also designed to meet the economic needs of the United States. Wartime production had lifted the country out of the Great Depression, but the end of the war in 1945 brought a recession and renewed fears of hard times. A rejuvenated western Europe furnished a market for U.S. goods. In effect, western Europe became a junior partner within a system of global trade that worked primarily to the advantage of the United States.

A high level of military spending in conjunction with several other factors, however, gradually weakened the position of the United States in the world economy.[21] Whereas the United States at one time could almost define international economic conditions, it is now also defined by them.[22] Germany and Japan have become powerful economic rivals of the United States. Today Japan, not the United States, is the world's leading exporter, and trade between the two countries results in a large surplus for Japan. The United States has also experienced a trade deficit with Germany. Japan particularly, but also Germany, benefited economically by spending less on the military than the United States. The Japanese yen and German Deutsche mark have at times been stronger currencies than the American dollar. In addition, western Europe as a whole has become a less receptive market for U.S. goods; European countries are now one another's best customers, trading among themselves through the European Union (EU).[23]

In economic terms, the world can best be described as tripolar—in other words, economic power is concentrated in three centers. One center is the United States, which produces nearly 20 percent of the world's goods and services. Another center is Japan, which accounts for 10 to 15 percent of the world's economy. The third and largest economy, with 25 to 30 percent of the world's gross product, is the EU, which includes the countries of Belgium, Denmark, France, Germany, Great Britain, Greece, Ireland, Italy, Luxembourg, the Netherlands, Portugal, Spain, Sweden, Finland, and Austria. These three centers, although they have less than 15 percent of the world's population, account for 60 percent of the world's economic output.

President Clinton meets with other G-7 leaders during a working session at their 1996 summit meeting in Lyon, France. The G-7 is a group of seven of the world's most economically powerful countries: the United States, Japan, Italy, Germany, France, Great Britain, and Canada. (Apesteguy-Benainous/Gamma-Liaison)

In a few respects, the United States is the weakest of the three economic centers: it has the largest national debt and the worst trade imbalance.

In other ways, however, the United States is the strongest of the three economic powers. Its economy is more well-rounded. Like the EU and Japan, the United States has a strong industrial base, but, unlike Japan, it also has a strong agricultural sector and, unlike both Japan and the EU, it has abundant natural resources. Its vast fertile plains have made it the world's leading agricultural producer. The United States ranks among the top three countries worldwide in production of wheat, corn, potatoes, peanuts, cotton, eggs, cattle, and pigs. As for natural resources, the United States ranks among the top five nations in copper, uranium, lead, sulfur, zinc, coal, gold, iron ore, natural gas, silver, and magnesium.[24]

As we discussed in Chapter 15, the United States also ranks highest in the world in terms of its global economic competitiveness. This ranking was assigned by the Switzerland-based Institute for Management Development, which bases its competitiveness surveys on countries' capacity to generate wealth. The United States owes its position to such factors as the strength of its domestic economy and its technological know-how. One area where the United States ranks below Japan and most of the EU countries is in "people skills"—the training and education of its work force.[25]

American Goals in the Global Economy

The United States depends on other countries for raw materials, finished goods, and capital to meet Americans' production and consumption demands. Meeting this objective requires the United States to have influence on world markets. The broad goals of the United States in the world economy include:

- Sustaining an open system of trade that will promote prosperity at home
- Maintaining access to energy and other resources that are vital to the regular functioning of the U.S. economy
- Keeping the widening gap between the rich and poor countries from destabilizing the world's economy[26]

GLOBAL TRADE The United States was most able to sustain domestic prosperity through global trade in the period after World War II. Industrialized Europe had been devastated by the war, but U.S. factories and farmlands emerged untouched by its effects and were producing more than a third of the world's goods. In terms of total goods and services, the United States is still the world's top exporting nation (see box: States in the Nation). But it is also leads the world in imports, and they exceed its exports by a substantial margin. In recent years, the United States has had a serious trade deficit (see Figure 17-2).

Not surprisingly, global trade has become an increasingly important domestic issue in the United States. Trade issues are a mixture of economics and politics. Protective tariffs and import restrictions, for example, are political responses to foreign economic competition. By placing a tariff or other restrictions on a product from abroad, and thereby increasing its price or limiting its availability, government can protect domestic producers of that product.

To oversimplify, the opposing sides on trade issues reflect the protectionism and the free trade positions. **Protectionism** emphasizes the immediate interests of domestic producers and includes measures necessary to give them an advantage in the domestic market over foreign competitors. The

S T A T E S   I N   T H E   N A T I O N

Foreign Exports and State Economies

The states differ considerably in the extent to which their economies depend on foreign exports. The state of Washington, with its aerospace, fishing, and logging industries and proximity to Canada and Asia, is the leading exporter. Trade with foreign countries accounts for 22 percent of the state's economy. Louisiana (16%), Alaska (11%), and Vermont (11%) are the only other states whose exports exceed 10 percent of the total state economy.

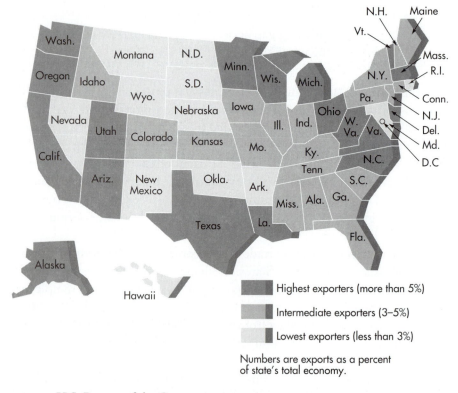

Highest exporters (more than 5%)

Intermediate exporters (3–5%)

Lowest exporters (less than 3%)

Numbers are exports as a percent of state's total economy.

SOURCE: U.S. Bureau of the Census.

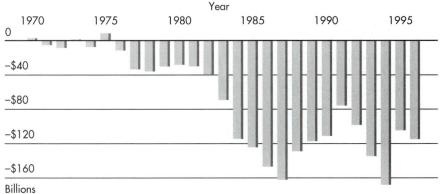

FIGURE 17-2 THE TRADE DEFICIT
Not since 1975 has the United States exported more goods and services than it imports. Source: U.S. Department of Commerce, 1997.

center of protectionist sentiment in the United States has been Congress. Many of its members are determined to protect locally operating firms that are adversely affected by foreign competitors. The protectionist position gains support from the view of most Americans that free trade results in a loss of jobs to low-wage countries (see Figure 17-3).

The **free trade** position assumes that the long-term economic interests of all countries are advanced when tariffs and other trade barriers are kept to a minimum. The leadership on free trade has usually come from the White House, although it is fair to say that most members of Congress, except on vital interests affecting their constituencies, support the principle of global free trade. Paradoxically, given their opinions on job loss, most Americans also say they generally favor free trade among countries.

These opposing positions clashed in 1993 over the issue of the North American Free Trade Agreement (NAFTA), which aims to create an EU-type market among the United States, Canada, and Mexico. Opponents of the agreement, who included organized labor, most environmental groups, and a majority of the Democrats in Congress, argued that it would result in the loss of countless jobs to Mexico. Its proponents, who included President Clinton, most large U.S. corporations, and most congressional Republicans, contended that the agreement would boost the economies of all three countries and was necessary if the United States was to maintain a leading position in global trade. The measure obtained majority support

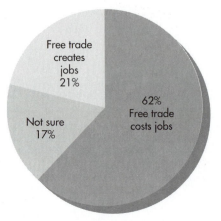

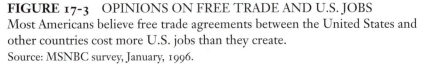

FIGURE 17-3 OPINIONS ON FREE TRADE AND U.S. JOBS
Most Americans believe free trade agreements between the United States and
other countries cost more U.S. jobs than they create.
Source: MSNBC survey, January, 1996.

in Congress, but only after side agreements were worked out to protect
some American producers from the adverse effects of open trade in North
America.

In its first year, NAFTA was a boon to all three countries involved (see
Figure 17-4). U.S. exports to Mexico rose sharply, while Mexico received an
inflow of capital and Canada increased its exports to both the United States
and Mexico. In late 1994, though, the value of the Mexican peso dropped
sharply, slowing U.S. exports and requiring the United States to provide
Mexico with billions of dollars to stabilize its currency. The long-term benefits of NAFTA apparently will depend mainly on the ability of Mexico to
stabilize its economy.

The new rules expanding the General Agreement on Tariffs and Trade
(GATT) may have an even greater impact than NAFTA on America's economy in the years to come. The rules received congressional approval in
1994 and aim at creating a nearly global free market: the rules lower worldwide tariffs by a third, strengthen protections for intellectual property (such
as patents and copyrights), and create panels that will arbitrate trade disputes
and establish standards in areas such as the environment, securities, and
worker safety. This multilateral trading system is coordinated by the World
Trade Organization (WTO), which was established in 1995 as the successor to GATT. The WTO's 124 member nations have basically committed

themselves to an open trade policy buttressed by regulations that are designed to ensure fair play among the participants.

ACCESS TO NATURAL RESOURCES   Although the United States is rich in natural resources, it is not self-sufficient. The major deficiency is oil; domestic production provides for only about half of the nation's use.

Outside the United States, most of the world's oil is found in the Middle East, Latin America, and Russia. Access to this oil has occurred mainly through the marketplace, but U.S. military force has also been instrumental. In the Middle East, for example, U.S. oil companies controlled one-tenth of Middle Eastern oil reserves before World War II began; just twenty years later, they controlled six-tenths.[27] This change was in part the result of the ability of U.S. firms after the war to furnish the capital to reopen oil fields damaged by the conflict and to open new fields. The United States also gained leverage through its support of reactionary regimes in Iran and other Middle Eastern countries, which responded by giving U.S. firms a larger role in their oil production.

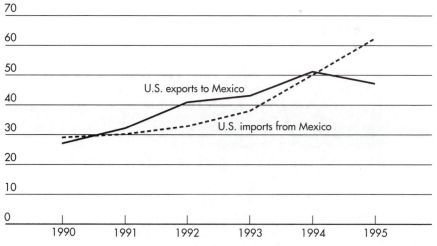

U.S. trade with Mexico, in billions

FIGURE 17-4   U.S. TRADE WITH MEXICO
In the first year of NAFTA, U.S. exports to Mexico increased sharply and the United States had a trade surplus. The surplus turned to a deficit in 1995 as a result of the collapse of the Mexican peso, which reduced Mexicans' purchasing power. Source: U.S. Department of Commerce.

The 1990–1991 war in the Persian Gulf is a more recent example of how U.S. military force has served the nation's resource needs. Iraq's invasion of oil-rich Kuwait threatened western supplies, and its defeat quelled the threat.

In general, however, military power has increasingly become a less effective means of preserving economic leverage.[28] Economic interdependence has made military intervention mostly counterproductive. For example, when Iranian fundamentalists took over the U.S. embassy in Teheran in 1979, one of the reasons the United States refrained from attacking Iran's oil fields was because the action would have substantially reduced the Middle East's oil-producing capacity.

RELATIONS WITH THE DEVELOPING WORLD   Political instability in the less developed countries, as in the case of Iraq's invasion of Kuwait, is disruptive to world markets. Less developed countries also offer marketplace opportunities. In order to progress, they need to acquire the goods and services that more industrialized countries can provide. To foster this demand, the United States and the other industrialized countries provide developmental assistance to poorer countries. These contributions include direct foreign aid and also indirect assistance through international organizations such as the IMF and the World Bank. Since World War II, the United States has been far and away the leading source of aid to the developing countries of the world. The United States is still near the top in terms of its total annual contributions but is now far down the list in terms of per capita contributions (see Table 17-1). The primary recipient of U.S. foreign aid is Israel, which, at $3 billion annually, gets more than a fourth of the total.

Foreign aid is a favorite target of politicians. Upon being named chair of the Senate Foreign Relations Committee, Jesse Helms (R-N.C.) said he would trim millions in aid "going down foreign ratholes."[29] Many Americans share the view that the United States ought not to be funding discretionary programs abroad when there are pressing needs at home. The unpopularity of foreign aid is also a consequence of the public's exaggerated notion of how much the United States spends in this area. In a 1994 poll that asked respondents to name the largest federal programs, foreign aid was at the top of the list (27 percent said it was the most expensive federal program). In fact, foreign aid is near the bottom, accounting for less than 1 percent of the total federal budget.[30]

Foreign assistance is only one source of the funds that flow from the United States to developing countries: private investment is the other major source. After trailing Japan for much of the 1980s, the United States has again emerged as the country whose firms invest most heavily abroad. In

TABLE 17-1   U.S. ASSISTANCE TO DEVELOPING COUNTRIES
The United States ranks high in terms of total amount spent on
development assistance but ranks low in terms of per capita expenditure

	Development Assistance	
	Total (Billion)	*Per Capita*
Canada	$ 2.6	$ 96
France	7.4	129
Germany	6.9	108
Great Britain	3.2	56
Italy	3.4	59
Japan	11.0	88
Sweden	2.1	245
United States	11.3	44

SOURCE: *OECD in Figures* (Paris: Organization for Economic Cooperation and Development, 1993).

1996, U.S. *multinational corporations* (firms that have major operations in more than one country) invested twice as much abroad as Japanese, French, German, or British firms. Foreign investment by U.S.-based multinationals works to America's advantage in at least two important ways. First, it sends a flow of overseas profits back to the United States, which strengthens the country's financial base. Second, it makes other nations dependent on the prosperity of the United States; their economies are linked to the condition of U.S. business.

The Politics of Global Economic Policy

The global economy has changed a great deal since America's halcyon days in the period immediately following World War II. It is greatly more competitive and less responsive to military power. Of course, the United States still derives economic advantages from its superpower status. Many countries prefer a militarily strong United States to the alternatives. China, for example, has not been highly critical of America's continued military presence in the Pacific, preferring it to the prospect of a remilitarized Japan. Such situations provide the United States with special opportunities for favorable economic relationships.[31]

Nevertheless, the United States necessarily depends more heavily than in the past on the strength of its own economy to forge a favorable position in world trade. This situation has caused U.S. corporations in recent years to launch cost-cutting measures in order to make their products more competitive in the global market.[32] The changes have also led U.S. policymakers to alter their approaches to business regulation, public education, and many other policies that affect the country's competitive position. Another indicator of a new approach is the emphasis that the United States has placed on the WTO, whose member nations are committed to lowering trade barriers so as to promote the type of world trading system that can benefit all participating countries.

Public opinion in recent years has consistently supported the idea that the United States should turn its attention away from military priorities toward economic ones. This opinion seems to reflect the lesson that American elites and officials have drawn from international experiences during the last half-century, particularly during the past decade or so. The consensus is broad enough to suggest that American politics in the 1990s will focus on reinvigorating the U.S. economy.

SUMMARY

From 1945 to 1990, U.S. foreign and defense policies were dominated by a concern with the Soviet Union. During most of this period the United States pursued a policy of containment based on the premise that the Soviet Union was an aggressor nation bent on global conquest. Containment policy led the United States into wars in Korea and Vietnam and to maintain a large defense establishment. U.S. military forces are deployed around the globe, and the nation has a large nuclear arsenal. The end of the cold war, however, has made some of this weaponry and much of the traditional military strategy less relevant to maintaining America's security. Cutbacks in military spending and a redefinition of the military's role are under way.

With the end of the cold war, the United States has taken a new approach to foreign affairs, which President George Bush labeled as a "new world order." It proposes that nations work together toward common goals and includes efforts to address global problems, such as drug trafficking and environmental pollution. The Persian Gulf war is the most notable example of the multilateralism that is a characteristic of the new world order.

Increasingly, national security is being defined in economic terms. After World War II, the United States helped establish a global trading system within which it was the leading partner. The nation's international economic position, however, has gradually weakened, owing to domestic problems and to the emergence of strong competitors, particularly Japan and Germany. Many analysts believe that a revitalized economic sector rather than military power holds the key to America's future position in international affairs.

The chief instruments of national security policy are diplomacy, military force, economic exchange, and intelligence gathering. These are exercised through specialized agencies of the U.S. government, such as the Departments of State and Defense, which are largely responsive to presidential leadership. Increasingly, national security policy has also relied on international organizations, such as the UN and WTO, which are responsive to the global concerns of major nations.

MAJOR CONCEPTS

cold war
containment
détente
deterrence
free trade
insurgency

internationalism
isolationism
military-industrial complex
multilateralism
protectionism

SUGGESTED READINGS

Barnet, Richard J., and John Cavanagh. *Global Dreams: Imperial Corporations and the New World Order.* New York: Simon & Schuster, 1994. Argues that the key players in today's world are large multinational corporations.

Greider, William. *One World, Ready or Not: The Manic Logic of Global Capitalism.* New York: Simon & Schuster, 1997. A critical analysis of the global economy, and its effect on Americans' lives.

Holsti, Ole. *Public Opinion and American Foreign Policy.* Ann Arbor: University of Michigan Press, 1996. An analysis that concludes public opinion has had a significant and positive impact on U.S. foreign policy.

Johnson, Loch K. *Secret Agencies: U.S. Intelligence Agencies in a Hostile World.* New Haven, Conn.: Yale University Press, 1996. A nuanced assessment of the record of U.S. intelligence agencies.

Karnow, Stanley. *Vietnam: A History.* New York: Penguin, 1983. A thorough history of American involvement in Vietnam.

Kenen, Peter B., ed. *Understanding Interdependence: The Macroeconomics of the Open Economy.* Princeton, N.J.: Princeton University Press, 1995. A survey of the organization and workings of the international monetary system.

Lindsay, James M. *Congress and the Politics of U.S. Foreign Policy.* Baltimore, Md.: Johns Hopkins University Press, 1994. An analysis of Congress's increasingly assertive role in foreign policy.

Nye, Joseph. *Bound to Lead: The Changing Nature of United States Power.* New York: Basic Books, 1990. An analysis of the U.S. role in world affairs in the aftermath of the cold war.

Ohmae, Kenichi. *The End of the Nation State: The Rise of Regional Economies.* New York: Free Press, 1995. An analysis of the impact of economic change on national sovereignty.

Oye, Kenneth A., Robert J. Lieber, and Donald Rothchild. *Eagle in a New World: American Grand Strategy in the Post–Cold War Era.* New York: HarperCollins, 1992. A collection of essays on the choices the United States faces now that the cold war has ended.

READING 17

A Borderless World
KENICHI OHMAE

A funny—and, to many observers, a very troubling—thing has happened on the way to former U.S. President Bush's so-called "new world order": the old world has fallen apart. Most visibly, with the ending of the Cold War, the long-familiar pattern of alliances and oppositions among industrialized nations has fractured beyond repair. Less visibly, but arguably far more important, the modern nation state itself—that artifact of the 18th and 19th centuries—has begun to crumble.

For many observers, this erosion of the long-familiar building blocks of the political world has been a source of discomfort at least and, far more likely, of genuine distress. They used to be confident that they could tell with certainty where the boundary lines ran. These are our people; those are not. These are our interests; those are not. These are our industries; those are not. It did not matter that little economic activity remained truly domestic in any sense that an Adam Smith or a David Ricardo would understand. Nor did it matter that the people served or the interests protected represented a small and diminishing fraction of the complex social universe within each set of established political borders.

The point, after all, was that everyone knew—or could talk and act as if he or she knew—where the boundary lines ran. Everyone's dealings could rest, with comfortable assurance, on the certain knowledge, as Robert Reich has put it, of who was "us" and who was "them." The inconvenient fact that most of the guns pointed in anger during the past two decades were pointed by national governments at some segment of the people those governments would define as "us"—well, that really did not matter, either. Boundaries are boundaries.

Politics, runs the time-worn adage, is the art of the possible. Translated, that means it is also the art of ignoring or overlooking discordant facts: guns pointed the wrong way, democratic institutions clogged to the point of paralysis by minority interests defended in the name of the majority—and, perhaps most important, domestic economies in an increasingly borderless world of economic activity. So what if average GNP per capita in China is $317 but, in Shenzhen, whose economy is closely linked with that of Hong Kong, it is $5,695? Boundaries are boundaries, and political dividing lines mean far more than demonstrable communities of economic interest.

No, they don't. Public debate may still be hostage to the outdated vocabulary of political borders, but the daily realities facing most people in the developed and developing worlds—both as citizens and as consumers—speak a vastly different idiom. Theirs is the language of an increasingly borderless economy, a true global marketplace. But the references we have—the maps and guides—to this new terrain are still largely drawn in political terms. Moreover, as the primary features on this landscape—the traditional nation states—begin to come apart at the seams, the overwhelming temptation is to redraw obsolete, U.N.-style maps to reflect the shifting borders of those states. The temptation is understandable, but the result is pure illusion. No more than the work of early cartographers do these new efforts show the boundaries and linkages that matter in the world now emerging. . . .

The uncomfortable truth is that, in terms of the global economy, nation states have become little more than bit actors. They may originally have been, in their mercantilist phase, independent, powerfully efficient engines of wealth creation. More recently, however, as the downward-ratcheting logic of electoral politics has placed a death grip on their economies, they have become—first and foremost—remarkably inefficient engines of wealth distribution. Elected political leaders gain and keep power by giving voters what they want, and what they want rarely entails a substantial decrease in the benefits, services, or subsidies handed out by the state.

Moreover, as the workings of genuinely global capital markets dwarf their ability to control exchange rates or protect their currency, nation states have become inescapably vulnerable to the discipline imposed by economic choices made elsewhere by people and institutions over which they have no practical control. Witness, for example, the recent, Maastricht-related bout of speculation against the franc, the pound, and the kronor. Witness, also, the unsustainable but self-imposed burden of Europe's various social programs. . . .

Second, and more to the point, the nation state is increasingly a nostalgic fiction. It makes even less sense today, for example, than it did a few years ago to speak of Italy or Russia or China as a single economic unit. Each is a motley combination of territories with vastly different needs and vastly different abilities to contribute. . . .

Third, when you look closely at the goods and services now produced and traded around the world, as well as at the companies responsible for them, it is no easy matter to attach to them an accurate national label. Is an automobile sold under an American marque really a U.S. product when a large percentage of its components comes from abroad? Is the performance of IBM's foreign subsidiaries or the performance of its R&D operations in Europe and Japan really a measure of U.S. excellence in technology? For that matter, are the jobs created by Japanese plants and factories in the Mississippi Valley really a measure of the health of the Japanese, and not the U.S., economy? The barbershop on the corner may indisputably be a part of the domestic American economy. But it is just not possible to make the same claim, with the same degree of confidence, about the firms active on the global stage. . . .

An arresting, if often overlooked, fact about today's borderless economy is that people often have better access to low-cost, high-quality products when they are not produced "at home." Singaporeans, for example, enjoy better and cheaper agricultural products than do the Japanese, although Singapore has no farmers—and no farms—of its own. Much the same is true of construction materials, which are much less expensive in Singapore, which produces none of them, than in Japan, which does. . . .

For more than a decade, some of us have been talking about the progressive globalization of markets for consumer goods like Levi's jeans, Nike athletic shoes, and Hermés scarves—a process, driven by global exposure to the same information, the same cultural icons, and the same advertisements, that I have elsewhere referred to as the "California-ization" of taste. Today, however, the process of convergence goes faster and deeper. It reaches well beyond taste to much more fundamental dimensions of worldview, mindset, and even thought process. There are now, for example, tens of millions of teenagers around the world who, having been raised in a multimedia-rich environment, have a lot more in common with each other than they do with members of older generations in their own cultures. For these budding consumers, technology-driven convergence does not take place at the sluggish rate dictated by yesterday's media. It is instantaneous—a nanosecond migration of ideas and innovations.

The speed and immediacy of such migrations take us over an invisible political threshold. In the post-Cold War world, the information flows underlying economic activity in virtually all corners of the globe simply cannot be maintained as the possession of private elites or public officials. They are shared, increasingly, by all citizens and consumers. This sharing does not, of course, imply any necessary similarity in how local economic choices finally get made. But it does imply that there is a powerful centripetal force at work, counteracting and counterbalancing all the centrifugal forces noted above.

The emotional nexus of culture, in other words, is not the only web of shared interest able to contain the processes of disintegration unleashed by the reappearance of older fault lines. Information-driven participation in the global economy can do so, too, ahead of the fervid but empty posturing of both cheap nationalism and cultural messianism. The well-informed citizens of a global marketplace will not wait passively until nation states or cultural prophets deliver tangible improvements in lifestyle. They no longer trust them to do so. Instead, they want to build their own future, now, for themselves and by themselves. They want their own means of direct access to what has become a genuinely global economy.

SOURCE: Kenichi Ohmae, *The End of the Nation State: The Rise of Regional Economies* (New York: Free Press, 1995). Reprinted by permission.
Dr. Kenichi Ohmae heads a citizens' political reform movement in Japan and was formerly a director of an international management consulting firm.

Appendixes

THE DECLARATION OF INDEPENDENCE

In Congress, July 4, 1776,

THE UNANIMOUS DECLARATION OF THE THIRTEEN UNITED STATES OF AMERICA

When, in the course of human events, it becomes necessary for one people to dissolve the political bands which have connected them with another, and to assume, among the powers of the earth, the separate and equal station to which the laws of nature and of nature's God entitle them, a decent respect to the opinions of mankind requires that they should declare the causes which impel them to the separation.

We hold these truths to be self-evident, that all men are created equal; that they are endowed by their Creator with certain unalienable rights; that among these, are life, liberty, and the pursuit of happiness. That, to secure these rights, governments are instituted among men, deriving their just powers from the consent of the governed; that, whenever any form of government becomes destructive of these ends, it is the right of the people to alter or to abolish it, and to institute a new government, laying its foundation on such principles, and organizing its powers in such form, as to them shall seem most likely to effect their safety and happiness. Prudence, indeed, will dictate that governments long established, should not be changed for light and transient causes; and, accordingly, all experience hath shown, that mankind are more disposed to suffer, while evils are sufferable, than to right themselves by abolishing the forms to which they are accustomed. But, when a long train of abuses and usurpations, pursuing invariably the same object, evinces a design to reduce them under absolute despotism, it is their right, it is their duty, to throw off such government and to provide new guards for their future security. Such has been the patient sufferance of these colonies, and such is now the necessity which constrains them to alter their former systems of government. The history of the present King of Great Britain is a history of repeated injuries and usurpations, all having, in direct object, the establishment of an absolute tyranny over these States. To prove this, let facts be submitted to a candid world:

He has refused his assent to laws the most wholesome and necessary for the public good.

He has forbidden his governors to pass laws of immediate and pressing importance, unless suspended in their operation till his assent should be obtained; and, when so suspended, he has utterly neglected to attend to them.

He has refused to pass other laws for the accommodation of large districts of people, unless those people would relinquish the right of representation in the legislature; a right inestimable to them, and formidable to tyrants only.

He has called together legislative bodies at places unusual, uncomfortable, and distant from the depository of their public records, for the sole purpose of fatiguing them into compliance with his measures.

He has dissolved representative houses repeatedly for opposing, with manly firmness, his invasions on the rights of the people.

He has refused, for a long time after such dissolutions, to cause others to be elected; whereby the legislative powers, incapable of annihilation, have returned to the people at large for their exercise; the state remaining, in the meantime, exposed to all the danger of invasion from without, and convulsions within.

He has endeavored to prevent the population of these States; for that purpose, obstructing the laws for naturalization of foreigners, refusing to pass others to encourage their migration hither, and raising the conditions of new appropriations of lands.

He has obstructed the administration of justice, by refusing his assent to laws for establishing judiciary powers.

He has made judges dependent on his will alone, for the tenure of their offices, and the amount and payment of their salaries.

He has erected a multitude of new offices, and sent hither swarms of officers to harass our people, and eat out their substance.

He has kept among us, in time of peace, standing armies, without the consent of our legislatures.

He has affected to render the military independent of, and superior to, the civil power.

He has combined, with others, to subject us to a jurisdiction foreign to our Constitution, and unacknowledged by our laws; giving his assent to their acts of pretended legislation:

For quartering large bodies of armed troops among us:

For protecting them by a mock trial, from punishment, for any murders which they should commit on the inhabitants of these States:

For cutting off our trade with all parts of the world:

For imposing taxes on us without our consent:

For depriving us, in many cases, of the benefit of trial by jury:

For transporting us beyond seas to be tried for pretended offences:

For abolishing the free system of English laws in a neighboring province, establishing therein an arbitrary government, and enlarging its boundaries, so as to render it at once an example and fit instrument for introducing the same absolute rule into these colonies:

For taking away our charters, abolishing our most valuable laws, and altering, fundamentally, the powers of our governments:

For suspending our own legislatures, and declaring themselves invested with power to legislate for us in all cases whatsoever.

He has abdicated government here, by declaring us out of his protection, and waging war against us.

He has plundered our seas, ravaged our coasts, burnt our towns, and destroyed the lives of our people.

He is, at this time, transporting large armies of foreign mercenaries to complete the works of death, desolation, and tyranny, already begun, with circumstances of cruelty and perfidy scarcely paralleled in the most barbarous ages, and totally unworthy the head of a civilized nation.

He has constrained our fellow citizens, taken captive on the high seas, to bear arms against their country, to become the executioners of their friends, and brethren, or to fall themselves by their hands.

He has excited domestic insurrections amongst us, and has endeavored to bring on the inhabitants of our frontiers, the merciless Indian savages, whose known rule of warfare is an undistinguished destruction of all ages, sexes, and conditions.

In every stage of these oppressions, we have petitioned for redress, in the most humble terms; our repeated petitions have been answered only by repeated injury. A prince, whose character is thus marked by every act which may define a tyrant, is unfit to be the ruler of a free people.

Nor have we been wanting in attention to our British brethren. We have warned them, from time to time, of attempts made by their legislature to extend an unwarrantable jurisdiction over us. We have reminded them of the circumstances of our emigration and settlement here. We have appealed to their native justice and magnanimity, and we have conjured them, by the ties of our common kindred, to disavow these usurpations, which would inevitably interrupt our connections and correspondence. They, too, have been deaf to the voice of justice and consanguinity. We must, therefore, acquiesce in the necessity which denounces our separation, and hold them as we hold the rest of mankind, enemies in war, in peace, friends.

We, therefore, the representatives of the United States of America, in general Congress assembled, appealing to the Supreme Judge of the world for the rectitude of our intentions, do, in the name, and by the authority of the good people of these colonies, solemnly publish and declare, that these united colonies are, and of right ought to be, free and independent states: that they are absolved from all allegiance to the British Crown, and that all political connection between them and the state of Great Britain is, and ought to be, totally dissolved; and that, as free and independent states, they have full power to levy war, conclude peace, contract alliances, establish commerce, and to do all other acts and things which independent states may of right do. And, for the support of this declaration, with a firm reliance on the protection of Divine Providence, we mutually pledge to each other our lives, our fortunes, and our sacred honor.

The foregoing Declaration was, by order of Congress, engrossed, and signed by the following members:

John Hancock

New Hampshire
Josiah Bartlett
William Whipple
Matthew Thornton

Massachusetts Bay
Samuel Adams
John Adams
Robert Treat Paine
Elbridge Gerry

Rhode Island
Stephen Hopkins
William Ellery

Connecticut
Roger Sherman
Samuel Huntington
William Williams
Oliver Wolcott

New York
William Floyd
Philip Livingston
Francis Lewis
Lewis Morris

New Jersey
Richard Stockton
John Witherspoon
Francis Hopkinson
John Hart
Abraham Clark

Pennsylvania
Robert Morris
Benjamin Rush
Benjamin Franklin
John Morton
George Clymer
James Smith
George Taylor
James Wilson
George Ross

Delaware
Caesar Rodney
George Read
Thomas M'Kean

Maryland
Samuel Chase
William Paca
Thomas Stone
Charles Carroll, of
    Carrollton

Virginia
George Wythe
Richard Henry Lee
Thomas Jefferson
Benjamin Harrison
Thomas Nelson, Jr.
Francis Lightfoot Lee
Carter Braxton

North Carolina
William Hooper
Joseph Hewes
John Penn

South Carolina
Edward Rutledge
Thomas Heyward, Jr.
Thomas Lynch, Jr.
Arthur Middleton

Georgia
Button Gwinnett
Lyman Hall
George Walton

Resolved, That copies of the Declaration be sent to the several assemblies, conventions, and committees, or councils of safety, and to the several commanding officers of the continental troops; that it be proclaimed in each of the United States, at the head of the army.

THE CONSTITUTION
OF THE UNITED STATES[1]

We the People of the United States, in Order to form a more perfect Union, establish Justice, insure domestic Tranquility, provide for the common defence, promote the general Welfare, and secure the Blessings of Liberty to ourselves and our Posterity, do ordain and establish this CONSTITUTION for the United States of America.

Article I

Section 1.
All legislative Powers herein granted shall be vested in a Congress of the United States, which shall consist of a Senate and House of Representatives.

Section 2.
The House of Representatives shall be composed of Members chosen every second Year by the People of the several States, and the Electors in each State shall have the Qualifications requisite for Electors of the most numerous Branch of the State Legislature.

No Person shall be a Representative who shall not have attained to the Age of twenty-five Years, and been seven Years a Citizen of the United States, and who shall not, when elected, be an Inhabitant of that State in which he shall be chosen.

[Representatives and direct Taxes[2] shall be apportioned among the several States which may be included within this Union, according to their respective Numbers, which shall be determined by adding to the whole Number of free Persons, including those bound to Service for a Term of Years, and excluding Indians not taxed, three fifths of all other Persons.][3] The actual Enumeration shall be made within three Years after the first Meeting of the Congress of the United States, and within every subsequent Term of ten Years, in such Manner as they shall by Law direct. The Number of Representatives shall not exceed one for every thirty

---

[1] This version, which follows the original Constitution in capitalization and spelling, was published by the United States Department of the Interior, Office of Education, in 1935.
[2] Altered by the Sixteenth Amendment.
[3] Negated by the Fourteenth Amendment.

Thousand, but each State shall have at Least one Representative; and until such enumeration shall be made, the State of New Hampshire shall be entitled to chuse three, Massachusetts eight, Rhode-Island and Providence Plantations one, Connecticut five, New York six, New Jersey four, Pennsylvania eight, Delaware one, Maryland six, Virginia ten, North Carolina five, South Carolina five, and Georgia three.

When vacancies happen in the Representation from any State, the Executive Authority thereof shall issue Writs of Election to fill such Vacancies.

The House of Representatives shall chuse their Speaker and other Officers; and shall have the sole Power of Impeachment.

Section 3.

The Senate of the United States shall be composed of two Senators from each State, chosen by the Legislature thereof, for six Years; and each Senator shall have one Vote.

Immediately after they shall be assembled in Consequence of the first Election, they shall be divided as equally as may be into three Classes. The Seats of the Senators of the first Class shall be vacated at the Expiration of the second Year, of the second Class at the Expiration of the fourth Year, and of the third Class at the Expiration of the sixth Year, so that one-third may be chosen every second Year; and if Vacancies happen by Resignation, or otherwise, during the Recess of the Legislature of any State, the Executive thereof may make temporary Appointments until the next Meeting of the Legislature, which shall then fill such Vacancies.

No Person shall be a Senator who shall not have attained to the Age of thirty Years, and been nine Years a Citizen of the United States, and who shall not, when elected, be an Inhabitant of that State for which he shall be chosen.

The Vice President of the United States shall be President of the Senate, but shall have no vote, unless they be equally divided.

The Senate shall chuse their other Officers, and also a President pro tempore, in the absence of the Vice President, or when he shall exercise the Office of President of the United States.

The Senate shall have the sole Power to try all Impeachments. When sitting for that purpose they shall be on Oath or Affirmation. When the President of the United States is tried, the Chief Justice shall preside: And no person shall be convicted without the Concurrence of two thirds of the Members present.

Judgment in Cases of Impeachment shall not extend further than to removal from Office, and disqualification to hold and enjoy any Office of honor, Trust, or Profit under the United States: but the Party convicted shall nevertheless be liable and subject to Indictment, Trial, Judgment, and Punishment, according to Law.

Section 4.

The Times, Places and Manner of holding Elections for Senators and Representatives, shall be prescribed in each State by the Legislature thereof; but the Congress may at any time by Law make or alter such Regulations, except as to the Places of Chusing Senators.

The Congress shall assemble at least once in every Year, and such Meeting shall be on the first Monday in December, unless they shall by Law appoint a different Day.

Section 5.

Each House shall be the Judge of the Elections, Returns and Qualifications of its own Members, and a Majority of each shall constitute a Quorum to do Business; but a smaller number may adjourn from day to day, and may be authorized to compel the Attendance of absent Members, in such Manner, and under such Penalties, as each House may provide.

Each House may determine the Rules of its Proceedings, punish its Members for disorderly Behaviour, and, with the Concurrence of two thirds, expel a Member.

Each House shall keep a Journal of its Proceedings, and from time to time publish the same, excepting such Parts as may in their Judgment require Secrecy; and the Yeas and Nays of the Members of either House on any question shall, at the Desire of one fifth of those Present, be entered on the Journal.

Neither House, during the Session of Congress, shall, without the Consent of the other, adjourn for more than three days, nor to any other Place than that in which the two Houses shall be sitting.

Section 6.

The Senators and Representatives shall receive a Compensation for their Services, to be ascertained by Law, and paid out of the Treasury of the United States. They shall in all Cases, except Treason, Felony, and Breach of the Peace, be privileged from Arrest during their Attendance at the Session of their respective Houses, and in going to and returning from the same; and for any Speech or Debate in either House, they shall not be questioned in any other Place.

No Senator or Representative shall, during the Time for which he was elected, be appointed to any civil Office under the Authority of the United States, which shall have been created, or the Emoluments whereof shall have been increased, during such time; and no Person holding any Office under the United States shall be a Member of either House during his continuance in Office.

Section 7.

All Bills for raising Revenue shall originate in the House of Representatives; but the Senate may propose or concur with Amendments as on other bills.

Every Bill which shall have passed the House of Representatives and the Senate, shall, before it become a Law, be presented to the President of the United States; If he approve he shall sign it, but if not he shall return it, with his Objections, to that House in which it shall have originated, who shall enter the Objections at large on their Journal, and proceed to reconsider it. If after such Reconsideration two thirds of that House shall agree to pass the bill, it shall be sent, together with the objections, to the other House, by which it shall likewise be reconsidered, and if approved by two thirds of that House, it shall become a Law. But in all such Cases the Votes of both Houses shall be determined by Yeas and Nays, and the Names of the Persons voting for and against the Bill shall be entered on the Journal of each House respectively. If any Bill shall not be returned by the President within ten Days (Sundays excepted) after it shall have been presented to him, the Same shall be a Law, in like Manner as if he had signed it, unless the Congress by their Adjournment prevent its Return, in which Case it shall not be a Law.

Every Order, Resolution, or Vote to which the Concurrence of the Senate and House of Representatives may be necessary (except on a question of Adjournment) shall be presented to the President of the United States; and before the Same shall take Effect, shall be approved by him, or being disapproved by him, shall be repassed by two thirds of the Senate and House of Representatives, according to the Rules and Limitations prescribed in the Case of a Bill.

Section 8.
The Congress shall have Power To lay and collect Taxes, Duties, Imposts and Excises, to pay the Debts and provide for the common Defence and general Welfare of the United States; but all Duties, Imposts and Excises shall be uniform throughout the United States;

To borrow money on the credit of the United States;

To regulate Commerce with foreign Nations, and among the several States, and with the Indian Tribes;

To establish an uniform rule of Naturalization, and uniform Laws on the subject of Bankruptcies throughout the United States;

To coin Money, regulate the Value thereof, and of foreign Coin, and fix the Standard of Weights and Measures;

To provide for the Punishment of counterfeiting the Securities and current Coin of the United States;

To establish Post Offices and post Roads;

To promote the Progress of Science and useful Arts, by securing for limited Times to Authors and Inventors the exclusive Right to their respective Writings and Discoveries;

To constitute Tribunals inferior to the Supreme Court;

To define and punish Piracies and Felonies committed on the high Seas, and Offenses against the Law of Nations;

To declare War, grant Letters of Marque and Reprisal, and make Rules concerning Captures on Land and Water;

To raise and support Armies, but no Appropriation of Money to that Use shall be for a longer Term than two Years;

To provide and maintain a Navy;

To make Rules for the Government and Regulation of the land and naval forces;

To provide for calling forth the Militia to execute the Laws of the Union, suppress Insurrections and repel Invasions;

To provide for organizing, arming, and disciplining the Militia, and for governing such Part of them as may be employed in the Service of the United States, reserving to the States respectively, the Appointment of the Officers, and the Authority of training the Militia according to the discipline prescribed by Congress;

To exercise exclusive Legislation in all Cases whatsoever, over such District (not exceeding ten Miles square) as may, by Cession of particular States, and the acceptance of Congress, become the Seat of the Government of the United States, and to exercise like Authority over all Places purchased by the Consent of the Legislature of the State in which the Same shall be, for the Erection of Forts, Magazines, Arsenals, Dock-yards, and other needful Buildings;—And

To make all Laws which shall be necessary and proper for carrying into Execution the foregoing Powers, and all other Powers vested by this Constitution in the Government of the United States, or in any Department or Officer thereof.

Section 9.

The Migration or Importation of such Persons as any of the States now existing shall think proper to admit, shall not be prohibited by the Congress prior to the Year one thousand eight hundred and eight, but a tax or duty may be imposed on such Importation, not exceeding ten dollars for each Person.

The privilege of the Writ of Habeas Corpus shall not be suspended, unless when in Cases of Rebellion or Invasion the public Safety may require it.

No bill of Attainder or ex post facto Law shall be passed.

No capitation, or other direct, Tax shall be laid unless in Proportion to the Census or Enumeration herein before directed to be taken.

No Tax or Duty shall be laid on Articles exported from any State.

No Preference shall be given by any Regulation of Commerce or Revenue to the Ports of one State over those of another: nor shall Vessels bound to, or from, one State, be obliged to enter, clear, or pay Duties in another.

No Money shall be drawn from the Treasury, but in Consequence of Appropriations made by Law; and a regular Statement and Account of the Receipts and Expenditures of all public Money shall be published from time to time.

No Title of Nobility shall be granted by the United States: And no Person holding any Office of Profit or Trust under them, shall, without the Consent of the Congress, accept of any present, Emolument, Office, or Title, of any kind whatever, from any King, Prince, or foreign State.

Section 10.

No State shall enter into any Treaty, Alliance, or Confederation; grant Letters of Marque and Reprisal; coin Money; emit Bills of Credit; make any Thing but gold and silver Coin a Tender in Payment of Debts; pass any Bill of Attainder, ex post facto Law, or Law impairing the Obligation of Contracts, or grant any Title of Nobility.

No State shall, without the Consent of the Congress, lay any Imposts or Duties on Imports or Exports, except what may be absolutely necessary for executing its inspection Laws; and the net Produce of all Duties and Imposts, laid by any State on Imports or Exports, shall be for the use of the Treasury of the United States; and all such Laws shall be subject to the Revision and Control of the Congress.

No state shall, without the Consent of Congress, lay any duty of Tonnage, keep Troops, or Ships of War in time of Peace, enter into any Agreement or Compact with another State, or with a foreign Power, or engage in War, unless actually invaded, or in such imminent Danger as will not admit of delay.

Article II

Section 1.
The executive Power shall be vested in a President of the United States of America. He shall hold his Office during the Term of four years, and, together with the Vice President, chosen for the same Term, be elected, as follows:

Each State shall appoint, in such Manner as the Legislature thereof may direct, a Number of Electors, equal to the whole Number of Senators and Representatives to which the State may be entitled in the Congress: but no Senator or Representative, or Person holding an Office of Trust or Profit under the United States, shall be appointed an Elector.

[The Electors shall meet in their respective States, and vote by Ballot for two persons, of whom one at least shall not be an Inhabitant of the same State with themselves. And they shall make a List of all the Persons voted for, and of the Number of Votes for each; which List they shall sign and certify, and transmit sealed to the Seat of the Government of the United States, directed to the President of the Senate. The President of the Senate shall, in the Presence of the Senate and House of Representatives, open all the Certificates, and the Votes shall then be counted. The Person having the greatest Number of Votes shall be the President, if such Number be a Majority of the whole Number of Electors appointed; and if there be more than one who have such Majority, and have an equal Number of Votes, then the House of Representatives shall immediately chuse by Ballot one of them for President; and if no Person have a Majority, then from the five highest on the List the said House shall in like Manner chuse the President. But in chusing the President, the Votes shall be taken by States, the Representation from each State having one Vote; a quorum for this Purpose shall consist of a Member or Members from two-thirds of the States, and a Majority of all the States shall be necessary to a Choice. In every Case, after the Choice of the President, the Person having the greatest Number of Votes of the Electors shall be the Vice President. But if there should remain two or more who have equal votes, the Senate shall chuse from them by Ballot the Vice President.][4]

[4]Revised by the Twelfth Amendment.

The Congress may determine the Time of chusing the Electors, and the Day on which they shall give their Votes; which Day shall be the same throughout the United States.

No person except a natural-born Citizen, or a Citizen of the United States, at the time of the Adoption of this Constitution, shall be eligible to the Office of President; neither shall any Person be eligible to that Office who shall not have attained to the Age of thirty-five years, and been fourteen Years a Resident within the United States.

In Case of the Removal of the President from Office, or of his Death, Resignation, or Inability to discharge the Powers and Duties of the said Office, the same shall devolve on the Vice President, and the Congress may by Law provide for the Case of Removal, Death, Resignation, or Inability, both of the President and Vice President, declaring what Officer shall then act as President, and such Officer shall act accordingly, until the disability be removed, or a President shall be elected.

The President shall, at stated Times, receive for his Services a Compensation, which shall neither be increased nor diminished during the Period for which he shall have been elected, and he shall not receive within that Period any other Emolument from the United States, or any of them.

Before he enter on the execution of his Office, he shall take the following Oath or Affirmation:—"I do solemnly swear (or affirm) that I will faithfully execute the Office of President of the United States, and will, to the best of my Ability, preserve, protect, and defend the Constitution of the United States."

Section 2.
The President shall be Commander in Chief of the Army and Navy of the United States, and of the Militia of the several States, when called into the actual Service of the United States; he may require the Opinion, in writing, of the principal Officer in each of the executive Departments, upon any subject relating to the Duties of their respective Offices, and he shall have Power to Grant Reprieves and Pardons for Offenses against the United States, except in Cases of Impeachment.

He shall have Power, by and with the Advice and Consent of the Senate, to make Treaties, provided two-thirds of the Senators present concur; and he shall nominate, and by and with the Advice and Consent of the Senate, shall appoint Ambassadors, other public Ministers and Consuls, Judges of the supreme Court, and all other Officers of the United States, whose Appointments are not herein otherwise provided for, and which shall be established by Law: but the Congress may by Law vest the Appointment of such inferior Officers, as they think proper, in the President alone, in the Courts of Law, or in the Heads of Departments.

The President shall have Power to fill up all Vacancies that may happen during the Recess of the Senate, by granting Commissions which shall expire at the End of their next Session.

Section 3.
He shall from time to time give to the Congress Information of the State of the Union, and recommend to their Consideration such Measures as he shall judge

necessary and expedient; he may, on extraordinary occasions, convene both Houses, or either of them, and in Case of Disagreement between them, with respect to the Time of Adjournment, he may adjourn them to such Time as he shall think proper; he shall receive Ambassadors and other public Ministers; he shall take care that the Laws be faithfully executed, and shall Commission all the Officers of the United States.

Section 4.
The President, Vice President and all civil Officers of the United States, shall be removed from Office on Impeachment for, and Conviction of, Treason, Bribery, or other high Crimes and Misdemeanors.

Article III

Section 1.
The judicial Power of the United States, shall be vested in one supreme Court, and in such inferior Courts as the Congress may from time to time ordain and establish. The Judges, both of the supreme and inferior Courts, shall hold their Offices during good Behaviour, and shall, at stated Times, receive for their Services, a Compensation, which shall not be diminished during their Continuance in Office.

Section 2.
The judicial Power shall extend to all Cases, in Law and Equity, arising under this Constitution, the Laws of the United States, and Treaties made, or which shall be made, under their Authority;—to all Cases affecting ambassadors, other public ministers and consuls;—to all cases of admiralty and maritime Jurisdiction;—to Controversies to which the United States shall be a Party;—to Controversies between two or more States;—between a State and Citizens of another State;[5]—between Citizens of different States—between Citizens of the same State claiming Lands under Grants of different States, and between a State, or the Citizens thereof, and foreign States, Citizens, or Subjects.

In all Cases affecting Ambassadors, other public Ministers and Consuls, and those in which a State shall be Party, the supreme Court shall have original Jurisdiction. In all the other Cases before mentioned, the supreme Court shall have appellate Jurisdiction, both as to Law and Fact, with such Exceptions, and under such Regulations as the Congress shall make.

The trial of all Crimes, except in Cases of Impeachment, shall be by Jury; and such Trial shall be held in the State where the said Crimes shall have been committed; but when not committed within any State, the Trial shall be at such Place or Places as the Congress may by Law have directed.

[5]Qualified by the Eleventh Amendment.

Section 3.

Treason against the United States, shall consist only in levying War against them, or in adhering to their Enemies, giving them Aid and Comfort. No Person shall be convicted of Treason unless on the Testimony of two Witnesses to the same overt Act, or on Confession in open Court.

The Congress shall have power to declare the Punishment of Treason, but no Attainder of Treason shall work Corruption of Blood, or Forfeiture except during the Life of the Person attained.

Article IV

Section 1.

Full Faith and Credit shall be given in each State to the public Acts, Records, and judicial Proceedings of every other State. And the Congress may by general Laws prescribe the Manner in which such Acts, Records and Proceedings shall be proved, and the Effect thereof.

Section 2.

The Citizens of each State shall be entitled to all Privileges and Immunities of Citizens in the several States.

A Person charged in any State with Treason, Felony, or other Crime, who shall flee from Justice, and be found in another State, shall on demand of the executive Authority of the State from which he fled, be delivered up, to be removed to the State having Jurisdiction of the crime.

No Person held to Service or Labour in one State, under the Laws thereof, escaping into another, shall, in Consequence of any Law or Regulation therein, be discharged from such Service or Labour, but shall be delivered up on Claim of the Party to whom such Service or Labour may be due.

Section 3.

New States may be admitted by the Congress into this Union; but no new State shall be formed or erected within the Jurisdiction of any other State; nor any State be formed by the Junction of two or more States, or parts of States, with-out the Consent of the Legislatures of the States concerned as well as of the Congress.

The Congress shall have Power to dispose of and make all needful Rules and Regulations respecting the Territory or other Property belonging to the United States; and nothing in this Constitution shall be so construed as to Prejudice any Claims of the United States, or of any particular State.

Section 4.

The United States shall guarantee to every State in this Union a Republican Form of Government, and shall protect each of them against Invasion; and on Application of the Legislature, or of the Executive (when the Legislature cannot be convened) against domestic Violence.

Article V

The Congress, whenever two-thirds of both Houses shall deem it necessary, shall propose Amendments to this Constitution, or, on the Application of the Legislatures of two-thirds of the several States, shall call a Convention for proposing Amendments, which, in either Case, shall be valid to all Intents and Purposes, as part of this Constitution, when ratified by the Legislatures of three-fourths of the several States, or by Conventions in three-fourths thereof, as the one or the other Mode of Ratification may be proposed by the Congress; Provided that no Amendment which may be made prior to the Year One thousand eight hundred and eight shall in any Manner affect the first and fourth Clauses in the Ninth Section of the first Article; and that no State, without its Consent, shall be deprived of its equal Suffrage in the Senate.

Article VI

All Debts contracted and Engagements entered into, before the Adoption of this Constitution, shall be as valid against the United States under this Constitution, as under the Confederation.

This Constitution, and the Laws of the United States which shall be made in Pursuance thereof; and all Treaties made, or which shall be made, under the Authority of the United States, shall be the supreme Law of the Land; and the Judges in every State shall be bound thereby, any Thing in the Constitution or Laws of any State to the Contrary notwithstanding.

The Senators and Representatives before mentioned, and the Members of the several State Legislatures, and all executive and judicial Officers, both of the United States and of the several States, shall be bound by Oath or Affirmation to support this Constitution; but no religious Tests shall ever be required as a qualification to any Office or public Trust under the United States.

Article VII

The Ratification of the Conventions of nine States shall be sufficient for the Establishment of this Constitution between the States so ratifying the same.

Done in Convention by the Unanimous Consent of the States present the Seventeenth Day of September in the Year of our Lord one thousand seven hundred and Eighty seven, and of the Independence of the United States of America the Twelfth. In Witness whereof We have hereunto subscribed our Names.[6]

George Washington
President and deputy from Virginia

New Hampshire
John Langdon
Nicholas Gilman

Massachusetts
Nathaniel Gorham
Rufus King

Pennsylvania
Benjamin Franklin
Thomas Mifflin
Robert Morris
George Clymer
Thomas FitzSimons
Jared Ingersoll
James Wilson
Gouverneur Morris

Virginia
John Blair
James Madison, Jr.

North Carolina
William Blount
Richard Dobbs Spaight
Hugh Williamson

Connecticut
William Samuel Johnson
Roger Sherman

New York
Alexander Hamilton

Delaware
George Read
Gunning Bedford, Jr.
John Dickinson
Richard Bassett
Jacob Broom

South Carolina
John Rutledge
Charles Cotesworth
Pinckney
Charles Pinckney
Pierce Butler

New Jersey
William Livingston
David Brearley
William Paterson
Jonathan Dayton

Maryland
James McHenry
Daniel of St. Thomas
Jenifer
Daniel Carroll

Georgia
William Few
Abraham Baldwin

Articles in Addition to, and Amendment of, the Constitution of the United States of America, Proposed by Congress, and Ratified by the Legislatures of the Several States, Pursuant to the Fifth Article of the Original Constitution.[7]

Amendment I

Congress shall make no law respecting an establishment of religion, or prohibiting the free exercise thereof; or abridging the freedom of speech, or of the press; or the right of the people peaceably to assemble, and to petition the Government for a redress of grievances.

---

[6]These are the full names of the signers, which in some cases are not the signatures on the document.
[7]This heading appears only in the joint resolution submitting the first ten amendments.

Amendment II

A well regulated Militia, being necessary to the security of a free State, the right of the people to keep and bear Arms shall not be infringed.

Amendment III

No Soldier shall, in time of peace, be quartered in any house, without the consent of the Owner, nor in time of war, but in a manner to be prescribed by law.

Amendment IV

The right of the people to be secure in their persons, houses, papers, and effects, against unreasonable searches and seizures, shall not be violated, and no Warrants shall issue, but upon probable cause, supported by Oath or affirmation, and particularly describing the place to be searched, and the persons or things to be seized.

Amendment V

No person shall be held to answer for a capital or otherwise infamous crime, unless on a presentment or indictment of a Grand Jury, except in cases arising in the land or naval forces, or in the Militia, when in actual service in time of War or public danger; nor shall any person be subject for the same offence to be twice put in jeopardy of life or limb; nor shall be compelled in any criminal case to be a witness against himself, nor be deprived of life, liberty, or property, without due process of law; nor shall private property be taken for public use, without just compensation.

Amendment VI

In all criminal prosecutions, the accused shall enjoy the right to a speedy and public trial, by an impartial jury of the State and district wherein the crime shall have been committed, which district shall have been previously ascertained by law, and to be informed of the nature and cause of the accusation; to be confronted with the witnesses against him; to have compulsory process for obtaining witnesses in his favour, and to have the Assistance of Counsel for his defense.

Amendment VII

In suits at common law, where the value in controversy shall exceed twenty dollars, the right of trial by jury shall be preserved, and no fact tried by a jury, shall be otherwise reexamined in any Court of the United States, than according to the rules of the common law.

Amendment VIII

Excessive bail shall not be required, nor excessive fines imposed, nor cruel and unusual punishments inflicted.

Amendment IX

The enumeration of the Constitution, of certain rights, shall not be construed to deny or disparage others retained by the people.

Amendment X

The powers not delegated to the United States by the Constitution, nor prohibited by it to the States, are reserved to the States respectively, or to the people.
[Amendments I–X, in force 1791.]

Amendment XI[8]

The Judicial power of the United States shall not be construed to extend to any suit in law or equity, commenced or prosecuted against one of the United States by Citizens of another State, or by Citizens or Subjects of any Foreign State.

Amendment XII[9]

The Electors shall meet in their respective States and vote by ballot for President and Vice-President, one of whom, at least, shall not be an inhabitant of the same State with themselves; they shall name in their ballots the person voted for as President, and in distinct ballots the person voted for as Vice-President, and they shall make distinct lists of all persons voted for as President, and of all persons voted for as Vice-President, and of the number of votes for each, which lists they shall sign and certify, and transmit sealed to the seat of the government of the United States, directed to the President of the Senate;—The President of the Senate shall, in the presence of the Senate and House of Representatives, open all the certificates and the votes shall then be counted;—The person having the greatest num-

[8]Adopted in 1798.
[9]Adopted in 1804.

ber of votes for President, shall be the President, if such number be a majority of the whole number of Electors appointed; and if no person have such majority, then from the persons having the highest numbers not exceeding three on the list of those voted for as President, the House of Representatives shall choose immediately, by ballot, the President. But in choosing the President, the votes shall be taken by states, the representation from each state having one vote; a quorum for this purpose shall consist of a member or members from two-thirds of the states, and a majority of all the states shall be necessary to a choice. And if the House of Representatives shall not choose a President whenever the right of choice shall devolve upon them, before the fourth day of March next following, then the Vice-President shall act as President, as in the case of the death or other constitutional disability of the President.—The person having the greatest number of votes as Vice-President, shall be the Vice-President, if such number be a majority of the whole number of Electors appointed, and if no person have a majority, then from the two highest numbers on the list, the Senate shall choose the Vice-President; a quorum for the purpose shall consist of two-thirds of the whole number of Senators, and a majority of the whole number shall be necessary to a choice. But no person constitutionally ineligible to the office of President shall be eligible to that of Vice-President of the United States.

Amendment XIII[10]

Section 1.
Neither slavery nor involuntary servitude, except as a punishment for crime whereof the party shall have been duly convicted, shall exist within the United States, or any place subject to their jurisdiction.

Section 2.
Congress shall have power to enforce this article by appropriate legislation.

Amendment XIV[11]

Section 1.
All persons born or naturalized in the United States, and subject to the jurisdiction thereof, are citizens of the United States and of the State wherein they reside. No State shall make or enforce any law which shall abridge the privileges or immunities of citizens of the United States; nor shall any State deprive any person of life, liberty, or property, without due process of law; nor deny to any person within its jurisdiction the equal protection of the laws.

[10]Adopted in 1865.
[11]Adopted in 1868.

Section 2.

Representatives shall be apportioned among the several States according to their respective numbers, counting the whole number of persons in each State, excluding Indians not taxed. But when the right to vote at any election for the choice of electors for President and Vice-President of the United States, Representatives in Congress, the Executive and Judicial officers of a State, or the members of the Legislature thereof, is denied to any of the male inhabitants of such State, being twenty-one years of age, and citizens of the United States, or in any way abridged, except for participation in rebellion, or other crime, the basis of representation therein shall be reduced in the proportion which the number of such male citizens shall bear to the whole number of male citizens twenty-one years of age in such State.

Section 3.

No person shall be a Senator or Representative in Congress, or elector of President and Vice-President, or hold any office, civil or military, under the United States, or under any State, who, having previously taken an oath, as a member of Congress, or as an officer of the United States, or as a member of any State legislature, or as an executive or judicial officer of any State, to support the Constitution of the United States, shall have engaged in insurrection or rebellion against the same, or given aid or comfort to the enemies thereof. But Congress may by a vote of two-thirds of each House, remove such disability.

Section 4.

The validity of the public debt of the United States, authorized by law, including debts incurred for payment of pensions and bounties for services in suppressing insurrection or rebellion, shall not be questioned. But neither the United States nor any State shall assume or pay any debts or obligation incurred in aid of insurrection or rebellion against the United States, or any claim for the loss or emancipation of any slave; but all such debts, obligations, and claims shall be held illegal and void.

Section 5.

The Congress shall have the power to enforce, by appropriate legislation, the provisions of this article.

Amendment XV[12]

Section 1.

The right of citizens of the United States to vote shall not be denied or abridged by the United States or by any State on account of race, color, or previous condition of servitude—

[12]Adopted in 1870.

Section 2.
The Congress shall have power to enforce this article by appropriate legislation.

Amendment XVI[13]

The Congress shall have power to lay and collect taxes on incomes, from whatever source derived, without apportionment among the several States, and without regard to any census or enumeration.

Amendment XVII[14]

The Senate of the United States shall be composed of two Senators from each State, elected by the people thereof, for six years; and each Senator shall have one vote. The electors in each State shall have the qualifications requisite for electors of the most numerous branch of the State legislatures.

When vacancies happen in the representation of any State in the Senate, the executive authority of such State shall issue writs of election to fill such vacancies: *Provided,* That the legislature of any State may empower the executive thereof to make temporary appointments until the people fill the vacancies by election as the legislature may direct.

This amendment shall not be so construed as to affect the election or term of any Senator chosen before it becomes valid as part of the Constitution.

Amendment XVIII[15]

Section 1.
After one year from the ratification of this article the manufacture, sale, or transportation of intoxicating liquors within, the importation thereof into, or the exportation thereof from the United States and all territory subject to the jurisdiction thereof for beverage purposes is hereby prohibited.

Section 2.
The Congress and the several States shall have concurrent power to enforce this article by appropriate legislation.

Section 3.
This article shall be inoperative unless it shall have been ratified as an amendment to the Constitution by the legislatures of the several States, as provided in the Con-

---

[13]Adopted in 1913.
[14]Adopted in 1913.
[15]Adopted in 1918.

stitution, within seven years from the date of the submission hereof to the States by the Congress.

Amendment XIX[16]

The right of citizens of the United States to vote shall not be denied or abridged by the United States or by any State on account of sex.

Congress shall have power to enforce this article by appropriate legislation.

Amendment XX[17]

Section 1.
The terms of the President and Vice-President shall end at noon on the 20th day of January, and the terms of Senators and Representatives at noon on the 3d day of January, of the years in which such terms would have ended if this article had not been ratified; and the terms of their successors shall then begin.

Section 2.
The Congress shall assemble at least once in every year, and such meeting shall begin at noon on the 3d day of January, unless they shall by law appoint a different day.

Section 3.
If, at the time fixed for the beginning of the term of the President, the President elect shall have died, the Vice-President elect shall become President. If a President shall not have been chosen before the time fixed for the beginning of his term or if the President elect shall have failed to qualify, then the Vice-President elect shall act as President until a President shall have qualified; and the Congress may by law provide for the case wherein neither a President elect nor a Vice-President elect shall have qualified, declaring who shall then act as President, or the manner in which one who is to act shall be selected, and such person shall act accordingly until a President or Vice-President shall have qualified.

Section 4.
The Congress may by law provide for the case of the death of any of the persons from whom the House of Representatives may choose a President whenever the right of choice shall have devolved upon them, and for the case of the death of any of the persons from whom the Senate may choose a Vice-President whenever the right of choice shall have devolved upon them.

[16]Adopted in 1920.
[17]Adopted in 1933.

Section 5.
Sections 1 and 2 shall take effect on the 15th day of October following the ratification of this article.

Section 6.
This article shall be inoperative unless it shall have been ratified as an amendment to the Constitution by the legislatures of three-fourths of the several States within seven years from the date of its submission.

Amendment XXI[18]

Section 1.
The eighteenth article of amendment to the Constitution of the United States is hereby repealed.

Section 2.
The transportation or importation into any State, Territory, or possession of the United States for delivery or use therein of intoxicating liquors, in violation of the laws thereof, is hereby prohibited.

Section 3.
This article shall be inoperative unless it shall have been ratified as an amendment to the Constitution by conventions in the several States, as provided in the Constitution, within seven years from the date of the submission hereof to the States by the Congress.

Amendment XXII[19]

No person shall be elected to the office of the President more than twice, and no person who has held the office of President, or acted as President, for more than two years of a term to which some other person was elected President shall be elected to the office of the President more than once.

But this Article shall not apply to any person holding the office of President when this Article was proposed by the Congress, and shall not prevent any person who may be holding the office of President, or acting as President, during the term within which this Article becomes operative from holding the office of President or acting as President during the remainder of such term.

This article shall be inoperative unless it shall have been ratified as an amendment to the Constitution by the legislatures of three-fourths of the several states within seven years from the date of its submission to the states by the Congress.

[18]Adopted in 1933.
[19]Adopted in 1961.

Amendment XXIII[20]

Section 1.
The District constituting the seat of Government of the United States shall appoint in such manner as the Congress may direct:

A number of electors of President and Vice-President equal to the whole number of Senators and Representatives in Congress to which the District would be entitled if it were a State, but in no event more than the least populous State; they shall be in addition to those appointed by the States, but they shall be considered, for the purposes of the election of President and Vice-President, to be electors appointed by a State; and they shall meet in the District and perform such duties as provided by the twelfth article of amendment.

Section 2.
The Congress shall have power to enforce this article by appropriate legislation.

Amendment XXIV[21]

Section 1.
The right of citizens of the United States to vote in any primary or other election for President or Vice President, for electors for President or Vice President, or for Senator or Representative in Congress, shall not be denied or abridged by the United States or any state by reason of failure to pay any poll tax or other tax.

Section 2.
The Congress shall have the power to enforce this article by appropriate legislation.

Amendment XXV[22]

Section 1.
In case of the removal of the President from office or of his death or resignation, the Vice President shall become President.

Section 2.
Whenever there is a vacancy in the office of the Vice President, the President shall nominate a Vice President who shall take office upon confirmation by a majority vote of both Houses of Congress.

Section 3.
Whenever the President transmits to the President Pro Tempore of the Senate and the Speaker of the House of Representatives his written declaration that he is un-

[20]Adopted in 1961.
[21]Adopted in 1964.
[22]Adopted in 1967.

able to discharge the powers and duties of his office, and until he transmits to them a written declaration to the contrary, such powers and duties shall be discharged by the Vice President as Acting President.

Section 4.
Whenever the Vice President and a majority of either the principal officers of the executive departments or of such other body as Congress may by law provide, transmit to the President Pro Tempore of the Senate and the Speaker of the House of Representatives their written declaration that the President is unable to discharge the powers and duties of his office, the Vice President shall immediately assume the powers and duties of the office as Acting President.

Thereafter, when the President transmits to the President Pro Tempore of the Senate and the Speaker of the House of Representatives his written declaration that no inability exists, he shall resume the powers and duties of his office unless the Vice President and a majority of either the principal officers of the executive departments or of such other body as Congress may by law provide, transmit within four days to the President Pro Tempore of the Senate and the Speaker of the House of Representatives their written declaration that the President is unable to discharge the powers and duties of his office. Thereupon Congress shall decide the issue, assembling within forty-eight hours for that purpose if not in session. If the Congress, within twenty-one days after receipt of the latter written declaration, or, if Congress is not in session, within twenty-one days after Congress is required to assemble, determines by two-thirds vote of both Houses that the President is unable to discharge the powers and duties of his office, the Vice President shall continue to discharge the same as Acting President; otherwise, the President shall resume the powers and duties of his office.

Amendment XXVI[23]

Section 1.
The right of citizens of the United States, who are eighteen years of age or older, to vote shall not be denied or abridged by the United States or by any State on account of age.

Section 2.
The Congress shall have power to enforce this article by appropriate legislation.

Amendment XXVII[24]

No law varying the compensation for the services of Senators and Representatives shall take effect until an election of Representatives shall have intervened.

[23]Adopted in 1971.
[24]Adopted in 1992.

Glossary

accountability The ability of the public to hold government officials responsible for their actions.

affirmative action A term that refers to programs designed to ensure that women, minorities, and other traditionally disadvantaged groups have full and equal opportunities in employment, education, and other areas of life.

agency point of view The tendency of bureaucrats to place the interests of their agency ahead of other interests and ahead of the priorities sought by the president or Congress.

agenda setting The power of the media through news coverage to focus the public's attention and concern on particular events, problems, issues, personalities, and so forth.

alienation A feeling of personal powerlessness that includes the notion that government does not care about the opinions of people like oneself.

apathy A feeling of personal non-interest or unconcern with politics.

appellate jurisdiction The authority of a given court to review cases that have already been tried in lower courts and are appealed to it by the losing party; such a court is called an appeals court or appellate court. (See also **original jurisdiction.**)

authority The recognized right of an official or institution to exercise power. (See also **power.**)

bill A proposed law (legislative act) within Congress or another legislature. (See also **law.**)

Bill of Rights The first ten amendments to the Constitution, which set forth basic protections for individual rights to free expression, fair trial, and property.

block grants Federal grants-in-aid that permit state and local officials to decide how the money will be spent within a general area, such as education or health. (See also **categorical grants.**)

bureaucracy A system of organization and control based on the principles of hierarchical authority, job specialization, and formalized rules. (See also **formalized rules; hierarchical authority; job specialization.**)

cabinet A group consisting of the heads of the (cabinet) executive departments, who are appointed by the president, subject to confirmation by the Senate. The cabinet was once the main advi-

A-27

sory body to the president but no longer plays this role. (See also **cabinet departments.**)

cabinet (executive) departments The major administrative organizations within the federal executive bureaucracy, each of which is headed by a secretary (cabinet officer) and has responsibility for a major function of the federal government, such as defense, agriculture, or justice. (See also **cabinet; independent agencies.**)

candidate-centered politics Election campaigns and other political processes in which candidates, not political parties, have most of the initiative and influence. (See also **party-centered politics.**)

capitalism An economic system based on the idea that government should interfere with economic transactions as little as possible. Free enterprise and self-reliance are the collective and individual principles that underpin capitalism.

categorical grants Federal grants-in-aid to states and localities that can be used only for designated projects. (See also **block grants.**)

checks and balances The elaborate system of divided spheres of authority provided by the U.S. Constitution as a means of controlling the power of government. The separation of powers among the branches of the national government, federalism, and the different methods of selecting national officers are all part of this system.

citizens' (noneconomic) groups Organized interests formed by individuals drawn together by opportunities to promote a cause in which they believe but which does not provide them significant individual economic benefits. (See also **economic groups; interest group.**)

civic duty The belief of an individual that civic and political participation is a responsibility of citizenship.

civil liberties The fundamental individual rights of a free society, such as freedom of speech and the right to a jury trial, which in the United States are protected by the Bill of Rights.

civil (equal) rights The right of every person to equal protection under the laws and equal access to society's opportunities and public facilities.

civil service system See **merit system.**

clear-and-present-danger test A test devised by the Supreme Court in 1919 in order to define the limits of free speech in the context of national security. According to the test, government cannot abridge political expression unless it presents a clear and present danger to the nation's security.

clientele groups Special-interest groups that benefit directly from the activities of a particular bureaucratic agency and are therefore strong advocates of the agency.

cloture A parliamentary maneuver which, if a three-fifths majority votes for it, limits Senate debate to 100 hours and has the effect of defeating a filibuster. (See also **filibuster.**)

cold war The lengthy period after World War II when the United States and the USSR were not engaged in actual combat (a "hot war") but were nonetheless locked in a state of deep-seated hostility.

collective (public) goods Benefits that are offered by groups (usually citizens' groups) as an incentive for membership but that are nondivisible (e.g., a clean environment) and therefore are available to nonmembers as well as members of the particular group. (See also **free-rider problem; private goods.**)

commerce clause The clause of the Constitution (Article I, section 8) that empowers the federal government to regulate commerce among the states and with other nations.

common-carrier role The media's function as an open channel through which political leaders can communicate with the public. (See also **public representative role; signaler role; watchdog role.**)

comparable worth The idea that women should get pay equal to men for work that is of similar difficulty and responsibility and that requires similar levels of education and training.

compliance The issue of whether a court's decisions will be respected and obeyed.

concurring opinion A separate opinion written by a Supreme Court justice who votes with the majority in the decision on a case but who disagrees with their reasoning. (See also **dissenting opinion; majority opinion; plurality opinion.**)

confederacy A governmental system in which sovereignty is vested entirely in subnational (state) governments. (See also **federalism; unitary system.**)

conference committee A temporary committee that is formed to bargain over the differences in the House and Senate versions of a bill. The committee's members are usually appointed from the House and Senate standing committees that originally worked on the bill.

conservatives Those who emphasize the marketplace as the means of distributing economic benefits but look to government to uphold traditional social values. (See also **liberals; libertarians; populists.**)

constituency The individuals who live within the geographical area represented by an elected official. More narrowly, the body of citizens eligible to vote for a particular representative.

constitutional democracy A government that is democratic in its provisions for majority influence through elections and constitutional in its provisions for minority rights and rule by law.

constitutionalism The idea that there are definable limits on the rightful power of a government over its citizens.

containment A doctrine developed after World War II, based on the assumptions that the Soviet Union was an aggressor nation and that only a determined United States could block Soviet territorial ambitions.

cooperative federalism The situation in which the national, state, and local levels work together to solve problems.

de facto **discrimination** Discrimination on the basis of race, sex, religion, ethnicity, and the like that results from social, economic, and cultural biases and conditions. (See also *de jure* **discrimination.**)

de jure **discrimination** Discrimination on the basis of race, sex, religion, ethnicity, and the like that results from a law. (See also *de facto* **discrimination.**)

dealignment A situation in which voters' partisan loyalties have been substantially and permanently weakened. (See also **party identification; realignment.**)

decision A vote of the Supreme Court in a particular case that indicates which party the justices side with and by how large a margin.

delegates The idea of elected representatives as obligated to carry out the expressed wishes of the electorate. (See also **trustees.**)

demand-side economics A form of fiscal policy that emphasizes "demand" (consumer spending). Government can use increased spending or tax cuts to place more money in consumers' hands and thereby increase demand. (See also **fiscal policy; supply-side economics.**)

democracy A form of government in which the people govern, either directly or through elected representatives.

demographic representativeness The idea that the bureaucracy will be more responsive to the public if its employees at all levels are demographically representative of the population as a whole.

denials of power A constitutional means of limiting governmental action by listing those powers that government is expressly prohibited from using.

deregulation The rescinding of regulations then in force for the purpose of improving efficiency.

détente A French word meaning "a relaxing" and used to refer to an era of improved relations between the United States and the Soviet Union that began in the early 1970s.

deterrence The idea that nuclear war can be discouraged if each side in a conflict has the capacity to destroy the other with nuclear weapons.

devolution The passing down of authority from the national government to states and localities.

direct primary See **primary election.**

dissenting opinion The opinion of a justice in a Supreme Court case that explains the reasons for disagreeing with the majority position. (See also **concurring opinion; majority opinion; plurality opinion.**)

diversity The principle that individual differences should be respected, are a legitimate basis of self-interest, and are a source of strength for the American nation.

dual federalism A doctrine based on the idea that a precise separation of national power and state power is both possible and desirable.

economic groups Interest groups that are organized primarily for economic reasons but which engage in political activity in order to seek favorable policies from government. (See also **citizens' groups; interest group.**)

economy A system of production and consumption of goods and services, which are allocated through exchange among producers and consumers.

efficiency The relationship of inputs (the labor and material that go into making a product or service) to outputs (the product or service itself). The greater the output for a given input, the more efficient the production process.

elastic clause See **"necessary and proper" clause.**

elitism The view that the United States is essentially run by a tiny elite (composed of wealthy or well-connected individuals) who control public policy through both direct and indirect means.

entitlement programs Individual-benefit programs, such as social security, that require government to provide a designated benefit to any person who meets the legally defined criteria for eligibility.

enumerated powers (expressed powers) The seventeen powers granted to the national government under Article I, section 8 of the Constitution. These powers include taxation and the regulation of commerce as well as the authority to provide for the national defense.

equal-protection clause A clause of the Fourteenth Amendment that forbids any state to deny equal protection of the laws to any individual within its jurisdiction.

equal rights See **civil rights.**

equality The principle that all individuals have moral worth and are entitled to fair treatment under the law.

equality of opportunity The idea that all individuals should be given an equal chance to succeed on their own.

equality of result The objective of policies intended to reduce or eliminate the effects of discrimination so that members of traditionally disadvantaged groups will have the same benefits of society as do members of advantaged groups.

equity (in relation to economic policy) The situation in which the outcome of an economic transaction is fair to each party. An outcome can usually be considered fair if each party enters into a transaction freely and is not knowingly at a disadvantage.

establishment clause The First Amendment provision that government may not favor one religion over another, or religion over no religion, and that prohibits Congress from passing laws respecting the establishment of religion.

exclusionary rule The legal principle that government is prohibited from using in trials evidence that was obtained by unconstitutional means (for example, illegal search and seizure).

executive departments See **cabinet departments.**

executive leadership system An approach to managing the bureaucracy that is based on presidential leadership and presidential management tools, such as the president's annual budget proposal. (See also **merit system; patronage system.**)

expressed powers See **enumerated powers.**

externalities Burdens that society incurs when firms fail to pay the full cost of resources used in production. An example of an externality is the pollution that results when corporations dump industrial wastes into lakes and rivers.

facts (of a court case) The relevant circumstances of a legal dispute or offense as determined by a trial court. The facts of a case are crucial because they help to determine which law or laws are applicable in the case.

federalism A governmental system in which authority is divided between two sovereign levels of government: national and regional. (See also **confederacy; unitary system.**)

filibuster A procedural tactic in the U.S. Senate whereby a minority of legislators prevent a bill from coming to a vote by holding the floor and talking until the majority gives in and the bill is withdrawn from consideration. (See also **cloture.**)

fiscal federalism The expenditure of federal funds on programs run in part through state and local governments.

fiscal policy A tool of economic management by which government attempts to maintain a stable economy through its taxing and spending decisions. (See also **demand-side economics; monetary policy; supply-side economics.**)

formalized rules A basic principle of bureaucracy that refers to the standardized procedures and established regulations by which a bureaucracy conducts its operations. (See also **bureaucracy.**)

free-exercise clause A First Amendment provision that prohibits the government from interfering with the practice of religion or prohibiting the free exercise of religion.

free-rider problem The situation in which the incentives offered by a group to its members are also available to nonmembers. The incentive to join the group and to promote its cause is reduced because nonmembers (free riders) receive the benefits without having to pay any of the group's costs. (See also **collective goods.**)

free trade The view that all countries benefit to the degree that trade between them is not impeded by tariffs and other forms of protectionism. (See also **protectionism.**)

freedom of expression Americans' freedom to communicate their views, the foundation of which is the First Amendment rights of freedom of conscience, speech, press, assembly, and petition.

gender gap The tendency of women to vote more heavily Democratic than men do.

government The effort of people to find agreeable ways of living together.

government corporations Bodies, such as the U.S. Postal Service and Amtrak, that are similar to private corporations in that they charge for their services, but different in that they receive federal funding to help defray expenses. Their directors are appointed by the president with Senate approval.

grants of power The method of limiting the U.S. government by confining its scope of authority to those powers expressly granted in the Constitution.

grassroots lobbying A form of lobbying designed to persuade officials that a group's policy position has strong constituent support.

hierarchical authority A basic principle of bureaucracy that refers to the chain of command within an organization, whereby officials and units have control over those below them. (See also **bureaucracy**.)

honeymoon period The president's first months in office, a time when Congress, the press, and the public are more inclined than usual to support presidential initiatives.

ideology A consistent pattern of opinion on political issues that stems from a basic underlying belief or set of beliefs.

implied powers The federal government's constitutional authority (through the "necessary and proper" clause) to take action that is not expressly authorized by the Constitution but which supports actions that are so authorized. (See also **"necessary and proper" clause**.)

in-kind benefit A government benefit that is a cash equivalent, such as food stamps or rent vouchers. This form of benefit ensures that recipients will use public assistance in a specified way.

inalienable (natural) rights Those rights which persons theoretically possessed in the state of nature, prior to the formation of governments. These rights, including those of life, liberty, and property, are considered inherent and as such are inalienable. Since government is established by people, government has the responsibility to preserve these rights.

independent agencies Bureaucratic agencies that are similar to cabinet departments but usually have a narrower area of responsibility. Each such agency is headed by a presidential appointee who is not a cabinet member. An example is the National Aeronautics and Space Administration (NASA). (See also **cabinet departments.**)

individual goods See **private goods.**

individualism A philosophical belief that stresses the values of hard work and self-reliance and holds that the individual should be left to succeed or fail on his or her own.

inside lobbying Direct communication between organized interests and policymakers, which is based on the assumed value of close ("inside") contacts with policymakers.

insurgency A type of military conflict in which irregular soldiers rise up against an established regime.

interest group A set of individuals who are organized to promote a shared political interest. (See also **citizens' groups; economic groups.**)

interest-group liberalism The tendency of public officials to support the policy demands of self-interesed groups (as opposed to judging policy demands according to whether or not they serve a larger conception of "the public interest").

internationalism The view that the country should involve itself deeply in world affairs. (See also **isolationism.**)

interpretive style of reporting The style of reporting that aims to explain *why* something is taking place or has occurred.

iron triangle A small and informal but relatively stable group of well-positioned legislators, executives, and lobbyists who seek to promote policies beneficial to a particular interest. (See also **issue network.**)

isolationism The view that the country should deliberately avoid a large role in world affairs and, instead, concentrate on domestic concerns. (See also **internationalism.**)

issue network An informal network of public officials and lobbyists who have a common interest and expertise in a given area and who are brought together by a proposed policy in that area. (See also **iron triangle.**)

job specialization A basic principle of bureaucracy which holds that the responsibilities of each job position should be explicitly defined and that a precise division of labor within the organization should be maintained. (See also **bureaucracy.**)

judicial activism The doctrine that the courts should develop new legal principles when judges see a compelling need, even if this action places them in conflict with the policy decisions of elected officials. (See also **judicial restraint.**)

judicial conference A closed meeting of the justices of the U.S. Supreme Court to discuss the points of the cases before them; the justices are not supposed to discuss conference proceedings with outsiders.

judicial restraint The doctrine that the judiciary should be highly respectful of precedent and should defer to the judgment of legislatures. The doctrine claims that the job of judges is to work within the confines of laws set down by tradition and law-making majorities. (See also **judicial activism.**)

judicial review The power of courts to decide whether a governmental institution has acted within its constitutional powers and, if not, to declare its action void.

jurisdiction (of a court) A given court's authority to hear cases of a particular kind. Jurisdiction may be original or appellate.

jurisdiction (of a congressional committee) The policy area in which a particular congressional committee is authorized to act.

laissez-faire doctrine A classic economic philosophy which holds that owners of businesses should be allowed to make their own production and distribution decisions without government regulation or control.

law (as enacted by Congress) A legislative proposal, or bill, that is passed by both the House and Senate and is either signed or not vetoed by the president. (See also **bill.**)

lawmaking function The authority (of a legislature) to make the laws necessary to carry out the government's powers. (See also **oversight function; representation function.**)

laws (of a court case) The constitutional provisions, legislative statutes, or judicial precedents that apply to a court case.

legitimacy (of judical power) The issue of the proper limits of judicial authority in a political system based in part on the principle of majority rule.

liberals Those who favor activist government as an instrument of economic security and equitable redistribution of resources but reject the notion that government should favor a particular set of social values. (See also **conservatives; libertarians; populists.**)

libertarians Those who oppose government as an instrument of traditional values and of economic security. (See also **conservatives; liberals; populists.**)

liberty The principle that the people are the ultimate source of governing authority and that their general welfare is the only legitimate purpose of government.

limited government A government that is subject to strict limits on its lawful uses of powers and hence on its ability to deprive people of their liberty.

lobbying The process by which interest-group members or lobbyists attempt to influence public policy through contacts with public officials.

majoritarianism The idea that the majority prevails not only in elections but also in determining policy.

majority opinion A Supreme Court opinion that results when a majority of the justices are in agreement on the legal basis of the decision. (See also **concurring opinion; dissenting opinion; plurality opinion.**)

means test The requirement that applicants for public assistance must demonstrate they are poor in order to be eligible for the assistance. (See also **public assistance.**)

merit (civil service) system An approach to managing the bureaucracy whereby people are appointed to government positions on the basis of either competitive examinations or special qualifications, such as professional training. (See also **executive leadership system; patronage system.**)

military-industrial complex The three components (the military establishment, the industries that manufacture weapons, and the members of Congress from states and districts that depend heavily on the arms industry) that mutually benefit from a high level of defense spending.

momentum A strong showing by a candidate in early presidential nominating contests, which leads to a buildup of public support for the candidate.

monetary policy A tool of economic management, available to government, based on manipulation of the amount of money in circulation. (See also **fiscal policy.**)

multilateralism The situation in which nations act together in response to problems and crises.

multiparty system A system in which three or more political parties have the capacity to gain control of government separately or in coalition.

natural rights See **inalienable rights.**

"necessary and proper" clause (elastic clause) The authority granted Congress in Article I, section 8 of the Constitution "to make all laws which shall be necessary and proper" for the implementation of its enumerated powers. (See also **implied powers.**)

negative government The philosophical belief that government governs best by staying out of people's lives, thus giving individuals as much freedom as possible to determine their own pursuits. (See also **positive government.**)

neutral competence The administrative objective of a merit-based bureaucracy. Such a bureaucracy should be "competent" in the sense that its employees are hired and retained on the basis of their expertise and "neutral" in the sense that it operates by objective standards rather than partisan ones.

news The news media's version of reality, usually with an emphasis on timely, dramatic, and compelling events and developments.

news media See **press.**

nomination The designation of a particular individual to run as a political party's candidate (its "nominee") in the general election.

noneconomic groups See **citizens' groups.**

objective journalism A model of news reporting which is based on the communication of "facts" rather than opinions and which is "fair" in that it presents all sides of partisan debate. (See also **partisan press.**)

open party caucuses Meetings at which a party's candidates for nomination are voted upon and which are open to all of the party's rank-and-file voters who want to attend.

opinion (of a court) A court's written explanation of its decision which serves to inform others of the legal basis for the decision. Supreme Court opinions are expected to guide the decisions of other courts. (See also **concurring opinion; dissenting opinion; majority opinion; plurality opinion.**)

original jurisdiction The authority of a given court to be the first court to hear a case. (See also **appellate jurisdiction.**)

outside lobbying A form of lobbying in which an interest group seeks to use public pressure as a means of influencing officials.

oversight function A supervisory activity of Congress that centers on its constitutional responsibility to see that the executive carries out the laws faithfully and spends appropriations properly. (See also **lawmaking function; representation function.**)

partisan press Newspapers and other communication media that openly support a political party and whose news in significant part follows the party line. (See also **objective journalism.**)

party-centered politics Election campaigns and other political processes in which political parties, not individual candidates, hold most of the initiative and influence. (See also **candidate-centered politics.**)

party coalition The groups and interests that support a political party.

party competition A process in which conflict over society's goals is transformed by political parties into electoral competition in which the winner gains the power to govern.

party identification The personal sense of loyalty that an individual may feel toward a particular political party. (See also **dealignment; realignment.**)

party leaders Members of the House and Senate who are chosen by the Democratic or Republican caucus in each chamber to represent the party's interests in that chamber and who give some central direction to the chamber's deliberations.

party organizations The party organizational units at national, state, and local levels; their influence has decreased over time due to many factors. (See also **candidate-centered politics; party-centered politics; primary election.**)

patronage system An approach to managing the bureaucracy whereby people are appointed to important government positions as a reward for political services they have rendered and because of their partisan loyalty. (See also **executive leadership system; merit system; spoils system.**)

pluralism A theory of American politics which holds that society's interests are substantially represented through the activities of groups.

plurality opinion A court opinion that results when a majority of justices agree on a decision in a case but do not agree on the legal basis for the decision. In this instance, the legal position held by most of the justices on the winning side is called a plurality opinion. (See also **concurring opinion; dissenting opinion; majority opinion.**)

policy Generally, any broad course of governmental action; more narrowly, a specific government program or initiative.

policy implementation The primary function of the bureaucracy is policy implementation, which refers to the process of carrying out of the authoritative decisions of Congress, the president, and the courts.

political action committee (PAC) The organization through which an interest group raises and distributes funds for election purposes. By law, the funds must be raised through voluntary contributions.

political culture The characteristic and deep-seated beliefs of a particular people.

political movements See **social movements.**

political participation A sharing in activities designed to influence public policy and leadership, such as voting, joining political parties and interest groups, writing to elected officials, demonstrating for political causes, and giving money to political candidates.

political party An ongoing coalition of interests joined together to try to get their candidates for public office elected under a common label.

political socialization The learning process by which people acquire their political opinions, beliefs, and values.

political system The various components of American government constitute a political system. The parts are separate, but they connect with each other, affecting how each performs.

politics The process through which society makes its governing decisions.

population In a public opinion poll, the term *population* refers to the people (for example, the citizens of a nation) whose opinions are being estimated through interviews with a sample of these people.

populists Those who favor activist government as a means of promoting both economic security and traditional values. (See also **conservatives; liberals; libertarians.**)

pork barrel projects Laws whose tangible benefits are targeted at a particular legislator's constituency.

positive government The philosophical belief that government intervention is necessary in order to enhance personal liberty when individuals are buffeted by economic and social forces beyond their control. (See also **negative government**.)

poverty line As defined by the federal government, the poverty line is the annual cost of a thrifty food budget for an urban family of four, multiplied by three to allow also for the cost of housing, clothes, and other expenses. Families below the poverty line are considered poor and are eligible for certain forms of public assistance.

power The ability of persons or institutions to control policy. (See also **authority**.)

precedent A judicial decision in a given case that serves as a rule of thumb for settling subsequent cases of a similar nature; courts are generally expected to follow precedent.

presidential approval rating A measure of the degree to which the public approves or disapproves of the president's performance in office.

presidential commissions These organizations within the bureaucracy are headed by commissioners appointed by the president. An example of such a commission is the Commission on Civil Rights.

press (news media) Those print and broadcast organizations that are in the news-reporting business.

primary election (direct primary) A form of election in which voters choose a party's nominees for public office. In most primaries, eligibility to vote is limited to voters who are registered members of the party.

prior restraint Government prohibition of speech or publication before the fact, which is presumed by the courts to be unconstitutional unless the justification for it is overwhelming.

private (individual) goods Benefits that a group (most often an economic group) can grant directly and exclusively to the individual members of the group. (See also **collective goods**.)

probability sample A sample for a poll in which each individual in the population has a known probability of being selected randomly for inclusion in the sample. (See also **public opinion poll**.)

procedural due process The constitutional requirement that government must follow proper legal procedures before a person can be legitimately punished for an alleged offense.

proportional representation A form of representation in which seats in the legislature are allocated proportionally according to each political party's share of the popular vote. This system enables smaller parties to compete successfully for seats. (See also **single-member districts**.)

prospective voting A form of electoral judgment in which voters choose the candidate whose policy promises most closely match their own preferences. (See also **retrospective voting**.)

protectionism The view that the immediate interests of domestic producers should have a higher priority (through, for example, protective tariffs) than free trade between nations. (See also **free trade.**)

public assistance A term that refers to social welfare programs funded through general tax revenues and available only to the financially needy. Eligibility for such a program is established by a means test. (See also **means test; social insurance.**)

public goods See **collective goods.**

public opinion Those opinions held by ordinary citizens that they express openly.

public opinion poll A device for measuring public opinion whereby a relatively small number of individuals (the sample) are interviewed for the purpose of estimating the opinions of a whole community (the population). (See also **probability sample.**)

public representative role A role whereby the media attempt to act as the public's representatives. (See also **common-carrier role; signaler role; watchdog role.**)

purposive incentives Reasons for joining a citizens' group. Purposive incentives are opportunities to promote a cause in which an individual believes.

realignment An election or set of elections in which the electorate responds strongly to an extraordinarily powerful issue that has disrupted the established political order. A realignment has a lasting impact on public policy, popular support for the parties, and the composition of the party coalitions. (See also **dealignment; party identification.**)

reapportionment The process, after a new census of the population, of redistributing House seats so that the number of seats in each state more closely reflects the size of the population of each state.

reasonable-basis test A test applied by courts to laws that treat individuals unequally. Such a law may be deemed constitutional if its purpose is held to be "reasonably" related to a legitimate government interest.

redistricting The process of altering election districts in order to make them as nearly equal in population as possible. Redistricting takes place every ten years, after each population census.

registration The practice of placing citizens' names on an official list of voters before they are eligible to exercise their right to vote.

regulation A term that refers to government restrictions on the economic practices of private firms.

regulatory agencies Administrative units, such as the Federal Communications Commission and the Environmental Protection Agency, that have responsibility for the monitoring and regulation of ongoing economic activities.

representation function The responsibility of a legislature to represent various interests in society. (See also **lawmaking function; oversight function.**)

representative democracy A system in which the people participate in the decision-making process of government not directly but indirectly, through the election of officials to represent their interests.

republic Historically, the form of government in which representative officials met to decide on policy issues. These representatives were expected to serve the public interest but were not subject to the people's immediate control. Today, the term *republic* is used interchangeably with *democracy*.

reserved powers The powers granted to the states under the Tenth Amendment to the Constitution.

retrospective voting A form of electoral judgment in which voters support the incumbent candidate or party when their policies are judged to have succeeded and oppose the candidate or party when their policies are judged to have failed. (See also **prospective voting.**)

sample In a public opinion poll, the relatively small number of individuals who are interviewed for the purpose of estimating the opinions of an entire population. (See also **public opinion poll.**)

sampling error A measure of the accuracy of a public opinion poll. The sampling error is mainly a function of sample size and is usually expressed in percentage terms. (See also **probability sample.**)

selective incorporation The absorption of certain provisions of the Bill of Rights (for example, freedom of speech) into the Fourteenth Amendment so that these rights are protected from infringement by the states.

self-government The principle that the people are the ultimate source and proper beneficiary of governing authority; in practice, a government based on majority rule.

senatorial courtesy The tradition that a U.S. senator from the state in which a federal judicial vacancy has arisen should have a say in the president's nomination of the new judge if the senator is of the same party as the president.

seniority A member of Congress's consecutive years of service on a particular committee.

separated institutions sharing power The principle that, as a way to limit government, its powers should be divided among separate branches, each of which also shares in the power of the others as a means of checking and balancing them. The result is that no one branch can exercise power decisively without the support or acquiescence of the others.

service relationship The situation where party organizations assist candidates for office but have no power to require them to accept or campaign on the party's main policy positions.

service strategy Use of personal staff by members of Congress to perform services for constituents in order to gain their support in future elections.

signaler role The accepted responsibility of the media to alert the public to important developments as soon as possible after they happen or are discovered. (See also **common-carrier role; public representative role; watchdog role.**)

single-issue politics The situation in which separate groups are organized around nearly every conceivable policy issue and press their demands and influence to the utmost.

single-member districts A form of representation in which only a single candidate is elected to a particular office by the voters of that district. This system favors major parties because only candidates who can gain a large proportion of votes in an election district have a realistic chance of winning. (See also **proportional representation.**)

social insurance Social welfare programs based on the "insurance" concept, so that individuals must pay into the program in order to be eligible to receive funds from it. An example is social security for retired people. (See also **public assistance.**)

social (political) movements Active and sustained efforts to achieve social and political change by groups of people who feel that government has not been properly responsive to their concerns.

sovereignty The ultimate authority to govern within a certain geographical area.

split-ticket voting The pattern of voting in which the individual voter in a given election casts a ballot for one or more candidates of each major party. This pattern is the opposite of straight-ticket voting, in which the voter supports only candidates of one party in a particular election. (See also **straight-ticket voting.**)

spoils system The practice of granting public office to individuals in return for political favors they have rendered. (See also **patronage system.**)

standing committee A permanent congressional committee with responsibility for a particular area of public policy. An example is the Senate Foreign Relations Committee.

stewardship theory A theory that argues for a strong, assertive presidential role, with presidential authority limited only at points specifically prohibited by law. (See also **Whig theory.**)

straight-ticket voting When a voter in an election casts a ballot that includes only candidates of the same party. (See also **split-ticket voting.**)

strict-scrutiny test A test applied by courts to laws that attempt a racial or ethnic classification. In effect, the strict-scrutiny test eliminates race or ethnicity as a legal classification when it places minority group members at a disadvantage. (See also **suspect classifications.**)

suffrage The right to vote.

supply-side economics A form of fiscal policy that emphasizes "supply" (production). An example of supply-side economics would be a tax cut for business. (See also **demand-side economics; fiscal policy.**)

supremacy clause Article VI of the Constitution, which makes national law supreme over state law when the national government is acting within its constitutional limits.

suspect classifications Legal classifications, such as race and national origin, that have invidious discrimination as their purpose and are therefore unconstitutional. (See also **strict-scrutiny test.**)

transfer payment A government benefit that is given directly to an individual, as in the case of social security payments to a retiree.

trustees The idea of elected representatives as obligated to act in accordance with their own consciences as to what policies are in the best interests of the public. (See also **delegates.**)

two-party system A system in which only two political parties have a real chance of acquiring control of the government.

tyranny of the majority The potential of a majority to monopolize power for its own gain and to the detriment of minority rights and interests.

unitary system A governmental system in which the national government alone has sovereign (ultimate) authority. (See also **confederacy; federalism**)

unity The principle that Americans are one people who form an indivisible union.

voter turnout The proportion of persons of voting age who actually vote in a given election.

watchdog role The accepted responsibility of the media to protect the public from deceitful, careless, incompetent, and corrupt officials by standing ready to expose any official who violates accepted legal, ethical, or performance standards. (See also **common-carrier role; public representative role; signaler role.**)

Whig theory A theory that prevailed in the nineteenth century and held that the presidency was a limited or restrained office whose occupant was confined to expressly granted constitutional authority. (See also **stewardship theory.**)

whistle-blowing An internal check on the bureaucracy whereby individual bureaucrats report instances of mismanagement that they observe.

writ of *certiorari* Permission granted by a higher court to allow a losing party in a legal case to bring the case before it for a ruling; when such a writ is requested of the U.S. Supreme Court, four of the Court's nine justices must agree to accept the case before it is granted *certiorari*.

Notes

CHAPTER ONE

[1]Alexis de Tocqueville, *Democracy in America* (1835–1840), ed. J. P. Mayer and A. P. Kerr (Garden City, N.Y.: Doubleday/Anchor, 1969), 640.

[2]See Jay Fliegelman, *Declaring Independence: Jefferson, Natural Language and the Culture of Performance* (Stanford, Calif.: Stanford University Press, 1993).

[3]See Peter Lawler and Robert Schaefer, *American Political Rhetoric*, 2d ed. (Totowa, N.J.: Rowman & Littlefield, 1990).

[4]See William Fischer, David Gerber, Jorge Guitart, and Maxine Seller, *Identity, Community, and Pluralism in American Life* (New York: Oxford University Press, 1996); Rogers M. Smith, "The American Creed and American Identity: The Limits of Liberal Citizenship in the United States," *Western Political Quarterly* 41 (1988): 225–252; Robert S. Erikson, John P. McIver, and Gerald C. Wright, Jr., "State Political Culture and Public Opinion," *American Political Science Review* 81 (September 1987): 797–813.

[5]Clinton Rossiter, *Conservativism in America* (New York: Vintage, 1962), 67.

[6]James Bryce, *The American Commonwealth*, vol. 2 (New York: Macmillan, 1960), 247–254. First published in 1900.

[7]Ralph Barton Perry, *Puritanism and Democracy* (New York: Vanguard, 1944), 124–125; see also Peter D. Salins, *Assimilation, American Style* (New York: Basic Books, 1996).

[8]See Gabriel Almond and Sidney Verba, *The Civic Culture* (Boston: Little, Brown, 1965); Richard Merelman, *Making Something of Ourselves: On Culture and Politics in the United States* (Berkeley: University of California Press, 1984).

[9]Tocqueville, *Democracy in America*, 310.

[10]Times Mirror Center for the People and the Press survey, 1990–1991.

[11]See Douglas Muzzio and Richard Behn, "Thinking about Welfare," *The Public Perspective*, February/March 1995, 35–38; Stanley Feldman and John Zaller, "The Political Culture of Ambivalence: Ideological Responses to the Welfare State," *American Journal of Political Science*, 36 (1992): 268–307.

[12]See Seymour Martin Lipset, *American Exceptionalism: A Double-Edged Sword* (New York: Norton, 1996); Claude Levi-Strauss, *Structural Anthropology* (Chicago: University of Chicago Press, 1983); Clifford Geertz, *Myth, Symbol, and Culture* (New York: Norton, 1974).

[13]U.S. Census Bureau figures.

[14]Quoted in Ralph Volney Harlow, *The Growth of the United States*, vol. 2 (New York: Henry Holt, 1943), 497.

[15]Quoted in Michael Harrington, *Socialism* (New York: Bantam, 1973), 142.
[16]Harold D. Lasswell, *Politics: Who Gets What, When, How* (New York: McGraw-Hill, 1938).
[17]Theodore Lowi, *Incomplete Conquest: Governing America* (New York: Holt, Rinehart & Winston, 1981), ch. 1; see also William Hudson, *American Democracy in Peril*, rev. ed. (Chatham, N.J.: Chatham House, 1996).
[18]Harold D. Lasswell and Abraham Kaplan, *Power and Society* (New Haven, Conn.: Yale University Press, 1950), 75–77.
[19]*Federalist* No. 47.
[20]See Charles H. McIlwain, *Constitutionalism: Ancient and Modern* (Ithaca, N.Y.: Cornell University Press, 1983).
[21]Alan S. Rosenbaum, ed., *Constitutionalism: The Philosophical Dimension* (Westport, Conn.: Greenwood, 1988), 4.
[22]Tocqueville, *Democracy in America*, ch. 6.
[23]Benjamin I. Page and Robert Shapiro, "Effects of Public Opinion on Policy," *American Political Science Review* 77 (March, 1983): 178; see also Urie Bronfenbrenner, Peter McClelland, Stephen Leci, Phyllis Moen, and Elaine Wethington, *The State of Americans* (New York: Free Press, 1996).
[24]See Robert Dahl, *Democracy and Its Critics* (New Haven, Conn.: Yale University Press, 1989).
[25]C. Wright Mills, *The Power Elite* (New York: Oxford University Press, 1965); William Domhoff, *The Power Elite and the State: How Policy Is Made in America* (New York: Aldine de Gruyter, 1990).
[26]David Easton, *The Political System* (New York: Knopf, 1965), 97.
[27]E. E. Schattschneider, *Two Hundred Million Americans in Search of a Government* (New York: Holt, Rinehart & Winston, 1969), 42.

CHAPTER TWO

[1]Woodrow Wilson, *Constitutional Government in the United States* (New York: Columbia University Press, 1908), 173.
[2]Thomas E. Patterson, *The 1996 Election and Other Recent Developments* (New York: McGraw-Hill, 1997), 29.
[3]Richard H. Leach, *American Federalism* (New York: Norton, 1970), 1.
[4]George Bancroft, *History of the Formation of the Constitution of the United States of America*, 3d ed., vol. 1 (New York: D. Appleton, 1883), 166.
[5]Catherine Drinker Bowen, *Miracle at Philadelphia* (Boston: Little, Brown, 1986), 10.
[6]William Wirt Henry, *Patrick Henry: Life, Correspondence, and Speeches*, vol. 3 (New York: Scribner's, 1891), 431.
[7]Alfred H. Kelly, Winifred A. Harbison, and Herman Belz, *The American Constitution*, 7th ed. (New York: Norton, 1991), 122.
[8]*Federalist* No. 45.

[9]See Stanley Elkins and Eric McKitrick, *The Age of Federalism: The Early American Republic, 1788–1800* (New York: Oxford University Press, 1993).

[10]*McCulloch v. Maryland*, 4 Wheaton 316 (1819).

[11]See also *Martin v. Hunter's Lessee*, 1 Wheaton 304 (1816); Elkins and McKitrick, *The Age of Federalism*.

[12]Oliver Wendell Holmes, Jr., *Collected Legal Papers* (New York: Harcourt, Brace, 1920), 295–296.

[13]John C. Calhoun, *The Works of John C. Calhoun* (New York: Russell & Russell, 1968).

[14]See *Cooley v. Board of Wardens of the Port of Philadelphia*, 53 Howard 299 (1851).

[15]Alan Brinkley, *The Unfinished Nation* (New York: McGraw-Hill, 1993), 371.

[16]*U.S. v. Cruikshank*, 92 U.S. 452 (1876).

[17]*Santa Clara County v. Southern Pacific Railroad Co.*, 118 U.S. 394 (1886).

[18]*U.S. v. E. C. Knight Co.*, 156 U.S. 1 (1895).

[19]*Hammer v. Dagenhart*, 247 U.S. 251 (1918).

[20]*Lochner v. New York*, 198 U.S. 25 (1905).

[21]William G. Ross, *Muted Fury: Populists, Progressives, and Labor Unions Confront the Courts* (Princeton, N.J.: Princeton University Press, 1993).

[22]Kelly, Harbison, and Belz, *The American Constitution*, 529.

[23]James E. Anderson, *The Emergence of the Modern Regulatory State* (Washington, D.C.: Public Affairs Press, 1962), 2–3.

[24]*Schechter Poultry Co. v. United States*, 295 U.S. 495 (1935).

[25]*NLRB v. Jones and Laughlin Steel*, 301 U.S. 1 (1937).

[26]*American Power and Light v. Securities and Exchange Commission*, 329 U.S. 90 (1946); see also Richard A. Maidment, *The Judicial Response to the New Deal* (New York: Manchester University Press, 1992).

[27]Louis Fisher, *American Constitutional Law* (New York: McGraw-Hill, 1990), 384.

[28]Richard A. Maidment, *The Judicial Response to the New Deal: The U.S. Supreme Court and Economic Regulation* (New York: Manchester University Press, 1992).

[29]*Garcia v. San Antonio Transit Authority*, 469 U.S. 528 (1985).

[30]See Thomas Anton, *American Federalism and Public Policy* (Philadelphia: Temple University Press, 1989).

[31]Morton Grodzins, *The American System: A New View of Government in the United States* (Chicago: Rand McNally, 1966).

[32]John E. Chubb, "The Political Economy of Federalism," *American Political Science Review* 79 (December 1985): 994–1015.

[33]See Paul A. Peterson, *The Price of Federalism* (Washington, D.C.: Brookings Institution, 1995).

[34]See Rosella Levaggi, *Fiscal Federalism and Grants-in-Aid* (Brookfield, Vt.: Avebury, 1991).

[35]See David L. Shapiro, *Federalism: A Dialogue* (Evanston, Ill.: Northwestern University Press, 1995); Douglas D. Rose, "National and Local Forces in State Politics," *American Political Science Review* 67 (December 1973): 1162–1173.

[36]Thomas R. Dye, "The Devolution Revolution," *Madison Review* 1 (Winter 1996): 2–3; Tommy Thompson, *Power to the People* (New York: HarperCollins, 1996).

[37]See Richard Nathan and Fred Doolittle, *Reagan and the States* (Princeton, N.J.: Princeton University Press, 1987); Timothy J. Conlan, *New Federalism* (Washington, D.C.: Brookings Institution, 1988).

[38]Richard Lacayo, "They Can Multiply without Dividing," *Time*, November 21, 1994, 66.

[39]Andrew W. Dobelstein, *Politics, Economics, and Public Welfare* (Englewood Cliffs, N.J.: Prentice-Hall, 1980), 5.

[40]Lloyd A. Free and Hadley Cantril, *The Political Beliefs of Americans* (New York: Simon & Schuster, 1968), 21; see also William Lunch, *The Nationalization of American Politics* (Berkeley: University of California Press, 1987).

[41]Survey for the Times Mirror Center for the People and the Press by Princeton Survey Research Associates, July 12–27, 1994.

CHAPTER THREE

[1]*Federalist* No. 51.

[2]John Locke, *The Two Treatises of Government*, ed. Thomas I. Cook (New York: Hafner, 1947), 159–186, 228–247; see also A. John Simmons, *The Lockean Theory of Rights* (Princeton, N.J.: Princeton University Press, 1994).

[3]Max Weber, "Politics as a Vocation," in Hans H. Gerth and C. Wright Mills, eds., *From Max Weber: Essays in Sociology* (New York: Oxford University Press, 1958), 78.

[4]Gaillard Hunt, ed., *The Writings of James Madison* (New York: Putnam, 1904), 274.

[5]*Federalist* No. 47.

[6]See *Federalist* Nos. 47 and 48.

[7]Richard Neustadt, *Presidential Power and the Modern Presidents* (New York: Free Press, 1990), 29.

[8]Henry J. Abraham, *The Judicial Process*, 6th ed. (New York: Oxford University Press, 1993), 320–322.

[9]*Marbury* v. *Madison*, 1 Cranch 137 (1803).

[10]Joan Biskupic and Elder Witt, *The Supreme Court and the Powers of the American Government* (Washington, D.C.: Congressional Quarterly Press, 1996), chs. 2–3.

[11]Robert A. Dahl, *Pluralist Democracy in the United States* (Chicago: Rand McNally, 1967), 370.

[12]Quoted in Richard M. Johnson, *The Dynamics of Compliance*, (Evanston, Ill.: Northwestern University Press, 1967), 3.

[13]See Charles S. Hyneman, "Republican Government in America," in George J. Graham, Jr., and Scarlett G. Graham, eds., *Founding Principles of American Government*, rev. ed. (Chatham, N.J.: Chatham House, 1984), 19.

[14]*Federalist* No. 10.

[15]Ibid.

[16]Leslie F. Goldstein, "Judicial Review and Democratic Theory: Guardian Democracy vs. Representative Democracy," *Western Political Quarterly* 40 (1987): 391–412.

[17]Richard Henry Lee, "Letters from the Federal Farmer," in Forrest McDonald, ed., *Empire and Nation* (Englewood Cliffs, N.J.: Prentice-Hall, 1962), 103–117.

[18]See Paul W. Kahn, *Legitimacy and History: Self-Government in American Constitutional History* (New Haven, Conn.: Yale University Press, 1993).

[19]Hannah Arendt, *On Revolution* (New York: Viking, 1963), ch. 6.

[20]Benjamin Ginsberg, *The Consequences of Consent* (New York: Random House, 1982), 22.

[21]Dahl, *Pluralist Democracy*, 92.

[22]This interpretation is taken from Walter Lippmann, *Public Opinion* (New York: Free Press, 1965), 178–179; for a general discussion of the uncertain meaning of the Constitution, see Lawrence H. Tribe and Michael C. Dorf, *On Reading the Constitution* (Cambridge, Mass.: Harvard University Press, 1991).

[23]James MacGregor Burns, *The Vineyard of Liberty* (New York: Knopf, 1982), 368.

[24]See William Allen White, "The Boss System," in Richard Hofstadter, ed., *The Progressive Movement, 1900–1915* (Englewood Cliffs, N.J.: Prentice-Hall, 1963), 104–107.

[25]Charles S. Beard, *An Economic Interpretation of the Constitution* (1913; New York: Macmillan, 1941).

[26]See Gerald Benjamin and Michael J. Malbin, eds., *Limiting Legislative Terms* (Washington, D.C.: Congressional Quarterly Press, 1992).

[27]*United States* v. *Thornton*, No. 95–265 (1995).

Chapter Four

[1]Julian P. Boyd, ed., *The Papers of Thomas Jefferson*, vol. 12 (Princeton, N.J.: Princeton University Press, 1955), 440.

[2]*Anderson* v. *Creighton*, 483 U.S. 635 (1987).

[3]See Paul L. Murphy, *The Shaping of the First Amendment: 1791 to the Present* (New York: Oxford University Press, 1991).

[4]See *Madsen* v. *Women's Health Center, Inc.*, 115 S. Ct. 23 (1994); *National Org. for Women* v. *Schneidler*, 114 S. Ct. 798 (1994).

[5]*Schenck* v. *United States*, 249 U.S. 47 (1919).

[6]*Dennis* v. *United States*, 341 U.S. 494 (1951).

[7]See, for example, *Yates* v. *United States*, 354 U.S. 298 (1957); *Noto* v. *United States*, 367 U.S. 290 (1961); *Scales* v. *United States*, 367 U.S. 203 (1961).

[8]*United States* v. *Carolene Products Co.*, 304 U.S. 144 (1938).

[9]*United States* v. *O'Brien*, 391 U.S. 367 (1968).

[10]*United States* v. *Eichman*, 496 U.S. 310 (1990).

[11]*Texas v. Johnson*, 109 S. Ct. at 2544 (1989).

[12]*New York Times Co. v. United States*, 403 U.S. 713 (1971).

[13]*Nebraska Press Assn. v. Stuart*, 427 U.S. 539 (1976).

[14]*Barron v. Baltimore*, 7 Peters 243 (1833).

[15]*Gitlow v. New York*, 268 U.S. 652 (1925).

[16]*Fiske v. Kansas*, 274 U.S. 30 (1927) (speech); *Near v. Minnesota*, 283 U.S. 697 (1931) (press); *Cantwell v. Connecticut*, 310 U.S. 296 (1940) (religion); and *DeFonge v. Oregon*, 299 U.S. 253 (1937) (assembly and petition).

[17]*Near v. Minnesota*.

[18]*Brandenburg v. Ohio*, 395 U.S. 444 (1969).

[19]*National Socialist Party v. Skokie*, 432 U.S. 43 (1977).

[20]*R.A.V. v. St. Paul*, No. 90-7675 (1992).

[21]*Wisconsin v. Mitchell*, No. 92-515 (1993).

[22]*Forsyth County v. Nationalist Movement*, No. 91-538 (1992).

[23]*New York Times Co. v. Sullivan*, 376 U.S. 254 (1964).

[24]*Milkovich v. Lorain Journal*, 497 U.S. 1 (1990); see also *Masson v. The New Yorker*, No. 89-1799 (1991).

[25]*Miller v. California*, 413 U.S. 15 (1973).

[26]*Barnes v. Glen Theatre*, No. 90-26 (1991).

[27]*Stanley v. Georgia*, 394 U.S. 557 (1969).

[28]*Osborne v. Ohio*, 495 U.S. 103 (1990).

[29]*Denver Area Consortium v. Federal Communications Commission*, No. 95-124 (1996).

[30]See Mary Segers and Ted G. Jelen, *A Wall of Separation?* (Lanham, Md.: Rowman & Littlefield, 1997).

[31]Ibid.

[32]*Lemon v. Kurtzman*, 403 U.S. 602 (1971).

[33]*Board of Regents v. Allen*, 392 U.S. 236 (1968).

[34]*Engel v. Vitale*, 370 U.S. 421 (1962).

[35]*Abington School District v. Schempp*, 374 U.S. 203 (1963).

[36]*Wallace v. Jaffree*, 472 U.S. 38 (1985).

[37]*Lee v. Weisman*, No. 90-1014 (1992).

[38]*Wisconsin v. Yoder*, 406 U.S. 295 (1972); see also *Church of the Lukumi Babalu Aye v. City of Hialeah*, No. 91-948 (1993).

[39]*Griswold v. Connecticut*, 381 U.S. 479 (1965).

[40]*Roe v. Wade*, 401 U.S. 113 (1973).

[41]*Webster v. Reproductive Health Services*, 492 U.S. 490 (1989); see also *Rust v. Sullivan*, No. 89-1391 (1991).

[42]*Planned Parenthood v. Casey*, No. 91-744 (1992).

[43]Charles H. Franklin and Liane C. Kosacki, "Republican Schoolmaster: The U.S. Supreme Court, Public Opinion, and Abortion," *American Political Science Review* 83 (1989): 751–772; see also Barbara Hinkson Craig and David M. O'Brien, *Abortion and American Politics* (Chatham, N.J.: Chatham House, 1993).

[44]*McNabb v. United States*, 318 U.S. 332 (1943).

[45] *Powell* v. *Alabama*, 287 U.S. 45 (1932).

[46] *Mapp* v. *Ohio*, 367 U.S. 643 (1961).

[47] *Gideon* v. *Wainwright*, 372 U.S. 335 (1963).

[48] *Malloy* v. *Hogan*, 378 U.S. 1 (1964).

[49] *Miranda* v. *Arizona*, 384 U.S. 436 (1966); see also *Escobedo* v. *Illinois*, 378 U.S. 478 (1964).

[50] *Pointer* v. *Texas*, 380 U.S. 400 (1965).

[51] *Klopfer* v. *North Carolina*, 386 U.S. 213 (1967).

[52] *Duncan* v. *Louisiana*, 391 U.S. 145 (1968).

[53] *Benton* v. *Maryland*, 395 U.S. 784 (1969).

[54] *Weeks* v. *United States*, 232 U.S. 383 (1914).

[55] *Nix* v. *Williams*, 467 U.S. 431 (1984); see also *United States* v. *Leon*, 468 U.S. 897 (1984).

[56] *Michigan* v. *Sitz*, No. 88-1897 (1990).

[57] *Whren* v. *United States*, No. 95-5841 (1996); see also *California* v. *Hodari D.*, No. 89-1632 (1991).

[58] *Townsend* v. *Sain*, 372 U.S. 293 (1963).

[59] *Keeney* v. *Tamaya-Reyes*, No. 90-1859 (1992); see also *Coleman* v. *Thompson*, No. 89-7662 (1991).

[60] *Brecht* v. *Abrahamson*, No. 91-7358 (1993); see also *McCleskey* v. *Zant*, No. 89-7024 (1991).

[61] *Felker* v. *Turpin*, No. 95-8836 (1996).

[62] See David M. O'Brien, "The High Court Changes Course," *The Public Perspective* 2 (July/August 1991): 6–7.

[63] See *Batson* v. *Kentucky*, 476 U.S. 79 (1986); *Edmonson* v. *Leesville Concrete Company*, No. 89-7743 (1991); *Powers* v. *Ohio*, 499 U.S. 400 (1991).

[64] *Minnick* v. *Mississippi*, 498 U.S. 146 (1991).

[65] *Jaffee* v. *Redmond*, No. 95-266 (1994).

[66] Kurt Heine, "Philadelphia Cops Beat One of Their Own," *Syracuse Herald-American*, January 15, 1995, A13.

[67] *Wilson* v. *Seiter*, No. 89-7376 (1991).

[68] *Harmelin* v. *Michigan*, No. 89-7272 (1991).

[69] Alpheus T. Mason, *The Supreme Court: Palladium of Freedom* (Ann Arbor: University of Michigan Press, 1962); but see also Robert F. Nagel, *Judicial Power and American Character* (New York: Oxford University Press, 1996).

Chapter Five

[1] Speech of Martin Luther King, Jr., in Washington, D.C., August 2, 1963.

[2] *Washington Post* wire story, May 14, 1991.

[3] Reported on *CBS Evening News*, January 16, 1989.

[4] Robert Nisbet, "Public Opinion versus Popular Opinion," *Public Interest* 41 (1975): 171.

[5]The classic analysis of this system of legalized segregation is C. Vann Woodward, *The Strange Career of Jim Crow*, 3d rev. ed. (New York: Oxford University Press, 1974).

[6]*Plessy* v. *Ferguson*, 163 U.S. 537 (1896).

[7]See, for example, *Missouri ex rel. Gaines* v. *Canada*, 305 U.S. 57 (1938).

[8]See Richard Kugler, *Simple Justice: The History of Brown v. Board of Education and Black America's Struggle for Equality* (New York: Knopf, 1977).

[9]*Brown* v. *Board of Education of Topeka*, 347 U.S. 483 (1954).

[10]See Taylor Branch, *Parting the Waters* (New York: Simon & Schuster, 1988).

[11]See Steven A. Shull, *The President and Civil Rights Policy: Leadership and Change* (Westport, Conn.: Greenwood, 1989).

[12]See Gerald Rosenberg, *The Hollow Hope* (Chicago: University of Chicago Press, 1991).

[13]See Derrick Bell, *And We Are Not Saved: The Elusive Quest for Racial Justice* (New York: Basic Books, 1987); Robert C. Smith and Richard S. Hzer, *Race, Class, and Culture* (Albany: State University of New York Press, 1992).

[14]Study cited on "The Law Show," New York State Public Radio, August 5, 1996.

[15]Verne E. Smith and Mare Peyser, "Terror in the Night Down South," *Newsweek* June 3, 1996, 34.

[16]See Carol M. Swain, *Black Faces, Black Interests* (Cambridge, Mass.: Harvard University Press, 1993).

[17]*Tinker* v. *Colwell*, 193 U.S. 473 (1904).

[18]See Eleanor Flexner, *Century of Struggle*, rev. ed. (Cambridge, Mass.: Harvard University Press, 1975); Ellen Carol DuBois, *Feminism and Suffrage: The Emergence of an Independent Women's Movement in America, 1848–1869* (Ithaca, N.Y.: Cornell University Press, 1978).

[19]See Jane Mansbridge, *Why We Lost the ERA* (Chicago: University of Chicago Press, 1986).

[20]See Kathleen Hall Jamieson, *Beyond the Double Bind* (New York: Oxford University Press, 1995).

[21]Linda Witt, Karen M. Paget, and Glenna Matthews, *Running as a Woman* (New York: Free Press, 1994).

[22]Mary Lou Kendrigan, *Political Equality in a Democratic Society: Women in the United States* (Westport, Conn.: Greenwood, 1984).

[23]Timothy Bledsoe and Mary Herring, "Victims of Circumstance: Women in Pursuit of Political Office," *American Political Science Review* 84 (1990): 213–224.

[24]"The Gender Story," *The Public Perspective*, August/September 1996, 1–33; Sue Tolleson Rinehart, *Gender Consciousness and Politics* (New York: Routledge, 1992).

[25]"The Gender Gap at the State Level," *The Public Perspective*, January/February 1993, 100.

[26]*County of Washington* v. *Gunther,* No. 80-429 (1981).

[27]See, however, Sara M. Evans and Barbara Nelson, *Wage Justice* (Chicago: University of Chicago Press, 1989).

[28]See Ellen Frankel Paul, *Equity and Gender* (New Brunswick, N.J.: Transaction Books, 1989).

[29]See Rudulfo O. de la Garza, Louis DeSipio, F. Chris Garcia, John Garcia, and Angelo Falcon, *Latino Voices* (Boulder, Colo.: Westview Press, 1992); David G. Gutiérrez, *Walls and Mirrors: Mexican Americans, Mexican Immigrants, and the Politics of Ethnicity* (Berkeley: University of California Press, 1995); Hans Stavans, *The Hispanic Condition* (New York: HarperPerennial, 1996).

[30]*De Canas* v. *Bica*, 424 U.S. 351 (1976).

[31]Nancy Gibbs, "Keep Out, You Tired, You Poor . . .," *Time*, October 3, 1994, 46–47.

[32]James Truslow Adams, *The March of Democracy*, vol. 4 (New York: Scribner's, 1933), 284–285.

[33]*Lau* v. *Nichols*, 414 U.S. 563 (1974).

[34]Mary Johnson, "Overcoming the Social Barriers," *The Nation*, April 9, 1988, 489–494.

[35]*Romer* v. *Evans*, No. 94-1039 (1996).

[36]See, for example, *Plyler* v. *Doe*, 457 U.S. 202 (1982).

[37]See *Reed* v. *Reed*, 404 U.S. 71 (1971); see also Joseph Ignagni and Thomas R. Marshall, "Gender Equality and the Supreme Court: Taking Another Look," *American Review of Politics* 16 (Fall/Winter 1995): 239–252.

[38]*Craig* v. *Boren*, 429 U.S. 190 (1976).

[39]*Rostker* v. *Goldberg*, 453 U.S. 57 (1980).

[40]*United States* v. *Virginia*, No. 94-1941 (1996).

[41]Federal Reserve Bank data, 1991.

[42]See J. Morgan Kousser, *The Shaping of Southern Politics: Suffrage Restriction and the Establishment of the One-Party South, 1880–1910* (New Haven, Conn.: Yale University Press, 1974).

[43]V. O. Key, Jr., *Southern Politics* (New York: Knopf, 1949), 495.

[44]*Smith* v. *Allwright*, 321 U.S. 649 (1944).

[45]*Bush* v. *Verg*, No. 94-805 (1996); *Shaw* v. *Hunt*, No. 94-923 (1996); *Muller* v. *Johnson*, No. 94-631 (1995).

[46]See Terry Eastland, *Ending Affirmative Action* (New York: Basic Books, 1997); but see also Barbara A. Bergmann, *In Defense of Affirmative Action* (New York: Basic Books, 1997).

[47]"The Quiet Race War," *Newsweek*, April 8, 1996, 38.

[48]*University of California Regents* v. *Bakke*, 438 U.S. 265 (1978).

[49]*Steelworkers* v. *Weber*, 443 U.S. 193 (1979); *Fullilove* v. *Klutnick*, 448 U.S. 448 (1980).

[50]*Local No. 28, Sheet Metal Workers* v. *Equal Employment Opportunity Commission*, 478 U.S. 421 (1986); see also *Local No. 93, International Association of Firefighters* v. *Cleveland*, 478 U.S. 501 (1986); *Firefighters* v. *Stotts*, 459 U.S. 969 (1984); *Wygant* v. *Jackson*, 476 U.S. 238 (1986).

[51]*Adarand* v. *Pena*, No. 94-310 (1995).

[52]See *Wards Cove Packing* v. *Antonio*, 490 U.S. 642 (1989).

[53]Gunnar Myrdal, *An American Dilemma: The Negro Problem and Modern Democracy* (New York: Harper, 1944).

[54]James S. Kunen, "The End of Integration," *Time*, April 29, 1996, 39.

[55]*Swann* v. *Charlotte-Mecklenburg County Board of Education*, 402 U.S. 1 (1971).

[56]*Milliken* v. *Bradley*, 418 U.S. 717 (1974).

[57]*Missouri* v. *Jenkins* (1995); see also *Board of Education (Oklahoma City)* v. *Dowell*, 498 U.S. 237 (1991).

[58]Jennifer Hochschild, *The New American Dilemma* (New Haven, Conn.: Yale University Press, 1984); Jennifer Hochschild, *Facing Up to the American Dream* (Princeton, N.J.: Princeton University Press, 1996).

CHAPTER SIX

[1]V. O. Key, Jr., *Public Opinion and American Democracy* (New York: Knopf, 1961), 8.

[2]See Benjamin I. Page and Robert Shapiro, *The Rational Public* (Chicago: University of Chicago Press, 1992), 285–288.

[3]Jerry L. Yeric and John R. Todd, *Public Opinion*, 2d ed. (Itasca, Ill.: Peacock, 1989), 3.

[4]Elisabeth Noelle-Neumann, *The Spiral of Silence*, 2d ed. (Chicago: University of Chicago Press, 1993), ch. 1.

[5]Sidney Verba and Norman H. Nie, *Participation in America: Political Democracy and Social Equality* (New York: Harper & Row, 1972), 281–284.

[6]See Michael W. Traugott and Paul J. Lavrakas, *The Voters' Guide to Election Polls* (Chatham, N.J.: Chatham House, 1996).

[7]Ibid.

[8]Steven A. Peterson, *Political Behavior: Patterns in Everyday Life* (Newbury Park, Calif.: Sage, 1990), 28–29.

[9]Ibid.

[10]See Murray Edelman, *Politics as Symbolic Action* (Chicago: Markham, 1971).

[11]See M. Kent Jennings and Richard Niemi, "The Transmission of Political Values from Parent to Child," *American Political Science Review* 62 (March 1968): 169–184.

[12]M. Kent Jennings and Richard G. Niemi, *Generations and Politics* (Princeton, N.J.: Princeton University Press, 1981), 91.

[13]See David O. Sears, "Whither Political Socialization Research?" in Orit Ichilov, ed., *Political Socialization, Citizenship Education, and Democracy* (New York: Teachers College Press, 1990), 69–97.

[14]Ichilov, *Political Socialization, Citizenship Education, and Democracy.*

[15]Noelle-Neumann, *The Spiral of Silence.*

[16]See Shanto Iyengar, *Is Anyone Responsible? How Television Frames Political Issues* (Chicago: University of Chicago Press, 1991); Shanto Iyengar and Donald Kinder, *News That Matters: Television and American Opinion* (Chicago: University of Chicago Press, 1987).

[17]Thomas E. Patterson, *Out of Order* (New York: Vintage, 1994), ch. 2; see also Marion R. Just, Ann N. Crigler, Dean E. Alger, Timothy E. Cook, Montague Kern, and Darrell M. West, *Crosstalk: Citizens, Candidates, and the Media in a Presidential Campaign* (Chicago: University of Chicago Press, 1996).

[18]See David Green, *Shaping Political Consciousness: The Language of Politics in America from McKinley to Reagan* (Ithaca, N.Y.: Cornell University Press, 1988); for the view that the public also shapes the positions of leaders, see Paul Brace and Barbara Hinckley, *Follow the Leader: Opinion Polls and Modern Presidents* (New York: Basic Books, 1992).

[19]See Richard Merelman, *Making Something of Ourselves* (Berkeley: University of California Press, 1984); John White, *The New Politics of Old Values* (Hanover, N.H.: University Press of New England, 1988); Richard J. Ellis, *American Political Cultures* (New York: Oxford University Press, 1993).

[20]Philip Converse, "The Nature of Belief Systems in Mass Publics," in David Apter, ed., *Ideology and Discontent* (New York: Free Press, 1965), 206; John L. Sullivan, James E. Pierson, and George E. Marcus, "Ideological Constraint in the Mass Public," *American Journal of Political Science* 22 (May 1978): 233–249; Eric R. A. N. Smith, *The Unchanging American Voter* (Berkeley: University of California Press, 1989).

[21]See E. J. Dionne, *Why Americans Hate Politics* (New York: Simon & Schuster, 1992); E. J. Dionne, *They Only Look Dead* (New York: Simon & Schuster, 1996); David Frum, *What's Right?* (New York: Basic Books, 1996).

[22]CNN/USA Today poll conducted by the Gallup Organization, 1994.

[23]"The Gender Story," *The Public Perspective*, August/September 1996, 1–33; Sue Tolleson Rinehart, *Gender Consciousness and Politics* (New York: Routledge, 1992).

[24]Susan A. MacManus, *Young v. Old: Generational Combat in the 21st Century* (Boulder, Colo.: Westview Press, 1996).

[25]See Angus Campbell, Philip Converse, Warren Miller, and Donald Stokes, *The American Voter* (New York: Wiley, 1960), chs. 3–4.

[26]Martin P. Wattenberg, *The Decline of American Political Parties, 1952–1984* (Cambridge, Mass.: Harvard University Press, 1990).

[27]See E. E. Schattschneider, *The Semisovereign People* (New York: Holt, Rinehart & Winston, 1980), ch. 8.

[28]See G. William Domhoff, *The Power Elite and the State* (New York: Aldine de Gruyter, 1990).

[29]Benjamin I. Page and Robert Y. Shapiro, "Effects of Public Opinion on Policy," *American Political Science Review* 77 (March 1983): 178.

[30]See Benjamin Ginsberg, *The Consequences of Consent* (New York: Random House, 1982); but also see Samuel L. Popkin, *The Reasoning Voter: Communication and Persuasion in Presidential Campaigns* (Chicago: University of Chicago Press, 1991).

CHAPTER SEVEN

[1]Walter Lippmann, *Public Opinion* (1922; New York: Free Press, 1965), 36.

[2]"Congress's Sour Finish," *The New York Times*, October 8, 1994, 22.

[3]See Steven J. Rosenstone and John Mark Hansen, *Mobilization, Participation and Democracy in America* (New York: Macmillan, 1993).

[4]Quoted in Ralph Volney Harlow, *The Growth of the United States* (New York: Henry Holt, 1943), 312.

[5]See William H. Flanigan and Nancy Zingale, *The Political Behavior of the American Electorate*, 8th ed. (Washington, D.C.: Congressional Quarterly Press, 1994), 24–26.

[6]Example from Gus Tyler, "One Cheer for the Democrats," *New Leader*, November 3, 1986, 6.

[7]Turnout figures provided by Washington, D.C., embassies of the respective countries, 1995.

[8]Ivor Crewe, "Electoral Participation," in David Butler, Howard R. Penniman, and Austin Ranney, eds., *Democracy at the Polls* (Washington, D.C.: American Enterprise Institute, 1981), 249.

[9]Juliet Eilperin, "Talking 'Bout the 'X' Generation," *Roll Call*, June 6, 1995, 13.

[10]Richard Boyd, "Decline of U.S. Voter Turnout," *American Politics Quarterly* 9 (April 1981): 142.

[11]Ruy A. Teixeira, *The Disappearing American Voter* (Washington, D.C.: Brookings Institution, 1992).

[12]Crewe, "Electoral Participation," 251–253.

[13]G. Bingham Powell, "Voting Turnout in Thirty Democracies," in Richard Rose, ed., *Electoral Participation: A Comparative Analysis* (Beverly Hills, Calif.: Sage, 1980), 6.

[14]CNN exit polls, 1996.

[15]Sidney Verba, Kay Schlozman, and Henry Brady, *Voice and Equity* (Cambridge, Mass.: Harvard University Press, 1995).

[16]Jerry L. Yeric and John R. Todd, *Public Opinion*, 2d ed. (Itasca, Ill.: Peacock, 1989), 226.

[17]See, for example, Norman H. Nie, G. Bingham Powell, and Kenneth Prewitt, "Social Structure and Political Participation," *American Political Science Review* 63 (September 1969): 808–832.

[18]John M. Strate, Charles J. Parrish, Charles D. Elder, and Coit Ford III, "Life Span Civic Development and Voting Participation," *American Political Science Review* 83 (June 1989): 443–465.

[19]Norma Nie, Jane Junn, and Kenneth Stehlik-Barry, *Education and Democratic Citizenship in America* (Chicago: University of Chicago Press, 1996).

[20]Ibid.

[21]M. Margaret Conway, *Political Participation in the United States*, 2d ed. (Washington, D.C.: Congressional Quarterly Press, 1991), 23–25.

[22]Mark Kesselman and Joel Kreiger, *European Politics in Transition* (Lexington, Mass.: Heath, 1987), 87.

[23]Edie N. Goldenberg and Michael W. Traugott, *Campaigning for Congress* (Washington, D.C.: Congressional Quarterly Press, 1984), ch. 9.

[24]Thomas E. Patterson, *The Mass Media Election* (New York: Praeger, 1980), chs. 7–10.

[25]D. Roderick Kiewiet, *Macro-Economics and Micro-Politics* (Chicago: University of Chicago Press, 1983), 154–158; Gallup Reports, 1936–1994.

[26]V. O. Key, Jr., *The Responsible Electorate* (Cambridge, Mass.: Belknap Press of Harvard University Press, 1966), ch. 1.

[27]Rosenstone and Hanson, *Mobilization, Participation, and Democracy in America*.

[28]Joseph Schumpeter, *Capitalism, Socialism, and Democracy* (New York: Harper Torchbooks, 1950), 269.

[29]Craig A. Rimmerman, *The New Citizenship* (Boulder, Colo.: Westview Press, 1997).

[30]W. Russell Neuman, *The Paradox of Mass Politics* (Cambridge, Mass.: Harvard University Press, 1986), 176.

[31]Samuel H. Barnes et al., eds., *Political Action* (Beverly Hills, Calif.: Sage, 1979), 541–542.

[32]Russell J. Dalton, *Citizen Politics in Western Democracies*, 3d. ed. (Chatham, N.J.: Chatham House, 1996), 43.

[33]Barnes et al., *Political Action*, 541–542.

[34]Patterson, *Mass Media Election*, ch. 4.

[35]Survey of Times Mirror Center for People and the Press, 1990.

[36]See Benjamin Ginsberg, *The Consequences of Consent* (New York: Random House, 1982), ch. 2.

[37]See Laura R. Woliver, *From Outrage to Action* (Urbana: University of Illinois Press, 1993).

[38]See Katherine Tate, *From Protest to Politics* (Cambridge, Mass.: Harvard University Press, 1994).

[39]Dalton, *Citizen Politics in Western Democracies*, 38.

[40]Edward N. Mueller and Mitchell A. Seligson, "Inequality and Insurgency," *American Political Science Review* 81 (1987): 425–451.

[41]William Watts and Lloyd A. Free, eds., *The State of the Nation* (New York: University Books, Potomac Associates, 1967), 97.

[42]Robert E. Lane, "Market Justice, Political Justice," *American Political Science Review* 80 (1986): 383; see also Jennifer Nedelsky, *Private Property and the Limits of American Constitutionalism* (New York: Oxford University Press, 1990).

[43]Ginsberg, *Consequences of Consent*, 49.

[44]Stephen Earl Bennett and David Resnick, "The Implications of Nonvoting for Democracy in the United States," *American Journal of Political Science* (August 1990): 771–802.

CHAPTER EIGHT

[1]E. E. Schattschneider, *Party Government* (New York: Rinehart, 1942), 1.

[2]E. E. Schattschneider, *The Semisovereign People: A Realist's View of Democracy in America* (New York: Holt, Rinehart & Winston, 1961), 140.

[3]Leon D. Epstein, *Political Parties in Western Democracies* (New York: Praeger, 1967), 9.

[4]L. Sandy Maisel, *Parties and Elections in America*, 2d ed. (New York: McGraw-Hill, 1993), 9–18.

[5]See John Aldrich, *Why Parties? The Origin and Transformation of Political Parties in America* (Chicago: University of Chicago Press, 1995).

[6]See Richard P. McCormick, *The Second American Party System: Party Formation in the Jacksonian Era* (Chapel Hill: University of North Carolina Press, 1966).

[7]Alexis de Tocqueville, *Democracy in America* (1835–1840), ed. J. P. Mayer and A. P. Kerr (Garden City, N.Y.: Doubleday/Anchor, 1969), 60.

[8]Aldrich, *Why Parties?*, 151.

[9]See Kristi Andersen, *The Creation of a Democratic Majority, 1928–1936* (Chicago: University of Chicago Press, 1979).

[10]See Kevin Phillips, *The Emerging Republican Majority* (New Rochelle, N.Y.: Arlington House, 1969).

[11]See Harold W. Stanley, "Southern Partisan Changes: Dealignment, Realignment or Both?" *Journal of Politics* 50 (1988): 64–88; Earl Black and Merle Black, *Politics and Society in the South* (Cambridge, Mass.: Harvard University Press, 1987); Robert H. Swansbrough and David M. Brodsky, eds., *The South's New Politics: Realignment and Dealignment* (Columbia: University of South Carolina Press, 1988); Dewey L. Grantham, *The Life and Death of the Solid South* (Lexington: University of Kentucky Press, 1988); Alexander P. Lamis, ed., *The Two-Party South* (New York: Oxford University Press, 1988).

[12]William H. Flanigan and Nancy Zingale, *Political Behavior of the American Electorate*, 8th ed. (Washington, D.C.: Congressional Quarterly Press, 1994), 58–63.

[13]Frederick G. Dutton, *Changing Sources of Power* (New York: McGraw-Hill, 1971), ch. 6.

[14]See E. J. Dionne, Jr., *Why Americans Hate Politics* (New York: Simon & Schuster, 1992); Everett Carll Ladd, "On Mandates, Realignments, and the 1984 Presidential Election," *Political Science Quarterly*, Spring 1985, 1–16.

[15]The classic account of the relationship of electoral and party systems is Maurice Duverger, *Political Parties* (New York: Wiley, 1954), bk. II, ch. 1; see also Giovanni Sartori, *Parties and Party Systems* (Cambridge, England: Cambridge University Press, 1976); Arend Lijphardt, *Electoral Systems and Party Systems* (New York: Oxford University Press, 1994).

[16]Clinton Rossiter, *Parties and Politics in America* (Ithaca, N.Y.: Cornell University Press, 1960), 11.

[17]Gerald M. Pomper, *Passions and Interests: Political Party Concepts of American Democracy* (Lawrence: University of Kansas Press, 1992), ch. 1.

[18]Ibid.

[19]John F. Bibby, *Politics, Parties, and Elections in America*, 2d ed. (Chicago: Nelson-Hall, 1992), 275–283.

[20]Steven J. Rosenstone, Roy L. Behr, and Edward H. Lazarus, *Third Parties in America*, 2d ed. (Princeton, N.J.: Princeton University Press, 1996).

[21]Daniel Mazmanian, *Third Parties in Presidential Elections* (Washington, D.C.: Brookings Institution, 1984), 143–144.

[22]See Lawrence Goodwyn, *The Populist Movement* (New York: Oxford University Press, 1978).

[23]Anthony King, *Running Scared* (New York: Free Press, 1997).

[24]See Alan Ehrenhalt, *The United States of Ambition* (New York: Times Books, 1991).

[25]See Paul S. Herrnson, *Party Campaigning in the '80s* (Cambridge, Mass.: Harvard University Press, 1988); Aldrich, *Why Parties?*, 253.

[26]See James L. Gibson, John P. Frendreis, and Laura L. Vertz, "Party Dynamics in the 1980s: Change in County Party Organizational Strength, 1980–1984," *American Journal of Political Science* 33 (1989): 67–90.

[27]James L. Gibson, Cornelius P. Cotter, John F. Bibby, and Robert J. Huckshorn, "Assessing Party Organizational Strength," *American Journal of Political Science* 27 (May 1983): 200; John F. Bibby, Cornelius P. Cotter, James L. Gibson, and Robert L. Huckshorn, "Parties in State Politics," in Virginia Gray, Herbert Jacob, and Kenneth N. Vines, eds., *Politics in the American States* (Boston: Little, Brown, 1983), 77.

[28]See, for example, Sarah McCally Morehouse, "Money versus Party Effort: Nominating for Governor," *American Journal of Political Science* 34 (1990): 706–724.

[29]*Cousins* v. *Wigoda*, 419 U.S. 477 (1975); *Democratic Party of the United States* v. *La Follette*, 450 U.S. 107 (1975).

[30]Frank J. Sorauf, *Money in American Elections* (Glenview, Ill.: Scott, Foresman, 1988), 132.

[31]Joseph Napolitan, *The Election Game and How to Win It* (New York: Doubleday, 1972).

[32]David B. Magleby and Candice J. Nelson, *The Money Chase: Congressional Campaign Finance Reform* (Washington, D.C.: Brookings Institution, 1990).

[33]John F. Bibby, *Politics, Parties, and Elections in America*, 3d ed. (Chicago: Nelson-Hall, 1996), 205.

[34]Ibid.

[35]David Chagall, *The New King-Makers* (New York: Harcourt Brace Jovanovich, 1981).

[36]Michael W. Traugott and Paul J. Lavrakas, *The Voters' Guide to Election Polls* (Chatham, N.J.: Chatham House, 1996).

[37]Kiku Adatto, "Sound Bite Democracy," Joan Shoronstein Center on the Press, Politics, and Public Policy, Research Paper R-2, Harvard University, Cambridge, Mass., June 1990.

[38]Darrell M. West, *Air Wars: Television Advertising in Election Campaigns, 1952–1992* (Washington, D.C.: Congressional Quarterly Press, 1993), 140–146.

[39]Ibid.

[40]Stephen Ansolabehere and Shanto Iyengar, *Going Negative* (New York: Free Press, 1995), ch. 5.

[41]West, *Air Wars*, 12.

[42]Ibid., 143.

[43]Thomas E. Patterson, *Out of Order* (New York: Vintage, 1994), ch. 2.

[44]David Adamany, "Political Parties in the 1980s," in Michael J. Malbin, ed., *Money and Politics in the United States* (Chatham, N.J.: Chatham House, 1984), 114.

[45]Aldrich, *Why Parties?*, 269.

[46]David E. Price, *Bringing Back the Parties* (Washington, D.C.: Congressional Quarterly Press, 1984), 116.

[47]See James P. Pfiffner, *The Modern Presidency* (New York: St. Martin's Press, 1994), ch. 6.

CHAPTER NINE

[1]E. E. Schattschneider, *The Semisovereign People: A Realist's View of Democracy in America* (New York: Holt, Rinehart & Winston, 1960), 35.

[2]Quoted in Norman J. Ornstein and Shirley Elder, *Interest Groups, Lobbying, and Policymaking* (Washington, D.C.: Congressional Quarterly Press, 1978), 11.

[3]Alexis de Tocqueville, *Democracy in America* (1835–1840), ed. J. P. Mayer and A. P. Kerr (Garden City, N.Y.: Doubleday/Anchor, 1969), bk. II, ch. 4.

[4]See Jack L. Walker, Jr., *Mobilizing Interest Groups in America: Patrons, Professions, and Social Movements* (Ann Arbor: University of Michigan Press, 1991).

[5]E. Pendleton Herring, *Group Representation before Congress* (Washington, D.C.: Brookings Institution, 1929), 78.

[6]Kay Lehman Schlozman and John T. Tierney, *Organized Interests and American Democracy* (New York: Harper & Row, 1986), 41.

[7]See Robert H. Salisbury, John P. Heinz, Edward O. Leumann, and Robert L. Nelson, "Who Works with Whom? Interest Group Alliances and Opposition," *American Political Science Review* 81 (December 1987): 1217–1234.

[8]Terry Moe, "A Calculus of Group Membership," *American Journal of Political Science* 24 (November 1980): 593–632.

[9]See Lawrence Rothenberg, *Linking Citizens to Government: Interest Group Politics at Common Cause* (New York: Cambridge University Press, 1992).

[10]Mancur Olson, *The Logic of Collective Action* (Cambridge, Mass.: Harvard University Press, 1965), 64.

[11]See Ernest Wittenberg and Elisabeth Wittenberg, *How to Win in Washington* (Cambridge, Mass.: Blackwell, 1989), 81.

[12]Walker, *Mobilizing Interest Groups in America*, ch. 1.

[13]Christopher J. Bosso, "The Color of Money: Environmental Groups and the Pathologies of Fund Raising," in Allan J. Cigler and Burdett Loomis, *Interest Group Politics*, 4th ed. (Washington, D.C.: Congressional Quarterly Press, 1995), 101–103.

[14]See Allen D. Hertzke, *Representing God in Washington* (Knoxville: University of Tennessee Press, 1988); Matthew Moen, *The Christian Right and Congress* (Tuscaloosa: University of Alabama Press, 1989).

[15]Schlozman and Tierney, *Organized Interests and American Democracy*, 54; see also Ronald J. Hrebenar and Ruth K. Scott, *Interest Group Politics in America* (Englewood Cliffs, N.J.: Prentice-Hall, 1990), 167.

[16]Ornstein and Elder, *Interest Groups, Lobbying, and Policymaking*, 82–86.

[17]See John Mark Hansen, *Gaining Access* (Chicago: University of Chicago Press, 1991).

[18]Robert H. Salisbury and Paul Johnson, "Who You Know versus What You Know," *American Journal of Political Science* 33 (February 1989): 175–195.

[19]Ornstein and Elder, *Interest Groups, Lobbying, and Policymaking*, 70.

[20]Quoted in ibid, 77.

[21]Bruce C. Wolfe and Bertram J. Levine, *Lobbying Congress*, 2d ed. (Washington, D.C.: Congressional Quarterly Press, 1996).

[22]See Marver Bernstein, *Regulating Business by Independent Commission* (Princeton, N.J.: Princeton University Press, 1955).

[23]Paul J. Quirk, *Industry Influence in Federal Regulatory Agencies* (Princeton, N.J.: Princeton University Press, 1981).

[24]John E. Chubb, *Interest Groups and the Bureaucracy: The Politics of Energy* (Stanford, Calif.: Stanford University Press, 1983), 200–201.

[25]Lee Epstein and C. K. Rowland, "Interest Groups in the Courts," *American Political Science Review*, 85 (1991): 205–217; Joseph Stewart, Jr., and James F. Sheffield, Jr., "Does Interest Group Litigation Matter? The Case of Black Political Mobilization in Mississippi," *Journal of Politics* 49 (August 1987): 780–798; Joseph F. Kobylka, "A Court-Related Context for Group Litigation," *Journal of Politics* 49 (November 1987): 1061–1078.

[26]See Hansen, *Gaining Access.*

[27]Hugh Heclo, "Issue Networks and the Executive Establishment," in Anthony King, ed., *The New American Political System* (Washington, D.C.: American Enterprise Institute, 1978), 87–124.

[28]Ornstein and Elder, *Interest Groups, Lobbying, and Policymaking*, 88–93.

[29]Wittenberg and Wittenberg, *How to Win in Washington*, 81.

[30]Quoted in Mark Green, "Political PAC-Man," *The New Republic*, December 13, 1982, 20.

[31]Frank J. Sorauf, *Inside Campaign Finance* (New Haven, Conn.: Yale University Press, 1992).

[32]Quoted in Larry Sabato, *PAC Power: Inside the World of Political Action Committees* (New York: Norton, 1984), 72.

[33]Federal Elections Commission (FEC) Report, April 29, 1993.

[34]See Michael J. Malbin, "Of Mountains and Molehills," in Michael J. Malbin, *Parties, Interest Groups, and Campaign Finance Laws* (Washington, D.C.: American Enterprise Institute, 1981), 157–177.

[35]See Thomas L. Gatz, *Improper Influence* (Ann Arbor: University of Michigan Press, 1996); Dan Clawson, Alan Neustadtl, and Denise Scott, *Money Talks* (New York: Basic Books, 1992).

[36]Walker, *Mobilizing Interest Groups in America.*

[37]See Robert Dahl, *Dilemmas of Pluralist Democracy* (New Haven, Conn.: Yale University Press, 1982).

[38]Walker, *Mobilizing Interest Groups in America,* 112.

[39]Theodore J. Lowi, *The End of Liberalism: The Second Republic of the United States* (New York: Norton, 1979).

[40]Jeffrey Berry, *The Interest Group Society* (Boston: Little, Brown, 1984), 172.

[41]See G. William Domhoff, *The Power Elite and the State* (New York: Aldine de Gruyter, 1990).

[42]See Lawrence S. Rothenberg, *Linking Citizens to Government* (New York: Cambridge University Press, 1992).

[43]Benjamin Ginsberg, *The Consequences of Consent* (New York: Random House, 1982), 214.

[44]See, for example, Walker, *Mobilizing Interest Groups in America.*

[45]Jonathan Rauch, *Demosclerosis: The Silent Killer of American Government* (New York: Times Books, 1994).

CHAPTER TEN

[1]Theodore H. White, *The Making of the President, 1972* (New York: Bantam, 1973), 327.

[2]See Richard Davis, *The Press and American Politics* (New York: Longman, 1992), 24–27.

[3]Comment at the annual meeting of the American Association of Political Consultants, Washington, D.C., 1977.

[4]Culver Smith, *The Press, Politics, and Patronage* (Athens: University of Georgia Press, 1977), 2, 15, 39–55.

[5]Frank Luther Mott, *American Journalism, a History: 1690–1960* (New York: Macmillan, 1962), 114–115.

[6]Smith, *Press, Politics, and Patronage,* 163–168.

[7]Doris A. Graber, *Mass Media and American Politics,* 4th ed. (Washington, D.C.: Congressional Quarterly Press, 1993), 36; Mark Wahlgren Summers, *The Press Gang* (Chapel Hill: University of North Carolina Press, 1994).

[8]See Michael Schudson, *Discovering the News* (New York: Basic Books, 1978).

[9]Commission on Freedom of the Press, *A Free and Responsible Press* (Chicago: University of Chicago Press, 1974), 62–63.

[10]Mott, *American Journalism,* 220–227, 241, 243.

[11]Edwin Emery, *The Press and America: An Interpretive History of the Mass Media* (Englewood Cliffs, N.J.: Prentice-Hall, 1977), 350.

[12]Quoted in Mott, *American Journalism,* 529.

[13]See Dean A. Alger, *The Media and Politics*, 2d ed. (Belmont, Calif.: Wadsworth, 1996), 122–123.

[14]Quoted in David Halberstam, *The Powers That Be* (New York: Knopf, 1979), 208–209.

[15]Leo Bogart, *The Age of Television* (New York: Unger, 1956), 213.

[16]Theodore H. White, *America in Search of Itself: The Making of the President, 1956–1980* (New York: Harper & Row, 1982), 172–173.

[17]Quoted in Michael Robinson and Margaret Sheehan, *Over the Wire and on TV* (New York: Russell Sage Foundation, 1983), 226.

[18]Jean Gaddy Wilson, "For a New Nation, The New Future," *Nieman Reports* 46 (Spring 1992): 17.

[19]Figures from *Standard Rate and Data Service* and *Electronic Media*, various dates.

[20]Graber, *Mass Media and American Politics*, 36.

[21]Ben H. Bagdikian, *The Media Monopoly*, 4th ed. (Boston: Beacon, 1992).

[22]Paul H. Weaver, *News and the Culture of Lying* (New York: Free Press, 1994).

[23]Herbert J. Gans, *Deciding What's News* (New York: Vintage, 1980).

[24]James Fallows, *Breaking the News* (New York: Pantheon, 1996).

[25]Thomas Patterson, *Out of Order* (New York: Vintage, 1994), ch. 2.

[26]Walter Lippman, *Public Opinion* (New York: Macmillan, 1922), 214.

[27]Stephen Hess, "A Washington Perspective," paper presented at the Donald S. Mc-Naughton Symposium, sponsored by Syracuse University, New York City, April 1985.

[28]Bernard C. Cohen, *The Press and Foreign Policy* (Princeton, N.J.: Princeton University Press, 1963), 13.

[29]See John Anthony Maltese, *Spin Control* (Chapel Hill: University of North Carolina Press, 1994).

[30]S. Robert Lichter and Richard E. Noyes, *Good Intentions Make Bad News*, updated ed. (Lanham, Md.: Rowman & Littlefield, 1997), ii.

[31]Kiku Adatto, "Sound Bite Democracy," Joan Shorenstein Center on the Press, Politics, and Public Policy, Research Paper R-2, Harvard University, Cambridge, Mass., June 1990.

[32]Kenneth Walsh, *Feeding the Beast* (New York: Random House, 1996).

[33]Patterson, *Out of Order*, ch. 3.

[34]Thomas E. Patterson, "Bad News, Bad Governance," *ANNALS* 546 (July 1996): 97–108.

[35]Data from Center for Media and Public Affairs, Washington, D.C., 1996.

[36]Quoted in Max Kampelman, "The Power of the Press," *Policy Review* 6 (1978): 19.

[37]Ibid.

[38]Quoted in Edward J. Epstein, *News from Nowhere: Television and the News* (New York: Random House, 1973), ix; see also Paul Weaver, *News and the Culture of Lying* (New York: Free Press, 1994).

[39]Lippmann, *Public Opinion*, 221.

CHAPTER ELEVEN

[1]Roger H. Davidson and Walter J. Oleszek, *Congress and Its Members*, 2d ed. (Washington, D.C.: Congressional Quarterly Press, 1985), 7.

[2]See Paul S. Herrnson, *Congressional Elections: Campaigning at Home and in Washington* (Washington, D.C.: Congressional Quarterly Press, 1995).

[3]See Gary C. Jacobson, *The Politics of Congressional Elections*, 4th ed. (New York: Longman, 1996).

[4]See Jonathan S. Krasno, *Challenges, Competition, and Reelection: Comparing House and Senate Campaigns* (New Haven, Conn.: Yale University Press, 1995).

[5]David R. Mayhew, *Congress: The Electoral Connection* (New Haven, Conn.: Yale University Press, 1974), 16; Richard F. Fenno, Jr., *Home Style: House Members in Their Districts* (Boston: Little, Brown, 1978), 167.

[6]James L. Payne, "The Personal Electoral Advantage of House Incumbents, 1936–1976," *American Politics Quarterly* 8 (October 1980): 465–482.

[7]Lawrence C. Dodd, "A Theory of Congressional Cycles," in Gerald Wright, Leroy Rieselbach, and Lawrence C. Dodd, *Congress and Policy Change* (New York: Agathon, 1986).

[8]Bruce Cain, John Ferejohn, and Morris P. Fioring, *The Personal Vote* (Cambridge: Harvard University Press, 1987).

[9]Information provided by Clerk of the House, 1997.

[10]Harold W. Stanley and Richard G. Niemi, *Vital Statistics on American Politics*, 5th ed. (Washington, D.C.: Congressional Quarterly Press, 1995), 217.

[11]See Diana Evans Yiannakis, "House Members' Communication Styles," *Journal of Politics* 44 (November 1982): 1049–1073.

[12]*Congressional Quarterly Guide to Congress*, 3d ed. (Washington, D.C.: Congressional Quarterly Press, 1982), 666; see also David A. Leuthold, *Electioneering in a Democracy* (New York: Wiley, 1968).

[13]See Jacobson, *The Politics of Congressional Elections*.

[14]See Thomas E. Mann, *Unsafe at Any Margin: Interpreting Congressional Elections* (Washington, D.C.: American Enterprise Institute, 1978); see also Gary C. Jacobson, *The Electoral Origins of Divided Government* (Boulder, Colo.: Westview Press, 1990).

[15]Quoted in "A Tale of Myths and Measures: Who Is Truly Vulnerable?" *Congressional Quarterly Weekly Report*, December 4, 1993, 7.

[16]James E. Campbell, *The Presidential Pulse of Congressional Elections* (Lexington: University Press of Kentucky, 1993).

[17]Linda L. Fowler and Robert D. McClure, *Political Ambition* (New Haven, Conn.: Yale University Press, 1989).

[18]Thomas Kazee, "Recruiting Challengers in U.S. House Elections," *Legislative Studies Quarterly* (August 1983): 469–480.

[19]Keith R. Poole and Howard Rosenthal, "Patterns of Congressional Voting," *American Journal of Political Science*, 35 (February 1991): 228.

[20]Linda Witt, Karen M. Paget, and Glenna Matthews, *Running as a Woman: Gender and Power in American Politics* (New York: Free Press, 1993); see also Sue Thomas, *How Women Legislate* (New York: Oxford University Press, 1994).

[21]Ronald M. Peters, Jr., *The American Speakership* (Baltimore: Johns Hopkins University Press, 1990).

[22]Fred R. Harris, *Deadlock or Decision: The U.S. Senate and the Rise of National Politics* (New York: Oxford University Press, 1993), 182.

[23]Ibid., ch. 4.

[24]Quoted in Frank H. Mackamar, *Understanding Congressional Leadership* (Pekin, Ill.: Dickson Center, 1981), 9.

[25]See Barbara Sinclair, *Legislators, Leaders, and Lawmaking* (Baltimore: Johns Hopkins University Press, 1995).

[26]See David W. Rohde, *Parties and Leaders in the Postreform House* (Chicago: University of Chicago Press, 1991).

[27]Jonathan D. Salant, "New Chairman Swing to Right: Freshmen Get Choice Posts," *Congressional Quarterly Weekly Report*, December 10, 1994, 3493.

[28]See Richard L. Hall and C. Lawrence Evans, "The Power of Subcommittees," *Journal of Politics*, May 1990, 335–355.

[29]See Steven S. Smith and Christopher J. Deering, *Committees in Congress*, 2d ed. (Washington, D.C.: Congressional Quarterly Press, 1990).

[30]David W. Rhode and Kenneth A. Shepsle, "Domestic Committee Assignments in the House of Representatives," *American Political Science Review* 73 (September 1973): 889–905.

[31]Steven S. Smith, *The American Congress* (Boston: Houghton Mifflin, 1995), 189–198.

[32]See Stephen E. Frantzich and Steven E. Schier, *Congress: Games and Strategies* (Dubuque, Iowa: Brown & Benchmark, 1995), 127.

[33]See Gerald S. Strom, *The Logic of Lawmaking* (Baltimore: Johns Hopkins University Press, 1990).

[34]See Robert Spitzer, *President & Congress* (New York: McGraw-Hill, 1993).

[35]See Paul C. Light, *The President's Agenda*, rev. ed. (Baltimore: Johns Hopkins University Press, 1991).

[36]See Richard Davis, "News Media Coverage of National Political Institutions," Ph.D. dissertation, Syracuse University, 1986.

[37]Quoted in Martin Tolchin, "How Senators View the Senate," *New York Times*, November 25, 1984, 40.

[38]Walter J. Oleszak, *Congressional Procedures and the Policy Process*, 4th ed. (Washington, D.C.: Congressional Quarterly Press, 1995), ch. 10.

[39]See Gary Orfield, *Congressional Power: Congress and Social Change* (New York: Harcourt Brace Jovanovich, 1975); Charles O. Jones, *Clean Air: The Policies and Politics of Pollution Control* (Pittsburgh: University of Pittsburgh Press, 1975).

[40]James L. Sundquist, "Congress and the President: Enemies or Partners?" in Lawrence C. Dodd and Bruce I. Oppenheimer, eds., *Congress Reconsidered* (New York: Praeger, 1977), 240.

[41]See Paul C. Light, *Forging Legislation* (New York: Norton, 1992).

[42]See Gary W. Cox and Mathew D. McCubbins, *Legislative Leviathan* (Berkeley: University of California Press, 1993).

[43]Eric M. Uslaner, *The Decline of Comity in Congress* (Ann Arbor: University of Michigan Press, 1994).

[44]See Joel D. Aberbach, *Keeping a Watchful Eye* (Washington, D.C.: Brookings Institution, 1990).

[45]See William F. West, *Controlling the Bureaucracy* (Boulder, Colo.: Westview Press, 1994).

CHAPTER TWELVE

[1]Woodrow Wilson, *Constitutional Government in the United States* (New York: Columbia University Press, 1908), 67.

[2]Robert Hirschfield, ed., *The Power of the Presidency*, 3d ed. (New York: Aldine, 1982), 3.

[3]James W. Davis, *The American Presidency* (New York: Harper & Row, 1987), 13.

[4]See Barry M. Blechman and Stephen S. Kaplan, *Force without War* (Washington, D.C.: Brookings Institution, 1978).

[5]*United States* v. *Belmont*, 57 U.S. 758 (1937).

[6]Robert DiClerico, *The American President*, 4th ed. (Englewood Cliffs, N.J.: Prentice-Hall, 1995), 47.

[7]Quoted in Wilfred E. Binkley, *President and Congress*, 3d ed. (New York: Vintage, 1962), 142.

[8]Theodore Roosevelt, *An Autobiography* (New York: Scribner's, 1931), 383.

[9]See Richard M. Pious, *The American Presidency* (New York: Basic Books, 1979), 83.

[10]Robert J. Spitzer, *President and Congress* (New York: McGraw-Hill, 1993), 35–37.

[11]Kenneth A. Oye, Robert J. Lieber, and Donald Rothchild, *Eagle in a New World* (New York: HarperCollins, 1992).

[12]Spitzer, *President and Congress*, 137–232.

[13]James Bryce, *The American Commonwealth* (New York: Commonwealth Edition, 1908), 230.

[14]Davis, *American Presidency*, 20.

[15]See Mark A. Peterson, *Legislating Together: The White House and Capitol Hill from Eisenhower to Reagan* (Cambridge, Mass.: Harvard University Press, 1990).

[16]Thomas R. Marshall, *Presidential Nominations in a Reform Age* (New York: Praeger, 1981); James W. Ceaser, *Presidential Selection: Theory and Development* (Princeton, N.J.: Princeton University Press, 1979).

[17]Thomas E. Patterson, *Out of Order* (New York: Vintage, 1994).

[18]See Michael Nelson, ed., *The Elections of 1992* (Washington, D.C.: Congressional Quarterly Press, 1993), 2–4.

[19]See Hugh Winebrenner, *The Iowa Precinct Caucuses* (Ames: Iowa State University Press, 1987); Gary R. Orren and Nelson W. Polsby, eds., *Media and Momentum: The New Hampshire Primary and Nomination Politics* (Chatham, N.J.: Chatham House, 1987).

[20]Myron A. Levine, *Presidential Campaigns and Elections* (Itasca, Ill.: Peacock, 1995), 30.

[21]Kiku Adatto, "Sound Bite Democracy," Joan Shorenstein Center on the Press, Politics, and Public Policy, Research Paper R-2, Harvard University, Cambridge, Mass., June 1990.

[22]Sidney Kraus, ed., *The Great Debates* (Bloomington: Indiana University Press, 1962), 190.

[23]Kathleen Hall Jamieson, *Packaging the Presidency*, 2d ed. (New York: Oxford University Press, 1992).

[24]John P. Burke, *The Institutional Presidency* (Baltimore: Johns Hopkins University Press, 1992); Charles E. Walcott and Karen M. Hult, *Governing the White House* (Lawrence: University Press of Kansas, 1995).

[25]Davis, *American Presidency*, 240; see also Bradley Patterson, *The Ring of Power* (New York: Basic Books, 1988), 90–91.

[26]James Pfiffner, *The Modern Presidency* (New York: St. Martin's Press, 1994), 91–96.

[27]Quoted in Stephen J. Wayne, *Road to the White House, 1996* (New York: St. Martin's Press, 1996), 156.

[28]Shirley Anne Warshaw, *Powersharing: White House–Cabinet Relations in the Modern Presidency* (Albany: State University of New York Press, 1995).

[29]See Jeffrey E. Cohen, *The Politics of the United States Cabinet* (Pittsburgh: University of Pittsburgh Press, 1988).

[30]Pfiffner, *Modern Presidency*, 123.

[31]Quoted in James MacGregor Burns, "Our Super-Government—Can We Control It?" *The New York Times*, April 24, 1949, 32.

[32]See Paul C. Light, *Thickening Government: Federal Hierarchy and the Diffusion of Accountability* (Washington, D.C.: Brookings Institution, 1995).

[33]James Pfiffner, "The President's Chief of Staff: Lessons Learned," *Presidential Studies Quarterly* 22 (Winter 1993): 77–102.

[34]See Richard Rose, *The Postmodern Presidency* (Chatham, N.J.: Chatham House, 1991).

[35]Pfiffner, *Modern Presidency*, 117–122.

[36]Michael Mezey, *Congress, the President, and Public Policy* (Boulder, Colo.: Westview Press, 1989), 110–115.

[37]George Edwards III, *At the Margins* (New Haven, Conn.: Yale University Press, 1989), 39–46.

[38]Erwin Hargrove, *The Power of the Modern Presidency* (New York: Knopf, 1974).

[39]James P. Pfiffner, *The Strategic Presidency: Hitting the Ground Running*, 2d ed. (Chicago: Dorsey Press, 1996).

[40]Thomas P. (Tip) O'Neill, with William Novak, *Man of the House: The Life and Political Memoirs of Speaker Tip O'Neill* (New York: Random House, 1987), 297.

[41]Fred I. Greenstein, ed., *Leadership in the Modern Presidency* (Cambridge, Mass.: Harvard University Press, 1988), ch. 10.

[42]Robert J. Spitzer, *The Presidential Veto: Touchstone of the American Presidency* (Albany: State University of New York Press, 1988).

[43]Richard Neustadt, *Presidential Power and the Modern Presidents* (New York: Free Press, 1990), 71–72.

[44]*Congressional Quarterly Weekly Reports*, December 19, 1992, 3896.

[45]Mary E. Stuckey, *The President as Interpreter-in-Chief* (Chatham, N.J.: Chatham House, 1991).

[46]See Neustadt, *Presidential Power.*

[47]Gallup Polls, November 2–5, 1979, and November 30–December 3, 1979.

[48]John E. Mueller, "Presidential Popularity from Truman to Johnson," *American Political Science Review* 64 (March 1970): 18–34.

[49]See John Anthony Maltese, *Spin Control* (Chapel Hill: University of North Carolina Press, 1994); Michael Baruch Grossman and Martha Joynt Kumar, *Portraying the President* (Baltimore: Johns Hopkins University Press, 1981).

[50]Samuel Kernell, *Going Public: New Strategies of Presidential Leadership* (Washington, D.C.: Congressional Quarterly Press, 1986), 1.

[51]Jeffrey Tulis, *The Rhetorical Presidency* (Princeton, N.J.: Princeton University Press, 1987); see also Craig Allen Smith, *The White House Speaks* (Westport, Conn.: Greenwood, 1994).

[52]Stuckey, *The President as Interpreter-in-Chief*

[53]Heclo, "Introduction: The Presidential Illusion," 2.

[54]Theodore J. Lowi, *The "Personal" Presidency: Power Invested, Promise Unfulfilled* (Ithaca, N.Y.: Cornell University Press, 1985).

CHAPTER THIRTEEN

[1]Norman Thomas, *Rule 9: Politics, Administration, and Civil Rights* (New York: Random House, 1966), 6.

[2]Opening section of chapter based on James P. Pfiffner, "The National Performance Review in Perspective," working paper, 94-4, The Institute of Public Policy, George Mason University, 1994, 12.

[3]Quoted in Albert Gore, Jr., *From Red Tape to Results: Creating a Government That Works Better and Costs Less* (Washington, D.C.: U.S. Superintendent of Documents, 1993), 1.

[4]Max Weber, *Economy and Society*, trans. Guenther Roth and Claus Wittich (New York: Bedminster, 1968), 23.

[5]*Rutan* v. *Republican Party of Illinois*, 497 U.S. 62 (1990).

[6]Sar A. Levitan and Alexandra B. Noden, *Working for the Sovereign* (Baltimore: Johns Hopkins University Press, 1983), 28–29, 39.

[7]See Cornelius M. Kerwin, *Rulemaking: How Government Agencies Write Law and Make Policy* (Washington, D.C.: Congressional Quarterly Press, 1994).

[8]Michael Lipsky, *Street-Level Bureaucracy* (New York: Russell Sage Foundation, 1980); see also George Serra, "Citizen-Initiated Contact and Satisfaction with Bureaucracy," *Journal of Public Administration* 5 (April 1995): 175–188.

[9]Jay M. Shafritz, *Personnel Management in Government* (New York: Marcel Dekker, 1981), 9–13.

[10]James Q. Wilson, "The Rise of the Bureaucratic State," *Public Interest* 41 (Fall 1975): 77–103.

[11]David Nachmias and David H. Rosenbloom, *Bureaucratic Government: U.S.A.* (New York: St. Martin's Press, 1980), 39.

[12]David H. Rosenbloom, *Federal Service and the Constitution* (Ithaca, N.Y.: Cornell University Press, 1971), 83.

[13]For insights on this and other civil service mechanisms, see Patricia Ingraham and David Rosenbloom, *The Promise and Paradox of Civil Service Reform* (Pittsburgh: University of Pittsburgh Press, 1992); Pfiffner, "The National Performance Review in Perspective."

[14]Herbert Kaufman, "Emerging Conflicts in the Doctrine of Public Administration," *American Political Science Review* 50 (December 1956): 1060.

[15]Ibid., 1062.

[16]See Richard W. Waterman, *Presidential Influence and the Administrative State* (Knoxville: University of Tennessee Press, 1989).

[17]Norton E. Long, "Power and Administration," *Public Administration Review* 10 (Autumn 1949), 269; Joel D. Aberbach, Robert A. Putnam, and Bert A. Rockman, *Bureaucrats and Politicians in Western Democracies* (Cambridge, Mass.: Harvard University Press, 1980).

[18]See Herbert Kaufman, *The Administrative Behavior of Federal Bureaucrats* (Washington, D.C.: Brookings Institution, 1981), 4.

[19]See John Brehon and Scott Gates, *Working, Shirking and Sabotage* (Ann Arbor: University of Michigan Press, 1996).

[20]Quoted in Aaron Wildavsky, *The Politics of the Budgetary Process*, 4th ed. (Boston: Little, Brown, 1984), 19.

[21]Joel D. Aberbach and Bert A. Rockman, "Clashing Beliefs within the Executive Branch," *American Political Science Review* 70 (June 1976): 461.

[22]Aberbach, Putnam, and Rockman, *Bureaucrats and Politicians in Western Democracies*, 52.

[23]Jonathan Bendor, Serge Taylor, and Roland Van Gaalen, "Stacking the Deck: Bureaucratic Missions and Policy Design," *American Political Science Review* 81 (September 1987): 873–896.

[24]See Jack L. Walker, Jr., *Mobilizing Interest Groups in America* (Ann Arbor: University of Michigan Press, 1991).

[25]Herbert Kaufman, *Are Government Organizations Immortal?* (Washington, D.C.: Brookings Institution, 1976), 76; see also Jonathan Rauch, *Demosclerosis* (New York, Times Books, 1994).

[26]Long, "Power and Administration," 269.

[27]See William P. Browne, *Cultivating Congress* (Lawrence: University Press of Kansas, 1995).

[28]Hugh Heclo, "Issue Networks and the Executive Establishment," in Anthony King, ed., *The New American Political System* (Washington, D.C.: American Enterprise Institute, 1978), 102.

[29]See John Mark Hansen, *Gaining Access* (Chicago: University of Chicago Press, 1991).

[30]Martin Laffin, "Reinventing the Federal Government," in Christopher Peele, Christopher J. Bailey, Bruce Cain, and B. Guy Peters, eds., *Developments in American Politics 2* (Chatham, N.J.: Chatham House, 1995), 172–176; Harry W. Reynolds, Jr., ed., *Ethics in American Public Service* (Philadelphia: Annals of the American Academy, 1995).

[31]Phillip B. Heymann, *The Politics of Public Management* (New Haven, Conn.: Yale University Press, 1988); James G. Benze, Jr., *Presidential Power and Management Techniques* (New York: Greenwood, 1987).

[32]James G. March and Johan P. Olson, "Organizing Political Life: What Administrative Reorganization Tells Us about Government," *American Political Science Review* 77 (June 1983): 281–296.

[33]B. Dan Wood and Richard W. Waterman, "Political Control of the Bureaucracy," *American Political Science Review* 85 (September 1991): 810, figure 2.

[34]Paul C. Light, *Thickening Government: Federal Hierarchy and the Diffusion of Accountability* (Washington, D.C.: Brookings Institution, 1995).

[35]See Hugh Heclo, *A Government of Strangers* (Washington, D.C.: Brookings Institution, 1977), 117–118.

[36]Aaron Wildavsky, *The New Politics of the Budgetary Process*, 2d ed. (New York: HarperCollins, 1992).

[37]See Donald Kettl, *Deficit Politics* (New York: Macmillan, 1992).

[38]See Joel D. Aberbach, *Keeping a Watchful Eye* (Washington, D.C.: Brookings Institution, 1990).

[39]Wood and Waterman, "Political Control of the Bureaucracy," 820–821; see also Cathy Marie Johnson, *The Dynamics of Conflict between Bureaucrats and Legislators* (Armonk, N.Y.: Sharpe, 1992).

[40]See Johnson, *The Dynamics of Conflict between Bureaucrats and Legislators*.

[41]David Rosenbloom, "The Evolution of the Administrative State, and Transformations of Administrative Law," in David Rosenbloom and Richard Schwartz, eds., *Handbook of Regulation and Administrative Law* (New York: Marcel Dekker, 1994), 3–36.

[42]See *Vermont Yankee Nuclear Power Corp.* v. *National Resources Defense Council, Inc.*, 435 U.S. 519 (1978); *Chevron* v. *National Resources Defense Council*, 467 U.S. 837 (1984); *Heckler* v. *Chaney*, 470 U.S. 821 (1985).

[43]Roberta Ann Johnson and Michael E. Kraft, "Bureaucratic Whistleblowing and Policy Change," *Western Political Quarterly* 43 (December 1990): 849–874.

[44]"Way, Way Off in the Wild Blue Yonder," *Time*, May 29, 1995, 32–33.

⁴⁵See Kathleen Staudt, *Women, Foreign Assistance, and Advocacy Administration* (New York: Praeger, 1985); Frederick C. Mosher, *Democracy and the Public Service,* 2d ed. (New York: Oxford University Press, 1982), 13.

⁴⁶See B. Dan Wood and Richard M. Waterman, *Bureaucratic Dynamics* (Boulder, Colo.: Westview Press, 1994).

⁴⁷David Osborne and Ted Gaebler, *Reinventing Government: How the Entrepreneurial Spirit Is Transforming the Public Sector* (New York: Addison-Wesley, 1992); see also Michael Barzelay and Babak J. Armajani, *Breaking through Bureaucracy* (Berkeley: University of California Press, 1992); Robert D. Behn, *Leadership Counts* (Cambridge, Mass.: Harvard University Press, 1991).

⁴⁸Ronald C. Moe, "The 'Reinventing Government' Exercise: Misinterpreting the Problem, Misjudging the Results," *Public Administration Review* (March/April, 1994): 125–136.

⁴⁹Tom Shoop, "From Citizens to Customers," *Government Executive* (May 1994): 27–30.

⁵⁰See Mark Goldstein, *America's Hollow Government: How Washington Has Failed the People* (Homewood, Ill.: Business One Irwin, 1992); but see also James Pinkerton, *What Comes Next?* (New York: Hyperion, 1995.

CHAPTER FOURTEEN

¹*Marbury* v. *Madison,* 1 Cranch 137 (1803).

²*Planned Parenthood* v. *Casey,* No. 91–744 (1992).

³*Roe* v. *Wade,* 401 U.S. 113 (1973).

⁴See Michael J. Perry, *The Constitution, the Courts, and Human Rights: An Inquiry into the Legitimacy of Constitutional Policymaking by the Judiciary* (New Haven, Conn.: Yale University Press, 1982).

⁵Raoul Berger, *Government by Judiciary: The Transformation of the Fourteenth Amendment* (Cambridge, Mass.: Harvard University Press, 1977).

⁶Rebecca Mae Salokar, *The Solicitor General: The Politics of Law* (Philadelphia: Temple University Press, 1992); see also Cornell W. Clayton, *The Politics of Justice: The Attorney General and the Making of Legal Policy* (Armonk, N.Y.: Sharpe, 1992).

⁷See Bernard Schwartz, *Decision: How the Supreme Court Decides Cases* (New York: Oxford University Press, 1996).

⁸Lawrence Baum, *The Supreme Court,* 5th ed. (Washington, D.C.: Congressional Quarterly Press, 1995), 117.

⁹*Gideon* v. *Wainwright,* 372 U.S. 335, (1963).

¹⁰From a letter to the author by Frank Schwartz of Beaver College. This section reflects substantially Professor Schwartz's recommendations to the author, as does the later section that addresses the "federal-court myth."

¹¹*Hutto* v. *Davis,* 370 U.S. 256 (1982).

¹²*Roe* v. *Wade.*

[13]David M. O'Brien, *Storm Center: The Supreme Court in American Politics*, 4th ed. (New York: Norton, 1996), 69–76.

[14]See Robert A. Carp and Ronald Stidham, *The Federal Courts*, 2d ed. (Washington, D.C.: Congressional Quarterly Press, 1990).

[15]Stephen L. Wasby, *The Supreme Court in the Federal Judicial System*, 4th ed. (Chicago: Nelson-Hall, 1993), 75.

[16]Henry J. Abraham, *The Judicial Process*, 6th ed. (New York: Oxford University Press, 1993), 24–26.

[17]Robert Scigliano, *The Supreme Court and the Presidency* (New York: Free Press, 1971), 146; see also David Savage, *Turning Right: The Making of the Rehnquist Supreme Court* (New York: Wiley, 1992).

[18]Quoted in Baum, *The Supreme Court*, 37.

[19]See Robert A. Carp and Ronald Stidham, *Judicial Process in America*, 3d ed. (Washington, D.C.: Congressional Quarterly Press, 1996), ch. 8.

[20]John Gottschall, "Reagan's Appointments to the U.S. Courts of Appeals," 70 *Judicature* 48 (1986): 54.

[21]See George L. Watson and John Alan Stookey, *Shaping America: The Politics of Supreme Court Appointments* (New York: Longman, 1995).

[22]People for the American Way data, 1994.

[23]Henry J. Abraham, "The Judicial Function under the Constitution," *News for Teachers of Political Science* 41 (Spring 1984): 14.

[24]Sheldon Goldman, "Should There Be Affirmative Action for the Judiciary?" *Judicature* 62 (May 1979): 494.

[25]Quoted in Louis Fisher, *American Constitutional Law* (New York: McGraw-Hill, 1990), 5.

[26]Baum, *The Supreme Court*, 117.

[27]Quoted in Charles P. Curtis, *Law and Large as Life* (New York: Simon & Schuster, 1959), 156–157.

[28]See Joan Biskupic and Elder Witt, *The Supreme Court and the Powers of the American Government* (Washington, D.C.: Congressional Quarterly Press, 1996), ch. 1.

[29]Wasby, *The Supreme Court in the Federal Judicial System*, 53.

[30]See Lee Epstein, *Conservatives in Court* (Knoxville: University of Tennessee Press, 1985), 80–88.

[31]See Watson and Stookey, *Shaping America*.

[32]John Schmidhauser, *The Supreme Court* (New York: Holt, Rinehart & Winston, 1964), 6.

[33]Jeffrey A. Segal and Harold J. Spaeth, *The Supreme Court and the Attitudinal Model* (New York: Cambridge University Press, 1993).

[34]Linda Greenhouse, "In Supreme Court's Decisions, A Clear Voice, and a Murmur," *The New York Times*, July 3, 1996, 19.

[35]See Robert F. Nagel, *Judicial Power and American Character* (New York: Oxford University Press, 1996).

[36]O'Brien, *Storm Center*, 56–61.

[37]See Harry H. Wellington, *Interpreting the Constitution* (New Haven, Conn.: Yale University Press, 1990).

[38]Abraham, "The Judicial Function under the Constitution," 14.

[39]Alexander M. Bickel, *The Supreme Court and the Idea of Progress* (New Haven, Conn.: Yale University Press, 1978), 173–181.

[40]Louis Lusky, *By What Right? A Commentary on the Supreme Court's Power to Revise the Constitution* (Charlottesville, Va.: Michie, 1975), 214–216.

[41]*Romer* v. *Evans*, No. 94-1039 (1996).

[42]See Larry W. Yackle, *Reclaiming the Federal Courts* (Cambridge, Mass.: Harvard University Press, 1994).

[43]See Michael J. Perry, *The Constitutional and the Courts* (New York: Oxford University Press, 1994).

[44]Quoted in "Good for the Left, Now Good for the Right," *Newsweek*, July 8, 1991, 22.

CHAPTER FIFTEEN

[1]This section relies substantially on Alan Stone, *Regulation and Its Alternatives* (Washington, D.C.: Congressional Quarterly Press, 1982).

[2]See Marc Allen Eisner, *Regulatory Politics in Transition* (Baltimore: Johns Hopkins University Press, 1993).

[3]See Walter A. Rosenbaum, *Environmental Politics and Policy*, 3d ed. (Washington, D.C.: Congressional Quarterly Press, 1994); Ronald Shaiko, "Greenpeace, U.S.A.," *ANNALS* 528 (July 1993): 89–103.

[4]Paul Portney, "Beware of the Killer Clauses inside the GOP's 'Contract,' " *The Washington Post National Weekly Edition*, January 23–29, 1995, 21.

[5]See Richard A. Harris and Sidney M. Milkis, *The Politics of Regulatory Change* (New York: Oxford University Press, 1996).

[6]See Larry N. Gerston, Cynthia Fraleigh, and Robert Schwab, *The Deregulated Society* (Pacific Grove, Calif.: Brooks/Cole, 1988); Donald F. Kettl, "The Savings and Loan Bailout: The Mismatch between the Headlines and the Issues," *PS: Political Science and Politics* 23 (September 1991): 441–447.

[7]H. Peyton Young, *Equity: In Theory and Practice* (Princeton, N.J.: Princeton University Press, 1995).

[8]David E. Vogel, "The 'New' Social Regulation in Historical and Comparative Perspective," in Thomas McGraw, ed., *Regulation in Perspective* (Cambridge, Mass.: Harvard University Press, 1981), 162.

[9]Molly Ivins, "GOP Job Bill Is Truly Bad," *Syracuse Post-Standard*, February 15, 1995, A10.

[10]Vogel, " 'The 'New' Social Regulation," 173.

[11]See Thomas Streeter, *Selling the Air* (Chicago: University of Chicago Press, 1996).

[12] See Robert Lekachman, *The Age of Keynes* (New York: Random House, 1966).

[13] See Donald F. Kettl, *Deficit Politics* (New York: Macmillan, 1992).

[14] See Bruce Bartlett, *Reaganomics: Supply-Side Economics* (Westport, Conn.: Arlington House, 1981); Kenneth Hoover and Raymond Plant, *Conservative Capitalism in Britain and the United States* (New York: Routledge, 1989).

[15] House Ways and Means Committee data, 1991.

[16] See Aaron Wildavsky, *The New Politics of the Budgetary Process*, 2d ed (New York: HarperCollins, 1992).

[17] Seymour Martin Lipset, "The Economy, Elections, and Public Opinions," *Tocqueville Review* 5 (Fall 1983): 431.

[18] D. Roderick Kiewiet, *Macro-Economics and Micro-Politics* (Chicago: University of Chicago Press, 1983), 154–158.

[19] Milton Friedman and Walter Heller, *Monetary vs. Fiscal Policy* (New York: Macmillan, 1969).

[20] Steven Pearlstein, "The Man Who Really Runs America," *The Washington Post National Weekly Edition*, February 6–12, 1995, 23.

CHAPTER SIXTEEN

[1] See Jennifer Hochschild, *Facing Up to the American Dream* (Princeton, N.J.: Princeton University Press, 1996).

[2] Michael Harrington, *The Other America: Poverty in the United States* (New York: Macmillan, 1962); see also Sheldon H. Danziger, Gary D. Sandefur, and Daniel H. Weinberg, eds., *Confronting Poverty* (Cambridge, Mass.: Harvard University Press, 1994); William Julius Wilson, *The Truly Disadvantaged: The Inner City, the Underclass, and Public Policy* (Chicago: University of Chicago Press, 1987).

[3] James D. Wright, *Address Unknown: The Homeless in America* (New York: Aldine de Gruyter, 1989).

[4] Charles Murray, *Losing Ground: American Social Policy, 1950–1980* (New York: Basic Books, 1984).

[5] John J. Dilulio, "True Welfare Reform," *The Washington Post National Weekly Edition*, January 23–29, 1995, 20.

[6] See David T. Ellwood and Lawrence H. Summers, "Is Welfare Really the Problem?" *Public Interest* 83 (Spring 1986): 57–78.

[7] *Five Thousand American Families* (Ann Arbor: University of Michigan Institute for Social Research, 1977); see also *Panel Study of Income Dynamics* (Ann Arbor: University of Michigan Institute for Social Research, 1996 and other years).

[8] Everett Carll Ladd, *American Political Parties* (New York: Norton, 1970), 205.

[9] David B. Walker, *Toward a Functioning Federalism* (Cambridge, Mass.: Winthrop, 1981), 102.

[10] V. O. Key, Jr., *The Responsible Electorate* (Cambridge, Mass.: Belknap Press of Harvard University, 1966), 43.

[11] See Jill Quadrangle, *The Transformation of Old Age Security* (Chicago: University of Chicago Press, 1988).

[12] Paul Light, *Artful Work: The Politics of Social Security* (New York: Random House, 1985), ch. 9.

[13] For a general overview of 1950s and 1960s policy disputes, see James Sundquist, *Politics and Policy* (Washington, D.C.: Brookings Institution, 1968).

[14] "Welfare: Myths, Reality," Knight-Ridder News Service story, *Syracuse Post-Standard*, December 5, 1994, A1, A6.

[15] Quoted in Malcolm Gladwell, "The Medicaid Muddle," *The Washington Post National Weekly Edition*, January 16–22, 1995, 31.

[16] Herbert McClosky and John Zaller, *American Ethos: Public Attitudes toward Capitalism and Democracy* (Cambridge, Mass.: Harvard University Press, 1984), 18.

[17] Karl A. Lamb, *As Orange Goes: Twelve California Families and the Future of American Politics* (New York: Norton, 1974), 178.

[18] Based on Organization for Economic Co-Operation and Development (OECD) data, 1993.

[19] Laurel Shaper Walters, "World Educators Compare Notes," *Christian Science Monitor*, September 7, 1994, 8.

[20] See John E. Chubb and Terry M. Moe, *Politics, Markets, and America's Schools* (Washington, D.C.: Brookings Institution, 1990); Jeffrey R. Henig, *Rethinking School Choice* (Princeton, N.J.: Princeton University Press, 1995).

[21] See Phillip Longman, *Return of Thrift: How the Collapse of the Middle Class Welfare System in the United States Will Reawaken Values in America* (New York: Free Press, 1996).

CHAPTER SEVENTEEN

[1] "Lyon or Mouse," *The Economist*, July 6, 1996, 64.

[2] See Peter B. Kenen, ed., *Understanding Interdependence: The Macroeconomics of the Open Economy* (Princeton, N.J.: Princeton University Press, 1995).

[3] American Assembly Report (cosponsored by the Council on Foreign Relations), *Rethinking America's Security* (New York: Harriman, 1991), 8.

[4] For an overview of Soviet policy, see Alvin Z. Rubenstein, *Soviet Foreign Policy since World War II*, 4th ed. (New York: HarperCollins, 1992); for an assessment of U.S. policy, see Robert Dallek, *The American Style of Foreign Policy* (New York: Oxford University Press, 1990).

[5] See John Lewis Gaddis, *Strategies of Containment* (New York: Oxford University Press, 1982).

[6] Mr. X. (George Kennan), "The Sources of Soviet Conduct," *Foreign Affairs* 25 (July 1947): 566–582.

[7] See Stanley Karnow, *Vietnam: A History* (New York: Penguin, 1983); David M. Barrett, *Uncertain Warriors: Lyndon Johnson and His Vietnam Advisors* (Lawrence: University of Kansas Press, 1993).

[8]Charles Kegley and Eugene Wittkopf, *American Foreign Policy*, 2d ed. (New York: St. Martin's Press, 1982), 48.

[9]See Keith L. Nelson, *The Making of Détente* (Baltimore: Johns Hopkins University Press, 1995).

[10]See Russell J. Ling, "Reagan and the Russians," *American Political Science Review* 78 (June 1984): 338–355.

[11]For a general view of America's new world role, see Kenneth A. Oye, Robert J. Lieber, and Donald Rothchild, *Eagle in a New World: American Grand Strategy in the Post-Cold War Era* (New York: HarperCollins, 1992).

[12]See Loch K. Johnson, *Secret Agencies: U.S. Intelligence in a Hostile World* (New Haven, Conn.: Yale University Press, 1996).

[13]See Robert Jervis, *The Illogic of American Nuclear Strategy* (Ithaca, N.Y.: Cornell University Press, 1984).

[14]Richard J. Barnet, "Reflections: The Disorders of Peace," *The New Yorker*, January 20, 1992, 61.

[15]"What Is Terrorism?" *The Economist*, March 2, 1996, pp. 23–25.

[16]See Ole Holsti, *Public Opinion and American Foreign Policy* (Ann Arbor: University of Michigan Press, 1996).

[17]See James M. Lindsay, *Congress and the Politics of U.S. Foreign Policy* (Baltimore: Johns Hopkins University Press, 1994); William Conrad Gibbons, *The U.S. Government and the Vietnam War* (Washington, D.C.: U.S. Government Printing Office, 1994).

[18]Seymour Melman, *Pentagon Capitalism* (New York: McGraw-Hill, 1970), 175; Paul A. Koistinen, *The Military-Industrial Complex* (New York: Praeger, 1980).

[19]See Elie Abel, *The Shattered Bloc: Beyond the Upheaval in Eastern Europe* (Boston: Houghton Mifflin, 1990).

[20]Paul Kennedy, *The Rise and Fall of the Great Powers* (New York: Random House, 1988); for an alternative view, see Joseph Nye, *Bound to Lead: The Changing Nature of American Power* (New York: Basic Books, 1990).

[21]William Diebold, Jr., "The United States in the World Economy: A Fifty-Year Perspective," *Foreign Affairs* 62 (Fall 1983): 81–104; see also Walter Russell Mead, *Mortal Splendor: The American Empire in Transition* (Boston: Houghton Mifflin, 1987).

[22]See William Greider, *One World, Ready or Not: The Manic Logic of Global Capitalism* (New York: Simon & Schuster, 1997).

[23]See Kenichi Ohmae, *The End of the Nation State: The Rise of Regional Economies* (New York: Free Press, 1995).

[24]U.S. government data, various agencies, 1996.

[25]*The World Competitiveness Yearbook* (Luasanne, Switzerland: International Institute for Management Development, 1996).

[26]American Assembly, *Rethinking America's Security*, 9; see also Robert O. Keohane, Joseph S. Nye, and Stanley Hoffmann, eds., *After the Cold War* (Cambridge, Mass.: Harvard University Press, 1993).

[27]Harry Magdoff, *The Age of Imperialism: The Economics of U.S. Foreign Policy* (New York: Monthly Review Press, 1969), 43.

[28]See Robert O. Keohane and Joseph S. Nye, *Power and Interdependence: World Politics in Transition*, 2d ed. (Boston: Little, Brown, 1989).

[29]Quoted in Tom Masland, "Going Down the Aid 'Rathole'?" *Newsweek*, December 5, 1994, 39.

[30]Hobart Rowen, "The Budget: Fact and Fiction," *The Washington Post National Weekly Edition*, January 16–22, 1995, 5.

[31]See Gerald L. Houseman, *America and the Pacific Rim: Coming to Grips with New Realities* (Lanham, Md.: Rowman & Littlefield, 1995).

[32]See Richard J. Barnet and John Cavanagh, *Global Dreams: Imperial Corporations and the New World Order* (New York: Simon & Schuster, 1994).

Acknowledgments

Chapter 1 Reading 1: From Jennifer L. Hochschild, "The Future of the American Dream," *Facing Up to the American Dream: Race, Class, and the Soul of the Nation*, pp. 250, 256–260. Copyright © 1984. Reprinted by permission of Princeton University Press.

Reading 2: From R. Kent Weaver, "Deficits and Revolution in the 104th Congress," pp. 45–48. Reprinted with permission of *Publius: The Journal of Federalism* 26:3 (Summer 1996).

Chapter 4 Figure, Chapter 4: From "Locking People Up around the World," *U.S. News & World Report*, p. 17. Copyright, Sept. 19, 1966, U.S. News & World Report.

Figure 4–1: From Wall Street Journal Poll, 1996. Reprinted by permission of *The Wall Street Journal*, © 1996 Dow Jones & Company, Inc. All Rights Reserved Worldwide.

Figure 4–2: From Time/CNN Survey by Yankelovich Partners, Inc., January 17–18, 1994.

Chapter 5 Table 5–1: Table reported in Rudolpho O. de la Garza, Angelo Falcon, F. Chris Garcia, and John A. Garcia, "Hispanic Americans in the Mainstream of U.S. Politics," © *The Public Perspective*, a publication of the Roper Center for Public Opinion Research, University of CT, Stoors. July/August 1992, p. 19. Reprinted by permission.

Chapter 6 Figure 6–3: First part of figure from Los Angeles Times survey, January 19–22, 1995. Copyright © 1995 Los Angeles Times. Reprinted with permission.

Reading 6: From Benjamin I. Page and Robert Y. Shapiro, "Democracy, Information, and the Rational Public," *The Rational Public: Fifty Years of Trends in Americans' Policy Preferences*. Copyright © 1992. Reprinted by permission of The University of Chicago Press.

Chapter 7 Figure 7–2: Data from National Opinion Research Center, 1990, and Roper Surveys, 1993. Reprinted by permission of National Opinion Research Center and the Roper Organization.

Figure 7–3: From Pew Research Center, 1995. Reprinted with permission from Pew Research Center for The People & The Press.

Reading 7: Reprinted by permission of the publisher from *Voice and Equality: Civic Voluntarism in American Politics* by Sidney Verba, Kay Lehman Schlozman, and Henry E. Brady. Harvard University Press, copyright © 1995 by the President and Fellows of Harvard College.

Chapter 8 Figure 8–3: From CBS News/New York Times poll, September 8–11, 1994. Reprinted by permission of New York Times Graphics.

Reading 8: From Alan Ehrenhalt, "The Politics of Amtition" from *The United States of Ambition* by Alan Ehrenhalt. Copyright © 1991 by Alan Ehrenhalt. Reprinted by permission of Times Books, a division of Random House, Inc.

Chapter 9 Figure, Chapter 9: From Helmut L. Anheier, Lester M. Salamon, and Edith Archambault, "Participating Citizens: U.S.-Europe Comparisons in Volunteer Action," © *The Public*

Perspective, a publication of the Roper Center for Public Opinion Research, University of CT, Stoors. March/April 1994, p. 19. Reprinted by permission.

Reading 9: From Jonathan Rauch, "The Paralyzing Effect of Group Politics" from *Demonsclerosis* by Jonathan Rauch. Copyright © 1994 by Jonathan Rauch. Reprinted by permission of Times Books, a division of Random House, Inc.

Chapter 10 Figure 10.1: From *Out of Order* by Thomas E. Patterson. Copyright © 1993 by Thomas E. Patterson. Reprinted by permission of Alfred A. Knopf, Inc.

Figure 10–2: From "Sound Bite News: Television Coverage of Elections 1968–1988," *Journal of Communication,* vol. 42 (Spring 1992), p. 6 and from the Center for Media and Public Affairs, 1992 and 1996. Reprinted by permission.

Figure 10–3: From *Out of Order* by Thomas E. Patterson. Copyright © 1993 by Thomas E. Patterson. Reprinted by permission of Alfred A. Knopf, Inc.

Reading 10: From Thomas E. Patterson, "The Miscast Institution" from *Out of Order* by Thomas E. Patterson. Copyright © 1993 by Thomas E. Patterson. Reprinted by permission of Alfred A. Knopf, Inc.

Chapter 11 Figure 11–1: From *Congressional Quarterly Weekly Report,* various dated. Reprinted by permission of Congressional Quarterly, Inc.

Figure 11–5: From *Congressional Quarterly Weekly Report,* various dated. Reprinted by permission of Congressional Quarterly, Inc.

Reading 11: Adapted from Paul S. Hernson, "Running for Congress," *Congressional Elections: Campaigning at Home and in Washington.* Congressional Quarterly Press, 1995, pp. 2–17. Used by permission of Congressional Quarterly Press.

Chapter 12 Figure 12–2: From *Congressional Quarterly Weekly Report,* December 31, 1994, p. 3620. Reprinted by permission of Congressional Quarterly, Inc.

Reading 12: From Richard Rose, "The Postmodern President," *The Postmodern President,* 1991. Reprinted by permission of Chatham House Publishers.

Chapter 13 Figure 13–3: Adapted from B. Dan Wood and Richard W. Waterman, "Political Control of the Bureaucracy," *American Political Science Review,* 85(3), 1991, p. 821, fig. 7. Reprinted by permission of American Political Science Association.

Table, Chapter 13: Adapted from *The Politics of Bureaucracy,* 3rd Edition, by B. Guy Peters, 1989, pp. 102–103, ch. 3, table 3.7. Reprinted by permission of Addison-Wesley Educational Publishers, Inc.

Reading 13: From David Osborne and Ted Gaebler, "Reinventing Government," *Reinventing Government: How the Entrepreneurial Spirit Is Transforming the Pubic Sector,* Addison-Wesley, 1992.

Chapter 14 Table, Chapter 14: Table from *Comparative Constitutional Law* by Mauro Cappelletti and William Cohen, 1979, Chapter 4. The Michie Company. Reprinted by permission, copyright Michie, 1979. All rights reserved.

Table 14–2: From People for the American Way. Reprinted by permission.

Reading 14: From William J. Brennan, Jr., "Judicial Interpretation." Address to the Text and Teaching Symposium, Georgetown University, October 12, 1985. Reprinted by permission.

Chapter 15 Reading 15: From *Reviving the American Dream: Congress, the States and the Federal Government* by Alice M. Rivlin, 1992. Reprinted by permission of the Brookings Institution.

Chapter 16   Figure 16–2: Figure from Time/CNN survey by Yankelovich Partners, December 7–8, 1994.

Reading 16: From B. Guy Peters, "Social Policy," in *Developments in American Politics 2*, edited by G. Peele, C. H. Bailey, B. C. Cain, and B. G. Peters, 1995. Reprinted by permission of Chatham House Publishers.

Chapter 17   Figure 17–3: Figure from MSNBC survey, January, 1966.

Index